'*Human Resource Management: A Critical Approach* (Third Edition) is unparalleled in its depth and breadth, offering a comprehensive and incisive exploration of HRM frameworks, strategies, and emerging challenges. This exceptional text equips students with the analytical tools needed to navigate the complexities of HRM, and also serves as an invaluable reference for professionals and researchers alike. I confidently assign it to my students and rely on it frequently in my own research and teaching'.

Anthony Nyberg, *Director, Center for Executive Succession and Chaired Professor in the Darla Moore School of Business, University of South Carolina, USA*

'This book brings together an international team of experts to deliver a critical analysis of core HRM activities and significant developments in people management. This is an invaluable resource for HRM students, scholars, and managers who are looking for an in-depth and engaging discussion about the context and content of HRM'.

Helen De Cieri, *Professor of Management, Monash University, Australia*

'The third edition again offers a rich exploration of HRM's evolving landscape, blending foundational theories with critical perspectives on contemporary challenges such as AI, gig work, and sustainability. This essential resource equips scholars and practitioners with the ideas needed to innovate in HRM, fostering deeper insights into ethical, strategic, and global dimensions'.

Elaine Farndale, *Professor of Human Resource Management, The Pennsylvania State University, USA*

Human Resource Management

Written by an international team of respected scholars, *Human Resource Management: A Critical Approach*, 3rd edition, adopts a critical perspective to examine the core management function of human resource management (HRM) in all its complexity – including its darker sides.

Despite over three decades of debate around the nature of HRM, its intellectual boundaries and its application in practice, the field continues to be dogged by several theoretical and practical limitations. This textbook opens with a critique of the very concept of HRM, tracing its development over time, and then systematically analyses the context of HRM, practice of HRM and international perspectives on HRM.

New chapters commissioned for this third edition examine HRM and consider issues including diversity and inclusion, employee well-being, digitalisation and AI, sustainable HRM and gig work and job deconstruction.

This textbook is essential reading for advanced and inquisitive students of HRM, and for HRM professionals seeking to deepen their understanding of the complexities of their field.

David G. Collings holds Chair of Sustainable Business at Trinity Business School, Trinity College Dublin, Ireland. He previously held academic appointments at the University of Sheffield, Dublin City University and the University of Galway. He has held visiting positions at King's College London, Cornell Univeristy and Nanyang Business School in Singapore.

Geoffrey Wood is Professor and DanCap Private Equity Endowed Chair, and Department Chair DAN Management at Western University in Canada, and also holds adjunct professorships at the University of Bath and Cranfield University, both in the UK. Previously, he served as Dean and Professor of International Business, at Essex Business School and before then as Professor of International Business at Warwick Business School, UK.

Leslie T. Szamosi is Professor and Director of the Pan-European MBA programme at CITY College, University of York Europe Campus. He is also Accreditor and Panel Chair for the International Faculty of the Association of MBAs (AMBA) and a regular evaluator and assessor of European Union-funded projects. He has worked in both the private and public sectors in Canada.

Human Resource Management

A Critical Approach

Third Edition

Edited by David G. Collings, Geoffrey Wood and Leslie T. Szamosi

Routledge
Taylor & Francis Group
LONDON AND NEW YORK

Designed cover image: Getty Images

Third edition published 2025
by Routledge
4 Park Square, Milton Park, Abingdon, Oxon, OX14 4RN

and by Routledge
605 Third Avenue, New York, NY 10158

Routledge is an imprint of the Taylor & Francis Group, an informa business

First edition published by Routledge 2009

Second edition published by Routledge 2019

British Library Cataloguing-in-Publication Data
A catalogue record for this book is available from the British Library

ISBN: 978-1-032-62554-6 (hbk)
ISBN: 978-1-032-62561-4 (pbk)
ISBN: 978-1-032-62556-0 (ebk)

DOI: 10.4324/9781032625560

Typeset in Galliard
by Deanta Global Publishing Services, Chennai, India

To Aoife and Orlaith my brave, strong, beautiful and smart girls x

DC

To Katerina, my three angels (Maria-Lorna, Margarita, Dimitris), Dad (Gabor) and Giagia (Maroula) – family is everything.

LTS

To Vicky and Alice, thanks for everything.

GW

Contents

Tables

Figures

About the Editors

David G. Collings holds Chair of Sustainable Business at Trinity Business School, Trinity College Dublin, Ireland. He is Member of the Royal Irish Academy and Fellow of the Academy of Social Sciences, the Chartered Institute of Personnel and Development and Trinity College Dublin. He was 2021/22 Chair of the HR Division of Academy of Management. He previously held academic appointments at the University of Sheffield, Dublin City University and the University of Galway and visiting appointments at King's College London, Nanyang Business School, Singapore, Simon Fraser University and Cornell University as a Fulbright Research Scholar.

His research and teaching interests focus on sustainable work, talent management and global mobility. A particular focus of his recent work is the future of work and sustainable performance. He has published numerous papers in leading international outlets such as *Academy of Management Journal*, *Academy of Management Discoveries*, *Journal of Management*, *Journal of Management Studies*, *Organization Science* and *Personnel Psychology*. He has also published in leading applied outlets such as *Harvard Business Review* and *MIT Sloan Management Review*. He has edited 12 books, including *The Oxford Handbook of Talent Management* with Wayne Cascio and Kamel Mellahi. He is an Associate Editor at *Journal of Management* and former Editor in Chief at *Journal of World Business*, *Human Resource Management Journal* and the *Irish Journal of Management*. He also currently sits or has sat on a dozen editorial boards including *Academy of Management Review*, *Journal of International Business Studies*, *Journal of Management*, and *Journal of Management Studies*.

Geoffrey T. Wood is Professor and DanCap Private Equity Endowed Chair and Department Chair DAN Management at Western University in Canada, and also holds adjunct professorships at the University of Bath and Cranfield University, both in the UK. Previously, he served as Dean and Professor of International Business at Essex Business School and before then as Professor of International Business at Warwick Business School, UK. He has authored/co-authored/edited 18 books, and over 220 articles in peer-reviewed journals. Geoff's research interests centre on the relationship between institutional setting, corporate governance, firm finance and firm level work and employment relations. He is a Fellow of the Academy of Social Sciences and a Fellow of the British Academy of Management and is also in receipt of an Honorary Doctorate in economics from Aristotle University, Greece. Geoffrey Wood is Editor in *Chief of Human Resource Management Journal.* He also edits the Chartered ABS Journal Guide ranking list. Previously he has served as Editor in Chief of *Academy of Management Perspectives*, the *British Journal of Management* (official journal of the British Academy of Management) and of the *Annals of Corporate Governance* (official journal of the ICGS). He is the outgoing Editor in Chief of the *Academy of Management Perspectives* (official journal of the Academy of Management). He has had numerous research grants, including funding councils (eg ESRC), government departments (eg US Department of Labor; UK Department of Works and Pensions), charities (eg Nuffield Foundation), the labour movement (eg the ITF) and the European Union.

Leslie T. Szamosi is Professor and Director of the Pan-European MBA programme at CITY College, University of York Europe Campus. He is also Accreditor and Panel Chair for the International Faculty of the Association of MBAs (AMBA) and a regular evaluator and assessor of European Union-funded projects. He has worked both in the private and public sectors in Canada.

Prof. Szamosi worked as a private consultant and seminar leader for diverse organisations such as the European Union (ERASMUS, KOMVER II), Digital Electronics (now part of Compaq Computers), Human Resources Development Canada, International Finance Corporation, INECCOBANK, Industry Canada, KPMG Management, the Canadian Imperial Bank of Commerce (C.I.B.C.) and TELUS (formerly British Columbia Telecom). He is a highly sought-after presenter and has run numerous seminars and workshops for a variety of organisations and institutions throughout the region and North America including: ARCA, Heineken, Deutsche Telecom, A1 (Bulgaria), the International Finance Corporation, Oracle, the Ministry of Health (R. of North Macedonia), USAID, the World Bank, the Romanian Bankers' Association and Hemofarm. He has widely published over 70 papers in highly-ranked international journals and conferences.

About the Contributors

Rami Al-Sharif is Lecturer in Human Resource Management, at the Adam Smith Business School, University of Glasgow, UK.

Debby Bonnin is Associate Professor, University of Pretoria, Pretoria, South Africa.

Corine Boon is Professor of HRM and People Analytics, University of Amsterdam, The Netherlands.

Kieran M. Conroy is Reader in International Business, Queen's Business School, Queen's University Belfast, UK.

John Cullen is Emeritus Professor of Management Accounting, Sheffield University Management School, University of Sheffield, UK.

Pauline Dibben is Professor of Employment Relations, Sheffield University Management School, University of Sheffield, UK.

James Duggan is Lecturer in HRM, at Cork University Business School, University College Cork, Ireland.

Tony Dundon is Professor of HRM and Employment Relations, Kemmy Business School, University of Limerick, Ireland.

Yseult Freeney is Professor of Organisational Psychology, Dublin City University Business School, Dublin City University, Ireland.

Mick Fryer is Teacher in Business Ethics and Business Environment at Cardiff Business School, Cardiff University, UK.

Claire Gubbins is Professor of HRM and OB, Dublin City University Business School, Dublin City University, Ireland.

Patrick Gunnigle is Emeritus Professor of Business Studies, Kemmy Business 4School, University of Limerick, Ireland.

Novika Grasiaswaty is Junior Lecturer in Psychology, Universitas YARS, Jakarta, Indonesia.

Irena Grugulis is Chair in Work and Skills, Leeds University Business School, University of Leeds, UK.

Frank Horowitz is Professor International Human Resource Management – Emerging Markets, Cranfield School of Management, University of Cranfield, UK.

Phil Johnson was Professor of Organisation Studies, Sheffield University Management School, University of Sheffield, UK.

Steven Kilroy is Associate Professor of HRM, Trinity Business School, Trinity College Dublin, Ireland.

Zsuzsanna Kispál-Vitai is Full Professor, University of Pécs, Hungary.

Gilton Klerck is Professor of Industrial and Economic Sociology, Rhodes University, South Africa.

Dimitrios Koukourdinos is Head of Student Affairs, Swiss University of Applied Science Institute, Switzerland.

Caroline Linhares is Senior Lecturer in Accounting, Sheffield Hallam University, UK.

Ashish Malik is Professor of HRM, Queen's Business School, Queen's University Belfast, UK

Brian Matthews is a researcher at Institute for Human Resource Management, WU Vienna University of Economics and Business, Austria.

Anthony McDonnell is Dean and Professor of Management, Cork University Business School, University College Cork, Ireland.

Juliana Meira is Lecturer in Management Accounting, Sheffield University Management School, University of Sheffield, UK.

Luiz Miranda is Professor of Accounting, Federal University of Pernambuco, Recife, Brazil.

Michael Muller-Camen is Professor and Head, Institute for Human Resource Management, WU Vienna University of Economics and Business, Austria.

Kevin R. Murphy is Kemmy Chair of Work and Employment Studies, Kemmy Business School, University of Limerick, Ireland.

Hillary O'Leary is a PhD researcher at Dublin City University Business School, Dublin City University, Ireland.

Jaap Paauwe is Professor of HRM at Tilburg University, the Netherlands.

Riccardo Peccei is Professor of Organisational Behaviour and Human Resource Management at King's Business School, King's College London, UK.

Erik Poutsma is (Emeritus) Associate Professor International Labour Studies, Institute for Management Research, Radboud University, the Netherlands.

Alexandros Psychogios is Professor of Human Resource Management and Organisational Behaviour at Loughborough Business School, University of Loughborough, UK.

Suzanne Richbell was Senior Lecturer in HRM at Sheffield University Management School, UK.

Philip Rogiers is Assistant Professor of Organizational Behavior and Organization Theory, Esade Business School, Ramon Llull University, Spain.

Jill Rubery is Professor of HRM, Alliance Manchester Business School, The University of Manchester, UK.

Rosalind Searle is Professor of Human Resource Management and Organisational Psychology, at the Adam Smith Business School, University of Glasgow, UK.

Giovanni Oscar Serafini is Associate Professor Human Resource Management at the Business Administration and Economics Department, CITY College, University of York Europe Campus, Greece.

Karina van de Voorde is Associate Professor at the Department of Human Resource Studies, Tilburg University, the Netherlands.

Stephen Wood is Professor of Management, University of Leicester School of Business, University of Leicester, UK.

Adrian Wilkinson is Professor and Director, Centre for Work, Organisation and Wellbeing and the Department of Employment Relations, Griffith Business School, Griffith University, Australia.

1 Human Resource Management

A Critical Introduction

David G. Collings, Geoffrey Wood and Leslie T. Szamosi

Introduction

Much has changed since the first edition of this book was published in 2009. In reflecting on these changes, we are reminded of Harney and Collings' (2021: 3) assertion that 'the global economy is at an inflection point with significant implications for how we conceptualize and understand HRM [human resource management]'. They point to a range of factors including the impact of the COVID-19 pandemic, resurgent nationalism, technological disruption, changing demographics and diversity, asymmetry and wealth disparity, declining trust in institutions, and the ecological crisis confronting the globe, as amongst the biggest influences on human resources [HR]. Since then, the rapid emergence of generative AI has also significantly disrupted work and organisation (Budhwar et al, 2023; Nyberg et al, 2025).

Take, for example, the impact of the COVID-19 pandemic. There is little doubt that the pandemic has had significant impacts on the human resource (HR) profession and the management of employees globally. The pandemic was, at its core, a human crisis, and it positioned HR leaders as central to the response in organisations globally and, thus, elevated the status of the HR profession as a whole (Collings et al, 2021a). The pandemic also had significant implications for how work is organised for many employees. Key amongst these implications was the shift to working from home. While this was initially a necessity to ensure the health of workers without front-line responsibilities, it has become a taken-for-granted expectation in many professions (Bloom, Han & Liang, 2024). Indeed, it is hard to imagine a return to full-time, on-site working for many employees and various forms of hybrid work have become the norm. A second key impact of COVID-19 was the digitalisation of many industries that had traditionally relied on face-to-face interaction with customers at physical premises (Collings et al, 2021b). These, and other changes, fundamentally shifted the skill required by employees and managers alike and had significant implications for how people are managed in organisations.

Notwithstanding these recent evolutions, and despite nearly three decades of debate in the mainstream literature around the nature of human resource management (HRM), its intellectual boundaries, and its application in practice

DOI: 10.4324/9781032625560-1

the field continues to be dogged by a number of theoretical and practical limitations (Harney and Collings, 2021). This book is intended to provide readers with an advanced and critical discussion of the key debates and themes around HRM as it is conceptualised and operationalised in the current environment. We see the volume's contribution in the tradition of Storey (2007) and Legge (1995), and our aim is to provide a well-grounded and intellectually rewarding critical overview of the key issues surrounding HRM from theoretical and practical perspectives that combine theory with practice. In doing so, the volume draws on contributions from leading scholars in the field who provide detailed discussions on key debates in their respective offerings.

In this introduction, we provide the context for the book through considering a number of overarching themes within which key debates in the field of HRM are also grounded. Specifically, we provide a summary discussion of the theoretical and intellectual boundaries of HRM, consider its emergence in historical context and identify some of the pervasive contradictions and limitations prevailing in the literature. Finally, we provide a short outline of the structure and content of this volume.

HRM Defined

Our discussion begins by considering what HRM actually means today. Although in the broadest sense it may be taken to denote all aspects of recruitment and hiring, planning, development and reward, the human side of the organisation of work, and of the employment contract, HRM has also been taken to incorporate a much more involved, strategic dimension. In other words, it is not just about the choice and implementation of particular policies and practices towards the management of people but the adoption of a dynamic and adaptive (as adverse to purely administrative) purpose, in line with wider organisational strategic choices (Wilkinson et al. 2014). Yet, there remains much debate as to how much HRM really involves strategic choices, as opposed to the implementation of strategies imposed from higher up the organisational – and ownership – hierarchy. Others have argued that HRM has an ideological dimension; recognising people as an active resource may be superior to one that simply sees them as passive subjects. It also suggests, however, that as with any other resources, they should be deployed of and dispensed with, in line with perceived organisational priorities, rather than individuals who should be treated with a degree of empathy, in both their interests and for the longer-term sustainability of the organisation. Yet, implicit or explicit in much of the HRM literature is that there is value to treating employees in an enlightened manner, whether because this is ultimately better for the bottom line or because it is a good thing *per se*. Given the importance of definition in understanding the boundaries of a field, this issue is clearly an important point of departure, given that since its emergence HRM has continued to be 'dogged' by the still largely unresolved ambiguity surrounding its definition. As Blyton and Turnbull (1992: 2) note, 'The ways in which the term is used by academics and practitioners indicates both variations in meaning and significantly different emphases on what constitutes its core components'.

One of the dominant characterisations has been to define HRM as a contested domain, with rival soft and hard approaches towards people management (e.g., Johnstone, 2023). The soft approach to HRM is generally associated with the Harvard School, and in particular, the writings of Michael Beer and colleagues, and with a later tradition of UK scholarship, associated with the *Human Resource Management Journal* (see Beer et al., 1984; Beer, Boselie and Brewster, 2015; Beer and Spector, 1985; Walton and Lawrence, 1985). As with the hard school, the soft school emphasises the importance of aligning HR policies with organisational strategy, but it also emphasises the role of employees as a valuable asset and source of competitive advantage through their commitment adaptability and quality, rather than being treated simply in instrumental terms (Legge, 1995; D'Art, 2002; Wood and Vitai 2014). It stresses gaining employee commitment to the organisation through adopting a congruent suite of HRM policies. Soft HRM may itself be subdivided into two strands. The first strand, soft HRM, draws on behavioural sciences in particular, building on with strong resonance with the *Human Relations* school. The latter emphasised the importance of communication and recognising the need to give employees the opportunity to grow while the concept of human growth, which is central to its theory, echoes 'all-American' bowdlerised theories of motivation, from McGregor's *Theory Y* to Maslow's *Hierarchy of Needs* (Legge, 1995). Hence, it is sometimes conceptualised as 'developmental humanism' (Storey, 1989; Legge, 1995).

Sceptics have conceptualised soft HRM as the 'iron fist in the velvet glove', arguing that this theory of soft HRM 'reduced … the complex debate about the role of people in work organisations to the simplistic dogma of an economic model, which even its "creator" Adam Smith would probably not have wished applied in such an indiscriminate manner' (Hart, 1993: 29–30). Another uncharitable definition of soft HRM is that it constituted a desperate rearguard action by liberal academics and practitioners, mostly writing in the United States, to sell more humane forms of managing people to essentially conservative owner interests that have, in increasing numbers, ruthlessly pressed for a maximisation of short-term profits, regardless of the cost to both employees and the long-term good of the organisation (Wilkinson et al. 2014; Mellahi et al. 2010). In other words, soft HRM is about trying to encourage firms to be 'nicer' to their people, on the basis that such 'niceness' is likely to translate into greater commitment and productivity, and hence, even more profits, and moral issues take a 'back-seat'.

A second substrand of soft HRM has been one associated with a body of scholars rooted in the industrial relations tradition (which, in turn, focused on the employment contract with the inherent tensions surrounding the amount employees are paid and how the contract is enforced) (Wilkinson et al. 2014). This strand is inherently pragmatic; rather than rejecting the notion of HRM on the basis that it is management-, rather than employee-centred, it accepts that HRM has become the main broad framework through which firms manage and engage with their people. This approach seeks to synthesise the industrial relations tradition (with its interest in the nature and extent of workplace tensions and imbalances, the role of unions and the interplay between conflict and compromise) with the insights provided by empirical research on other aspects of people management, for example, human resource development and planning (Brewster et al. 2012). The result is an analytical framework that seeks to draw connections between different areas of HR policy and practice (for example, between the degree of training and employment security provided). This approach recognises the possibility of providing solutions to particular issues and challenges, without denying inherent tensions and imbalances.

Soft HRM stands in contrast with the hard variant generally associated with the Michigan School (Forbrun et al., 1984). Hard HRM places a strong emphasis on the use of human resource (HR) systems to 'drive' the attainment of the strategic objectives of the organisations (Forbrun et al., 1984). While soft HRM emphasises the human element of HRM, the emphasis of the hard approach is very much on the resource as a means of maximising shareholder value over the short term. The duty of managers is quite simply to create value for owners, and a focus on other issues such as employee rights is simply a distraction: rather, by focusing on returns, the organisation will perform most efficiently, which ultimately is in the interests of all.

It has been argued that, in the tradition of Taylorism and Fordism, employees are viewed as a factor of production that should be rationally managed and deployed in quantitative and calculative terms in line with business strategy (Tyson and Fell, 1986; Storey, 1992). Rather different to classic Taylorism or Fordism, however, job security in the new hard HRM is seen as an unnecessary luxury, whilst pay rates are to be kept to the lowest level the external labour market would permit. There is little mention in the literature illustrating how hard HRM echoes Henry Ford's famous commitment to a (then very generous) $5/day wage (however hardline Ford was towards trade unions, and indeed, concerned with managing the personal lives of employees). In other words, hard HRM is far removed from past notions of paternalist management, which, whilst assuming that decision-making should be centralised in the hands of senior management, also acknowledged that the firm had long-term responsibilities to its workers; however, hard HRM also embodies an element of sophistication. For example, it would allow for quite sophisticated reward systems to align the interests of senior managers and shareholders (Wood and Vitai 2014). Again, there is an implicit assumption of trickle-down (a prosperous organisation will be better equipped to provide jobs and have the capacity to pay genuinely hardworking and effective employees well), and there is a basis for enthusing employees around this (Brewster et al. 2011). Indeed, many employers associated with hard HRM (eg McDonald's, Walmart) set great stores around collective employee expressions of enthusiasm, whether those marshalled are happy or not (c.f. Smith 2011). In contrast, under the traditional sweatshop model, there would be no such underlying assumptions nor any commitment to developing or refining HR systems; rather, the focus would be around ensuring the maximum amount of labour is extracted from employees and pay is kept as low as possible.

Hard human resource variants are designed to be both internally consistent and externally aligned with the organisational strategy. These interventions seek to ensure full utilisation of the labour resource, not merely in terms of physical output but also in ensuring that employees excel (Wood and Vitai 2014; Storey, 1992). It is legitimised and finds its impetus from a market-responsive frame of reference (Storey, 2007). At the extreme, implicit contracts regarding pensions and tenure are seen as hampering effective management: these should, if possible, be jettisoned, with employee rights being pared back as much as possible. Critics of this point of view have argued that such a focus is likely to generate higher staff turnover rates, with the inevitable loss of job-specific skills and accumulated wisdom, low trust, low levels of organisational commitment, and hence, higher transaction costs (see Marsden, 1999). Cascio's (2006) comparison of Walmart, an archetype of hard HRM, with Costco, a company defined by high ethical standards and a softer approach to HRM, confirms the limitations of the former approach. Walmart, which prioritises shareholders as stakeholders and maximises the labour extracted from employees, has been consistently outperformed by Costco over several decades (Blinn, 2013; Cascio, 2006). This translates into significantly stronger sales and profit per employee and shareholder returns. Similar results are evidenced in organisations such as QuikTrip, Mercadona and Trader Joe's where investment in employees means larger labour budgets but translates into stellar operational execution and higher sales and profits. Employees also work more efficiently and find work more fulfilling while delivering improved customer service (Collings, 2014; Ton, 2023). In other words, hard HRM is likely to make organisations less efficient, and in practice, differences from the sweatshop model are not always clear-cut. It could be argued that most successful, incrementally innovative, high-value-added manufacturing firms have shunned hard HRM. In contrast, hard HRM has been more widely deployed in more volatile areas of economic activity, such as financial services and across the service economy, although, in the case of the latter it often appears to degenerate towards the sweatshop model.

A second and arguably simpler way of viewing things is that for HRM, the soft/hard divide, in the narrow sense, can be defined as a strategic approach to managing employees, which came to the forefront in the liberal market economies, particularly the US and the UK, in the 1980s. Whilst having both soft ('people friendly') and hard ('people as a resource to be deployed, utilized and, if need be, disposed of') variations, common to this approach was an emphasis on optimal shareholder outcomes, with enhancing outcomes for other stakeholders being at best, a secondary objective, and at worst, an unnecessary distraction. This 'two sides of the same coin' point of view argues that since the end of the long boom that lasted from the post-World War II period up until the 1970s, there has been a period of erratic and unstable growth and recession. This period has been characterised by employers gaining the upper hand over employees, due to the very much weaker bargaining position of the latter (cf. Kelly 1998). Given this, managers – particularly in the liberal market economies, such as the US and UK, where workers have historically had fewer rights under both law and convention – have taken the opportunity to fundamentally change the way they manage people. This has taken the form of systematic attempts to undermine collective bargaining with unions, replacing this with weak forms of consultation with individual employees. Collective employment contracts – where workers performing similar jobs are rewarded according to a pre-agreed pay scale – are replaced with individual ones, with employees being rewarded based on regularly appraised performance and/or through pay rates simply being linked to outputs. In other words, the role of the employee in the firm is not a dynamic and, in some sense, negotiated relationship but rather simply the deployment of a resource, in the same way a firm would deploy other physical resources, such as raw materials.

A third perspective is to simply conceptualise HRM as little more than a renaming of personnel management. In this vein, writers such as Armstrong (1987) describe HRM as 'old wine in new bottles', while Guest (1987) pointed to the fact that when HR emerged as a more modern name for people management, many personnel departments simply changed their names to HRM departments, with little evidence of any change in role. In practice, this would suggest that much HR work really concerns the administration of systems governing the administration of pay, promotion and recruitment procedures, etc. In turn, this would imply that HR managers are likely to lack power within the organisation and have little say in setting real organisational strategies.

Finally, HRM may be defined broadly in terms of including all aspects of managing people in organisations and the ways in which organisations respond to the actions of employees, either individually or collectively. The value of this 'catch-all term' is that it describes the wide range of issues surrounding both the employment contract, situations where an employment contract has yet to be agreed on (recruitment and selection), and ways in which employees may be involved and participate in areas not directly governed by the employment contract to make working life more agreeable and/or to genuinely empower people. In other words, it goes beyond simply 'industrial relations' or 'employment relations'. The terms 'personnel administration' or 'personnel management' would not provide a totally accurate label, given their administrative and non-strategic connotations. Although this would be in line with the pragmatic strand of soft HRM, this approach is somewhat broader in that it does assume that any type of relationship between employers and employees is optimal.

HRM is operationalised in terms of strategic interventions designed to develop resourceful employees and to elicit their commitment to the organisational goal (Storey, 1992). Critics have charged that this sometimes leads to assumptions that many or most problems may be solved by good communication and through reducing the space for misunderstandings, and discounts

Table 1.1 Definitions of HRM

Definition	*Implication*
Contested domain	HRM is a contested domain, with two rival paradigms, hard and soft HRM
Two sides of the same coin	Whether hard or soft, HRM is about the management of people in a particular, new way. This may involve the use of strategy to manage people or simply reflect structural changes that have strengthened management at the expense of employees
'New wine in old bottles'	HRM is little more than the extension of traditional personnel management
Collective noun	HRM is a commonly reflected description for a range of practices associated with managing work and employment relations

the impact of pay on productivity and motivation, and indeed, any benefits that might flow from giving employees a genuine say in the running of the enterprise (Wilkinson et al. 2014). Yet, central to HRM is the recognition that it is about *management*, and hence, about hierarchies and that the exercise of managerial power is never totally smooth or effective. Again, even if the importance of wages may sometimes be discounted, it is recognised that the employment relationship is central to people management, with attendant – for good or ill – inherent imbalances between contracting parties. As such, it is very distinct from organisational psychology that focuses on individual and group behaviours, rather than *management* of relationships that embody material inequality. Again, HRM tends to view the firm as historically and spatially rooted, suggesting that contextual circumstances need to be taken into explicit account to a greater extent than would typically be the case in organisational psychology.

The preceding discussion highlights the ambiguity around the boundaries of HRM. These differences are summarised in Table 1.1. The tension around definition persists in the literature and a central theme in this volume is highlighting the contradictions between these two broad understandings of HRM. We argue that for ethical and sustainability reasons, more stakeholder-oriented approaches to people management are preferable, with shareholder-dominant approaches facing both quotidian microcrises at firms (encompassing problems of human capital development and commitment) and at macroeconomic (encompassing problems of excessive speculation-driven volatility, industrial decline and chronic balance of payments problems) levels (see also Harney and Collings, 2021).

HRM and Personnel Management Compared

As noted, a key point of reference in definitions on HRM is through comparing it with its predecessor – personnel management. Although this debate is somewhat dated, it remains important. Thus, it merits summary discussion.

During the early days of HRM's emergence as a mainstream approach to people management, several commentators were sceptical about the extent to which it represented something different to its predecessor – personnel management. Over time it has become apparent that there are substantive differences between the two, at least at a theoretical level. In illuminating these differences, a brief discussion on personnel management is merited (for a full discussion, see Legge, 1995).

While there are several accepted definitions of personnel management, some of which in the US context are closer to accepted definitions of HRM (see Kaufman, 2001; Strauss, 2001), there is a degree of consensus as to its key characteristics. First, personnel management is largely conceived as a downstream activity with a limited strategic impact. And, despite the rhetoric, HRM is often not that strategic: after all, both hard and soft HRM ultimately depict HRM as a transmission belt, passing down an agenda of shareholder value. Further, personnel management is generally considered to be reactive and piecemeal with little integration between its various elements. One of the greatest management thinkers – if popular management writing can be considered thought at all – of the last century, Peter Drucker (1961: 269), neatly summarised the personnel role as

> a collection of incidental techniques with little internal cohesion. As personnel administration conceives the job of managing worker and work, it is partly a file clerk's job, partly a housekeeping job, partly a social worker's job and partly firefighting to head off union trouble or to settle it.

Of course, what many organisations claim is HRM has much akin with old style personnel management. Yet, in pointing to its shortfalls, it is easy to forget that the approach also had some merits. In emphasising administration, it highlighted continuity and procedurality, which, of course, holds advantages for employees in making working for the organisation a much more predictable affair. Again, in lowering transaction costs in the operationalisation of the employment relationship, it may also impart greater efficiencies to the firm, when compared to the constant strategic churn that characterised many organisations, and, indeed, which inevitably follows on overusage of consultants.

Of course, what went on in the personnel function in the past was – as with present-day HRM – bound up with contextual circumstances. Hence, Legge's (1995: 88) observation that 'in the UK "personnel management" evokes images of do-gooding specialists trying to constrain line managers, of weakly kowtowing to militant unions, of both lacking power and having too much power'. Indeed, it has been argued that the perceived welfare role of the personnel function was one aspect of it that limited its credibility as a managerial function. It also resulted in females playing a key role in personnel in its formative years in the UK context (Legge, 1995). A scrutiny of the gender composition of classes at many Chartered Institute of Personnel and

Development approved training centres provides some corroboration for the gendered nature of much HR work and how it has changed since the 1970s. A further dimension of the historical personnel role in the UK was its key role in negotiating with trade unions up until the 1980s, even if it was often firefighting. Indeed, it was this element of the role that brought increasing numbers of males into the profession (Gunnigle et al., 2006). Evidence in the UK, however, points to a return towards a greater feminisation of the HR function (Kersley et al., 2006: 69).

The historical engagement with trade unions points to a collectivist orientation and, owing to the historical prominence of trade unions, particularly in the UK and Ireland, personnel management became infused with a pluralist frame of reference (Flanders, 1964). Given the importance of bargaining, managing the industrial relationship gained a distinct identity: it is worth noting that the divide between basic personnel management and industrial relations persists in the academic literature, with, as a general rule, those academic journals focusing on the former having low prestige, and on the latter, higher prestige. Newer, explicitly HR journals represent something of a crossover and incorporate aspects of both, as well as insights from other disciplines.

The preceding discussion suggests that HRM and personnel management – and industrial relations – may differ in several, substantive, ways. The first is that HRM is conceived as having a more strategic role and, hence, elevated to the top management table, suggesting a more upstream role, even if, in practice, this has been little more than wishful thinking. For example, researchers at the University of Southern California found little difference in how HR practitioners spent their time between 1996 and 2016 (Lawler, 2017). HR practitioners continued to be overwhelmed by managing poor performers, implementation of HR policies and supporting change initiatives, spending less than 15 per cent of their time on strategic issues. Nonetheless, HRM does concern attempts to develop an integrated and congruent set of HR policies as opposed to the piecemeal approach apparent in the traditional personnel role. Furthermore, HR policy and practice is also targeted at the individual level reflected in the preference for individual performance-related pay, individual communication mechanisms, employee opinion surveys and the like. A final key distinguishing factor is that, reflective of the individualist orientation, HRM is premised on a unitarist understanding of conflict, suggesting that there are no intrinsic conflicts of interest in the employment relationship as all within the organisation are working towards a common goal for the success of the organisation. The common goal is reflected in the idea that there is a single source of authority within the organisation – management. Given that there are argued to be no conflicts of interest within the organisation, conflicts are caused by breakdowns in communication or by troublemakers. Conflict should be suppressed by improving communication or removing troublemakers from the organisation. Unions are opposed on two grounds: (1) there are no conflicts of interest within the workplace and thus they are unnecessary, and (2) they would represent an alternative source of authority. Alternatively, unions may be co-opted to the managerial agenda, through 'partnership', with unions trading off militancy for continued recognition and the benefits that would arguably flow from greater organisational competitiveness. More critical strands of the HR literature suggest that this focus is mistaken, that employees often retain a collective identity and that managerial power will inevitably continue to be challenged in ways that would make new accommodations necessary if the organisation is to work in the most effective way.

HRM Enters the Mainstream

It is generally agreed that HRM gained mainstream acceptance as an approach towards people management, particularly in the UK and the US, in the 1980s, although it should be noted that its roots can be traced some 20 years earlier in the US context (see Strauss, 2001). It was during the 1980s, however, that HRM became widely embraced by practitioners and academics alike. For practitioners, it offered a new agenda to replace the lacklustre image of personnel management and the adversarial rhetoric of industrial relations; not only did it hold out the prospect of less conflictual ways of resolving workplace issues, but it also adopted that of a more professional status for its adherents. Yet for academics it represented an opportunity for rebranding and reorienting careers away from industrial relations and personnel management, topics which many feared were losing their import as academic subjects (Guest, 2001; Strauss, 2001). The emergence of HRM is generally traced to a confluence of factors. The impact of the external context on HR function is reflected in Beer et al.'s (1984: 34) observation that 'HRM policies and practices are not and cannot be formed in a vacuum. They must reflect the governmental and societal context in which they are embedded', and it is generally recognised that several political, economic and social factors prompted the emergence of HRM at this time.

Guest (1990) argues that the most significant of these factors were external pressures on industry, of which the most important were increasing competition – and the UK and the US's decline of industrial competitiveness – in the US and international marketplace, combined with concerns over the retarded rate of productivity growth in the US. The greatest competitive threat, to the US and UK in particular, at this time, came from the rise of the Pacific economies, most notably Japan but also South Korea, Taiwan and Singapore, who competed through technological advantages and initially cheaper labour costs but also from the increasingly outward orientation of German manufacturing. These trends and notably, Japanese firms' entry into the US market threatened traditional strongholds of US industry; in particular, the automakers who had previously enjoyed an oligopolistic position in the US marketplace. The same could be said for German automakers in the case of the UK. Japanese competitors could provide high quality products at a very competitive price. In the UK, similar threats were experienced from other large European economies and the shift from 'command' to 'market' economies in central and eastern Europe (Legge, 1995). This increasing competition was reflective of the growing globalisation of the marketplace, a trend facilitated by improvements in information technology and transportation and free-trade agreements, meaning that the barriers traditionally created by national borders were being broken down. Concomitantly, levels of technological differentiations blurred as technological advances limited the potential of technology as a source of competitive advantage. There was a gradual recognition that part of the recipe of the German and Japanese successes were highly-skilled and motivated workforces; as indicated earlier, firms were subject to far greater competitive pressures than they had been historically accustomed to. These factors influenced the shift in emphasis towards employees as a source of competitive advantage. This view was very much consistent with the 'excellence literature' in the US (Peters and Waterman, 1982). Their work traced the success of high-performing companies to the motivation of employees through involved management styles, which were responsive to market changes (Beardwell, 2001) This excellence literature was very influential and influenced the shift towards HRM in organisations.

Increasing competition should also be considered in the context of the difficult economic conditions of the early 1980s. Specifically, the oil crises of the latter part of the 1970s and early 1980s precipitated a global economic recession, which further influenced the climate in which organisations operated. At a political level, the Reagan government in the US and the Thatcher government in the UK certainly facilitated the emergence of a new individualist approach to management of employees, which gave impetus to the declining role of trade unions in these countries. The free-market ideology of these governments was most visible in Reagan's showdown with the air traffic controllers in the US, which ultimately resulted in the dismissal of the striking employees. In the UK, Thatcher's high-profile standoff with striking miners had broadly similar connotations. This led to mine workers being defeated, but also the wilful destruction of much of the mining industry, overexploitation of North Sea oil and gas reserves and the frittering away of revenues to support tax cuts and the various ideological projects. These conditions, along with an overvalued currency (with, in turn, seriously adverse consequences for manufacturing) reflect the extent to which breaking organised labour – and the pursuit of a broader, right-wing ideology – was prioritised over basic economic logic and the well-being of the country at large. Indeed, it has been argued that the policy of privatisation of elements of the public sector, combined with a raft of anti-union legislation under Thatcher's Conservative government in the UK, 'encouraged firms to introduce new labour practices and to re-order their collective bargaining arrangements' (Hendry and Pettigrew, 1990: 19). The unitarist underpinning of HRM certainly resonated more closely with these ideals compared with pluralist industrial relations traditions, with its focus on understanding and managing industrial conflict. The developments have left an enduring legacy in the UK context. Whilst union rights have increased under the Labour governments of the late 1990s and 2000s, the government has been reluctant to extend comprehensive employment rights to the growing body of agency workers and has ruthlessly privatised, partially privatised or otherwise outsourced the provision of public infrastructure and services to politically well-connected private contractors who have generally tended to practice far tougher HR than their public sector counterparts (Dibben et al. 2007). This is not to suggest that the UK has turned into an island of sophisticated HRM, even of the hard variety. Rather, it appears the sweatshop model is gaining ground. For example, efforts to rein in the gang-masters that supply cheap (and, in alarmingly many cases, coerced) labour to agriculture, catering and frontline service industries – and, indeed, to properly enforce labour law in the latter – have been half-hearted at best. Although commentators in the popular media suggest that robotics have been a threat to jobs, it is telling that wages have become so low that in some areas of the economy, previous automation has been abandoned in favour of manual labour, the most obvious example would be the case of carwashes.

A final factor which facilitated the emergence of HRM as an integral part of mainstream management practice was a fundamental restructuring of the economies of developed countries. This shift was reflected in a decline in significance of traditional industries and a rise in new industrial sectors such as high-tech industries and a significant shift in employment towards the services sector. Many of these industries were less tied to the established patterns of traditional old-style industrial relations (Beardwell, 2001); although there have been islands of success in organising some workers in these areas, in most instances, unions have been unable to make significant inroads (Dibben and Wood, 2011). More critical accounts have, as noted earlier, suggested that all these economic and industrial changes represented one of many historical periods where the relative power of management vis-à-vis employees had disproportionately increased; in time, this will be reversed, with employees fighting back, clawing back some of the gains of previous decades (Kelly, 1998). In this regard, HRM is conceived to be the current incarnation of management's ongoing search for the 'best' method to manage the employment relationship (D'Art, 2002).

Thus, while the precise antecedents of the emergence of HRM can be very dependent on the analyst's interpretation of events (Beardwell, 2001), it is clear that a range of factors combined to facilitate the emergence of HRM as a mainstream approach to the management of employees. Notwithstanding the aforementioned examples of factors in the UK environment that facilitated the emergence of HRM, for some, HRM as a concept is rooted in US traditions (Brewster 2007; Guest, 1990), and hence, may have limited applicability abroad. We now consider this perspective.

HRM: An American Concept with Little Applicability Abroad?

As we have demonstrated, HRM as an approach to people management is generally seen to have its roots in the US context. In this regard, much of the heritage of HRM in the US context long predates the mainstream emergence of HRM in the 1980s. Particularly prominent in the US context has been the dominance of non-union industrial relations, which clearly resonates with HRM. This anti-union ideology is generally attributed to the development of American industry. Most notable in this regard is, as Leidner (2002) notes, the fact that the balance of power in the US workplace favours capital more than in most other countries. Arguably, this is most apparent in terms of the doctrine of 'Employment at Will', which underscores all aspects of the employment relationship in American industry. This widely accepted doctrine means that, in the absence of contracts or legislation, employment contracts are 'at-will', and thus can be terminated by either party without explanation or cause; thus, workers have no ongoing right to employment and no legal obligation for fairness is placed on employers (Leidner, 2002). The evolution of the power relationship alluded to can be traced to the evolution of US industry. In this regard, the lack of legislative support of worker collectives prior to the 1930s resulted in non-union practices prevailing for many US employees (Kochan et al., 1986). Guest (1990) posits that at this stage, individualism became ingrained in US culture. This individualism is often characterised in terms of a meritocracy, where ambition predominates (ibid.). This is reflected in articulations of the 'American Dream', which Guest (1990) posits was first formally articulated in the context of the New Deal in the 1930s. While different variations have been presented over the years, Guest (1990) postulates that several common themes emerge. Most significant in terms of our consideration of the context of people management in US industry is the view of America as a land of opportunity, where through self-improvement and hard work anyone can become a success. Thus, the emphasis in US culture is on individuals grasping opportunities as they present themselves and making the most of them, with government and employers aiding simply in terms of providing a context (Guest, 1990). This is significant for several reasons. First, it intensifies managements' perceived right to manage; and second, it amplifies individualistic tendencies and notions of meritocracy ingrained in US culture. Leidner (2002: 27), when examining the nature of employment relations in the US fast-food industry, highlights this cultural idiosyncrasy thus:

> The American values of individualism and meritocracy suggest that workers should improve their lot by moving out of fast-food jobs rather than by improving the compensation and working conditions of the jobs.

Thus, from a cultural point of view at least, the obligation is placed on the individual to improve their situation by exiting the unsatisfactory working situation and moving on to a more rewarding or satisfactory job. This highlights the individual focus in HRM theory and is consistent with the shift away from collective employment relations.

Clearly reflective of this ideology is the welfare capitalist movement, which developed during the late nineteenth century. This involved America's large corporations developing a uniquely American response to the 'labour question', which was private and managerial as opposed to governmental and labourist (Jacoby, 1997). This movement viewed the industrial enterprise as the source of stability and security in modern society as opposed to government or trade unions (Jacoby, 1997). These firms emphasised job security (achieved through an emphasis on internal labour markets), good rates of pay, a variety of welfare benefits and non-union forms of employment relations (ibid.). Clearly these characteristics, combined with the later influence of 'all-American' theories of motivation, from McGregor's Theory Y to Maslow's hierarchy of needs (Legge, 1995) referred to previously, were also influential in the emergence of HRM in the US context.

For some (e.g., Guest, 1990; Brewster, 2007) the US heritage of HRM thinking and practice means that its application in practice in other countries may be questionable. As Brewster (2007: 771) notes, 'Whether the US-derived visions of HRM apply everywhere in the world is an important question for both theory and practice'. Based on a large body of empirical work, Brewster (2007) concludes that many aspects of HRM practice are different in the European context. It is worth noting that, for example, how many UK employers chose *not* to get rid of unions in the 1980s, at a time when they certainly would have enjoyed much government support: hence, to a degree at least, pluralist ways of doing things remain surprisingly embedded in many UK workplaces. The comparability of HRM systems across countries is a key theme in the literature, and this is taken up by Chris Brewster and Wolfgang Mayrhofer in their contribution to the current volume.

The Credibility Gap?

A final theme which we explore in this introduction is the challenge that HRM has long since faced in establishing its value as a managerial activity. In Legge's (1995: 9) words, this 'obsession with [establishing] their credibility' has dogged personnel, and more recently, HRM practitioners throughout their history. In this regard, Tyson's (1985: 22) oft-cited comment is illustrative of this credibility gap:

> If all the managers were to write in their diaries each day 'What have I done today to make the business successful?' would the personnel manager have an embarrassingly short entry to make?

To a degree, these credibility challenges relate to the traditional downstream role that personnel management occupied in firms, combined with the established welfare role that the function performed in many organisations. Thus, as we noted earlier, practitioners were quick to embrace HRM as it offered the potential to replace the uninspiring image of personnel management. Further, rhetorically at least, it offered the possibility of bringing HRM to the top management table and a role in developing corporate strategy. In the UK context, the Workplace Employee Relations Surveys (WERS) have provided key insights into the changing role of the HR profession over recent decades. Some earlier surveys in the series concluded that 'HR managers are a new breed of managers, and that the increase in their numbers is not the product of a re-labelling exercise' (Kersley et al., 2006: 70) as some early critics of HRM purported. Thus, the WERS studies provide evidence of substantial differences in role between those with 'HR' in their job titles and their counterparts who retain 'Personnel'. The former tended to spend more time on employment relations issues, were more qualified, were more likely to have responsibility for pay and pension and tended to have been in their posts for a shorter period than the latter. HR professionals also appeared to have more autonomy, particularly in relation to pay (see Kersley et al., 2006: 70). However, the picture presented by the WERS data on the influence of the HR/personnel function at board level is less optimistic. Specifically, personnel representation at board level displayed a marked decline in the private sector from 1984 onwards – from 76 per cent in 1984 to 71 per cent in 1990 to 64 per cent in 1998 (Millward et al., 2000: 76). Similarly, the 2004 study found that HR managers were even less likely to be involved in the development of strategic business plans than in 1998 (Kersley et al., 2006). This trend did not abate in the 2011 data with a decline in HR representation at board level to 56 per cent (van Wanrooy et al, 2013). However, it would be wrong to suggest that HR does not have a strategic role in any organisations and in the UK, the decline of the strategic role of the HR function was largely confined to smaller firms. Board level representation remained relatively stable in UK-based multinational corporations (MNCs), while it actually rose in the largest organisations and those recognising trade unions (Millward et al., 2000: 77). Indeed, large MNCs such as Procter & Gamble, Pitney Bowes, Goldman Sachs and General Electric are often cited as truly embracing the potential of HR as a strategic partner within the organisation (see Hammonds, 2005). It is important to note, however, that global data suggest a more pessimistic landscape on this question. As noted previously, researchers found little difference in how HR practitioners spent their time between 1996 and 2016 (Lawler, 2017). HR practitioners continued to be overwhelmed by managing poor performers, implementation of HR policies and supporting change initiatives, meaning they spent less than 15 per cent of their time on strategic issues.

Since then, however, there has been an increasing focus on matters that both concern managing people, yet are of little real importance. Graeber (2019) notes that economic change has shrunk the number of frontline jobs engaged in productive activities, but this has been counterbalanced by the rise of the large number of managerial and administrative jobs that add little in the way of value; there is little doubt that HRM has not been immune to such tendencies. This includes a focus on strategy retreats, trivial yet compulsory training and development activities, staff engagement exercises that facilitate lengthy yet forcibly positive discussion around supposedly important matters on which the key decisions have already been made, and the even more complex appraisal systems, amongst other ultimately worthless activities. The adoption of new technologies (eg AI) has, if anything, accelerated this tendency as the amassing of new and more data requires additional people to monitor and make sense of. Indeed, the rapidity with which AI can analyse information and generate reports of varying quality would suggest that, rather than simply doing away with labour per se, it may well shrink productive employment even further, yet generate even more 'bullshit' jobs in both line and HR management (c.f. Graeber, 2019).

Hence, some feel that there is a significant gap between the rhetoric and reality of HRM in terms of its strategic contribution. As Hammonds (2005) neatly summarised in his provocative contribution, 'Why We Hate HR':

> After close to 20 years of hopeful rhetoric about becoming 'strategic partners' with a 'seat at the table' where the business decisions that matter are made, most human-resources professionals aren't nearly there. They have no seat, and the table is locked inside a conference room to which they have no key. HR people are, for most practical purposes, neither strategic nor leaders.

Over almost a decade later, Lawler (2014) came to the same conclusion:

> Unfortunately, my data suggest that HR rarely plays a major role in the development and implementation of business strategies. They are most active in helping design the organization for change, and least active when it comes to working with the corporate board. When I look at whether their role has changed in the recent years, the answer is, "No." HR seems to be about as involved in business strategy today as it was a decade ago.

Perhaps this outcome has something to do with how performance is conceptualised in the modern firm. This is illustrated in the tension between the hard and soft variants of HRM in the literature: a central theme in this volume is highlighting the contradictions between these two broad understandings of HRM. We argue that for ethical and sustainability reasons, more stakeholder-oriented approaches to people management are preferable, with shareholder-dominant approaches facing both quotidian microcrises at firms (encompassing problems of human capital development and commitment) and at macroeconomic (encompassing problems of excessive speculation-driven volatility, industrial decline and chronic balance of payments problems) levels. As Stephen Wood discusses in his contribution to the current volume, this search for legitimacy of the HR function has long since been premised on the illumination of a link between HRM and the firm's financial performance, as evidenced by Mark Huselid and colleagues' seminal contributions (Huselid, 1995; Huselid et al., 1997). While acknowledging the importance of the bottom line of financial performance, a broader conceptualisation of the HR role in terms of, perhaps, social legitimacy (as advanced by Lees, 1997; Boxall and Purcell, 2008, etc.), emphasising the moral legitimacy or ethical standing of the firm in the societies in which they operate (Paauwe and Farndale, 201704), or on governance, 'the establishment of appropriate "rules of the game" involved in successfully managing the employment relationship' (as advanced by Sisson, 2007), may be more appropriate in establishing the credibility of the HR function (see also Matthews and Muller-Camen's contribution to the current volume).

A recurring feature through the HRM literature is the extent to which HR really can make a measurable contribution to the bottom line. Empirical evidence on this is mixed, which, at least in part, would reflect that rival points of view rarely measure the same things, at the same point of time, with genuinely comparable data. In recent years, there has been growing interest in the role and potential of High Performance Work Systems (HPWS). These involve closer engagement and collaboration between management and workers that aim to enhance the level of the contribution of employees that may be fostered through co-determination and skills development (Cafferkey and Dundon, 2015). It may also be seen as a mechanism that enhances employee capabilities, productivity and commitment (Zhang et al., 2014; Datta et al., 2023). Other work adds agility and effective adoption of technological advances (Kaushik and Mukherjee, 2022; c.f. Darwish et al., 2020). Of course, HPWS is a composite phenomena, and it may be hard to measure how genuinely committed employees are to the organisation's success; hence, there has been a tendency to focus on which of its dimensions and consequences are easily measurable (Cafferkey and Dundon, 2015).

In practical terms, it could be argued that the old soft/hard HRM debate is being replayed in the HPWS literature, with those inclined to the former school of thought praising its co-determinative elements, and the latter the maximising of employee potential and output. This raises the question as to how different HPWS is to the 'old' strategic HR. Clearly advances in technology (ranging from AI through to enhanced employee monitoring) and new forms of working (eg remote and hybrid working) have challenged many assumptions regarding what makes for enhanced employee performance. This might suggest there is a need for a more rigorous understanding of what HPWS is and what it could become.

One positive trend over recent years is the elevated status of HR professionals during the COVID-19 pandemic (Collings et al, 2021b). Arguably, given that the pandemic was a people issue at its core, HR's role became central to navigating firms' responses to the crisis. HR leaders assumed responsibility for areas that were traditionally far beyond their remits and were heavily relied upon by other leaders (Collings, 2021a). In line with the stakeholder approach advocated for, noted previously, we are seeing an increasing emphasis on stakeholder management in HR. The pandemic forced organisations to better manage the trade-offs between employees, customers and shareholders as stakeholders (Collings et al, 2021a). Despite being initially slow to embrace the wider economic, social and governance (ESG) agenda in terms of organisations' wider impact on society (Stahl et al, 2020), HR is increasingly stepping into the role of leading organisations' ESG agenda, which, again, potentially raises the profile of the function internally and externally.

The Disciplinary Foundations of HRM

Any introduction of HRM would be incomplete without some discussion as to the disciplinary foundations of HRM. Personnel management may have emphasised procedures, but it also emphasised processes and objectivity. The latter included formal mechanisms for selection and recruitment, and in the deployment of individuals within organisations, that encompassed the use of tools and techniques from psychology such as aptitude testing, manpower planning formula and the application of theories of motivation based on assumed human needs and concerns. The latter would include, of course, both Maslow's theories of motivation – including the infamous triangular depiction of his hierarchy of needs much beloved by intellectually challenged undergraduates – to more sophisticated developments, extensions and counterdevelopments. To its proponents, the use of scientific knowledge could ensure that the most suitable workers were allocated to the most appropriate jobs. To its critics, the use of such tools often constitute 'pseudo science', with very ambitious claims of universal applicability being constantly belied by organisational reality and applied research. Nonetheless, psychological approaches remain influential in serious debates by both academics and practitioners. Many concepts have also been appropriated by pop management 'gurus', whose works, linking bowdlerised theory with homespun wisdom and wilful stupidity, remain persistently well represented amongst the 'twit lit' to be found in any airport bookstore.

In contrast, industrial relations has tended to draw on industrial sociology (itself a synthesis of sociology and aspects of thinking from the discipline of engineering), a critical discipline that has sought to understand work and employment in terms of social group formation and dynamics, the role of institutions and the interface between humans and technology. Particularly influential political economy perspectives analyse work and employment relations from a basic starting point: that the employment contract represents an open-ended exchange with a readily quantifiable cash wage being exchanged for an ultimately indeterminate amount of labour power (Hyman, 1989). Employers will naturally try and quantify the latter, with a view to maximising the amount of labour extracted, be it through structuring and routinisation, measuring of the quantity and quality of output, and regularly reviewing performance, whilst trying to circumscribe wage rates. Employees will, in turn, naturally seek to maximise wages and try to limit and/or enhance the pleasure of labour time. To its proponents, such a perspective provides both a realistic assessment of what really goes on in organisations and critical tools for analysis.

However, aspects of the industrial relations literature – notably in the US – have also drawn on the tools and techniques of rational choice economics to understand dimensions of employment, such as the operation of labour markets. However, scientific claims are often belied by the complexities of social reality and the tendency of both managers and workers to view the world from both an individual and a communitarian (or social) perspective. Nonetheless, rational choice economics' emphasis on 'economic man', of society and organisations as being composed of rational profit maximising individuals has infused much of the thinking behind shareholder value conceptualisations of HRM. More recent developments in heterodox economics, that take account of the effects of social collectives (associations) and institutions, have resulted in the application of what has been termed 'socio-economics' to studying people management. In practice, however, proponents of such thinking have tended to have close links to industrial sociology, with individuals often moving between such groupings.

It is worth noting that those approaching people management from these different perspectives are often antipathetic to each other, in theory if not in practice, and, with some notable exceptions, make little effort to engage with each other's ideas. A scrutiny of HR and related departments in the UK will find some predominantly composed of psychologists, others of industrial sociologists and a few of rational choice economists. Each publish in their 'own' journals and are dismissive of the quality of others. For example, the *British Journal of Industrial Relations* is widely held by industrial relations experts and industrial sociologists as one of the finest academic journals – if not the finest – in the field, but is routinely ranked as second flight in journal rankings listings compiled by psychologists.

The Structure and Content of the Book

The book is structured in three distinct sections, each drawing on contributions from leading academics in the respective areas who engage with the respective topics in a critical way. Following this introduction, in Section One, the Context of HRM, readers are introduced to some of the key foundational concepts of HRM and the overarching issues that help to frame modern discussions on HRM and its implications within ever-changing, many times chaotic, situations.

The first chapter in this section, Chapter 2, by Phil Johnson and Leslie T. Szamosi, reviews the organisational context of HRM from bureaucratic through to post-bureaucratic forms. Issues relate to the economic crisis and changing organisational forms and are utilised to illustrate an array of social and economic influences that continue to influence HR practice in organisations.

In Chapter 3, Jaap Paauwe and Corine Boon introduce the concept of strategic HRM through analysing the link between strategy and HRM, including different strategic approaches, one of which is 'strategic fit'. The authors also present alternative approaches that seek to balance the implementation and dynamics of traditional approaches through a synthesis of recent conceptual frameworks.

Chapter 4, by Stephen Wood, considers the linkage between HRM and organisational performance to assess claims that HRM can be decisive for organisational performance or that HRM centred on employee involvement or development justifies the same.

Chapter 5, by Mick Fryer, Dimitrios Koukourdinos and Alexandros Psychogios analyses key debates around ethics and its implications for underscoring HRM, a topic often neglected by mainstream books. With a focus on participative HRM practices, the discussion is grouped according to different ways of thinking about ethics: ethical absolutism, ethical relativism and ethical intersubjectivism including a historical upgrade to the discussion.

In Chapter 6, Hilary O'Leary and Yseult Freeney provide a bird's eye, critical evaluation of equality, diversity and inclusion (EDI) from a HR perspective. Building on an expanding body of literature around EDI, this chapter highlights the complexities in EDI thinking and implementation. The authors caution against the assumption that doing something is better than doing nothing.

In Chapter 7, Geoffrey Wood, Pauline Dibben, John Cullen, Juliana Meira, Debby Bonnin, Luiz Miranda and Caroline Linhares develop a unique interdisciplinary perspective (from HRM to global value and supply chains, to employment relations) to evaluate the evolving nature of HRM in supply chains. They consider the impacts of economic and pandemic crises, labour repression down supply chains, how up-and-down supply chains have impacted HR practices and the impact of formal and informal regulation.

Chapter 8, by Claire Gubbins, debates the management of knowledge and organisational learning through HR practices. A variety of scientific and social paradigms and critiques, and the convergence and divergence debate is evaluated with a critical evaluation of the role of individual, interpersonal or social and organisational HR practices for knowledge circulation and organisational learning.

The final chapter in this section, Chapter 9, analyses the increasing and evolving significance of SMEs in the global economy. Tony Dundon and Adrian Wilkinson evaluate the application of HRM in such organisations. Following the analysis of the polarising perspectives of 'small is beautiful' versus 'bleak house' in the literature, the key dimensions of HRM in SMEs are evaluated (e.g., recruitment, training).

In Section Two, the focus of analysis and discussion moves more towards the Practice of HRM. This section reflects the management of HR flows within organisations and looks at specific aspects of HR practice.

In Chapter 10, Rosalind Searle, Rami-Al-Sharif and Novika Grasiaswaty evaluate the key debates around recruitment and selection of employees within organisations in the age of artificial intelligence. Aspects of attraction and selection and the associated tools and instruments are evaluated, and three distinct paradigms for examining these processes are introduced along with emergent issues in the area, including demographic changes, global recruitment and selection and the role of trust.

Chapter 11, by Zsuzsa Kipal-Vitai and Geoff Wood, outlines the nature of HR planning in organisations and introduces the role of institutions in influencing HR activities within the firm. Two distinct areas are analysed herein: the meaning of HR planning and how it is applied in different contexts and locales, and an analysis of the different applied tools and techniques of HR planning.

Chapter 12, by Anthony McDonnell, Patrick Gunnigle and Kevin R. Murphy, critically evaluates contemporary performance appraisal and performance management systems in organisations. An analysis of the various debates in the context of performance management in organisations is also provided.

Chapter 13, reward management in organisations, is considered by Erik Poutsma. This chapter outlines both the function and form of rewards in the contemporary employment relationship. Together with performance management, reward management systems are concerned with motivating and engaging employees and compelling them to express desired behaviours; this chapter seeks to push the debate forward.

In Chapter 14, Irena Grugulis engages with human resource development, which is often emphasised as a means of developing individual competence in organisations. The realities of labour market practice are culled from the rhetoric of enthusiasm in considering the way skills are changing and the differences in various work environments, drawing conclusions that are not always positive but very much in line with COVID-era experiences of HRM.

Chapter 15, by Gilton Klerck, presents a useful counterpoint to the unitary underpinning of HRM through an industrial relations critique. The focus is on an assessment of the 'crisis' of IR in practice, the theoretical critiques of IR by various approaches and concludes with a discussion of the challenges of IR going forward.

The final chapter in this section, Chapter 16, by Kieran Conroy and Ashish Malik, explores three overarching international HRM themes: global staffing, HRM practice transfer and global talent management. Building on emerging and future debates on the increased digitisation of the disruptive world of work, the authors discuss how International Human Resource Management (IHRM) practitioners and scholars might adopt an artificial intelligence (AI) perspective of IHRM as a comprehensive way to manage an increasingly younger crossborder workforce.

The final section of the book, Section Three, examines HRM in the context of emerging contemporary trends globally.

Chapter 17, by Giovanni Serafini and Leslie T. Szamosi, critically evaluates the evolution (or revolution) of HRM from digitalisation through to the integration of artificial intelligence and its impact on all of the critical strategic functions. These developments are considered in such a way as to pave the way for the development of 4IR workplace ecosystems where humans and AI work together seamlessly.

In Chapter 18, David Collings, Philip Rogiers and James Duggan consider emerging trends and their impact on how work is designed and organised in organisations. In considering the historical context of jobs, they show how jobs have been a central reference point for work in organisations for almost two centuries. However, they argue that over recent years, we have witnessed a breakdown in how we think about and understand jobs. They highlight the gig economy and internal job deconstruction as key examples of this breakdown and consider what this means for work and employment.

In Chapter 19, Brian Matthews and Michael Muller-Camen revisit past critiques and position the debate on sustainable HRM in the context of recent crisis developments. They explore the implications of the new emerging influence of common good values (CGVs), relational collective action approaches and overall implementation with the notion of gaining insights regarding the future role HRM can play in unifying the discipline towards a sustainable agenda.

The final chapter of our book, Chapter 20, by Karina van de Voorde, Steven Kilroy and Riccardo Peccei, critically examines the extant research on worker physical and mental health in the context of HRM and link to broader discussions of hedonic and eudaimonic well-being while evaluating the aspects of overall welfare at work. They set out an ambition of HRM to influence worker well-being by qualitatively reviewing the evolution of employee-centred HRM research and contemporary developments that aim to provide a more nuanced understanding of worker health in the context of HRM.

Conclusion

Whatever its meaning, it has become common practice for organisations to label their people management function 'HRM'. This may mean a wide range of things in practice, that it could be argued that the term HRM should now be simply taken as a common noun to denote all aspects of managerial practice devoted to the management of employees, and, indeed, encompass dynamic ways in which employees may respond to the latter. Although there is much evidence that different types of HRM are concentrated in different places, no national system is so effective as to impose a single uniform model (Wood et al. 2014). Again, although investors tend to follow different time horizons in different settings, much of the diversity in HRM can be understood in terms of the latter's agendas and how effective they are in imposing them. By the same measure, there has been a growing recognition that what is good for short-term activist investors is often not only bad for employees but for sustaining the organisation and, indeed, other investors with longer term horizons (Collings, 2014; Wood et al. 2014). Although HR managers often lack the power, ability and sometimes will to impact on the way in which the organisation is governed, it is important that, at least, they retain an awareness of such issues and the manner in which this will impact how they discharge their own roles.

Around the time of the emergence of HRM, many contributors were convinced that HRM was a 'fragile plant', which they predicted would not survive. Within a short time, however, the signs were that its position was more positive than such an interpretation would suggest (see Storey, 2007); others were quick to dismiss it as a noxious weed. However, despite the unresolved issues regarding its intellectual boundaries, HRM has endured and gained an important place in managerial practice in organisations, even if as little more than a collective noun to describe many practices. For Keith Sisson (2007: 79) HRM 'appears to have firmly established its supremacy over personnel management'. While another key UK contributor, John Storey (2007: 17), eloquently summarises the position of HRM in modern organisations thus:

> Clearly, HRM is no panacea; no set of employment policies ever will be. But, as a persuasive account (or narrative) of the logic underpinning choice in certain organizations and as an aspiration pathway for others, it is an idea worthy of examination.

We hope that the contributions in the current text go some way towards introducing students to some of the key debates in the field of HRM. Further, the leading edge contributors advance debates in this key area of management practice.

References

Armstrong, M. (1987). Human Resource Management: A case of the emperor's new clothes. *Personnel Management,* 19(8), 30–35.

Beardwell, I. (2001). An introduction to human resource management: Strategy, style or outcome. In I. Beardwell and L. Holden (Eds.), *Human Resource Management: A Contemporary Approach,* 3rd ed, (pp. 4–31). Harlow: Prentice Hall.

Beer, M. and Spector, B. (1985). Corporate wide transformations in human resource management. In R. E. Walton and P. R. Lawrence (Eds.), *Human Resource Management, Trends and Challenges.* Boston, MA: Harvard Business School Press.

Beer, M., Boselie, P. and Brewster, C. (2015). Back to the future: Implications for the field of HRM of the multistakeholder perspective proposed 30 years ago. *Human Resource Management,* 54(3), 427–438.

Beer, M., Spector, B., Lawrence, P. R., Quinn Mills, D., and Walton, R. E. (1984). *Managing Human Assets.* New York: Free Press.

Blinn, P. J. (2013). Which retailer is the socially responsible one? http://beta.fool.com/pjblinn/2013/03/05/costco-vs-wal-mart-socially-responsible-pick/25492/.

Bloom, N., Han, R. and Liang, J. (2024). Hybrid working from home improves retention without damaging performance. *Nature,* 630, 920–925.

Blyton, P. and Turnbull, P. (1992). HRM: Debates, dilemmas and contradictions. In P. Blyton & P. Turnbull (Eds.), *Reassessing Human Resource Management.* London: Sage.

Boxall, P. and Purcell, J. (2008). *Strategy and Human Resource Management,* 2nd ed. Basingstoke: Palgrave Macmillan.

Brewster, C. (2007). Human Resource Management: European views and perspectives. *International Journal of Human Resource Management,* 18, 769–787.

Brewster, C., Goergen, M. and Wood, G. (2011). Corporate governance systems and employment relations. In A. Wilkinson and M. Townshend (Eds.), *The Future of Employment Relations: New Paradigms, New Developments.* London: Palgrave Macmillan.

Brewster, C., Goergen, M., Wood, G. and Wilkinson, A. (2012). Varieties of capitalism and investments in human capital. *Industrial Relations*, 51(s1), 501–527.

Budhwar, P., Chowdhury, S., Wood, G., Aguinis, H., Bamber, G. J., Beltran, J. R., Boselie, P., Lee Cooke, F., Decker, S., DeNisi, A. and Dey, P. K. (2023). Human resource management in the age of generative artificial intelligence: Perspectives and research directions on ChatGPT. *Human Resource Management Journal*, 33(3), 606–659.

Cafferkey, K. and Dundon, T. (2015). Explaining the black box: HPWS and organisational climate. *Personnel Review*, 44(5), 666–688.

Cascio, W. F. (2006). Decency means more than 'Always Low Prices': A comparison of Costco to Wal-Mart's Sam's Club. *Academy of Management Perspectives*, 20(3), 26–37.

Collings, D. G. (2014). Toward mature talent management: Beyond shareholder value. *Human Resource Development Quarterly*, 25(3), 301–319.

Collings, D. G., McMackin, J., Nyberg, A. J. and Wright, P. M. (2021a). Strategic human resource management and COVID-19: Emerging challenges and research opportunities. *Journal of Management Studies*, 58(5), 1378.

Collings, D. G., Nyberg, A. J., Wright, P. M. and McMackin, J. (2021b). Leading through paradox in a COVID-19 world: Human resources comes of age. *Human Resource Management Journal*, 31(4), 819–833.

D'Art, D. (2002). Managing the employment relationship in a market economy. In D. D'Art and T. Turner (Eds.), *Irish Employment Relations in the New Economy.* Dublin: Blackhall.

Darwish, T. K., Wood, G., Singh, S. and Singh, R. (2020). Human resource management in India: Performance and complementarity. *European Management Review*, 17(2), 373–389.

Datta, S., Budhwar, P., Agarwal, U. A. and Bhargava, S. (2023). Impact of HRM practices on innovative behaviour: Mediating role of talent development climate in Indian firms. *The International Journal of Human Resource Management*, 34(6), 1071–1096.

Dibben, P., James, P., Roper, I. and Wood, G. (2007). *Modernising Work in Public Services: Redefining Roles and Relationships in Britain's Changing Workplace.* London: Palgrave Macmillan.

Dibben, P. and Wood, G. (2011). Union renewal: Objective circumstances and social action. In G. Gall, A. Wilkinson, and R. Hurd (Eds.), *The International Handbook of Labour Unions.* Cheltenham: Edward Elgar.

Drucker, P. (1961). *The Practice of Management.* London: Mercury Books.

Flanders, A. (1964). *Industrial Relations: What is Wrong with the System.* London: Faber and Faber.

Forbrun, C., Tichy, N. M. and Devanna, M. A. (Eds.) (1984). *Strategic Human Resource Management.* New York: Wiley.

Graeber, D. (2019). *Bullshit Jobs: A Theory.* New York: Simon and Schuster.

Guest, D. E. (1987). Human resource management and industrial relations. *Journal of Management Studies*, 24, 503–521.

Guest, D. E. (1990). Human resource management and the American dream. *Journal of Management Studies*, 27, 977–987.

Guest, D. E. (2001). Human resource management and the American dream. *Journal of Management Studies*, 27, 377–397.

Gunnigle, P., Heraty, N. and Morley, M. J. (2006). *Human Resource Management in Ireland*, 3rd ed. Dublin: Gill and Macmillan.

Hammonds, K. H. (2005). Why we hate HR. *Fast Company*, 97, 40.

Harney, B. and Collings, D. G. (2021). Navigating the shifting landscapes of HRM. *Human Resource Management Review*, 31(4), 100824.

Hart, T. (1993). Human resource management – Time to exorcise the militant tendency. *Employee Relations*, 15(3), 29–36.

Hendry, C. and Pettigrew, A. (1990). Human resource management: An agenda for the 1990s. *International Journal of Human Resource Management*, 1, 17–43.

Huselid, M. A. (1995). The impact of human resource management practices on turnover, productivity, and corporate financial performance. *Academy of Management Journal*, 38, 635–672.

Huselid, M. A., Jackson. S. E. and Schuler, R. S. (1997). Technical and strategic human resource management effectiveness as determinants of firm performance. *Academy of Management Journal*, 40, 171–188.

Hyman, R. (1989). *The Political Economy of Industrial Relations: Theory and Practice in a Cold Climate*. London: Macmillan.

Jacoby, S. M. (1997). *Modern Manors: Welfare Capitalism Since the New Deal*. Princeton, NJ: Princeton University Press.

Johnstone, S. (2023). Hard and soft HRM. In *Encyclopedia of Human Resource Management* (pp. 165–166). Cheltenham: Edward Elgar Publishing.

Kaufman, B. E. (2001). The theory and practice of strategic HRM and participative management: Antecedents in early industrial relations. *Human Resource Management Review*, 11, 505–533.

Kaushik, D. and Mukherjee, U. (2022). High-performance work system: A systematic review of literature. *International Journal of Organizational Analysis*, 30(6), 1624–1643.

Kelly, J. (1998). *Rethinking Industrial Relations*. London: Routledge.

Kersley, B., Alpin, C., Forth, J., Bryson, A., Brewley, H., Dix, G. and Oxenbridge, S. (2006). *Inside the Workplace: Findings from the 2004 Workplace Employment Relations Survey*. London: Routledge.

Kochan, T. A., Katz, H. C. and McKersie, R. B. (1986). *The Transformation of American Industrial Relations*. New York: Basic Books.

Lawler, E. E. (2014). HR should own organizational effectiveness. *Forbes*. https://www.forbes.com/sites/edwardlawler/2014/02/11/hr-should-own-organizational-effectiveness/#586a66261e46.

Lawler, E. E. (2017). *Reinventing Talent Management: Principles and Practices for the New World of Work*. Oakland, CA: Berrett-Koehler.

Lees, S. (1997). HRM and legitimacy market. *International Journal of Human Resource Management*, 8, 226–243.

Legge, K. (1995). *Human Resource Management: Rhetorics and Realities*. Basingstoke: Palgrave Macmillan.

Leidner, R. (2002). Fast food in the United States of America. In T. Royle and B. Towers (Eds.), *Labour Relations in the Global Fast Food Industry*. London: Routledge.

Marsden, D. (1999). *A Theory of Employment Systems.* Oxford: Oxford University Press.

Mellahi, K., Morell, K. and Wood, G. (2010). *The Ethical Business: Challenges and Controversies.* London: Palgrave Macmillan.

Millward, N., Bryson, A. and Forth, J. (2000). *All Change at Work? British Employment Relations 1980–1998, as Portrayed by the Workplace Industrial Relations Surveys Series.* London: Routledge.

Nyberg, A.J., Schleicher, D.J., Bell, B., Boon, C., Cappell, P., Collings, D.G., Dalle Molle, J.E., Feuerriegel, S., Gerhart, B., Jeong, Y., Korsgaard, A., Minbaeva, D., Ployhart, R. Tambe, P., Weller, I., Wright, P. & Yakubovich, V. (2025) "A Brave New World of HR Research: Identifying Grand Challenges of the GenAI Revolution", *Journal of Management*

Paauwe, J. and Farndale, E. (2004). *Strategy, HRM and Performance: Achieving Long Term Viability a Contextual Approach*, 2nd ed. Oxford: Oxford University Press.

Peters, T. J. and Waterman, R. H., Jr. (1982). *In Search of Excellence: Lessons from America's Best Run Companies.* New York: Harper and Row.

Sisson, K. (2007). Facing up to the challenges of success: Putting 'governance' at the heart of HRM. In J. Storey (Ed.), *Human Resource Management: A Critical Text*, 3rd ed. London: Thompson Publishing.

Smith, K. (2011). What do 1.5 million Wal-Mart women have in common?: Dukes v. Wal-Mart class action certification. *Boston College Law Review*, 52, 149.

Stahl, G. K., Brewster, C. J., Collings, D. G. and Hajro, A. (2020). Enhancing the role of human resource management in corporate sustainability and social responsibility: A multi-stakeholder, multidimensional approach to HRM. *Human Resource Management Review*, 30(3), 100708.

Storey, J. (1992). *Developments in the Management of Human Resources.* Oxford: Blackwell.

Storey, J. (2007). Human resource management today: An assessment. In J. Storey (Ed.), *Human Resource Management: A Critical Text*, 3rd ed. London: Thompson Publishing.

Strauss, G. (2001). Human resource management in the USA: Correcting some British impressions, *International Journal of Human Resource Management*, 12, 873–897.

Ton, Z. (2023). *The Case for Good Jobs: How Great Companies Bring Dignity, Pay, and Meaning to Everyone's Work.* Cambridge, MA: Harvard Business Review Press.

Tyson, S. (1985). Is this the very model of a modern personnel manager? *Personnel Management*, 17(5), 22–25.

Tyson, S. and Fell, A. (1986). *Evaluating the Personnel Function.* London: Hutchinson.

van Wanrooy, B., Bewley, H., Bryson, H., Forth, J., Freeth, S., Stokes, L., and Wood, S. (2013) *The 2011 Workplace Employment Relations Survey: First Findings.* London: WERS.

Walton, R. E. and Lawrence, P. R. (Eds.) (1985). *Human Resource Management, Trends and Challenges.* Boston, MA: Harvard Business School Press.

Wilkinson, A., Wood, G., and Deeg, R. (Eds.). (2014). *Oxford Handbook of Employment Relations: Comparative Employment Systems.* Oxford: Oxford University Press.

Wood, G., Brewster, C., and Brookes, M. (2014). *Human Resource Management and the Institutional Perspective.* New York: Routledge.

Wood, G. and Vitai, Z. (2014). *Strategic Human Resource Management*, G. Rees and P. Smith, Eds. London: Sage.

Zhang, M., Di Fan, D., and Zhu, C. J. (2014). High-performance work systems, corporate social performance and employee outcomes: Exploring the missing links. *Journal of Business Ethics*, 120, 423–435.

Section One

Context of HRM

2 HRM in Changing Organisational Contexts

Phil Johnson and Leslie T. Szamosi

Introduction

The management of human resources (HR) in contemporary organisations is very often prescriptively presented as an interrelated set of activities aimed at systematically enhancing the task performance of employees in a manner commensurate with the strategic aims of the organisation. Numerous researchers (Jacoby, 1985; Langbert, 2002; Townley, 1989; Mueller and Carter, 2005) have noted that how, and under what circumstances, these managerial practices are accomplished varies in response to an array of social and economic influences of which one key source is the broader organisational context in which they take place.

In recent years, the impact of economic crises (eg Psychogios et al, 2014) and the COVID-19 pandemic (eg Haque, 2023) are illustrative of the extrinsic influences that have impacted on people management. Here we are immediately confronted as well by the often rather optimistically presented forecast that work organisations are progressively changing through the evolution of what are described as post-bureaucratic, flexible, high-performance forms of organisation and management (Heckscher, 1994; Osbourne and Plastrik, 1998; Volberda, 1998; Applebaum et al, 2000; Maravelias, 2003; Hendry, 2006; Josserand et al. 2006) as well as changes in economic and political systems (eg Serafini et al, 2020). These 'new' (Hastings, 1993) organisational forms arise out of the recasting of roles, relationships and tasks within organisations at the expense of traditional bureaucratic modes of control related more directly to employee task performance, yet there continues to be conflicting evidence about its success (Dischner, 2015; Daood and Giustiniano, 2024).

In this chapter we take a historical exploration of the implications of these developments, with a particular focus on the economic crisis and digitalisation (including artificial intelligence as a precursor to an entire chapter in this book) that has been reshaped for the practice of HRM. We first review the key characteristics of the bureaucratic form and the various conditions perceived as necessary for its successful implementation. We then evaluate the pressures faced by contemporary work organisations that are often deemed to be undermining the viability of the bureaucratic form and ostensibly encouraging the

DOI: 10.4324/9781032625560-3

evolution of post-bureaucratic systems. Then, we outline the nature of the post-bureaucratic form of organisation as presented by various authors before moving on to the possible implications for HRM praxis, and we conclude by considering alternative views of contemporary organisational change that cast some doubt upon the claims of this post-bureaucratic thesis.

The Bureaucratic Organisational Form

It has been well documented that bureaucratic forms of organisation arose on a large scale in western Europe and the USA, during the late 19th and early 20th centuries, as a means of replacing earlier forms of work organisation (eg Clawson, 1980; Littler, 1982). Weber (1947) suggested that one of the most distinctive features of such administrative systems was the development of a framework of intentionally established and impersonal rules to govern task performance. For Weber, this 'required' the subordination of workers to the precise calculation of the means by which specific ends may be achieved. Through the exercise of formal rationality, these rules (ie, orders from above) were designed by superiors who occupied their posts based on merit (eg higher levels of expert knowledge, experience and/or expertise) and they possessed formal-legal authority. The creation of rules and procedures, supported by various means of monitoring, evaluating, rewarding and sanctioning compliance, served to pre-programme task performance, remove most, if not all, choice or discretion with regard to how work would be accomplished and increased the probability that perceived organisational requirements would dominate that behaviour. The result is that ...

> *... the fully developed bureaucratic apparatus compares with other organizations exactly as does the machine with the non-mechanical modes of production. Precision, speed, unambiguity, knowledge of the files, continuity, discretion, unity, strict subordination, reduction of friction and of material and personal costs – these are raised to the optimum point in the strictly bureaucratic organization ...*
>
> *(Weber, 1947: 973)*

Whilst Weber thought that the development of bureaucracy was progressive given that it did away with earlier organisation forms he regarded as irrational, he was fearful of its potential for creating an imprisoning 'iron cage' (1904: 1264) and the danger that people whose aims were not founded in the best interests of society as a whole could gain command and misdirect the purpose of the bureaucratic machine. In bureaucracies, the routine application of discipline, through members' mundane complicitness with the rules, becomes progressively sanctified and normalised (eg Bos and Willmott, 2001), thereby causing various levels of organisational stagnation or systems which fail to comprehend the ethical severity of their actions. As such, the means come to dominate the ends and workers fail to morally evaluate the ends to which their everyday activities in organisations are working towards. For writers such as Bauman (1989), bureaucracies may enable, rationalise, distance and render banal engagement in horrific acts such as those associated with the Holocaust. In opposition to Bauman's portrayal of bureaucracy as dehumanising, du Gay has pointed to how 'objectivity' required by the bureaucrat to follow rule-based frameworks can result in the virtuous 'trained capacity to treat people as individual cases ... so that the partialities of patronage and the dangers of corruption might be avoided' (2000: 42). As such, if bureaucracy evolves in step with society, and the changes in society, this dehumanising aspect can be somewhat downgraded.

As in the case of Taylorism, bureaucratic control processes resulted in various levels of job fragmentation and specialisation as a means towards simplifying tasks to enable the measurement of effort expended and the administration of incentives to encourage greater effort (reward and punishment orientations). As such, it is closely associated with the development of modern forms of work study and industrial engineering, which use a variety of scientific techniques for deriving standard times and methods for undertaking tasks, planning and standardising work flows with detailed divisions of labour and creating precise job descriptions: the operation of piecework payment systems (Littler, 1982; Hales, 1993; Kamei, 2017). As in Fordism and McDonaldisation, bureaucratisation entails the application and integration of technology into the organisational system (eg the assembly line and the use of single-purpose machine tools) as a means towards simplifying tasks and pre-programming the pace and sequencing of labour processes (eg Cooley, 1980; Ritzer, 2006) where the rules governing task performance are built into, and operationalised by, the technology in use. If one considers this in relation to the speed to technological adoption today (AI, digitalisation etc.), the rules are being changed daily.

Given the nature of today's work systems and the inherent reliance on technology-driven systems of production, bureaucratic principles may be seen as a key point of inflection. Yet, despite bureaucracy's dominance throughout much of the 20th century as a form of control over labour processes, it is no longer considered as viable (eg Maravelias, 2003; Becker et al., 2016). The underlying rationale for this presumed demise centres upon a key characteristic of bureaucratic superstructures, namely, that they are somehow dependent upon a hierarchical ordering of knowledge, in the form of 'task continuity', as the basis of rational-legal authority. Task continuity generally refers to the requirement that in order to write and administer the rules necessary for pre-programming and standardising tasks, superiors must be able to conceptualise or rationalise what their subordinates should be doing, how, where and when, to achieve the required efficiency and effectiveness sought. This is only achievable when superiors have gained the knowledge required and then applied it through reconfiguring and standardising the execution of those tasks by operatives; however, when tasks are complex, unpredictable and unanalysable, knowledge for acquisition, reconfiguration and regulation is not readily available. Thus, the complexities of such tasks do not easily adhere themselves to bureaucratic hierarchical ordering to identify the 'best' way of doing tasks and thereby enable the divorce of task conception from its execution. In today's 'creative' and open-innovation workplace environments, such bureaucratic systems could be highly problematic. In situations of task discontinuity, it becomes necessary to develop alternative forms of control that leave task conceptualisation and the identification of how best to undertake tasks to the discretion and intuition of the experienced operative by (re)uniting all aspects of task performance into a coherent whole.

In sum, it has been argued that the application of formal rationality to mould collective behaviour is applicable in conditions of environmental stability where there is a relatively constant and homogeneous throughput of goods and/or services (eg provisioning of a standardised product such as cheese or a mobile phone or public services). In these circumstances, task requirements and transformation processes are already known, and by their very nature, predictable; therefore, it becomes possible to assert control through hierarchically generated rules and procedures that standardise, pre-programme, monitor and enforce/reinforce the required task performance (Mintzberg, 1979; Drucker, 1993; Daft, 1998). Regardless of the specific form of bureaucracy adopted, Human Resource Management (HRM), or given such circumstances, more accurately termed Personnel Management (PM) (Guest, 1991), is geared towards servicing such bureaucratic requirements. According to Guest (ibid.), in such circumstances, PM is primarily associated with external and instrumental 'compliance-based' systems of control, largely dependent upon collectively negotiated systems of extrinsic rewards, thus ensuring efficiency and cost minimisation within a centralised, mechanistic, organisational structure. Hence, the management of personnel within bureaucracies is centred on the creation of detailed job descriptions and specifications; the negotiation and implementation of payment systems to support the effort-reward nexus; minimal operative training for undertaking de-skilled tasks; the administration of management development with a focus upon succession planning through the dissemination of requisite technical skills and the maintenance of related promotion and career structures; and the procedural regulation of industrial relations in concert with elected employee representatives.

A wide cross-section of authors have argued that control through the monitoring of subordinate compliance with bureaucratic rules and procedures becomes increasingly difficult if tasks are, or become, non-routine (Perrow, 1967), emergent (Mohrman et al., 1990), deconstructed (Rogiers & Collings, 2024) and differentiated (Clegg, 1990), since the task behaviour required for efficient and effective task performance becomes, unknowable to, and therefore not pre-programmable by, those elevated in the meritocratic hierarchies of rational-legal authority (Ouchi, 1979; 1980). It is precisely the relatively recent emergence of these conditions that are thought to threaten the viability and sanctity of bureaucratic forms of work organisation today and, hence, changing the form that the management of HR should take.

Changing Organisational Environments and the Development of Post-Bureaucracy

Various authors have claimed that the social, economic, political and technological environment in which organisations operate have fundamentally changed more dramatically in some areas of the world than others (eg Annosi and Brunetta, 2017; Innocenti et al, 2017; Serafini et al, 2020). It has been argued that the production, distribution, exchange and consumption of goods and services have dramatically accelerated and become increasingly diverse, specialised and temporary: a destabilised 'casino capitalism' (Bluestone and Harrison, 1988; Strange, 2015) or 'hypercapitalism' (Rifkind, 2000) of 'globalization and relativisation' (Robertson, 1992), of 'intensified risk and reflexivity' (Beck, 2000a, b), of 'heterogenization' (Daudi, 1990) and 'time-space compression'. Commentators have also called this period the end of organised capitalism (Lash and Urry, 1987), the age of unreason (Handy, 1989), post-capitalist society (Drucker, 1993) and a runaway world (Giddens, 1999). Regardless of the label used, their uniting axiom is that we have entered an unstable socio-historical configuration, which is, by definition, pushing organisations towards new designs as managers try to cope with irreversible dramatic changes that are thought to be gaining speed, characterised by volatility, uncertainty, complexity and ambiguity (VUCA) (Bennett and Lemoine, 2014). According to this 'fast capitalism' view, the main casualties here are, or should be, bureaucratic organisations that are seen as incapable of efficiently coping with this new world order (eg Heckscher, 1994; Castells, 1996).

In his analysis of Western society, Beck (1992; 1997; 2000a, b) argues that we have moved into a risk-driven society that has evolved into something inherently more complex, dynamic and uncertain (2000b) where along with the continued accumulation of knowledge and its application through scientific and technological innovation comes an awareness of 'the incalculability of their consequences' (Beck, 1992: 22). At the more macro level, Beck draws attention to the ecological implications of these developments and the unsettling consequences of globalisation (2000b) while at the micro level, concerns rest with the need for individuals to reconcile themselves to an enduring sense of insecurity wherein individuals are required to create, live and take responsibility for their own lives (Beck and Beck-Gernsheim, 2002). At the meso level, he draws attention to how institutions are developing in a society dominated by our collective awareness of the unintended consequences of institutions calling into question the legitimacy of said institutions. His view is that social changes are occurring that are 'opening up Weber's bureaucratic iron cage' (2000a: 222) through the requirement to balance and cope reflexively with risk that escapes bureaucratic control and to respond to a more chaotic and uncertain world. Beck is cautious here, however, as he suggests that these processes have not seen an end to bureaucracy through its replacement by more responsive institutional configurations. This drives towards the displacement and restoration of bureaucratic features as outcomes of ongoing internal struggles in which institutions attempt to gain and maintain trust in authority and hierarchy while providing levels of flexibility and tolerance to changes (Pahi et al, 2024; de Laat, 2023).

In contrast, much of management literature is less circumspect regarding the institutional outcomes of these processes. For instance, as Osbourne and Gaebler summarised it in their highly influential book, bureaucratic organisations 'increasingly fail us' because what is demanded are institutions that are extremely flexible and adaptable, 'that [are] lead by persuasion and incentives rather than commands; that give their employees a sense of meaning and control, even ownership' (1992:15). The reasoning behind such claims relates directly to the earlier argument: knowledge and information are no longer hierarchically ordered and distributed in contemporary organisations. This is because the destabilising disturbances caused by what is classified as either late modernity (Giddens, 1990; 1991) or post-modernity (Lyon, 1994; Wagner, 1992) make the world less comprehensible to various actors. Due to their top-down mode of command and control, bureaucracies are 'condemned' as being sclerotic, especially when faced with demands for constant innovation and change caused by unstable and unpredictable organisational environments and other disturbances such as rapid technological change. These destabilising forces are seen to be endemic and thus affect all organisations (Peters, 1992; Quinn, 1992; Savage, 1996). Such an organisational situation requires employees who are capable of using their intuition, discretion and often superior local or international knowledge to creatively and flexibly deal with unpredictable variations in production and service demands, as and when they arise, rather than merely complying with pre-formulated rules and procedures or waiting for the direct supervisory commands or permission of managers. The result has been an emerging organisational literature couched largely in terms of post-bureaucracy which has direct implications for how the management of human resources could be undertaken, as can be seen in the digitalisation era (eg Mustafa et al, 2022).

Although the language used does vary, a key argument has been to point to both the demise of bureaucratic organisations and to celebrate their replacement by emergent alternative organisational forms that go 'beyond bureaucracy' (Laffin, 1998), even 'banishing' it (Osbourne and Plastrik, 1998) to constitute an ostensibly 'new work order' (Gee et al., 1996) – the post-bureaucracy. This is presented as a necessary response to conditions of continual change and uncertainty: a flatter, more networked and flexible organisation wherein 'empowered' employees are vested with high degrees of 'responsible autonomy' and self-management so that they can immediately respond to unpredictable demands in an efficient and effective manner.

This post-bureaucratic view has tacitly appropriated and redirected several important concepts previously deployed by organisation theorists including, for example, organic versus mechanistic structures (Burns and Stalker, 1961); the implications of environmental uncertainty and instability (Lawrence and Lorsch, 1967); the flexible firm (Atkinson, 1984); flexible specialisation (Piore and Sable, 1984); adhocracy (Mintzberg, 1979) and network organisations

(Miles and Snow, 1986). The relatively nuanced and contextualised theoretical use of many of these concepts, usually under the aegis of a perspective derived from contingency theory, has been superseded by what amounts to a universalistic prescription as it is assumed that conditions of uncertainty and instability now affect all organisations. Indeed, the term post-bureaucracy often signifies a perceived rupture with the organisational tenets of a bygone age. Here the bureaucratic 'paradigm' is (re)presented as something that is 'outmoded' as it is now judged to be obsolete and counterproductive rather than contingently viable according to circumstances (eg Barzelay with Armajani, 1992; Heckscher, 1994), oftentimes encompassing the moral dimension. For instance, the presumed 'defunct' bureaucracies are often presented as being oppressive and patriarchal, whereas post-bureaucracies are nuances to be empowering and involving everyone in decision-making and, hence, are presumed to be inherently morally 'superior' as they are more likely to meet the needs of today's employees; healthy adults through how they are organised (eg Savage, 1996; Melnic, 2022).

Implications of Post-Bureaucracy for HRM

The post-bureaucratic organisational form seeks to liberate employees from the increasingly dysfunctional hierarchical constraints engendered by bureaucracies and enhance their ability to deal with the requirements of an increasingly destabilised working environment (Adler, 2001; Beneviste, 1994). As Castells typically summarises, post-bureaucratic organisations must cope with uncertainty through a 'greater need for an autonomous educated worker able and willing to program and decide entire sequences of work' (1996: 241). Thus, the intention is to create a workforce capable of adaptation rather than dependent upon routinised repertoires (Stark, 2001) and one which is customer-driven yet empowered to make judgements on how to improve customer service and value (Kernaghan, 2000). This is achieved by the creation of functionally flexible high-performance workforces (Kalleberg, 2003; Shin and Konrad, 2017), where multiskilled employees are empowered to exercise discretion and cope with discontinuous change by continuously (re)developing their organisational roles in the face of shifting demands (Volberda, 1998; Wood, 1999) made increasingly unpredictable due to the destabilising disturbances outlined. This leads us to a central tenet of the post-bureaucratic thesis, shared general principles, rather than rules, guide and integrate members' actions (Heckscher, 1994). The 'master concept' here is the replacement of bureaucratic controls with 'structures that develop informed consent' where command replaces feelings of mutuality and commitment, embedded in organisational processes that produce dialogue, persuasion and trust (eg Osbourne and Plastrik, 1998).

A key characteristic of post-bureaucracy is employee empowerment, usually defined in terms of management ceding to employees the capacity to determine cooperatively certain aspects of their work (Englehardt and Simmons, 2002; Maravelias, 2003; Wilkinson, 1998), without waiting for 'permission and direction from top management' (Quinn and Spreitzer, 1997: 45) and identifying and removing 'conditions that promote powerlessness' (Conger and Kanungo, 1988: 474) while enabling senior managers to retain a measure of overall control. Empowerment is generally aimed at engendering employees' 'directed' autonomous self-management anchored in a sense of purpose and direction often provided by the systematic dissemination of an entrepreneurial ethic articulated and propagated by the strategic goals of the enterprise (Black and Porter, 2000). Thus, the extension and reconfiguration of roles is restricted to their local involvement in deciding the means by which the strategic agenda set may be more effectively implemented through their exercise of discretion over how tasks are completed (see also Kochan and Osterman, 2002; Menon, 2001; Wallach and Mueller, 2006). Through a range of HRM practices that stimulate, support and sustain self-discipline, self-determination and self-development, whilst instilling a sense of organisational commitment and enhancing motivation, it is purported that an empowered workforce becomes a source of competitive advantage through improved employee task performance (Aarthi and Sujatha, 2022) Applebaum et al., 2000; Patterson et al., 2004) and job satisfaction (Mathew and Nair, 2022; Seibert et al., 2004).

This form of employee participation is not just about broader task design but it is also usually operationalised through the creation of autonomous teamwork where empowered teams 'make decisions, implement them and are held accountable' (Randolph, 1994: 28). The result is a workforce organised through temporary team-based and project-related activities that appear and disappear according to ever-shifting organisational requirements (Neff and Stark, 2003) with enhanced horizontal collaborations implemented as a means towards improving communication and speed up decision-making (Kellogg et al., 2006). Advocates present such team-working as a means of facilitating and enhancing amongst employees: lateral communication; information sharing between and within organisational levels; cooperative problem ownership and resolution through critical evaluation of existing organisation processes channelled by a commitment to continuous improvement (eg Brodbeck, 2002; Ozaralli, 2003; Seibert et al., 2004; Beirne, 2006).

According to some authors (eg Applebaum et al., 1999; Mills and Ungson, 2003; Quinn and Spreitzer, 1997), however, cascading decision-making power may create centrifugal tendencies and the need to reconcile a possible loss of management control with the requirement for integration of a loosely-coupled system through ensuring goal congruence. This requires a shift from bureaucratic modalities of control to less obtrusive culturally-based, normative, ideational or clan modalities as a more viable means of disciplining employees by reconstructing employee subjectivity so that it is commensurate with senior management's perceived requirements (eg Serafini and Szamosi, 2015; Alvesson and Willmott, 2002; Beirne, 2006; Hodgson, 2004; Menon, 2001). Whilst cultural forms of control are often deployed alongside bureaucratic modalities to create chimerical forms of control or to reduce reliance upon the bureaucracy (eg Hales, 2002), it is the high level of reliance upon culture management as a mode of control that is usually presented as one of the distinguishing characteristics of the post-bureaucratic ideal-type.

As Kunda (1992) notes, instead of overtly focusing upon members' actual behaviour, or the outcomes as such, normative or cultural control is a more hidden and insidious type of formal control which focuses upon the basic value premises that surround members' behaviour and decision-making to normatively regulate the employee's consciousness. For Kunda, the concept of culture has both cognitive and affective dimensions referring to what members know and emotionally feel about their organisation and their work. Thus, normative cultural control is based upon establishing 'intense emotional attachment and the internalisation of clearly enunciated company values' (ibid.: 10). As such, controllers must attempt to ensure that subordinates internalise, or have already internalised, the values, beliefs and attitudes that are deemed to be supportive of the organisational goals set by hierarchical superiors. As Kunda observes,

> ... *under normative control, membership is founded not on the behavioural or economic transaction traditionally associated with work organizations, but, more crucially, on an experiential transaction, one in which symbolic rewards are exchanged for a moral orientation to the organization.*
> (1992: 2)

In a similar vein, Anthony (1994: 92) observes that 'bureaucratic control, from the perspective of the controllers, unfortunately leaves subordinates free, partly because they possess their own cultural defences. So the defences must be broken down'. Once these cultural defences are lowered, informal peer group pressure upon the individual member is redirected and begins to marshal management approved norms (eg Barker, 1997). A possible result is 'an overcoming of the division between the 'personal life', values and beliefs of employees and the impersonal demands of corporations for greater productivity and quality' (Willmott, 1993: 523). So, if the appropriate values are subscribed to, a common sense of purpose or 'moral involvement', activated through emotion and sentiment, develops which makes the constant surveillance and supervision of employees by managers, as a means of external control, redundant. Ironically, this alternative source of discipline and control over the employee through the management of culture could, in principle, reduce the need for some tiers of management, thereby contributing to the delayering of organisations, among other HRM implications.

An important means by which culture management may be attempted is through the deployment of sophisticated recruitment and selection procedures aimed at pre-emptive control of the attitudinal and behavioural characteristics of new organisational members (Brannan and Hawkins, 2007; Kochan and Osterman, 2002). Thus, through the use of assessment centres, psychometric tests, personal history inventories and indices of loyalty etc. a systematic attempt is made to help ensure that the attitudinal and behavioural characteristics of new employees match the prescribed organisational culture, thereby trying to exclude the introduction of alternative sources of social influence deriving from, for instance, communities outside the organisation; trade unions, professional groupings and so on. Simultaneously, redundancy may be used as a tool to minimise alternative values by removing those who appear unable, or unwilling, to embrace the specified culture (Dobson, 1988). Besides attempting to alter the composition of the workforce using recruitment, selection and redundancy, there may also be concerted managerial attempts to influence the value premises of members' behaviour by trying to restructure attitudes and beliefs through the use of an array of related HRM practices (eg Wood et al., 2012; Hope and Hendry, 1995; Legge, 1995; Guest, 1998). For instance, induction, training, appraisal and reward systems may be formally realigned to disseminate and reinforce displays of culturally acceptable behaviour.

Thus, HRM praxis may play a key role in attempting to resolve the control-consent dilemma created by empowerment programmes and their diffusion of elements of management prerogative downwards, through directing (Waterman, 1988) employees' exercise of initiative and self-management including through the development of 'responsible autonomy' that harnesses 'their loyalty to the firm's ideals (the competitive struggle) ideologically' (Friedman, 1977: 5; 1990; Harley 2005). In this fashion, the control-consent dilemma is resolved through the delineation of how, where and when employees may exercise autonomy and power through reconstructing their subjectivity in line with management's requirements (Knights and McCabe, 2004; Elmes and Smith, 2001; Maravelias, 2003). Where this strategy is effective, the means by which employees constitute their own identities is merged with how they exercise self-regulation, and as Miller and Rose (1990: 26) suggest, 'the 'autonomous' subjectivity of the productive individual ... [becomes] ... a central economic resource'. The result is that employee evaluation processes then become a (contentious) matter of assessing members' behaviour through reference to the observable manifestation of sanctioned cultural mores and sentiments in the performance of their tasks and their relationships with other members, customers, clients and so on.

By extending employees' participation in deciding the means by which strategic decisions are implemented through enabling/allowing them to exercise discretion over how, when and at what pace work is undertaken, certain management functions usurped through the development of bureaucracy are reappropriated by operatives and the traditional division between management and 'labour' becomes blurred. In order to support these developments. managers must change according to many advocates. No longer can management practice be founded upon an authoritative articulation of (usually incalculable and inevitably dysfunctional) rules aimed at controlling subordinates' workplace behaviours. Instead, what is required are managers capable of deploying 'learning leadership' (Senge, 1990) in the form of horizontal communication and dialogue in mutually therapeutic relationships (Tucker; 1999). As such, managerial roles such as *coach* (Lyons and Bandura, 2023; Ben-Hador, 2023), *mentor* (Garvey and Alred, 2001) and *co-learner* (Marquardt, 1996) become crucial – roles that require managers with a knowledge and skill base substantially different to those required by bureaucracies (see Hendry, 2006).

There is also an increasing emphasis upon leadership at the expense of management where leadership is construed in terms of articulating, promulgating and inculcating in others an organisational vision and mission often driven by some form of strategic analysis of the 'big picture' that confronts the 'business' (eg Dubrin, 2001). In essence, leaders are presented as visionaries who anticipate and initiate changes through communicating and sharing their visions and enthusing their subordinates: 'leadership' we are told 'creates new patterns of action and new belief systems' (Barker, 1997: 349). Management, on the other hand, is recast and construed as being much more mundane, if not virtually banal. Management becomes about interpreting the leaders' vision and practically implementing it through various organisational processes whilst maintaining and enhancing productivity. According to this discourse, whilst leadership becomes the primary focus of senior managers, individual managers are expected, to some degree, to undertake aspects of both leadership and management in their performance. As Dubrin starkly puts it 'without being led as well as managed, organisations face the threat of extinction' (2001: 4).

Pattinson (1997) describes how the ascription of a special leadership status to managers often entails the deployment of quasi-religious metaphors whereby senior managers are somehow bestowed with mystical capacity akin to latter-day prophets. Here the connotation is that executives are somehow blessed by a higher power because they can see things that others cannot. Such a view of management sets the (senior) manager at the centre stage of organisations and as a crucial influencer upon organisational culture and performance. To do this they must become 'transformational', 'charismatic' leaders – messianic visionaries in the sense that they can invoke, and energetically disseminate to 'followers', a compelling image of an idealised future organisational state, which, through stimulating emotional attachment to, and trust in, the leader, inspires followers to become highly committed to the leader's vision and prepared to make sacrifices towards this (Tourish and Pinnington, 2002).

Although the articulation of these new modes of management and leadership may entail the search for new bases of legitimacy when rational-legal authority is threatened, the ostensible reason for this reconfiguration is to support and facilitate the hallmarks of the post-bureaucracy era: the participation of self-directed employees in decision-making and the dissemination of culturally approved values as a form of commitment-based control. As Hope and Hendry have observed, the required management behaviour also demands 'an investment of "self" rather dogged mimicry of behaviour and values set down in the corporate handbook. If the self is not engaged then power is reduced, for the required behaviour is distanced from the person itself' (1995: 63). Moreover, employees may be alert to disparity between management's cultural rhetoric and their apparent everyday behaviour to the extent that employees may use the espoused values underpinning prescribed cultural change to challenge the inauthenticity signified by such lapses in managerial performance of their corporate script (eg Rosenthal et al., 1997; Linstead, 1999). The dissemination of the prescribed culture often entails reorganisation of the workplace to ensure that those with the required values (at least at the public level of testimony) are in positions of influence, as role models, so that they can communicate these symbolically in their everyday leadership (see Pattinson, 1997; Grugulis et al. 2000) and through their establishment of corporate rites, ceremonies, slogans, stories and myths that indicate appropriate behaviour. Other processes of communication and social interaction might, as Dent (1995) observed, entail some spatial reorganisation by physically locating managers close to those they wish to influence so as enable them to informally nurture and sustain the desired cultural changes. Other means of cultural dissemination and maintenance may include team briefings, quality circles, house journals and the organisation of various social activities that entail 'cultural extravaganza' (Deal and Kennedy: 1982: 74) inside and outside the workplace.

As discussed, employee empowerment, the evolution of new managerial roles etc. must be supported by an array of HRM practices and may be seen as potential post-bureaucratic solutions to the uncertainties created by an array of destabilising disturbances. We have focused, thus far, upon one key means of responding to these demands, through the development of one type of 'labour-led' flexibility where the emphasis is upon the development of a functionally flexible and multiskilled internal workforce capable of exercising their discretion so as to cope with high degrees of task uncertainty. An alternative, yet often complementary way of variably using labour, is via the external labour market which relates to the ease with which employee numbers can be varied to meet fluctuations in demand through the use of temporary employment contracts (Manelkar et al, 2023 Atkinson, 1984; Kalleberg, 2001; 2003). The result may be a division of the workforce into 'peripheral' numerically flexible temporary employees, organised around a numerically stable 'core' of permanent employees, willing and able to learn new skills according to requirements. Thus, increasing levels of internal and external uncertainty, by demanding various forms of flexibility in organisations, may result in a mixture of bureaucratic and post-bureaucratic modalities of control within one organisation (eg Kalleberg, 2001; 2003). One need look no further than the current debate around 'zero-hours contracts' to see the new frontier of flexible organisations and worker uncertainty (Mantouvalou, 2022; Rubery, 2015). Bureaucratic modalities may still be appropriate for numerically flexible peripheries doing relatively unskilled tasks, since the uncertainty of their tasks is around (eg seasonal) fluctuations in the amount of this work, rather than the nature of the tasks themselves being unpredictable. In contrast, the functionally flexible cores may exhibit 'post-bureaucratic' modalities.

An alternative to labour-led flexibility is that of market-led flexibility engendered by network type organisations (Miles and Snow, 1986) characterised by disaggregated operations spread between loosely-coupled clusters of firms (or individuals) distributed throughout the value chain, which are coordinated primarily through contractual arrangements. One need look no further than the post-pandemic movement to what have been termed 'digital nomads' (Shawkat et al, 2021). Such workers are attracted by the combination of lifestyles and co-workation experiences that come with such systems (Chevtaeva and Denizci-Guillet, 2021) and the creation of a neoliberal order thus breaking the aforementioned traditional models (Mancinelli, 2020).

The development of networks entail, to varying degrees, the 'unbundling' of large, vertically integrated organisations through 'downsizing' to a core of value-add competencies (Jarillo, 1993), which include a brokerage role for coordinating the network and the 'outsourcing' or 'externalisation' of other activities that can be done more efficiently by others. Therefore, to varying degrees, networks entail vertical disintegration with individual participatory organisations specialising in the provision of a narrower range of goods and services. Here it is the network as a whole that is flexible, rather than the individual participatory organisation, since it is the mixture of goods and services available that can be altered. As such, networks are seen to constitute 'lean', 'flexible', low-cost structures particularly suited to the ostensible demands of current organisational environments by 'unblocking' organisational learning, innovation and change through the creation of more porous interfaces with their environments (Child and McGrath, 2001; Josserand, 2004). Relationships with, and control over, contractors to whom specific tasks have been outsourced may vary according to the nature of the forms of contractual network governance in place (Powell, 1990; see also Chapter 18 in the current volume on gig-work and job deconstruction).

Conclusions

We have sought to demonstrate that at the heart of the post-bureaucratic thesis are issues of control and changes in how management exercises direction, surveillance and discipline over subordinates in response to increasing levels of uncertainty caused by an array of destabilising disturbances. The thesis claims that there is an ongoing shift in control modalities from those associated with the 'direct' control of subordinates to those more associated with the establishment of 'responsible autonomy' (Harley, 2005), and this has been accelerated largely in part due to the pandemic (Holleran and Notting, 2023). This control shift is usually idealised as the development of empowered, self-regulated members, who, having internalised management, derived cultural norms and then proceeded to exercise 'commitment-based' self-control in a manner commensurable with senior management's strategic aims and objectives. These processes have direct implications for HRM practice as control moves towards purposefully shaping the identities and attitudes of employees, albeit often in a reactive manner (eg Evans, 1999). This shift in control is illustrated and summarised by Table 2.1.

Table 2.1 Bureaucracy and post-bureaucracy compared

Bureaucracy: *Vertical hierarchy*	*Post-Bureaucracy:* *Delayered with team-based heterarchies*
Low trust chains of command	High trust, dialogue/persuasion
Search for predictability and efficiency	Search for flexibility and effectiveness through members' commitment and empowerment
Low-discretion tasks: obedience valued	High-discretion tasks: creativity valued
Control through calculative compliance via rules and incentives	Control through responsible autonomy based on principles anchored in moral involvement
Leadership-based rational-legal authority	Learning-leadership often based on charisma

The shift from bureaucratic to post-bureaucratic modes of organisation and HRM has been presented largely as a demand that has to be accommodated if we accept that increasing levels of turbulence and uncertainty mean that organisational settings are becoming too complex and ambiguous to be managed through bureaucratic modalities of control. There is a tendency in the literature to present post-bureaucracy as unproblematically superior because it is taken to generate, through emotional and sentimental manipulation, internalised self-discipline expressed as feelings of commitment to 'the organisation': employee behavioural outcomes that bureaucratic forms of control, with their focus upon compliance to external sources reward and punishment, cannot systematically deliver. So in relation to its bureaucratic alternatives, post-bureaucracy is often presented as generally, rather than contingently, more effective and efficient because they can reduce bureaucratic impedimenta, flatten hierarchies, cut administrative costs, increase productivity, and crucially increase the agility and responsiveness of organisations to an increasingly destabilised business environment.

As Jaques pointed out, however, 'It appears to be a condition of modernity for every generation to believe it is in the midst of revolutionary change' (1996: 18–19). Here there is an inherent danger of overly rationalising management decision-making and the choices that are made with regard to different organisational forms: that senior managers, by deploying economically rational calculation, consciously seek out and implement efficiency-optimising solutions to secure unambiguous organisational goals in the discharge of their fiduciary shareholder responsibilities, in the case of private sector, (or elected representatives in the case of the public sector). Such assumptions about managerial behaviour are dubious as they treat managers as if they were all-knowing, yet servile, agents of capital's interests – a characterisation that has been widely questioned and exposed by both theoretical and empirical research (eg Jackall, 1988; Watson, 1994; Cappelli, et al., 1997; Grint 1995; Buchanan and Badham, 1999). A result of this characterisation is that the description of changes in organisational form and prescription about these processes become entangled. As well, an analysis that theoretically explains the evolution of post-bureaucracy as a necessary progressive response to demands arising from the need for efficiency and competitive advantage in changing organisational circumstances propelled by the destabilising disturbances previously is also too simplistic.

In contrast, Barley and Kunda (1992) eschew such determinism by pointing to how the propagation of managerial 'ideologies of control' come in repeated historical 'surges'. In defining what they mean by ideology, Barley and Kunda point out how theorists have to draw on assumptions, often unwittingly, about the nature of the phenomena with which they deal. In management theory, the resultant discourses refer to corporations, employees and managers and the 'means by which the latter can direct the other two' (ibid.: 364). With reference to North America, Barley and Kunda use historical information to document how management discourse has oscillated no fewer than five times since the 1870s, between what they call normative and rational rhetoric of control.

Rational control is defined as bureaucratising work processes and a utilitarian appeal to what was construed as the employee's economically rational self-interest. Rational modes of theorising surged from 1900 to 1923 with scientific management, and again with systems rationalisation from 1955 to 1980. In contrast, normative control is defined as the idea that managers could regulate employee behaviour by attending to their thoughts and emotions through some form of culture management. Normative modes of theorising surged from 1870–1900 with industrial betterment, again from 1925–1955 with human relations and again from 1980 to the (then) present day with organisation culture and quality. During each surge to prominence, the particular ideology being propagated is considered to be at the cutting edge of managerial thought, *if not necessarily* at the level of management practice.

Barley and Kunda proceed to argue that the different ideologies of control themselves express culturally based assumptions that have conceptually constrained the imagination of managerial community to what amounts to a dichotomy. They do demonstrate, however, how economic cycles have determined when new surges in management theorising happen. While each surge was championed by specific groups 'whose interests were thereby advanced' (ibid.: 393), they conclude that, in practice, rationalist thinking is usually dominant, but normative factors receive more attention at certain points in time. Generally they hypothesise that '... one might argue that rational rhetoric should surge when profitability seems most tightly linked to the management of capital. Conversely, normative rhetoric should surge when profitability seems to depend more on the management of labour' (ibid., 389). They suggest that managers will be 'attracted to rhetoric that emphasise rational procedures and structures when profits hinge easily on capital investment and automation' (ibid.: 391) but will shift to normative rhetoric, emphasising the motivation of labour, when returns on capital seem to be in decline during economic downswings.

They also emphasise that they do not claim that rational and normative ideologies alternately become dominant according to economic cycles, but rather that the rational has always tended to be theoretically prevalent and more closely linked to practice. Moreover, rationalism will sometimes fuel an interest in, and be tempered by, normative theorising, as it may be seen to provide a means of reducing employees' negative reactions to scientific management or Fordism and other attempts at bureaucratising labour processes. Hence, it is important to temper any consideration of the emergence of new organisational forms and their impact upon HRM with the possibility that we may be witnessing waves of shifting rhetoric, that confuse prescription and description, whose relationship to organisational praxis is ambiguous yet nevertheless legitimise and possibly energise an evolving array of HRM practices that, when implemented, impact upon social relationships within the workplace. Perhaps it is here that Beck's (2000a) caution, referred to earlier, gains even more power when he warns that the displacement, retention and restoration of bureaucratic organisational features are outcomes of ongoing political struggles in which vested interests attempt to maintain and justify our trust in authority and hierarchy.

References

Aarthi, G., and Sujatha, S. (2022) Future team leadership and empowerment in the performance of measuring virtual team productivity with information technology. *International Journal of Professional Business Review, 7*(2), 6.

Adler, P. (2001) Market, hierarchy and trust: The knowledge economy and the future of capitalism. *Organization Science, 12*, 215–234.

Alvesson, M., and Willmott, H. (2002) Identity regulation as organizational control: producing the appropriate individual. *Journal of Management Studies,* 39(5): 619–644.

Annosi, M. C., and Brunetta, F. (2017) *New Organizational Forms, Controls, and Institutions: Understanding the Tensions in 'Post-Bureaucratic' Organizations.* New York: Springer.

Anthony, P. (1994) *Managing Culture.* Buckingham: Open University Press.

Applebaum, E., Bailey, T., Berg, P., and Kalleberg, A. L. (2000) *Manufacturing Advantage; Why High-Performance Work Systems Pay Off.* Ithaca, NY: ILR Press.

Applebaum, S. H., Herhert, D. and Leroux, S. (1999) Empowerment: Power, culture and leadership: A strategy or fad for the millennium. *Journal of Workplace Learning, 11*(7), 233–254.

Atkinson, J. (1984) Manpower strategies for flexible organizations. *Personnel Management, 16*(8), 28–31.

Barker, R. (1997) How can we train leaders if we don't know what leadership is? *Human Relations, 50*, 343–362.

Barley, S. R., and Kunda, G. (1992) Design and devotion: Surges of rational and normative ideologies of control in managerial discourse. *Administrative science Quarterly, 37*, 363–399.

Barzelay, M., with Armajani, B. J. (1992) *Breaking Through Bureaucracy*. Berkeley, CA: University of California Press.

Bauman, Z. (1989) *Modernity and the Holocaust*. London: Polity Press.

Beck, U. (1992) *Risk Society*. London: Sage.

Beck, U. (1997) *The Reinvention of Politics*. Cambridge: Polity Press.

Beck, U. (2000a) Risk society revisited. Theory Politics and Research. In B. Adam, U. Beck, and J. van Loon (Eds.) (pp. 68–90), London: Sage.

Beck, U. (2000b) *What is Globalization?* Cambridge: Polity Press.

Beck, U., and Beck-Gernsheim, E. (2002) *Individualization*. London: Sage.

Becker, S. O., Boeckh, K., Hainz, C., and Woessmann, L. (2016) The empire is dead, long live the empire! Long-run persistence of trust and corruption in the bureaucracy. *The Economic Journal, 126*(590), 40–74.

Beirne, M. (2006) *Empowerment and Innovation*. Cheltenham: Edward Elgar.

Ben-Hador, B. (2023). The practice of manager as coach (MAC): Unequal power relations and their effect on feelings toward the organization. *Human Resource Development Quarterly, 35*(1), 67–88.

Beneviste, G. (1994) *Twenty-First Century Organization: Analyzing Current Trends*. San Francisco, CA: Jossey-Bass.

Bennett, N., and Lemoine, G. J. (2014) What a difference a word makes: Understanding threats to performance in a VUCA world. *Business Horizons, 57*(3), 311–317.

Black, S., and Porter, L. (2000) *Management: Meeting New Challenges*. New York: Prentice-Hall.

Bluestone, B., and Harrison H. (1988) *The Great U-Turn*. New York: Basic Books.

Bos, R. T., and Willmott, H. (2001) Towards post dualistic business ethics: Interweaving reason and emotion in working life. *Journal of Management Studies, 38*(6), 769–793.

Brannan, M. J., and Hawkins, B. (2007) London calling: Selection as a pre-emptive strategy for cultural control. *Employee Relations, 29*(2), 178–191.

Brodbeck, P. (2002) Implications for organization design: Teams as pockets of excellence. *Team Performance Management: An International Journal, 8*(1/2), 21–38.

Buchanan, D., and Badham, R. (1999) *Power, Politics and Organizational Change: Winning the Turf Game*. London: Sage.

Burns T., and Stalker, G. (1961) *The Management of Innovation*. London: Tavistock.

Cappelli, P., Bassi, L., Kahtz, H., Knoke, D., Osterman, P., and Useem, M. (1997) *Change at Work*. Oxford: Oxford University Press.

Castells, M. (1996) *The Rise of the Network Society*. Malden MA: Blackwell.

Chevtaeva, E., and Denizci-Guillet, B. (2021). Digital nomads' lifestyles and coworkation. *Journal of Destination Marketing & Management, 21*.

Child J., and McGrath, R. (2001) Organizations unfettered: Organizational form in an information intensive economy. *Academy of Management Journal, 44*(6), 1135–1148.

Clawson, D. (1980) *Bureaucracy and the Labour Process: The Transformation of US Industry, 1860–1920*. New York: Monthly Review Press.

Clegg, S. R. (1990) *Modern Organizations: Organization Studies in the Postmodern World*. London: Sage.

Conger, J. A., and Kanungo, R. N. (1988) The empowerment process: Integrating theory and practice. *Academy of Management Review, 13*(3), 471–482.

Cooley, M. (1980) *Architect or Bee*. Slough: Langley Technical Services.

Daft, R. L. (1998) *Essentials of Organization Theory and Design*. Cincinnati, OH: South-Western College Publishing.

Daood, A., and Giustiniano, L. (2024). Improvising around and about boundaries in open organizations. In *The Routledge Companion to Improvisation in Organizations* (pp. 357–366). London: Routledge.

Daudi, P. (1990) Con-versing in management's public place. *Scandinavian Journal of Management, 6*(3), 285–307.

Deal, T., and Kennedy, A. (1982) *Corporate Cultures: The Rites and Rituals of Corporate Life*. Reading, MA: Addison-Wesley.

de Laat, K. (2023). Remote work and post-bureaucracy: Unintended consequences of work design for gender inequality. *ILR Review, 76*(1), 135–159.

Dent, M. (1995) The new national health service: A case of postmodernism? *Organization Studies, 16*(5), 875–899.

Dischner, S. (2015) Organizational structure, organizational form, and counterproductive work behavior: A competitive test of the bureaucratic and post-bureaucratic views. *Scandinavian Journal of Management, 31*(4), 501–514.

Dobson, P. (1988) Changing culture. *Employment Gazette*, pp. 647–650.

Drucker, P. (1993) *Post-Capitalist Society*. New York: Harper and Row.

du Gay, P. (2000) *In Praise of Bureaucracy: Weber, Organization and Ethics*. London: Sage.

Dubrin, A. (2001) *Leadership. Research Findings, Practice and Skills*. Boston, MA: Houghton Mifflin.

Elmes M., and Smith, C. (2001) Marked by the spirit: Contextualizing workplace empowerment in American spiritual ideals. *Journal of Applied Behavioural Science, 37*(1), 33–50.

Englehardt, M., and Simmons, P. (2002) Organizational flexibility for a changing world. *Leadership and Organizational Development Journal, 23*(3), 113–121.

Friedman, A. (1977) *Industry and Labour*. London: Macmillan.

Friedman, A. (1990) Management strategies, techniques and technology: Towards a complex theory of the labour process. In D. Knoghts and H. Willmott (Eds.), *Labour Process Theory* (pp. 177–208). London: Macmillan.

Garvey, B., and Alred, G. (2001) Mentoring and the tolerance of complexity. *Futures, 33*, 519–530.

Gee, J. P., Hull, G., and Lankshear, C. (1996) *The New Work Order*. St. Leonards: Allen and Unwin.

Giddens, A. (1990) *The Consequences of Modernity*. Cambridge: Polity.

Giddens, A. (1991) *Modernity and Self-Identity*. Cambridge: Polity

Giddens, A. (1999) *Runaway World: How Globalization is Re-Shaping Our Lives*. London: Profile Books.

Grint, K. (1995) *Management: A Sociological Introduction*. London: Taylor Francis.

Grugulis, I. Dundon, T., and Wilkinson, A. (2000) Culture control and the 'culture manager': Employment practices in a consultancy. *Work Employment and Society, 14*(1), 97–116.

Guest, D. (1991) Personnel Management: The end of orthodoxy. *British Journal of Industrial Relations, 29*(2), 149–175.

Guest, D. E. (1998) Beyond HRM: Commitment and the contract culture. In P. Sparrow and M. Marchington (Eds.), *Human Resource Management: The New Agenda* (pp. 37–51). London: Pitman Publishing.

Hales, C. (1993) *Managing Through Organization*. London: Routledge.

Hales, C. (2002) Bureaucracy-lite and continuities in managerial work. *British Journal of Management, 13*, 51–66.

Handy, C. (1989) *The Age of Unreason*. Boston: Harvard Business School.

Haque, A. (2023). The impact of the COVID-19 pandemic on employee motivation and organisational resilience and the role of strategic HRM: Renewal of a resource-based conceptual model. *Management Matters, 20*(2), 117–133.

Harley, B. (2005) Hope or hype: High performance work systems. In B. Harley, J. Hyman, and P. Thompson (Eds.), *Participation and Democracy* (pp. 313–327). Basingstoke: Palgrave Macmillan.

Hastings, C. (1993) *The New Organization*. London: McGraw-Hill.

Heckscher, C. (1994) Defining the post-bureaucratic type. In C. Heckscher and A. Donnellon (Eds.), *The Post-Bureaucratic Organization: New Perspectives on Organizational Change* (pp. 14–62). Newbury Park, CA: Sage.

Hendry, J. (2006) Educating managers for post-bureaucracy: The role of the humanities. *Management Learning, 37*(3), 267–281.

Hodgson, D.E. (2004) Project work. *Organization, 11*(1), 81–100.

Holleran, M., and Notting, M. (2023). Mobility guilt: Digital nomads and COVID-19. *Tourism Geographies, 25*(5), 1341–1358.

Hope, V., and Hendry, J. (1995) Corporate culture - Is it relevant for organizations of the 1990s. *Human Resource Management Journal, 5*(4), 61–73.

Innocenti, L., Sammarra, A., and Profili, S. (2017) From control to commitment work systems: The role of HRM in the post-bureaucratic transition. In *Evolution of the Post-Bureaucratic Organization* (pp. 274–296). Hershey: IGI Global.

Jackall, R. (1988) *The World of Corporate Managers*. Oxford: Oxford University Press.

Jacoby, S. (1985) *Employing Bureaucracy*. New York: Columbia University Press.

Jaques, R. (1996) *Manufacturing Consent*. London: Sage.

Jarillo, J. C. (1993) *Strategic Networks: Creating the Borderless Organization*. Oxford: Butterworth-Heinemann.

Josserand, E. (2004) *The Network Organization: The Experience of Leading French Multinationals*. Cheltenham: Edward Elgar.

Josserand, E., Teo, S., and Clegg, S. R. (2006) From bureaucratic to post-bureaucratic: The difficulties of transition. *Journal of Organizational Change Management, 19*(1), 54–64.

Kalleberg, A. L. (2001) Organizing flexibly: The flexible firm in a new century. *British Journal of Industrial Relations, 39*(4), 479–504.

Kalleberg, A. L. (2003) Flexible firms and market segmentation: Effects of workplace restructuring on jobs and workers. *Work and Occupations, 30*(2), 154–175.

Kamei, K. (2017) Trade induced firm productivity and division of labor in a general equilibrium with oligopoly. *Economics Bulletin, 37*(4), 2384–2393.

Kellogg, K. C., Orlikowski, W. J., and Yates, J. (2006) Life in the trading zone: Structuring coordination across boundaries in post-bureaucratic organizations. *Organization Science, 17*(1), 22–44.

Kernaghan, K. (2000) The post-bureaucratic organization and public service values. *International Review of Administrative Sciences, 66*(1), 91–104.

Knights, D., and McCabe, D. (2004) 'Ain't misbehavin?' Opportunities for resistance under new forms of quality management. *Sociology, 34*(3), 421–436.

Kochan, T., and Osterman, P. (2002). The mutual gains enterprise. In C. Mabey, G. Salamon, and J. Storey (Eds.), *Strategic Human Resource Management* (pp. 63–97). London: Sage.

Kunda, G. (1992) *Engineering Culture: Control and Commitment in a High Tech Corporation*. Philadelphia, PA: Temple University Press.

Laffin, M. (1998) Beyond bureaucracy: Understanding recent changes in the public sector professions. In M. Laffin (Ed.), *Beyond Bureaucracy? New Approaches in Public Sector Management* (pp. 1–17). Aldersot: Avebury.

Langbert, M. (2002) Continuous improvement in the history of human resource management. *Management Decision, 40*(10), 932–937.

Lash, S., and Urry J. (1987) *The End of Organized Capitalism*. Cambridge: Polity Press.

Lawrence, P., and Lorsch, J. (1967) *Organization and Environment: Managing Differentiation and Integration*. Homewood, IL: Richard D. Irwin.

Legge, K. (1995) *Human Resource Management: Rhetorics and Reality*. Basingstoke: Macmillan.

Linstead, S. (1999) Managing culture. In L. Fulop and S. Linstead (Eds.), *Management: A Critical Text* (pp. 82–121). Basingstoke: Macmillan Press.

Littler, C. R. (1982) *The Development of the Labour Process in Capitalist Societies*. London: Heinemann Education Books.

Lyon, D. (1994) *Postmodernity*. Buckingham: Open University Press.

Lyons, P., and Bandura, R. P. (2023). Manager-as-coach and use of scientific tools for instruction. *European Journal of Training and Development, 47*(5/6), 473–486.

Mancinelli, F. (2020). Digital nomads: Freedom, responsibility and the neoliberal order. *Information Technology & Tourism, 22*(3), 417–437.

Manelkar, K. A., Iyer, R., Gupta, K., and Sampat, B. (2023). A relationship between perceived investment in temporary employee development and organizational performance: An empirical study. *Journal of Organizational Effectiveness: People and Performance, 10*(2), 265–292.

Mantouvalou, V. (2022). Welfare-to-work, zero-hours contracts and human rights. *European Labour Law Journal, 13*(3), 431–449.

Maravelias, C. (2003) Post-bureaucracy - Control through professional freedom. *Journal of Organizational Change Management, 16*(5), 547–566.

Marquardt, M. J. (1996) *Building the Learning Organization: A Systems Approach to Quantum Improvement and Global Success*. New York: McGraw-Hill.

Mathew, J., and Nair, S. (2022). Psychological empowerment and job satisfaction: A meta-analytic review. *Vision, 26*(4), 431–440.

Melnic, A. (2022). Generational theories as a way of understanding the structure of work potential. *Contemporary Economy Journal, 7*(2), 74–79.

Menon, S. T. (2001) Employee empowerment: An integrative psychological approach. *Applied Psychology: An International Review, 50*(1), 153–180.

Miles, R. E., and Snow, C. C. (1986) Organizations: New concepts for new forms. *California Management Review, 28*(3), 62–73.

Miller, P., and Rose, N. (1990) Governing economic life. *Economy and Society, 19*(1), 1–31.

Mills, P. K., and Ungson, G. (2003) Reassessing the limit of structural empowerment: Organization constitutions trusts controls. *Academy of Management Review, 28*(1), 143–151.

Mintzberg, H. (1979) *The Structuring of Organizations: A Synthesis of Research*. Englewood Cliffs, NJ: Prentice-Hall.

Mohrman, S. A., Ledford, G. E., and Mohrman, A. M. (1990) *Large-Scale Organizational Change*. San Francisco CA: Jossey-Bass

Mueller, F., and Carter, C. (2005) The HRM project and managerialism: Or why some discourses are more powerful than others. *Journal of Organizational Change Management, 18*(4), 369–382.
Mustafa, G., Solli-Sæther, H., Bodolica, V., Håvold, J. I., and Ilyas, A. (2022). Digitalization trends and organizational structure: Bureaucracy, ambidexterity or post-bureaucracy? *Eurasian Business Review, 12*(4), 671–694.
Neff, G. D. and Stark, D. (2003) Permanently beta: Responsive organization in the internet era. In P. Howard and S. Jones (Eds.), *Society on-Line: The Internet in Context* (pp. 173–188). Thousand Oaks, CA: Sage.
Osbourne, D., and Gaebler, T. (1992) *Re-Inventing Government.* Reading, MA': Addison-Wesley.
Osbourne, D., and Plastrik, D. (1998) *Banishing Bureaucracy: Five Strategies for Reinventing Government.* New York: Plume.
Ouchi, W. G. (1979) A conceptual framework for the design of management control systems. *Management Science, 25*, 833–848.
Ouchi, W. G. (1980) Markets, bureaucracies and clans. *Administrative Science Quarterly, 25*, 129–141.
Ozarallı, N. (2003) Effects of transformational leadership on empowerment and team effectiveness. *Leadership and Organizational Development Journal, 24*(5/6), 335–344.
Pahi, M. H., Ahmed, U., Imroz, S. M., Shah, S. M. M., and Yong, I. S. C. (2024). The flexible HRM and firm performance nexus: Can empowering leadership play any contingent role? *International Journal of Productivity and Performance Management, 73*(2), 629–647.
Patterson, M. G., West, M. A., and Wall, T. D. (2004) Integrating manufacturing, empowerment and company performance. *Journal of Organizational Behaviour, 25*, 641–665.
Pattinson, S. (1997) *The Faith of Managers.* London: Cassell.
Perrow, C. A. (1967) A framework for the Comparative analysis of Organizations. *American Sociological Review, 32*, 194–208.
Peters, T. (1992) *Liberation Management.* London: Macmillan.
Piore, M. J., and Sable, C. F. (1984) *The Second Industrial Divide: Possibilities for Prosperity.* New York: Basic Books.
Powell, W. W. (1990) Neither market nor hierarchy: Network forms of organization. In G. Thompson, J. Frances, R. Levacic, and J. Mitchell (Eds.), *Markets, Hierarchies and Networks* (pp. 265–276). London: Sage.
Psychogios, A., Szamosi, L. T., and Brewster, C. (2014) Work organization, human resource management and the economic crisis. In C. F. Machado and J. P. Davim (Eds.), *Work Organization and Human Resource Management* (pp. 1–19). Heidelberg: Springer.
Quinn, J. (1992) *Intelligent Enterprise.* New York: Free Press.
Quinn, R. E., and Spreitzer, G. M. (1997) The road to empowerment: Seven questions every leader should consider. *Organizational Dynamics, 26*, 37–49.
Randolph, W. A. (1994) Navigating the journey to empowerment. *Organizational Dynamic, 23*(4), 19–32.
Rifkind, J. (2000) *The Age of Access: The New Culture of Hypercapitalism, Where All of Life Is a Paid-For Experience.* New York: Tarcher Putnam.
Ritzer, G. (2006) *McDonaldization: The Reader*, 2nd ed. Thousand Oaks, CA: Pine Forge Press.

Robertson, R. (1992) *Globalization*. London: Sage.
Rogiers, P., and Collings, D. G. (2024) The end of jobs? Paradoxes of job deconstruction in organizations. *Academy of Management Perspectives*, *38*(2), 177–196.
Rosenthal, P., Hill, S., and Peccei, R. (1997) Checking out service: Evaluating excellence, HRM, and TQM in retailing. *Work, Employment and Society, 11*(3), 481–503.
Rubery, J. (2015) Change at work: Feminisation, flexibilisation, fragmentation and financialisation. *Employee Relations*, *37*(6), 633–644.
Savage, C. (1996) *5th Generation Management, Cocreating through Virtual Enterprising, Dynamic Teaming and Knowledge Networking*. Boston, MA: Butterworth Heineman.
Seibert, S., Silver, S., and Randolph, W. (2004) Taking power to the next level: A multiple-level model of empowerment performance and satisfaction. *Academy of Management Journal*, *47*, 332–50.
Senge, P. M. (1990) *The Fifth Discipline: The Art and Practice of the Learning Organization*. London: Century.
Serafini, G. O., and Szamosi, L. T. (2015) Five star hotels of a Multinational Enterprise in countries of the transitional periphery: A case study in human resources management. *International Business Review*, *24*(6), 972–983.
Serafini, G. O., Wood, G., and Szamosi, L. T. (2020). People management after state socialism: A literature review and research agenda. *Human Resource Management Review*, *30*(4), 100741.
Shawkat, S., Abd Rozan, M. Z., Salim, N. B., and Shehzad, H. M. F. (2021). Digital nomads: A systematic literature review. In *7th International conference on research and innovation in information systems (ICRIIS)* (pp. 1–6). Johor Bahru, Malaysia: IEEE.
Shin, D., and Konrad, A. M. (2017) Causality between high-performance work systems and organizational performance. *Journal of Management*, *43*(4), 973–997.
Stark, D. (2001) Ambiguous assets for uncertain environments: Hierarchy in post-socialist firms. In P. DiMaggio (Ed.), *The 21st Century Firm: Changing Organization in International Perspective* (pp. 69–104). Princeton NJ: Princeton University Press.
Strange, S. (2015) *Casino Capitalism: With an Introduction by Matthew Watson*. Oxford: Oxford University Press
Tourish, D. and Pinnington, A. (2002) Transformational leadership, corporate cultism and the spirituality paradigm: Aan unholy trinity in the workplace?, *Human Relations, 55*(2), 147–172.
Tucker, J. (1999) *The Therapeutic Corporation*. New York: Oxford University Press.
Volberda H. (1998) *Building the Flexible Firm: How to Remain Competitive*. Oxford: Oxford University Press.
Wagner, P. (1992) Liberty and discipline: Making sense of postmodernity, or, once again, towards a sociohistorical understanding of modernity. *Theory and Society, 21*(4), 467–492.
Wallach, V. A., and Mueller, C. W. (2006) Job characteristics and organizational predictors of psychological empowerment within human service organizations: an exploratory study. *Administration in Social Work, 30*(1), 95–113.
Waterman, R. H. (1988) *The Renewal Factor*. London: Bantam.
Watson, T. (1994) *In Search of Management*. London: Routledge.

Weber, M. (1904) On Protestantism and Capitalism. In T. Parsons, E. Shils, K. D. Naegele, and J. R. Pitts (Eds.), (1965) *Theories of Society: Foundations of Modern Sociological Theory* (pp. 1253–1264). New York: Free Press.

Weber, M. (1947) *The Theory of Social and Economic Organization*. New York: Oxford University Press.

Wilkinson, A. (1998) Empowerment: Theory and practice. *Personnel Review, 27*(1), 40–56.

Willmott, H. C. (1993) Strength is ignorance; Slavery is freedom: Managing culture in modern organizations. *Journal of Management Studies, 30*(4), 515–552.

Wood, G., Psychogios, A., Szamosi, L. T., and Collings, D. G. (2012) Institutional approaches to comparative HRM. In C. Brewster, W. Mayrhofer, and E. Farndale (Eds.), *Handbook of Research on Comparative Human Resource Management* (pp. 27–50). Cheltenham: Edward Elgar Publishing.

Wood, S. (1999) Human resource management and performance. *International Journal of Management Reviews, 1*, 367–413.

3 Strategic HRM

A Critical Review

Corine Boon and Jaap Paauwe

Introduction

Since the development of Human Resource Management (HRM) as a field of scientific research in the 1980s, many changes have taken place in this area. An important development has been the integration of HRM into the strategic management process. This growing area of research has been labelled strategic HRM in that it emphasises the strategic role of HRM in meeting business objectives (Delery, 1998). Strategic HRM draws attention to the contribution of HRM towards the performance of organisations; in other words, what is the added value of HRM for organisations? To achieve this, the integration between strategy and HRM is emphasised; the basic premise underlying strategic HRM is that organisations that adopt a particular strategy require HR practices that may differ from those required by organisations adopting alternative strategies (Delery and Doty, 1996), assuming an important link between organisational strategy and HR practices that are implemented in that organisation.

Therefore, we need to make sure that we shed some clear light on the issue of whether strategy matters (either at corporate or business level) and in what sense does it matter to (the effectiveness of) HRM? In this chapter, we begin with an introduction as to what strategy means and shift towards different strategy approaches that have been used in the field. Then we will explain the link between strategy and HRM, whereby we introduce the concept of 'strategic fit'. As existing approaches to strategic fit have been highly criticised, we will present an alternative approach, taking into account the implementation and dynamics of nontraditional approaches focused on processes and content of strategy and HRM. The chapter concludes with a step towards a synthesis of strategic HRM research by presenting two recent conceptual frameworks (Paauwe & Farndale, 2017; Snell & Morris, 2021), considering the different perspectives and interests of a variety of stakeholders involved in strategic HRM.

DOI: 10.4324/9781032625560-4

Strategy

There are many different meanings of strategy, resulting in an enormous variety of approaches to a particular strategy. The most well-known of these, and still dominantly present in all the strategic management textbooks, is the rational planned approach, also referred to as the so-called classical approach. Its main characteristics show resemblance with the military setting (based on Mintzberg, 1990 and Whittington, 1993):

- A controlled and conscious process of thought directly derived from the notion of rational economic man;
- For which the prime responsibility rests with the chief executive officer;
- Who is in charge of a fully formulated, explicit and articulated decision-making process;
- In which there is a strict distinction between formulation and implementation.

The classical approach to strategy places great confidence in the readiness and capacity of managers to adopt profit-maximising strategies through rational long-term planning, as Whittington (1993: 17) critically remarks. In the early notions on strategic HRM, we find a striking similarity with the previously mentioned premises of the classical approach. For example, Hendry and Pettigrew (1986) state that the call or plea for strategic HRM implies:
The use of planning

- A coherent approach to the design and management of personnel systems based on an employment policy and manpower strategy, often underpinned by a philosophy;
- HRM activities are matched to some explicit strategy;
- The people of the organisation are seen as a strategic resource for achieving a competitive advantage.

In reality, however, the concept of strategy has many different meanings. Mintzberg was one of the first to demonstrate this. He distinguished five meanings of the strategy concept (based on Mintzberg, 1987; and see also Mintzberg et al., 1998):

- Strategy as a plan (intended): A direction, a guide or course of action into the future, which implies looking ahead;
- Strategy as a pattern (realised): Consistency in behaviour over time, which implies looking at past behaviour;
- Strategy as a ploy: A specific manoeuvre intended to outwit an opponent or competitor;
- Strategy as a position: The way in which the organisation positions its products and or services in particular markets in order to achieve a competitive advantage;

- Strategy as a perspective: An organisation's fundamental way of doing things, the way in which the members of the organisation perceive their environment, their customers etc.

In order to integrate the many available perspectives on strategy, several authors have proposed an overview of different approaches (Mintzberg, 1998; Volberda, 2004; Whittington, 2001). Mintzberg, Ahlstrand and Lampel (2009) categorise the different strategic management perspectives into ten 'schools'. The *design* school, *planning* school and *positioning* school are *outside-in* approaches (Stopford & Baden-Fuller, 1994). They see the environment as a stable factor which can be studied objectively (Paauwe & Farndale, 2017). The organisation's market environment is taken as a starting point, based on which the organisation develops a strategy. The *design* school sees strategy formation as a deliberate process of conscious thought (Tampoe & MacMillan, 2000). An example is the 'SWOT' (strengths, weaknesses, opportunities, threats) analysis. The *planning* school is more formalised and more detailed than the design school. It includes a stepwise approach to creating an all-encompassing strategy. The *positioning* school analyses the competitive position of an organisation using economic modelling. Examples are Porter's (1980, 1985) well-known five forces model which identifies five forces that make up the competitive environment (competitive rivalry, supplier power, buyer power, threat of substitution and threat of new entry), Porter's (1980, 1985) generic strategies (cost leadership, differentiation and focus) and the Boston Consulting Group's growth-share matrix and experience curve.

Particularly the positioning school has been applied to the field of HRM, by linking competitive strategies to HR policies and practices (Paauwe & Farndale, 2017). For example, Porter's (1980) generic strategies (cost leadership, differentiation, focus) have been linked to desired employee role behaviours, and in turn, to HR policies and practices by Schuler and Jackson (1987). Other studies, including more recent work, have linked Miles and Snow's (1984) strategy typology (prospectors, defenders, analysers, reactors) to strategic HRM (eg Boy Akdag & Ekmekci, 2023; Guest, 1997; Schultz, Bennett, & Ketchen, 2015).

Mintzberg et al. (2009) further distinguishes the *entrepreneurial* school by emphasising the importance of the active role of a visionary leader in searching for new ways to speed up a company's growth (emanating originally from Schumpeter, 1934). The *cognitive* school sees the viewpoint of the strategist and considers strategy formulation as a cognitive process, where strategies emerge as perspectives that influence people's reactions to environmental factors and change (Paauwe & Farndale, 2017). In the *learning* school, incremental steps in strategy formulation are taken as a result of mutual adjustment between factors outside (outside forces or events) and inside (internal decisions) the organisation. This reflects a collective learning process wherein strategy formulation and implementation overlap (Mintzberg et al., 2009: 217). The *power* (or *political*) school opts for a power perspective and focuses on the bargaining process between power blocks inside and outside the organisation, which results in a strategy. The resulting strategies reflect the outcome of negotiating particular interests of the different stakeholders (Mintzberg et al., 2009). Next, the *cultural* school centres around the norms and beliefs of organisational members and regards strategy formulation as a process of social interaction between organisational members, resulting in a strategy that reflects the deeply embedded resources or capabilities of the organisation (Mintzberg et al., 2009: 281). The *environmental* school – rooted in contingency theory – argues that organisations should respond to the environment in order to achieve a competitive advantage, thus seeing the environment as a central actor in the process of strategy formulation. Finally, the *configurational*

Table 3.1 Three modes of strategy synthesis

The 'boundary' school	*The 'dynamic capabilities' school*	*The 'configurational school'*
Questions Where to draw the boundary How to manage across the divide	With whom and how do firms compete How do they sustain their competitive advantage over time	What are the contingencies Which strategy configurations are effective What are the underlying dimensions of strategy configurations
Base disciplines/ theories Agency theory (economics/ psychology) Transaction costs theory Industrial organisation Control theories (sociology) Decision-making theories (psychology)	Resource-based theory of the firm (economics) Entrepreneurship (economics) Innovation theories (organisation theory) Learning theories (organisational behaviour)	Social sciences History equilibrium model (biology) Catastrophe theories (mathematics)
Problem-solving tools The strategy sourcing process (Venkatesan 1992) Porter's value chain (Porter 1980)	The roots of competitiveness (Prahalad and Hamel 1990) The capability matrix (Schoemaker 1992)	Archetypes (Miller and Friesen 1980) Strategic type (Miles and Snow 1978) FAR method (Volberda 1998)
New directions Strategising Joint value creation Building trust Learning across boundaries	Coevolution of capabilities and competition Managerial dimensions of dynamic capabilities	Conceptually derived typology Empirically based taxonomies Configurations as source of competitive advantage

Source: Volberda and Elfring (2001).

school integrates the other nine schools and emphasises that the ideal strategy depends on the circumstances. Depending on the specific context, organisations can find an effective strategy 'configuration', and when the context changes, a new configuration is needed in order to remain effective.

Other authors have proposed similar and somewhat broader perspectives in order to synthesise the range of different strategy schools. For example, Volberda and Elfring (2001: 11-12) propose the boundary school, the dynamic capabilities school, and the configurational school as three different modes of strategy synthesis with associated challenges and underlying theories (see Table 3.1).

These three modes of strategy synthesis (which also include several strategy approaches discussed earlier) have had an important impact on strategic HRM. For example, the boundary school hints at the issue of the fragmented organisation, whereby different suppliers are involved in the delivery of services or in the manufacturing of products. This implies that different categories of workers are involved of which only some are employed by the focal organisation. This raises issues of governance, control, risk, compliance, also from an HR perspective (see Farndale, Paauwe, Boselie, 2010). The dynamic capabilities school focuses on the need for continuous adaptation of HRM systems and practices in order to make sure that the human capital capabilities are up to date with the organisational capabilities as required by changing market circumstances. For example, increasing online selling at the expense of physical retail outlets requires new skills from existing staff, etc. Finally, the configurational school refers to the unique combination of market circumstances, technology, business strategy, human capital, HRM systems etc. which – when properly managed – will result in a unique and hopefully sustained competitive advantage. Our two theoretical frameworks, in the final section, titled 'In Search of a Synthesis', gives a comprehensive overview of all the factors and antecedents which play a role in achieving such a unique configuration. Next we will describe how the field of strategic HRM has applied theories and insights using varied approaches.

Traditional Approaches in Strategic HRM

In describing the traditional approaches used in the area of strategic HRM, we need to distinguish between process and content models. The *process* of strategy refers to the way strategies come about, whereas the *content* is concerned with the product of strategy in terms of the 'what' of strategy.

A mixture of both process and content is the so-called Harvard model by Beer et al. (1984a), one of the most well-known models in HRM theorising, which starts from a situational perspective (see Figure 3.1). Besides market and strategic considerations, it takes into account the interests of the various stakeholders in both the external and internal environment. Besides performance in its strict economic sense, individual well-being and societal consequences are also included. The framework is both descriptive and prescriptive. It gives

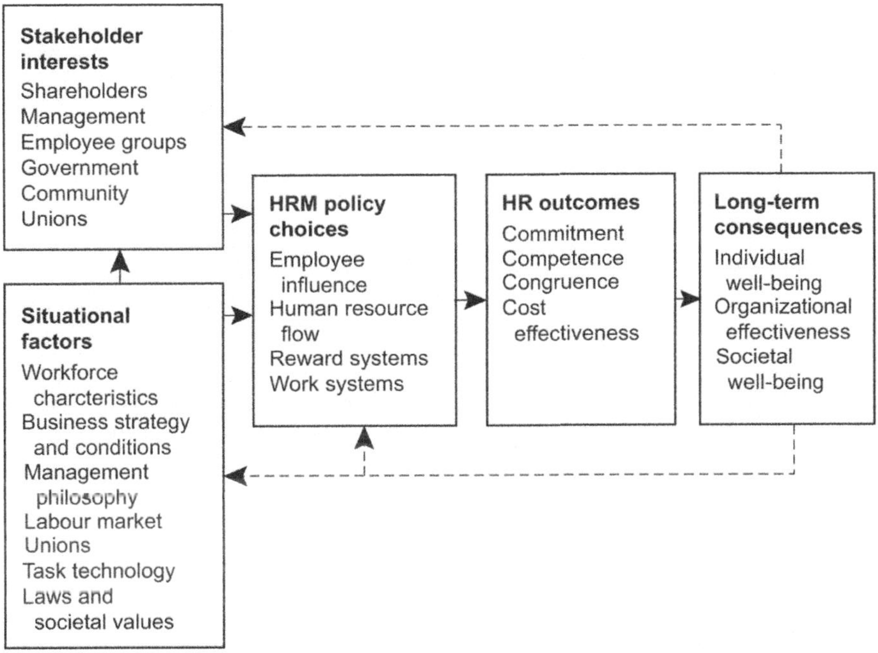

Figure 3.1 The Harvard approach (Source: Beer et al., 1984a. Reprinted with permission of Michael Beer.)

an overview of the factors that are important in shaping HRM policies, but at the same time it is quite conclusive in prescribing to what kind of outcomes these choices – once made – should lead. In 2014, a special issue of *Human Resource Management* was dedicated to the 30 years' existence of this framework and based on the reviews in that special issue (among which Beer et al., 2015), it is still relevant for those authors who believe in a contextual approach and a variety of stakeholders interested in the outcomes of the relationship between strategy and HRM (see Paauwe & Farndale, 2017).

Fombrun et al. (from Michigan Business School) published their competing approach in the same year as their counterparts from Harvard (Figure 3.2). Achieving a tight fit between strategy, structure and HRM policies takes place amid economic, political and cultural forces. More focused on the functional level of HRM itself, they emphasise the so-called human resource cycle, which can be considered as one of the first content models. In their cycle, performance is dependent upon selection, appraisal, rewards and development.

Strategic Fit

As shown in the aforementioned conceptual models, the nature of the link between strategy and HRM has been a central issue to strategic HRM. The

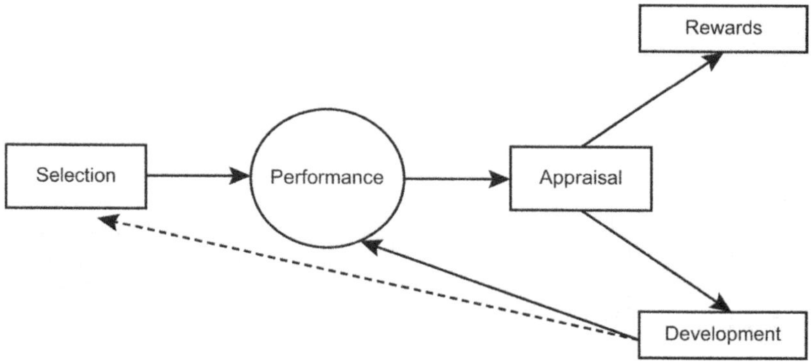

Figure 3.2 The Michigan approach – the human resource cycle (Source: Fombrun et al., 1984. Reprinted with permission of John Wiley & Sons Inc.)

basic premise underlying strategic HRM is that organisations adopting a particular strategy require HRM practices that may differ from those required by organisations adopting alternative strategies (Delery and Doty, 1996), assuming an important link between organisational strategy and HRM practices, which has been labelled *strategic fit* (also *vertical fit*). Strategic fit stresses the importance of linking business objectives and HRM. The assumption is that HR systems, which 'simultaneously exploit the potential for complementarities or synergies among such practices and help to implement a firm's competitive strategy, are sources of sustained competitive advantage' (Huselid, 1995).

In testing strategic fit, most researchers use the 'classical' strategy typologies of Porter (1985) or Miles and Snow (1978) to operationalise strategy (Kehoe, 2021; Schuler and Jackson, 1987; Montemayor, 1996; Youndt, Snell, Dean, & Lepak, 1996). For example, Schuler and Jackson (1987) were among the first to present how strategy and HRM policies could be related. They used Porter's generic strategies (cost effectiveness, innovation and quality), and linked each of these strategies to a repertoire of role behaviours. Subsequently, HRM policies and practices are used to reinforce the required role behaviours (ie, the behavioural view). For example, for an innovation strategy, HRM practices are aimed at facilitating cooperative interdependent behaviour that is oriented towards the longer term and at fostering exchange of ideas and risk-taking, such as variable pay rates and broad career paths. Collins and Kehoe (2017) focused more specifically on innovation strategies, and suggest that exploration and exploitation strategies require different types of HR systems to support required role behaviours. An exploration strategy is focused on innovation, whereas an exploitation strategy focuses on using past knowledge or refinement of existing products (Collins & Kehoe, 2017; Gupta, Smith, & Shalley, 2006). Collins and Kehoe (2017) show that an exploration strategy requires an 'engineering' HR system, characterised by selection focused on broad capabilities to perform a range of tasks that will change over time, challenging work, development opportunities and autonomy. An exploitation strategy requires a 'bureaucratic' HR system, characterised by selection for abilities to perform specific tasks right away, competitive compensation tied to individual performance and tight control. A better fit between the strategies and HR systems is associated with higher firm performance.

Many classic models of strategic HRM make use of strategy typologies from Porter (1985) or Miles and Snow (1978), which reflects an outside-in approach (Baden-Fuller and Stopford, 1994), as strategic decisions are made based on the external environment. This corresponds with the strategic contingency approach (ie, Lawrence and Lorsch, 1967; Mintzberg, 1979), which emphasises the influence of contextual factors inside and outside the organisation on HRM. In the 1990s, a shift in strategic thinking was represented by the introduction of the resource-based view (RBV) (Barney, 1991), representing an inside-out perspective. Internal resources (such as finance, organisational systems and physical assets but also people) and how these contribute to a sustained competitive advantage are the starting point in this approach. This shift in strategic management has had major implications on the field of HRM. Wright and McMahan state:

> This RBV of competitive advantage differs from the traditional strategy paradigm in that the emphasis of the resource-based view of competitive advantage is on the link between strategy and internal resources of the firm. The RBV is firm-focused whereas the traditional strategic analysis paradigm has had an industry-environment focus.
>
> (Wright and McMahan, 1992)

In this approach, the unique strengths and capabilities of the employees determine the range of possible business strategies to be implemented. 'The resource-based view may demonstrate the fact that strategies are not universally implementable but are contingent on having the human resource base necessary to implement them' (Wright and McMahan, 1992: 303). The RBV states that internal resources (for example, human resources) which are scarce, valuable, inimitable and non-substitutable serve as the basis for a sustained competitive advantage (for an overview, see Gerhart & Feng, 2021). Table 3.2 presents an overview of the outside-in versus the inside-out perspective.

These two perspectives seem contradictory but can both be relevant for strategic HRM. On the one hand, HRM is dependent on the strategic positioning of the firm as it attempts to fit with the market environment; on the other hand, (human) resources can be cultivated and developed in order to enable strategies that will result in a sustainable competitive advantage. Reviews and meta-analyses of strategic HRM suggest that both perspectives are relevant for strategic HRM (Boselie et al., 2005; Paauwe, 2009; Jackson et al., 2014; Jiang, Lepak, Hu & Baer, 2012; Jiang, Takeuchi & Lepak, 2013; Wright & Ulrich, 2017); both contingency theory and RBV have been widely used as theoretical framework underlying strategic HRM models. The

Table 3.2 Outside-in versus inside-out perspective

	Outside-in perspective	*Inside-out perspective*
Emphasis on	Markets over resources	Resources over markets
Orientation	Market-/industry-driven	Resource-driven
Starting point	Market/industry structure	Firm's resource infrastructure
Fit through	Adaptation to environment	Adaptation of environment
Strategic focus	Attaining advantageous position	Attaining distinctive resources
Strategic moves	Market/industry positioning	Developing resource base
Tactical moves	Industry entry and positioning	Attaining necessary resources
Competitive weapons	Bargaining power and mobility barriers	Superior resources and imitation barriers

Source: De Wit, B. and Meyer, R. (1998). Reprinted with permission of Thomson Publishing Services.

behavioural view, rooted in contingency theory, has gained importance in recent years. Also, human capital theory (taking an inside-out perspective) has been applied often to strategic HRM (Jackson et al., 2014; Jiang et al., 2012; Wright & Ulrich, 2017). Human capital theory emphasises that the organisation's human capital, which is the composition of employees' skills, abilities and knowledge, helps to achieve a competitive advantage. HRM practices can be used to optimise the organisation's human capital pool (Jackson et al., 2014; Jiang et al., 2012). Building on these ideas, the field of strategic human capital has emerged, which combines strategy with HR and focuses on the antecedents and consequences of human capital in organisations (Boon, Eckardt, Lepak, & Boselie, 2018; Ray, Essman, Nyberg, Ployhart, & Hale, 2023; Wright, 2021; Wright, Coff, & Moliterno, 2014).

Building on the behavioural perspective on HRM, human capital theory and the RBV, the so-called AMO model draws our attention to the importance of a bundle of HRM practices which focuses on Abilities, Motivation and Opportunity to participate in order to improve performance. The AMO model has become increasingly popular among HRM academics and can now be considered as the most dominant theoretical framework (Bos-Nehles, Townsend, Cafferkey, & Trullen, 2023; Paauwe, 2009). This is due to the interest in the past few decades in so-called High Performance Work Systems (HPWS), being a set of related HR practices such as training and development, contingent pay and reward schemes, performance management (including appraisal) and careful recruitment and selection (Boselie et al., 2005: 72) focused on enhancing performance. These practices are often bundled under the three headings of the AMO framework (Appelbaum et al., 2000), such as the AMO bundles distinguished by Subramony (2009) (see Table 3.3). Two meta-analyses that both make use of the AMO framework for bundling HRM

Table 3.3 The content of HRM bundles

Skill-enhancing bundles
Job descriptions/requirements generated through job analysis
Job-based skill training
Recruiting to ensure availability of large applicant pools
Structured and validated tools/procedures for personnel selection
Motivation-enhancing bundles
Formal performance appraisal process
Incentive plans (bonuses, profit-sharing, gain-sharing plans)
Linking pay to performance
Opportunities for internal career mobility and promotions
Health care and other employee benefits
Empowerment-enhancing bundles
Employee involvement in influencing work process/outcomes
Formal grievance procedure and complaint resolution systems
Job enrichment (skill flexibility, job variety, responsibility)
Self-managed or autonomous work groups
Employee participation in decision-making
Systems to encourage feedback from employees

Source: Subramony (2009: 746).

practices (Jiang, et al., 2012; Subramony, 2009) show that the three bundles (A: skill-enhancing, M: motivation-enhancing and O: empowerment-enhancing) have significant and positive relationships with outcomes like employee retention, operating performance (eg labour productivity, reduction of waste) and financial performance. Moreover, similar to the conclusion by Combs et al. (2006), Subramony finds that bundles/systems have a stronger effect than individual HRM practices. Jiang et al. (2012) find that skill-enhancing (A) and motivation-enhancing (M) HRM practices are selected as '...the most critical mediating factors' (Jiang et al., 2012: 10), resulting in decreased staff turnover, increased operational productivity and improved financial performance. More recently, Bos-Nehles et al. (2023) reviewed 104 quantitative HRM articles published between 1997 and 2022 and found – in line with Jiang et al. (2012) – that ability and motivation act as mediators in the relationship between AMO-enhancing HRM practices and performance. In addition, their results suggest that the relationships between ability (A) and motivation (M) and performance outcomes depend on the extent to which opportunity-enhancing (O) practices are in place.

Problems with 'Fit': Best Practice or Best Fit?

Conceptually, the idea of fit is convincing, which is why it continues to play an important role in strategic HRM research (Becker and Huselid, 2006; Gerhart, 2004; Kehoe, 2021). However, originally, more evidence was found for the counterpart of the 'fit' approach, the 'best practice' approach. This touches on the issue of the universalistic approach of 'best practices' versus the contingent approach of 'best fit'. While the 'best fit' approach assumes that the effectiveness of HR practices is context-specific, the best practice approach assumes that certain HR practices universally outperform others and acknowledges that a set of 'best practices' exists which will lead to organisational effectiveness, regardless in which organisation it is implemented.

To date, although theoretically the 'best fit' approach is more convincing, still only modest evidence has been found for 'best fit' (Paauwe & Farndale, 2017). Much attention has been paid to high performance, high commitment and high involvement work systems, which have been successfully applied in a range of industries. Most studies on high performance work systems do not distinguish between different strategies and show that such systems are universally effective. However, other studies do show that HRM is highly context dependent. Different sectors, institutional contexts and cultures need different HRM systems. For example, Toh, Morgeson and Campion (2008) show that HRM bundles are related to organisational values and structures; studies also show differences in HRM systems between national cultures (Rabl, Jayasinghe, Gerhart, & Kühlmann, 2014), (relational) climates (Batistič & Poell, 2022; Mohammed, Batistic, Cerne, & Poell, 2023) and public and private sectors (Kalleberg, Marsden, Reynolds, & Knoke, 2006; Bach and Kessler, 2007) between manufacturing and services (eg Combs et al., 2006), and show that specific HRM practices are used in hospitals (Veld, Paauwe & Boselie, 2010), call centres (Batt et al., 2009) and agriculture (Kroon & Paauwe, 2014).

More recently, besides sectoral differences in HRM, there is increasing attention for strategically targeted HRM systems which target specific strategic objectives, such as customer service or safety (Jackson et al., 2014, Alingh et al., 2015), personal initiative (Hong, Liao, Raub, & Han, 2016) or ethics (Guerci, Radaelli, Battisti, & Siletti, 2017). Collins and Kehoe (2017), for example, argue that broad HRM systems only provide a limited perspective on what an effective HR system is. As a result, it is difficult to determine which HR investments are needed to improve performance in a specific context. They study the alignment between three different HR systems (engineering, commitment and bureaucratic HRM systems) and innovation strategies (exploration or exploitation strategy). Each HRM system represents a different underlying philosophy. The engineering HRM system focuses on attracting diverse talent with specialised knowledge and creating an environment in which they share, test and challenge ideas. The commitment HRM system focuses on building long-term relationships with employees by creating a work environment characterised by employee loyalty and strong internal ties. The bureaucratic HRM system focuses on narrow jobs for which employees with narrow skill sets and experience are needed, and formal coordination and control are used to manage those employees. In a sample of 230 software firms, they show that a fit between an engineering HRM system and an exploration strategy, and a fit between a bureaucratic HRM system and an exploitation strategy were both associated with higher profit growth. No results were found for the commitment HRM system (Collins & Kehoe, 2017).

Han, Kang, Oh, Kehoe and Lepak (2019) take a more nuanced approach to vertical (or strategic) fit by focusing on a specific element of strategy: organisations' market-entry timing mode. The high performance work systems – product sales relationship was positive and significant for fast followers (who wait and learn from first movers' successes and failures) but not for first movers (who are focused on producing new-to-market products) and fence-sitters (who are focused on maintaining their current markets).

Overall this suggests increasing evidence for the best fit approach. However, still the majority of studies support the best practice approach. How can we explain the lack of empirical support for strategic fit? A reason might be that the real nature of fit is not captured in these research projects. For example, most researchers use the 'classical' strategy typologies of Porter (1985) or Miles and Snow (1978) to operationalise strategy (eg Schuler and Jackson, 1987; Montemayor, 1996; Youndt et al., 1996), whereas in reality, competitive strategies are more complex and tend to consist of more elements than those captured in these classic strategy typologies (Paauwe, 2004, Gerhart, 2004; Kehoe, 2021). Also, one company can have multiple strategic goals at the same time (Snell & Morris, 2021). In such a case, the required role behaviours are highly mixed. Strategy typologies are thus unable to capture the uniqueness and complexity of business strategies. Yet, this uniqueness is seen as the potential source of sustainable competitive advantage (Becker and Huselid, 2006; Snell & Morris, 2021).

Moreover, most studies adopt a narrow focus on HRM systems, which does not reflect the variety of employee role behaviours that may be required when pursuing different strategies (Collins & Kehoe, 2017). Becker and Huselid (2006: 910) argue that fit is 'inherently multidimensional and not easily captured by simple bivariate statements'. Boxall and Purcell (2003) formulate three main critiques on the 'classical' approaches for measuring strategic fit: they overlook employee interests, lack sophistication in their description of competitive strategy and devote insufficient attention to dynamics. Moreover, empirical studies mainly do not take into account changes and time lags (Boon, Den Hartog, & Lepak, 2019; Paauwe and Boselie, 2005); it takes 12 to 18 months for an HRM strategy to be developed and implemented, and another three to four years before a relationship with performance could be observed (Wright and Haggerty, 2005). In addition, changes might occur in the strategy and/or the HRM system. As both strategy and HRM systems are dynamic, fit at one moment in time does not guarantee fit at another moment in time and besides fit, flexibility is needed (Wright & Snell, 1998; Wright & Ulrich, 2017). Following these criticisms, there is a need for a more advanced approach for measuring strategic fit, which will be described in the next section.

Towards a More Advanced Approach to Strategic Fit

Some steps have been made in developing more extensive strategic fit approaches. For example, Gratton et al. (1999a), when using a content approach to strategy, use a set of strategic objectives, which are unique to the organisation rather than a strategy typology. Besides the content approach, establishing fit also involves – as already indicated earlier – a process dimension (De Wit and Meyer, 1998; Paauwe, 2004). The idea of process approaches is that the integration of strategy, HRM processes and functions result in a fit between human resource needs (following strategy) and employee skills and behaviours (elicited by HRM practices) (Bennett et al., 1998). Boon and colleagues (Boon et al., 2007; Boon, 2008) build on the work of Golden and Ramanujam and Gratton et al. and propose an operationalisation of strategic fit consisting of *three* elements: a content element, a process element *and* an implementation element. The *content* element, following Gratton et al. (1999a), covers the extent to which different HR practices aim at achieving business objectives and the number of HRM practices that are linked with strategy. The *process* element focuses on the role of the HRM function in strategy formulation, following Golden and Ramanujam (1985). They discuss the extent to which the HR function is involved in strategy formulation and whether the HR director and HR managers are a member of the management team on different levels in the organisation. Achieving a strong fit would imply full integration of strategy and HR processes, which enables the design of HRM practices that fit well with strategy in terms of content.

Building on research on HR process, strategy *implementation* has also been stressed. Classic approaches to strategic fit focus on designing HR practices which fit with the strategy, without paying attention to implementation of those practices within organisations. Becker and Huselid (2006), for example, argue that strategy implementation should be given more attention in strategic HRM. Implementation is no longer seen as the process that automatically follows strategy formulation but they are co-dependent (Grant, 2005). 'A strategy that is formulated without regard to its implementation is likely to be fatally flawed' (Grant, 2005: xii). RBV researchers state that 'the ability to implement strategies is, by itself, a resource that can be a source of competitive advantage' (Barney, 2001: 54).

Applied to HRM, a potentially effective HRM system may still fail to generate the desired results if it is not consistently implemented (Bowen & Ostroff, 2004). Similarly, Guest and Bos-Nehles (2013) argue that most research assumes that HRM practices are universally and consistently implemented and thus effectiveness is uniform. However, this is rarely the case. In line with this idea, a growing stream of research examines HR implementation. Nishii and Wright (2008) make a distinction between HRM practices 'on paper' (intended HRM), HRM practices that are actually implemented in an organisation (actual HRM) and how employees perceive these HRM practices (perceived HRM). They argue that variation in actual HRM will likely occur between different departments or teams because line managers differ in whether and how they implement HRM practices, and variation in perceived HRM will even be larger, because employees within these departments or teams differ in their needs, preferences and attributions (Nishii, Lepak, & Schneider, 2008; Nishii & Wright, 2008). Effective implementation would mean that intended, actual and perceived HRM are similar. Research has, indeed, shown that there is a disconnect between intended, actual and perceived HRM (eg Boon, Den Hartog, & Lepak, 2019; Den Hartog, Boon, Verburg, & Croon, 2013; Liao, Toya, Lepak, & Hong, 2009). At the same time, research has shown that employee perceptions of HRM are most strongly related to employee attitudes and behaviours, and performance (Guest, 1999). This approach thus emphasises the importance of consistent implementation of HRM by line managers, in order to maximise alignment and minimise variation between intended, actual and perceived HRM in organisations, such that the intended goals are likely to be achieved. Similarly, Bowen and Ostroff (2004; 2016) introduced the concept of 'HRM strength', which refers to the process through which consistent messages about the content of the HR system is communicated to employees.

Huselid and Becker (2011) also argue that a key component of successful strategy implementation is workforce differentiation, and that differentiation is a way to address the complexity inherent in strategic fit. They argue that 'some jobs are more valuable (strategic) than others, and they should be managed accordingly' (Huselid & Becker, 2011: 424). They focus on key strategic business processes which fit with a differentiated HR architecture that consists of the systems, practices, competencies and employee performance behaviours that reflect the development and management of the firm's strategic human capital (Becker & Huselid, 2006; Huselid & Becker, 2011). Related to this perspective is also the increased attention for developing HRM systems for different categories of employees. Lepak and Snell (1999; 2002) propose the HR architecture, a framework which distinguishes different categories of workers according to degree ***of added value*** of human capital and ***degree of uniqueness*** of human capital. Two recent reviews of HR differentiation and the HR architecture show that many researchers have assessed a differentiated HR architecture and showed the benefits of this approach (Marescaux, De Winne, & Brebels, 2021; Luo, Sun, Lin, Luo, Qin, & Pan, 2022). For example, Huselid, Beatty and Becker (2005) build on Lepak and Snell (1999) by developing a portfolio approach to workforce management. They identify strategic positions: (A positions) – those positions that contribute most to strategy and competitive advantage – and making sure that these are being fulfilled by the best possible employees (A players); and, secondly, that these are accompanied by good performers (B players) in essential support positions (B positions). The final step is making sure that non-performing employees (C players) and positions/jobs (C positions) that do not add value are eliminated.

In sum, we argue that strategic fit includes the following three dimensions:

- *Content*: to what degree are HR practices really focused on achieving business objectives as stated by the organisation?
- *Process*: to what degree is the HR function involved in the process of strategy formulation?
- *Implementation*: to what degree are HR practices consistently implemented in the organisation such that the intended goals can be achieved?

Dynamics and Agility

Besides the three elements that make up fit, Boon et al. (Boon et al., 2007; Boon, 2008) also propose to add a dynamic element to strategic fit, labelled *adaptation*. Adaptation focuses on how supportive of change and how proactive or reactive organisations and their HR systems are, which is important for maintaining strategic fit in changing environments. Organisations operate in dynamic environments and have to cope with change by continually adapting their business strategy to the turbulent environment. Yet, most HR researchers take a static approach in measuring fit, and researchers have just started to pay attention to dynamics (Boxall and Purcell, 2003; Kehoe, 2021). Some researchers such as Wright and Snell (1998) and Boxall and Purcell (2008) do draw attention to the importance of flexibility in strategic HRM, optimising adaptability and efficiency simultaneously. Miles and Snow (1994) see fit as a process of continuously adapting to changes in the environment and stress that 'unless a firm is alert and adept, today's fit becomes tomorrow's misfit'. While tight fit implies a close linkage between strategy and HRM, early fit is even more proactively oriented. Early fit is a tight fit that is achieved before competitors do and aims at gaining a leading position (Miles & Snow, 1994). Similarly, Lengnick-Hall and Beck (2005: 742) stress that organisations do not move from one equilibrium to another and argue that organisations should have a close connection to the environment in order to achieve long-term successfulness.

Building on the fit-flexibility framework of Wright and Snell (1998), the concept of HR flexibility was introduced (eg Beltrán-Martín, Bou-Llusar, & Salvador-Gómez, 2021; Beltrán-Martín, Roca-Puig, Escrig-Tena, & Bou-Llusar, 2008; Evans & Davis, 2005; Way et al., 2015; Way, Wright, Tracey, & Isnard, 2018). The realisation that strategic HRM should not only focus on achieving short-term results, but should also help organisations to be able to cope with future changes led to this line of research. In line with this, scholars extended the RBV and human capital theory beyond a focus on a firm's current human resource pool, to a focus on a firm's future human resource pool. HR flexibility can be defined as the 'organisational capabilities focused on adapting employee attributes – such as knowledge, skills and behaviours – to changing environmental conditions' (Beltrán-Martín et al., 2021: 2), and consists of resource flexibility (the extent to which resources can be used in a variety of contexts) and coordination flexibility (the ability to quickly acquire and deploy resources) (Way et al., 2015). Studies show that HR systems affect outcomes via increasing HR flexibility (eg Beltrán-Martín et al., 2008 and that HR flexibility is particularly helpful in enhancing firm performance in dynamic industries, but HR flexibility can be negatively related with performance when industry dynamism is low (Way et al., 2018).

The concept of *agility* goes a step further than adaptation or flexibility. An agile organisation (Dyer and Shafer, 1999, Nijssen and Paauwe, 2010) aims to develop a built-in capacity to shift, flex and adjust, either alone or with alliance partners, as circumstances change, and to do so as a matter of course. While adaptation focuses on strategic changes to cope with changing environments, agility implies that the whole firm should be flexible (Ahammad, Glaister, & Gomes, 2020). Strategy as such is not important; instead, all work processes should be organised such that they can move along with changes in the environment, and the role of HRM within agility is vital (Ahammad et al., 2020). In line with this, Paauwe (2004: 99) even goes one step further by suggesting 'agile' HRM systems, which – once achieved – can act as an enabling device for a whole range of strategic alternatives. As the dynamics in the marketplace increase for a range of sectors, we should not be bothered with trying to align HRM practices and policies with the business strategy, as it simply takes too long before the HRM practices start to take effect. The very moment the HRM practices are finally in place, the business strategies from which they were derived are already outmoded and replaced by new insights. So, in these circumstances, it might be better to focus on creating a workforce characterised by agility, which means the creation of a workforce which is eager to learn, able to handle changes as a normal way of life and is able to work in both virtual configurations as well as in reconfigurable real-life teams, which can easily be resolved and reformatted into another composition, dependent on the demands put forward by the marketplace.

Dyer and Ericksen (2006: 11) refer in this respect to the concept of workforce scalability as the capacity of an organisation to keep its human resources aligned on an ongoing basis by constantly transitioning from one human resource configuration to another etc. Workforce scalability consists of organisational/HRM practices aimed at workforce alignment (fit) and workforce fluidity (flexibility). Workforce alignment refers to a static steady state, yet workforce fluidity refers to the speed and ease with which transitions are made from one aligned human resource configuration to another … ad infinitum (Dyer and Ericksen, 2006: 12), which is relevant for organisations operating in highly dynamic markets. Nijssen and Paauwe have developed this concept further by referring to the following enabling practices:

- Building relations with suppliers of human resources as well as potential employers of the workforce;
- Competence-based training;

- Training aimed at building a broad skill set (eg cross-training and job-rotation);
- Discretionary work design (relying on own initiative);
- Allowing organisational slack.

(Nijssen and Paauwe, 2012: 3323)

Recently the concept of Agile working has gained momentum. Agile or agility originally stems from the software development sector, but nowadays the concept of agile ways of working has become increasingly popular in other areas (such as banking, health care, education) and in other functional domains than just ICT. Examples include marketing and human resources (Steegh, 2024). The so-called Scrum approach has become a popular practice of working agile at the team level. A recent literature review study defines the agile way of working at the team level by the following five key dimensions (Steegh, 2024):

- Agile team orientation: The members share a collectivistic attitude and commitment towards the team and its way of working;
- Customer collaboration: Agile teams closely collaborate with customers;
- Cross-functional collaboration: Due to the complexity of the task, the Agile teams consists of team members with diverse knowledge, skills and abilities;
- Reflexivity: Teams reflect, plan and adapt their plans if required and do this in cycles of two–four weeks, including input from and interaction with customers and stakeholders;
- Shared leadership: The teams are characterised by low levels of hierarchical differentiation, which results in a distribution of leadership roles.

Needless to say that the Agile way of working, once applied on a large scale, will have consequences for strategy development, leadership and the way in which performance management will be applied.

In sum, on the one hand, HRM is dependent on the strategic positioning of the firm; on the other hand, human resources can be cultivated and developed in order to build strategic capability that will result in a competitive advantage. So the apparently conflicting perspectives of 'outside-in' and 'inside-out' are, in reality, a paradox; a situation in which two seemingly contradictory or even mutually exclusive factors are both true at the same time. We will now reconcile the two perspectives (outside-in and inside-out) in our search for a synthesis.

In Search of a Synthesis

Apart from the Beer et al. model (1984b), most early USA-based models and research designs that focus on the link between HRM and performance were often based on financial performance indicators such as profit, shareholders' value, ROI etc. This was in sharp contrast with European-based (especially mainland European) models, which used more stakeholder-oriented approaches, balancing the needs, interests and aspirations of the various stakeholders both inside and outside the organisation. These two different perspectives contrast profitability and responsibility. Paauwe and Boselie (2003, 2005), for example, draw attention to the importance of legitimacy and responsibility of organisations. They apply institutional theory to strategic HRM to incorporate pressures of the institutional context on HRM. Nowadays, many approaches shift towards a focus on the contextual nature of HRM, change and paying more attention to a variety of stakeholders.

By way of synthesis we present two recent conceptual frameworks that take into account the broader context of strategic HRM. The first one we present here is the HR ecosystem framework as developed by Snell and Morris (2021) who argue that most research on fit does not fully take into account the complex and dynamic realities of today's organisations; the increasingly diverse workforce, work environments and necessary skills that are quickly changing, the increase in types of work relationships (eg including temporary work and gig work) and quickly evolving technologies. To account for this increased variability, they propose the HR ecosystem framework.

The HR ecosystem is defined as 'a purposeful work arrangement among two or more worker communities to create value for a common set of customers' (Snell, Swart, Morris, & Boon, 2023: 5) and consists of a range of different elements, including strategy, workforce composition, capabilities and culture, that are interacting with each other and coevolving with the organisation. The HR ecosystem includes processes of both convergence and divergence: 'the system needs to hold the organisation together while at the same time forming and reforming its composition' (Snell & Morris, 2021: 227). Also, it explicitly includes both complexity and adaptation. Taken together, the HR ecosystem framework offers insight in the processes of alignment and highlights the need to approach fit in an evolutionary way, and trying to find a balance between divergence and convergence in order to achieve a better fit over time. For an extensive description of all the elements of this framework and underlying theorising/argumentation, we refer to Snell and Morris (2021).

The second framework we would like to present here as a form of synthesis originates from the *contextually based human resource theory* of Paauwe (2004), which took into account the importance of the internal and external context of organisations. The model incorporated inside-out and outside-in approaches, institutionalism, demonstrates a stakeholder perspective, and included both content and processes of HRM. In 2017, Paauwe and Farndale revised this model, based on doing research, consultancy and executive training, which resulted into the 'Contextual SHRM Framework' (Paauwe and Farndale, 2017: 103). (See Figure 3.3.)

The Contextual SHRM Framework helps to analyse the connection between the firm's context, the business strategy, required organisational capabilities and legitimacy claims, the resulting design of HRM and subsequent organisational performance. It incorporates elements of the contingency and configurational models (Delery & Doty, 1996), new institutional theory

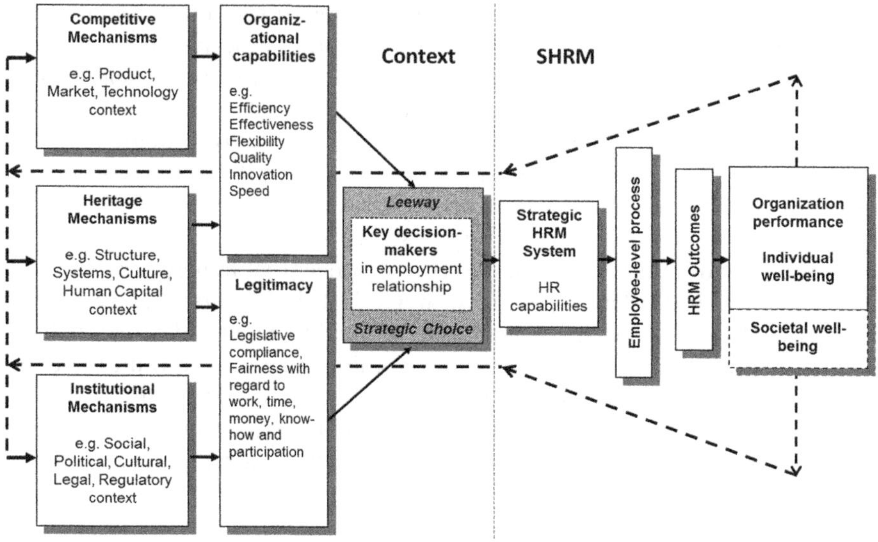

Figure 3.3 The contextual SHRM framework

(DiMaggio & Powell, 1983), RBV (Barney, 1991), and is inspired by the Harvard approach (Beer, Spector, Lawrence, Mills, & Walton, 1984a). It does not only encompass a systems approach, but also actors (agency). Whereas a systems approach might give the impression of a functionalistic and deterministic approach, adding an actor's perspective to it implies leeway, agency for making choices for the relevant actors involved, such as the management team, HR director, works councils, trade union representatives etc.

The first point to note is that there are two sides to the Contextual SHRM Model as depicted in Figure 3.3: the 'context' side and the 'SHRM' side. According to Paauwe and Farndale, the context side focuses on the three dominant factors in an organisation's context: competitive mechanisms, institutional mechanisms (including social, political, legal and regulatory elements) and the organisation's heritage mechanisms. The actors' perspective or the role of agency is reflected by the 'key decision-makers' in the employment relationship who have leeway for strategic choice in any given organisational context.

The outcomes of the competitive, institutional and heritage mechanisms are, on the one hand, 'organisational capabilities'; and on the other hand, claims for legitimacy and fairness. These describe how the firm is dealing with its reality, often describing a desired state. Paauwe and Farndale (2016:11/12) mention the following example:

> ... from an institutional mechanisms perspective, there may be legislation in place requiring employee involvement in corporate decision-making (eg a system of codetermination). In order to achieve legitimacy, the

organisation may set up a works council to achieve the required level of employee voice. The legislation is part of the institutional mechanisms affecting the firm, but the means to achieving legitimacy is the firm's response to meet the demands for legitimacy (defined at the exchange level as between an organisation and society, and at the fairness level as between employee and employer).

The same kind of reasoning can be developed with respect to the competitive mechanisms: A company might be faced with ever-changing customer demands, which require a high degree of flexibility and/or agility as an organisational capability in order to deal with the dynamics in the marketplace. Based on the demands resulting from the three context dimensions, the key decision-makers face the challenge of developing proper HRM systems in order to meet with the demands for organisational capabilities as well as legitimacy and fairness claims.

Different forms of fit or alignment are represented in the Contextual SHRM Framework. First, there is the organisational fit between the organisation's heritage and its SHRM system, aimed at establishing an appropriate linkage between the HRM system and other relevant systems in the organisation including technological, production and control systems (Wood, 1999). Second, there is the 'strategic' (vertical) fit between the competitive mechanisms and the SHRM system in order to make sure that the HRM system is aligned with business strategy. At the same time, this also emphasises the importance of implementation capability, which to a large degree will be determined by the quality of the HR department and its interaction with line management. Third, 'environmental' or 'institutional' fit, which entails ensuring an appropriate alignment of the HRM system with the institutional environment of the organisation, including the social, cultural, political and legal contexts. Finally, 'internal' (horizontal) fit should be is present in the HRM system itself. Its various components must fit together to maximise the synergies of the system (Farndale & Paauwe, 2018: 206).

Having explored the context side of the Contextual SHRM Model, Paauwe and Farndale build on the notion of internal alignment to uncover the SHRM side of the model. Here they explore the key decision-makers who are responsible for devising a strategic HRM system. The aim here is to create HRM capabilities that can support the organisational capabilities arising from the competitive, institutional and heritage mechanisms. HRM capabilities are defined as 'the routines embedded in the tacit and implicit knowledge of members of an organisation functioning to acquire, develop, nurture, deploy and redeploy human resources in a dynamic, competitive environment' (Park, Gardner, & Wright, 2004: 262).

The next part of the framework, HRM outcomes, are the result of employee-level processes in the organisation – employee attitudes and behaviours that are reactions to the SHRM system, such as employee job satisfaction, turnover, absenteeism, engagement, organisational citizenship behaviours and commitment. HRM outcomes are a result of the application of a range of HRM practices affected by a variety of moderating and mediating contextual factors, such as organisational justice, climate, leadership style, involvement of line management etc. For an extensive treatment, see Paauwe and Farndale (2017).

As far as the final outcomes are concerned, Paauwe and Farndale emphasise in the *Contextual SHRM Model*, the overall firm performance as being 'a balancing act between financial performance, employee well-being and societal well-being. We argue that it is important to offset a managerial perspective that focuses on financial performance indicators (organisation outcomes) such as productivity, customer satisfaction, sales and profit, with an employer perspective that pays greater attention to employee well-being' (Paauwe and Farndale, 2016: 15/16). Finally, through societal well-being, the Contextual SHRM Framework emphasises that the performance of a firm consequently impacts on the society in which it is embedded. Firms do not operate in a vacuum. Firms both react to and help to create the context in which they are embedded. The societal implications of firm performance, in turn, feed back into the context in which the organisation is operating, becoming an antecedent to the institutional, competitive and heritage mechanisms the firm faces. (Paauwe and Farndale, 2017).

In Conclusion

By presenting these two frameworks, we aligned a variety of perspectives that are all important in strategic HRM: outside-in and inside-out approaches, strategic contingency theory, RBV and institutional theory, HR differentiation, systems' approach and actors' approach by including the key decision-makers as well as the capability of the HR department. Also, we emphasised a broad performance concept, composed of organisational performance, individual well-being and societal well-being, all amid of a complex and changing, dynamic context.

At the same time, we need to be aware of the fact that, reflecting on reality, in many cases HRM is not strategic at all. The strategic role of HRM largely varies between companies and sectors and can depend on market conditions. Sometimes HRM is very reactive and short-term oriented. For example, in case of a sudden drop in sales – caused by an energy crisis – the HR function is involved in the termination of labour contracts, cutting the outsourcing of activities and stops making use of temporary work agencies, just in order to cut expenses and help to restore a proper balance between cash inflow and cash outflow. Sometimes in highly stable situations, HR is only concerned with the administration and control of regular inflow and outflow of people based on acceptable degrees of labour turnover. However, due to fierce and very often international competition and the introduction of market mechanisms in former public sectors (think of energy, water, health care, etc.), increasingly more companies are faced with competitive demands which necessitate a strategic, dynamic and even agile approach to the management of people.

References

Ahammad, M. F., Glaister, K. W., & Gomes, E. (2020). Strategic agility and human resource management. *Human Resource Management Review, 30*(1), 100–700.

Alingh, R. A., Hoekstra, F., van der Schans, C. P., Hettinga, F. J., Dekker, R., & van der Woude, L. H. (2015). Protocol of a longitudinal cohort study on physical activity behaviour in physically disabled patients participating in a rehabilitation counselling programme: ReSpAct. *BMJ Open, 5*(1), e007591.

Appelbaum, E., Bailey, T., Berg, P., & Kalleberg, A. (2000). *Why High-Performance Work Systems Pay Off.* Ithaca, NY: Cornell University Press.

Bach, S., & Kessler, I. (2007). HRM and the new public management. In Boxall, P. F., Purcell, J., & Wright, P. M. (Eds.). *The Oxford Handbook of Human Resource Management.* Oxford Handbooks Online, (pp. 200–240)..

Baden Fuller, C., & Stopford, J. M. (1994). Creating corporate entrepreneurship. *Strategic Management Journal, 15*(7), 521–536.

Barney, J. B. (1991). Firm resources and sustained competitive advantage. *Journal of Management, 17*(1), 99–120.

Barney, J. B. (2001). Is the resource-based 'view' a useful perspective for strategic management research? Yes. *Academy of Management Review, 26*(1), 41–56.

Batistič, S., & Poell, R. F. (2022). Do HR systems and relational climates affect knowledge hiding? An experiment and two-source multi-level study. *Journal of Business Research, 147*, 82–96.

Batt, R., Holman, D., & Holtgrewe, U. (2009). The globalization of service work: Comparative institutional perspectives on call centers: Introduction to a special issue of Industrial & Labor Relations Review. *ILR Review, 62*(4), 453–488.

Becker, B., & Huselid, M. A. (2006). Strategic human resource management: Where do we go from here? *Journal of Management, 32*(6), 898–925.

Beer, M., Boselie, P., & Brewster, C. (2015). Back to the future: Implications for the field of HRM of the multistakeholder perspective proposed 30 years ago. *Human Resource Management, 54*(3), 427–438.

Beer, M., Spector, B., Lawrence, P.R., & Mills, D.Q. (1984b). *Managing Human Assets: The Groundbreaking Harvard Business School Program.* New York: Free Press.

Beer, M., Spector, B., Lawrence, P., Quinn Mills, D., & Walton, R. (1984a). *Human Resource Management: A General Manager's Perspective.* New York: Free Press.

Beltrán-Martín, I., Bou-Llusar, J. C., & Salvador-Gómez, A. (2021). HR flexibility and firm performance in professional service firms. *Journal of Management & Organization, 30*(6) 1–22.

Beltrán-Martín, I., Roca-Puig, V., Escrig-Tena, A., & Bou-Llusar, J. C. (2008). Human resource flexibility as a mediating variable between high performance work systems and performance. *Journal of Management, 34*(5), 1009–1044.

Bennett, N., Ketchen, D. J. Jr., & Schultz, E. B. (1998). An examination of factors associated with the integration of human resource management and strategic decision making. *Human Resource Management, 37*(1), 3–16.

Boon, C. (2008). *HRM and Fit: Survival of the Fittest!* Rotterdam: ERIM/Erasmus University Rotterdam.

Boon, C., Boselie, P., Paauwe, J., & Den Hartog, D. N. (2007). *Measuring strategic and internal fit in HRM: An alternative approach.* Proceedings of The Academy of Management Annual Meeting, Philadelphia, PA, August.

Boon, C., Den Hartog, D. N., & Lepak, D. P. (2019). A systematic review of human resource management systems and their measurement. *Journal of Management, 45*(6), 2498–2537.

Boon, C., Eckardt, R., Lepak, D. P., & Boselie, P. (2018). Integrating strategic human capital and strategic human resource management. *The International Journal of Human Resource Management, 29*(1), 34–67.

Bos-Nehles, A., Townsend, K., Cafferkey, K., & Trullen, J. (2023). Examining the Ability, Motivation and Opportunity (AMO) framework in HRM research: Conceptualization, measurement and interactions. *International Journal of Management Reviews, 25*(4), 725–739.

Boselie, P., Dietz, G., & Boon, C. (2005). Commonalities and contradictions in HRM and performance research. *Human Resource Management Journal, 15*(3), 67–94.

Bowen, D. E., & Ostroff, C. (2004). Understanding HRM–firm performance linkages: The role of the "strength" of the HRM system. *Academy of Management Review, 29*(2), 203–221.

Boxall, P., & Purcell, J. (2003). *Strategy and Human Resource Management.* New York: Palgrave Macmillan.

Boxall, P., & Purcell, J. (2008). *Strategy and Human Resource Management* (2nd edn.). New York: Palgrave Macmillan.

Boy Akdag, L., & Ekmekci, Ö. T. (2023). Exploring the black box of human resource and business strategy linkage: The effect of strategic fits on organisational performance. *International Journal of Manpower, 44*(5), 859–879.

Collins, C., & Kehoe, R. (2017). Examining strategic fit and misfit in the management of knowledge workers. *ILR Review, 70*(2), 308–335.

Combs, J., Liu, Y., Hall, A., & Ketchen, D. (2006). How much do high-performance work practices matter? A meta-analysis of their effects on organisational performance. *Personnel Psychology, 59*(3), 501–528.

Delery, J. E. (1998). Issues of fit in strategic human resource management: Implications for research, *Human Resource Management Review, 8*(3), 289–309.

Delery, J. E., & Doty, D. H. (1996). Modes of theorizing in strategic human resource management: Tests of universalistic, contingency, and configurational performance predictions, *Academy of Management Journal, 39*(4), 802–835.

De Wit, B., & Meyer, R. (1998). *Strategy: Process, Content, Context: An International Perspective* (2nd edn.). London: Thomson.

Den Hartog, D. N., Boon, C., Verburg, R. M., & Croon, M. A. (2013). HRM, communication, satisfaction, and perceived performance: A cross-level test. *Journal of Management, 39*(6), 1637–1665.

DiMaggio, P., & Powell, W. W. (1983). The iron cage revisited: Collective rationality and institutional isomorphism in organisational fields. *American Sociological Review, 48*(2), 147–160.

Dyer, L. and Ericksen, J. (2006). *Dynamic Organizations: Achieving Marketplace Agility through Workforce Scalability.* Ithaca, NY: Cornell University, School of Industrial and Labor Relations, Center for Advanced Human Resource Studies.

Dyer, L., & Shafer, R. A. (1999). From human resource strategy to organisational effectiveness: Lessons from research on organisational agility. *Research in Personnel and Human Resource Management, 4*, 145–174.

Evans, W. R., & Davis, W. D. (2005). High-performance work systems and organisational performance: The mediating role of internal social structure. *Journal of Management, 31*(5), 758–775.

Farndale, E. & Paauwe, J. (2018). SHRM and context: Why firms want to be as different as legitimately possible. *Journal of Organizational Effectiveness: People and Performance, 5*(1), 202–210.

Farndale, E., Paauwe, J., & Boselie, P. (2010). An exploratory study of governance in the intra-firm human resources supply chain. *Human Resource Management, 49*(5), 849–868.

Fombrun, C. J., Tichy, M. M., & Devanna, M. A. (1984). *Strategic Human Resource Management.* New York: John Wiley.

Gerhart, B. (2004). *Research on human resources and effectiveness: Selected methodological challenges, HRM: What's Next?* Rotterdam: Erasmus University.

Gerhart, B., & Feng, J. (2021). The resource-based view of the firm, human resources, and human capital: Progress and prospects: *Journal of Management, 47*(7), 1796–1819.

Golden, K. A., & Ramanujam, V. (1985). Between a dream and a nightmare: On the integration of the human resource management and strategic business planning processes, *Human Resource Management, 24*(4), 429–452.

Grant, R. M. (2005). *Contemporary Strategy Analysis* (5th Rev Edn). Oxford: Blackwell Publishing.

Gratton, L., Hope-Hailey, V., Stiles, P., & Truss, C. (1999a). Linking individual performance to business strategy: The people process model. *Human Resource Management, 38*(1), 17–31.

Guerci, M., Radaelli, G., De Battisti, F., & Siletti, E. (2017). Empirical insights on the nature of synergies among HRM policies—An analysis of an ethics-oriented HRM system. *Journal of Business Research, 71*, 66–73.

Guest, D. E. (1997). Human resource management and performance: A review and research agenda. *International Journal of Human Resource Management, 8*(3), 263–276.

Guest, D. E. (1999). Human resource management–the workers' verdict. *Human Resource Management Journal, 9*(3), 5–25.

Guest, D. E., Bos-Nehles, A. C., Paauwe, J., & Wright, P. (2013). HRM and performance: The role of effective implementation. In *HRM and Performance: Achievements and Challenges* (pp. 79–96).

Gupta, A. K., Smith, K. G., & Shalley, C. E. (2006). The interplay between exploration and exploitation. *Academy of Management Journal, 49*(4), 693–706.

Han, J. H., Kang, S., Oh, I.-S., Kehoe, R. R., & Lepak, D. (2019). The goldilocks effect of strategic human resource management? Optimizing the benefits of a high performance work system through the dual alignment of vertical and horizontal fit. *Academy of Management Journal, 62*(5), 1388–1412.

Hendry, C., & Pettigrew, A. (1986). The practice of strategic human resource management. *Personnel Review, 15*(5), 3–8.

Hong, Y., Liao, H., Raub, S., & Han, J. H. (2016). What it takes to get proactive: An integrative multilevel model of the antecedents of personal initiative. *Journal of Applied Psychology, 101*(5), 687–701.

Huselid, M. A. (1995). The impact of human resource management practices on turnover, productivity, and corporate financial performance. *Academy of Management Journal, 38*(3), 635–672.

Huselid, M. A., Beatty, R. W., & Becker, B. E. (2005). 'A players' or 'A positions'? *Harvard Business Review, 83*(12), 110–117.

Huselid, M. A., & Becker, B. E. (2011). Bridging micro and macro domains: Workforce differentiation and strategic human resource management. *Journal of Management, 37*(2), 421–428.

Jackson, S. E., Schuler, R. S., & Jiang, K. (2014). An aspirational framework for strategic human resource management. *Academy of Management Annals, 8*(1), 1–56.

Jiang, K., Lepak, D. P., Hu, J., & Baer, J. C. (2012). How does human resource management influence organisational outcomes? A meta-analytic investigation of mediating mechanisms. *Academy of Management Journal, 55*(6), 1264–1294.

Jiang, K., Takeuchi, R., & Lepak, D. P. (2013). Where do we go from here. New perspectives on the Black Box in strategic human resource management research. *Journal of Management Studies, 50*(8), 1448–1480.

Kalleberg, A. L., Marsden, P. V., Reynolds, J., & Knoke, D. (2006). Beyond profit? Sectoral differences in high-performance work practices. *Work and Occupations, 33*(3), 271–302.

Kehoe, R. R. (2021). Revisiting the concepts of vertical and horizontal fit in HRM: What we know, what we don't know, and where we might go. *Academy of Management Perspectives, 35*(2), 175–180.

Kroon, B., & Paauwe, J. (2014). Structuration of precarious employment in economically constrained firms: The case of Dutch agriculture. *Human Resource Management Journal, 24*(1), 19–37.

Lawrence, P. R., & Lorsch, J. (1967). *Organization and Environment*. Boston, MA: Harvard School of Business Administration Press.

Lengnick-Hall, C. A., & Beck, T. E. (2005). Adaptive fit versus robust transformation: How organisations respond to environmental change. *Journal of Management, 31*(5), 738–757.

Lepak, D. P., & Snell, S. A. (1999). The human resource architecture: Toward a theory of human capital allocation and development. *Academy of Management Review, 24*(1), 31–48.

Lepak, D. P., & Snell, S. A. (2002). Examining the human resource architecture: The relationships among human capital, employment, and human resource configurations. *Journal of Management, 28*(4), 517–543.

Liao, H., Toya, K., Lepak, D. P., & Hong, Y. (2009). Do they see eye to eye? Management and employee perspectives of high-performance work systems and influence processes on service quality. *Journal of Applied Psychology, 94*(2), 371–391.

Luo, B. N., Sun, T., Lin, C. H. V., Luo, D., Qin, G., & Pan, J. (2022). The human resource architecture model: A twenty-year review and future research directions. *Strategic Human Resource Management and Organizational Effectiveness*, 17–54.

Marescaux, E., De Winne, S., & Brebels, L. (2021). Putting the pieces together: A review of HR differentiation literature and a multilevel model. *Journal of Management, 47*(6), 1564–1595.

Miles, R. E., & Snow, C. C. (1978). *Organizational Strategy, Structure, and Process*. New York: McGraw-Hill.

Miles, R. E., & Snow, C. C. (1984). Designing strategic human resources systems. *Organizational Dynamics, 13*(1), 3652.–
Miles, R. E., & Snow, C. C. (1994). *Fit, Failure, and the Hall of Fame: How Companies Succeed or Fail.* New York: The Free Press.
Mintzberg, H. (1979). *The Structuring of Organizations.* London: Prentice Hall.
Mintzberg, H. (1987). Five p's for strategy. *California Management Review, 30,* 11–24.
Mintzberg, H. (1990). The design school: Reconsidering the basic premises of strategic management. *Strategic Management Journal, 11,* 171–195.
Mintzberg, H., Ahlstrand, B., & Lampel, J. (1998). *Strategy Safari: A Guided Tour Through the Wilds of Strategic Management.* New York: Free Press.
Mintzberg, H., Ahlstrand, B., & Lampel, J. (2009). *Strategy Safari: Your Complete Guide Through the Wilds of Strategic Management.* Upper Saddle River, NJ: Pearson Education.
Mirvis, P. H. (1997). Human resource management: Leaders, laggards, and followers. *Academy of Management Executive, 11*(2), 43–56.
Mohammed, S. S., Batistic, S., Černe, M., & Poell, R. F. (2023). Does the context matter? The interplay of HR systems and relational climates predicting individual and team creativity. *Creativity Research Journal, 35*(1), 63–81.
Montemayor, E. F. (1996). Congruence between pay policy and competitive strategy in high-performing firms. *Journal of Management, 22*(6), 889–908.
Nijssen, M., & Paauwe, J. (2010). *HRM, Dynamic Environments and Institutionalism: How to Achieve Organisational Agility.* Working Paper IIRA, Presented at the HR Study Group, Copenhagen.
Nijssen, M., & Paauwe, J. (2012). HRM in turbulent times: How to achieve organisational agility? *The International Journal of Human Resource Management, 23*(16), 3315–3335.
Nishii, L. H., Lepak, D. P., & Schneider, B. (2008). Employee attributions of the "why" of HR practices: Their effects on employee attitudes and behaviors, and customer satisfaction. *Personnel Psychology, 61*(3), 503545.–
Nishii, L. H., & Wright, P. (2008). Variability at multiple levels of analysis: Implications for strategic human resource management. In D. B. Smith (Ed.), *The People Make the Place.* New York: Taylor and Francis. (pp. 225–248).
Ostroff, C., & Bowen, D. E. (2016). Reflections on the 2014 decade award: Is there strength in the construct of HR system strength? *Academy of Management Review, 41*(2), 196–214.
Paauwe, J. (2004). *HRM and Performance: Achieving Long-Term Viability.* Oxford: Oxford University Press.
Paauwe, J. (2009). HRM and performance: Achievements, methodological issues and prospects. *Journal of Management Studies, 46*(1), 129–142.
Paauwe, J., & Boselie, P. (2003). Challenging 'strategic HRM' and the relevance of the institutional setting. *Human Resource Management Journal, 13*(3), 56–70.
Paauwe, J., & Boselie, P. (2005). HRM and performance: What's next? *Human Resource Management Journal, 15*(4), 68–83.
Paauwe, J., & Farndale, E. (2016). *Modelling the SHRM-performance relationship: The contextual SHRM model.* Paper presented at the Xth international workshop on HRM, October, Cadiz, Spain.
Paauwe, J., & Farndale, E. (2017). *Strategy, HRM and Performance: A Contextual Approach.* Oxford: Oxford University Press.

Park, H. J., Gardner, T. M., & Wright, P. M. (2004). HR practices or HR capabilities: Which matters? Insights from the Asia Pacific region. *Asia Pacific Journal of Human Resources, 42*(3), 260–273.

Porter, M.E. (1980). *Competitive Strategy.* New York: Free Press.

Porter, M. E. (1985). *Competitive Advantage: Creating and Sustaining Superior Performance.* New York: Free Press.

Rabl, T., Jayasinghe, M., Gerhart, B., & Kühlmann, T. M. (2014). A meta-analysis of country differences in the high-performance work system-business performance relationship: The roles of national culture and managerial discretion. *Journal of Applied Psychology, 99*(6), 1011–1041.

Ray, C., Essman, S., Nyberg, A. J., Ployhart, R. E., & Hale, D. (2023). Human capital resources: Reviewing the first decade and establishing a foundation for future research. *Journal of Management, 49*(1), 280–324.

Schuler, R. S., & Jackson, S. E. (1987). Linking competitive strategies with human resource management practices. *Academy of Management Executive, 1*(3), 207–219.

Schultz, E. B., Bennett, N., & Ketchen Jr, D. J. (2015). An examination of the relationship between strategy and human resource management practices among small businesses. *Journal of Small Business Strategy, 8*(1), 35–48.

Schumpeter, J. A. (1934). *The Theory of Economic Development.* Cambridge, MA: Harvard University Press, p. 19.

Snell, S. A., & Morris, S. S. (2021). Time for realignment: The HR ecosystem. *Academy of Management Perspectives, 35*(2), 219–236.

Snell, S. A., Swart, J., Morris, S., & Boon, C. (2023). The HR ecosystem: Emerging trends and a future research agenda. *Human Resource Management, 62*(1), 5–14.

Steegh, R (2024 *Adaptiveness in action: Exploring the processes ad outcomes of the agile way of working.* PhD Dissertation Tilburg University, Tilburg.

Stopford, J. M., & Baden-Fuller, C. W. (1994). Creating corporate entrepreneurship. *Strategic Management Journal, 15*(7), 521–536.

Subramony, M. (2009). A meta-analytic investigation of the relationship between HRM bundles and firm performance. *Human Resource Management, 48*(5), 745–768.

Tampoe, M., & MacMillan, H. (2000). *Strategic management, process, content and implementation.* Oxford: Oxford University Press.

Toh, S. M., Morgeson, F. P., & Campion, M. A. (2008). Human resource configurations: Investigating fit with the organisational context. *Journal of Applied Psychology, 93*(4), 864.

Veld, M., Paauwe, J., & Boselie, P. (2010). HRM and strategic climates in hospitals: Does the message come across at the ward level?. *Human Resource Management Journal, 20*(4), 339–356.

Volberda, H. W. (2004). *De flexibele onderneming: strategieën voor succesvol concurreren.* London: Kluwer.

Volberda, H. W., & Elfring, T. (Eds.). (2001). *Rethinking Strategy.* London: Sage.

Way, S. A., Tracey, J. B., Fay, C. H., Wright, P. M., Snell, S. A., Chang, S., & Gong, Y. (2015). Validation of a multidimensional HR flexibility measure. *Journal of Management, 41*(4), 1098–1131.

Way, S. A., Wright, P. M., Tracey, J. B., & Isnard, J. F. (2018). HR flexibility: Precursors and the contingent impact on firm financial performance. *Human Resource Management, 57*(2), 567–582.

Whittington, R. (1993). *What is Strategy, and Does It Matter?* London: Routledge.

Whittington, R. (2001). *What is Strategy-and Does it Matter?* London: Cengage Learning EMEA.

Wood, S. (1999). Human resource management and performance. *International Journal of Management Reviews, 1*(4), 367–413.

Wright, P. M. (2021). Rediscovering the "Human" in strategic human capital. *Human Resource Management Review, 31*(4), 100781.

Wright, P. M., Coff, R., & Moliterno, T. P. (2014). Strategic human capital: Crossing the great divide. *Journal of Management, 40*(2), 353–370.

Wright, P. M., & Haggerty, J. J. (2005). *Missing Variables in Theories of Strategic Human Resource Management: Time, Cause, and Individuals: 17.* Ithaca, NY: CAHRS at Cornell University.

Wright, P. M., & McMahan, G. C. (1992). Theoretical perspectives for strategic human resource management. *Journal of Management, 18*(2), 295–320.

Wright, P. M., & Snell, S. A. (1998). Toward a unifying framework for exploring fit and flexibility in strategic human resource management. *Academy of Management Review, 23*(4), 756–772.

Wright, P. M., & Ulrich, M. D. (2017). A road well traveled: The past, present, and future journey of strategic human resource management. *Annual Review of Organizational Psychology and Organizational Behavior, 4*(1), 45–65.

Youndt, M. A., Snell, S. A., Dean, J. W., & Lepak, D. P. (1996). Human resource management, manufacturing strategy, and firm performance. *Academy of Management Journal, 39*(4), 836–866.

4 HRM and Organisational Performance

Stephen Wood

Introduction

Strategic human resource management (HRM), which came to the fore in the liberal market economies in the 1980s, places primacy on the impact of the human resource and its management on strategic outcomes. It reflects what Collings, Wood and Szamosi refer to in the opening chapter as the use of the term HRM to indicate a 'more strategic role' for people management than it had under a regime of personnel management; the fulfilment of which is oriented to 'the agenda of shareholder value'. Other stakeholders' interests, including employees, are at best secondary or are to be reconciled with those of the shareholders. A contrasting stakeholder approach sees strategic HRM as more of a process of managing human resources in light of competing pressures and in which management reconciles competing tensions where possible or makes appropriate trade-offs where necessary.

At the extreme, the former, the shareholder approach, treats employees like any other commodity, as a resource to be used to maximise the profits of the firm or in the case of other organisations, the key performance indicators, and to be discarded when of no further use. While the latter, the stakeholder approach, treats employees' humanity as distinguishing them from other resources and giving them a prominent position with unique rights amongst stakeholders. The emphasis for HRM in the shareholder approach would be its direct effect on the profitability and asset value of the organisation; while in the stakeholder approach, its impact directly on employees would be a priority. Indeed, the stakeholder approach has arisen partly as a counteraction to the shareholder approach, as European writers in particular sought to rebalance priorities in HRM thinking.

Allied to the rise of strategic HRM was the development of new models of people management with an emphasis on employee involvement and development. It was argued that traditional methods of management often characterised as Taylorist, after the founder of the scientific management theory, with its focus on standardising work and narrowly defined job specifications, was no longer appropriate in an increasingly dynamic and competitive economy. Such Taylorism led to an under-utilisation and development of human skills; but in

DOI: 10.4324/9781032625560-5

the current context, approaches that involve workers more or enhance their skills ought to yield competitive advantages for firms or increase the efficiency and quality of public service provision.

Given this expectation, that innovative approaches that reverse certain features of Taylorism would guarantee higher levels of performance than would traditional systems, they have been widely labelled as high-performance systems. Moreover, it was widely assumed that increased opportunities for involvement and development would be beneficial for workers and deemed desirable by them. High-performance systems were thus portrayed as delivering the fulfilment of both employees' and employers' needs, offering mutual gains to both parties. An approach that satisfies stockholders' needs could yield employee satisfaction and well-being and, hence, a key tension that was thought to require managers to make trade-offs no longer existed and the distinction between the stockholder and shareholder approaches becomes redundant. However, it was also noted that when faced with economic crises, management as agents of shareholders may introduce cost-cutting measures such as wage and employment freezes, job restructuring and of work intensification, which undermine the efficacy of the new HRM (Cappelli, 1999; Godard, 2004).

In the wake of both the claims for HRM and questions surrounding it, a line of research developed in the early 1990s that examined whether particular HRM models are, indeed, associated with higher levels of organisational performance. This chapter introduces some of the key studies and assesses whether they support the claims made that HRM can be decisive for organisational performance, or more specifically, that an HRM centred on employee involvement or development justifies the high-performance tag.

The Concepts Underlying the HRM-Performance Studies

Human resource management increasingly replaced personnel management in organisations, professional circles and academia as a term to represent that part of an organisation's activities concerned with the recruitment, development and management of its employees in order to convey a modernisation of personnel management. At its simplest, modernisation entailed placing much more emphasis on the contribution of people to the key performance indicators, that is, on treating employees on a par with technology as an asset of the organisation rather than a cost that should be minimised.

Pfeffer (1998) indeed characterises the high-performance system as 'profits through people'. He saw this initially as involving 13 main practices: employment security, selectivity in recruiting, high wages, information sharing, teams and job redesign, training and skill development, symbolic egalitarianism, cross-utilisation and cross-training, incentive pay, employee ownership, participation and empowerment, wage compression and promotion from within. But in a subsequent listing he reduced these to a core, the first seven in that list (Pfeffer, 1998). These practices are contrasted with non-people-centred methods such as those associated with the control-centred Taylorist approach, the heavy use of contingent workers and piecework compensation systems.

The rationale underlying Pfeffer's listing (final or original) of practices appears to be that they represent sophisticated people management or HRM, much of which builds on behavioural science research, for example, on selection. However, in keeping with the emphasis on strategic HRM fulfilling stakeholders' objectives, Huselid et al. (1997) and others distinguish strategic practices from technical practices on the basis that the former contribute to profitability, innovation and the asset base of the organisation. In contrast, technical practices play a maintenance role, ensuring that the correct human resources are in place. Most of the practices in Pfeffer's list are in Huselid et al.'s terms, strategic, but selection method is the most prominent practice in Pfeffer's list, one that is treated as technical, playing a maintenance role.

The implication of Huselid et al.'s definition is that strategic practices are concerned with the development and utilisation of the people once they are in place in the organisation. This has been the key focus of the high-involvement modernisation agenda. Here the emphasis is on the advantages of involving all employees through giving them more discretion over how they do their job and engaging them in modes of involvement concerned with idea generation and managerial decision-making. Capturing this vision, Lawler (1986), Walton (1985) and others in the 1980s portrayed the HRM required for the future as what they termed the high-involvement or high-commitment model. It covers both job and organisational involvement, to use Wall et al.'s (2004) terms and includes job enrichment, teamwork, idea-capturing methods such as quality circles, functional flexibility, extensive training and development, as well as motivational methods to support these, such as internal promotion and contingent reward systems. The adoption of such practices involves the curtailment of certain Taylorist principles, which rested on a divorce of the conception of tasks from their execution, the former the prerogative of managers, the latter the role of workers.

It is claimed that increased uncertainty, competition and technological development are demanding that all employees should be more engaged and proactive in their jobs than they were in Taylorist mass production systems – the car assembly line being the paradigm case of these – if organisations are to survive in an increasingly competitive context. The participative philosophy underlying high-involvement management would demand and, by implication, successfully engender a greater level of employee commitment and involvement. Its core, the increasing employee involvement, would chime with employees' motivational needs for satisfying and challenging jobs and to identify with the organisations for which they work, as well as enhance their job security and income growth. In so doing, high-involvement management would guarantee effective sustained organisational performance in an increasingly competitive, uncertain and globalised economy.

A final influence on the modernisation agenda, particularly in the USA, was the perception that if employers were going to maximise their return on 'their' human resources, promotion and pay needed to be more strongly linked to performance than they had in the past. It was thought that in many organisations, seniority rules and other bureaucratic practices, often thought to be associated with trade union influence, resulted in a too loose connection between performance and key personnel decisions. As such, while employee voice is welcomed as an input to change programmes or organisational innovations, the kind of employee voice concerned with grievances and trade unions is less welcomed. In some circles this is seen as antithetical to successful high-performance HRM as it is thought to have detrimental effects on performance, when, in fact, Walton (1985) was at pains to stress that unionism is not necessarily antithetical to high-commitment or -involvement management.

We can see that there are a number of overlapping currents influencing the development of the HRM–performance field and the concepts underlying it, which can be summarised thus:

1. The consolidation of developments in personnel management, some based on behavioural science methods, into a coherent sophisticated HRM approach to people management that signifies employees are valued, as opposed to a more ad hoc or neglectful approach.
2. The quest for a personal management that could visibly contribute to the key performance indicators of organisations.
3. The importance of human capital to the organisation, focused on the investment in the human asset or employee development, and the involvement of employees in both their immediate job and the wider context in which it is embedded, reflecting the need for organisations to proactively respond to an increasingly dynamic environment.
4. An HRM centred on performance as the key criteria for selection, promotion, reward and evaluation, ie, in which seniority and other status criteria are not significant.

While these concerns overlap, distinguishing them helps us to understand the different foci of the studies within the HRM–performance research stream. They are, in fact, blended together in the Ability–Motivation–Opportunity (AMO) Framework (Boxall and Purcell, 2003; Gerhart, 2008: 318–22) that underpins some of the studies. This framework is based on a theory of individual performance that extends Vroom's (1964) earlier emphasis on ability and motivation by adding an 'opportunity to participate' in Appelbaum's (2000) terms, or 'opportunity to contribute to effectiveness' in Gerhart's terms (2008: 319). The trichotomy is reflected in a characterisation of high-performance systems as having three components, each of which correspond to the three elements of the AMO Framework, thus: (1) a work organisation element which is about the opportunities for employee involvement and participation, (2) a training and development component which is concerned with human capital or skill and knowledge acquisition and (3) a motivational-enhancement part concerned with incentives to perform in order to ensure that employees are motivated to use their discretion in line with the organisation's objectives (Appelbaum et al., 2000; Bailey, 1993; Kalleberg et al., 2006).

Boxall and Purcell (2003) suggest that the Ability–Motivation–Opportunity Framework is increasingly the performance theory that underlies the stream of research which emerged in the 1990s that tests the link between human resource management and performance. This may mislead people into inferring that the studies are more homogeneous than they are. There are clear differences in the sets of practices used in the studies, as Boxall and Purcell (2003) note, yet the diversity within the studies reflects more than this, as their underlying foci are often quite dissimilar. I will now consider some studies to illustrate the diversity.

Key HRM-Performance Studies

I present six studies, each of which illustrates one of the following concerns:

1. The profits (or performance) through people approach, through a coherent sophisticated approach that signifies employees are valued;
2. The quest for a personal management that could visibly contribute to the key performance indicators of organisations;
3. The importance of human capital to the organisation, focused on the investment in the human asset;
4. The high-involvement management approach that reverses Taylorism;
5. An HRM centred on performance;
6. The AMO Framework.

Consequently I will not present the studies in the oft-used chronological order.

The studies have been based on correlational analyses, in which HRM is measured through a method that captures the collective use of a set of human resource practices and is then correlated with measures of performance. This reflects an underlying current in the literature that human resource practices need to cohere if performance is to be optimised.

Performance through People: West, Guthrie, Dawson, Borrill and Carter's Use of Pfeffer's Practices in a Hospital Context

Our first study is atypical in that it is not dealing with profit-making organisations, as West et al. (2006) investigated the link between the human resource system and performance in a sample of 52 hospitals in England. A high-performance human resource system is taken to be one that uses the core practices in Pfeffer's framework and West et al. include six practices in their measure of it: training, performance management, participation, decentralisation, teams and employment security. Each of these was measured using several items. For example, for performance management, respondents (a) rated the priority the hospital placed on conducting performance appraisals for all employees, (b) indicated the percentage of staff in each occupational group receiving an appraisal in the past 12 months and the frequency of these appraisals, (c) estimated the percentage of staff in each occupational group that received training in the conduct of performance appraisals and (d) whether the appraisal system was subject to systematic evaluation. Through aggregating the answers to these dimensions, a measure of what West et al. (2006) call 'the sophistication and extensiveness of the performance management system' was created. Their overall index of a high-performance human management system was measured by standardising and aggregating such measures. They also included in their index, somewhat oddly as it is not a practice, a measure of whether the hospital had Investors in People accreditation, a national accreditation that organisations in the UK can apply for that looks at, among other things, their training and development (http://www.investorsinpeople.co.uk). Health care was measured by the standardised mortality ratio, which indicates whether more or less patients have died than one would expect, taking in account a set of standardising factors, or if, in fact, the amount is exactly as expected. The HRM system was found to be negatively associated with mortality rate even controlling for prior mortality.

Strategic 'Bottom-Line' Personal Management: Huselid, Jackson and Schuler's Study of Strategic and Technical HRM

Huselid et al.'s (1997) focus is on the differentiation between strategic and technical practices. The strategic, defined by their being connected directly with the achievement of business objectives, are associated with the kinds of practices that are prominent in the high-involvement, AMO or high-performance work systems models – team-based job designs, flexible workforces and employee empowerment. Huselid et al. also consider them to be 'relatively recent innovations' (p. 172). In contrast, they claim technical HRM activities are more established and it is precisely because they are institutionalised that they cannot give organisations a competitive advantage. They entail practices associated with recruiting, selection, performance measurement, training and the administration of compensation and benefits.

Using a sample of 293 US firms from ten different sectors, Huselid et al. (1997) studied the effectiveness of the HRM activities, and not just their use of practices, as the other studies we will consider do. The assessment of effectiveness was made by the respondents, senior managers (92 per cent of whom were in HRM positions) who answered a postal questionnaire. They were asked to rate their satisfaction with 'the results currently being achieved' (Huselid et al., 1997: 175) for individual practices. Factor analysis of the ratings confirmed a separation between the activities that Huselid et al. designated as 'Strategic HRM Effectiveness' from the technical. The strategic activities included a number of practices associated with their definition that cohere to some extent: teamwork, subordinate participation and empowerment, employee–manager communications, workforce flexibility and deployment and management development and succession planning. But it also included advance issue identification and strategic needs analysis, and work/family programmes. Compensation is mentioned as potentially important to strategic HRM, which might be taken to mean incentive systems as these are prominent in the high-performance literature, as Huselid et al. acknowledge. But these are identified along with items such as benefits and services, retirement strategies, recruiting and training (significantly treated together) and performance appraisal as technical practices.

Performance was measured by (a) productivity (sales per employee); and (b) two measures of profit, namely gross return on assets (GRATE) and a market value index (Tobin's *q*). The statistical analyses controlled for a large number of factors known to relate to performance, including firm size and industrial sector. The focus was on business performance subsequent to when the data on human resource practices was collected, in order to determine whether HRM practices in one year predicted performance in the following year, which strengthens the basis for causal inference.

The analyses revealed a positive relationship between strategic HRM effectiveness and gross return on assets and a marginal relationship ($p < 0.10$) for productivity and the Tobin's *q* measure of profit, which is the ratio of the total market value of a firm over total asset value. For technical HRM effectiveness, however, there was no statistically significant relationship with any measure of performance, thus supporting Huselid et al.'s differentiation of types of HRM.

Human Capital Focus: Koch and McGrath's Human Resource Management Sophistication

Koch and McGrath (1996) define HRM in terms of the identification and development of human capital. These practices, it is argued, 'are associated with the creation and maintenance of human capital as a strategic resource' (p. 336), that is, they may give the firm a competitive advantage. Three practices comprise sophisticated human resource management: investments in human resource planning (the accurate projection of human capital needs), investments in hiring (the identification of individuals that are best suited to meet organisational objectives) and investments in the development of employees (particularly in the mechanisms through which they realise their potential and reduce uncertainty about how well they will perform). Using indices created from multiple measures of these, which were gained from questionnaires sent to executives in 319 US business units, Koch and McGrath found that hiring was strongly related to labour productivity and that planning and development were related to it but not so strongly, ie, were significant only at the 5 per cent level. However, the association of all three was stronger in units with high levels of capital intensity, measured by the log of the assets per employee, ie, it was moderated by capital intensity. This moderation was greater for planning than for the others. An overall index of human resource sophistication, created by combining the three other indices, was also related to labour productivity, and this relationship intensified as the capital of the firm increased. Nonetheless, productivity gains from human resource management sophistication were apparent at all but the lowest levels of capital intensity.

High-Involvement Management: Arthur's Steel Mill Study

Arthur (1994) concentrates on employee involvement, using Walton's (1985) high-commitment management as its organising principle. This model, and its opposite, the control or Taylorist model, are seen as approaches to human resource management that have the effect of 'shaping ... employee behaviour and attitudes at work'. The control approach is defined by its goals 'to reduce labour costs, or improve efficiency, by enforcing compliance with specified rules and procedures and basing employee rewards on some measurable output criteria'. In contrast, the underlying orientation of the commitment approach is to develop committed employees who can be trusted to use their discretion to carry out their tasks in ways that are consistent with the organisation's goals. It is clear that Arthur sees high-commitment management as entailing organisational involvement, including employees thinking of better ways of doings their jobs, as the measure of it included high levels of employee involvement in managerial decisions, formal participation programmes and training in group problem-solving.

Other practices included in the study, some of which were less obviously central measures of high-commitment management, were general training, zero or low levels of incentive pay, formal grievance procedures, social gatherings, percentage of craft workers, supervisor/worker ratio, as well as wage and benefit measures such as the total employment cost per production and maintenance worker.

Arthur (1994) collected data on HRM practices and organisational performance by questionnaires completed by human resource managers in a sample of 30 small US steel mills. Using cluster analysis, he discriminated between those plants adopting high-commitment management from those using the high-control approach. For example, the commitment workplaces were characterised by employee involvement in managerial decisions, formal participation programmes, training in group problem-solving and an emphasis on skilled work. Fourteen of the mills fell into the commitment category, while the remaining 16 were of the control type, identified by low use of these involvement practices.

The commitment plants were found, controlling for such factors as plant size and degree of trade union membership, to be associated with higher labour efficiency (average number of labour hours required to produce one tonne of steel), lower scrap rates (tonnes of raw steel required to produce one tonne of finished product) and lower labour turnover (number of shop floor workers who had left in the last year).

A Performance-Based HRM: Delery and Doty's Study of Market and Internal Systems

Delery and Doty's (1996) focus is on differentiating a performance-based system – labelled the market-type of employment system – from one based on an internal labour market. The emphasis in the market system is on performance being gauged by results, while the internal system performance is judged by behaviour. Employee development, the human capital focus, is limited to the internal system as in the ideal type of the market system, no formal training and minimal induction is given. Practices associated with high involvement are, however, not consistently allocated to one of the systems: the key non-Taylorist practice of loose job definitions is associated with the market system, while jobs are very tightly defined in the internal system; but participation in decision-making and employee voice are seen to be part of the internal system and employees are given little voice in the market system. In many respects, the market system is the one that Pfeffer and others see as antithetical to the high-performance system.

In a study of 1,050 US banks, Delery and Doty concentrated on the management of one occupation, the loan officer. They acquired information on the human resource practices and business strategy from the bank's senior human resource manager and further 'general information' (Delery and Doty, 1996: 814) about the bank and its strategy from the bank's president.

Delery and Doty tested the association between their seven individual practices on performance. The main finding was that results-oriented appraisal, profit-sharing and employment security were positively associated with the return on average assets, while profit-sharing, and, though only marginally, results-oriented appraisal, were associated with return on equity. But the relationship between the results-oriented appraisal and both measures of performance was found to vary depending on the degree to which the bank adopted an innovation-oriented strategy, though it still had a pay-off in all circumstances. This offers some support for the contingency or 'best fit' (see Chapter 3) approach that a third factor, eg whether the organisation is following a particular business strategy, moderates the relationship between particular HRM practices and performance.

Examining the two systems of employment, the market and internal systems, Delery and Doty (1996) found that the more closely an organisation's employment system resembled the market type, the better its return on average assets and equity. In contrast, the greater the proximity to the internal ideal type, the lower the performance on these two measures. None of their tests for contingency theory showed that the association between the systems and performance depended on the strategic fit.

While the research suggests that the market system is positively associated with performance, the problem is how the concept relates to the high-involvement or -performance terminology, since, on the one hand, it contains the non-Taylorist job design but relies on the external labour market and is characterised by low degrees of training and participation.

Applying the Ability–Motivation–Opportunity Framework: Huselid's Study of Private Companies in the USA

Huselid (1995) studied a set of 968 organisations with over 100 employees by sampling firms from all major industries in the US private sector. He focuses on the three types of practices that make up the AMO framework, which he labels collectively, a high-performance work system. He argues that the use of such a system gives employees a high level of skill and motivation and structures their jobs so that they have the opportunity to use these skill and abilities. Having obtained information on the firms' human resource management practices by a questionnaire mailed to the senior human resources professional in each company, Huselid used principal component analysis to investigate the relationship between the practices and found that they formed two identifiable factors. He labelled these in terms of the AMO vocabulary. The first, he termed 'Employee Motivation', the second he argued captured the other two dimensions, skills and work organisation, together, and thus he termed this 'Employee Skills and Organisational Structure'. The motivation factor covered such practices as performance appraisal, compensation based on appraisals, staff recruitment and promotion on merit (rather than on seniority). The second factor, skills and organisation structure, included information sharing, formal job analysis, attitude surveys, training and selection testing, participation in quality circles or labour-management teams, and incentive payment schemes. The intelligibility of the factors is not perhaps as clear as Huselid takes them to be, particularly as one would expect incentive payment schemes to be under employee motivation, and there may be some overlap between it and appraisal (included in the motivation factor) being used to determine employee's compensation.

Huselid examined how each factor was related to labour turnover, productivity, measured by sales per employees, and two measures of corporate financial performance, a capital-market index of the value of the firm (Tobin's *q*, reflecting current and potential profitability) and gross rate of return on capital. Neither factor was significantly (below the 5 per cent level) related to labour turnover, the human resource outcome. Employee Motivation, but not Employee Skills and Organisational Structures, was significantly positively associated with productivity. It was also related to Tobin's *q* measure of market value, but not to the gross rate of return on assets. In contrast, the Employee Skills and Organisational Structures index was strongly related to the gross rate of return on assets but only weakly associated with Tobin's *q*. Underplaying the variation in the results across outcomes and dimensions of high-performance work systems, Huselid (1995: 667) concludes that 'The magnitude of the returns for investments in High Performance Work Practices is substantial'.

Comparing the Studies

The results of all the studies reviewed point in the direction of a link between HRM and performance. However, even in the same study the impact of HRM differs across performance outcomes. West et al. (2006) tested for one performance outcome and found a link between it and HRM. Of those that tested for multiple outcomes, Arthur's (1994) is the only study in which the measure of HRM is strongly related to all the performance measures considered, in this case, three. Huselid et al. (1997) found that the strategic mode of HRM had an impact on performance, albeit weakly on two of their measures, but the technical mode did not, as they predicted. In Huselid's (1995) study, for example, the motivation factor was related to productivity but the skills and organisation one was not, while the strength of the associations with the two profit measures varied between the two factors. Neither was related to labour turnover. Similarly, Delery and Doty (1996) identified seven aspects of HRM and two performance indicators. Only four of the 14 relationships were statistically significant. More generally, Wall and Wood (2005) oversaw 25 studies from refereed journals and in only three of these were all the tested performance effects supported by the data.

Moreover, the studies are disparate in terms of the concepts and measures they use. Though in broad terms they cover similar practices, their emphasis and specific measures differ considerably. Huselid et al. (1997) is an exception to the others as it measured the effectiveness of practices in terms of respondents' satisfaction with the use of each practice, whereas the others record whether or not a practice is used but not its effectiveness. For example, Huselid (1995) measures whether appraisal is used to determine employees' pay, but did not assess how frequently or how well the appraisal was done. In West et al.'s study, an index is used, whereas in Huselid's (1995) study, two or more dimensions of HRM have been identified. One of the starkest contrasts is in the treatment of performance-related pay, which for Arthur (1994) is associated with the control model, whereas for Huselid (1995) it is part of the high-performance work system that entails employee involvement. Indeed, he uses incentive pay to explain why the employee motivation factor is unrelated to labour turnover, suggesting it induces poor performers to leave. It is also significant that work enrichment or job empowerment is included in Arthur (1994) and Huselid et al. (1997) and omitted in Huselid (1995) and Koch and McGrath (1996), as this was a foundation of the original concept of high-involvement or -commitment management. The inclusion of loosely defined jobs in Delery and Doty's (1996) market system, when all the other items are almost antithetical to the high-involvement system, illustrates the diversity in the treatment of job design. Wood and Wall (2007) have, in fact, shown that an increasing tendency in the HRM–performance stream was to omit altogether job involvement from practices.

That there are differences in the performance effects and HRM systems defined in the studies is not a criticism of the individual studies, it is simply a statement about them as a whole. However, it makes it difficult to determine the nature and meaning of the overall pattern of results and implies that there are limits to what one can conclude from the studies. There is no clearly identifiable relationship between the types of practices included in the studies and the results. There is, thus, no stronger or weaker relationship between one set of practices than another. However, since the emphasis is on using indices or cluster analysis, few studies have tested whether certain practices have stronger effects than others, as Delery and Doty (1996) did.

The studies we have reviewed, and others, have a number of other weaknesses. First, there are methodological problems, the most fundamental of which is that they are cross-sectional. They only test an association between HRM and performance at one point in time. This, thus, limits the extent to which one can make causal inferences about HRM affecting performance. It could be that high performing organisations are the ones that introduce certain types of HRM. Other methodological problems include the researchers' reliance on a single respondent in the organisation for the measures of human resource practice and, in some cases, for performance measures. If the same person provides information on the practices and the performance, this may result in common method bias (systematic error variance shared among variables arising from their being measured from the same source) as some respondents may overestimate both their use of practices and their performance, while others may be systematically underestimating them. This may result in a positive relationship between the practices and performance being overestimated.

Second, the studies have concentrated on human resource practices, which means that there is no control for other types of managerial practices. It could be that organisations that use sophisticated human resource practices tend also to use the most sophisticated practice in one or more areas of management and it is either such practices or the synergistic relationship between these and human resource management that is most telling for performance. Moreover, HRM practices, particularly ones associated with high-involvement management, are widely associated with operational management methods such as total quality management or lean production, which is an American expression for the use of Japanese management methods that aim to produce on a just-in-time basis using total quality management procedures (Womack et al., 1990). In some accounts of these, human resource practices are, indeed, assumed to be an integral part of them (e.g. Shah and Ward, 2003).

Third, few studies have evaluated competing hypotheses or models of performance. Typically a composite measure of HRM is used. Studies like Huselid's that identify different dimensions (motivation, and skill and organisation factors), and tests of the interaction between them, are rare. Even scarcer in these studies are tests of the association between performance and individual practices or adequate tests of synergies between practices (Wall and Wood, 2005).

The significance given to measuring the collective use of HRM practices rests, so Appelbaum et al. (2000: 34) say, on the compelling 'argument that firms adopting a coherent set of workplace practices designed to maximize horizontal fit should have superior performance'. Yet there are three meanings of coherency referred to in the literature, namely: (a) the workplace practices are complementary, (b) synergies exist between the practices leading to positive interaction effects on performance and (c) the practices form an integrated system. These are nonetheless often treated as if they are the same, when – as Wood and de Menezes (2008) show – they are not and entail discrete models of performance.

A complement of practices consists of all those practices that individually have a positive association with performance. As such, a complement of high-performance practices would be made up of the practices that are best in each of the domains of HRM. Each would add something unique. Synergistic practices are those that enhance the effect on performance of each other. A high-performance synergistic set would be one in which all practices interact positively with each other, or at least with one other, so that the combined use of the practices has a greater effect than the sum of the effects of the individual practices. While, an integrated approach implies that the practices reflect an underlying orientation to HRM or distinctive approach, to use Arthur's term (1994), and it is this that is positively associated with performance. Orientations in general are organising principles for guiding people's judgements and behaviour, so in the case of high-involvement management, such an orientation reflects an organisation-wide concern for employee involvement. The core of this orientation is thus a philosophy, but it also entails the adoption of practices that are consistent with the high-involvement concept. The practices can thus be treated as manifestations of the underlying philosophy or orientation.

The three interpretations of coherency imply different models for measuring HRM. Indices based on what are known as formative indicators (Diamantopoulos and Siguaw, 2006) or cause indicators (Bollen, 1989) are appropriate for measuring systems of complementary practices. These are contrasted with those that measure an underlying construct created from items – in this case practices – that are assumed to reflect or be caused by it. Such scales are sometimes called reflective indicators (Diamantopoulos and Siguaw, 2006) or effect indicators (Bollen, 1989). The underlying assumption and essential requirement for creating scales is that the items are unidimensional, and hence, strongly associated with each other (Hattie, 1985). These scales are appropriate for measuring an orientation whose enactment means the design of practices reflects its focus. Practices are used as indicators of this underlying orientation, which explains their coexistence, rather than of their existence *per se*. In statistical terms, practices are manifest variables and orientations are latent variables. The synergistic approach is best tested by inserting interaction terms involving two or more practices in performance equations. An exponential relationship between the index and performance might indicate a synergistic relationship between the practices, but could also suggest that HRM signals are successfully used to indicate to employees that their employer is committed to their welfare, and that this effect intensifies with each additional practice.

Most, if not all, of the researchers using indices refer to the synergistic nature of the relationship between practices and performance. For example, Hoque (1999: 422) uses an index of practices to test what he refers to as 'the synergistic benefits resulting from the introduction of HRM as a … package of practices that cohere with and mutually reinforce each other'. This is not appropriate. Similarly, cluster analysis has been used (as in Arthur's [1994] study) on the assumption that testing the association between cluster membership and performance is a test of the synergistic model. But this is not an adequate test, as it simply compares groupings of organisations on the basis that they employ particular practices, not on the strength of the interaction effect.

Finally, in the initial wave of studies, no attempts were made to assess intermediate variables between HRM and performance that might mediate any relationship. Several factors have been mentioned as accounting for observed correlations, including job satisfaction, organisational commitment, organisation of work and methods of working, skill and knowledge levels and proactive behaviours (Wood and Wall, 2007). However, they were not explored, creating what has become known as the black-box problem (Elorza et al., 2011). West et al. (2006: 997) list identification of the mechanisms mediating the relationship between HRM systems and outcomes as the 'most obvious' of the 'important and intriguing theoretical questions arising from their research'. Several reviewers of the area (eg Delery, 1998), having concluded that the studies have shown a strong link between HRM and performance, go on to suggest that the next stage of research is to explore these mechanisms.

Although the four problems we have identified are widespread in the HRM–performance literature, more recent studies exist that have overcome one or more of these problems. We now introduce some of them.

Some Other Key HRM-Performance Studies

Cappelli and Neumark: Longitudinal Analysis

Cappelli and Neumark's (2001) study was the first that assessed the HRM–performance relationship using a longitudinal design. They use the high-performance work practices nomenclature, but place 'employee involvement' at its centre. They particularly highlight teamwork as 'the typical mechanism through which employee involvement operates', but argue that other practices such as suggestion schemes and job rotation can create a sense of involvement as well. They also identify training in teamwork, pay-for skill and gain-sharing as important supporting practices.

Cappelli and Neumark use a secondary data set, the National Employers Survey of the USA, which is administered by telephone interviews with the plant manager in the manufacturing sector or the local business manager in the service sector. The sample is of establishments in the private sector with 20 or more employees. Core work organisation practices included in the study are team meetings (including quality circles), self-managed teams and job rotation, while the other measures included are cross-training, teamwork training, pay for skill, profit sharing and total quality management, which is treated as a form of employee involvement.

Productivity was measured by sales per worker, while labour costs per workers and unit labour costs were also estimated. Cappelli and Neumark test the complementary and synergistic models of performance.

None of the practices was significantly positively related to productivity, as was expected. The one significant result was a negative association between job rotation and productivity. Nor was there any strong evidence of synergies between key practices, as measured by two-way interactions between practices. The interaction between profit-sharing and self-managed teams was significant in some specifications. Some of the practices were found to raise labour costs per worker – total quality management, team training and profit-sharing – but none of the key work organisation ones did. This suggests that these practices raise wages or other benefits of workers, and hence, compensation costs. But the effect on profitability was slight. Overall the study found no strong support for a relationship between HRM and performance, albeit with a limited range of HRM practices, making it distinctive within the research stream.

MacDuffie: Extending High-Involvement Management to Lean Production

MacDuffie (1995) conducted a study of 62 car assembly plants, the majority of which were in the USA, Europe and Japan. This study was the first to include measures of lean production. The data was collected as part of a wider project, MIT's The Future of the Automobile project, from which the concept of Lean Production was developed.

MacDuffie separated three systems. First, a work system, which is centred in AMO terms on the opportunity for involvement and is concerned with 'how work is organised, in terms of both formal work structures and the allocation of work responsibilities, and the participation of employees in production-related problem-solving activity' (p. 207). It was measured by an index (or formative scale) constituted by the percentage of the workforce involved in (a) teams, and (b) employee involvement groups, the number of production-related suggestions received from employees, the percentage of suggestions implemented, the extent of job rotation and the degree of worker involvement in quality tasks.

The second system is the human resource system, which is concerned with the HRM practices that provide ways for workers to acquire skills and the incentives to boost their motivation (p. 200), ie, the skill-acquisition and motivational dimensions of the AMO framework. It was measured by an index based on the following practices: staff selection was based on an openness to learning, rather than on previous relevant experience; minimal status barriers between managers and workers (ie, harmonisation across grades); training being provided for (a) new recruits, and (b) experienced production staff and other staff; and pay levels being dependent on plant performance.

The third system is the lean production system, which measured the extent to which the system is buffer-less using an index of buffer-use based on three items: the average number of vehicles held in work-in-progress buffers as a percentage of output, the average level of components kept in stock and the percentage of space dedicated to final repair. The lower the scores on each of these, the more lean is the plant.

In MacDuffie's study, plant performance was measured by labour productivity, defined as the labour hours to build a vehicle; and quality, the number of defects per vehicle. Labour productivity was made comparable across plants by adjustments to reflect differences due to the complexity of the product (eg number of components and welds).

MacDuffie found that the three indices were associated with productivity and moreover, the three-way interaction between them was likewise related, indicating a synergistic relationship between them. MacDuffie called such a system the flexible production system. In the case of quality, the work system index and the human resource policies index were associated with superior quality, but the lean index was not significantly related to it, and there was not a synergistic relationship amongst the three sets of practices. The results offered considerable support for the hypothesis that both high-involvement management and supporting motivational HRM practices are associated with superior performance or at least productivity and quality in manufacturing; and in the case of productivity. that these have a synergistic relationship with lean production. We, again, though, have a slight difference in results across performance measures.

Birdi, Clegg, Patterson, Robinson, Stride, Wall and Wood: Extending High-Involvement Management to Lean Production with Longitudinal Analysis

Birdi et al. (2008) examined both the complementary and synergistic models of performance. They focused on the impact of three human resource practices central to either the high-involvement or human capital perspective: empowerment, teamwork and extensive training. Each was measured by a single item – but the respondents were given a description of the practice by the interviewer (p. 480). In the case of empowerment, it was defined as 'Passing considerable responsibility for operational management to individuals or teams (rather than keeping all decision-making at the managerial level)'. The measure thus captured both the job involvement associated with enriched jobs that have high levels of discretion and the type of organisational involvement associated with problem-solving and idea generation, as in the high-involvement model. The teams factor was defined separately from empowerment as 'Placing employees into teams with their own responsibilities and given the freedom to allocate work between team members (rather than having everyone work as individuals)'. Extensive training was identified as 'Providing a range of development opportunities for all employees (rather than training people occasionally to meet specific job needs)'. Birdi et al. also included three operational management techniques associated with lean production – just-in-time, total quality management, supply-chain partnering – as well as advanced manufacturing technology.

Birdi et al.'s study involved analysing the performance of 308 UK companies over 22 years. During the 22-year period, the companies implemented some or all of these practices. The longitudinal research design enabled the researchers to assess the extent to which the introduction of a practice had some effect on their indicator of company performance, a key measure of productivity, value-added, which they derived from the companies' profit and loss accounts.

Using multilevel regression analysis, with time embedded in company, Birdi et al. found that, of the seven practices, only empowerment and extensive training had a clear impact on value-added in the years following their introduction, an effect that did not differ across types of manufacturing firms. Extensive training had a significant effect on productivity following its introduction, but the size of its effect varied across firms.

Highly significantly, Birdi et al. also found that the performance of all practices was enhanced by teamwork. Empowerment and extensive training thus had even more effect when firms used teamwork. Moreover, all the operational practices, just-in-time, total quality management (TQM), supply-chain partnering and advanced manufacturing technology had a positive effect on performance if teamwork was being adopted, when they did not have an effect where work was not organised on a team basis. Empowerment and extensive training also enhanced the effect of TQM, while empowerment had a similar effect on the impact of supply-chain partnering, as extensive training did on just-in-time.

Birdi et al.'s study thus showed that some. but not all. HRM practices have a unique association with productivity. Empowerment and, to a lesser extent, extensive training are crucial in their own right; while teamwork has a synergistic effect on all other practices, including the operational methods. As such, the study shows that relative to operational practices, human resource factors are more significant than operational practices, or at least are vital ingredients for making lean production work. Without empowerment or teamwork, the potential returns on investing in just-in-time, total quality management and supply-chain partnering will not be fully realised.

Wood and de Menezes: Testing Competing Hypotheses

Wood and de Menezes (2008) explicitly test the complementary, synergistic and integration perspectives, that is the associations between performance and (a) individual practices, (b) the joint use of individual practices and (c) a high-involvement orientation. They use data from the core of the UK's Workplace

Employee Relations Survey of 1998, its survey based on managerial respondents of 2,191 workplaces across the whole economy, private and public.

Because of their interest in the orientation perspective, they first assessed whether an orientation underlay the use of practices associated with organisational involvement such as teamwork, quality circles, functional flexibility, suggestion schemes and supports for these concerned with either skills acquisition and knowledge sharing such as training for team-working or motivational practices such as job security guarantees to aid the organisational involvement (reported in full by de Menezes and Wood, 2006). They showed that the correlation between the high-involvement practices concerned with work organisation and skill acquisition was explained by a common factor, which they treated as reflecting an underlying high-involvement orientation. The motivational practices were neither part of the high-involvement orientation nor formed a unified set. They also included measures of work enrichment practices, which were also discrete from high-involvement management or the individual motivational supports. This suggests that the use of high-involvement management is not limited to contexts where jobs have high levels of autonomy or variety. Also, the use of the motivational supports may be quite common without high-involvement management. Wood and de Menezes also found a strong association between high-involvement management and total quality management, which itself is an identifiable orientation.

Given this prior analysis, Wood and de Menezes (2008) assessed the association between high-involvement management, enriched jobs, motivational supports and total quality management on performance discretely. High-involvement management and total quality management were measured by a reflective scale, while enriched jobs and motivational supports were measured by individual practices.

Wood and de Menezes measured workplaces' performance on four dimensions: productivity, rate of change in productivity, labour turnover and absenteeism. The first two measures were based on an assessment by the managers responding to the survey, the other two on their reporting of actual levels. Tests of the complementary and synergistic perspective revealed that the individual practices that reflect the high-involvement orientation or two-way interactions between them were not related to any performance measure.

However, they found support for the orientations perspective: the high-involvement orientation was linked to both the level and rate of change in labour productivity. But it was not, however, a main effect, as its relationship with productivity was moderated by total quality management. Similarly, the high-involvement orientation's association with the rate of change in productivity was moderated by a motivational support – variable pay.

Total quality management was a main effect in both the level and rate of change of productivity equations while variable pay was a main effect in the productivity change models, suggesting it can aid the acceptance of change. Finally, and most significantly, the practices that were mostly strongly related to productivity were job variety and method control, both elements of enriched jobs.

The high-involvement orientation was not related to labour turnover and its association with absenteeism was the opposite of that predicted: the greater the level of the orientation, the higher the absence. Job security guarantees, a motivational practice, was however negatively related to labour turnover. But no motivational or work enrichment practice was associated with absence. The study shows the advantage of testing competing hypotheses and differentiating different aspects of HRM, as the links to performance vary across them and between performance measures.

Wood, van Veldhoven, Croon and de Menezes: Assessing Psychologically-Based Mediators of HRM–Performance Links

Wood et al. (2012) used the WERS survey of 2004, using data from the equivalent management survey to the 1998 one used by Wood and de Menezes and the employee survey that is conducted in the majority of those workplaces that responded to the management survey. They focus on the employee involvement dimension of the AMO model and distinguish between two types: role- and organisational-involvement management, the former they term enriched job design and the latter high-involvement management. Using multilevel regression analysis, they show that enriched job design is related to productivity, financial performance and quality and this is mediated by the level of job satisfaction in the workplace (using a measure based on eight facets of job satisfaction). Enriched job design was associated positively with job satisfaction. In contrast, high-involvement management, using the measure used in the noted Wood and de Menezes (2008) study, was negatively related to job satisfaction, and this has a mediating effect that reduces the extent of the positive relationship between high-involvement management and productivity, financial performance and quality.

That job satisfaction is an intervening variable between work enrichment and performance offers support for a mutual gains model of HRM. However, in the case of high-involvement management, the findings suggest that there may be a conflict between its effects on employers' outcomes and those on employees, as their concerns and anxieties may increase with its use. Wood et al. suggest that this is not because the quantitative demands have increased but rather that high-involvement management entails a qualitative change in demands, as employees are encouraged to be proactive and flexible. This may imply or be accompanied by pressures to improve performance, which may, in turn, raise concerns in the worker's mind about both their competencies, relations with others and psychological (and not just job) security. As such, high-involvement management may be perceived as a stressor and 'rather than creating an increased sense of coherency or a feeling of being valued by the organisation', employees may begin 'to question the organisation's valuation of them and the comprehensibility … of what surrounds them' (Wood et al., 2012: 437). Wood et al. imply that such effects may not be universal but reflect Britain's historical and economic context at the time. The study left open the question of what mediated the relationship between high-involvement management and performance.

Gittell, Seidner and Wimbush: Assessing Organisationally Based Mediators of HRM –Performance Links

Gittell et al. (2010) acknowledge AMO's emphasis on human capital and motivation and as explanations of the HRM–performance link, but posit a third mechanism, the relationships between employees. Using the high-performance work practices terminology, they argue that these support 'the development of relational coordination' which is 'a mutually reinforcing web of communication and relationships carried out in the purpose of task integration' (*op cit*: 491). Based on what they call post-bureaucracy theory, they argue that the network of relationships that aid the coordination of work, which are significant elements of the social capital of the organisation, are especially important for performance where work is highly interdependent, uncertain and time-constrained.

Gittell's et al. (2010) research was in nine orthopaedics units in the USA. They measured high-performance work systems by a measure that was slanted to cross-functionality in the way team meetings, selection, conflict resolution, performance measurement, rewards and boundary spanning were conducted. For example, cross-functional selection was measured by whether each of physicians, nurses and physical therapists are selected for cross-functional teamwork. Relational coordination was measured by seven items: frequency of communication, timeliness, accuracy and problem-solving focus of communication, and the extent to which relationships involve a) shared goals, b) shared knowledge, c) mutual respect. This measure was found to mediate the relationship between high-performance work systems and two (single-item) measures of performance; patient-perceived quality of care and efficiency measured by the length of stay controlling for patient characteristics. They conclude that performance-enhancing relationships can be designed and created through managerial practices and need not only emerge informally. The extent to which Gittell et al. see their approach as complementing other theories of the mediators of the HRM–performance relationship or as offering the main approach is unclear. For example, they argue that 'the high-performance work practices identified in this study are focused on building employee–employee relations' (p. 491), which leaves open the possibility that other practices, for example, concerned with fostering human capital, may contribute to high performance. Nonetheless, the study firmly places organisational factors as potential mediators of the HRM–performance relationship, and such factors may explain the effect of organisational-involvement management that Wood et al. left unexplained after the tests they conducted that were focused on employee outcomes.

Jiang, Lepak, Hu and Baer: Metanalysis That Differentiates Mediators of the HRM – Performance Link

Jiang et al. (2012: 1264), convinced that the evidence of a positive relationship between HRM and various organisational outcomes is robust, argue that the key remaining issue concerns 'the mechanisms through which HRM is associated with different organisational outcomes'. They use the AMO framework to differentiate three dimensions of HRM systems – skill-enhancing practices, motivation-enhancing practices and opportunity to contribute practices – and in turn, to argue that the mechanisms linking each will vary between the dimensions. They consider two mediators, human capital and employee motivation. They hypothesise that human capital is a stronger mediator of the relationship between skill-enhancing practices and performance outcomes than is employee motivation; while employee motivation is a stronger mediator of relationships between motivation-enhancing practices and opportunity-to-contribute practices.

Through a meta-analysis of 120 studies, covering a total of 31,463 organisations, reviewing the core relationships involved in the possible pathways between practices and outcomes (i.e. not simply those that tested their mediation model), they found support for their hypothesised relationships. All three dimensions were indirectly related to a composite measure of financial outcomes, operational outcomes (composed, for example, of productivity and quality service) and voluntary turnover through both human capital and employee motivation; but that human capital was more significant in the case of skill-enhancing practices and motivation more significant for the other two dimensions. There were also direct relationships between the subdimensions of HRM and the performance measures, which require, as Jiang et al. acknowledge, exploration of additional mediators. One such factor, we might suggest, is internal coordination, as highlighted by Gittell et al. (2010).

Overviewing the Research Stream

This chapter has painted a picture of considerable diversity in the HRM–performance research stream in terminology, foci, practices considered, measurement methods and results. This contrasts with earlier reviews that present it as a unified area (Becker and Gerhart, 1996; Becker and Huselid, 1998; Dyer and Reeves, 1995; Wall and Wood, 2005: exceptions include Wood 1999, and Wood and Wall, 2007). Diversity of practices and use of composite HRM measures were observed but not presented as a serious issue, while terms used to label the systems are treated as interchangeable and the complementary and synergistic approaches considered synonymous. These reviews created a narrative in which the two central concerns in the area – holistic use of practices and employee involvement – are linked, together forming a more strategic approach to HRM. The cumulative evidence that such an approach outperforms conventional personnel management is assumed to be strong – a positive relationship between use of these systems and organisational performance has, in effect, been established. On the assumption that the results are comparable and robust, the issue becomes one of explaining the relationship and examining its mediators, to get inside the black box that has often been referred to (Elorza et al., 2011; Messersmith et al., 2011; Paul and Anantharaman, 2003; Takeuchi et al., 2007). This conclusion has spawned a set of mediation studies, which have dominated the research stream during this century (e.g. Allen et al., 2013; Bartram et al., 2014; Beltrán-Martín et al., 2008; Bonias et al., 2010; Fu et al., 2015; Paul and Anantharaman, 2003; Takeuchi et al., 2007; Wood and Ogbonnaya, 2018), and together form what might be seen as a second wave of HRM–performance studies.

More recent reviews (Boon et al., 2019; Hauff et al., 2018; Wood, 2020, 2021) have been more critical, drawing attention to the heterogeneity across the field, and in particular, identifying the diverse ways that human resource practices are combined to create human resource systems and how different assumptions about the nature of the relationships between elements of the system and outcomes underlie these systems (echoing Wood and de Menezes [2008], reviewed earlier). Boon et al. (2019: 2498) hone in on the conflation of complementary and synergistic relationships between practices, treating the existence of such synergistic relationships as 'a fundamental assumption' of the area; they conclude that because the majority of studies use additive indices, the measurement method does not align with the theory. Consequently, all that can be inferred from the studies is that 'investments in some broad set of HR [human resource] practices yields returns' (p. 2516). However, if at least some studies combine best practices in their domain, the results are consistent with the complementary theory, and as Wood (2021) suggests, one could adjust the theory and conclude that such a system yields a positive performance premium. If the theory is not recalibrated, then testing for synergy – how practices strengthen each other's effect – requires examination of the interaction between pairs or larger combinations of practices (as Cappelli and Neumark [2001] did).

In a review centred on the black-box studies, Wood (2020) reinforces his earlier theme (Wood and Wall, 2007) that employee involvement has been neglected in HRM measures (the focus having instead been on the A and M of the AMO model), and concludes that the narrative linking the holistic and involvement themes is misleading. He identifies a divide between HRM as an orientation towards fostering involvement – a managerial philosophy – and as a set of practices constituting the high-performance work system – a managerial technology. Wood argues that high-involvement management must be decoupled from the high-performance work system. Their differences go beyond the emphases placed on types of practices; they include the performance theories underpinning them. In high-involvement management, the enactment of the approach explains the performance effect – it's the principles that explain performance, rather than the practices, as the principles do not just guide the design practices, but also reactions to key events and everyday leadership behaviours. Practices must be consistent with these principles, but their precise nature may vary. In contrast, in the high-performance work systems perspective, performance effects are the direct result of using a preformed set of practices in a coherent way. The practices must, if the concept is to make sense, be best in class, each practice playing a unique role that others do not. The achievement of high performance depends on the extent of their use or their interaction effects.

In a second review, Wood (2021) concentrates on mediation studies and shows that the research stream has crystalised around the holism concern and the concept of the high-performance work system – this label is given to the HRM system in 19 out of 34 mediation studies (56 per cent) reviewed, compared with five of the 27 black-box studies in Wood and Wall's (2007) review. This reduction in the diversity of terminology has, however, been superseded by a proliferation of mediators, as only three mediators appear in more than three studies – organisational commitment, job satisfaction and human capital. The mediators fall into two categories: psychological or behavioural mechanisms (e.g. job satisfaction, organisational citizenship and psychological empowerment), and organisational characteristic mechanisms (e.g. human capital, social capital, social exchange and relational coordination). Given all the studies report at least one positive mediation effect, it is impossible to judge which one is superior. The problems within the black-box studies remain in the mediation studies, including misalignment between the use of additive indices and the stress on synergy when introducing the theory, a diversity of practices with little justification for their inclusion in HRM measures, and the under-representation of involvement. In some cases, this partly reflects the use of measures from the black-box literature.

The few studies focused on high-involvement management (Fernandez and Moldogaziev, 2013; Gittell et al. 2010; Guerrero and Barraud-Didler, 2004; Wood et al., 2012; Wood and Ogbonnaya, 2018) are, Wood (2021) concludes, more consistent with their underlying theory, developing as they do appropriate reflective scales for measuring its existence based on involvement practices and their supports. These studies also re-emphasise the importance of job-level involvement through designing jobs with autonomy as the bedrock of high-involvement, as in the models of Lawler (1986) and Walton (1985). The nature of high-involvement management is more assured and theoretically grounded. The benefits of job-level involvement on performance and well-being are well established, and organisational-level involvement should improve how people connect what they do with what others do, develop shared understandings and learn from each other, akin to Gittell et al.'s relational coordination.

This reinforces calls to decouple the concepts of high-involvement management and high-performance work systems. As Wood (2021:108) says, 'The diversity in the HRM–performance literature reflects substantive – and not just methodological – differences between studies', and the next phase of research should acknowledge this. The two perspectives also have different policy implications. High-involvement management entails forensic design of practices to a high degree of specificity and managers internalising a value set. In contrast, the high-performance systems approach is technocratic, a literal, evidence-based view involving managers acquiring knowledge of best practices.

Conclusions

This review of the research on the HRM–performance relationship has highlighted how the studies differ in their foci, coverage of practices and performance measures, as well as samples and methods of data collection. The results vary significantly even across performance measures in the individual studies. The negative results in the longitudinal study of Cappelli and Neumark highlight that it cannot be taken for granted that some links between certain practices or dimensions of HRM will be found.

Nonetheless, collectively the studies show that it is a rich area of study. But it is premature to conclude that certain practices are superior to others or that a particular HRM system can be singled out as the high-performance approach. The emphasis in earlier reviews on the need to get inside the black box between HRM and performance has been heeded, as some of the studies in the latter half of the chapter illustrate and Wood (2021) reviewed extensively. Yet insufficient attention has been given to how the diversity in concepts of HRM contributes to the uncertainty about the overall pattern of results.

The variety of starting points of the studies, identified here, explains some of the diversity in concepts. The most marked such difference is between emphasising the holistic use of a set of sophisticated personnel practices and the power of a high-involvement approach centred on employee involvement. They overlap, in that organisational and role involvement are both sophisticated personnel practices. But they should be treated as different concerns, not as two sides of the same coin.

The holistic perspective leads to framing the issue in terms of the more practices the better and implies the use of formative indexes to capture this systemic use, while Jiang et al. (2012) and others have opened the possibility that the performance effects of subsystems of practices may result from different mechanisms. The high-involvement management perspective centres, á la Arthur (1994) and Wood et al. (2012), on the underlying approach that management takes to the involvement of employees in the organisation and how this is fostered and supported. The precise nature of the practices used to achieve this may vary, but generic measures of these can be treated as manifestations of the underlying approach which can be used to create reflexive measures. Again, the mechanisms linking high-involvement management may differ between dimensions, as Wood et al. (2012) suggests. Role-involvement management may be explained by psychologically-based processes, such as job satisfaction and well-being, while following Gittell et al. (2010), organisational processes may be more significant in the case of organisational involvement.

It is also too early to make hard-and-fast decisions about the merits of the shareholder and stakeholder models or whether they are reconcilable.

Positive effects on the well-being of employees have been found in a number of studies (Appelbaum et al., 2000; Macky and Boxall, 2007, 2008; Mohr and Zoghi, 2008), but Wood et al.'s (2012) results suggest that the conclusions may differ depending on the practice. Role-involvement management appears from their study and others' to benefit both shareholders and stakeholders, while organisational-involvement management may benefit shareholders but can have costs in the form of increased anxiety for workers. Such costs may vary over time and may reflect the liberal market context, but nonetheless, it may suggest that managements might need, in the long-run, to make trade-offs between profits and workers' well-being or find ways of reducing any anxiety associated with organisational involvement management.

The starting point for the next phase of the research stream is to acknowledge high-performance work systems and high-involvement management as alternatives, and either settle on a clear focus or assess them as competitors, much as Wood and de Menezes (2008) did. Either way, the neglect of employee involvement needs rectifying. Moreover, involvement has also been neglected in practice, at least in liberal market economies like the USA and UK, and the findings of the studies focused on involvement suggests awakening interest in it may yield benefits for employers and employees. The emphasis in the past decade or so has been on performance management – this is akin to a literal reading of the high-performance system, which stresses incentive systems, performance monitoring and appraisal. This chimes with the attention given to matching labour input more closely to demand for labour through work scheduling, zero-hours contracts and (potentially bogus) self-employment methods. Much of this work is fostered by the development of the digital economy, the shaping of which all too often does not involve employees or end users. This development, along with the increased use of remote working following COVID-19, provides opportunities to foster involvement; the focus would then switch to identifying new ideas, facilitators, constraints and stressors, rather than perfecting performance management systems or implementing training designed to embed imposed changes.

References

Allen, M. R., Ericksen, J., and Collins, C. J. (2013). Human resource management, employee exchange relationships, and performance in small businesses. *Human Resource Management*, 52: 153–174.

Appelbaum, E., Bailey, T., Berg, P., and Kalleberg, A. L. (2000). *Manufacturing Advantage: Why High-Performance Work Systems Pay Off.* Ithaca, NY: Cornell University Press.

Arthur, J. B. (1994). Effects of human resource systems on manufacturing performance and turnover. *Academy of Management Journal*, 7: 670–687.

Bailey, T. (1993). *Discretionary effort and the organization of work: employee participation and work reform since Hawthorne.* Mimeo, Teachers College, Columbia University, New York, NY.

Bartram, T., Karimi, L., Leggat, S. G., and Stanton, P. (2014). Social identification: Linking high performance work systems, psychological empowerment and patient care. *International Journal of Human Resource Management*, 25: 2401–2419.

Becker, B. E., and Gerhart, B. (1996). The impact of human resource management on organizational performance: Progress and prospects. *Academy of Management Journal*, 39: 779–801.

Becker, B. E., and Huselid, M. A. (1998). High performance work systems and firm performance: A synthesis of research and managerial implications. In G. R. Ferris (Ed.), *Research in Personnel and Human Resources Management* (Vol. 16, pp. 53–101). Stamford, CT: JAI Press.

Beltrán-Martín, I., Roca-Puig, V., Escrig-Tena, A., and Bou-Llusar, J. C. (2008). Human resource flexibility as a mediating variable between high performance work systems and performance. *Journal of Management*, 34: 1009–1044.

Birdi, K. C., Clegg, C., Patterson, M., Robinson, A., Stride, C., Wall, T., and Wood, S. (2008). Contemporary manufacturing practices and company performance: A longitudinal study. *Personnel Psychology*, 61: 467–501.

Bollen, K. A. (1989). *Structural Equations with Latent Variables.* New York: Wiley.

Bonias, D., Bartram, T., Leggat, S. G., and Stanton, P. (2010). Does psychological empowerment mediate the relationship between high performance work systems and patient care quality in hospitals? *Asia Pacific Journal of Human Resources*, 48: 319–337.

Boon, C., Den Hartog, D. N., and Lepak, D. P. (2019). A systematic review of human resource management systems and their measurement. *Journal of Management*, 45: 2498–2537.

Boxall, P. and Purcell, J. (2003). *Strategy and Human Resource Management.* Basingstoke: Palgrave Macmillan.

Cappelli, P. (1999). *The New Deal at Work.* Boston, MA: Harvard Business School Press.

Cappelli, P. and Neumark, D. (2001). Do "high performance" work practices improve establishment-level outcomes? *Industrial and Labor Relations Review*, 54: 737–775.

Delery, J. E. (1998). Issues of fit in strategic human resource management: Implications for research. *Human Resource Management Review*, 8(3): 289–309.

Delery, J. E., and Doty, D. H. (1996). Modes of theorizing in strategic human resource management: Tests of universalistic, contingency, and configurational performance predictions. *Academy of Management Journal*, 39(4): 802–835.

de Menezes, L. M., and Wood, S. (2006). The reality of flexible work systems in Britain. *International Journal of Human Resource Management*, 17: 1–33.

Diamantopoulos, A., and Siguaw, J. (2006). Formative versus reflective indicators in organizational measure development: A comparison and empirical illustration. *British Journal of Management*, 117: 263–282.

Dyer, L., and Reeves, T. (1995). Human resources strategies and firm performance: What do we know and where do we need to go? *International Journal of Human Resource Management*, 6: 656–670.

Elorza, U., Aritzeta, A., and Ayestarán, S. (2011). Exploring the black box in Spanish firms: The effect of the actual and perceived system on employees' commitment and organizational performance. *International Journal of Human Resource Management*, 22: 1401–1422.

Fernandez, S., and Moldogaziev, T. (2013). Employee empowerment, employee attitudes, and performance: Testing a causal model. *Public Administration Review*, 73: 490–506.

Fu, N., Flood, P. C., Bosak, J., Rousseau, D. M., Morris, T., and O'Regan, P. (2015). How do high performance work systems influence organizational innovation in professional service firms? *Employee Relations*, 37: 209–231.

Gerhart, B. (2008). Horizontal and vertical fit in human resource systems. In C. Otroff and T. A. Judge (Eds.), *Perspectives on Fit* (pp. 317–348). New York: Lawrence and Erlbaum.

Gittell, J. H., Seidner, R., and Wimbush, J. (2010). A relational model of how high-performance work systems work. *Organization Science*, 21: 490–506.

Godard, J. (2004). A critical assessment of the high-performance paradigm. *British Journal of Industrial Relations*, 53: 482–502.

Guerrero, S., & Barraud-Didler, V. (2004). High-involvement practices and performance of French firms. *International Journal of Human Resource Management*, 15: 1408–1423.

Hattie, J. (1985). Methodology review: Assessing unidimensionality of tests and items. *Applied Psychological Measurement*, 9: 139–164.

Hauff, S., Alewell, D., and Hansen, N. K. (2018). Further exploring the links between high-performance work practices and firm performance: A multiple-mediation model in the German context. *German Journal of Human Resource Management*, 32: 5–26.

Hoque, K. (1999). Human resource management and performance in the UK hotel industry. *British Journal of Industrial Relations*, 37: 419–443.

Huselid, M. A. (1995). The impact of human resource management practices on turnover, productivity, and corporate financial performance. *Academy of Management Journal*, 38: 635–672.

Huselid, M. A., Jackson, S. E., and Schuler, R. S. (1997). Technical and strategic human resource management effectiveness as a determinant of firm performance. *Academy of Management Journal*, 40: 171–188.

Jiang, K., Lepak, D. P., Hu, J., and Baer, J. C. (2012). How does human resource management influence organizational outcomes? A meta-analytic investigation of mediating mechanisms. *Academy of Management Journal*, 55: 1264–1294.

Kalleberg, A. L., Marsden, P. V., Reynolds, J., and Knoke, D. (2006). Beyond profit? Sectoral differences in high-performance work practices. *Work and Occupations*, 33: 271–302.

Koch, M. J., and McGrath, R. G. (1996). Improving labor productivity: Human resource management policies do matter. *Strategic Management Journal*, 17: 335–354.

Lawler, E. E. (1986). *High-Involvement Management*. San Francisco, CA: Jossey-Bass.

MacDuffie, J. P. (1995). Human resource bundles and manufacturing performance: Organizational logic and flexible production systems in the world auto industry. *Industrial and Labor Relations Review*, 48: 197–121.

Macky, K., and Boxall, P. (2007). The relationship between 'high-performance work practices' and employee attitudes: An investigation of additive and interaction effects. *International Journal of Human Resource Management*,, 18: 537–567.

Macky, K., and Boxall, P. (2008). High-involvement work processes, work intensification and employee well-being: A study of New Zealand worker experiences. *Asia Pacific Journal of Human Resources*, 46: 38–55.

Messersmith, J. G., Patel, P. C., Lepak, D. P., and Gould-Williams, J. S. (2011). Unlocking the black box: Exploring the link between high-performance work systems and performance. *Journal of Applied Psychology*, 96: 1105–1118.

Mohr, R. D., and Zoghi, C. (2008). High involvement management work design and job satisfaction. *Industrial and Labor Relations Review*, 61: 275–296.

Paul, A. K., and Anantharaman, R. N. (2003). Impact of people management practices on organizational performance: Analysis of a causal model. *International Journal of Human Resource Management*, 14: 1246–1266.

Pfeffer, J. (1998). *The Human Equation: Building Profits by Putting People First.* Boston, MA: Harvard Business School Press.

Shah, R., and Ward, P. T. (2003). Lean manufacturing: Context, practice bundles, and performance, *Journal of Operations Management*, 21: 129–149.

Takeuchi, R., Lepak, D. P., Wang, H., and Takeuchi, K. (2007). An empirical examination of the mechanisms mediating between high-performance work systems and the performance of Japanese organizations. *Journal of Applied Psychology*, 92: 1069–1083.

Vroom, V. H. (1964). *Work and Motivation.* New York: Wiley.

Wall, T. D., and Wood, S. (2005). The romance of human resource management and business performance and the case for big science. *Human Relations*, 58: 1–34. [Reprinted in Anderson, N. (Ed.). (2007). *Fundamentals in HRM: Sage's Major Works* (Volume 4, pp. 71–95). London: Sage].

Wall, T. D., Wood, S. J., and Leach, D. J. (2004). Empowerment and performance. In C. L. Cooper and I. T. Robertson (Eds.), *International Review of Industrial and Organizational Psychology* (Vol. 19, pp. 1–46). London: Wiley.

Walton, R. E. (1985). From 'control' to 'commitment' in the workplace. *Harvard Business Review*, 63: 77–84.

West, M. A., Guthrie, J. P., Dawson, J. F., Borrill, C. S., and Carter, M. (2006). Reducing patient mortality in hospitals: The role of human resource management. *Journal of Organizational Behaviour*, 27: 983–1002.

Womack, J., Jones, D. T., and Roos, D. (1990). *The Machine That Changed the World.* New York: Rawson.

Wood, S. (1999). Human resource management and performance. *International Journal of Management Reviews*, 1: 367–413.

Wood, S. (2020). The HRM–Performance Research Stream: Are we all on the same page? *International Journal of Management Reviews*, 22: 408–426.

Wood, S. (2021). Developments in the HRM–Performance Research Stream: The mediation studies. *German Journal of Human Resource Management*, 35: 83–113.

Wood, S., and de Menezes, L. M. (2008). Comparing perspectives on high involvement management and organizational performance across the British economy. *International Journal of Human Resource Management*, 19: 639–683.

Wood, S., and Ogbonnaya, C. (2018). High-involvement management, economic recession, well-being, and organizational performance. *Journal of Management*, 44: 3070–3095.

Wood, S., van Veldhoven, M., Croon, M., and de Menezes, L. M. (2012). Enriched job design, high involvement management and organizational performance: The mediating roles of job satisfaction and well-being. *Human Relations*, 65: 419–445.

Wood, S. J., and Wall, T. D. (2007). Human resource management and employee voice. *International Journal of Human Resource Management*, 18: 1335–1372.

5 HRM

An Ethical Perspective

Mick Fryer, Dimitrios Koukourdinos and Alexandros Psychogios

Introduction

It is tempting to assume that the ethics of HRM should be measured in relation to its tendency to promote employee well-being. An ethical premium is thus placed on those practices that protect employees' material interests, serve their emotional needs and promote their self-actualisation. Conversely, it is tempting to cast an ethical question mark over HRM practices that subordinate employees' well-being to the commercial success of the organisation for which they work.

However, such an approach is problematic in at least two respects. Firstly, there are some compelling moral arguments in favour of prioritising commercial success over and above the well-being of employees (some of which will be discussed later). Considering the merits of such arguments requires us to do more than highlight the intuitive allure of employee well-being. Secondly, even if we do wish to place employee well-being above all other considerations, spelling out the detail of such an agenda is no simple matter. This task is complicated by the possibility that the well-being of one group of employees may conflict with that of other groups (Stanworth, 2000). For example, tensions between the interests of core employees and agency workers, between those of a local workforce and remote employees, or between the well-being of junior and senior employees may introduce dilemmas. Furthermore, it is not always easy to build a clear understanding of an organisation's responsibilities even as they relate to the well-being of a specific group of employees. For instance, should feelings of paternalistic care take precedence over libertarian principles of self-determination, or does the apparent 'fairness' of performance-related pay justify a consequent intensification of risk for employees (Heery, 2000)?

Where, then, should we turn for guidance if we wish to move beyond the intuitive appeal of an employee well-being agenda and consider HRM ethics more systematically? Fortunately, there are plenty of philosophical resources available to inform such an undertaking. Even if we confine ourselves to the Western tradition, two and a half millennia of enquiry into the nature of right and wrong has offered an abundant reservoir of insights. The aim of this

DOI: 10.4324/9781032625560-6

chapter is to provide an introduction to some of the most influential ideas that have emerged from this tradition and to consider what they have to say to HRM.

To provide some structure to this task, these ideas will be arranged according to their *metaethical* presuppositions. In other words, ethics theories will be grouped according to three different ways of thinking about ethics: namely, *ethical absolutism, ethical relativism* and *ethical intersubjectivism*. It will become apparent that each group of theories offers some useful insights but that each provides, at best, an ambivalent guide to ethical HRM practice. We will also suggest that, while ethical absolutist and ethical relativist theory might be interpreted as offering a basis for unilateral management decision-making about ethically charged HR matters, each also contains fertile ground for ethical legitimation of participative HRM practices. This theme will be developed further during discussion of the third metaethical perspective, ethical intersubjectivism, which offers a more explicit endorsement of participative workplace arrangements. We will also describe how intersubjectivist theory might inform ethical evaluation of various instantiations of employee voice. Finally, this chapter takes a further step, introducing one more perspective to HRM ethics, which although close to intersubjectivism, represents a distinctive approach to ethics based on Christian East Orthodox philosophical tradition. By focusing on Yanaras' philosophical views, we suggest the perspective of *personhood* in ethics of HRM, a relational approach that understands employees in organisations as unique persons defined through their relations with other employees. Moreover, the concept of employee voice and its opposite, employee silence, is used in order to briefly elucidate this perspective.

Ethical Absolutism

Ethical absolutism is characterised by a belief that moral rightness and wrongness can be assessed in accordance with objective standards that are valid for all people, at all times and in all places. Although these universally valid standards need to be interpreted and applied in a manner that responds to each situation, ethical absolutism proposes that the standards themselves remain constant. Finding a recipe for ethical HRM practice would involve identifying those universally valid standards and applying them to specific work contexts. In seeking to identify the universal standards that should shape our moral evaluations, different ethical absolutist philosophers have followed different routes. Here, we will offer an overview of three of the most influential contributions: utilitarianism, rights theory and Kantian theory.

Utilitarianism: Maximising the Good

Some ethical absolutist theorists evaluate ethicality purely in relation to consequences. In other words, they consider an ethically desirable action to be one which brings about ethically desirable consequences, and an ethically undesirable action to be one which leads to ethically undesirable consequences.

This way of thinking about ethics is usually referred to as *consequentialism*. The most well-known consequentialist theory is *utilitarianism*, which judges consequences in relation to the total amount of good that is produced. When faced with a moral dilemma, utilitarians suggest that we should consider the likely consequences of the various courses of action available to us and select the option that will bring about the greatest amount of good for the greatest number of people. Maximisation of the good is, therefore, the objective standard that utilitarians apply to guide their ethical deliberations.

Utilitarianism offers a simple and intuitive guide to HRM ethics. This may be why it is popular amongst business managers, who often draw on utilitarian-style rationales to justify ethically contentions HR decisions (Legge, 1998; Parker, 2002; Fryer, 2011). For instance, when asked to justify employee redundancies, along with the hardship that this causes for those employees, their families and their local community, managers often point to the greater number of people – such as other employees, shareholders, suppliers and customers – who depend on the prosperity of their company and who, therefore, stand to gain from the cost reductions and efficiency enhancements associated with workforce restructuring. The hardship experienced by a small group is justified by the good consequences experienced by many more people.

However, the apparent simplicity of utilitarianism can be misleading. That it does not provide the straightforward guide to management decision-making that it seems to promise is evident from the contrasting business priorities that have been justified on utilitarian grounds. On the one hand, some commentators suggest that society will benefit most if each business focuses all its efforts on making as much money for its owners as possible (Smith, 1998/1776; Jensen, 2002). The rationale behind this argument is that, to maximise shareholder returns, businesses must maximise long-term profitability. Since this requires them to use scarce resources as efficiently as they can, it will, in the long term, be in everybody's best interests. If shareholder value maximisation entails hardship for some employees, then these writers consider this to be a price worth paying to achieve this greater good. Conversely, other writers have challenged this rationale on utilitarian grounds, arguing that the common good of society will only be achieved if businesses' managers seek to directly enhance the happiness of all those people, including its employees (Jones and Felps, 2013a, 2013b). According to this view, looking after all stakeholders is far more likely to maximise the good than prioritising shareholder returns.

Such disagreements may be due partly to complications surrounding the application of utilitarian principles to practical business scenarios. For one thing, it is not always easy to predict the consequences of business decisions with any degree of certainty, so we can never be quite sure what course of action will bring about the greatest good for the greatest number. Then there is the question of whether we should try to maximise the total amount of good, even if only a few very fortunate people benefit, or whether we should aim to disperse good things as widely as possible so that many people receive a small amount of the benefits (Audi, 2007). And what should count as 'the good' anyway? Should we just try to maximise pleasure and minimise pain, as suggested by Jeremy Bentham (2000/1789)? Should we follow John-Stuart Mill (1962/1861) in distinguishing between higher pleasures, which are associated with intellectual and cultural refinement, and lower pleasures, which appeal to people of less refined taste? Or should we agree with G.E. Moore (1993/1903) that certain states of mind, such as the appreciation of beauty and the acquisition of knowledge, have merit regardless of their pleasantness or unpleasantness. Or perhaps we should drop all attempts to define an objective list of 'good' things and just say that 'the good' consists of meeting people's preferences, whatever they may be (Hare, 1981).

Clearly, how we answer questions such as these will shape the way in which we apply utilitarianism to specific contexts. These complexities need not detract from the merits of the principle of good maximisation; nor do they mean that utilitarianism has no role to play in HRM ethics. However, these difficulties do indicate that maximising the good is not such a straightforward guide to ethical evaluation of HRM as it may seem at first sight.

Rights Theory: Respecting People's Rights

Whereas utilitarianism judges the moral desirability of the consequences of our actions, other ethical absolutist approaches focus on features that are intrinsic to those actions. One such approach is to think about the *rights* that are relevant to a particular situation. Focusing on rights accords with the way we frequently talk about ethics: we often speak about 'human rights', 'citizenship rights' or 'employment rights'. The assumption underpinning such talk is that people have certain rights, which carry intrinsic value and that others should respect those rights. Moreover, when we speak of rights we usually assume that they should be respected even when doing so may not lead to the greatest amount of good for the greatest number of people.

One of the most important expressions of human rights in recent times is the Universal Declaration of Human Rights (UDHR), which was proclaimed at a General Assembly of the United Nations in 1948. The UDHR lists a set of fundamental rights that apply to all people, in all places, at all times and that should be universally protected. It was mainly a politically-focused document. However, many of the rights that the UDHR upholds, such as the right to effective remedy, the right to equal pay for equal work, the right to form and join trade unions, the right to rest and leisure and the right to express opinions, are relevant to contemporary HRM contexts.

Within business contexts, discussions often revolve around of the rights of stakeholders. The thinking behind such discussions is that stakeholders – such as employees, suppliers, customers and shareholders – have certain rights because of their relationship with a business and that these rights should be respected by those in charge. In considering stakeholders' rights, it may be necessary to go beyond those formal, explicit rights that are laid down in written contracts. While contractual rights often carry legal force, ethical evaluation may also need to embrace tacit rights that are not contractually enshrined but which play an important part in shaping people's ethical expectations. Within HRM contexts, the 'psychological contract' (Guest and Conway, 2002; Conway and Briner, 2005) provides a useful framework for thinking about these tacit rights.

Different business ethics theorists have applied rights theory in diverse ways to arrive at contrasting conclusions. Milton Friedman (1970) argued that the only rights that should count in business contexts are the property rights of shareholders. Shareholders are the owners of firms, so their interests and expectations should be put above all other considerations by the business managers who run those firms on their behalf. Other business ethics writers (e.g. Donaldson and Preston, 1995) have argued that the involvement of other stakeholders in corporate activity confers on them rights that should also be respected in business decision-making. Notable amongst these other stakeholders are employees, who make a significant contribution to a firm's success and who are deeply affected by the decisions its senior managers make. Therefore, the rights of employees might be just as important to HRM decision-making as those of shareholders.

As with utilitarianism, then, rights theory highlights some important considerations that should be taken into account in business. However, like utilitarianism, it does do not offer an unequivocal guide to HRM ethics. The conclusions to which rights theory points depend very much on how we classify rights, how we weight them and, in particular, how we arbitrate between conflicting rights of different stakeholders.

Kantian (Deontological) Theory: Doing Our Duty

A third ethical absolutist approach is to think more about *duty* than about individual rights or the common good. Duty-based theories are usually referred to as *deontological* theories. Whereas rights theory directs attention to the moral entitlements of those affected by an ethically-charged decision, deontological theory focuses more on the duty of the decision-maker. The most influential deontological theorist was Immanuel Kant. Kant's discussion of duty (1948/1785, 1997/1788) placed a great deal of emphasis on human rationality and human freedom/autonomy. Kant believed that the key characteristics that differentiate human beings from all other species are our ability to reason and our autonomy. Whereas other species are inclined to act on physical or emotional urges, humans alone are able to think rationally about their actions and act accordingly. For Kant, the fact that we are able to act in opposition to physical and emotional urges means that we are also fundamentally free. That is, we are able to act autonomously.

Kant drew a number of conclusions from this celebration of human rationality and human freedom. The first is that he believed we can use our reason to work out what our duty consists of. He proposed that we do this by applying certain principles – as he put it, by applying certain formulations of the 'categorical imperative'. Perhaps the most important of these for HRM is the second formulation of Kant's categorical imperative, which is sometimes referred to as 'the formula of the end in itself' (e.g. Paton, 1948: 90). In his presentation of this principle, Kant observed that it would be irrational for a rational, autonomous being to use another rational, autonomous being merely as a means to an end. In other words, we should not use other people to achieve things we want to achieve without also treating them in ways that respect their freedom and rationality. To apply this thinking to an HRM context, it may be permissible for business managers to use employees as means to achieve corporate success – that is, to use them as a means to an end – but those employees should also be treated as an end in themselves. They should be treated in ways that respect their rationality and their autonomy.

Different business ethics writers have drawn on Kantian theory to justify contrasting sets of business priorities. On the one hand, Bowie (1998, 2002) applies Kant in ways that regulate some intuitively troubling excesses of corporate conduct whilst leaving the fundamental structures and priorities of US managerial capitalism, especially as they relate to HRM, largely untouched. On the other hand, Jones et al. (2005) find Bowie's interpretation and application of Kantian theory insufficiently rigorous. Instead, they find in Kant's writing ample grounds from which to challenge some of those structures and priorities that Bowie seeks to sanitise. As with utilitarianism and rights theory, then, although Kant's philosophy provides useful insights to HRM ethics, the conclusions to which it leads depend on the manner of its interpretation and application. Given the scope and complexity of Kant's writing, along with the interpretational disagreements that have long occupied Kant scholars, this problem should not be underestimated.

Applying Ethical Absolutist Theories

A general implication of ethical absolutist theories for HRM is that, when confronted with a moral dilemma, the universal principles upon which the respective theory is based should be applied so as to identify the morally correct course of action. However, as the earlier discussion reveals, this may not be easy. Despite the apparent simplicity of the decision-making principles offered by ethical absolutist theories, these theories still have to be interpreted and applied to specific situations. And in the act of interpretation and application there is considerable scope for ambivalence. Kaler (1999) goes so far as to suggest that such ambivalence means that ethics theory is more likely to be used for ethical justification than to inform ethical evaluation. In other words, the expedient flexibility of ethical absolutist theories means that they are more likely to be co-opted to support courses of action that we have already chosen than they are to help us choose those courses of action.

But perhaps we should not summarily dismiss the usefulness of ethical absolutist theory in the light of such problems. Even if we agree that they do not provide unequivocal prescriptions for action, we might nevertheless grant that different ethical absolutist theories can serve a useful purpose. Maybe the best way to think of these various theories is as separate lenses, each of which can be used to look at an ethically charged scenario in slightly different ways to help us appreciate dimensions of that scenario that we might otherwise have overlooked. Thus, the lens of utilitarianism may highlight the consequences of HRM practices and policies for employees, their families and others who may not spring readily to mind. Similarly, the lens of rights-based consideration might evoke sensitivity to the entitlements–explicit and tacit–of businesses' less obvious, less powerful or less strident stakeholders. And the lens of Kantian evaluation may foreground some ways in which HRM practices respect or fail to respect the dignity that is due to all employees as rational, autonomous beings. Even if we agree with Kaler that we usually make moral decisions by applying a sort of moral gut-feel, we might nevertheless argue that the quality of our decisions will be enhanced if that gut-feel is exposed to a certain amount of critical reflection; critical reflection that can be facilitated by viewing morally charged situations (Fryer, 2015, 2016).

Ethical Relativist Theory

Ethical relativism questions the existence of objective standards of moral right and wrong that apply to all people, in all places, at all times. It therefore casts doubt on the idea that the ethical legitimacy of HRM practice can be evaluated by applying universal principles. Ethical relativists highlight the plurality of ethical opinion and try to account for that plurality. Moreover, they emphasise the merits of acting in accordance with personal ethical conviction.

Nietzsche: Challenging the Legitimacy of 'Slave Morality'

One of the most controversial and influential proponents of ethical relativist theory was Friedrich Nietzsche. Nietzsche (2003/1887) proposed that the basis for any system of moral values lies in convention and that morality has no claim to legitimacy beyond the particular convention that underpins it. Furthermore, Nietzsche suggested that the moral standards that gain conventional acceptance within any society tend to be those that promote the interests of that society's dominant members. And interests, as Nietzsche defined them, are concerned primarily with power. According to Nietzsche, then, morality is all about power: a dominant morality is no more than a set of values that enables certain groups of people to assert power over others.

Nietzsche based these conclusions on a genealogical study of the origins of Western morality. He observed that ancient forms of morality, going back to the early times of Greek, Celtic and Nordic civilisations, had privileged the interests of the strong. Thus, moral legitimacy had been accorded to qualities possessed by powerful elites; qualities such as strength, courage, pride, endeavour, willingness to take risks and a capacity to endure hardship. However, Nietzsche also noted a reversal of values in more recent times. He described how, thanks to their superior numbers and inspired by power-seeking religious authorities, the masses have established the primacy of a very different form of morality: a 'slave morality' that upholds values that enable those masses to resist the power of their former 'masters'. This contemporary, slave morality celebrates qualities such as benevolence, meekness, sympathy, humility, caution and equality. Moreover, Nietzsche noted that in modern times we have come to experience sensations such as guilt and shame, which he believed to be no more than psychological artefacts that help us come to terms with the adversities and disappointments that inevitably characterise the human condition.

Nietzsche regretted this modern reversal of morality because, as he saw it, the human race can only progress if people are willing to take risks, endure hardship, act courageously and so on. He believed that the predominance of slave morality is constraining human beings and preventing us from realising our full potential. He therefore advocated a 'revaluation of values', in which we would cast off the shackles of slave morality and once again grasp our capacity for greatness.

Nietzsche's account of morality presents manifold implications for HRM ethics. For one thing, it seems to justify an elitist, competitive, organisational culture that applauds those who take risks and endure hardship in order to attain and hold on to power. Values such as egalitarianism and altruism would hold no currency in such a culture. Moreover, moral criticism of powerful people for their ruthless arrogance would lack justification because Nietzsche's rebuttal of the values of slave morality undermines its ethical foundations. From an HRM perspective, these ideas seem to point towards meritocratic, performance-based systems and practices, in which the most capable employees are encouraged to progress while their weaker colleagues are left to flounder.

However, although a literal reading of Nietzsche seems to justify elitist organisational structures, his refutation of ethical absolutism also offers other insights. As well as challenging the possibility of absolute moral standards, Nietzsche also celebrated the freedom that this gives to moral agents. Indeed, some scholars (e.g. White, 1994/1988) suggest that this is the key point that Nietzsche was trying to make: that his prime concern was to urge every individual to come to terms with the potency of their own, autonomous, ethical conviction. Nietzsche was railing against the human tendency to follow the herd rather than make up our own minds about right and wrong. Therefore, he is not telling his readers to abandon ethics. On the contrary, he is telling us to embrace it wholeheartedly. But he is also telling us that, ultimately, we must make our own moral decisions; that when it comes to ethical judgement, each of us has to grasp the power of our own sovereign will.

Sartre's Existentialism: Celebrating Moral Autonomy

Nietzsche's celebration of individual moral autonomy has been developed more explicitly by later philosophers of the *existentialist* school, such as Jean-Paul Sartre (2003/1943; 1973/1946). In *Existentialism and Humanism*,

Sartre offers a personal account that sums up nicely his metaethical stance. Sartre relates how he is approached by a student for advice about an agonising moral choice that the student faces. Confronted by two possible options, both of which have implications that are deeply troubling, the student asks Sartre what he should do. Sartre's response is: 'you are free, therefore, choose' (1973/1946: 38). The message entailed in Sartre's advice is that there are no absolute standards to which the student can refer in making his choice. Nor can anyone else make that choice on the student's behalf. The only legitimate criterion of moral choice, according to Sartre, is the student's personal commitment to that choice. Presumably, if Sartre had been confronted by an HR manager seeking advice on a particularly thorny work-related dilemma, his response would have been the same: he would have emphasised the manager's freedom to make their own moral choice and to act on that choice. For Sartre, to acknowledge and embrace this moral autonomy is an 'authentic' way to be.

Commentators who have explored the implications of Sartre's existentialism for HRM (Jackson, 2005; Ashman and Winstanley, 2006; West, 2007) suggest that, far from making HRM an ethics-free zone in which the powerful can assert their dominance uninhibited by the fetters of moral guilt, it accentuates the desirability of putting ethical considerations at the forefront of HRM decisions. Moreover, they point out that Sartre's writing problematises the current fashion for corporate codes of ethics, since, on an existentialist account, people should be encouraged to make their own decisions about ethics and accept responsibility for the consequences. These recent adapters also suggest that Sartre's celebration of ethical autonomy highlights the importance of encouraging imaginative engagement with a plurality of ethical perspectives, of emotional connection to the predicament of humanity in its various manifestations and of tolerance of moral ambivalence.

Bauman: The Importance of Exposure to Other People's Predicaments

These last points relate to a further important ethical relativist theme that has been explored by Zygmunt Bauman (1993). Bauman, drawing on the work of Emmanuel Levinas, highlights the importance of getting close to ethically charged scenarios and being exposed to the predicament of those who they affect. He points out that these close encounters are vital for stimulating our moral sensitivity and informing our moral convictions. Without them, we are likely to become inured to the ethical implications of our actions. Bauman also suggests that the 'denial of proximity' that tends to occur in large organisations is problematic in this respect, since it puts hierarchical and spatial distance between decision-makers and the consequences of their decisions.

Martin Parker (2002) echoes this theme when he discusses the tendency for globally dispersed organisational forms, in which electronic communication increasingly replaces face-to-face encounters, to undermine senior managers' sense of local responsibility. Parker also recounts deliberate actions taken by companies to distance senior managers from exposure to the consequences of their decisions, thus making it easier for them to 'down-size without looking employees in the eye' (2002: 85). On a similar note, Varman and Al-Amoudi (2016) draw on the work of Judith Butler to explain how distance encourages senior managers of a large corporation to treat its remote workers in ways that they would be disinclined to treat employees who were closer at hand. Varman and Al-Amoudi describe, in such situations, processes of 'derealisation' whereby the identities of remote employees cease to conform to familiar categories of ethical significance. As a result, their predicaments do not carry moral weight in corporate decisions and their lives become 'ungrievable'.

These ideas highlight the moral significance of direct encounters with the people and the predicaments that our actions and our decisions affect. In an HRM context, they draw attention to the ethical desirability of HR-related decisions being made by people who are in close proximity to the contexts and the people that are impacted by them.

Applying Ethical Relativist Theories

As with ethical absolutist theory, ethical relativism offers a range of insights into HRM ethics. On the one hand, Nietzsche's demolition of any solid ground for ethical evaluation suggests that perhaps we should just get on with life, business and the management of people in whatever way we choose, unconstrained by a misguided search for moral legitimation. However, other strands of ethical relativist theory indicate that such an abnegation of moral responsibility would be unwise. Sartre's existentialist philosophy suggests that, rather than ignoring its ethical implications, HRM should engage wholeheartedly with them. Far from pulling the rug from beneath any aspirations for ethical legitimation for HRM decisions, this strand of ethical relativism places the onus of legitimation fairly and squarely on the shoulders of the decision-maker.

This discussion of ethical relativism has also highlighted some ways in which the ethical quality of specific HRM decisions might be enhanced. For one thing, awareness of the formative influence of our circumstances and our aspirations on our moral convictions might encourage us to engage with perspectives that have been shaped by different contextual factors. Given the role that proximity plays in informing ethical reflection and arousing ethical sensitivity, these ideas underline the value of speaking to those whose lives will be most deeply affected by the courses of action that are under consideration.

Ethical Intersubjectivist Theory

Ethical absolutist theories seek to identify universally valid foundations of moral legitimacy, while ethical relativist theory questions the possibility of such universally valid foundations and applauds autonomous individual choice in ethical evaluation. On the face of it, ethical absolutist and ethical relativist metaethical stances are both supportive of unilateral HRM decisions. They seem to be consistent with the idea that one person – such as a senior manager – can stand apart from other people and make decisions that affect those people without consulting them. From an ethical absolutist perspective, all that person would need to do is apply the principles prescribed by their chosen theory – such as maximisation of the good, respect for fundamental human rights, or respect for persons – and follow the course of action thus indicated. Similarly, ethical relativism, with its emphasis on personal moral conviction, seems to call upon us to look within ourselves rather than engage with others when making ethically charged decisions.

However, there are features of both ethical approaches that also indicate the desirability of consultation. For a start, given disagreements about how 'the good' should be defined and how its maximisation should be achieved, it seems appropriate to engage with other people's perspectives before making utilitarian evaluations that concern them. Also, if HRM policies are to respect fundamental human rights in the workplace, then perhaps they should take account of the rights to democratic participation that formed such a crucial element in the evolution of rights theory. Moreover, it would seem inconsistent with Kant's celebration of human autonomy and human freedom for HR managers to make decisions about people without inviting their input to those decisions. As for ethical relativism, the importance that philosophers have placed on moral autonomy and proximity suggests that HRM decision-makers should do what they can to engage with the ethical perspectives and predicaments of others before making decisions.

But if ethical absolutist and ethical relativist theories offer some support for participative HRM practices, far less equivocal advocacy of democratic participation in the workplace is offered by a third metaethical perspective that will be considered in this section: ethical intersubjectivism. Ethical intersubjectivism challenges the ethical absolutist presupposition that objective standards of ethicality can be applied in all places at all times. However, it also challenges the ethical relativist conclusion that ethics is, therefore, a matter of individual conviction. According to the *Oxford English Dictionary*, the word 'intersubjective' means 'existing between conscious minds'. Ethical intersubjectivism thus relates to ethical standards that exist between conscious minds. It accords legitimacy to those shared standards and concerns itself with the processes by which they come about.

Habermas's Discourse Ethics

The most influential recent contributor to intersubjectivist thought is Jürgen Habermas, whose writings about communicative action (1979/1976; 1984/1981; 1987/1981) and discourse ethics (1990/1983; 1994/1991) have been particularly influential. Habermas bases his ideas on a social understanding of human beings. He emphasises the fact that people live in social groups, that they always have done so and that they probably always will do so. He believes that any plausible ethics theory must acknowledge that social characteristic of humanity. Habermas also points to the importance of discourse;

we need to engage in discourse to reach the shared understandings upon which the coordination of our social relationships depends.

Habermas places particular emphasis on reaching shared understanding in what he calls the *lifeworld*. Lifeworld, as Habermas understands it, has been described as:

> the substratum of our conscious worldviews and of all social action … [it] comprises the vast stock of taken-for-granted definitions and understandings of the world that give coherence and direction to our everyday actions and interactions.
>
> (Pusey, 1987: 58)

Importantly, it is in the realm of lifeworld that people seek ethical legitimation for practices that take place within economic and political systems. Habermas highlights the extent to which the perceived ethicality of money-oriented and power-oriented 'systems' relies on their compatibility with normative agreements that are achieved within a shared lifeworld. If economic and political systems get out of sync with those lifeworld understandings, they lose ethical legitimacy. The lifeworld shared by a particular social group is neither static nor monolithic. Rather, it constantly evolves and is comprised of a multiplicity of overlapping and interrelated elements. Moreover, although the understandings and definitions that comprise the lifeworld are taken for granted and, for the most part, operate below the level of conscious thought, we can relate to them through processes of critical reflection and rational argumentation. It is these processes that enable progressive evolution of the lifeworld as well as progressive legitimation of the associated economic and political systems. Habermas thus envisages a processual model of ethical legitimation, in which discourse enables: a) the definitions and understandings that circulate within a shared lifeworld to be interrogated and negotiated; and b) decisions that shape economic and political structures and priorities to be kept in sync with those shared lifeworld agreements.

Habermas explores the conditions that discourse must meet if it is to enable the shared understanding that is required for ethical legitimation. He suggests that a self-evident starting point is that any person who is in any way implicated in a situation under consideration should be able to participate in discourse about it. If our aim is to achieve shared understanding about a topic through discourse, it makes no sense to exclude from that discourse anyone who may be involved in, or affected by, the topic that we seek to understand. Moreover, each person must be able to participate in that discourse without constraint. Each should be able to say whatever they want to say. It is also important that, whenever one person makes a statement, others should be able to challenge that statement with respect to its factual accuracy, how well placed the speaker is to make it and what the speaker seeks to achieve in making it. Only when such challenges have been made and responded to, can shared understanding be achieved across all the dimensions of speech. Drawing on these insights, Habermas offers the following 'rules of discourse':

> 'every subject … is allowed to take part in the discourse
> 'everyone is allowed to question any assertion whatever
> 'everyone is allowed to introduce any assertion whatever into the discourse
> 'everyone is allowed to express [their] attitudes, desires and needs
> 'no speaker may be prevented, by internal or external coercion, from exercising [their] rights as laid down [by the noted principles]'
> (1990/1983: 89).

Applying Ethical Intersubjectivism

Applying Habermas's model for ethical legitimation to HRM clearly presents practical challenges. The most obvious is that work-related discussions may not always be conducted in the spirit of disinterested neutrality, which seems most appropriate to the achievement of shared lifeworld understanding. It might, therefore, be suggested that Habermas's model holds little relevance for practical HRM contexts. In anticipation of this criticism, Habermas acknowledges that 'ideal speech situations' (1984 /1981, 1987/ 1981), aimed purely at achieving understanding, are comparatively rare. He concedes that we generally have some form of vested interest in the outcome of those discourses in which we engage. However, he proposes that this need not undermine the morally legitimating potential of discourse as long as all participants openly declare any affiliations, personal interests or emotional attachments that may introduce a note of partiality. If this condition is met, and as long as all parties are free to challenge the assertions made by their others on the dimensions of factual accuracy, eligibility and intent, the quest for shared understanding can still proceed unimpeded.

To summarise, intersubjectivist ethics understands HRM to be ethical insofar as it facilitates and responds to discourse. That discourse should include all those who may be affected by the situations under discussion. Each participant should be able to contribute without constraint. Each should be free to introduce any assertion into the discourse that they see fit. Furthermore, each should be able to challenge any aspect of the assertions made by fellow participants in order to ensure a shared basis of understanding with regard to the factual accuracy of the assertion, the speaker's eligibility to make that assertion and the effect that the speaker seeks to bring about in making the assertion. All parties should also be committed to transparency with regard to any vested interests that they may have in the matter under the discussion. As long as these conditions are met, HRM discourse can play a part in negotiating shared lifeworld agreements between implicated parties and ensuring the consistency of money- and power-based workplace arrangements with those shared lifeworld agreements.

Ethical Intersubjectivism and Employee Voice

In an HRM context, Habermas's ethical intersubjectivism resonates strongly with notions such as organisational democracy, workplace participation, employee involvement and consultation at work. Each of these topics has inspired its own distinct field of enquiry, but all share some common ground that is relevant to this discussion. The term *employee voice* will be used here to denote that common ground. We choose this term partly because of its 'historical pedigree' (Wilkinson et al., 2014: 3), and partly because the word 'voice' captures an element of these various fields of enquiry that is particularly relevant to intersubjectivist ethics.

Employee voice has been defined as the 'expression of employee perspectives within [their] organisation' (Beardwell, 1998: 32). It might be viewed from within the pluralist industrial relations tradition (Ackers, 2007) as a mechanism for representing employees' interests, and for ensuring that those interests are taken into account in management decisions. At the other end of the spectrum of interpretations, the high-involvement/high-commitment literature understands employee voice as a means of building employee loyalty and driving improvements in commercial performance (Dundon et al., 2004). The range and diversity of employee voice practices is also emphasised by Wilkinson et al. (2014), who describe many forms that they might take. These include: the articulation of individual dissatisfaction through grievance and complaint procedures; the expression of collective organisation through union involvement and other forms of representative dialogue; contribution to management decision-making through various discursive forums; and demonstration of cooperative relations via partnership agreements, joint consultative committees and works councils.

However, despite the variety of meanings of employee voice, it is not these differences that are most relevant to its capacity for intersubjective ethical legitimation of HRM. For this purpose, it is instructive to consider employee voice across four dimensions highlighted by Mick Marchington et al. (2005: 27–29) in his discussion of employee involvement; that is, to consider employee voice practices in relation to their degree, scope, level and form of involvement.

Degree of involvement refers to 'the extent to which workers – or their representatives – are able to influence management decisions' (Marchington et al., 2005: 27). If employee voice practices are to provide intersubjective ethical legitimacy to HRM, they need to have a real impact on decision-making. 'Voice without muscle' (Kaufman and Taras, 2010, cited in Wilkinson et al., 2014: 7) will not suffice. Superficial, 'stage managed' (Dundon et al., 2004) employee voice practices, which are aimed purely at engendering a sense of belonging amongst employees but that have no real impact on decision-making, would be, at best, ethically neutral from an intersubjectivist perspective. Moreover, intersubjectivist theory would not accord ethical legitimacy to 'pseudo–participation' (Claydon, 2000) or 'pseudo-democracy' (Johnson,

2006), which is aimed purely at building commitment to organisational objectives and cultural norms.

The *scope* of involvement, as Marchington et al. defines it, relates to 'the type of matter dealt with in the participation arena, ranging from the trivial to the strategic' (2005: 28). To limit employee voice to the former whilst excluding broader operational and strategic issues would place an unwarranted restraint on its capacity to lend moral legitimacy to HRM policies, practices and structures. Intersubjectivist theory calls for people to be able to achieve lifeworld agreement about those matters that affect them. Although trivial, housekeeping issues such as the Christmas party arrangements or the colour of the wallpaper in the office (ibid), may well matter to employees, the long-term, strategic direction of the firm and the employment implications associated with it are likely to have a far more profound impact on their lives. It is, therefore, important that employee voice arrangements include discourse about the latter as well as the former.

Level of participation, for Marchington, refers to the setting within which decision-making is carried out. It varies from the 'workplace or departmental level through to establishment, division or headquarters' (2005: 28). Marchington notes a tendency for matters of trivial scope to be discussed at the local level while broader operational and strategic issues are decided at headquarters with little or no input from employees in dispersed locations. For employee voice to achieve intersubjective ethical legitimacy, discussions involving employees in local settings, no matter how remote from corporate head offices, must have the capacity to influence decisions taken at the HQ of even the largest and most dispersed corporation.

Marchington suggests that the fourth dimension of involvement, its *form*, might range from direct forms, in which employees participate as individuals, to indirect forms, which are more likely to operate through collective, representative arrangements. Although intersubjectivist ethics places a premium on direct democratic participation, it need not rule out representative arrangements so long as these conform to the rules of discourse outlined earlier. In this respect, Dundon et al. (2004) discuss various direct and indirect, individual and collective avenues. Of utmost importance, from an intersubjectivist perspective, is that no matter what form is chosen, all employees have the chance to express whatever opinions they wish to express and to challenge the opinions expressed by others. In particular, it is important that opportunities to raise and challenge 'validity claims', as Habermas would put it, are not constrained by considerations of hierarchy.

In addition to their degree, scope, level and form of involvement, one further dimension seems particularly relevant to the intersubjectively legitimating potential of employee voice practices. This dimension concerns whether such practices are put in place for *instrumental* reasons, in the expectation that they will enhance commercial performance, or for *normative* reasons, based on their capacity for ethical legitimation. A scan of the popular management literature indicates no shortage of instrumentally driven opportunities for the expression of employee voice. Indeed, Johnson describes a 'clarion call' (2006: 247) for apparently democratic practices in post-bureaucratic organisations that aim to flourish within dynamic business environments. Johnson points out that this is largely due to a growing (though debatable) perception that there is commercial gain to be made by relaxing hierarchical control, flattening organisational structures and encouraging innovative input from all parts of the organisation.

The fact that employee voice practices are initiated in the interests of commercial success rather than ethical legitimation need not necessarily undermine their capacity to provide the latter. Indeed, the two aims may be mutually supportive: Brewster et al. (2014) find that commercially driven participative practices are more likely to succeed when supported by broader participation structures. Thus, the instrumental case for participation may help to foster an environment in which ethically legitimating employee voice forums thrive. However, two points seem important here. The first point concerns transparency of intent, the significance of which was highlighted earlier. Although instrumentally driven employee voice practices may also offer the potential for ethical legitimation of HRM, the reasons why these practices are initiated needs to be openly stated. Failure to do so would comprise a hidden strategic agenda that would be problematic. The second point is that the purposes that drive employee voice mechanisms may shape their degree, scope, level and form of involvement. And while an instrumental purpose per se need not undermine the ethically legitimating capacity of employee voice, we should be alert to the possibility that it may entail limitations in degree, scope, level and form that would.

The Perspective of 'Personhood' in HRM Ethics

The examination of the previously noted different approaches to the ethical conduct in HRM recapitulates, in a concise manner, the modern Western philosophical tradition on ethics. Next to this tradition, however, lies a familiar yet different approach to ethics and morality as represented by the tradition of the Christian Orthodox East. A prominent scholar in this tradition is the Greek philosopher and theologian Christos Yannaras.[1] Although he does not address directly the subject of HRM, his philosophical ideas and the ontological framework that informs them, can provide useful insights to ethical perspectives in this context.

Yannaras' approach is closer to intersubjectivism. He rejects equally an absolutist and a relativistic approach to ethics. Instead, in his theological and philosophical work he emphasises the importance of 'personhood' vis-à-vis the concept of the individual, and of community of interpersonal relations vis-à-vis a contractual relationship based merely on utility. Yannaras argues that the basic orientation of the main ideologies of modernity remain *individual-centric*, an orientation that stems originally from the natural condition of humanity, its impulses for self-preservation, survival, dominance and pleasure.

> The individual-centric way of existence defines the created world. Nevertheless, the human being is vested with the capacity of free will, that is, the possibility of freedom from instinctive impulses of individual-centrism, from the way of created existence.
>
> (Yannaras, 2019: 116-7).

The Eastern Orthodox philosophical tradition exhibits a totally different understanding of the human subject: it is a different ontology and anthropology that has found expression in the theology of 'personhood'. The concept of the 'person', central in Orthodox theology after the 1960s, is seen as an expression of the human being truer than that of the 'individual'. 'Person' is not an ***individual*** in the sense of an autonomous, self-determining entity. 'Personhood' is a referential reality: the uniqueness of a person is always defined 'relatively', through relations with other people. In sharp contrast to the 'individual', in the notion of the person, the ontological principle is not a common essence, but a relation, a ***mode of being***. According to Yannaras, by thinking of the human being in terms of the 'individual', that is, equating the being of man with his nature, personal distinctiveness is obliterated. The person certainly represents an individual, but an individual ***in relation***, a dynamic actualisation of relationship (Yannaras, 2007: 5). 'Each person is a "unique," "dissimilar" and "unrepeatable" subject in dynamic relationship with other human beings and the natural world' (Yannaras, 2007: 17). Yet, this personal uniqueness is only revealed through relationships: only vis-à-vis the others will our own distinctiveness comes to light. Therefore, community and personhood are inextricably linked.

What does the perspective offered by Yannaras mean for the ethics of HRM? That neither the application of an 'objective' principle, be it utilitarianism or rights (with all the arbitrariness pertaining to the interpretation of what is 'good', 'useful' or 'right'), nor the relativistic abandoning of the decision to the solitary individual will and convictions of the manager can be a basis and a criterion for ethical conduct. In this respect, Yannaras' approach is closer to intersubjectivism and discourse ethics that may be useful as a means. However, within the intersubjectivism thinking we still need to address and overcome the essentially individual-centric participation of the different stakeholders in the process.

Hence, ethical, according to Yannaras' approach, is the conduct of a HR manager that:

a) respects the uniqueness and the holistic character of the persons participating; the employee should not be treated merely as a 'resource', a fragmented sum of talents, skills and experiences. Moreover, ethical HRM, influenced by this perspective, should extend beyond the material aspects of employment to consider the overall well-being of employees, acknowledging the interconnectedness of work and personal life.

b) facilitates the creation of interpersonal relations at all levels in an organisation, encourages respect but also mutual understanding and acknowledgement. In his still untranslated book *The Real and the Imaginary in Political Economy*, Yannaras reminds us that in the field of modern economics we talk about *profit*, *capital*, *labour*, *national product* without suspecting that the intellectual obviousness of these terms conceals a direct experiential reality of active relations, *ways* of correlating of personal human actions that are not reduced to a single interpretative code (Yannaras, 1996: 19–20). Ethical is the HR practice that prioritises the dignity and freedom of persons within the organisational community and that facilitates the creation of interpersonal communion.

c) understands the organisation as a community. Yannaras' emphasis on community and interrelationship resonates with the idea that organisations are not mere agglomerations of individuals but interconnected communities. The ethical conduct of HRM should foster a sense of community, promoting collaboration, mutual support and the well-being of all members. This, to a significant degree, challenges traditional hierarchical models and encourages a more participatory approach. Relationships based on 'necessity' and 'dependence,' i.e., exploitative and oppressive relationships, are 'non-relationships' because they lack the freedom that the 'unique', 'dissimilar' and 'unrepeatable' person requires to emerge and prosper (Cole, 2019: 306). This interpretation, however, does not equate to an abolition of hierarchy in organisations. For giving the basis to the formation of interpersonal relations does not level the real differences in talents and skills that each person uniquely bears (Yannaras, 2006).

Returning the discussion on employee voice, Yannaras' approach can be exemplified in the case of abstention from voicing individual opinions, to the benefit of the community. According to the personhood perspective, employee voice, that is, the ability or right of a person in an organisation to freely raise his/her concerns, is not independent from the fact that other people participate in the social entity too. Building on the outcome of a study by Prouska and Psychogios (2018), one may suggest a new form of employee silence, namely, *social empathy silence*. Employee silence, as an antithetical concept to voice, is traditionally used to describe the reluctance of employees to voice their concerns about organisational issues (Milliken, Morrison, & Hewlin, 2003). This is caused either by individual employee motivations (simply they do not want to) or/and or by management decisions that leave employees out of the voice process (Donaghey, Cullinane, Dundon, & Wilkinson, 2011). However, the conceptualisation of employee silence seems to reproduce the individualistic ideological basis of absolutism and relativism. In contrast, Prouska and Psychogios (2018) found that in a period of economic downturn and turbulence, what seems to prevail is a conceptualisation of silence based on empathetic approach of employees to each other. Empathetic silence draws on people's unwillingness to voice an opinion based solely on their self-interest, because this opinion, although useful to them, may negatively affect the situation of others in the community. This conceptualisation of silence offers an example of a personhood view of ethics in HRM, showing that employees shape reality and take actions (in the particular case, the conscious decision not to speak up) through their coexistence and relations to others. They perceive the crisis as posing an immediate threat to all, and their response to it takes into consideration others around them. In this respect, HR practitioners should not limit themselves in promoting the right of employee voice, but also to underline the benefits of using or not using this right taking into consideration the common good of all members.

In conclusion, this framework attempts to provide a new thinking towards ethics in HRM. The role of the ethical 'human resources' manager (a term that Yannaras would most probably reject as an oxymoron) would not be that of the responsible for the most useful, or effective use, of the fragmented talents and skill of an individual employee, but rather the facilitator of interrelationship between the different persons in an organisation, aiming at avoiding alienation of the employees from their work and at the orientation of the contribution of each participant (including the proprietors themselves) to the common flourishing of the organisation-community as a whole.

Conclusion

This chapter began by suggesting that we should go beyond the intuitive allure of employee well-being to find a basis for ethical evaluation of HRM. Accordingly, the chapter has introduced a range of ethics theories under three different metaethical headings and suggested some ways in which these might inform consideration of HRM ethics. Although ethical absolutist and ethical relativist theories do not provide simple and straightforward prescriptions for ethical HRM, this discussion has highlighted some insights that they offer to a comprehensive appreciation of the ethical implications of specific HRM scenarios.

The chapter has also highlighted the support that ethical absolutist and ethical relativist theories provide for participative HRM practices. Although neither metaethical perspective provides an unequivocal endorsement for employee participation, the theories that fall within each group provide fertile grounds for its legitimation. A more explicit affirmation of participative HRM practices is provided by ethical intersubjectivism. Moreover, ethical intersubjectivist theory offers a framework for evaluating the ethically legitimating potential of various forms of employee voice. Finally, the ideas stemming from the concept of personhood and the prioritisation of the criterion of interrelationship and the avoidance of alienation may provide intersubjectivism with the necessary flexibility and coherence to avoiding a lapsing back to a mere organised ethical relativism.

Perhaps the conclusion we should draw from this is that ethical HRM is a complex matter, which eludes precise definition. Nevertheless, practitioners who seek a compelling, theoretically grounded basis of ethical legitimation for HRM practice can find it in a comprehensive instantiation of employee voice that conforms to the principles suggested by ethical intersubjectivism.

Note

1 It would be difficult to give even a very brief description of the voluminous work of Yannaras, who until recently, due to the lack of translation of many of his books in English, was not known to the Anglophone academia. His work transcends the conventional academic field division between philosophy and theology. Yannaras' level of analysis is neither social science, nor historical per se; it is philosophical and theological, namely, an analysis at the level of ontology. Yet, it is not an abstract account, but it is rooted in a consistent comparison of two paradigms, one that was historically rooted in ancient Greece and further elaborated in the Orthodox Christian tradition and one represented by the paradigm of the 'West'.

References

Ackers, P. (2007). Collective bargaining as industrial democracy: Hugh Clegg and the political foundations of British industrial relations pluralism. *British Journal of Industrial Relations*, 45–1, 77–101.

Ashman, I. and Winstanley, D. (2006). Business ethics and existentialism. *Business Ethics: A European Review*, 15(3): 218–233.

Audi, R. (2007). Can utilitarianism be distributive? Maximization and distribution as criteria in managerial decisions. *Business Ethics Quarterly*, 17(4): 593–611.

Bauman, Z. (1993). *Postmodern Ethics*. Malden, MA: Blackwell.

Beardwell, I. (1998). Voices on. *People Management*, May, 32–36.

Bentham, J. (2000/1789). Principles of morals and legislation. In T. Griffin (Ed.), *Selected Writings on Utilitarianism*. Ware: Wordsworth.

Bowie, N. (1998). A Kantian theory of meaningful work. *Journal of Business Ethics*, 17: 1083–1092.

Bowie, N. (2002). A Kantian approach to business ethics. In R. E. Fredericks (Ed.), *A Companion to Business Ethics*, (pp.3–16). Oxford: Blackwell.

Brewster, C., Brookes, M., Johnson, P. and Wood, G. (2014). Direct involvement, partnership and setting: A study in bounded diversity. *The International Journal of Human Resource Management*, 25(6): 795–809.

Claydon, T. (2000). Employee participation and involvement. In D. Winstanley and J. Woodall (Ed.), *Ethical Issues in Contemporary Human Resource Management*, (pp. 208–233). Basingstoke: Macmillan.

Cole, J. (2019). Personhood, relational ontology, and the Trinitarian politics of eastern orthodox thinker Christos Yannaras. *Political Theology*, 20(4): 297–310

Conway, N. and Briner, R. B. (2005). *Understanding Psychological Contracts at Work: A Critical Evaluation of Theory and Research*. Oxford: Oxford University Press.

Donaghey, J., Cullinane, N., Dundon, T. and Wilkinson, A. (2011). Reconceptualising employee silence: Problems and prognosis. *Work, Employment and Society*, *25*(1), 51–67.

Donaldson, T. and Preston, L. (1995). The stakeholder theory of the corporation: Concepts, evidence and implications. *Academy of Management Review*, 20(1): 65–91.

Dundon, T., Wilkinson, A., Marchington, M. and Ackers, P. (2004). The meanings and purpose of employee voice. *International Journal of Human Resource Management*, 15–6, 1149–1170.

Friedman, M. (1970). The social responsibility of business is to increase its profits. *The New York Times Magazine*, September 13.

Fryer, M. (2011). *Ethics and Organizational Leadership: Developing a Normative Model.* Oxford: Oxford University Press.

Fryer, M. (2015). *Ethics Theory and Business Practice.* London: Sage.

Fryer, M. (2016). A role for ethics theory in speculative business ethics teaching. *Journal of Business Ethics*, 138(1): 79–90.

Guest, D.E. and Conway, N. (2002). *Pressure at Work and the Psychological Contract.* London: CIPD.

Habermas, J. (1979/1976). *Communication and the Evolution of Society.* London: Heinemann.

Habermas, J. (1984/1981). *The Theory of Communicative Action, Volume One: Reason and the Rationalisation of Society.* Boston, MA: Beacon Press.

Habermas, J. (1987/1981). *The Theory of Communicative Action, Volume Two: Lifeworld and System: A Critique of Functionalist Reason.* Boston, MA: Beacon Press.

Habermas, J. (1990/1983). *Moral Consciousness and Communicative Action.* Cambridge, MA: MIT Press.

Habermas, J. (1994/1991). *Justification and Application: Remarks on Discourse Ethics.* Cambridge, MA: MIT Press.

Hare, R. M. (1981). *Moral Thinking: Its Levels, Method and Point.* Oxford: Clarendon Press.

Heery, E. (2000). The new pay: Risk and representation at work. In D. Winstanley and J. Woodall (Eds.), *Ethical Issues in Contemporary Human Resource Management.* Basingstoke: Palgrave Macmillan.

Jackson, K. T. (2005). Towards authenticity: A Sartrean perspective on business ethics. *Journal of Business Ethics*, 58: 307–325.

Jensen, M. C. (2002). Value maximization, stakeholder theory, and the corporate objective function. *Business Ethics Quarterly*, 12(2): 235–256.

Johnson, P. (2006). Whence democracy? A review and critique of the conceptual dimensions and implications of the business case for organizational democracy. *Organization*, 13(2): 245–274.

Jones, C., Parker, M. and ten Bos, R. (2005). *For Business Ethics.* London: Routledge.

Jones, T. M. and Felps, W. (2013a). Stakeholder happiness enhancement: A neo-Utilitarian objective for the modern corporation. *Business Ethics Quarterly*, 23(3): 349–379.

Jones, T. M. and Felps, W. (2013b). Shareholder wealth maximization and social welfare: A Utilitarian critique. *Business Ethics Quarterly*, 23(2): 207–238.

Kaler, J. (1999). What's the good of ethical theory. *Business Ethics: A European Review*, 8(4): 206–213.

Kant, I. (1948/1785). Groundwork to the metaphysic of morals. In H. J. Paton (Ed.), *The Moral Law: Kant's Groundwork to the Metaphysic of Morals*. London: Hutchinson.

Kant, I. (1997/1788). *Critique of Practical Reason*. Cambridge: Cambridge University Press.

Kaufman, B. and Taras, D. (2010). Employee participation through non-union forms of employee representation. In A. Wikkinson, P. Gollan, M. Marchington and D. Lewin (Eds.), *The Oxford Handbook of Participation in Organizations*, (pp. 258–285). Oxford: Oxford University Press.

Legge, K. (1998). Is HRM ethical? Can HRM be ethical. In M. Parker (Ed.), *Ethics and Organizations*, (pp. 150–172). London: Sage.

Marchington, M. P., Harley, B., Hyman, J., & Thompson, P. (2005). Employee involvement: patterns and explanations. In *Participation and Democracy at Work: Essays in Honour of Harvie Ramsay*, (pp. 20–37). Basingstoke: Palgrave Macmillan Ltd.

Mill, J. S. (1962/1861). Utilitarianism. In M. Warnock (Ed.), *Utilitarianism*. London: Collins Fontana.

Milliken, F. J., Morrison, E. W. and Hewlin, P. F. (2003). An exploratory study of employee silence: Issues that employees don't communicate upward and why. *Journal of Management Studies*, *40*(6), 1453–1476.

Moore, G. E. (1993/1903). *Principia Ethica*. Cambridge: Cambridge University Press.

Nietzsche, F. (2003/1887). *The Genealogy of Morals*. New York: Dover.

Parker, M. (2002). *Against Management*. Cambridge: Polity.

Paton, H. J. (1948). *The Moral Law: Kant's Groundwork to the Metaphysic of Morals*. London: Hutchinson.

Prouska, R. and Psychogios, A. (2018). Do not say a word! Conceptualizing employee silence in a long-term crisis context. *The International Journal of Human Resource Management*, *29*(5), 885–914.

Pusey, M. (1987). *Jürgen Habermas*. London: Tavistock.

Sartre, J. P. (1973 /1946). *Existentialism and Humanism*. London: Methuen.

Sartre, J. -P. (2003/1943). *Being and Nothingness*. Oxford: Routledge.

Smith, A. (1998/1776). *Wealth of Nations*, K. Sutherland (Ed.). Oxford: Oxford University Press.

Stanworth, C. (2000). Flexible working patterns. In D. Winstanley and J. Woodall (Eds.), *Ethical Issues in Contemporary Human Resource Management*, (pp. 137–155). Basingstoke: Palgrave Macmillan.

Varman, R. and Al-Amoudi, I. (2016). Accumulation through derealisation: How corporate violence remains unchecked. *Human Relations*, 69(10): 1909–1935.

West, A. (2007). Sartrean existentialism and ethical decision-making in business. *Journal of Business Ethics*, 81(1): 15–25.

White, R. (1994/1988). The return of the master: An interpretation of Nietzsche's *Genealogy of Moral*. In R. Schacht (Ed.), *Nietzsche, Genealogy, Morality*. Berkeley, CA: University of California Press.

Wilkinson, A., Donaghey, J., Dundon, T. and Freeman, R. B. (2014). Employee voice: Charting new terrain. In A. Wilkinson, J. Donaghey, T. Dundon and R. B. Freeman (Eds.), *Handbook of Research on Employee Voice*, (pp. 3–16). Cheltenham: Edward Elgar.

Yannaras, C. (1996). *To pragmatiko kai to fantasiodes stin Politiki Oikonomia (Τὸ πραγματικὸ καὶ τὸ φαντασιῶδες στὴν Πολιτικὴ Οἰκονομία)*. Athens: Domos.

Yannaras, C. (2006). *Orthos logos kai koinoniki praktiki (Ὀρθὸς λόγος καὶ κοινωνικὴ πρακτική)*. Athens: Domos.

Yannaras, C. (2007). *Person and Eros*. Translated by N. Russell. Brookline, MA: Holy Cross Orthodox Press.

Yannaras, C. (2019). *Gia to noema tis politikis (Για το «νόημα» της πολιτικής)*. Athens: Ikaros.

6 Substance or Smokescreen

A Critical Evaluation of the Equality, Diversity and Inclusion Agenda in Organisations

Hilary T. O'Leary and Yseult Freeney

Introduction

Nurturing diverse, inclusive talent in organisations is imperative to maintaining a competitive advantage (Collings & Mellahi, 2009; Kaliannan et al., 2023). As a result, the field of equality, diversity and inclusion (EDI) has burgeoned over the past two decades, both in academia and practice, spanning multiple disciplines (Farndale et al., 2015; Randel, 2023). Yet, despite copious numbers of authors claiming it to be valuable to firm performance, whether through diversity of board membership or through crafting clear EDI policies (e.g. Brahma et al., 2021; Carter et al., 2003; Hossain et al., 2020), we still have a poor understanding of how to implement EDI programmes effectively, not least because EDI suffers from underdeveloped conceptualisation. What we know for certain is that EDI represents somewhat of a paradox for firms (Guillaume et al., 2017), comprising both challenges and opportunities for their workforces (Shore et al., 2018). Challenges arise where an ever-increasing expansion of social and demographic categories (e.g. gender, race, LGBTQ+, age, religion, disability, migrant populations amongst others) must all be accommodated within effective EDI policies, demanding a complex range of approaches. This expansion in remit may represent a double-edged sword, where broadening the scope of the diversity concept can be associated with a decreased representation of racial minority employees as found in US firms, for example (Akinola et al., 2024). In contrast, EDI promises great things – when organisations get it right, it supports innovation through diversity of thought (Yang and Konrad, 2011) and relational coordination, ultimately enhancing firm performance (Lee & Kim, 2020).

Despite its popularity as a concept and it being heralded as supporting firm profitability, EDI initiatives often fail (Dobbin & Kalev, 2016). A key reason for this is an overemphasis on the 'D' – diversity – and not enough on the 'I' – inclusion. Thus, effective EDI programmes must broaden their perspective beyond diversity of representation to create authentically inclusive organisations (Mor Barak et al., 2016) where employees experience a sense of psychological safety and belongingness. This requires Human Resource managers to develop clear and agile employee experience strategies that are continually

DOI: 10.4324/9781032625560-7

evolving to meet the needs of an increasingly diverse workforce (Shore et al., 2018). However, poor efficacy of such initiatives is not the only problem associated with the EDI industry. EDI can form a focal aspect of employer-branding strategies, where promotion of EDI values is used to attract talent, to the point it has become 'mainstreamed' (Jonsen et al., 2021). Scrutinising this branding further surfaces a deeper scepticism related to virtue-signalling or 'window-dressing', where inclusive practices fall far short of what many firms preach. While EDI initiatives are certainly well intended by some employers, often one-dimensional efforts, such as focusing on unconscious bias training, are unsurprisingly ineffective (Atewologun et al., 2018). For EDI to fulfil its purpose in building meaningful inclusive cultures, it demands wider, radical, systemic change (Dobbin & Kalev, 2016).

In this chapter, we provide a critical analysis of EDI as a concept, initiative and as a practice. Our goal is to surface the complexities in EDI thinking and implementation and to caution against the assumption that doing something is better than doing nothing. To commence, we first present the various definitions of each element and trace the origins of EDI as an ideology and movement. We illustrate tensions inherent within EDI where the 'business case' has supplanted social justice as a motive because, while this may incentivise firms to take note, this shift may ultimately dilute EDI efforts. This brings us to our analysis of why EDI initiatives fail, and we present three distinct but overlapping critical perspectives that challenge firms to take a more authentic approach, where programmes have real substance and where responsibility for EDI is shared across all members of the organisation. Despite a prolific level of scholarship in the area of EDI, the evidence base to inform practice remains frustratingly weak, and yet, our chapter gives pause for thought to practitioners who, rather than diving into the latest trends, are directed on developing a value-based strategy that is more likely to meet the core aspirations of the EDI agenda. Drawing on our analysis, we present three key principles for effective EDI practice while also pointing to an ongoing need for partnership between scholarship and practice to co-create meaningfully inclusive organisations.

Background

The origins of Equality, Diversity and Inclusion can be traced to social movements including the abolitionist movement (anti-slavery, c. 19th century); the women's suffrage movement (early 20th century) and the civil rights movement in the United States (mid-20th century), which all had equal opportunities for minority groups at their core (see Hellerstedt et al., 2024). Equal employment opportunities were ultimately incorporated through Title VII of the Civil Rights Act of 1964 in the USA (Kelly & Dobbin 1998) and legislation such as Article 13 of the Amsterdam Treaty 1997 in Europe, aimed at preventing discrimination and supporting equality in the workplace (Armstrong et al., 2010). Increasingly, affirmative actions, e.g. gender quotas to increase diverse representation in workplaces and gender representation in positions of decision-making, have been introduced in many countries (European Institute of Gender Equality, 2021). The use of quotas remains a thorny issue that is much debated but some activists make the case that coercion through quotas for recruiting minorities is fundamental to progressing representation (Köllen et al., 2018). The practices that fall within EDI management, however, have extended far beyond the use of quotas to encompass a wider array of initiatives in organisational settings.

EDI is often treated as one stream of work in organisations, however, while related, the E, D and 'I' are distinct concepts. The E in EDI can be used to refer to either Equality or Equity, which, although representing similar concepts, are not interchangeable. Equality can be conceptualised as 'sameness of treatment by asserting the fundamental equality of all persons' and Equity as 'fairness where an individual or group's circumstances are taken into consideration' (Lanfranconi Stamm & Basaran, 2023; Espinoza, 2007). Equity, as fairness or social justice, can also be defined as 'the absence of systematic disparities between groups with different levels of underlying social advantage/disadvantage ... wealth, power or prestige' (Braveman & Gruskin, 2003, p. 254). Equity, therefore, is at the systematic and structural level of the organisation. Diversity, which resides at the level of the individual, describes differences and dissimilarities among people (Yadav & Lenka, 2020), where employees can vary along social characteristics such as demographics (i.e. gender, age, ethnicity), values, beliefs or cultural backgrounds (Weber et al., 2018). Expanding on this, Mor Barak (2014: p.136) describes diversity in the workplace 'as the division of the workforce into distinct categories that a) have a perceived commonality within a given cultural or national context and b) impact potentially harmful or beneficial employment outcomes such as job opportunities, treatment in the workplace and promotion prospects – irrespective of job-related skills and qualifications'.

Equality and diversity may seem similar, allowing for equal employment access and representation of differences amongst individuals, with some researchers suggesting diversity management and employment opportunities are opposite ends of the same continuum (McDougall, 1998). While diversity focuses on differences between individuals, inclusion focuses on how people work together (Jonsen et al., 2021). Inclusion can be defined as when 'individuals of all backgrounds – not just members of historically powerful identity groups – are fairly treated, valued for who they are and included in core decision-making' (Nishii, 2013, p. 1754). Being included in organisational processes is a central component of inclusion 'to the degree to which individuals feel a part of critical organisational processes such as access to information and resources, involvement in work groups and ability to influence the decision process' (Mor Barak & Cherin, 1998 p.48).

Diversity management can be described as 'an approach to workplace equality [that] draws its distinctiveness largely from its focus on differences rather than "sameness"' (Gagnon & Cornelius, 2002, p. 36). However, the phrase 'diversity management' indicates managing diversity for organisational purposes in that managing diversity involves 'understanding that there are differences among employees and that these differences, if properly managed, are an asset to work being done more efficiently and effectively' (Bartz et al., 1990, p. 321). While diversity management aims to recognise the value of heterogeneity in organisations with a view to improve performance, it has been argued that it has evolved to focus on performance and the business case, shedding somewhat its original moral, emotive and legal motives (Özbilgin and Tatli, 2011; Urwin et al., 2013). Yet, it seems obvious to state that, first and foremost, there is a moral case for diversity and inclusion management within organisations. Work has a central role in people's lives and individuals have the right to be treated equally, fairly and with dignity and respect in all aspects of life (Hocking, 2017).

While diversity describes differences and dissimilarities amongst people, through the lens of intersectionality, it can be argued that we are all uniquely different, in that we can hold multiple social identities concurrently, e.g. a Black woman who is a manager, a disabled man who is a father. Intersectionality defined 'as the intertwined and multiplicative effects of multiple identity groups, considers how various combinations of individuals' social identities (e.g., gender, race/ethnicity, age) and their embedded meanings impact their lives, their employment and the organisations where they work' (Thatcher et al., 2023, p. 1). Through the lens of intersectionality, there is a compelling moral case for EDI management and practices. Nevertheless, the financial outcomes of EDI initiatives are important in order for organisations to invest resources into EDI management (CIPD, 2018). Evidence suggests that a diverse workforce contributes to a firm's competitive advantage (Richard, 2000) and that gender-diverse executive teams have greater likelihood of financial outperformance (McKinsey, 2023). However, the claims around the value of EDI to firms warrants further scrutiny.

Reputed Value of EDI to Firms and Employees

As noted earlier, EDI is increasingly regarded as an essential element of any organisation's strategic agenda (Theodorakopoulos and Budhwar, 2015) and scholars have evidenced the value of EDI through a number of academic studies (Hunt et al., 2018). There is quite a range of evidence on the purported value of EDI. Companies that embrace EDI better cater to the needs of more diverse customers (Steinfield et al., 2019) and better compete in the global marketplace (Jayne and Dipboye, 2004). The ability to embrace different viewpoints, talents and experiences can also boost a company's collective intellectual potential, leading to better business outcomes (Halvorson and Rock, 2015). Research reveals how a diverse workforce can improve a company's capacity to foster innovation, creativity and empathy in ways that environments lacking diversity often struggle (Eswaran, 2019). EDI can also inspire new ways of thinking and different perspectives, which can encourage employees to question their assumptions and work to keep their biases in check (Halvorson and

Rock, 2015). This, in turn, has been shown to improve decision-making and problem-solving, resulting in better team performance (Pollitt, 2005). Further, inclusive work environments can improve safety and drive employee engagement, commitment and pride, positively impacting customer satisfaction. These benefits allow companies the opportunity to realise additional strategic people capabilities that promote further financial performance (Pollitt, 2005).

Some scholars have demonstrated that organisations that adopt inclusive high performance work systems (a combination of traditional high performance work systems and diversity and equality management systems) demonstrate higher levels of labour productivity, increased workforce innovation and decreased voluntary turnover contributing to measurable monetary benefits at a firm level (Armstrong et al., 2010). Thus, in some quarters at least, there is little doubt as to the potential positive impact of investing in EDI.

In contrast to these value claims, however, other scholars argue that research shows only weak evidence supporting the claim that greater diversity contributes to bottom line performance (CIPD, 2018, 2019; Urwin et al., 2013). This may be due to the challenge in linking diversity variables or, indeed, other variables such as employee well-being to organisational performance (CIPD, 2019). Furthermore, while research has demonstrated the many benefits of diversity and inclusive management practices to innovation and problem-solving, it is clear that measuring the benefits of diversity management is highly context specific, e.g. both economically and organisationally (Urwin et al., 2013).

While there are opposing claims about the value of diversity for performance in firms (see Roberson et al., 2017), a narrow focus on the business case for EDI alone fails to address adequately deep-seated inequalities in the workplace (Tatli, 2011) and overshadows any genuine desire to see through progressive change (Tatli et al., 2015). Undoubtedly, the prominence of the business case presents somewhat of a tension for scholarship and practice. On the one side, we need to demonstrate value to firms because they often will invest energy in EDI only when they perceive it as a worthwhile endeavour, rather than merely as a means to meet legal requirements (Bhopal, 2018). In line with this, scholars may over-emphasise the need to link EDI practices explicitly to performance and profitability, which then becomes *the* priority for research (see Farndale et al., 2015; Roberson et al., 2017). However, an unintended consequence of this focus on profit may undermine genuine attempts to achieve inclusivity in organisations, resulting in misguided efforts that ultimately result in smokescreens or window-dressing, without achieving authentic and positive change for people within those organisations. It is important, therefore, to critically interrogate the EDI practices as they are typically implemented in organisations, while also evaluating the scholarly evidence base.

Critical Perspectives on EDI

In this section, we synthesise three critical perspectives on EDI. The first focuses on perception versus reality; the second on tunnel vision and lack of ambition; the third on siloisation. We consider each in turn before synthesising the joint negative impact these have on achieving genuine inclusivity and belonging for increasingly diverse workforces.

EDI: Authentic or Window-Dressing?

A key challenge related to EDI initiatives is their authenticity and the extent to which the values underpinning EDI strategies are enacted as much as they are espoused. In research and broader societal commentary, numerous accusations have been levelled at EDI that merit attention here. First, is the claim that EDI is window-dressing (Marques, 2010; Vassilopoulou, 2017), referring to false pretences of idealism when it comes to inclusivity. Such practices can be used to lure talent into the organisation with the promise of equal opportunities and a positive work environment. Second, EDI can represent a smokescreen (Kalev et al., 2006), which serves to obscure inequalities in the workplace and protect the organisation's reputation (Bhopal, 2023). Such approaches feign ethical principles to relevant stakeholders but the espoused values are not lived out inside the organisation. Third, is the argument that EDI is purely 'ceremonial' in approach (Dobbin & Kalev, 2017), presenting a multifaceted problem, where practices purportedly aimed at realising equality are frequently side-stepped to maintain the status quo.

Some critics have gone further to label EDI initiatives as institutional racism, where there is no authentic ambition to be all-inclusive but rather cynically use the terminology as legitimisation for not addressing the many forms of bias in employee recruitment and promotion practices (Steinmetz, 2021). To use one illustrative example, Dobbin and Kalev (2017) point to practices where supposed meritocracy is claimed to reward performance regardless of demographic differences but, in reality, research shows that performance ratings clearly favour white men. Recently there is evidence of a decrease in funding in EDI against a backdrop of inflation and cost-cutting, with EDI often first on the chopping board (Telford, 2024; Cave, 2024). Indeed, equality, diversity and inclusion teams, along with other support roles (e.g. recruitment), became casualties of the rightsizing and multiple layoffs most notable in technology firms in 2023, sending a potential message that these teams are not critical to business performance and, therefore, expendable.

EDI: The Implementation Gap

When embarking upon diversity and inclusion initiatives, organisations often begin with marking events e.g. Pride or International Women's Day or Eid, and with education and awareness training, for example, unconscious bias training. While well-intentioned, this overly narrow focus on calendar events and training can have unintended consequences. While events can be accompanied by much fanfare and a signal that minority groups matter, this one-dimensional approach can be seen as tokenistic, culminating in event fatigue. At worst, such approaches run the risk of being labelled 'woke' and ultimately being dismissed by the majority (Waldman and Sparr, 2023), thereby severely undermining the aspired objectives of EDI.

In relation to learning and development, it is no less problematic. Research suggests that placing an emphasis on individuals becoming educated in diversity issues sends a signal that the problem lies with the individuals (Dobbin & Kalev, 2022; 2016). Implementing diversity and inclusion training without following it up by putting the necessary structures or processes in place, runs the risk of little return (Dobbin & Kalev, 2018). The supposed benefits to firms have been questioned, particularly in terms of their validity and sustained long-term effects (Devine & Ash, 2022), with some going so far as to argue they are counterproductive (Dobbin & Kalev, 2021). Indeed, unintended outcomes of diversity training have been identified. For example, individuals who have attended training can feel virtuous having done what is required of them from a diversity and inclusion responsibility perspective and make no further efforts, which is also known as 'moral licensing' (Dobbin & Kalev, 2018; Bohnet, 2016). Training content can be easily forgotten (Dobbin & Kalev, 2016; Bezrukova et al., 2016), particularly if the training is not part of a wider diversity management programme of change (Dobbin & Kalev, 2018).

EDI: Siloisation and Passivity

A final critical issue we consider is the siloisation of EDI within organisations, where the principal change agents for EDI are confined to people holding roles such as 'Chief Diversity Officer'. Parallel to this is a weak evidence base supporting such EDI roles, where there is a considerable dearth of research investigating the impact of such roles in achieving EDI aspirations (Bhopal, 2023). Individuals holding these roles walk a tightrope in responding convincingly to the business case imperative set by the C-Suite, while at the same time championing the vision of their role to tackle inequalities and a lack of inclusivity meaningfully (Kirton et al., 2007). Nevertheless, some scholars do advocate for a task force or a role with specific EDI responsibilities. While this point may seem contradictory to the previous one, scholars (e.g. Dobbin & Kalev, 2022) suggest that while EDI efforts should be embedded in the organisation's strategy, systems, processes and culture, it should not negate the need for a senior EDI role or task force which encourages social accountability. Social accountability can hold behaviours to account (Dobbin & Kalev, 2022), for instance, sense checking recent hiring and promotion decisions and patterns with managers (Dobbin & Kalev, 2021). Thus, having a diversity manager or EDI taskforce is often well suited to carry out this role of social accountability, to overcome any diffusion of responsibility amongst the wider organisational community.

Shaping the Future of EDI through HRM

The multidisciplinary literature on EDI paints a complex picture, with many questions remaining unanswered. Devine and Ash (2022) reach a similar conclusion in their ambitious review of EDI where they argue that, given the current knowledge base in the literature, it is very challenging to derive evidence-based recommendations for diversity practice. That said, given the investment in EDI and the moral imperative behind getting it right, we summarise some key principles that should underpin EDI policy and practice in organisations. We start by positioning EDI as a major organisational change initiative with three main principles; we argue for the need to have a value-based strategy to support this change; we highlight employee agency as critical to meeting intended outcomes; and we call for better partnership between scholars and practitioners to build a stronger evidence base. We discuss each of these principles in turn.

EDI as Organisational Change

What should be clear at this stage is that having EDI initiatives in place will not automatically improve a firm's business performance. Research indicates that simply complying with the law and creating a more diverse talent pool through window-dressing can easily derail diversity initiatives (Pollitt, 2005). It is important that initiatives and supporting HR practices are developed and deployed in an integrated way (Waldman and Sparr, 2023) and underpinned by a clear change strategy. Often, initiatives can be reactive in response to a significant event. In the aftermath of the death of George Floyd in 2020, for example, organisations increased their diversity and inclusion efforts, keen to promote social justice and fairness in their organisations or in response to legislation in the US, notably the Supreme Court ruling against affirmative action in universities (Rios & Stein, 2023). For example, Delta Airlines took more action to advance Black talent in the organisation in 2020. In addition to joining the OneTen corporate coalition, (who aimed to collectively hire and advance 1 million Black employees without college degrees into 'family-sustaining jobs' in 10 years), Delta reclassified most roles that had previously required a college degree and began hiring on skill qualifications. They also expanded new apprenticeships and professional development programmes. (For full case study details, see Lambert, 2023.)

For workplace diversity to be truly embraced and to have a real positive impact on business performance takes a proactive, strategic and highly coordinated programme of activities to create a collaborative, supportive and respectful environment that encourages the participation and contribution of all employees. Waldman and Sparr (2023) refer to this approach as 'integrative'. The principle behind integrative strategies is to first acknowledge that differences exist and, drawing on paradox theory (Smith and Lewis, 2011), build a case for maintaining a meritocracy *while at the same time* valuing diversity. Communications must also be strategically framed, and the sensitivities surrounding EDI must be effectively and actively managed (Jayne and Dipboye, 2004). For example, research on the impact of demography on individual and group behaviour reveals that tension, competitiveness and distrust is felt amongst team members when their cultural experiences are not recognised as a resource, negatively impacting learning and limiting members' sense of self and group efficacy (Ely and Thomas, 2001). This points to the importance of understanding the breadth of diversity in an organisation and communicating effectively to those diverse groups to ensure they feel part of the EDI programme.

Evidence suggests it is better to create a culture of inclusion within the organisation and run training programmes on inclusiveness and building inclusive systems within organisations (Dobbin and Kalev, 2022). One such system could be how one attracts, retains and promotes employees. For example, in the UK, Zurich had an objective to do more to retain, develop and attract senior women. Engagement with staff revealed there was not enough flexible or part-time work available despite informal, flexible work policies already in place. In response, in 2019, it launched the Flexwork scheme, where they decided to advertise every role, including senior roles as flexible or part-time and has since seen positive results. (For further details, see Muller-Heyndyk, 2019.)

Within these inclusive systems, it is important to give managers autonomy to make their own decisions rather than following strict instructions. An inclusive culture also means managers are included in how policy is formed, as well as participating in the decision-making for their teams. An inclusive culture would mean that EDI would be 'baked in', built into the values of the organisation, that way it transcends all policy and decision-making processes and infuses challenge implementation effectively. In addition, having senior managers take the lead in the strategic development of EDI would shift the focus from compliance of EDI policies to value-based strategies (Hellerstedt et al., 2024). A value-based strategy that includes fairness and ethics would signal to members that they are valued and respected by the organisation. It would also encourage ethical HR practices including, for example, a transparent and fair recruitment and promotion process (Weaver & Treviño, 2001).

Research evidence suggests that investment in inclusion is central to the success of an EDI strategy, where it has been demonstrated that when inclusion as an outcome is emphasised, it captures both minority and majority employees' reality, benefitting everyone (Buengeler and Leroy and De Stobbeleir, 2018). Inclusion is also important in ensuring that employees feel accepted as valued members of their organisation, with the capacity to gain access to important networks and decision-making processes (Downey et al., 2015; Mor Barak, 2014). Three factors emerge as particularly significant in predicting the link between EDI and organisational performance (Sabharwal, 2014): i) Senior leadership commitment to fostering inclusion; ii) A belief that employees can influence organisational decisions; and iii) A belief that employees receive fair treatment. Achieving these outcomes requires leadership that is dedicated to creating a working culture that is characterised by a collective commitment to integrating diverse cultural identities as a source of insight and skill (Ely and Thomas, 2001; Holvino et al., 2004).

Managerial Implementation and Employee Agency in EDI

At a tactical level, leaders need effective people management capabilities in implementing diversity initiatives. This cannot be achieved by training programmes alone, such as unconscious bias training. A narrow focus can result in employees losing sight of the complex and nuanced nature of diversity issues resulting in a misplaced focus on the change (Steinfield et al., 2019). Leaders also need to support resources as well as authority and encouragement from the business to empower their employees to influence work-group decisions (Sabharwal, 2014). The role of the line manager is, hence, central. Dobbin and Kalev (2022) advocate for all managers to become 'change agents' within their organisations. It is through managers that organisational policies either live or die. Managers are those on the front line who live and breathe the policies from team personnel decision-making, to treating individuals with dignity and respect. Involving managers in inclusion initiatives, by ensuring that diversity and inclusion is embedded into the organisation's strategy, goals and objectives is key. Managers are critical to inclusion, through giving employees a voice, enabling their agency in realising change. Managers can also help close the gap between espoused and enacted HR practice, by translating HR practices into specific behavioural outcome expectancies to guide employees (Nishii & Paluch, 2018). Nishii and Paluch (2018) identify four behaviours that leaders/managers can adopt to close the implementation gap of HR practices; i) verbally articulate intended meanings and expectations; ii) role model desired behaviours; iii) reinforce preferred behaviours and; iv) assess followers' interpretations of the provided meanings so that adjustments can be made in the meaning-making process, if necessary.

While the involvement of managers in diversity and inclusion is vital, we discussed previously the importance of building social accountability for diversity and inclusion into the organisation through a specific EDI manager or EDI taskforce (Dobbin & Kalev, 2022). While it is important for managers to have some autonomy, it is vital for the organisation to hold behaviours to account, e.g. in promotion or recruitment to ensure a diverse and inclusive organisation. In short, if a company wishes to alter effectively the context within which diverse individuals interact (Nishii, 2013), EDI must be viewed as a strategic company-wide, ongoing investment. It also needs to be tailored to the unique needs and context of the company if it is to be successfully mobilised as a competitive tool (Jayne and Dipboye, 2004). This will ensure that areas deemed most relevant and meaningful for its employees are considered and that the company is best poised to realise tangible business results as well as benefits for employees themselves.

Evidence-Based Practice: Enabling EDI through Data Analytics

In creating an effective EDI strategy, the starting place (as with any strategy) is diagnosis, that is, to understand the current situation and analysing the gap between the current situation and the goal objective. To assess a situation, evidence is required, and to gauge the effectiveness of a course of action or strategy, data in all of its forms are required. Data-orientated approaches are recognised to expand opportunities to enhance knowledge and to inform HRM-driven solutions (Minbaeva, 2021). A lack of data can thwart EDI change management implementation, for example, when it comes to identifying a diverse leadership pipeline (e.g. Elliott et al., 2023). Hence, an evidence-based approach to implementing EDI policies and practices is key. Barends et al. (2014) describe evidence-based practice as about 'making decisions through the conscientious, explicit and judicious use of the best available evidence from multiple sources' (p.205). The sources of evidence or information Barends et al. (2014, p. 7) suggest are: 1. Scientific evidence (research outcomes from academic journals); 2. Organisational evidence (data, facts and figures gathered from the organisation); 3. Experiential evidence (the professional experience and judgement of practitioners); and 4. Stakeholder evidence (the values and concerns of people who may be affected by the decision). HR or people analytics that analyses people data and draws on technological tools, e.g. visual dashboards, to provide insights for HR (Fu et al., 2023) should be considered in the effective management of EDI.

There can be an assumption that people analytics relies on quantitative data alone. 'Hard' data systems of measuring and tracking diversity and equality equip organisations with important information for decision-making and, while valuable for driving EDI-related change, in isolation, such systems do little to explain experiences of inequality, exclusion or tokenism (Gagnon et al., 2022). Thus, systems for EDI that embrace data in both quantitative and qualitative forms – that are attuned to the direction of implementation and impact, and which make space for the employee voice – are essential for driving meaningful change that results in genuinely inclusive employee experiences. In short, organisations must have data to inform and evaluate their EDI initiatives, and yet deep understanding of the role of data analytics to assess the merits or unintended negative consequences of HR practices, including those aimed at strengthening EDI, remains limited (Marler & Boudreau, 2017). Few organisations exploit the power of data to inform practice (Minbaeva, 2018). This is problematic because EDI is still emerging and the impact of initiatives must be monitored. It is not enough simply to introduce initiatives – when stubborn or when moving in the wrong direction, EDI strategy must be revisited to inform sustainable, positive change.

Conclusion

In conclusion, our analysis has highlighted an EDI landscape that is intricate and dynamic. While there is some recognition of the value to firms of nurturing diverse talent, the journey towards genuine inclusivity is fraught with challenges and paradoxes. While the 'business case' for EDI has gained traction, it risks overshadowing the fundamental principles of social justice, potentially diluting the authenticity of EDI efforts. Despite the proliferation of initiatives and burgeoning research activity in the EDI space, the gap between scholarship and practice persists. Our critical analysis underscores the imperative for organisations to move beyond tokenistic gestures and commit to systemic change. Human Resource managers can play a central role in adopting agile, value-based strategies to meet the evolving needs of diverse workforces and commit to an ongoing transparent evaluation and regulation of EDI initiatives. In moving forward, we propose three guiding principles for effective EDI practice: EDI as strategic organisational change; managerial implementation that supports employee agency; and evidence-based, data-informed practice. By adhering to these principles, organisations can navigate the complexities of EDI, fostering inclusive cultures that nurture employee well-being and firm innovation. It is only through collaborative efforts that the promise of EDI can be realised, leading to more equitable workplaces, where all employees can thrive.

References

Akinola, M., Opie, T., Ho, G., Castel, S., Unzueta, M., Kristal, A., Stevens, F., Brief, A., & Zambrotta, N. D. 2024. Does Broadening the term "Diversity" Correlate with a Lowered Representation of Racial Minorities and Women in Organizations? *Academy of Management Discoveries*. https://doi.org/10.5465/amd.2020.0058.

Armstrong, C., Flood, P. C., Guthrie, J. P., Liu, W., MacCurtain, S., & Mkamwa, T. 2010. The impact of diversity and equality management on firm performance: Beyond high performance work systems. *Human Resource Management*, *49*(6), pp. 977–998.

Atewologun, D., Cornish, T., & Tresh, F. (2018). Unconscious bias training: An assessment of the evidence for effectiveness. *Equality and human rights commission research report series*. Manchester: Equality and Human Rights Commission. Research Report 113.

Barends, E., Rousseau, D. M., & Briner, R. B. 2014. Evidence-based management: The basic principles. *Centre for Evidence Based Management*. Available at https://www.cebma.org/wp-content/uploads/Evidence-Based-Practice-The-Basic-Principles.pdf [*Accessed* 13 March 2024].

Bartz, D. E., Hillman, L. W., Lehrer, S., & Mayhugh, G. M. 1990. A model for managing workforce diversity. *Management Education and Development, 21*(4), pp. 321–326. https://doi.org/10.1177/135050769002100406

Bezrukova, K., Spell, C. S., Perry, J. L., & Jehn, K. A. 2016. A meta-analytical integration of over 40 years of research on diversity training evaluation. *Psychological Bulletin*, *142*(11), p. 1227.

Bhopal, K. 2018. *White Privilege: The Myth of a Post-Racial Society*. Bristol: Policy Press.

Bhopal, K. 2023. 'We can talk the talk, but we're not allowed to walk the walk': The role of equality and diversity staff in higher education institutions in England. *Higher Education*, *85*(2), pp. 325–339.

Bohnet, I. 2016. *What Works*. Cambridge, MA: Harvard University Press.

Brahma, S., Nwafor, C., & Boateng, A. 2021. Board gender diversity and firm performance: The UK evidence. *International Journal of Finance & Economics*, *26*(4), pp. 5704–5719.

Braveman, P., & Gruskin, S. 2003. Defining equity in health. *Journal of Epidemiology and Community Health (1979-)*, *57*(4), pp. 254–258.

Buengeler, C., Leroy, H., & De Stobbeleir, K. 2018. How leaders shape the impact of HR's diversity practices on employee inclusion. *Human Resource Management Review*, *28*(3), pp. 289–303.

Carter, D. A., Simkins, B. J., & Simpson, W. G. 2003. Corporate governance, board diversity, and firm value. *Financial Review*, *38*(1), pp. 33–53.

Cave, D. 2024. The 'woke' debate: how valid are criticisms of the EDI agenda? *CIPD People Management*, February – April.

CIPD. 2018. Diversity and inclusion at work: Facing up to the business case. Available at https://www.cipd.org/uk/knowledge/evidence-reviews/diversity-inclusion/ [Accessed 20 February 2024].

CIPD. 2019. Diversity management that works: An evidence-based review. Available at https://www.cipd.org/uk/knowledge/reports/diversity-management-recommendations/ [Accessed 14 February 2024].

Collings, D. G., & Mellahi, K. 2009. Strategic talent management: A review and research agenda. *Human Resource Management Review*, *19*(4), pp. 304–313.

Devine, P. G., & Ash, T. L. 2022. Diversity training goals, limitations, and promise: A review of the multidisciplinary literature. *Annual Review of Psychology*, *73*, pp. 403–429.

Dobbin, F., & Kalev, A. 2016. Why diversity programs fail. *Harvard Business Review*, *94*(7), p. 14.

Dobbin, F., & Kalev, A. 2017. Are diversity programs merely ceremonial? Evidence-free institutionalization. In *The SAGE Handbook of Organizational Institutionalism* (pp. 808–828).

Dobbin, F., & Kalev, A. (2018). Why Doesn't Diversity Training Work? The Challenge for Industry and Academia. *Anthropology Now*, *10*(2), 48–55.

Dobbin, F., & Kalev, A. 2021. The civil rights revolution at work: What went wrong. *Annual Review of Sociology*, 47, pp. 281–303.

Dobbin, F., & Kalev, A. 2022. *Getting to Diversity: What Works and What Doesn't.* Cambridge, MA: Harvard University Press.

Downey, S. N., Van der Werff, L., Thomas, K. M., & Plaut, V. C. 2015. The role of diversity practices and inclusion in promoting trust and employee engagement. *Journal of Applied Social Psychology*, *45*(1), pp. 35–44.

Elliott, S., Simeone, M., Scott, K. A., & Wentz, E. 2023. Practices and typologies for using organizational data to identify potential leaders for equity, diversity, and inclusion within institutions. *International Journal of Leadership in Education*, pp. 1–12.

Ely, R. J., & Thomas, D. A. 2001. Cultural diversity at work: The effects of diversity perspectives on work group processes and outcomes. *Administrative Science Quarterly*, *46*(2), pp. 229–273.

Espinoza, O. 2007. Solving the equity–equality conceptual dilemma: A new model for analysis of the educational process. *Educational Research*, *49*(4), pp. 343–363. https://doi.org/10.1080/00131880701717198

Eswaran, V. 2019. The business case for diversity in the workplace is now overwhelming. Available at https://www.weforum.org/agenda/2019/04/business-case-for-diversity-in-the-workplace/ [Accessed 25 March 2024].

European Institute for Gender Equality. 2021. Quotas can turbocharge progress on gender balance in politics and business. Available at https://eige.europa.eu/

newsroom/news/quotas-can-turbocharge-progress-gender-balance-politics-and-business?language_content_entity=en [Accessed 13 March 2024].

Farndale, E., Biron, M., Briscoe, D. R., & Raghuram, S. 2015. A global perspective on diversity and inclusion in work organisations. *The International Journal of Human Resource Management*, *26*(6), pp. 677–687.

Fu, N., Keegan, A., & McCartney, S. 2023. The duality of HR analysts' storytelling: Showcasing and curbing. *Human Resource Management Journal*, *33*(2), pp. 261–286.

Gagnon, S., Augustin, T., & Cukier, W. 2022. Interplay for change in equality, diversity and inclusion studies. *Human Relations*, *75*(7), pp. 1327–1353.

Gagnon, S., & Cornelius, N. 2002. From equal opportunities to managing diversity to capabilities: A new theory of workplace equality? In N. Cornelius (Ed.), *Building Workplace Equality: Ethics, Diversity and Inclusion* (pp. 13–58). London: Thomson.

Guillaume, Y. R., Dawson, J. F., Otaye-Ebede, L., Woods, S. A., & West, M. A. 2017. Harnessing demographic differences in organizations: What moderates the effects of workplace diversity? *Journal of Organizational Behavior*, *38*(2), pp. 276–303.

Halvorson, H. G., & Rock, D. 2015. Beyond bias. *Strategy+ Business (PWC)*, *80*, pp. 1–10.

Hellerstedt, K., Uman, T., & Wennberg, K. 2024. Fooled by diversity? When diversity initiatives exacerbate rather than mitigate bias and inequality. *Academy of Management Perspectives*, *38*(1), pp. 23–42.

Hocking, C. 2017. Occupational justice as social justice: The moral claim for inclusion. *Journal of Occupational Science*, *24*(1), pp. 29–42. https://doi.org/10.1080/14427591.2017.1294016

Holvino, E., Ferdman, B. M., & Merrill-Sands, D. 2004. Creating and sustaining diversity and inclusion in organizations: Strategies and approaches. In M. S. Stockdale & F. J. Crosby (Eds.), *The Psychology and Management of Workplace Diversity* (pp. 245–276). Malden, MA: Blackwell Publishing.

Hossain, M., Atif, M., Ahmed, A., & Mia, L. 2020. Do LGBT workplace diversity policies create value for firms? *Journal of Business Ethics*, *167*, pp. 775–791.

Hunt, V., Prince, S., Dixon-Fyle, S., & Yee, L. 2018. Delivering through diversity. *McKinsey & Company*, *231*, pp. 1–39.

Jayne, M. E., & Dipboye, R.L. 2004. Leveraging diversity to improve business performance: Research findings and recommendations for organizations. *Human Resource Management*, *43*(4), pp. 409–424.

Jonsen, K., Point, S., Kelan, E. K., & Grieble, A. 2021. Diversity and inclusion branding: A five-country comparison of corporate websites. *The International Journal of Human Resource Management*, *32*(3), pp. 616–649.

Kalev, A., Dobbin, F., & Kelly, E. 2006. Best practices or best guesses? Assessing the efficacy of corporate affirmative action and diversity policies. *American Sociological Review*, *71*(4), pp. 589–617.

Kaliannan, M., Darmalinggam, D., Dorasamy, M., & Abraham, M. 2023. Inclusive talent development as a key talent management approach: A systematic literature review. *Human Resource Management Review*, *33*(1), p. 100926.

Kelly, E., & Dobbin, F. 1998. How affirmative action became diversity management: Eemployer response to antidiscrimination law, 1961 to 1996. *American Behavioral Scientist*, *41*(7), pp. 960–984. https://doi.org/10.1177/0002764298041007008

Kirton, G., Greene, A. M., & Dean, D. 2007. British diversity professionals as change agents–radicals, tempered radicals or liberal reformers? *The International Journal of Human Resource Management*, *18*(11), pp. 1979–1994.

Köllen, T., Kakkuri-Knuuttila, M. L., & Bendl, R. 2018. An indisputable "holy trinity"? On the moral value of equality, diversity, and inclusion. *Equality, Diversity and Inclusion: An International Journal*, *37*(5), pp. 438–449.

Lambert, L. 2023. Advancing Black talent: From the flight ramp to 'family-sustaining' careers at Delta. Harvard Business School Working Knowledge, 16 October. Available at https://hbswk.hbs.edu/item/advancing-black-talent-from-the-flight-ramp-to-family-sustaining-careers-at-delta [Accessed 22 July 2024].

Lanfranconi Stamm, L. M., & Basaran, A. 2023. Implementing equity and equality at the frontline in two contrasting Welfare-To-Work (WTW) organizations in California. *Human Service Organizations: Management, Leadership & Governance*, *47*(1), pp. 57–75. https://doi.org/10.1080/23303131.2022.2133037

Lee, H. W., & Kim, E. 2020. Workforce diversity and firm performance: Relational coordination as a mediator and structural empowerment and multisource feedback as moderators. *Human Resource Management*, *59*(1), pp. 5–23.

Marler, J. H., & Boudreau, J.W. 2017. An evidence-based review of HR Analytics. *The International Journal of Human Resource Management*, *28*(1), pp. 3–26.

Marques, J. F. 2010. Colorful window dressing: A critical review on workplace diversity in three major American corporations. *Human Resource Development Quarterly*, *21*(4), pp. 435–446.

McDougall, M. 1998. Devolving gender management in the public sector: Opportunity or opt-out? *International Journal of Public Sector Management*, *11*(1), pp. 71–80. https://doi.org/10.1108/09513559810199906

McKinsey. 2023. Diversity matters even more: The case for holistic impact. Available at https://www.mckinsey.com/featured-insights/diversity-and-inclusion/diversity-matters-even-more-the-case-for-holistic-impact#/

Minbaeva, D.B. 2018. Building credible human capital analytics for organizational competitive advantage. *Human Resource Management*, *57*(3), pp. 701–713.

Minbaeva, D.B., 2021. Disrupted HR? *Human Resource Management Review*, *31*(4), p. 100820.

Mor Barak, M. E. 2014. *Managing Diversity: Toward a Globally Inclusive Workplace* (3rd ed.). Thousand Oaks, CA: Sage.

Mor Barak, M. E., & Cherin, D. A. 1998. A tool to expand organizational understanding of workforce diversity: Exploring a measure of inclusion-exclusion. *Administration in Social Work*, *22*(1), pp. 47–64. https://doi.org/10.1300/J147v22n01_04

Mor Barak, M .E., Lizano, E. L., Kim, A., Duan, L., Rhee, M. K., Hsiao, H. Y., & Brimhall, K. C., 2016. The promise of diversity management for climate of inclusion: A state-of-the-art review and meta-analysis. *Human Service Organizations: Management, Leadership & Governance*, *40*(4), pp. 305–333.

Muller-Heyndyk, R. 2019. Case study: Shrinking the gender pay gap at Zurich through "FlexWork." *HR Magazine*, 4 September. Available at https://www.hrmagazine.co.uk/content/features/case-study-shrinking-the-gender-pay-gap-at-zurich-through-flexwork/ [accessed 22 July 2024].

Nishii, L. H. 2013. The benefits of climate for inclusion for gender-diverse groups. *Academy of Management Journal*, *56*(6), pp. 1754–1774. https://doi.org/10.5465/amj.2009.0823

Nishii, L. H., & Paluch, R. M. 2018. Leaders as HR sensegivers: Four HR implementation behaviours that create strong HR systems. *Human Resource Management Review*, *28*(3), pp. 319–323. https://doi.org/10.1016/j.hrmr.2018.02.007

Özbilgin, M., & Tatli, A. 2011. Mapping out the field of equality and diversity: Rise of individualism and voluntarism. *Human Relations, 64*(9), pp. 1229–1253. https://doi.org/10.1177/0018726711413620

Pollitt, D. 2005. Diversity is about more than observing the letter of the law. *Human Resource Management International Digest, 13*(4), p. 37.

Randel, A. E. 2023. Inclusion in the workplace: A review and research agenda. *Group & Organization Management*. https://doi.org/10.1177/10596011231175578

Richard, O. C. 2000. Racial diversity, business strategy, and firm performance: A resource-based view. *Academy of Management Journal, 43*(2), pp. 164–177. https://doi.org/10.2307/1556374

Rios, E., & Stein C. 2023. US supreme court rules against affirmative action in Harvard and UNC cases. *The Guardian*. Available at https://www.theguardian.com/law/2023/jun/29/us-supreme-court-affirmative-action-harvard-unc-ruling

Sabharwal, M. 2014. Is diversity management sufficient? Organizational inclusion to further performance. *Public Personnel Management, 43*(2), pp. 197–217.

Shore, L. M., Cleveland, J. N., & Sanchez, D. 2018. Inclusive workplaces: A review and model. *Human Resource Management Review, 28*(2), pp. 176–189. https://doi.org/10.1016/j.hrmr.2017.07.003

Smith, W. K., & Lewis, M. W. 2011. Toward a theory of paradox: A dynamic equilibrium model of organizing. *Academy of Management Review, 36*(2), pp. 381–403.

Steinfield, L., Sanghvi, M., Zayer, L. T., Coleman, C. A., Ourahmoune, N., Harrison, R. L., Hein, W., & Brace-Govan, J. 2019. Transformative intersectionality: Moving business towards a critical praxis. *Journal of Business Research, 100*, pp. 366–375.

Steinmetz, C. H. 2021. Criticism of the concepts of diversity and inclusion in Western countries. *Advances in Social Sciences Research Journal, 8*(9), pp. 116–132.

Tatli, A. 2011. A multi-layered exploration of the diversity management field: Diversity discourses, practices and practitioners in the UK. *British Journal of Management, 22*(2), pp. 238–253.

Tatli, A., Nicolopoulou, K., Özbilgin, M., Karatas-Ozkan, M., & Öztürk, M.B. 2015. Questioning impact: Interconnection between extra-organizational resources and agency of equality and diversity officers. *The International Journal of Human Resource Management, 26*(9), pp. 1243–1258.

Telford, T. 2024. As DEI gets more divisive, companies are ditching their teams. *Washington Post*. Available at https://www.washingtonpost.com/business/2024/02/20/corporate-diversity-job-cuts/ [accessed 18 February].

Thatcher, S.M.B., Hymer, C.B. and Arwine, R.P. (2023) Pushing Back Against Power: Using a Multilevel Power Lens to Understand Intersectionality in the Workplace. *Academy of Management Annals, 17*(2), pp. 710–750.

Theodorakopoulos, N., & Budhwar, P. 2015. Guest editors' introduction: Diversity and inclusion in different work settings: Emerging patterns, challenges, and research agenda. *Human Resource Management, 54*(2), pp. 177–197.

Urwin, P., Parry, E., Dodds, I., David, A. H., & Karuk, V. 2013. *The business case for equality and diversity: A survey of the academic literature*. London Department for Business, Innovation and Skills, London.

Vassilopoulou, J. 2017. Diversity management as window dressing? A company case study of a Diversity Charta member in Germany. *Management and Diversity, 3*, pp. 281–306.

Waldman, D.A., & Sparr, J. L. 2023. Rethinking diversity strategies: An application of paradox and positive organization behavior theories. *Academy of Management Perspectives, 37*(2), pp. 174–192.

Weaver, G. R., & Treviño, L. K. 2001. The role of human resources in ethics/compliance management: A fairness perspective. *Human Resource Management Review, 11*(1), pp. 113–134. https://doi.org/10.1016/S1053-4822(00)00043-7

Weber, T. J., Sadri, G., & Gentry, W. A. 2018. Examining diversity beliefs and leader performance across cultures. *Cross Cultural & Strategic Management, 25*(3), pp. 382–400. https://doi.org/10.1108/CCSM-11-2016-0200

Yadav, S., & Lenka, U. 2020. Diversity management: A systematic review. *Equality, Diversity and Inclusion: An International Journal,* 39(8), pp. 901–929. https://doi.org/10.1108/EDI-07-2019-0197

Yang, Y., & Konrad, A. M. 2011. Diversity and organizational innovation: The role of employee involvement. *Journal of Organizational Behavior, 32*(8), pp. 1062–1083.

7 HRM and Global Value Chains

Reconfiguration and Regulation in Times of Economic Crisis

Geoffrey Wood, Pauline Dibben, John Cullen, Juliana Meira, Debby Bonnin, Luiz Miranda and Caroline Linhares

Introduction

There has been a series of economic crises in recent years, including disruption to supply chains during the COVID-19 pandemic, preceded by the financial crisis of 2008. More generally, the global economy has suffered from volatile and uneven growth punctuated with recession since the early 1970s, in contrast to the long boom of the decades that preceded it. A feature of this long crisis has been the relative empowerment of owners and those leveraging highly-fungible assets over long-term investors and those with sunk capital – such as workers – in a specific firm and a particular locale (Wood 2013). Given this, and to greatly heightened global competition, many firms have shifted larger components of production towards suppliers. Prior to the COVID-19 pandemic, in many industries there had been a move towards a more contingent, remote and arms-length approach to contracting with suppliers. Free and Hecimovic (2021) argue that the move to disaggregate value-chain processes into smaller units capable of being performed anywhere in the world was motivated by a desire to reduce the costs of regulation. This behaviour by multinationals led to growing inequality between the Global North and Global South. While elites in the Global North gained from higher profits in high-priced markets, this was at the expense of the costs incurred in low-wage economies in the Global South. The pandemic disrupted this model of contracting, and, in the case of some firms at least, led to the pursuit of closer relationships, more so in geographical terms. At the same time, the pandemic also had multiple implications for HR, with a move to lockdowns and home-working for some (predominantly office workers) and increased risks to workplace health and safety for others (in manufacturing).

Supply disruption and demand contraction, as well as asymmetrical power relations across supply chains, meant that workers in the Global South faced job loss, insecurity and worsened employment conditions (Tejani and Fukuda-Parr 2021). Global Value Chain (GVC) theory explores the operation of supply networks across national boundaries: its core concern is not only the volume and geographic reach of supplier networks, but also the differences

DOI: 10.4324/9781032625560-8

in the relative value accrued at different stages of the production process and disparities in relative power and autonomy (Gereffi et al. 2005; Kano et al. 2020). It is these disparities and their causes and consequences for human resource management that form the core concern of this chapter. Prior to and since the pandemic, there has been growing interest in – and concern for – the variation in the nature and quality of employment relations and HR practices down supply chains (Donaghey et al. 2014; Outhwaite et al. 2019; Van Buren and Schrempf-Stirling 2022). In particular, concerns have been raised about the way in which prominent Western organisations may base their competitiveness on the ability to source ultra low-cost components or finished products through using suppliers that deploy extreme forms of labour repression (Donaghey et al. 2014; Anner, 2020). Major labour scandals, such as the Rana Plaza one, have resulted in negative publicity for large multinational firms (Butler and Begum, 2023). The standard corporate line of defence of dominant firms in global value chains (GVCs) in response to such scandals has been that of a claimed lack of knowledge about the excesses of their suppliers (Lund-Thomsen and Lindgreen 2014).

This chapter draws on a range of interdisciplinary perspectives from HRM, employment relations, GVC theory and applied research in supply chain management to ask three main questions. How and where do dominant suppliers explicitly, or implicitly, promote labour repression down their supply chains in hard times? How has the reconfiguration of supply chains affected the dissemination of practices up and down supply chains? And how might different – and in many instances, diminishing – forms of formal and informal regulation impact on both of these?

While reducing their direct responsibility for what happens further down the supply chain, firms have engaged in vertical unbundling, leading to a loss of direct ownership and an abrogation of control of operations. An integral component of this unbundling has been outsourcing and the subsequent development and extension of supply chain relations. The supply chain may be simply defined as a network of companies that combine in different ways to deliver goods and services to consumers, and in doing so, cross regional, national and continental boundaries (Christopher 2005; Kraus and Lind 2007). This creation of new 'intermediate markets' in formerly integrated production processes (Jacobides 2005, p. 465) has often been stimulated by intentions to focus more upon core high value-added competencies, knowledge rather than production, saving direct and indirect costs and developing greater flexibility with regard to demand swings and product or service innovation (see Kremic et al. 2006). In turn, this means more risk is borne by suppliers and, ultimately, their workers. The dominant firm reduces its own need for labour and the scale and scope of its HRM; in short, many HR problems are, at least partially, solved by doing away with them.

What has been termed as vertical disintegration has meant that traditional supply chain relations have become greatly extended across national boundaries, but with dominant parties retaining or deepening their influence over suppliers. These supply chain relations have been interlinked in what has been termed 'global value chains' (GVCs) to reflect disparities in power and relative resource allocations of value, and both geographical and organisational reconfiguration (Gibbon et al. 2008). Such developments have meant that, in practice, it is often no longer individual firms but supply chains that compete in particular markets. Therefore, the management of supply chain participants' inter-organisational relationships, as a basis of competitive advantage, has assumed ever-greater importance (Ageron et al. 2013). The resultant vertical disintegration of what Powell (1990) defined as conventional bureaucratically ordered production and control 'hierarchies', and the associated emergence of global value chains have together served to 'redefine the work and employment nexus' for many employees (Grimshaw and Rubery 2005, p.1027), and indeed, the relative advantages and challenges associated with HRM.

Reconfiguring of Supply Chain Networks and Competitive Advantage

Three major episodes of value chain development have occurred. The first was in response to the long crisis in the early 1970s and the second in response to its intensification from 2008 onwards. The third involved an initial isolationist reaction to the COVID-19 pandemic (Verbeke 2020) accompanied by supply disruption and demand contraction (Tejani and Fukuda-Parr 2021), followed by a contrasting push towards the disintegration of existing supply chains and pull towards strengthening pre-COVID GVCs (Mostafiz et al. 2022).

The first episode (from the 1970s) constituted a strategic response to the exigencies created by structural changes in input costs, technological change (and the unanticipated consequences thereof) and intensified global competition (Harland et al. 1999; Kraus and Lind 2007). The restructuring of operations implicit in the development and extension of supply chains entailed, to varying degrees, a vertically integrated bureaucracy: downsizing to a core of high value-added competencies that include a brokerage role for co-ordinating the network (Budros 2004), outsourcing upstream supply and downstream distribution activities and delayering, since internal hierarchical chains of command can become less important and possibly attenuated (Christopher 1998). Different strategic choices with regard to such organisational unbundling were thought to lead to different types of network. For instance, Miles and Snow (1986) first differentiated between internal network structures that rely on internally developed units to provide goods and services to a core organisational unit, stable network structures which utilise external providers selectively, and dynamic network structures which make extensive use of outsourcing through contracts with external providers. Other commentators classified networks according to variation in the inter-organisational relationships which evolve between participants in terms of: strategic alignment (Campbell and Wilson 1996); direction and orientation (Hinterhuber and Levin 1994);

the extent of collaboration (Cravens et al. 1996); the types of co-ordination mechanisms (Grandori and Soda 1995); the nature of the social and economic exchanges occurring (Rosenfeld 1996); the number of lateral links, reverse loops and two-way exchanges (Harland et al. 2001); and the degree of supply chain maturity (Tomkins 2001).

To varying degrees, supply chain networks can, therefore, entail the vertical disintegration of the agglomerated bureaucracy primarily associated with Fordism and the blurring of organisational boundaries (Amaeshi et al. 2008). Here, a range of participatory suppliers specialise in the provision of a range of usually relatively lower value-added goods and services to lead, or buyer firms who have usually retained higher value-added work (Kaplinsky 2005). In part enabled by technological developments in communication allowing the hypermobility of capital (Kraus and Lind 2007), networks were also seen to potentially enable lean, flexible, low-cost organisational structures (Krause 1997; Cooper and Slagmulder 2004) whist enabling risk-sharing (Blos et al. 2009) – perhaps more accurately described as risk offloading – and the leveraging of inter-firm network resources (Gulati 2007). Extended supply chain networks were seen as enabling faster access to new markets and speedier product development (Van der Meer-Kooistra and Kamminga 2010) so as to create long term competitive advantage, particularly suited to the contingencies arising in an increasingly globalised, uncertain and competitive environment (Antai 2011).

These organisational developments have been accompanied by numerous claims regarding the economic 'up-grading' of firm-level competitive advantage (Selwyn 2013, p.76) and improved flexibility. For instance, it has been argued that it is the network as a whole that is usually seen to be flexible rather than the individual supplier. Network flexibility is, due to the asymmetrical dependencies that are often created, it is the mixture of goods and services available to the buyer which can be reconfigured by either varying the combination of participants (Piore and Sable 1984; Christopher 1998) and/or by enhancing the ability of existing participants to alter their product or service offerings (Gosain et al. 2005). In either case, there is also the perceived potential for reducing the cost to the buyer of changing products or processes whilst seeking out lower, or squeezing extant, material and labour costs.

Reconfiguring of Global Supply Chains and HR Practices

The reconfiguration of supply chains in the second phase, from 2008 onwards, has been associated with the rise of more contingent and arm's-length contracting in many sectors, with important but complex implications for employer–employee relations and HR practices. Instead of vertically integrated bureaucracy, there has been the development of various combinations of post-bureaucratic, flexible, high-performance forms of organisation and management, wherein network development plays a significant role as a vehicle for further marketising the employment relationship and associated broader HR practices (Johnson et al. 2009). These organisational developments arguably reflect the opportunities conferred by a neoliberal institutional trajectory, thought to be shared in varying degrees, according to more pessimistic accounts, in most 'advanced' economies (Streeck 2009). Closely associated with this perceived trajectory is the demand to open organisations to the discipline and associated efficiencies provided by the logic of the free market (Vallas and Hill 2012). This trend towards more arm's-length employer–employee relations seems to have happened in two interrelated ways.

Firstly, global competition and capital mobility have exerted pressure to outsource particular elements of production processes in order to exploit cost-saving differentials in employment conditions, whilst simultaneously increasing the pressure upon retained employees to be competitive vis-à-vis the prospective offerings of alternative external lower-cost sub-contractors (Flecker and Meil 2010). In this context, agglomerated, vertically integrated bureaucracies have traditionally protected many employees from the operation of market forces. However, post-bureaucratic developments are characterised by 'relationships between firms and their employees, and relationships between employees, ... governed quite openly, by rules of the market rather than those of traditional obligation' (Hendry 2001, p.213). Secondly, it has been widely noted that as an alternative to, or as a complement for, bureaucratic control, management may actively attempt to imprint retained direct employees with the ethos and logic of free market enterprise as part of various culture management initiatives which blur the distinction between the identities of consumer and employee (Mäkelä 2013).

It is also evident that through redefining organisational boundaries between internal and external labour markets, a significant outcome of vertical disintegration has been the further development of segmented labour markets. These processes appear to potentially entail three interrelated developments. First, it has led to the retention of a relatively stable, functionally flexible core of employees doing high added-value work, and to a degree, being relatively sheltered from the negative consequences of such change (Hassel 2014). Second, it has resulted in the direct employment of usually less skilled employees sometimes located in numerically flexible peripheries undertaking more precarious and vulnerable jobs (Holst 2014). Third, it has contributed towards the outsourcing of lower added-value work to smaller external organisations, which, to varying degrees, compete in the open market to provide a range of goods and services (Masters and Miles 2002; Kalleberg 2003). Within these supplier firms, there are sometimes also moves to develop relatively stable and skilled core workforces (Selwyn 2012, p.206). Therefore, the implications for employment conditions are complex, with the potential for a range of different employer–employee relationships and HR practices to emerge in response to variable supply chain network configurations (Kalleberg 2003; Doellgast and Greer 2007).

Whilst the potential for variation cannot be ignored, Kalleberg (2009) has argued that with the push for flexibility by governments and employers, there has been a general move towards more precarious employment contracts. It is thought that by encouraging the proliferation of non-standard employment, the organisational developments noted earlier have served to reduce job security and increase feelings of insecurity (Fullerton and Wallace 2007; Hacker 2008), eroded wage rates and extended low-wage sectors in Western economies (Gautié and Schmitt 2010), intensified work (Wills 2009), increased inequality (Wilkinson and Pickett 2010; Emmenegger et al. 2012), encouraged anomie (Sennett 1998, 2006; Johnson and Duberley 2011) and individualised work (Gheradi and Murgai 2013). Moreover, these tendencies have been associated with the expectation that management and employees must act as competitive free agents who are often required to sell their labour, directly or indirectly, in multiple organisational sites to any available bidder with the responsibility for maintaining their own employability being delegated to the self-investing individual (Dardot and Laval 2013). Here, following neoliberal logic regarding the efficiency-maximising attributes of competition, employees are subjected to the discipline of market forces: something that emphasises their instrumental value for companies and their ever-present potential for disposability (Boltanski and Chiapello 2007; Flecker 2009). This situation is sometimes exacerbated by deteriorating employment conditions caused by opportunistic employers eschewing or undermining labour standards and ILO conventions (Locke 2013), often in response to the buyer's lack of commitment to long-term supply chain relationships (Kaufman and Saravanamuthu 2009) and their strategy of exploiting competition between multiple suppliers to reduce costs. Nevertheless, it has been argued that in some situations, the search for lower labour costs has served to relatively improve the extant employment conditions of some suppliers, although this may have been primarily motivated by branding concerns (Bartley 2007).

The degree to which HR practices are influenced may be mediated or intensified by the nature of buyer–supplier relationships. The nature of relationships has increasingly been conceptualised in terms of transactional and relational contracting, both among organisations (Bolton et al. 1994; Pittaway et al. 2004; Cadden et al. 2013) and within them (see, for example, Rousseau and Parks 1993). As with other conceptualisations, such as coercive and enabling (Free 2007), or arm's length and obligational (Sako 1992), the transactional–relational classification seems to largely derive from MacNeil's (1978, 1985) ideal-type formulation of contract governance. In this formulation, the transactional approach to contract governance is conceptualised in terms of a formal adversarial relationship between buyers and suppliers. The relationship is furthermore characterised by a short-term economic exchange and zero-sum conflict of interest in which integration and control are achieved through the implementation of binding, legalistic, contractual specifications and the discipline of quasi-market forces where there is an expectation of no altruistic behaviour between parties, and communication is limited and formal. In contrast, a relational approach entails a long-term, collaborative, social and economic exchange between parties that is characterised by informality, mutual trust, the assumption of mutual gains, interpersonal attachments, commitment to specific partners, reciprocal altruism, co-operative problem-solving and extensive formal and informal communication. In principle, any firm may manage inter-organisational relationships within supply chains using either strategy, or some blend of these ideal types in any particular contract, or different contractual forms with different suppliers (Blois 2002). The nature of buyer–supplier relationships may affect employment conditions by, for example, either moderating or exacerbating the operation of marketisation and either enabling or disabling regulation (Grimshaw and Rubery 2005). Where firms and their suppliers work closely together, there might be transfer of knowledge, which could potentially result in the supplier mimicking the good HR practices of the lead firm. However, the extent to which knowledge transfer of HR practices is likely to happen may be affected by the supplier's own cost-cutting agenda and external factors such as global competition and national legislation (Wood et al, 2016).

During the third episode, the COVID-19 pandemic from 2019 onwards severely disrupted the flow of supply chains due to border closures, lockdowns and social distancing of workers within manufacturing. Attenuated supply chains were marked by a lack of social interactions, information ambiguity and opportunistic behaviours. Future resilience might entail nearshoring, local sourcing or domestic production and/or the better development of supply chain collaboration and relationships, and improved knowledge management (Chowdhury et al 2021). Informed by concerns about supply-chain resilience, one key point of contention during the pandemic was whether companies should continue with just-in-time inventory practices or revert back to more just-in-case philosophies in order to ensure that customer demands could be met (Choi et al. 2023). Switching to just-in-case would more than likely mean an increase in inventory costs whilst continuing with just-in-time practices could result in lost sales due to inventory shortages. This debate has important implications for the location of manufacturing facilities and the operation of global supply chains going forward. However, it is arguably too early to be able to assess the long-term impacts of the COVID-19 pandemic on supply chains. Hence, some have ventured to suggest that there has been paradoxically a push to disintegrate existing supply chains, with moves towards localisation and the seeking of new/alternative buyers and suppliers (supported by national governments) on the one hand; yet, on the other, a reverting to the status quo pre-COVID (Mostafiz et al 2022), making for a somewhat indeterminate future (see also Ramani et al 2022; Scully et al 2023).

This disruption of supply chains and contraction of demand has had multiple impacts on workers. Given the unequal power relationships between the Global North and Global South, workers in the latter regions have been exposed to job losses, insecurity and worse conditions of employment, with unequal outcomes across different industries (Tejani and Fukuda-Parr, 2021), reflecting the offloading of risk onto workers. The future for such workers will depend on the relationships between key players – buyers and suppliers – across supply chains as well as national industrial policy and the broader institutional and regulatory context.

The Regulation of Employment Conditions in Supply Chains

Where employment conditions are adversely affected, there have been calls for increased regulation. One of the key actors potentially involved in regulation is the trade union. However, vertical disintegration and marketisation creates considerable operational problems for trade unions that could undermine their ability to regulate employment conditions through collective bargaining (Doellgast and Greer, 2007). Since outsourcing usually moves employment to smaller organisations that are often located abroad, it undermines prior approaches to employment regulation as it disrupts mutual dependencies between workers and employers, crucial for meaningful collective bargaining. As Wills (2009, pp. 444–5) argues, vertical disintegration creates 'spatial and emotional distance' between many workers and their 'real' employer at the top of the contracting chain who ultimately determines their employment conditions. As Riisgaard and Hammer (2011 p.168) also note, the result is that 'power in the employment relationship now transcends organisational boundaries'. Simultaneously, the threat of outsourcing has also been used to wring concessions out of retained employees (see Flecker 2009). In some cases, this has led to the adoption of what amounts to a defensive position by trade unions with a focus upon protecting core workers to the exclusion of others, thereby increasing labour market segmentation (Emmenegger et al. 2012). Nevertheless, in some sectors trade union pressure and demands from wider society have promoted better labour standards and employment practices amongst suppliers (Hassel 2014; Marslev et al, 2022), although the extent to which social up-grading has happened has been increasingly questioned (Barrientos et al. 2011; Anner, 2020). Here, much may depend upon the prevailing form of network governance which can influence the 'vulnerability' of employers to trade union action (Riisegaard and Hammer 2011, pp.185–6).

Another potential form of regulation is internal to the firm. There have been some institutional attempts to articulate voluntary labour standards aimed at influencing contractors' employment practices, especially in global supply chains, to militate against the evident potential for a rush to the bottom, possibly encouraged by what may be seen as a governance deficit (Locke 2013). Generally, the form that these attempts at supply chain regulation takes varies considerably (Reinecke et al. 2012). Such interventions could include voluntary codes of conduct, training programmes and supplier audits; international framework agreements between MNCs and global union federations in specific industries; labour clauses in Generalised Systems of Preferences (GSP) and free-trade agreements; and international guidelines and voluntary labour standards. Company codes are often derived from more general codes of practice, such as the ICFTU/ITS basic code of labour practice, the ILO conventions, or Standard SA 8000, a management system tool aimed at regulating working conditions. However, if voluntary labour standards are to deliver long-term benefits to employees, they require long-term sustainable relationships between buyers and suppliers with added market-based incentives for improved social performance and have to be based upon informed worker participation in their design, implementation and monitoring (Kaufman and Saravanamuthu 2009). Worker participation at the local level is not sufficient on its own: worker-driven supply chain governance requires worker involvement at both the workplace and transnational levels (Reinecke and Donaghey 2021). If not used to bring about real change, codes of conduct are arguably the weakest form of private regulation (Donaghey et al. 2014). Moreover, voluntary labour standards are constantly undermined by the cost-minimisation pressures present in highly-competitive global markets (Anner et al. 2013; Barrientos et al. 2011). Thus, labour standards can often decline down the supply chain. However, the extent of decline may vary, influenced by factors such as supply-chain strategies of multinationals and their fear of reputational damage, trade union and consumer pressure and industry and ownership form (Donaghey et al. 2014).

The implications for HR practices can, therefore, vary according to a range of extra-, intra- and inter-organisational factors including the firm's location in the supply chain, the nature of the work being undertaken, the availability of alternative sources of labour, forms of internal and external governance and, significantly, the nature of the social and economic relationships between customers and suppliers. Although the broad process of liberalisation and contingent contracting may have intensified since 2008, it can be argued that variation persists according to sector and locale. As Jessop (2012) notes, whilst neoliberalism has attained global eco-systemic dominance, its consequences are unevenly spread, with the persistence of different types of national mediation. In terms of global value chains, low-cost production in some locales may undermine higher value-added production paradigms elsewhere, and in others, help to shore them up. The complexity of factors influencing the reconfiguration and regulation of supply chains and the resulting impacts on HR are outlined in Figure 7.1.

Conclusions

A series of crises has influenced the configuration and regulation of supply chains, involving both pulls towards integration and pushes towards disintegration. Even where firms are seeking to embrace a high-quality paradigm, trends such as outsourcing represent a weakening of the cognitive capabilities of organisation, reflecting the cumulative knowledge and understanding of groupings of employees working closely together; hence, they may have

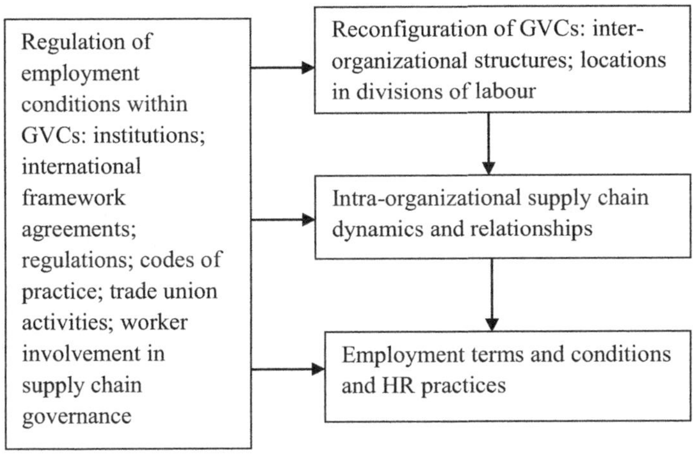

Figure 7.1 Reconfiguration and regulation of supply chains and HR practices

negative consequences for firms seeking an advantage based on quality or incremental innovation (Aoki 2010). Moreover, outsourcing is one of the main mechanisms driving precarity: this constitutes part and parcel of a move away from relational and towards ever-more transactional employment relationships, with some workers being regarded as core to the business function and others as peripheral, reflected in changes to conditions of service and job security (Kalleberg 2009). The focus on numerical flexibility through outsourcing down supply chains can lead to unintended outcomes and costs, the monitoring of contingent labour and outsourced work further down supply chains is necessary if reputational scandals are to be avoided and quality upheld (c.f. Wilkinson and Pickett 2010; Dibben et al. 2016).

Yet, there are significant counter-pressures and potential alternatives to this low-road scenario: consumers have exerted some degree of influence on the practices of a number of high-profile firms. Meanwhile, major coordinated markets such as Germany and Scandinavia have revitalised since the shocks of 2008 and the COVID-19 pandemic, and in contrast to the period of neoliberal triumphalism in the 1990s and early 2000s, their convergence with liberal-market, shareholder-dominant models no longer seems inevitable or likely. Further afield, the fastest growing emerging markets are generally distinguished by not following the liberal market model. This does not mean that they are necessarily associated with high-labour standards, but rather that there is a capacity and appetite for regulation that is absent in the liberal markets. Therefore, the lessons from the most recent crisis suggest that the patterns identified in much of the existing literature on HRM and value chains – that of contingent contracting and worsening labour standards – may not necessarily represent the inevitable global norm.

References

Ageron, B., Lavastre, O., and Spalanzani, A. (2013). Innovative supply chain practices: the state of French companies. *Supply Chain Management: An International Journal*, **18**, pp. 265–276.

Amaeshi, K. M., Osuji, O. K., and Nnodim, P. (2008). Corporate social responsibility in supply chains of global brands; a boundaryless responsibility? Clarifications, exceptions and implications. *Journal of Business Ethics*, **81**, pp. 223–234.

Anner, M. (2020). Squeezing workers' rights in global supply chains: Purchasing practices in the Bangladesh garment export sector in comparative perspective. *Review of International Political Economy*, **27**, pp. 320–347.

Anner, M., Blair, J., and Biasi, J. (2013). Towards joint liability in global supply chains: Addressing the root causes of labour violations in international subcontracting networks. *Comparative Labour Law and Policy Journal*, **9**, pp. 153–180.

Antai, I. (2011). A theory of the competing supply chain: alternatives for development. *International Business Review*, **4**, pp. 74–85.

Aoki, M. (2010). *Corporations in Evolving Diversity*. Oxford: Oxford University Press.

Barrientos, S., Gereffi, G., and Rossi, A. (2011). Economic and social up-grading in global production networks: A new paradigm for a changing world. *International Labour Review*, **15**, pp. 320-340.

Bartley, T. (2007). Institutional emergence in an era of globalization: The rise of transnational private regulation of labor and environmental conditions. *American Journal of Sociology*, **113**, pp. 297–351.

Blois, K. (2002). Business to business exchanges: A rich descriptive apparatus derived from MacNeil's and Menger's analyses. *Journal of Management Studies*, **39**, pp. 523–551.

Blos, M. F., Quaddus, M., Wee, H. M., and Wantabe, K. (2009). Supply chain risk management: A case study on the automotive and electronic industries in Brazil. *Supply Chain Management: An International Journal*, **14**, pp. 247–252.

Boltanski, L. and Chiapello, E. (2007). *The New Spirit of Capitalism*. London: Verso Books.

Bolton, M., Malmrose, R., and Ouchi, W. (1994). The organization of innovation in the US and Japan: Neoclassical and relational contracting. *Journal of Management Studies*, **21**, pp. 653–679.

Budros, A. (2004). Causes of early and later organizational adoption: The case of corporate downsizing. *Sociological Inquiry*, **74**, pp. 355–380.

Butler, S. and Begum, T. (2023). Abuses 'still rife': 10 years on from Bangladesh's Rana Plaza disaster. *The Guardian*, 24 April. https://www.theguardian.com/world/2023/apr/24/10-years-on-bangladesh-rana-plaza-disaster-safety-garment-workers-rights-pay.

Cadden, T., Marshall, D., and Cao, G. (2013). Opposites attract: Organizational culture and supply chain performance. *Supply Chain Management: An International Journal*, **1**, pp. 86–103.

Campbell, A. J. and Wilson, D. (1996). Managed networks: Creating strategic advantage. In D. Iaccobucci (Ed.), *Networks in Marketing*. London: Sage, pp. 125–144.

Choi, T. Y., Netland, T. H., Sanders, N., Sodhi, M. S., and Wagner, S. M. (2023). Just-in-time for supply chains in turbulent times. *Production and Operations Management*, **32**, pp. 2331–2340.

Chowdhury, P., Paul, S. K., Kaisar, S., and Moktadir, M. A. (2021). COVID-19 pandemic related supply chain studies: A systematic review. *Transportation Research Part E: Logistics and Transportation Review*, **148**. https://doi.org/10.1016/j.tre.2021.102271.

Christopher, M.G. (1998). *Logistics and Supply Chain Management.* London: Pitman.

Christopher, M. G. (2005). *Logistics and Supply Chain Management: Creating Added Value Networks.* Harlow: Pearson Publications.

Cooper, R. and Slagmulder, R. (2004). Interorganizational cost management and relational context. *Accounting, Organizations and Society*, *29*(1), 1–26.

Cravens, D. W., Piercy, N. F., and Shipp, S. H. (1996). New organizational forms for competing in highly dynamic environments: The network paradigm. *British Journal of Management*, 7, pp. 203–218.

Dardot, P. and Laval, C. (2013). *The New Way of the World: On Neoliberal Society.* London: Verso Books.

Dibben, P., Meira, J., Linhares, C., Bruce, R., and Wood, G. (2016). Vanishing value chains, industrial districts and HRM in the Brazilian automotive industry. *International Journal of Human Resource Management*, **27**, pp. 2398–2414.

Doellgast, V., and Greer, I. (2007). Vertical disintegration and the disorganization of German industrial relations. *British Journal of Industrial Relations*, **45**, pp. 55–76.

Donaghey, J., Reinecke, J., Noforou, C., and Lawson, B. (2014). From employment relations to consumption relations: Balancing labour governance in global supply chains. *Human Resource Management*, **53,** pp. 229–252.

Emmenegger, P., Haeusermann, S., Palier, B., and Seeleib-Kaiser, M. (2012). *The Age of Dualization: The Changing Face of Inequality in Deindustrializing Societies.* Oxford: Oxford University Press.

Ezzamel, M. and Wilmott, H. (2008). Strategy as discourse in a global retailer: A supplement to rationalist and interpretive accounts. *Organization Studies*, **9**, pp. 1–27.

Flecker, J. (2009). Outsourcing, spatial relocation and the fragmentation of employment. *Competition and Change*, **13**, pp. 251–266.

Flecker, J. and Meil, P. (2010). Organisational restructuring and emerging service value chains: Implications for work and employment. *Work, Employment and Society*, **24**, pp. 680–698.

Free, C. (2007). Supply chain accounting practices in the UK retail sector: Enabling or coercive collaboration? *Contemporary Accounting Research*, **24**, pp. 897–933.

Free, C. and Hecimovic, A. (2021). Global supply chains after COVID-19: The end of the road for neoliberal globalisation? *Accounting Auditing & Accountability Journal*, **34**, pp. 58–84.

Fullerton, A. S. and Wallace, M. (2007). Traversing the flexible turn: US workers' perceptions of job security. *Social Science Research*, **36**, pp. 201–221.

Gautié, J. and Schmitt, J. (2010). *Low-Wage Work in the Wealthy World.* New York: Russell Sage Foundation.

Gereffi, G., Humphrey, J., and Sturgeon, T. (2005). The governance of global value chains. *Review of International Political Economy*, **12**, pp. 78–104.

Gherardi, S., & Murgia, A. (2013). By hook or by crook: Flexible workers between exploration and exploitation. *Research in the Sociology of Organisations*, 37, 75–103.

Gibbon, P. Blair, J., and Ponte, S. (2008). Governing global value chains: An introduction. *Economy and Society,* **27,** pp. 315–338.

Gosain, S., Malhotra, A., and El Sawy, O. A. (2005). Coordinating for flexibility in e-business supply chains. *Journal of Management Information Systems*, **21**, pp. 7–45.

Grandori, A. and Soda, G. (1995). Inter-firm networks: Antecedents, mechanisms and forms, *Organization Studies*, **16**, pp. 183–214.

Grimshaw, D. and Rubery, J. (2005). Inter-capital relations and the network organisation. *Cambridge Journal of Economics*, **29**, pp. 1027–1051.

Gulati, R. (2007). *Managing Network Resources: Alliances, Affiliations, and Other Relational Assets.* Oxford: Oxford University Press.

Hacker, J. (2008). *The Great Risk Shift: The New Economy of Insecurity and the Decline of the American Dream* (Revised and expanded edition). Oxford: Oxford University Press.

Harland, C. M., Lamming, R. C., & Cousins, P. D. (1999). Developing the concept of supply strategy. *International Journal of Operations & Production Management, 19*(7), 650–674.

Harland, C. M., Lamming, R. C., Zeng, J., and Johnson, T. E. (2001). A taxonomy of supply networks. *International Journal of Operations and Production Management*, **37**, pp. 21–7.

Hassel A. (2014). The paradox of liberalization: Understanding dualism and the recovery of the German political economy. *British Journal of Industrial Relations*, **52**, pp. 57–81.

Hendry, J. (2001). After Durkheim: An agenda for the sociology of business ethics. *Journal of Business Ethics*, **34**, pp. 209–218.

Hinterhuber, H. H. and Levin, B. M. (1994). Strategic networks: The organization of the future. *Long Range Planning*, **27**, pp. 43–53.

Holst, H. (2014). Commodifying institutions: Vertical disintegration and institutional change in German labour relations. *Work, Employment and Society*, **28**, pp. 3–20.

Jacobides, M. G. (2005). Industry change through vertical disintegration: How and why markets emerged in mortgage banking. *Academy of Management Journal*, **48**, pp. 465–498.

Jessop, B. (2012). Rethinking the diversity and variability of capitalism: On variegated capitalism in the world market. In C. Lane and G. Wood (Eds.), *Institutions, Internal Diversity and Change*. London: Routledge, pp. 209–237.

Johnson, P. and Duberley, J. (2011). Anomie and culture management: Reappraising Durkheim. *Organization*, **18**, pp. 563–584.

Johnson, P., Wood, G., Brewster, C., and Brooks, M. (2009). The rise of post-bureaucracy. Theorists' fancy or organizational praxis? *International Sociology*, **24**, pp. 37–61.

Kalleberg A. L. (2003). Flexible firms and market segmentation: Effects of workplace restructuring on jobs and workers. *Work and Occupations*, **30**, pp. 154–175.

Kalleberg, A. L. (2009). Precarious work, insecure workers: Employment relations in transition. *American Sociological Review*, **74**, pp. 1–22.

Kano, L., Tsang, E. W. K., and Yeung, H.W-C. (2020). Global value chains: A review of the multi-disciplinary literature. *Journal of International Business Studies*, **51**, pp. 577–622

Kaplinsky, R. (2005). *Globalization, Poverty and Inequality: Between a Rock and a Hard Place*. Cambridge: Polity.

Kaufman, A. and Saravanamuthu, K. (2009). The dilemma of monitoring voluntary labour standards: Labour's 'muted' consent to exploit itself. *Advances in Public Interest Accounting*, **14**, pp. 297–319.

MacNeil, I. R. (1978). Contracts: Adjustment of long-term economic relations under classical, neoclassical and relational contract. *Northwestern University Law Review*, **72**, pp. 854–905.

MacNeil, I. R. (1985). Relational contract: What we do and do not know. *Wisconsin Law Review*, **4**, pp. 483–525.

Mäkelä, H. (2013). On the ideological role of employee reporting. *Critical Perspectives on Accounting*, *24*(4–5), 360–378.

Marslev, K., Staritz, C., and Raj-Reichert, G. (2022). Rethinking social upgrading in global value chains: Worker power, state–labour relations and intersectionality. *Development and Change*, **53**, pp. 827–859.

Masters, J. K. and Miles, G. (2002). Predicting the use of external labour arrangements: A test of the transaction costs perspective. *Academy of Management Journal*, **45**, pp. 431–442.

Miles, R. E. and Snow, C. C. (1986). Organizations: New concepts for new forms. *California Management Review*, **28**, pp. 62–73.

Mostafiz, M. I., Musteen, M., Saiyed, A., and Ahsan, M. (2022). COVID-19 and the global value chain: Immediate dynamics and long-term restructuring in the garment industry, *Journal of Business Research*, **139**, pp. 1588–1603.

Outhwaite, O. and Martin-Ortega, O. (2019). Worker-driven monitoring – Redefining supply chain monitoring to improve labour rights in global supply chains. *Competition & Change*, **23**, pp. 378–396.

Piore, M. J. and Sable, C. F. (1984). *The Second Industrial Divide.* New York: Basic Books.

Pittaway, L., Robertson, M., Munir, K. Denyer, D., and Neely, A. (2004). Networking and innovation: A systematic review of the evidence. *International Journal of Management Reviews*, **5–6**, pp. 137–168.

Powell, W.W. (1990). Neither market nor hierarchy: Network forms of organization. *Research in Organizational Behaviour*, **12,** pp. 295–336.

Ramani, V., Debabrata Ghosh, D., and Sodhi, M. S. (2022). Understanding systemic disruption from the Covid-19-induced semiconductor shortage for the auto industry. *Omega*, **113**. https://doi.org/10.1016/j.omega.2022.102720 0305–0483.

Reinecke, J. and Donaghey, J. (2021). Towards worker-driven supply chain governance: Developing decent work through democratic worker participation. *Journal of Supply Chain Management*, **57**, pp. 14–28.

Reinecke, J., Manning, S., and Von Hagen, O. (2012). The emergence of a standards market: Multiplicity of sustainability standards in the global coffee industry. *Organization Studies,* **33**, pp. 791–814.

Riisegaard, L. and Hammer, N. (2011). Prospects for labour in global value chains: Labour standards in the cut flower and banana industries. *British Journal of Industrial Relations,* **49**, pp. 168–190.

Rosenfeld, S. A. (1996). Does co-operation enhance competitiveness? Assessing the impacts of inter-firm collaboration. *Research Policy*, **25**, pp. 247–263.

Rousseau, D. M. and Parks, J. M. (1993). The contracts of individuals and organizations. *Research in Organization Behaviour*, **15**, pp. 1–43.

Sako, M. (1992). *Prices, Quality and Trust: Inter-firm Relations in Britain and Japan.* Cambridge: Cambridge University Press.

Scully, B., Mvundura, W., Nyirenda, T., Tambulu, B., and Zikalala, U. (2023). Cars and clothes in South Africa's Covid experience: The contrasting fortunes of two manufacturing sectors in South Africa. Working Paper No. 223/2023, Hochschule für Wirtschaft und Recht Berlin, Institute for International Political Economy (IPE), Berlin. https://www.econstor.eu/bitstream/10419/277754/1/1860169236.pdf.

Selwyn, B. (2012). Beyond firm-centrism: Re-integrating labour and capitalism into global commodity chain analysis. *Journal of Economic Geography,* **12,** pp. 205–226.

Selwyn, B. (2013). Social upgrading and labour in global production networks: A critique and an alternative conception. *Competition & Change*, *17*(1), 75–90.

Sennett, R. (1998). *The Corrosion of the Character.* New York: Norton.

Sennett, R. (2006). *The Culture of the New Capitalism.* New Haven CT: Yale University Press.

Streeck, W. (2009). *Re-forming capitalism: Institutional change in the German political economy.* Oxford University Press.

Tejani, S. and Fukuda-Parr, S. (2021). Gender and COVID-19: Workers in global value chains. *International Labour Review*, **160**, pp. 649–667.

Tomkins, C. (2001). Interdependencies, trust and information in relationships, alliances and networks. *Accounting, Organizations and Society*, **26**, pp. 161–191

Vallas, S. P. and Hill, A. (2012). Conceptualizing power in organizations. In D. Courpasson, D. Golsorkhi, and J. Sallaz (Eds.), *Rethinking Power in Organizations, Institutions, and Markets* (Research in the Sociology of Organizations, Volume 34), pp. 165–197. London: Emerald Group Publishing Limited.

Van Buren, H. J., III and Schrempf-Stirling, J. (2022). Beyond structural injustice: Pursuing justice for workers in post-pandemic global value chains. *Business Ethics, the Environment & Responsibility*, **31**, pp. 969–980.

Van der Meer-Kooistra, J. and Kamminga, P. E. (2010). The role of management accounting in joint venture relationships: A dynamic perspective. In H. Hakansson, K. Kraus, and J. Lind (Eds.), *Accounting in Networks* (Routledge Studies in Accounting), pp. 80–112. London: Routledge.

Verbeke A. (2020). Will the COVID-19 pandemic really change the governance of global value chains? *British Journal of Management*, **31**, pp. 444–446.

Wilkinson, R. and Pickett, K. (2010). *The Spirit Level: Why Equality is Better for Everyone.* Harmondsworth: Penguin.

Wills, J. (2009). Subcontracted employment and its challenges to labour. *Labour Studies Journal*, **34**, pp. 441–460.

Wood, G. (2013). Institutional diversity: Current issues and future contestations. *The Journal of Comparative Economic Studies*, **8**, pp. 3–20.

Wood, G., Dibben, P., and Meira, J. (2016). Knowledge transfer within strategic partnerships: The case of HRM in the Brazilian motor industry supply chain. *International Journal of Human Resource Management*, **8,** pp. 2398–2414.

8 Knowledge and Organisational Learning and Its Management through HR Practices

A Critical Perspective

Claire Gubbins

Introduction

The interest in knowledge stems from recognition that knowledge, particularly tacit knowledge, is a key source of sustainable competitive advantage (Lyles and Salk 1996; Tsai 2002; Zahara et al. 2000). It is argued that the turbulence of the business environment, or the VUCA (volatile, uncertain, complex and ambiguous) context in which organisations now operate, is the driver of this increasing interest in knowledge and its management. Furthermore, an exponential increase in new working models such as remote and hybrid working, about which there is limited empirical research, has also raised questions about the consequences for knowledge and its management. Without negating evidence that knowledge transfer is shown to positively impact organisational performance and innovation (van Wijk et al. 2008), a degree of cynicism is worth adding to this debate. First, more knowledge is not always better. Some research highlights that too much knowledge results in rigidities that tend to be counter-productive (Leonard-Barton 1992; Levinthal and March 1993; March 1991), diverse perspectives being ignored (Bowker and Star 1999) and may produce unwanted accountability (Schultze and Stabell 2004). Second, not all learning produces positive changes in behaviour where incorrect learning is shared.

Irrespective of these questions, the knowledge movement, remains a strong academic and practitioner discourse and a key business concern, and there is evidence that knowledge has value for organisations (van Wilk et al. 2008); too little produces inefficiencies and results in uncertainty and expensive mistakes (Schultze and Stabell 2004). Consequently, the knowledge discussion focuses on how to manage such a valuable resource. The early work in this area of knowledge and its management was centred in the information technology and practitioner-oriented literatures (Scarbrough and Swan 2005). The organisational learning view on knowledge received much less attention (Scarbrough and Swan 2005). Indeed, the knowledge management (KM) and organisational learning (OL) fields traditionally failed to acknowledge each other's domains, despite the similarities in the underpinning concepts (Vera and Crossan 2005). This is not surprising, as the KM field alone is rife with

DOI: 10.4324/9781032625560-9

debate and disagreement, with the fundamental issues revolving around definitions of knowledge and whether it can be managed. However, the fields have evolved more recently with greater integration of concepts and cross-fertilisation of ideas (Vera et al. 2011).

This chapter explores the key elements of these debates. Specifically, it first outlines the key scientific and social paradigms in the KM discourses and the implications of the choice of paradigm on definitions of knowledge, strategies for its management and associated critique. This section concludes with consideration of how the paradigms may more usefully be considered in tandem and possibly unified. This chapter also illuminates the similarities between the social paradigm of KM and OL discourse. Finally, the chapter draws on recognition that the social paradigm of KM and OL discourse points to the value of HR practices for the purposes of knowledge circulation and organisational learning. A critical perspective is utilised to examine the role of individual, interpersonal and organisational HR practices for knowledge circulation and organisational learning. This section also considers these practices in the context of the varying working models from in-person to remote and hybrid.

Knowledge and Its 'Management'

Defining what knowledge is and what forms of it are available, and consequently defining knowledge management, is challenging because a complete and agreed-upon definition of knowledge and knowledge management is still contested and debated (Collins 1993). Additionally, the KM field and concept are considered prescriptive, whereas the organisational knowledge (OK) field is theoretical, rooted in the resource-based view of the firm (Barney 1991). The reasons for this lack of alignment and debate lie in the particular set of assumptions and theoretical lens adopted by specific researchers.

At opposite sides of these debates lie, first, the KM researchers who identify that tacit knowledge, as opposed to explicit knowledge, is a source of sustainable competitive advantage and assume that in order to manage it, it must be explicit or codified (e.g. Nonaka and Takeuchi 1995). As such, researchers adopting this lens assume that knowledge can exist in the form of an object or entity, separate from people, and can be codified, and that tacit and explicit knowledge are separate and distinct types of knowledge (Hansen and Haas 2001). At the other side of the debate are KM researchers who assume that knowledge is deeply personal and embodied in people, embedded in and inseparable from their work practices and cultures and socially constructed; and as such, tacit and explicit knowledge are interlinked and inseparable (Tsoukas 1996). These researchers shift the debate away from knowledge as a commodity and towards a focus on knowledge and knowing as something that individuals and organisations do (Polanyi 1967; Blackler 1995; Cook and Brown 1999).

An alternative debate argues that when KM researchers adopt a position of either of these extremes, they miss the opportunities and implications of considering, and possibly integrating, the alternative perspective. Schultze and Stabell (2004) argue that contradictions are an intricate part of everyday life and a source of dynamic change, and so they seek not to resolve the contradictions but to engage with each of the perspectives and discuss the legitimacy of all perspectives. Similarly, Hazlett et al. (2005) discusses the need to break the paradigm mentality (Wilmott 1993) in relation to 'one right way' and recognise epistemological continuums and how multiple paradigms provide enhanced ability to analyse organisation phenomena (Palmer and Dunford 1996; Gioia and Pitre 1990), identify syntheses (Nonaka and Takeuchi 1995) and facilitate cross-disciplinary debate and learning (Hassard 1995). Adopting this position in the knowledge field, Ambrosini and Bowman (2002) connect the perspectives on the issue of tacit and explicit knowledge being separate or inseparable by proposing that there are degrees of tacitness ranging from explicit, to tacit that could be articulated, to tacit that can be imperfectly articulated, to the deeply ingrained, personally-held, inarticulable tacit knowledge. Acknowledging some of Ambrosini and Bowman's arguments, Tsoukas (2011) argues that tacit and explicit knowledge are not two ends of a continuum but two sides of the same coin and that the most explicit knowledge is still underpinned by tacit knowledge. With respect to knowledge 'management', Alvesson and Karreman (2001) present a framework of approaches to manage knowledge that reflects the diversity of perspectives on knowledge and its management. Their framework enables the selection of a suitable approach based on a researcher or practitioner's prior assumptions and theoretical lens.

Discourses/Paradigms on Knowledge and Implications for Defining and 'Managing' Knowledge

Two metalevel paradigms of knowledge are the scientific view and the social view (Hazlett et al. 2005). Schultze and Stabell (2004) label these paradigms the neo-functionalist discourse (discourse is used instead of paradigms to reflect the extent of debate within them and that the views are not clearly demarcated) and the constructivist discourse, respectively. The scientific view identifies 'knowledge is truth', as a body of facts and rational laws (Alvesson and Willmott 1996: Swan and Scarborough 2001), as an asset; something that can be owned, bought, sold to maintain competitive advantage. Neo-functionalist discourse identifies knowledge in binary, mutually-exclusive terms (Schultze and Stabell 2004) such as tacit–explicit, individual–collective, declarative–procedural (e.g. Kogut and Zander 1992; Nonaka 1994; Henderson and Clark 1990). It is also referred to as the computational paradigm where knowledge is viewed as rational, static and acontextual, and based on heuristics and mathematical models that aim to capture 'preferred' solutions and 'best practices' in response to organisational problems.

Knowledge and its 'management' in the neo-functionalist discourse is centred on converting knowledge into explicit knowledge (Dougherty 1992; Hedlund 1994) or managing the people who possess it (Hansen et al. 1999).

It concentrates on hardware and software and, as such, adopts a system-/techno-concentric approach. It stresses the need for technology, identifying knowledge, classifying it, categorising it, coding it, storing it explicitly and retrieving it (Hansen et al. 1999). This techno-structural form of management can be enacted via weak or strong management control, as illustrated in Alvesson and Karreman's (2001) framework, via extended libraries or enacted blueprints, respectively. Extended libraries implies KM that 'involves blending a company's internal and external information and turning it into actionable knowledge via a technology platform'. The stronger form of KM via enacted blueprints, requires knowledge to be carefully codified and stored in databases where it can be accessed and used easily by anyone in the company. The idea is that knowledge can be extracted from individuals and converted into databases. The stored knowledge provides templates for thinking as well as action, thus making relatively unskilled workers productive on a higher skill level nearly instantaneously. As Hansen et al. (1999) point out, the idea of codification is typically motivated by an economics of reuse, where organisational members are encouraged/forced to reuse codified knowledge rather than develop new solutions/knowledge.

This discourse and the associated KM approaches are not without critique. First, if tacit knowledge is managed through making it explicit, it can be imitated and thereby no longer a source of competitive advantage, so managing it destroys an organisational knowledge advantage (Barney 1991; Kogut and Zander 1992). Second, if KM focuses only on the capture and storage of facts and best practices, there is likely to be only limited organisational transformation other than increased efficiency, rather than the reframing necessary to produce innovation (Pitt 1998). Third, to attempt to manage workers' tacit knowledge is managerial exploitation of workers aimed at extracting power from and exerting control of workers, further exacerbating the management–employee divide (Smith and Willmott 1991). Finally are the criticisms levelled at the definition of knowledge adopted by those of the scientific paradigm by those of opposing paradigms – 'tacit knowledge has been greatly misunderstood in management studies' (Tsoukas 2001: 15), 'tacit knowledge cannot be "captured", "translated" or "converted" but only displayed, manifested in what we do' (Tsoukas 2001: 16).

The corollary to the scientific neo-functionalist discourse is the social paradigm or constructivist discourse of knowledge, which views knowledge as being socially constructed, complexly intertwined and mutually constitutive (Burgoyne et al. 1994; Schultze and Stabell 2004). This is also an organic paradigm and places emphasis not on computer science but on group dynamics (Malhotra 1998), people and organisational context such as people's interactions, work structures, processes and organisational culture. Proponents of this view don't reject technology but rather an overly technological view without concern for social networks of individual knowledge workers (Moffett et al. 2002). Constructivist discourse contends that knowledge is continuously shaped and being shaped by the social practices of individuals in communities and, thus, there can be no separation between individual and social knowledge (Pentland 1992; Von Krogh and Roos 1995). This view is people-centric, recognises both tacit and explicit knowledge and, thus, is of the view that often knowledge cannot be explicitly elicited and modelled. Tacit and explicit knowledge are mutually constituted and should not be viewed as separate types of knowledge, as explicit knowledge is always grounded on a tacit component (Tsoukas 1996). Constructivist discourse also challenges the notion that knowledge can be managed as an object separate from human action. It argues that the locus of knowing is not in the head but in practice (Tsoukas 1996; Brown and Duguid 1991). As such, knowledge and its 'management' through the lens of the organic paradigm would adopt a personalisation strategy based on person-to-person contact (Hansen et al. 1999). Alvesson and Karreman (2001) identify the community and normative control KM approaches as reflecting this paradigm. The community approach specifies that KM requires human and information systems that make information available and help people think together; developing communities that share knowledge and maintain diversity; creating an environment that truly values sharing knowledge; and developing individuals to be open to the ideas of others and to share ideas (McDermott 1999). Managing tacit knowledge through the lens of the constructivist discourse implies imitation through participation in communities of practice (Lave and Wenger 1991), perspective-making and perspective-taking (Boland and Tenkasi 1995) and through social capital (Cohen and Prusak 2001). The normative-control approach to knowledge and its 'management' is also socially grounded but adopts a stronger form of managerial intervention in the form of attempts to exercise normative control, possibly through creating an organisational culture which values knowledge sharing.

Criticisms levelled at this paradigm and its management approaches come from both sides of the debate. It is argued that the community approach to KM is weak and sometimes devoid of 'management', with more emphasis on community, sharing, caring and nurturing social relations (Alvesson and Karreman 2001). As such, this weak form of managerial control does not reflect organisational needs to identify, replicate, protect, develop and capitalise on any source of competitive advantage. An organisation which does not manage its critical tacit knowledge is unlikely to grow or dominate (Schultze and Stabell 2004). The fact that management in this paradigm is focused on the people who possess tacit knowledge points to an organisational vulnerability. When people to whom the tacit knowledge is bound leave an organisation or are re-located within an organisation, the competitive edge is lost (Schultze and Stabell 2004). The normative control approach with its emphasis on culture attracts criticism from those that argue that tacit knowledge is a more complex, inaccessible phenomena than organisational culture and, further still, that engineering culture is a difficult undertaking (Alvesson 2001; Alvesson and Karreman 2001).

Knowledge and Learning: Towards Convergence of the Paradigms

The ultimate focus in the knowledge management field, irrespective of whether the chosen paradigm is scientific or social, is on the content of the processes discussed, which is knowledge. The processes required are, in fact, learning processes, but the knowledge management (KM) and organisational learning (OL) fields failed to acknowledge each other's domains (Vera and Crossan, 2005) despite the relationships and similarities in the underpinning concepts. There is emerging convergence in the fields and concepts and cross-fertilisation of ideas (Vera et al. 2011) grounded in the basic recognition that learning occurs, first and foremost, at the individual level (Sadler-Smith 2006) and that it is processes of learning that develop knowledge for both individuals and organisations. Vera et al. (2011) neatly summarise the relationships and differences between knowledge, knowing and learning. Knowledge can be obtained through the mind and through the body by reflection and by doing. Knowledge is accumulated in our minds and in our bodies as declarative or procedural knowledge. Knowing is practice or knowledge that is part of action (Cook and Brown 1999). Learning is the change in knowledge and in knowing through changes in cognition and behaviour. Additionally, the definitions of learning illuminate that the products of learning are knowledge, skills, values and worldviews (Vera and Crossan 2005). Davenport and Prusak (1998) define knowledge as information acquired through implicit or explicit learning means and in the process combined with experience, context, interpretation and reflection. Argote (1999) defines learning as 'knowledge acquisition' and states that learning involves the processes through which members share, generate, evaluate and combine knowledge. KM authors adopt process or life-cycle definitions such as the creation (acquisition), refinement, storage, transfer or sharing of knowledge (King et al. 2008; Argote, 2021).

The most evident overlap in the KM and OL fields is through the social paradigm on KM. The social paradigm on KM illuminates people, social interaction, sharing knowledge, knowledge in action and practice, thinking together and imitation. Fundamental to these processes is that individuals have learnt and thereby possess knowledge to share and that through processes of sharing, practice, imitation and social interaction they further learn, and this knowledge develops and changes. However, the underlying learning process is not explored or referred to typically within the KM field. The KM field focuses on knowledge processing, whereas OL focuses on people processing (Scarbrough and Swan 2005). KM focuses on how to mobilise the knowledge base, whereas OL focuses on how to create the conditions in which individual and collective learning may flourish through people and values, attitudes, beliefs, languages and discourses (Scarbrough and Swan 2005). Broadly, the OL literature emphasises culture management and leadership as a means of encouraging socialisation and internalisation of explicit knowledge into the values and tacit understandings of employees.

Thus, while the dominant KM paradigm is the scientific paradigm (Scarbourough and Swan 2003), when the concept of knowledge is considered dynamic and not static and when discussions about knowledge and its management move from managing knowledge assets to managing knowledge associated processes, such as creation, transfer and sharing, there is significant opportunity to unify the insights from both the OL and OK fields (Vera et al. 2011). Schendel (1996) emphasises a need to understand learning as a process, as the capacity to develop organisational capability may be more important in creating competitive advantage than the specific knowledge gained. In this vein, the OL field is also valuable in that it recognises the dynamic multilevel nature of knowledge circulation. Crossan et al.'s (1999) OL framework is of the social paradigm and views learning at multilevel ie individual, social and organisational. However, most management research uses a single level of analysis (Hitt et al., 2007). Consequently, there is limited understanding of multilevel learning processes (Crossan et al., 2011; Swart and Harcup, 2013), though interest in multilevel learning, and specifically linkages between the levels, has increased (Wiewiora et al., 2019).

The value in better unifying the OL and OK fields is possibly even more pronounced with the increase in the prevalence of remote- and hybrid-working models. Empirical evidence on the impact of these working models is mixed, but it seems that the effects of remote work are predominantly negative in terms of collaboration, communication and knowledge sharing (eg Jackowska and Lauring, 2021). Pre-pandemic meta-analyses that explored knowledge sharing in remote teams report negative but nuanced effects. Specifically, Ortiz de Guinea et al. (2012) found that remoteness negatively influenced frequency of communications and level of knowledge sharing and that this negative effect was stronger for the teams that worked together for a short time compared to longer-term teams. Mesmer-Magnus et al.'s (2011) meta-analysis found that the effects of remoteness on knowledge sharing in teams is curvilinear rather than linear. This means that low levels of remoteness in teams improves information sharing, but high levels hinder it. Furthermore, working in remote teams (spatial separation from one's colleagues) negatively influences frequency of knowledge sharing among employees and temporal separation (when an employee's working times differ from their colleagues) decreases their awareness of the knowledge those colleagues have to offer. Additionally, employees who remain in the office can also experience a decrease in collaboration when their colleagues go remote (Rockmann and Pratt, 2015). Existing evidence also suggests that remote- or hybrid-work arrangements alter not only the quantity of collaboration and communication, but also the patterns regarding with whom people collaborate (Bloom et al., 2023).

Conversely, Choudhury et al. (2022) found that employees who worked in a hybrid mode (specifically, those who spend from 23 per cent to 40 per cent of their time working remotely) had the highest quantity of email communications with colleagues and the highest novelty of work output. However, Mulcahy & Andreeva (2023) argue that the Choudhury et al. (2022) study is signalling more about the increased coordination and collaboration challenges experienced by hybrid employees.

In light of this evidence, it seems intuitive to suggest that these working models require even greater attention be paid to both the scientific and social paradigm of knowledge in tandem. On one side, the scientific paradigm is increasingly important with the need for effective initiatives and technology which codify, store and action knowledge such that it is available to those whom need it irrespective of their work location. On the other hand, the social paradigm is important to ensure identification of interventions that support social interaction, group dynamics and communities to enable the social construction of knowledge, person-to-person interaction and practice which are cognisant of varied working models and combinations of working models. Integration of the OL and OK fields recognises the dynamic nature of knowledge circulation, the role of people in KM and OL discourse and concomitantly the organisational imperative to try to 'manage' the knowledge resource in either physical co-location-, remote- or hybrid-working models. Recognising that a learning organisation continuously transforms itself by developing its people, the HR perspective is a useful lens through which to identify initiatives to facilitate knowledge 'management' and organisational learning (Pedler et al. 1991; Dovey 1997).

HR Practices for Knowledge Circulation and Organisational Learning in In-Person/Remote/Hybrid Working Models

Rather than reviewing HR practices for knowledge 'management' due to the criticisms levelled at the idea of managing knowledge and the fundamentally scientific connotation and assumptions attached to it, this section focuses on an alternative term representing the various knowledge and learning processes ie knowledge circulation. However, this too is a rather ambitious term as the majority of empirical research on knowledge management or knowledge circulation processes focuses narrowly on only knowledge sharing or transfer (Gubbins & Dooley, 2021; Kennedy et al. 2015). By doing so, the literature focuses only on the unidirectional exchange of knowledge from the knowledge provider to the knowledge seeker/recipient (Gubbins & Kennedy, 2024; Gubbins & Dooley, 2021; Kennedy et al. 2015; Hansen et al. 2005) ie the 'push' perspective (Kim et al. 2011; Lin et al. 2005; McElroy 2003). However, knowledge which is 'pushed' or 'shared' will not necessarily be transferred or learnt if it is not what the 'recipient' requires (Quigley et al. 2007). Knowledge is only learnt from others when people have the need, motivation or opportunity for learning (Marsick and Watkins 2001; Eraut 2000; Le Clus 2011). This is the focus of the seeking perspective (Argote and Ingram 2000; Quigley et al. 2007). This section will review empirical research on HR practices for organisational learning and knowledge *sharing* and *transfer*.

The plethora of HR initiatives which can facilitate knowledge sharing can broadly be classified as organisational, interpersonal and individual. In a comprehensive systematic review drawing on the fields of information systems, psychology, organisational behaviour and strategic management, Wang and Noe (2010) identify the key initiatives, at these three levels. This framework and the initiatives illuminated will be used for the purposes of structuring this section.

'Managing' the Organisational Context and Knowledge Sharing

Four aspects of organisational context emerge as central in HR efforts to manage knowledge processes: organisational culture, management support, rewards and incentives and organisational structure (Wang and Noe 2010).

Organisational Culture and Norms and Knowledge Sharing

Developing a culture where knowledge sharing is valued and seen as a norm is one suggested strategy for 'managing' knowledge (Pan and Scarbrough 1999; Cabrera et al. 2006). This is most evident in the normative control approach to KM (Alvesson and Karreman 2001). The evidence available provides some support that a culture which supports knowledge sharing is necessary for knowledge-sharing technologies to be beneficial (De Long and Fahey 2000). Subjective norms and norms of reciprocity also encourage knowledge sharing, but the results are inconsistent, suggesting that other factors are also at play (Wang and Noe 2010). Norms are positively related to knowledge-sharing behaviour in communities of practice (Brown and Duguid 1991; Chiu et al. 2006). Research on online communities or electronic knowledge-sharing repositories finds that social norms and related concepts (ie pro-sharing norms, norms of reciprocity and collaborative norms) have significant positive effects on knowledge transfer (Gopalakrishnan and Santoro 2004; Chang and Chuang 2011) and intentions to share knowledge (Bock et al. 2005). Quigley et al. (2007) found that mutual norms for knowledge sharing enhanced the impact of incentives for knowledge sharing and, consequently, knowledge sharing.

However, there is also contradictory or more nuanced research findings on the relationship between norms and knowledge sharing. Wasko and Faraj (2005) found a negative relationship between norms of reciprocity and knowledge sharing. Kankanhalli et al. (2005) found perceived reciprocity to be positively related to participants' likelihood to contribute knowledge to the community under weak rather than strong pro-sharing norms. There are also mixed results with respect to learning culture and knowledge sharing (Taylor and Wright 2004; Lee et al. 2006). Organisational climates that emphasise competition pose a barrier to knowledge sharing, whereas cooperative climates help create trust and consequently facilitate knowledge sharing (Schepers and Van den Berg 2007; Wang 2004; Willem and Scarbrough 2006).

Evident from the available research on culture and norms, as a KM strategy, is a lack of consistency and clarity on how and when culture effectively facilitates KM. Critical perspectives on organisational culture more generally identify that organisational culture is difficult to 'manage' in itself (Ogbonna and Harris 2002) and that many organisations do not have one culture but rather many sub-cultures (Currie and Kerrin 2003; Alavi et al. 2005). Exasperating this is the increasing prevalence of remote- and hybrid-working models with recent research (Arena et al. 2023) comparing in-person-, remote- and hybrid-working models identifying challenges with transmitting cultural behaviours in remote-working models, which is subsequently likely to impact knowledge sharing.

Management Support and Knowledge Sharing

Management support, specific to knowledge sharing, is found to positively impact knowledge-sharing level, quality, perceptions of a knowledge-sharing culture, willingness to share knowledge, perceptions of the usefulness of knowledge sharing and knowledge exchange (see Wang and Noe 2010). In the remote-work context, of the limited evidence, there are studies indicating that leadership is relevant for the performance of remote teams (Chen, 2011). In one study it was identified that transformational leadership styles, which would include supportive behaviours, enhance social cohesion and qualitative/creative performance (See CEBMa, 2020).

Critics argue that some management support-type HR practices are simply packaged to present the illusion of support when, in fact, they are just another form of control and exploitation (Legge 1995). Management supports employees to share and codify their knowledge for the interests of the organisation. However, in doing so, employees may lose their valuable knowledge and potentially the associated power and status, thus widening the management–employee divide. It can also make it easier for the organisation to let the employee go or for another employee to gain power and status (Currie and Kerrin 2003).

Organisational Incentives and Knowledge Sharing

Incentives including recognition and rewards are often recommended as practices to facilitate knowledge sharing and help build a supportive knowledge-sharing culture; however, empirical support for the effects of extrinsic incentives is mixed. Rewards and perceptions of a high level of incentives positively influenced knowledge contributions to a knowledge management system and knowledge sharing (Kankanhalli et al. 2005; Kim and Lee 2006; Minbaeva et al. 2012). However, studies (Bock and Kim 2002; Bock et al. 2005) found that anticipated extrinsic rewards had a negative effect on attitudes towards knowledge sharing. Other studies reported no relationship (Kwok and Gao 2005; Lin, H. F. 2007; Chang et al. 2007). Research on how different types of reward systems influence knowledge sharing finds that cooperative rewards systems positively influence knowledge sharing, whereas competitive systems have a negative effect (Ferrin and Dirks 2003). Furthermore, group-based incentives generally produce more positive knowledge-sharing effects compared to individual incentives (Quigley et al. 2007; Taylor 2006).

Critics argue that to attach incentives to knowledge sharing and thereby encourage employees to give up their knowledge power can endanger their status and jobs. It may be a source of stress for employees in either trying to identify knowledge that they can share and so meet the knowledge-sharing objectives or stress in considering the cost/benefit of sharing or not sharing. It also possibly stimulates unhealthy competition between employees. On the other hand, however, it is providing a reward for knowledge gained and shared and a sense of achievement and value in being acknowledged as a source or provider of valuable knowledge.

Organisational Structures and Knowledge Sharing

Segmented organisational structures and strong divisional or group identities are generally found to inhibit knowledge sharing across their boundaries (Lam 1996; Tagliaventi and Mattarelli 2006; Liebowitz 2003; Yang and Chen 2007). Socially identified groups are likely to have greater solidarity, reciprocity norms, trust and sanctions against self-serving behaviours (Granovetter 1985; Krackhardt 1992; Inkpen and Tsang 2005; Huysman and De Wit 2004; Inkpen and Tsang 2005). Consequently, individuals who identify with a group hold attitudes and behave in ways that benefit the group (see Brewer and Brown 1998; de Cremer and Van Vugt 1999). A different challenge emerges in remote working contexts. It was found that the positive effects of social cohesion are even stronger within remote teams (See CEBMa, 2020), and that in remote teams, social cohesion has a positive effect on the development of team trust (Webber, 2008). However, social cohesion is harder to develop in remote teams because computer-mediated communication reduces social cues required to build relationships (Lin, 2008). In the context of knowledge sharing, such group identification and connection enables ease of knowledge flow between members of the in-group, is significantly positively related to intention to share knowledge (Liu and Phillips 2011) and enables social learning (Ashforth and Mael 1989; Bandura, 1977).

Concomitantly, excessive group closure can also lead to strong norms against associating with the out-group (Brewer 1979). Attributing membership to an out-group can be based on something as simple as a different department, role, rank or even demographic factors such as age group (Tajfel and Turner 1985). The consequences of strong levels of group identification include lower levels of knowledge sharing between groups (Gargiulo and Benassi 2000; Burt 1992) because it prompts competition between groups (Argote and Ingram 2000; Fisher et al. 1997; Moreland and Levine 2000; Tsai 2002). The trust literature also acknowledges this issue but points to how group closure enables the development of other forms of trust such as deterrence-based trust (Shapiro et al. 1992). This type of trust is developed and sustained through fear of punishment (e.g. loss of reputation, relationships) and provision of rewards for preserving it (Lewicki and Bunker 1996). Internal opportunism is unlikely to occur in closed groups due to the penalties or negative repercussions imposed by the group for corruptive behaviour (Inkpen and Tsang 2005). However, the overall impact of excessively demarcated organisational structures, group boundaries, social identification and group closure is limited knowledge shared outside the group and failures to accept knowledge from those outside the group. These actions, in turn, inhibit the organisational knowledge-circulation processes.

'Managing' Interpersonal Relationships and Knowledge Sharing

Two aspects of interpersonal relationships are central in HR initiatives to manage knowledge processes: diversity and social networks (Wang and Noe 2010).

Diversity and Knowledge Sharing

Diversity of team members, based on such characteristics as gender, marital status or education, influences knowledge-sharing behaviour. Individuals who consider themselves a minority are less likely to share knowledge with team members (Ojha 2005), teams with higher female–male ratios are more likely to engage in knowledge sharing (Sawng et al. 2006) and socially isolated members are more likely to disagree with others and less likely to contribute unique knowledge (Phillips et al. 2004; Thomas-Hunt et al. 2003).

Social Networks and Knowledge Sharing

Social network research on knowledge searching and transfer finds that by virtue of connecting unconnected social groups, weak ties provide access to non-redundant knowledge ie have greater search benefits (Hansen et al. 1999) as compared to strong ties, which are more likely to provide access to similar others who reside in the same social groups and so have access to knowledge already circulating. Levin and Cross (2004) furthered this line of research by identifying that weak ties are more beneficial for transferring valuable knowledge where competence and benevolence-based trust exist. However, a study by Maurer et al. (2011), which separates knowledge transfer into the more nuanced processes of knowledge mobilisation, assimilation and use, finds that trusted strong ties enhance the extent of knowledge transfer. In research focused on where the knowledge is flowing from and to, Tortoriello and Krackhardt (2010) found that individuals were more likely to demonstrate higher innovative performance when they maintained cross-unit knowledge transfer relationships that were characterised by closure (ie network cohesion). Equally, this study identified that tie strength, network cohesion and network range had a positive effect on the amount of knowledge acquired in cross-unit transfers.

In the remote- or hybrid-working contexts, the limited empirical research illustrates changes to social network structures and employee behaviour that likely impact knowledge flows and organisational learning. Bloom et al. (2023) found that employees that worked in hybrid mode (two days per week remotely) focus more on communicating with close contacts. Also, in remote working models, collaboration networks of employees became more static and siloed, with fewer bridges between disparate parts (Yang et al. 2021; Dahlander et al. 2021). Zappa et al. (2023) studied hybrid-working models and found that informal sharing networks shrunk and became more siloed with employees mostly going for work-related advice to those who work in the same work arrangement. Arena et al. (2023) found that overall social network connectivity dropped when comparing in-person working models to remote working models and the majority of the network erosion occurred between work groups. Consequently, cultural tacit behaviours that require interaction, modelling, practice and reinforcement to be understood and learnt, were learnt by fewer people in remote-working models due to reduced core connectivity overall and between-group connectivity in particular. Strong ties enabled greater transmission of tacit behaviours most especially in remote-working models. However, given the parallel decrease in connectivity, between-group connectivity and number of strong ties in remote-working models, the overall levels of transmission of tacit behaviours declined. However, with moves to hybrid-working models, some of the erosion in network connectivity declined alongside its consequences for transmission of cultural behaviours. Previous research suggests that these changes in collaboration patterns may impede the transfer of knowledge (Reagans & McEvily, 2003; Argote & Ingram, 2000; Hansen, 1999).

The social network perspective in general, and on knowledge sharing more specifically, has received limited critique despite some obvious issues and, according to Granovetter's (1985), original recognition of the duality within social structures, they can be a source of both opportunity and constraint for individual behaviour. Economists argue that the maintenance of social capital entails honouring obligations that may conflict with the pursuit of self-interest. Changing contextual circumstances such as changes in the environment or task in which one operates may necessitate new relationships. However, pressure to maintain current relationships that are no longer advantageous may hinder the ability to cultivate new relationships due to the time and energy involved and the reciprocal promises made in past or current relationships (Gargiulo and Benassi 1999). From a knowledge-sharing perspective, an individual's knowledge requirements are likely to change over time and with changing contextual circumstances; however, the need to concomitantly alter one's social network is not as easy as research and practice guidelines would imply.

'Managing' Individual Characteristics and Knowledge Sharing

The most evident individual level characteristics and components in research on knowledge sharing include trust, self-efficacy and perceived benefits and costs about knowledge sharing (Wang and Noe 2010).

Trust and Knowledge Sharing

There is a solid body of research focused on trust and knowledge sharing. Affect and cognition-based trust are shown to have positive influences on knowledge sharing at dyadic and team level (Chowdhury 2005; Mooradian et al. 2006; Wu et al. 2007). It is found that individuals tend to share less knowledge with others who are perceived to be very capable and share more knowledge with those who are perceived to be honest and fair and who followed principles (Bakker et al. 2006). Andrews and Delahaye (2000) found that knowledge sharing was based on the perceived trustworthiness of the knowledge recipient. Levin and Cross (2004) found that competence-based trust had a more significant impact on tacit over explicit knowledge sharing. They also found benevolence-based trust to be significant in both tacit and explicit knowledge exchanges.

In remote work contexts, it was found, that intra-team trust is even more important for teams with a high level of virtuality, as the trust–performance relationship is stronger when virtuality is high (De Jong, 2016; Lin, 2008; Capiola, 2019). More specifically, it was found that remote teams with high intra-team trust display higher levels of team information sharing, and team learning (Breuer, 2016). In addition, high intra-team trust heightens team members' willingness to trust in each other's knowledge and share information (De Jong, 2016).

Self-Efficacy and Knowledge Sharing

With regard to self-efficacy, research finds that it positively impacts attitudes towards knowledge sharing (Bock and Kim 2002), willingness to share knowledge (Liu and Liu 2011), intention to share knowledge (Cho and Li 2007; Cho et al. 2015), tacit knowledge-sharing intention (Yang and Farn 2009) and knowledge contribution or sharing behaviour, both within and outside of electronic repositories (Cabrera et al. 2006; Kankanhalli et al. 2005; Lu et al. 2006). Studies on confidence to share knowledge generally identify that individuals who are more confident in their ability to share knowledge have more positive intentions towards, and engagement in, knowledge sharing (Cabrera et al. 2006; Lin, H. F. 2007).

Benefits and Costs and Knowledge Sharing

Drawing on social exchange theory, which suggests that individuals evaluate the perceived ratio of benefits to costs and base their decision on the expectation that it will lead to rewards (Blau 1964; Emerson 1976), perceived benefits and costs are one of the most studied antecedents of knowledge sharing. Perceived benefits are positively associated with knowledge sharing (Lin, C. P. 2007: Hew and Hara 2007; Wasko and Faraj 2000, 2005), while perceived costs are negatively associated (Kankanhalli et al. 2005; Hew and Hara 2007). More specifically, some research identifies that where individuals believe that their shared knowledge is useful to others is more strongly related to knowledge sharing over the personal benefits they gain (Chiu et al. 2006; Siemsen et al. 2007: Wasko and Faraj 2000).

Hislop (2009) compares this cost/benefit decision-making process to a public good dilemma where individuals may feel they need to contribute to the public good, the organisational knowledge bank, as otherwise the resource will diminish. However, individuals are also concerned with negative personal consequences from sharing their knowledge, such as it is time consuming; giving away sources of individual power and status; and the fear of ridicule. Such fears negatively impact knowledge sharing (Empson 2001; Ardichvili et al. 2003; Martin 2006; Mooradian et al. 2006; Renzl 2008). However, by sharing knowledge, the benefits to individuals include intrinsic and extrinsic rewards, enhanced status, being perceived as an expert and gaining recognition for what they know.

Conclusion

Notwithstanding the high level of debate and controversy in the organisational knowledge field about what knowledge is and the extent to which it is manageable, this chapter aims to illuminate, through critical examination, the opportunities in acknowledging, and in cases, finding convergence in the discourses and with the field of organisational learning. This chapter emphasises the social paradigm of knowledge and its management as a means to illustrate the role of HR practices. It aims to demonstrate, with a degree of caution, how HR can facilitate knowledge circulation and organisational learning at a number of levels. The critical perspective adopted illustrates how HR can be useful but also that there are challenges with implementation, contradictions contained within the solutions due to the complex nature of knowledge and, effectively, there is no one 'best way'. More generally, empirical research that can inform HR practices aimed at facilitating knowledge circulation suffers from a number of other gaps. There is generally insufficient research on the plethora of possible HR initiatives which address the knowledge-circulation challenge; inconsistency of results; small effect sizes, an excessive focus on knowledge management in the form of information technologies; a failure to acknowledge both tacit and explicit knowledge (however defined) and, thus, an emphasis on the more measurable explicit knowledge; and a failure to explore all phases in the knowledge-sharing process from the perspective of both the knowledge provider and the recipient (Gubbins & Dooley, 2021; Kennedy et al. 2015). With the increasing prevalence of remote- and hybrid-working models, more nuanced research is required to identify what HR practices work when, where and for whom as available research suggests some HR practices that are particularly effective in physically co-located-working models are less effective in remote- or hybrid-working models and other HR practices are significantly more important and need to be implemented with greater intentionality.

References

Alavi, M., Kayworth, T. R. and Leidner, D. E. (2005). An empirical examination of the influence of organizational culture on knowledge management practices, *Journal of Management Information Systems*, 22(3): 191–224.

Alvesson, M. (2001). Knowledge work: Ambiguity, image and identity, *Human Relations*, 54(7): 863–886.

Alvesson, M. and Karreman, D. (2001). Odd couple: Making sense of the curious concept of knowledge management, *Journal of Management Studies*, 38(7): 995–1018.

Alvesson, M. and Willmott, H. (1996). *Making Sense of Management*. London: Sage.

Ambrosini, V. and Bowman, C. (2002). Tacit knowledge: Some suggestions for operationalization, *Journal of Management Studies*, 38(6): 811–829.

Andrews, K. M. and Delahaye, B. L. (2000). Influences on knowledge processes in organisational learning: the psychosocial filter, *Journal of Management Studies*, 37(6): 797–810.

Ardichvili, A., Page, V. and Wentling, T. (2003). Motivation and barriers to participation in virtual knowledge-sharing communities of practice, *Journal of Knowledge Management*, 7(1): 64–77.

Arena, M., Hines, S. and Golden, J. (2023). The three Cs for cultivating organizational culture in a hybrid world, *Organizational Dynamics*, 52(1). https://doi.org/10.1016/j.orgdyn.2023.100958

Argote, L. (1999). *Organizational Learning: Creating, Retaining and Transferring Knowledge*. Norwell, MA: Kluwer.

Argote, L. and Ingram, P. (2000). Knowledge transfer: A basis for competitive advantage in firms, *Organizational Behavior and Human Decision Processes*, 82(1): 150–169.

Argote, L., Lee, S. and Park, J. (2021). Organizational learning processes and outcomes: Major findings and future research directions, *Management Science*, 67(9): 5399–5429. https://doi.org/10.1287/mnsc.2020.3693

Ashforth, B. E. and Mael, F. (1989). Social identity theory and the organization, *Academy of Management Review*, 14: 20–39.

Bakker, M., Leenders, R. T. A. J., Gabbay, S. M., Kratzer, J. and Van Engelen, J.M. L. (2006). Is trust really social capital? Knowledge sharing in product development projects, *The Learning Organization*, 13(6): 594–605.

Bandura, A. (1977). *Social Learning Theory*. Englewood Cliffs, NJ: General Learning Press.

Barney, J. B. (1991). Firm resources and sustained competitive advantage, *Journal of Management*, 17(1): 99–120.

Blackler, F. (1995). Knowledge, knowledge work, and organizations: An overview and interpretation, *Organization Studies*, 16: 1021–1046.

Blau, P. M. (1964). *Exchange and Power in Social Life*. New York: John Wiley.

Bloom, N., Barrero, J. M., Davis, S., Meyer, B. and Mihaylov, E. (2023) Where managers and employees disagree about remote work, *Harvard Business Review*, 5 January. Available at https://hbr.org/2023/01/research-where-managers-and-employees-disagree-about-remote-work

Bock, G. W. and Kim, Y. (2002). Breaking the myths of rewards: An exploratory study of attitudes about knowledge sharing, *Information Resources Management Journal*, 15(2): 14–21.

Bock, G. W., Zmud, R. W., Kim, Y. G. and dan Lee, J. N. (2005). Behavioral intention formation in knowledge sharing: Examining the roles of extrinsic motivators, social-psychological forces, and organizational climate, *MIS Quarterly*, 29(1): 87–111.

Boland, R. J., Jr. and Tenkasi, R. V. (1995). Designing information technology to support distributed cognition, *Organization Science*, 5(3): 456–475.

Bowker, G. and Star, S. L. (1999). *Sorting Things Out: Classification and Its Consequences (Inside Technology)*. Boston, MA: MIT Press.

Breuer, C., Hüffmeier, J., & Hertel, G. (2016). Does trust matter more in virtual teams? A meta-analysis of trust and team effectiveness considering virtuality and documentation as moderators. *Journal of Applied Psychology*, *101*(8), 1151.

Brewer, M. B. (1979). In-group bias in the minimal intergroup situation: A cognitive-motivational analysis, *Psychological Bulletin*, 86: 307–324.

Brewer, M. B. and Brown, R. J. (1998). Intergroup relations, in D. Gilbert, S. Fiske and G. Lindzey (Eds.), *Handbook of Social Psychology*, 4th edition, pp. 554–594. Boston, MA: McGraw-Hill.

Brown, J. S. and Duguid, P. (1991). Organizational learning and communities of practice: Toward a unified view of working, learning and innovation, in E. L. Lesser, M. A. Fontaine and J. A. Slusher (Eds.), *Knowledge and Communities*. Oxford: Butterworth Heinemann.

Burgoyne, J., Pedler, M. and Boydell, T. (1994). *Towards the Learning Company: Concepts and Practices*. London: McGraw-Hill.

Burt, R. S. (1992). *Structural Holes: The Social Structure of Competition*, 1st edition. Cambridge, MA: Harvard University Press.

Cabrera, A., Collins, W. C. and Salgado, J. F. (2006). Determinants of individual engagement in knowledge sharing, *The International Journal of Human Resource Management*, 17(2): 245–264.

Capiola, A., Alarcon, G. M., Lyons, J. B., Ryan, T. J., & Schneider, T. R. (2019). Collective efficacy as a mediator of the trustworthiness–performance relationship in computer-mediated team-based contexts. *The Journal of Psychology*, *153*(7), 732–757.

CEBMa. (2020) Attributes of effective virtual teams: Rapid evidence assessment of scientific literature, CIPD, London. Available at https://www.cipd.org/en/knowledge/evidence-reviews/developing-virtual-teams/

Chang, H. H. and Chuang, S. S. (2011). Social capital and individual motivations on knowledge sharing: Participant involvement as a moderator, *Information & Management*, 48(1): 9–18.

Chang, T. J., Yeh, S. P. and Yeh, I. J. (2007). The effects of joint reward system in new product development, *International Journal of Manpower*, 28(3/4): 276–297.

Chen, C. C., Wu, J., Ma, M. and Knight, M. B. (2011). Enhancing virtual learning team performance: A leadership perspective. *Human Systems Management*, 30(4): 215.

Chiu, C. M., Hsu, M. H. and Wang, E. T. (2006). Understanding knowledge sharing in virtual communities: An integration of social capital and social cognitive theories, *Decision Support Systems*, 42(3): 1872–1888.

Cho, I., Park, H. and Kim, J. K. (2015). The relationship between motivation and information sharing about products and services on Facebook, *Behaviour & Information Technology*, 34(9): 858–868.

Cho, N. and Li, G. (2007). An empirical study on the effect of individual factors on knowledge sharing by knowledge type, *Journal of Global Business and Technology*, 3(2): 1–16.

Choudhury, S. (2005). The role of affect and cognition based trust in complex knowledge sharing cultures, *Journal of Managerial Issues*, 17(3): 310–326.

Choudhury, P., T. Khanna, C. Makridis and K. Schirmann (2022) Is Hybrid Work the Best of Both Worlds? Evidence from a Field Experiment, Working Paper 22–63, Boston: Harvard Business School.

Cohen, D. and Prusak, L. (2001). *In Good Company: How Social Capital Makes Organizations Work*. Boston, MA: Harvard Business School Press.

Collins, H. M. (1993). The structure of knowledge, *Social Research*, 60(1): 95–116.

Constant, D., Sproull, L. and Kiesler, S. (1996). The kindness of strangers: The usefulness of electronic weak ties for technical advice, *Organization Science*, 7(2): 119–135.

Cook, S. and Brown, J. S. (1999). Bridging epistemologies: The generative dance between organizational knowledge and organizational knowing, *Organization Science*, 10: 381–400.

Crossan, M. M., Lane, H. and White, R. (1999). An organisational learning framework: From intuition to institution. *Academy of Management Review*, 24(3): 522–537. https://doi.org/10.5465/amr.1999.2202135

Crossan, M. M., Maurer, C. C. and White, R. E. (2011). Reflections on the 2009 AMR decade award: Do we have a theory of organizational learning? *Academy of Management Review*, 36(3): 446–460.

Currie, G. and Kerrin, M. (2003). Human resource management and knowledge management: Enhancing knowledge sharing in a pharmaceutical company, *The International Journal of Human Resource Management*, 14(6): 1027–1045.

Dahlander, L., Wallin, M., Carnabuci, G. and Quintane, E. (2021). Forming new collaborations in remote work', *California Management Review*, 29 April. Available at https://cmr.berkeley.edu/2021/04/forming-new-collaborations-in-remote-work/

Davenport, T. and Prusak, L. (1998). *Working Knowledge: How Organisations Manage What They Know*. Cambridge, MA: Harvard Business School Press.

De Cremer, D. and Van Vugt, M. (1999). Social identification effects in social dilemmas: A transformation of motives, *European Journal of Social Psychology*, 29: 871–893.

De Jong, B. A., Dirks, K. T., & Gillespie, N. (2016). Trust and team effectiveness: a meta-analysis of critical contingencies and mediating mechanisms. *J Appl Psychol*, *101*, 1134–1150.

De Long, D. W. and Fahey, L. (2000). Diagnosing cultural barriers to knowledge management, *The Academy of Management Executive*, 14(4): 113–127.

Dougherty, D. (1992). A practice-centered model of organizational renewal through product innovation, *Strategic Management Journal*, 13: 77–92.

Dovey, K. (1997). The learning organisation and the organisation of learning: Learning, power, transformation and the search for form in learning organisation, *Management Learning*, 28: 331–349.

Emerson, R. M. (1976). Social exchange theory, *Annual Review of Sociology*, 2: 335–362.

Empson, L. (2001). Fear of exploitation and fear of contamination: Impediments to knowledge transfer in mergers between professional service firms, *Human Relations*, 54(7): 839–862.

Eraut, M. (2000). Non-formal learning and tacit knowledge in professional work, *British Journal of Educational Psychology*, 70: 113–136.

Ferrin, D. L. and Dirks, K. T. (2003). The use of rewards to increase and decrease trust: Mediating processes and differential effects, *Organization Science*, 14(1): 18–31.

Fisher, R., Maltz, E. and Jaworski, B. (1997). Enhancing communication between marketing and engineering: The moderating role of relative functional identification, *Journal of Marketing*, 61: 54–70.

Gargiulo, M. and Benassi, M. (1999). The dark side of social capital, in R. Th. A. J. Leenders and S. M. Gabbay (Eds.), *Corporate Social Capital and Liability*, pp. 298–322. New York: Springer.

Gargiulo, M. and Benassi, M. (2000). Trapped in your own net? Network cohesion, structural holes, and the adaptation of social capital, *Organization Science*, 11: 183–196.

Gioia, D. and Pitre, E. (1990). Multiparadigm perspectives on theory building, *Academy of Management Review*, 15: 584–603.

Gopalakrishnan, S. and Santoro, M. D. (2004). Distinguishing between knowledge transfer and technology transfer activities: The role of key organisational factors, *Engineering Management, IEEE Transactions on*, 51(1): 57–69.

Granovetter, M. S. (1985). Economic action and social structure: The problem of embeddedness, *American Journal of Sociology*, 91: 481–510.

Gubbins, C. and Dooley L. (2021) Delineating the tacit knowledge-seeking phase of knowledge sharing: The influence of relational social capital components, *Human Resource Development Quarterly*, 32: 319–348. https://doi.org/10.1002/hrdq.21423

Gubbins, C. and Kennedy, J. (2024), Knowledge management: Focusing on tacit knowledge circulation & learning, in T. S. Rocco, M. L. Morris and R. Poell (Eds.), *Sage Handbook of Human Resource Development*, Chapter 18, 205–221. London: Sage.

Hansen, M. and Haas, M. (2001). Competing for attention in knowledge markets: Electronic document dissemination in a managing consulting company, *Administrative Science Quarterly*, 46(1): 1–39.

Hansen, M. Mors, M. L. and Lovas, B. (2005). Knowledge sharing in organizations: Multiple networks, multiple phases, *Academy of Management Journal*, 48: 776–793.

Hansen, M., Nohria, N. and Tierney, T. (1999). What's your strategy for managing knowledge?, *Harvard Business Review*, 77(2): 106–112.

Hassard, J. (1995). *Sociology and Organisation Theory,* Cambridge: Cambridge University Press.

Hazlett, S., McAdam, R. and Gallagher, S. (2005). Theory building in knowledge management: In search of paradigms, *Journal of Management Inquiry*, 14(1): 31–42.

Hedlund, G. (1994). A model of knowledge management and N-Form Corporation, *Strategic Management Journal*, 15: 73–90.

Henderson, R. M. and Clark, K. B. (1990). Architectural innovation: The reconfiguration of existing product technologies and the failure of established firms, *Administrative Science Quarterly*, 35(1): 9–30.

Hew, K. F. and O'Hara, N. (2007). Knowledge sharing in online environments: A qualitative case study, *Journal of the American Society for Information Science and Technology*, 58(14): 2310–2324.

Hislop, D. (2009). *Knowledge Management in Organizations.* 2nd edition, Oxford: Oxford University Press.

Hitt, M. A., Beamish, P. W., Jackson, S. E. and Mathieu, J. E. (2007). Building theoretical and empirical bridges across levels: Multilevel research in management, *Academy of Management Journal*, 50(6), 1385–1399.

Huysman, M. and De Wit, D. (2004). Practices of managing knowledge sharing: Towards a second wave of knowledge management, *Knowledge and Process Management*, 11(2): 81–92.

Inkpen, A. C. and Tsang, E. W. (2005). Social capital, networks, and knowledge transfer, *Academy of Management Review*, 30(1): 146–165.

Jackowska, M., & Lauring, J. (2021). What are the effects of working away from the workplace compared to using technology while being at the workplace? Assessing work context and personal context in a global virtual setting. *Journal of International Management*, *27*(1), 100826.

Kankanhalli, A., Tan, B. and Wei, K. (2005). Contributing knowledge to electronic knowledge repositories: An empirical investigation, *MIS Quarterly*, 29(1): 113–143.

Kennedy, J., Gubbins, C. and Buckley, F. (2015). *Conceptualising knowledge seeking as part of the knowledge sharing process.* Organisational Learning and Knowledge Capabilities Conference (OLKC), Universita Cattolica del Sacro Cuore, Milan, Italy, 9–11 April.

Kim, J., Song, J. and Jones, D. R. (2011). The cognitive selection framework for knowledge acquisition strategies in virtual communities, *International Journal of Information Management*, 31(2): 111–120.

Kim, S. and Lee, H. (2006). The impact of organizational context and information technology on employee knowledge-sharing capabilities, *Public Administration Review*, 66(3): 370–385.

King, W. R., Chung, T. R. and Haney, M. H. (2008). Knowledge management and organizational learning, *Omega-International Journal of Management Science*, 36: 167–172.

Kogut, B. and Zander, U. (1992). Knowledge and the firm, combinative capabilities and the replication of technology, *Organization Science*, 3(5): 383–397.

Krackhardt, D. (1992). The strength of strong ties: The importance of philos in organizations, in N. Nohria and R. G. Eccles (Eds.), *Networks and Organizations: Structures, Form and Action*, pp. 216–239. Boston, MA: Harvard Business School Press.

Kwok, S. H. and Gao, S. (2005). Attitude towards knowledge sharing behavior, *Journal of Computer Information Systems*, 46(2): 45–51.

Lam, A. (1996). Engineers, management and work organization: A comparative analysis of engineers' work roles in British and Japanese electronics firms, *The Journal of Management Studies*, 33(2): 183–212.

Lave, J. and Wenger, E. (1991). *Situated Learning: Legitimate Peripheral Participation.* New York: Cambridge University Press.

Le Clus, M. (2011). Informal learning in the workplace: A review of the literature. *Australian Journal of Adult Learning*, 51(2): 355.

Lee, J. H., Kim, Y. G. and Kim, M. Y. (2006). Effects of managerial drivers and climate maturity on knowledge-management performance: Empirical validation, *Information Resources Management Journal*, 19(3): 48–60.

Legge, K. (1995). *Human Resource Management: Rhetorics and Realities*, Basingstoke: Macmillan.

Leonard-Barton D. (1992). Core capabilities and core rigidities: A paradox in managing new product development, *Strategic Management Journal*, 13: 111–125 (special issue).

Levin, D. Z. and Cross, R. (2004). The strength of weak ties you can trust: The mediating role of trust in effective knowledge transfer, *Management Science*, 50: 1477–1490.

Levinthal D. A. and March J. G. (1993). The myopia of learning, *Strategic Management Journal*, 14: 95–112 (special issue).

Lewicki, R. J. and Bunker, B. B. (1996). Developing and maintaining trust in work relationships, in R. Kramer and T. R. Tyler (Eds.), *Trust in Organizations: Frontiers of Theory and Research*, pp. 114–139. Thousand Oaks, CA: Sage.

Liebowitz, J. (2003). A knowledge management strategy for the Jason organization: A case study, *Journal of Computer Information Systems*, 44(2): 1–5.

Lin, C. P. (2007). To share or not to share: Modeling knowledge sharing using exchange ideology as a moderator, *Personnel Review*, 36(3): 457–475.

Lin, C. P., Standing, C. and Liu, Y.-C. (2008) A model to develop effective virtual teams, *Decision Support Systems*, 45(4): 1031.

Lin, H. F. (2007). Effects of extrinsic and intrinsic motivation on employee knowledge sharing intentions, *Journal of Information Science*, 33(2): 135–149.

Lin, L., Geng, X. and Whinston, A. B. (2005). A sender-receiver framework for knowledge transfer, *MIS Quarterly*, 29(2): 197–219.

Liu, N. and Liu, M. S. (2011). Human resource practices and individual knowledge-sharing behavior – An empirical study for Taiwanese R&D professionals, *The International Journal of Human Resource Management*, 22(4): 981–997.

Liu, Y. and Phillips, J. S. (2011). Examining the antecedents of knowledge sharing in facilitating team innovativeness from a multilevel perspective, *International Journal of Information Management*, 31: 44–52.

Lu, L., Leung, K. and Koch, P. T. (2006). Managerial knowledge sharing: The role of individual, interpersonal and organizational factors, *Management and Organization Review*, 2(1): 15–41.

Lyles, M. A. and Salk, J. E. (1996). Knowledge acquisition from foreign parents in international joint ventures: An empirical examination in the Hungarian context, *Journal of International Business Studies*, 27(5): 877–903.

Malhotra, Y. (1998). *Toward a knowledge ecology for organisational white- waters*. Paper presented at the Knowledge Ecology Fair 98: Beyond Knowledge Management, February. ONLINE event.

March J. G. (1991). Exploration and exploitation in organizational learning, *Organisation Science*, 2: 71–87 (special issue).

Marsick, V. J. and Watkins, K. E. (2001). Informal and incidental learning, *New Directions for Adult & Continuing Education*, 89: 25–34.

Martin, J. (2006). Multiple intelligence theory, knowledge identification and trust, *Knowledge Management Research and Practice*, 4: 207–215.

Maurer, I., Bartsch, V. and Ebers, M. (2011). The value of intra-organizational social capital: How it fosters knowledge transfer, innovation performance and growth, *Organization Studies*, 32(2): 157–185.

McDermott, R. (1999). Nurturing three dimensional communities of practice: How to get the most out of human networks, *Knowledge Management Review*, Fall edition, 26–29.

McElroy, M. W. (2003). *The New Knowledge Management: Complexity, Learning, and Sustainable Innovation*, Burlington, MA: Butterworth-Heinemann.

Minbaeva, D., Makela, K. and Rabbiosi, L. (2012). Linking HRM and knowledge transfer via individual-level mechanisms, *Human Resource Management*, 51(3): 387–405.

Moffett, S., McAdam, R. and Parkinson, S. (2002). Developing a model for technology and cultural factors in knowledge management: A factor analysis, *Knowledge Process and Management Journal*, 9(4): 237–255.

Mooradian, T., Renzl, B. and Matzler, K. (2006). Who trusts? Personality trust and knowledge sharing, *Management Learning*, 37(4): 523–540.

Moreland, R. and Levine, J. (2000). Socialization in organizations and groups, in M. Turner (Ed.), *Groups at Work: Advances in Theory and Research*, pp. 60–112. Mahwah, NJ: Lawrence Erlbaum.

Mulcahy, D. and Andreeva, T. (2023) Employer perspectives on employee work location: Collaboration, culture & control, Working Paper, 05/2023, Bruegel. Available at https://www.bruegel.org/working-paper/employer-perspectives-employee-work-location-collaboration-culture-and-control

Nonaka, I. (1994). A dynamic theory of organisational knowledge creation, *Organisation Science*, 5(1): 14–37.

Nonaka, I. and Takeuchi, H. (1995). *The Knowledge-Creating Company: How Japanese Companies Create the Dynamics of Innovation*. New York: Oxford University Press.

Ogbonna, E. and Harris, L. (2002). Managing organisational culture: Insights from the hospitality industry, *Human Resource Management Journal*, 12(1): 33–53.

Ojha, A. K. (2005). Impact of team demography on knowledge sharing in software project teams, *South Asian Journal of Management*, 12(3): 67–78.

Palmer, I. and Dunford, R. (1996). Interrogating reframing: Evaluating metaphor-based analyses of organizations, in S. Clegg and G. Palmer (Eds.), *The Politics of Management Knowledge*, pp. 141–154, London: Sage.

Pan, S. L. and Scarbrough, H. (1999). Knowledge management in practice: An exploratory case study, *Technology Analysis & Strategic Management*, 11(3): 359–374.

Pedler, M., Burgoyne, J. and Boydell, T. (1991). *The Learning Company: A Strategy for Sustainable Development*. London: McGraw-Hill.

Pentland, B. T. (1992). Organizing moves in software support hot lines, *Administrative Science Quarterly*, 37(4): 527–548.

Phillips, K. W., Mannix, E. A., Neale, M. A. and Gruenfeld, D. H. (2004). Diverse groups and information sharing: The effects of congruent ties, *Journal of Experimental Social Psychology*, 40(4): 497–510.

Pitt, M. (1998). The knowledge creating company: How Japanese companies create the dynamics of innovation, *Human Relations*, 51(4): 547–563.

Polanyi, M. (1967). *The Tacit Dimension*. London: Routledge.

Quigley, N. R., Tesluk, P. E., Locke, E. A. and Bartol, K. M. (2007). A multilevel investigation of the motivational mechanisms underlying knowledge sharing and performance, *Organisation Science*, 18(1): 71–88.

Reagans, R. and McEvily, B. (2003). Network structure & knowledge transfer: The effects of cohesion & range, *Administrative Science Quarterly*, 48(2): 240–267.

Renzl, B. (2008). Trust in management and knowledge sharing: The mediating effects of fear and knowledge documentation. *Omega*, 36: 206–220.

Rockmann, K. W., & Pratt, M. G. (2015). Contagious offsite work and the lonely office: The unintended consequences of distributed work. *Academy of Management Discoveries*, *1*(2), 150–164.

Sadler-Smith, E. (2006). *Learning and Development for Managers: Perspectives from Research and Practice*. Oxford: Blackwell Publishing.

Sawng, Y. W., Kim, S. H. and Han, H. S. (2006). R&D group characteristics and knowledge management activities: A comparison between ventures and large firms, *International Journal of Technology Management*, 35(1–4): 241–261.

Scarbrough, H. and Swan, J. (2003). Discourses of knowledge management and the learning organization: Their production and consumption, in M. Easterby Smith and M. Lyles (Eds.), *Handbook of Organizational Learning and Knowledge Management*, pp. 495–512. Oxford: Blackwell.

Schendel, D. (1996). Knowledge and the firm, *Strategic Management Journal*, 17: 1–4.

Schepers, P. and Van den Berg, P. T. (2007). Social factors of work-environment creativity, *Journal of Business and Psychology*, 21(3): 407–428.

Schultze, U. and Stabell, C. (2004) Knowing what you don't know? Discourses and contradictions in knowledge management research, *Journal of Management Studies*, 41(4): 549–573. https://doi-org.dcu.idm.oclc.org/10.1111/j.1467-6486.2004.00444.x

Shapiro, D., Sheppard, B. H. and Cheraskin, L. (1992). Business on a handshake, *Negotiation Journal*, 8: 365–377.

Siemsen, E., Balasubramanian, S. and Roth, A. V. (2007). Incentives that induce task-related effort, helping, and knowledge sharing in workgroups, *Management Science*, 53(10): 1533–1550.

Smith, C. and Willmott, H. (1991). The new middle class and the labour process, in C. Smith, D. Knights and H. Willmott (Eds.), *WhiteCollar Work: The Non- Manual Labour Process*, pp. 13–34. London: Macmillan.

Swan, J. and Scarborough, H. (2001). Knowledge management: Concepts and controversies, *Journal of Management Studies*, 38(7): 913–922.

Swart, J., & Harcup, J. (2013). 'If I learn do we learn?': The link between executive coaching and organizational learning, *Management Learning*, 44(4): 337–354.

Tagliaventi, M. R. and Mattarelli, E. (2006). The role of networks of practice, value sharing, and operational proximity in knowledge flows between professional groups, *Human Relations*, 59(3): 291–319.

Tajfel, H. and Turner, J. C. (1985). The social identify theory of group behavior, in S. Worchel and W. G. Austin (Eds.), *Psychology of Intergroup Relations*, pp. 7–24, Chicago, IL: Nelson-Hall.

Taylor, E. Z. (2006). The effect of incentives on knowledge sharing in computer-mediated communication: An experimental investigation, *Journal of Information Systems*, 20(1): 103–116.

Taylor, W. A. and Wright, G. H. (2004). Organizational readiness for successful knowledge sharing: Challenges for public sector managers, *Information Resources Management Journal*, 17(2): 22.

Thomas-Hunt, M. C., Ogden, T. Y. and Neale, M. A. (2003). Who's really sharing? Effects of social and expert status on knowledge exchange within groups, *Management Science*, 49(4): 464–477.

Tortoriello, M. and Krackhardt, D. (2010). Activating cross-boundary knowledge: Simmelian ties and the generation of innovation, *Academy of Management Journal*, 53(1): 167–181.

Tsai, W. (2002). Social structure of 'coopetition' within a multiunit organization: Coordination, competition and intraorganizational knowledge sharing, *Organization Science*, 13(2): 179–190.

Tsoukas, H. (1996). The firm as a distributed knowledge system: A constructionist approach, *Strategic Management Journal*, 17 (Winter Special Issue): 11–25.

Tsoukas, H. (2001). Where does new organizational knowledge come from? Keynote address at the International Conference Managing Knowledge: Conversations and Critiques, Leicester University, 10–11 April.

Tsoukas, H. (2011). How should we understand tacit knowledge? A phenomenological view, in M. Easterby-Smith and M. Lyles (Eds.), *Handbook of organizational learning and knowledge management,* 2nd edition, pp. 453–476, Chichester: John Wile & Sons.

Van Wijk, R., Jansen, J. P. and Lyles, M. A. (2008). Inter- and intra-organizational knowledge transfer: A meta-analytic review and assessment of its antecedents and consequences, *Journal of Management Studies*, 45(4): 830–853. https://doi.org/10.1111/j.1467-6486.2008.00771.x

Vera, D. and Crossan, M. (2005). Organisational learning and knowledge management: Toward an integrative framework, in M. Easterby-Smith and M. Lyles (Eds.), *The Blackwell Handbook of Organizational Learning and Knowledge Management*, pp. 122–142. Oxford: Blackwell Publishing.

Vera, D., Crossan, M. and Apaydin, M. (2011). A framework for integrating organizational learning, knowledge, capabilities, and absorptive capacity, in M. Easterby-Smith and M. Lyles (Eds.), *The Blackwell Handbook of Organizational Learning and Knowledge Management*, pp. 153–180. Oxford: Blackwell Publishing.

Von Krogh, G. and Roos, J. (1995). A perspective on knowledge, competence and strategy, *Personnel Review*, 24(3): 56–76.

Wang, C. C. (2004). The influence of ethical and self-interest concerns on knowledge sharing intentions among managers: An empirical study, *International Journal of Management*, 21(3): 370–381.

Wang, S. and Noe, R. A. (2010). Knowledge sharing: A review and directions for future research, *Human Resource Management Review*, 20(2): 115–131.

Wasko, M. M. and Faraj, S. (2000). 'It is what one does': Why people participate and help others in electronic communities of practice, *The Journal of Strategic Information Systems*, 9(2–3): 155–173.

Wasko, M. M. and Faraj, S. (2005). Why should I share? Examining social capital and knowledge contribution in electronic networks of practice, *MIS Quarterly*, 29: 35–57.

Webber, S. S. (2008). Development of cognitive and affective trust in teams: A longitudinal study, *Small Group Research,* 39(6): 746–769.

Wiewiora, A., Smidt, M. and Chang, A. (2019). The 'how' of multilevel learning dynamics: A systematic literature review exploring how mechanisms bridge learning between individuals, teams/projects and the organization, *European Management Review*, 16: 93–115.

Willem, A. and Scarbrough, H. (2006). Social capital and political bias in knowledge sharing: An exploratory study, *Human Relations*, 59(10): 1343–1370.

Willmott, H. (1993). Breaking the paradigm mentality, *Organisation Studies*, 14(5): 681–720.

Wu, W. L., Hsu, B. F. and Yeh, R. S. (2007). Fostering the determinants of knowledge transfer: A team-level analysis, *Journal of Information Science*, 33(3): 326–339.

Yang, C. and Chen, L. C. (2007). Can organizational knowledge capabilities affect knowledge sharing behaviour?, *Journal of Information Science*, 33(1): 95–109.

Yang, L., Holtz, D., Jaffe, S., Suri, S., Sinha, S., Weston, J., Joyce, C., Shah, N., Sherman, K., Hecht, B. and Teevan, J. (2021). The effects of remote work on collaboration among information workers, *Nature Human Behaviour*, 6: 43–54.

Yang, S. C. and Farn, C. K. (2009). Social capital, behavioural control, and tacit knowledge sharing – A multi-informant design, *International Journal of Information Management*, 29(3): 210–218.

Zahara, S. A., Ireland, R. D. and Hitt, M. A. (2000). International expansion by new venture firms: International diversity, mode of market entry, technological learning, and performance, *Academy of Management Journal*, 43: 925–950.

Zappa, P., Andreeva, T. and Dávila, G. (2023). Asymmetries in the hybrid workplace and their impact on knowledge network churn, Paper for the Academy of Management Annual Meeting, Boston, MA.

9 HRM in Small- and Medium-Sized Enterprises (SMEs)

Tony Dundon and Adrian Wilkinson

Introduction

Small-and Medium-sized Enterprises (SMEs) are often deemed critical to the economy of many countries. The reasons for this are twofold: first, there are so many smaller firms that make up a large proportion of employment; and second, because the way people are managed is regarded as central to the competitive standing of firms and industries (Boxall and Purcell, 2022). Such recognition has provoked debate about the role of human resource management (HRM) as a means to enhance organisational effectiveness (Kinnie et al., 2024). Within OECD economies, SME businesses employ more than 60 per cent of the labour force and generate around 55 per cent of national gross domestic product, accounting for 99 per cent of all business enterprises (OECD, 2019). Smaller firms are also established as global enterprises, operating in international markets and feature as important supply chain network agents with larger global partners in many parts of the less developed world (Tarique et al., 2022). Thus, SMEs are important in terms of engines of growth, international trade and numbers employed.

However, much of the HRM literature and normative models tends to be based on large-firm settings. Indeed, it is often assumed that the lessons from these larger mainstream organisations can be applied to people management practices of SMEs, writ large. Yet larger firms tend to be structured much more formally with bureaucratic command and control arrangements (Edwards and Ram, 2019). Large firms can be shaped directly by their national environment and business systems in a particular country with formalised institutional regimes; whereas among smaller enterprises, informality is much more common. Many SMEs tend to have a very particularistic approach to HRM, with varying management styles ranging from authoritarian to personnel and friendly relations, influenced as much by the values of founding owners than formal policies or notions of best practice HRM (Tarique et al., 2022).

The purpose of this chapter is to review the nature and extent of HRM among SMEs. We adopt a generalist approach to HRM, which includes employment relations broadly defined. In this way the chapter can report on various practices while providing an analysis about the meanings and

DOI: 10.4324/9781032625560-10

interpretations of management action in the context of a smaller rather than larger firm. The chapter starts by asking what an SME is, commenting on the importance of SMEs in a global and local economy and for human resource management specifically. Traditional approaches to HRM are then considered, assessing how they have been applied to smaller businesses. From this it is suggested that much theorising about HRM in SMEs is limited in that analysis often gravitates around one of two polarised perspectives: the 'small is beautiful' versus 'bleak house' scenario (Wilkinson 1999). The remainder of the chapter then reviews current research evidence concerning the core dimensions of HRM among SMEs (e.g. informality, recruitment, training, employee involvement/voice and related management practices).

What is an SME?

There is no 'single or acceptable definition of a small firm' (Storey, 1994:8). The US Small Business Administration once defined a small- to medium-sized firm if it employed fewer than 1,500 people! Today, most definitions tend to define a smaller firm as one employing 250 workers (OECD, 2019). Other similar bodies such as the European Commission (2015) categorise firm size as either *micro* (less than 10 employees), *small* (10–49 employees) or *medium*-sized enterprises (50–249 employees), and which have an annual turnover not exceeding €50 million (European Commission, 2015:3). However, as a definition for SMEs, such technical classifications based on numbers employed and financial turnover can be problematic (Dundon and Wilkinson, 2004). Small firms differ considerably in terms of what they do and who they employ: for example, a hairdressing shop employing ten or 12 people would be quite large for this segment of retail. Furthermore, the nature of each firm differs not only in terms of market sector and conditions but also social relations and whether an enterprise is family run. Some firms are dependent on larger organisations for their survival through outsourcing and contract services, while others operate in discrete and niche markets, such as hi-tech or business consultancy. Arguably, many studies fail to capture the specific economic position and social norms that govern management actions in each firm, and models of HRM tend to be applied to smaller firms as though they are the same as larger organisations (Harney and Alkhalaf, 2021). Moreover, SMEs are not homogenous but differ in terms of context, family and kinship along with variable labour and product markets (Edwards and Ram, 2019). It is often pointed out that such characteristics are underrepresented in academic scholarship surrounding HRM among SMEs (Harney et al., 2022).

There is a long pedigree of literature about employment and social relations in smaller work settings (Bolton Report, 1971; Rainnie, 1989; Ritchie, 1993; Ram, 1994; Ritchie, 1993; Goss, 1991; Wilkinson, 1999; Edwards et al., 2006 – among others). We do know a great deal about SMEs and, in particular, how important they are for economic growth, stability and employment. As noted, in most Westernised economies, smaller firms account for as much as 99 per cent of all business, which represents around 40 per cent of non-government employment. In 2024, in Britain, there were 5.45 million small- and medium-sized enterprises: a 0.8 per cent growth on the previous year (FSB, 2024). Across Europe as a whole, nine out of ten enterprises are an SME which, cumulatively, employ two out of every three workers (European Commission, 2015:3).

However, there are dangers in using such figures in a general or deterministic way, which may signal how scholars have underrepresented the nature and scope of HR activity among SMEs. For example, a number of smaller firms are not actually 'companies', but rather 'sole proprietorships' (FSB, 2023). And there are concerns about bogus self-employment in areas such as the platform economy, where workers are defined as independent contractors yet subject to control by the platforms and have been reported as lacking a voice about their work futures (Wilkinson et al., 2022a). SMEs that do have employees tend to be prominent in key sectors of the economy such as retail, hotels and restaurants, transport and communications, financial services and business services. Many SMEs are also family-owned (69 per cent), with the majority managed by first- or second-generation family members (BIS, 2016:36). Indeed, the role of familial relations has been noted as one of the more important set of factors that can influence how a small firm manages its human resource (Ram, 1994). In particular, the prevalence of dominant family values is crucial to understand HR arrangements at a workplace level (Edwards and Ram, 2019). Key challenges limiting the diffusion of more sophisticated HRM among SMEs can be a lack of professional in-house managerial skill and owner-managers having to rely on external sources for information (Harney et al., 2022; EU, 2015).

Theorising HRM in SMEs: From 'Bleak House' to 'Small Is Beautiful'

Some of the earlier studies about employment and HRM among SMEs tended to conflate the characteristics of smaller firms along opposite ends of a continuum (see Table 9.1). At one end, the 'small is beautiful' view argues that informal communication flows between employees and owner-manager helps to generate commitment and loyalty. This perspective was epitomised in the

Table 9.1 From small is beautiful to bleak house

Small is beautiful perspective	*Bleak house perspective*
Positive HR	Negative HR
Harmonious	Hidden conflict
Good HR	Hostile IR
Little bureaucracy	Instability
Family style	Authoritarianism

Adapted from Wilkinson 1999: 207.

findings of the Bolton Commission (1971), suggesting that SMEs provide a better [sic] employee relations environment than that found in larger firms. SMEs were believed to have a more committed and motivated workforce accompanied by lower levels of conflict.

The opposite end of this continuum paints a Dickensian picture of employment conditions in many SMEs (Wilkinson, 1999). According to this view, employees suffer poor working conditions, inadequate health and safety and have less access to union representation than employees in larger establishments. Conflict is not so much lacking but rather expressed through higher levels of absenteeism and labour turnover (Rainnie, 1989). The argument posits that the 'happy family' image of many SMEs hides a form of authoritarian management with few employees capable of challenging management decisions without reprisals or that workers become bound by a network of family and kinship ties that govern employment relations or without strategies that enhance entrepreneurship among ethnic minority supply chain companies (Ram et al., 2011).

As might be expected, these polarised perspectives are the subject of much debate and criticism. While there is the possibility of some truth to each extreme, in reality SMEs are best characterised by a complex web of social and familial norms, economic conditions and sector variability (Edwards et al., 2003). Informality, for example, cannot be automatically associated with harmonious work relations (Marchington and Suter, 2013); nor should the formalisation of management techniques indicate a measure of the substance of HRM within the smaller enterprise.

Theorising about HRM in SMEs in these 'either/or' terms can simplify practices that are much more complicated in reality (Wilkinson 1999). Studies show that employees who work in smaller firms display a high degree of satisfaction in relation to their counterparts in larger establishments (Forth et al., 2006). However, what is more difficult to explain is whether such satisfaction is attributable to the size of the firm or because of other contributory factors such as the role of management, leadership style or familial culture (Tsai et al., 2007). The work of Rainnie (1989) and Goss (1991) addressed the issue of variability among different types of SMEs. *Dependent* and *dominated* small firms are those that rely on large firms for their main customer base, responding to market pressures with low-cost differentiation strategies. Smaller supply chain firms embedded in larger firm supply networks can be vulnerable in many parts of the world (Taylor et al., 2013). As such, employees tend to experience low wages and generally poor conditions, although there can be variation between these types of firms. Examples are often found in subcontracting or retail outlets competing with larger firms. In contrast, *isolated* and *innovative* small firms tend to operate in markets that large firms avoid due to limited or minimal financial returns. *Isolated* SMEs often have to compete on the basis of low costs, whereas *innovative* SMEs may be competing in high-risk markets that require specialist expertise or high employee skills.

While these typologies offer a greater degree of specificity about the wide range of SMEs that exist, they have been criticised for being too deterministic by reducing factors to external market influences and neglecting internal social relations at the enterprise level. It is certainly evident that many smaller firms are dependent upon larger organisations for their economic survival, with the larger firm often holding a degree of market power over the actions and decisions of mangers (Harney and Dundon, 2006). These sorts of debates have led to some rich and varied studies concerning SMEs. One school of thought suggests that it is not size *per se* which best explains HRM in SMEs but rather the specificity of sector and market economy in which smaller firms have to operate (Curran, 2006). In contrast, other commentators argue that it is the type of management style or entrepreneurial support systems associated explaining a more universal HRM approach among SMEs (Hayton, 2003). Of course, employee satisfaction and business unit size may not be related at all. Tsai et al. (2007: 1780), for example, explain job satisfaction in SMEs may be a function of closer and more 'personal' relationships that exist across the SME sector. Kroon and Paauwe (2021: 3224) see HRM as needing to control the human side of work as well as the differentiation and integration of tasks and develop a configurational model of eight ideal types of HRM. Based on different positions along the hierarchy, formalities and input- or output-oriented dimensions of control, they identify craft employers, traditional owner-managers and strategic, knowledge and bleak house entrepreneurs from subcontracted work, alliances and partnerships and suggest this offers a new analytical starting point for comparing and contextualising empirically observed HRM configurations in SMEs.

A recent characterisation of HR in SMEs seeks to delineate differences by the acronym RECIPE (Harney et al, 2022: 3178–80). First, *Resource constraints* signal that SMEs do not have same capacity as larger firms for HR sophistication, with many owner-managers limited by time and lacking in dedicated HR personnel. Thus recruitment may be informal and *ad hoc* (see Carrol et al., 1999). Next, *Environmental vulnerability* means that SMEs are poorly placed to influence the business environment in which they operate (Wapshott & Mallett, 2024) and can, at times, be dependent upon larger supplier firms. Harney et al. (2022) outline *Concentrated control* as a third characteristic of the RECIPE acronym for SMEs. The feature is that dominant individuals such as owner-managers project a highly unitarist ideology as to what people management might entail, with little interest in getting wider voices or involvement across the firm. Fourth, *Informality*, which has been a recurring theme in scholarship about management and employment relations in smaller work settings (see Ram et al., 2001). Fifth, and related, the smaller size of the work settings means that there are *Proximal* and spatial relations between employees and owner-mangers. The firm is typically flatter and built around informal relations including familial type concerted control. Finally in the RECIPE acronym is *Employee dynamics*, extending the idea of a unique employee experience within an SME setting, including regular job rotation and working across multiple work tasks. While the RECIPE acronym signals a more refined understanding of the multiple and, at times, overlapping characteristics associated with how HR may be unique to an SME setting, they are contested ideas; as Harney et al. (2022: 3180) note, such features may infer a degree of work intensification by employers of employee effort.

In the next section, we paint a broad picture of the key practice areas for HRM in SMEs. These include: the prevalence of informality; recruitment practices and training; union membership and employee involvement; and the emergence of so-called 'newer' management techniques.

HRM in Practice in SMEs

Informality and People Management

It is generally accepted that an informal rather than bureaucratised relationship is a key defining characteristic of HRM in SMEs, as noted in the RECIPE acronym. Small firms rarely consider formalising their working practices and rely on an emergent approach with an absence of structured or professional HR management (Marlow, 2005). This is partly the result of a lack of resources, with 'informal routinisation' playing a large part in the day-to-day running of the firm. Nevertheless, Guerrero et al. (2021) show how HR professionals in SMEs can bundle and leverage their human capital to foster SME performance, implying that HR professionals can provide valuable additions to the management team .

Informality, however, does not imply a particular view of the substance or quality of HRM: it could be associated with an autocratic as much as a harmonious enterprise. This results in a situation where management policy and practice is 'unpredictable' and at times 'indifferent' to the human resource needs of a firm (Ritchie, 1993: 20). The significance of informality on any subsequent HR approach cannot be overstated. One implication is that personalisation and family ties can overlap and shape the nature of employment contracts and management actions in very informal ways.

In terms of HRM, informal interactions offer both the owner-manager workers a range of advantages, such as speed of decision-making, clarity of instruction and opportunities for employees to voice their ideas and concerns (Marchington and Suter, 2013). It is evident that these informal arrangements are much more challenging to sustain as a firm grows in size (Hann, 2012). One study found that an informal people management approach is more problematic when a firm employs more than 20 or more workers (Roberts et al., 1992: 255). This fits with the view that once the organisation grows above a certain size, management needs to become more professional and structured (Loan-Clarke et al., 1999). In many smaller firms during a growth stage, the owner-manager simply becomes 'harassed' with the day-to-day work pressures of customer demands and find little 'spare time' to handle the varied and emerging range of people management issues (Roberts at al, 1992: 242, Wilkinson et al., 2022b). In such situations, HRM is often accorded a low priority over meeting targets and production schedules.

There is some evidence to suggest a degree of diversity between small- and medium-sized enterprises, and between family-run and non-family-owned businesses (Forth et al,, 2006:26). At one level it is evident that the absence of HR specialists or formalised strategies is because many owner-managers see such policies as burdensome (Harney et al., 2022). The owners' particular sensitivity to market pressures and the need for speedy operational decisions has been employed as an argument against formalised procedures. It is generally advanced that matters such as employment legislation is problematic to smaller businesses, that is restricting expansion or constraining entrepreneurial innovation because of 'red-tape' or costly bureaucracy (Hann, 2012). Indeed, owner-manager ideologies and values to HRM tend to be unitarist with the (often incorrect) assumption that happy employees relate to a successful or profitable firm. At a practical level, it is also feasible that many managers in SMEs recognise the need for a policy to control employees, while at the same time realising they want to solicit cooperation in tandem with informal relations. Therefore, procedures need to be understood alongside owner-manager preferences for informality and the social action networks in which they are situated.

In fast growing SMEs, Wilkinson et al, (2022b: 1399–1400) saw firms moving to a point where they were thinking about introducing more formality. The motivation for building this formality was a recognition of the weaknesses inherent in informal relations in new, smaller companies. As the principal at one organisation observed:

> I am at the stage where I have got the policies drafted for the most part so I can say, well, you can, or you cannot get your phone reimbursed.

Equally, a manager in another firm commented that the existence of policy gave him a degree of distancing from other (older) staff:

> Guys, there is nothing personal. But we need to get through A, B, C, because it is in the policy. And I find by saying that it is nothing personal then they do not think it is ... personal.

Recruitment and Training in SMEs

Smaller firms are less likely to use personality tests when recruiting new staff and place a lower priority on off-the-job training than do larger firms. Arguably, difficulties of labour supply can be magnified for smaller firms compared to the experiences of many larger organisations given the lack of available recourses and the absence of HR specialists (Hann, 2012). While there is a preference for informality, recruitment methods have also shown to vary between industries and sectors. What is almost self-evident for SMEs is that because they have fewer employees to begin with, it is extremely difficult to maintain or develop an internal labour market based on recruitment and career development (Taylor, 2005, Wilkinson et al., 2022a). For most SMEs, recruitment of new staff is via *closed* and *responsive* methods that rely on informal networks (Carrol et al., 1999).

The implications of how SMEs recruit people can lead to potential problems of discrimination. For example, owner-managers can lack knowledge about equality regulations or diversity best practice options, with around one-third of SMEs seeking external advice, most asking for financial advice followed by employment law (BIS, 2016:116). We do know that very few SMEs monitor their recruitment methods with regard to equal opportunities (Forth et al., 2006). Further problems can arise with an *ad hoc* and informal approach to recruitment. For example, 'indirect' discrimination can be evident when workers are recruited from the same ethnic group or from within a particular familial and social milieu (Ram et al., 2011). Indeed, the use of family and ethnic labour can be extremely gendered, with women occupying positions of subordination in smaller (ethnic and family-run) firms: 'roles are rewarded accordingly, influenced by the "male-breadwinner" and female "actual or potential wife and mother" ideology' (Ram and Holliday, 1993:644). Over time, evidence reiterates that owner-managers prefer informal practices (Hann, 2012). Carrol et al. (1999:24) concluded that:

> [W]ord-of-mouth recruitment methods are potentially discriminatory. On the other hand, given the lack of in-house expertise in human resource management techniques and the nature of the labour market, it could be argued that these methods are the most appropriate. Hiring 'known quantities' could be seen as a very effective way of reducing uncertainty in recruitment decisions.

The recruitment of new employees also has the potential to inject new skills and experiences into the organisation. Thus, recruitment can, to some extent, substitute for training, which tends to be lower in SMEs. However, there is also the argument that training could be based on informal learning and the development of tacit skills. Therefore, the lower incidence of formal off-the-job training among SMEs may not be the same as a lack of learning and skill development found in larger organisations (Kitching and Blackburn, 2002). This debate aside, it seems that many owner-managers are either 'ignorant' of the softer people skills such as training, or they are too busy and pre-occupied with 'getting the products out the door' that they have little time to consider training needs in a coherent manner (Westhead and Storey, 1997). A further explanation for the lack of formal training in SMEs is that managers simply fear they will lose newly trained employees to competitors (Hann, 2012). Wynarczyk et al. (1993), for example, found that many small business owners expected line managers to leave the company if they wanted to advance their career.

In summary, SMEs have a different approach to recruitment and training than do larger organisations. It is an approach that is less formal and based on owner-manager views about what is appropriate for the business at a particular time (Taylor, 2005). Smaller firms have little internal labour market movement through promotion or career development, and recruitment can be one way to inject new skills into the organisation. Yet such recruitment methods raise a number of concerns about the potential discrimination surrounding informal and *ad hoc* processes.

Trade Union Membership and Employee Participation in SMEs

The available data on union membership in SMEs is patchy and disjointed. It is generally understood that union membership among SMEs is much lower than in larger organisations, although there is some international variation. For example, in the UK, around 7 per cent of workers in small *firms* are union members, rising to 10 per cent in *medium*-sized (50–249 employees) organisations. (Forth et al., 2006: 47). In the US, workers in smaller private-sector firms are unlikely to be union members, although they do tend to be paid more: the union wage premium can be an extra $200 per week more (BLS, 2023). In contrast, in Germany, union membership is 8 per cent in *micro* firms (0–9 employees) rising to 14 per cent in *small* (10–49 employees) establishments. In Norway, union density is around 30 per cent in *small*- and 51 per cent in *medium*-sized, respectively (Broughton, 2011). Further to this is that a greater proportion of employees in SMEs have never been a trade union member (in the UK): 71 per cent compared to 55 per cent in larger firms (Forth et al., 2006:47).

As might be expected, owner-managers are less likely to recognise a union for bargaining purposes than is the situation for larger companies. Compared to 31 per cent of large firms, only 3 per cent of SMEs recognise a union (Forth et al., 2006: 48). There is only a modest variation between sectors: 5 per cent for manufacturing firms and 3 per cent for service sector establishments. Given the absence of collective representation for workers employed in SMEs, it is perhaps not surprising that most owner-managers prefer to communicate with employees directly. For example, 86 per cent of managers said they would rather consult with employees than deal with a trade union (Forth et al., 2006:45). While most managers (72 per cent) say they have a 'neutral' attitude towards unions at their establishment, a growing proportion indicate they either 'actively discourage' union membership or are 'not in favour' of unions

Despite the informal nature of communication flows, noted earlier as a characteristic feature of smaller organisations, we know that most rely on informal meetings with employees, typically via face-to-face meetings between (owner)-manager and employee. In this regard, the utility of information sharing from management can be favourably received by employees in small firms compared to those employed in medium-sized and large organisations. One particular feature seems to be that in SMEs without an owner-manager on site, employees have been reported as being more positively disposed towards management communications than in those firms that are run by the owner (Forth et al., 2006:55). This may suggest that owner-managers have a tendency to guard company information as privy to them or their immediate family rather than sharing this or consulting with employees (Wilkinson et al, 2007). Nevertheless, a recent study showed that giving employees control over their own work roles and involving them in co-creating the future of the firm is positively related to their job satisfaction (Wikhamn et al., 2021).

A problem in much extant literature is that reliance on large-scale surveys to examine HRM cannot capture the complexity and unevenness associated with people management processes. Importantly, when practices are determined by an owner-manager or an owner who may also be the head of a family unit, then the outcomes can be very different for workers. For example, a paternalistic- or friendly-managerial approach does not negate the fact that owner-managers discriminate against workers and devise soft HR strategies to ensure the firm remains union-free (Dobbins and Dundon, 2020). In one study concerned with the extent to which SMEs are prepared for European employee information and consultation regulations, most owner-managers inform staff but fall short of the consultative requirements (Wilkinson et al., 2007). Adding to the complexity is what Ram (1994) describes as a 'negotiated order' between owner and employee that serves to constrain the power of owner-managers, especially when influenced by family and kinship links that override the formalised structures of an employment contract. It is these sorts of qualitative studies that suggest the meanings ascribed to specific HR practices may not be the same as the picture derived from large-scale surveys. In a study of SMEs, for example, Cullinane and Dundon (2014) report the prevalence of a strong unitarist ideology among owner-managers, with a distinctive anti-union posture concerning social dialogue or collective bargaining. Furthermore, reporting the existence of teamworking in a smaller firm is not the same as a team-based structure in a large organisation. In SMEs, employees tend to work together by definition of the smaller work environment: this is not a team as conventionally understood in much of the mainstream literature on HRM (Boxall and Purcell, 2022).

Pay among Small Firms

As already noted, pay tends to be lower among SMEs than in larger firms. Surprisingly, research has shown that many SMEs have benefitted from statutory National Minimum Wage (NMW) and the Real Living Wage may better support staff retention for the firm, have positive spillover effects into the local economy and help individuals when facing a cost-of-living crisis (see Prowse and Dobbins, 2022). The Real Living Wage is premised on what a person is supposed to need in order to meet minimum living standards. While exact numbers are difficult to quantify, it seems some SMEs that do pay the higher recommended (as opposed to the lower statutory) Real Living Wage do so for a mix of strategic and moral reasons (Werner, 2021).

Notwithstanding progressive SME living wage employers, only a small proportion of workers (5 per cent) have the opportunity to discuss and negotiate their pay by collective bargaining (Forth et al., 2006). Around 20 per cent of SMEs utilise a performance- or incentive-based system for employee remuneration (Forth et al., 2006:61). However, these have also proved to be difficult for SMEs, with a desire for more informal approaches overriding formalised variable pay schemes (Cox, 2005). Much more common are *ad hoc* wage-payment and wage-negotiation systems which can lack transparency about what other employees earn, even in the same firm (Gilman et al., 2015). Arguably, pay determination in the context of an SME is often based on managerial 'gut instinct', 'prejudice' by owner-managers or 'market pressures' at a given moment in time. In our own research (Dundon et al., 1999), one garage mechanic explained the procedure for a pay increase:

> I know when we get a rise. It's each Christmas. It's not automatic though, you only get a rise if they think you should have a pay rise [and] ... that's based on not dropping a bollock in the year ... It's a letter in the Christmas card saying we're getting a rise ... it really pisses the lads off. I mean a little card, 'all the best and all that', but nought about your money and so and so next to you gets something.

Overall, pay remains lower for workers in smaller firms, even though many report a higher rate of satisfaction than their counterparts in larger organisations (Forth et al., 2006). It is also important to be critical of wide-sweeping generalisations, as a great deal can depend on the precise occupational category or sector in which employees work. For some owner-managers, statutory instruments such as the Living Wage have limited their freedom to impose unilateral decisions. In other SMEs, variable-pay schemes have been implemented, although they are not without difficulties when they formalise an established informal routine (Cox, 2005). Moreover, many variable-pay schemes in smaller firms seem to be based on managerial 'gut instinct' rather than clear systematic and objective performance criteria (Gilman et al., 2002).

High-Performance HRM in SMEs

One of the more contradictory images of HRM in smaller firms is the apparent coexistence of 'informality' with particular 'bundling' of HR practices that are claimed to support organisational performance (Boxall and Purcell, 2022; see chapter 4 this volume). Examples include devolved managerial responsibilities, sophisticated and formalised recruitment and selection techniques, contingent rewards, team working and a range of employee involvement initiatives. According to Bacon et al. (1996), the use of such strategies among many SMEs may not necessarily be 'new', but rather less formal. Initiatives such as quality and cultural change programmes may have been present for as long, if not longer, in many SMEs but based on informal arrangements. In a study by

Downing-Burn and Cox (1999), for example, smaller engineering firms used various high-commitment practices such as quality audits, team working, job rotation and communication techniques. Harney and Dundon (2006) show that smaller firms had a range of innovative practices including employee voice and reward systems based on contingency-market strategies. However, Peetz et al. (2017) reported that while emerging firms were more casualised, less unionised and experiencing higher levels of market expansion and unpredictability, they showed remarkable similarity to older firms across a range of ER practices. WERS found that around one-fifth of SMEs use five or advanced management practices. Ogunyomi and Bruning (2016) report an association in SMEs between HRM practices and what are defined as some of the non-financial performance outcomes, such as employee satisfaction and health and safety. Other studies show the degree to which innovative HR strategies and cultural change programmes based on informal engagement tend to dominate in particular small-firm settings, often dependent on owner-manager personal preferences (Grugulis et al., 2000). It is suggested that many SMEs utilise some advanced HR techniques that may signal a degree of institutional isomorphism; that is to say, what is believed to be good practice in larger organisations is replicated among those SMEs that are aware of such practice complementarity (Bacon and Hoque 2005). More recently, Zhang and Edgar (2021) showed that an HR system as a source of human capital in SMEs is beneficial to employee capability through facilitating a proactivity mechanism. Haar et al. (2021) illustrated how SMEs can leverage their HPWS to achieve performance but that firm size was more important than the business context, pointing to larger-sized SMEs being better able to leverage their HPWS to achieve innovation.

However, how these practices actually translate to a smaller firm is debatable (Harney et al., 2022). In terms of the diffusion of sophisticated bundles of HRM practices that are claimed to underscore high-performing work systems, international data tends to suggest there is at best a moderate to low take-up among smaller-type firms in the UK (Forth et al., 2006), the US (Hayton, 2003), Australia (Wiesner et al., 2015) or Ireland (Harney and Nolan, 2014). The possible explanations are multiple. First, as is often the case in larger organisations, it is unclear why these managerial techniques should be viewed as positive. Many of these so-called new managerial practices can implicitly and explicitly rely on more traditional 'harder' employment conditions of work intensification, which ensures a degree of managerial control over employee effort. Second, it is often 'assumed' that communication flows in small firms are automatically good because of the flexibility and close proximity between employee and owner-manager. However, this may be 'one-way' communication and based upon a 'need-to-know' approach defined by the owner-manager. There is always a danger that samples reporting such change are self-selecting and, therefore, give a misleading impression of what is going on among SMEs as a whole (Curran et al., 1997). A third concern is that many SMEs can be dependent on larger organisations for business survival.

In these situations, owner-managers may feel obliged to conform to certain (new) managerial practices deemed desirable by the larger firm and adopted in name only in order to pacify (large firm) customer relations (Kinnie et al., 1999). For example, Heffernan and Dundon (2016) found that HR performance was in part mediated by pressures that engendered work intensification. Other examples have reported a shift in risk from a large firm to small supplier: in catering, cleaning, security and transport in which a significant proportion of the employees work part-time, they experience casual and temporary contracts and are low-paid women workers (MacMahon, 1996).

Yet the exploitative bleak house perspective can be equally misleading. Reports from workers employed in smaller establishments have been surprisingly positive. Tsai et al. (2007) argue that satisfaction among employees is best understood in the light of the personal relationships between employee and owner-manager: a factor evident across different economic sectors. One possible explanation is the way in which employees in smaller organisations experience and perceive their psychological contract (Cullinane and Dundon, 2006). Employee perceptions of trust and mutual obligations can have a greater resonance in a small social setting where friendly relations can develop over time (Harney & Alkhalaf, 2021).

Notwithstanding the utility in a social and psychological contract explanation, there remains a contradictory image of how employees experience their work environment in SMEs. Of course, this is also evident in larger firms. The idea that workers are satisfied in smaller firms and that relationships are friendlier is not always just a matter of size. HRM is often mediated on systems of 'unbridled individualism' with informality the central *modus operandi* in the day-to-day management of people. Many employees in smaller firms experience work-related illness, face dismissal and have less access to union representation than their counterparts in larger organisations: the fact they also seem highly satisfied is what challenges the discipline in seeking meaningful explanations that transcend polarised perspectives or static typologies of managerial action.

Conclusion

The numerical significance of SMEs to the economy, both nationally and internationally, means they warrant serious study and analysis. As Storey (1994: 160) has argued: 'any consideration of the small-firm sector which overlooked employment issues would be like *Hamlet* without the prince'. This importance has begun to be addressed by a range of earlier classic studies as well as more contemporary developments into HRM theory (Harney et al., 2022). It still remains debatable about the extent to which the size of a firm is more or less important than other contextual factors, such as labour and product markets, ownership, familial features, management ideology or industrial subculture; or the combinations thereof. Given that we do understand that in large firms HRM is not simply a function of them being large, the task of unravelling the relationship between factors in small firms should not be beyond us. If what constitutes 'smallness' is contextual and possibly subjective and interpretational, then we need to examine what factors come together to explain patterns of employment relations rather than assume one particular type, be it either small is beautiful, sweatshop or the innovative, high-risk SME.

Given the general overview of this chapter, there are a number of concluding comments to the issues and debates raised thus far. To begin with, much of the extant literature on HRM in SMEs tends to be characterised by size determinism. Arguably this represents a simplistic labelling of HRM that has been perpetuated by the absence of a theoretical framework to understand and prioritise particular contextual influences (Wapshott, and Mallett 2024). Smaller firms may manage their human resources differently than larger organisations, although in itself, size by the numbers employed is not a very good predictor as to 'why' they are different. In this chapter, attention has been given to charting the extent of various HR and newer-type managerial practices. By combining evidence from large-scale surveys and case study analysis, it is argued here that size is best viewed as a variable that mediates various priorities such as labour and product market pressures, supply chain relationships or inter-firm networks along with the political and familial environment for SMEs. In short, the context in which SMEs operate remains a crucial factor in explaining people management outcomes, be they employee job satisfaction or more hostile managerial attitudes towards collective representation. Issues concerning gender, industrial sector, occupational class and family ideologies are important explanatory factors that help unravel the nature and logic of management actions among a diverse range of small social settings. Which of these factors are more or less important is likely to vary over time and space. It is this dynamic that represents a key challenge for HRM.

References

Bacon, N., Ackers, P., Storey, J. and Coates, D. (1996), It's a small world: Managing human resources in small businesses, *International Journal of Human Resource Management*, 7(1): 83–100.

Bacon, N. and Hoque, K. (2005), HRM in the SME sector: Valuable employees and coercive networks, *International Journal of Human Resource Management*, 16(11): 1976–1999.

BIS (2016), *Longitudinal Small Business Survey Year 1 (2015): SME Employers.* BIS Research Paper No. 289, London: Department for Business, Innovation and Skills (BIS).

BLS (2023), *Union Members – 2022*, Bureau of Labor Statistics, US Department of Labor, 19th January. Available at www.bls.gov/news.release/pdf/union2.pdf.

Bolton Report (1971), *Report of the Commission of Inquiry on Small Firms*, chaired by J. E. Bolton, Cmnd 4811, London: HMSO.

Boxall, P. and Purcell, J. (2022) *Strategy and Human Resource Management,* 5th edition, London: Bloomsbury Academic.

Broughton, A. (2011), *SMEs in the Crisis: Employment, Industrial Relations and Local Partnership*, Dublin: European Foundation for the Improvement of Living and Working Conditions Report.

Carrol, M., Marchington, M., Earnshaw, J. and Taylor, S. (1999), Recruitment in small firms: Processes, methods, and problems, *Employee Relations*, 21(3): 236–250.

Cox, A. (2005), Managing variable pay in smaller workplaces, in S. Marlow, D. Patton and M. Ram (Eds.), *Labour Management in Small Firms*, London, Routledge.

Cullinane, N. and Dundon, T. (2006), The psychological contract: A critical review, *International Journal of Management Reviews*, 8(2): 113–129.

Cullinane, N. and Dundon, T. (2014), Unitarism and employer resistance to trade unionism, *International Journal of Human Resource Management*, 25(18): 2573–2590.

Curran, J. (2006), "Specificity" and "denaturing" the small business, *International Small Business Journal* 24(2): 205–210.

Curran, J., Blackburn, R., Kitching, J. and North, J. (1997), Small firms and workforce training: Some results, analysis and policy implications from a national survey, in M. Ram, D. Deakins and D. Smallbone (Eds.), *Small Firms: Enterprising Futures*, London: Paul Chapman Press.

Dobbins, T. and Dundon, T. (2020), Non-union employee representation, in A. Wilkinson, J. Donaghey, T. Dundon and R. B. Freeman (Eds.), *Handbook of Research on Employee Voice*, 2th edition, pp. 378–396, Cheltenham: Edward Elgar.

Downing-Burn, V. and Cox, A. (1999), Does size make a difference?, *People Management*, 5(2): 50–53.

Dundon T. and Wilkinson, A. (2004), Employment relations in small and medium sized enterprises', in B. Towers (Ed.), *Handbook of Employment Relations and Employment Law*, pp. 288–307, London: Kogan Press.

Dundon, T., Grugulis, I. and Wilkinson, A. (1999), Looking out of the black hole: Non-union relations in an SME, *Employee Relations*, 21(3): 251–266.

Edwards, P., Gilman, P., Ram, M. and Arrowsmith, J. (2003), Public policy, the performance of firms and the 'missing middle': The case of employment regulation and the role of local business networks, *Policy Studies*, 23(1): 5–20.

Edwards, P. and Ram, M. (2019), HRM in small firms: Respecting and regulating informality, in A. Wilkinson, D. Lepak, S.A. Snell and N. Bacon (Eds.), *Sage Handbook of Human Resource Management*, pp. 522–542, London: Sage.

Edwards, P., Ram, M., SenGupta, S. and Tsai, C. (2006), The structuring of working relationships in small firms: Towards a formal framework, *Organization*, 13(5): 701–724.

European Commission (2015), *User Guide to the SME Definition: Internal Market, Industry, Entrepreneurship and SMEs (Ref: Ares(2016)956541-24/02/2016).* Luxembourg: Publications Office of the European Union.

Forth, J., Bewley, H. and Bryson, A. (2006), *Small and Medium-Sized Enterprises: Findings from the 2004 Workplace Employment Relations Survey*, London: Routledge.

FSB. (2024), *UK Small Business Statistics: Business Population Estimates for the UK and Regions in 2024*, London: Federation of Small Business. Available at www.fsb.org.uk/uk-small-business-statistics.html

Gilman, M., Raby, S. and Pyman, A. (2015), The contours of employee voice in SMEs: The importance of context, *Human Resource Management Journal*, 25(4): 563–579.

Gilman, M., Edwards, P., Ram, M., & Arrowsmith, J. (2002). Pay determination in small firms in the UK: the case of the response to the National Minimum Wage. *Industrial Relations Journal*, *33*(1), 52–67.

Goss, D. (1991), *Small Business and Society*, London: Routledge.

Grugulis, I., Dundon, T. and Wilkinson, A. (2000), Cultural control and the 'culture manager': Employment practices in a consultancy, *Work, Employment & Society,* 14(1): 97–116.

Guerrero, S., Cayrat, C. and Cossette, M. (2021), Human resource professionals' human and social capital in SMEs: Small firm, big impact, *The International Journal of Human Resource Management*, 33(16): 1–23.

Haar, J., O'Kane, C. and Daellenbach, U. (2021), High performance work systems and innovation in New Zealand SMEs: Testing firm size and competitive environment effects, *The International Journal of Human Resource Management*, 33(16): 1–29.

Hann, A. (2012), *Employment Relations in SMEs: Day-to-Day Advice-Seeking and the Role of Intermediaries*, ACAS Research Report Ref 13/12: London, ACAS.

Harney, B. and Alkhalaf, H. (2021), A quarter-century review of HRM in Small and Medium Sized Enterprises (SMEs): Capturing what we know, and exploring where we need to go, *Human Resource Management*, 60(1): 5–29.

Harney, B. and Dundon T. (2006), Capturing complexity: Developing an integrated approach to analysing HRM in SMEs, *Human Resource Management Journal*, 16(1): 48–73.

Harney, B. and Nolan, C. (2014), HRM in small and medium-sized firms, in B. Harney and K. Monks (Eds.), *Strategic HRM: Research and Practice in Ireland*, pp. 157–190, Dublin: Orpen Press.

Harney. B., Gilman, M., Mayson, S. and Raby, S. (2022), Advancing understanding of HRM in small and medium-sized enterprises (SMEs): Critical questions and future prospects, *International Journal of Human Resource Management*, 33(16): 3175–3196.

Hayton, J. (2003), Strategic human capital management in SME, *Human Resource Management*, 42(4): 375–391.

Heffernan, M. and Dundon, T. (2016), Cross-level effects of High-Performance Work Systems (HPWS) on employee well-being: The mediating role of organisational justice, *Human Resource Management Journal,* 26(2): 211–231

Kinnie, N., Purcell, J., Hutchinson, S., Terry, M., Collinson, M. and Scarborough, H. (1999), Employment relations in SMEs: Market-driven or customer shaped?, *Employee Relations*, 21(3): 218–235.

Kinnie, N., Swart, J. and Cross, D. (2024), Human resource management and organisational performance: In search of the HR advantage, in A. Wilkinson, T. Dundon and E. Yate (Eds.), *Contemporary Human Resource Management: Text and Cases*, 7th edition, London: Sage.

Kitching, J. and Blackburn, R. (2002), The nature of training and motivation to train in small firms, Research Report 330, London: Department for Education and Skills.

Kroon, B. and Paauwe, J. (2021), HRM in 21st century small organizations: A midrange typology to describe, contrast and contextualize the phenomenon, *The International Journal of Human Resource Management*, 33(16): 1–28.

Loan-Clarke, J., Boocock, G., Smith, A. and Whittaker, J. (1999), Investment in management training and development by small businesses, *Employee Relations*, 21(3): 296–311.

MacMahon, J. (1996), Employee relations in small firms in Ireland: An exploratory study of small manufacturing firms, *Employee Relations*, 18(5): 66–80.

Marchington, M. and Suter, J. (2013), Where informality really matters: Patterns of employee involvement and participation in a non-union firm, *Industrial Relations*, 52(S1): 284–313.

Marlow, S. (2005), Introduction, in S. Marlow, D. Patton and M. Ram (Eds.), *Labour Management in Small Firms,* London: Routledge.

OECD. (2019), *Small and Medium Sized Enterprises and Entrepreneurship Outlook 2019*, Paris: Organisation for Economic Co-Operation and Development (OECD). Available at http://www.oecd.org/industry/smes/SME-Outlook-Highlights-FINAL.pdf

Ogunyomi, P. and Bruning, N. S. (2016), Human resource management and organizational performance of small and medium enterprises (SMEs) in Nigeria, *International Journal of Human Resource Management*, 27(6): 612–634.

Peetz, D., Muurlink, O., Townsend, K., Wilkinson, A. and Brabant, M. (2017), Are new organisations at the cutting edge of employment relations innovation? *Personnel Review*, 46(7), 1397–1413.

Prowse, P. and Dobbins, T. (2022), The real living wage and 'the good employer' in UK football clubs, in T. Dobbins and P. Prowse (Eds.), *The Living Wage: Advancing a Global Movement*, pp. 23–37, London: Routledge.

Rainnie, A, (1989), *Industrial Relations in Small Firms*, London: Routledge.

Ram, M. (1994), *Managing to Survive: Working Lives in Small Firms*, Oxford: Blackwell.

Ram, M. and Holliday, R. (1993), Relative merits: Family culture and kinship in small firms, *Sociology*, 27(4): 629–648.

Ram, M., Edwards, P, Gilman, M. and Arrowsmith, J. (2001), The dynamics of informality: Employment Relations in small firms and the effects of regulatory change, *Work, Employment and Society*, 15(4): 845–861.

Ram, M., Woldesenbet, K. and Jones, T. (2011), Raising the table stakes: Ethnic minority businesses and supply chain relationships, *Work, Employment and Society*, 25(2): 309–326.

Ritchie, J. (1993), Strategies for human resource management: Challenges in smaller and entrepreneurial organisations, in R. Harrison (Ed.), *Human Resource Management*, pp. 111–135, London: Addison-Wesley.

Roberts, I., Sawbridge, D. and Bamber, G. (1992), Employee relations in smaller enterprises, in B. Towers (Ed.), *Handbook of Industrial Relations Practice*, London: Kogan Press.

Storey, D. (1994), *Understanding the Small Business Sector*, London: Routledge.

Tarique, I., Briscoe, D. R. and Schuler, R. S. (2022), *International Human Resource Management: Policies and Practices for Multinational Enterprises*, New York: Routledge

Taylor, P., Newsome, K. and Rainnie. A (2013), 'Putting labour in its place': Global value chains and labour process analysis, *Competition & Change*, 17(1): 1–5.

Taylor, S. (2005), The hunting of the snark, in S. Marlow, D. Patton and M. Ram (Eds.), *Labour Management in Small Firms,* London: Routledge.

Tsai, C., SenGupta, S. and Edwards, P. (2007), When and why is small beautiful? The experience of work in the small firm, *Human Relations*, 60(12), 1779–1807.

Wapshott, R. and Mallett, O. (2024), HRM in small and medium-sized enterprises, in A. Wilkinson, T. Dundon and E. Yates (Eds.), *Contemporary Human Resource Management: Text and Cases*, 7th edition, pp. 469-485, London: Sage.

Werner, A. (2021), Why do managers of small and mediumsized businesses seek voluntary Living Wage accreditation? – An exploration of choice rationales, *European Journal of Work and Organizational Psychology*, 30(6), 778–789.

Westhead, P. and Storey, D. (1997), *Training Provision and the Development of Small and Medium Sized Enterprises*, Department for Education and Employment, Research Report No. 65, London: DfEE/HMSO.

Wiesner, R., McDonald, J. and Banham, H. C. (2015), Australian small and medium sized enterprises (SMEs): A study of high performance management practices, *Journal of Management & Organization*, 13(3), 227–248

Wikhamn, W., Wikhamn, B. R. and Fasth, J. (2021), Employee participation and job satisfaction in SMEs: Investigating strategic exploitation and exploration as moderators, T*he International Journal of Human Resource Management*, 33(16), 1–27.

Wilkinson, A. (1999), Employment relations in SMEs, *Employee Relations*, 22(3), 206–217.

Wilkinson, A., Dundon, T. and Grugulis, I. (2007), Information but not consultation: Exploring employee involvement in SMEs, *International Journal of Human Resource Management*, 18(7), 1279–1297.

Wilkinson, A., Dundon, T., Mowbray, P. K. and Brooks, S. (Eds.). (2022a), *Missing Voice? Worker Voice and Social Dialogue in the Platform Economy*, Cheltenham: Edward Elgar.

Wilkinson, A., Muurlink, O., Townsend, K. and Peetz, D. (2022b), The dual pressures of youth and expansion: Revisiting stage theories of growth in SMEs, *Employee Relations*, 44(6), 1393–1409.

Wynarczyk, P., Watson, R., Storey, D., Short, H. and Keasey, K. (1993), *The Managerial Labour Market in Small and Medium Sized Enterprises*, London: Routledge.

Zhang, J. A. and Edgar, F. (2021). HRM systems, employee proactivity and capability in the SME context, *The International Journal of Human Resource Management*, 33(16), 1–26.

Section Two

HRM Practice

10 Recruitment and Selection

The Age of Artificial Intelligence

Rosalind H. Searle, Rami Al-Sharif and Novika Grasiaswaty

Introduction

This chapter focuses on recruitment and selection processes, which often represent a job applicant's first formal interaction with organisations. We discuss the significant impacts in attracting and selecting staff, staff retention and the attitudes of rejected applicants towards an organisation. We look at the tools and instruments involved in recruitment and selection. Three distinct paradigms for examining these initial HR processes are raised and how they have shaped both research and practice are explored. We also consider the role of artificial intelligence and advanced technologies in recruitment and selection and explore how these innovations are reshaping traditional methods. Finally, emergent concerns are discussed, including demographic changes, global recruitment and selection, bias and ethical issues and the role of trust in shaping perceptions and behaviours of selectors and applicants.

What Is Recruitment and Selection?

Recruitment and selection are two different yet interlinked processes. Recruitment concerns the activities and practices utilised to attract desirable applicants, and selection pertains to the techniques used to select the most suitable ones (Klotz et al., 2013). These processes form the key opportunities for an organisation to change the type of staff it employs; however, such changes may need to attend also to attrition levels to see precisely who is leaving (Sissons and Green, 2017). As a result, HR professionals strive to attract and retain quality employees and face pivotal challenges (Ryan and Derous, 2016). These include meeting organisational innovation and efficiency desires and demands; presenting consistent and transparent information to attract those who fit or who can add a new skill set into the organisation, especially those from minority groups. Inherent in this challenge is a balance between attracting demographically diverse suitable applicants and standardising recruitment and selection processes without enforcing stereotype threat that adversely impacts certain groups.

DOI: 10.4324/9781032625560-12

Recruitment and selection are critical stages in the HRM cycle of a firm (Searle and Skinner, 2011), significantly affecting the organisation's future effectiveness and productivity. Choices of recruitment and selection tools not only send signals about the organisation (Guest et al., 2021) but also shape the workforce diversity due to their ability to attract certain groups (Ingold and Valizade, 2017). Attracting potential applicants is vital as limited applicant pools can hinder organisational flexibility and innovation.

As a central process at the start of employment, recruitment and selection has broad implications for other HR processes, including organisational development, change and attrition. Evaluating the effectiveness of these policies involves assessing the quality of new recruits, their integration, retention, impacts on existing employees and overall organisational performance (Searle and Skinner, 2011). Properly integrating new recruits into teams and aligning them with the organisation's brand is crucial for enhancing performance (Russell and Brannan, 2016).

Three Paradigms for Recruitment and Selection

Organisational and occupational psychology has much to say about the effective enactment of different selection activities; however, before we examine these processes in depth, it is important to step back and look at three distinct paradigms that determine the focus and the questions that researchers used to arrive at these findings. Through understanding these distinct perspectives, we can respond more meaningfully to the question, such as: why is there a gap between research and practice?

Psychometric Paradigm

The most well-established approach to recruitment and selection is the *psychometric or predictivist paradigm* (Schmitt and Chan, 1998). Implicitly in this approach is the dominance of the organisation that can identify, measure and select the applicant with the best knowledge, skills and abilities (KSA) for the job. Central to this paradigm are three key factors: *individual difference* in which applicants are regarded as having discernible and stable differences (Sackett, et al., 2017); *job roles* that can be performed only one way and can be objectively captured and quantified to create a criterion space; and finally, that there is *rationality in the decision-making* of organisations and their agents. Despite much being known about the cognitive limitations of individuals and the bounded rationality of our decisions (Simon, 1960), especially in a selection context (Chiavaroli et al., 2024), the impartiality of organisations remains unchallenged by this approach.

In this paradigm, applicants play a passive role, providing data through tests and tools to assess their knowledge, skills and abilities (KSA) for suitability. Much of the research undertaken in this framework is of high-volume multiple-vacancy positions, such as government agencies, armed forces or accountancy. In such situations, recruitment involves a large-scale process with multiple applicants being screened. These processes, frequently outsourced, hinge on having a qualified applicant pool and reducing job requirements to specific KSAs. The success of such routine processes depends on a consistently large candidate pool (LaHuis et al., 2007). Candidates who are rejected may reapply after enhancing their skills (Lievens et al., 2005), or, more cynically, gaining familiarity with the process and may have learnt some tricks to help them succeed. As a result, the ongoing attractiveness of the employing organisation and the job can become a significant concern (Lievens and Slaughter, 2016).

Over the past few years, artificial intelligence (AI) and significant technological developments have made it possible to utilise 'big data' (i.e. large volumes of data generated by organisations) to support better HR-related decision-making (Campion and Campion, 2024; Fisher et al., 2024; Stone et al., 2024). Sometimes, data from previous organisational datasets are used as benchmarks to refine employee selection criteria by analysing job performance indicators, such as time to productivity and retention rates. This approach can predict which candidates are likely to remain with the company long-term. Candidate information is then quantitatively analysed using computational methods to better forecast their potential behaviour and performance as employees (Pessach et al., 2020).

A central critique of the effectiveness and validity of this paradigm is the assumption of stable job roles, challenged by several factors such as rapid change in the structure and location of organisations, increasing flexibility in forms of organising, further uptake of team-based working and a rising unpredictability about the future (Stone et al., 2024). These rapid changing developments and the increasing shift of job into other parts of the globe undermine the stability of the criterion space used to identify applicants (Anderson et al., 2004). Recruitment and selection specialists need first to identify which job role components are likely to change to more accurately identifying job criteria. This has led to Future-Oriented Job Analysis (Landis et al., 1998) and recognition of adaptive work behaviours including organisational citizenship and pro-social behaviour (Borman et al., 1997; Motowidlo and Kell, 2003). However, the predictive validity of this approach has been challenged.

Social Process Paradigm

An alternative paradigm, and one that holds increasing importance in a rapidly changing, more global context, with labour scarcity for certain roles, is the *social process approach* (Herriot, 1987). This paradigm shifts the focus of recruitment and selection on to the social interaction between applicants and organisations. In this perspective, applicants are active participants, co-creating the recruitment process. It acknowledges applicants' multifaceted skills and potential to reshape their roles and influence others. This approach emphasises importance of developing a relationship between the applicant and the employing organisation, to foster trust.

This approach is more effective for unique vacancies, particularly in senior professional roles, where specific skills and approaches are sought. It highlights how every interaction in the selection process can provide valuable information. Therefore, during recruitment process, both the applicant and the organisation are continually assessing and adjusting the symmetry between each other (Bangerter et al., 2012; Walker et al., 2014).

It suggests value in research and practitioners viewing each selection event as a distinct occurrence. While this approach does not provide an alternative to how employees might be selected, it identifies new research topics and practical implications for organisations to consider in the design and implementation of their recruitment and selection processes (McCarthy et al., 2017). Increasingly, this paradigm is challenging researchers to look afresh at the pre-entry process (Ryan, et al., 2000), especially the challenges to those from different ethnicities (Derous et al., 2017). This position regards applicants as already having perceptions about the organisation, and identified some salience in their social identities prior to applying (Kaplan, et al., 2016; Searle, 2006), rather than these being formed due to the selection process. This perspective makes more prominent issues, such as trust development and maintenance, which may not only enhance the selection process but also can lead to more committed and motivated new employees for the organisation (Celani et al., 2008; Cropanzano et al., 2007).

A key and under researched insight from this approach is the role of social identity. Applicants are argued to have a repertoire of social identities, some of which they bring to a selection context (Banks et al., 2015). During the selection process, they are searching for clues as to the identity of the organisation, especially the beliefs, values and behavioural norms of the organisation, in order to evaluate the congruence between the two. For example, such research suggests that organisations have an identity and attract, recruit and retain employees who match a prototype in terms of personality (Schneider et al., 1998; Russell and Brannan, 2016) and values (O'Reilly et al., 1991). Therefore, if we are to understand selection processes better, it is important to study how identities are formed and developed, as well as the planned events/ practices that contribute to identity development (Ashforth et al., 2014). For example, which is more important in identity and, therefore, job attraction, organisation-produced advertising or more independent social contacts and their testimonials? Are there differences in the identity formation between new job seekers and more experienced recruits?

Importantly, this paradigm offers some valuable insights into research-practice differences, such as why there might be resistance to certain scientifically tested selection tools. While validity studies indicate biographical questionnaires are an effective selection tool, there is reluctance to use them, possibly because of the hostility of applicants who regard them as irrelevant and intrusive (Robertson et al., 1991). In contrast, evidence suggests applicants are far more comfortable with unstructured interviews (Cropanzano et al., 2007; Kohn and Dopboye, 1998) and focus on the propriety of the questions they are asked when discerning the procedural justice of the selection process (Celani et al., 2008; Gilliland, 1995; Searle and Billsberry, 2011). Thus, the choice of test or tool used by an organisation can alter applicants' perceptions of the organisation (Carless, 2006; Hausknecht et al., 2004).

Person-Organisation (P-O) Fit

A third paradigm highlights the multidimensionality of these processes – *Person-Organisation* (P-O) *Fit* (Bowen et al.,1991; Levesque, 2005). This approach centres on the interaction between an individual and their surroundings. Mischel (1968) argued that the environment in which people find themselves dictates their behaviour. This is an indirect contrast with trait theory and the psychometric view, which contends that individual traits shape individuals' behaviour and how they respond to the situations. Following Bower's (1973) study, which identified that the interaction of person and situation factors was approximately twice as powerful as a predictor of behaviour as either person or situation factors. Interactional psychology emerged as the most accepted explanation of human behaviour (Krahé, 1992). Similarly to the social interaction perspective, this approach focuses on a balance between both the individual and the organisation, with a unique emphasis on achieving a mutually beneficial goodness of fit. Results from two meta-analyses show the significant role P-O Fit plays in applicant attraction (Chapman et al., 2005; Uggerslev et al., 2012). For instance, study of minority applicants shows they pursue organisations that value diversity and thus affirm their identity (Avery et al., 2013; Walker et al., 2012). Despite the ongoing importance of P-O Fit, there remains a concerning paucity of studies in recruitment and selection (Abraham et al., 2015).

In the next two sections, two processes; attraction and selection, will be summarised with Hough and Oswald (2000) or Searle (2003) providing more comprehensive and in-depth reviews.

Attraction

A two-tier job market has emerged over the last few years with increased competition amongst employers to attract the most qualified applicants (Roberson, 2019; Stewart, 2016), while those without qualifications find it increasingly difficult to be shortlisted for vacancies. Research on the predictors of applicant attractions revealed that, unlike perceived alternativeness, aspects including perceived fit, recruiter behaviours, hiring expectancies and the characteristics of the job, organisation and recruitment process all contribute at different points in recruitment (Chapman et al., 2005; Uggerslev et al., 2012). Surveys from the CIPD (e.g. 2015) suggested that a majority of organisations (+77 per cent) experience ongoing difficulty in recruiting staff. Thus, there is ongoing interest in attempts to understand the reasons behind job seekers' behaviours (Barber and Roehling, 1993; Carless and Imber, 2007; Imus and Ryan, 2005).

Organisations must both attract and keep a pool of potential applicants for their vacancies. Therefore, selection using tools such as realistic job previews (RJPs) may be vital in some types of occupations (e.g. study of dirty work; Lopina, et al., 2012). For instance, applicants with high levels of cognitive ability and motivation to scrutinise the information provided by organisations exploit any available opportunity to assess the quality and veracity of such information (Uggerslev et al., 2012). This shows how unfulfilled promised expectations that breach trust perceptions can create subsequent deleterious work attitudes and behaviours (Breaugh, 2008; Klotz et al., 2013). Organisation image as an employer, or employer branding (Backhaus & Tikoo, 2004), plays a crucial role in attracting and retaining talent. Within the framework of person-organisation fit, the company's image serves as a significant signal to candidates about the organisation's values.

There are several tools that we will now explore that are utilised in the attraction of applicants, including paper media and internet job advertisements; word-of mouth with existing or previous employees; or the use of specialist third-party recruiters, known as head-hunters.

Media and Internet

Over the last ten years, there has been a change in the processes used to attract and recruit staff with increased deployment of the internet. A CIPD (2015) survey showed that, across all sectors, 65 per cent of the responding organisations had developed and enhanced their corporate websites to improve their corporate brand and applicant attraction. The internet provides organisations with a very cost-effective and efficient means of reaching applicants globally rather than through a printed medium (Baum and Kabst 2014; Holm 2012). E-recruiting can reduce hiring costs by 87 per cent compared to traditional recruiting (Maurer and Liu, 2007). In addition, it offers a portal for organisations to provide relevant and dynamic job information in a far more consistent manner than in the past (Pisano et al., 2017) and the opportunity to showcase the organisation, its achievements and credentials. They allow jobs to be previewed more effectively, and, therefore, organisational fit to be assessed more effectively, deterring unsuitable applicants in a way that maintains their positive view that the organisation that has done them a service by saving them wasting their time, effort and face for unsuitable roles (Dineen et al., 2002). Therefore, the content of websites, including job attributes, P-O Fit information and page design and functionality, are all crucial in creating positive impressions and in encouraging the right applications (Allen et al., 2013; Walker et al., 2012).

The rapidity of technology development has resulted in dual systems with companies developing both their own hosted sites on which vacancies appear and the creation of an additional presence on other sites such as LinkedIn, and

Facebook, amongst others (Pisano et al., 2017), which appeal and raise their profile to an IT literate youth market. Such sites offer organisations potential access to information about applicants through the use of personal postings on these sites (Nikolaou, 2014). This is a new application of the technology whose impact remains under research, but also more broadly for us to understand how and why technology changes the way people communicate with each other (McFarland and Ployhart, 2015).

Applicants have never had such an immediate, quality and plethora of sites to assist them in their job search, plus the speedy dissemination of job vacancies from different networks (Uggerslev et al., 2012). This has resulted in a change in the way information is used in the job search, with more attention being given to independent non-company sites (Talmage, 2012). The internet has provided the digitisation of job search systems with message systems designed to enable the posting of vacancies by firms, and C.V. by those seeking new job opportunities, wherever they may be. Potentially, this technology has removed previous geographical barriers to applicant attraction. However, it is also offering organisations new developments in the identification of desirable candidates with the potential to use both legitimate 'spiders' or 'bots' to search for candidates, plus more covert and surveillance-based processes, such as 'flipping' and 'peeling' to gather such data (Searle, 2006).

Word of Mouth

One of the most enduring sources of job seekers' information is word of mouth (Breaugh, 2008). Evidence suggests that it remains a highly credible and important source, especially when it is focused on the organisation (Van Hoye and Lievens, 2007). Its application, therefore, is not merely in supplying independently credible information about the potential employer (dependent on the reliability of the source) (Fisher et al., 1979), but also to discern organisational attractiveness and enabling insight into person-organisation fit.

The internet has given a new means of communicating this type of more personal information, and so word of mouth remains a significant tool for applicants. Organisations have attempted, with some success, to mimic the type of process through the development of employee testimonials on their websites (Fisher et al., 1979; Van Hoye and Lievens, 2007). However, its role as a source of information remains under-researched (Stoughton et al., 2015), although some have speculated as to its more significant role amongst experienced applicants who have wider networks they can draw upon (Searle, 2006).

Headhunters

Increasingly, third parties, such as headhunters, are becoming an important part of the recruitment process, especially for experienced staff. Shortages in key skill areas have created more opportunities for headhunters to use their in-depth knowledge of previous candidates to identify other potential candidates and provide shortlists for clients. This area is a key difference between experienced and inexperienced applicants. Given the bespoke nature of the process, it remains under-researched, with a fresh scrutiny of these processes because of calls for greater gender and ethnic diversity at the top of organisations (Doldor et al., 2016). We can, therefore, only speculate as to its role in the attraction process. However, those interested in the social process of recruitment need to pay more attention to the potentially negative impact these third parties can have on the recruitment relationship (Searle and Billsberry, 2011).

The Selection Process

The psychometric paradigm has long dominated research into the selection process. Seminal papers have identified and differentiated between the effectiveness of distinct selection tools. Amongst such research is the central role of intelligence testing as the best predictor of job performance, above that of personality assessment or value fit (Schmidt and Hunter, 1998). However, senior HR professionals either challenge or remain unaware of such clear scientific findings (Rynes et al., 2007). Indeed, recent attention has shown a significant gap between research evidence and HR practices regarding selection tools. We now explore distinct tools commonly used in selection processes, including ability tests, work sample tests or situational judgement tests, integrity tests, interviews and personality assessment.

Cognitive Ability Tests

In examining the evidence from this psychometric perspective, cognitive ability testing remains one of the most effective means of selection to enhance job performance (for example, Robertson and Smith, 2001). The job performance validity of cognitive ability tests alone is around 0.51, but taken together with structured interviews, in which the format of the interview is focused on the job criterion, it increases to 0.63. Ability tests assess the maximum performance a candidate can currently achieve, as such they are timed tests, which comprise multiple-choice items based on abstracted situations, focusing on key skills, such as numerical and comprehension skills. Test developers have produced an array of different instruments designed for distinct job levels, such as graduate, managerial, clerical or craft apprentices. While evidence shows that these tests can differentiate between individuals, concerns remain as to the lower performance of ethnic minority groups (Bobko et al., 1999; Schmitt and Mills, 2001). In addition, evidence suggests that the shift of many of these tools onto internet delivery platforms may serve to further advantage those who are more familiar with this new technology, such as young, more highly educated, white males (Lin et al., 2015; Sanchiz et al., 2017; van Deursen and Helsper, 2015). As selection processes potentially become more global in their applicant pool, care must be taken to ensure that the best candidate is indeed identified, and that build-it biases do not continue to result in the false rejection of otherwise effective candidates.

The link between assessment and job performance has been identified as complex, but given the more dynamic nature of job roles and the aforementioned compromised criterion space, how certain can we be that the ability tools chosen can effectively differentiate and identify the best candidates? A factor in answering this question concerns what ability tests actually measure. Cognitive ability can be categorised into two distinct elements: fluid intelligence, which involves the application of reasoning skills into novel situations; and crystallised intelligence, which focuses on more culturally specific reasoning skills. An instrument may measure either or both dimensions. Much has been written about how tests are constructed and the problems associated with different development techniques (Searle, 2003). Kline (1993) has long highlighted the role of statistical convenience rather than the underlying rationale in determining item inclusion. Frequently, such measures are validated against other general intelligence instruments rather than through external work-related outcomes, such as on-the-job performance. In addition, the scores obtained from any assessment instrument are only part of the answer, because any result has to be assessed against the relevant norm group in order to interpret its meaning. Test manuals provide details of these norm groups, which should reflect the applicant population in terms of ethnicity, age, gender etc., however, this might not always be possible, particularly where selection is being used as a tool to increase employee heterogeneity and so neither similar composition nor job performance data exists.

There are three important factors which may influence, to different degrees, the effective measurement of ability. One may be the failure of tests to actually measure fluid intelligence and instead concentrate on the assessment of more culturally specific crystallised knowledge. Research consistently shows minority group members underperform on ability tests, particularly when their identity becomes salient (Casad & Bryant, 2016; Kalokerinos et al., 2014). There is a significant body of research showing differences across race (Chan, 1997; Chan and Schmitt, 2002; Chan et al., 1997; Ryan, 2001). In addition, demographic studies suggest that assessment problems also emerge amongst older applicants (Bertolino et al., 2013; Rau et al., 2014), who are more likely to use culturally specific crystallised skills in their problem-solving (Horn and Noll, 1994). Finally, while having a good brain permits intelligent performance, it does not dictate it (Hunt, 1999), and motivation to perform to your maximum remains a central underlying component in any assessment (Goff and Ackerman, 1992). Some argue that the impact of these motivational differences is so significant that its elimination could reduce race-related cognitive ability test differences (Ployhart and Ehrhart, 2002). Motivation remains an important but under-researched component to understanding the effectiveness and fairness of assessment.

Attention has shifted onto the applicant and the exploration of perception in shaping organisational attractiveness and performance motivation. Including information, such as the use of ability tests within selection procedures, has been found to raise suspicion and reduce organisational attractiveness for some applicants, regardless of their personal experience of these tools (Reeve and Schultz, 2004). While including test validity data can positively enhance and alter such perceptions (Holtz et al., 2005), evidence shows that accumulated historical experiences of certain groups, such as black applicants, may significantly reduce the effort they extend in recruitment and selection because they simply do not believe they will be offered a job even if they score well (Sanchez et al., 2000). The complexity of these disparate group differences remains a significant research topic if we are to improve the effectiveness and ultimately the fairness and veracity of these tools. This issue has clear and important society-wide applications too, given growing concerns about radicalisation.

Work Sample

One of the central tools that appears to reduce the negative impact for ethnic minority groups, and are perceived to have higher face validity, are work sample or situational judgement tests (Lievens and Klimoski, 2001; Rockstuhl, et al., 2015; Schmitt and Mills, 2001). These selection instruments offer a more complex assessment focusing on applicants' work based judgements, abilities and behaviours. Used alone in selection, they show consistently high job performance validity (0.56), which increases when coupled with ability tests (0.60) (Robertson and Smith, 2001). One of the central ways these tests differ from ability tools is through the contextualisation of the content into a specific work situation. These tools can, therefore, provide data on the applicants' specific skills, but also provide an insight into their cultural fit. This is an important development as increasingly there is a shift in emphasis, particularly within key professions, such as medicine, away from *what* is done, i.e. skill and ability assessment, towards an inclusion of *how* such job tasks are performed. With the incremental validity these instruments provide, above that of cognitive and personality testing (Chan and Schmitt, 2002; Clevenger et al., 2001), their ease and cost-effective delivery through the internet, they are rapidly replacing the multiple-assessor, multiple-task approach of the assessment centre or being used as a pre-screening devise. This type of assessment provides a strong fidelity or relationship between the assessment and the actual work, which appeals to both applicant and recruiter (Kanning et al., 2006).

Work sampling is, however, not without its drawbacks. These types of instruments can require more in-depth job knowledge than those required to develop more generic ability tests. As a result, despite their obvious utility benefits, they can be time consuming and costly to produce, offering limited transportability to different contexts. Given their contextualised skill assessment, they may be difficult to use with applicants who have limited work experience, such as graduates. Of more concern, however, is the increase in response bias or faking found with these tools. Despite the ease with which faking can occur, altering the instruction from behavioural-tendency (e.g. what are you most likely to do?) to knowledge-based formats (e.g. what is the best answer?) can help reduce it. This shift also adversely affects the racial discrimination of such tools (Nguyen et al., 2005). Finally, evidence suggests a higher level of shrinkage found in these tests over more generic ability tools (Siegel and Bergman, 1975). However, this latter issue might be because of an erroneous assumption that jobs are static. These tools provide not just an assessment of how and what a candidate can perform, but they also contain job preview information for applicants enabling them to make more informed career decisions.

Integrity Tests

A more recent introduction into the suite of tools available to recruiters is integrity testing. Together with ability testing it shows high job performance validity (0.65) (Robertson and Smith, 2001) and the ability to predict undesirable work behaviours, such as theft, absence or other behaviour which takes advantage of the employer without discriminating against ethnic minority groups (Ones and Viswesvaran, 1998; Van Iddekinge et al., 2012). However, the reason we include them here is that they typify the gap between theory and practice through their limited adoption in recruitment despite strong research. Integrity tests are a tool in which the potential for faking is high because of the clear social cues about the preferred response in a hiring context. Therefore, including integrity tests as a tool can reduce both their accuracy and value and raise questions for candidates about the organisation's ethos. They are likely to be found in situations where their inclusion may act as a legal safety net for employers should a violation occur. They raise interesting questions about the perceived trustworthiness of staff.

Personality Tests

Personality testing is an increasingly common technique used to discern candidates' behavioural style and disposition. Its predictive validity varies considerably (Barrick and Mount, 1991; Gardner and Martinko, 1996). Its job performance validity is, however, quite low, between 0.21 (Schmidt et al., 1984) to 0.40 (Robertson and Smith, 2001). There has been an ongoing debate within the literature concerning the breadth of factors, or bandwidth, which personality can be meaningfully reduced to. Some favour a multiple factorial design of tools going into 30 factors (although there can be limited agreement as to their labelling), while others argue for the role of five main dimensions, including: openness, conscientiousness, extraversion, agreeableness and neuroticism (Costa and McCrea, 1985). A further contention concerns the prominence of one dimension, conscientiousness, as the main predictor of job performance validity (0.22). The increasing use of meta-analytic studies ensures this debate will continue.

Popular personality tools continue to divert into novel fields, especially those related to candidates' derailment potential (Hogan, 1992) and the more nefarious dimensions of personality (O'Boyle et al., 2012) or differentiating between behavioural styles and motivation to deploy them (Saville, 2006).

As with other psychometric tools, they discriminate unfavourably for ethnic minorities; however, through contextualising them to work, some of these differences can be reduced (Holtz et al., 2005).

Interviews

Interviews remain one of the most common methods of selection, although their criterion-related validity can vary widely from 0.19 (Schmidt and Radar, 1999) to 0.62 (Wiesner and Cronshaw, 1988). Bias and discrimination remain ongoing concerns with this selection tool (Billsberry, 2008). Researchers have identified a wide range of biases, including race, gender, appearance, age, attitude, non-verbal behaviour, physical setting and job-market situation (Avery and Campion, 1982). On average, white applicants perform 0.25 SD above those from ethnic groups, although the magnitude of difference can be reduced using structured formats with recruiters asking pre-defined questions and assessing responses against pre-defined responses (Huffcutt and Roth, 1998). This type of structured approach can, however, place interviewing on a par with cognitive tests alone (0.51) (Robertson and Smith, 2001), reducing the quality of the interaction to a verbally administered ability test.

Herriot (1993) identified the interview as the most important social process tool in an assessment, representing an opportunity for both parties to meet and formally assess each other. This perspective has received further corroboration by recognising the role of recruiters in influencing the decision-making of applicants (Carless, 2003; Herriot, 1993). Researchers have found that the behaviour of interviewers significantly influences the attractiveness of the organisation and the acceptance of job offers (Carless and Imber, 2007; [Other sources]). In particular, recruiter characteristics such as empathy, friendliness, positive affect and showing of interest have been found to have a positive impact (Chapman et al., 2005). However, attention has also considered how applicants might use impression management with interviewers (Chen et al., 2010) and in assessment centres (Klehe et al., 2014).

There can be important cultural differences in how interviews are used in selection. For example, French recruiters favour them by involving everyone who would work with the applicant, compared to a more Anglo-American approach to one or two interviews (Shackleton and Newell, 1994). Increasingly, some Anglo-American organisations, such as Google, are favouring a multiple-interview format with talks ascending right up to the director level for even fairly low-level vacancies. This reflects an increased attention on organisational and employee fit. These preferences as to the interview highlight both different approaches to selection and also how candidates' *expectations* of the process might vary. This is also an increasing use of technology to allow an internationalisation of applicant pools (Baker and Demps II, 2009).

Assessment Centres

Assessment centres remain the most in-depth form of selection, comprising multiple exercises and assessors evaluating multiple criteria. They involve many of the selection tools, including psychometric tests, interviews and more work sample-type exercises, such as group exercises, presentations, role plays or in-tray exercises. These approaches are more commonly deployed for managerial and graduate level vacancies, although they have wider scale applications. However, their high development and running costs can focus their use on high-volume and -level vacancies. Ongoing debate surrounds what is being measured in this topic and how it can be improved and made more ethical (Lievens et al., 2009; Rupp, 2009). The process offers many advantages, allowing potential observation in a far fairer way in which the candidate can preview the roles involved in the job and be seen by multiple assessors.

Advanced Technology

The Applicant Tracking System (ATS) is one of the earliest and most widely adopted advanced technologies in the recruitment and selection process. This system efficiently processes hundreds or even thousands of job applicants' resumes, helping employers identify the best candidates for a position by using algorithms to sort and prioritise them based on specific criteria. Its main focus is on recruitment and talent acquisition, rather than broader employee management and task assignment. According to (Laumer et al. 2015), ATS significantly reduces the recruitment cycle time, enhancing employer efficiency. A data-driven approach not only boosts efficiency but also effectiveness. A 2017 PwC report indicates that such algorithms, drawing on data from past recruitment decisions, have enabled L'Oréal recruiters to handle the high volume of approximately 5 million annual visitors to their job site more efficiently (Charlier & Kloppenburg, 2017). Additionally, advancements in technology have facilitated the use of other tools for assessment in selection processes. For instance, Laumer, Eckhard, and Weitzel (2012) demonstrated that online gaming could be incorporated into the recruitment process as a part of self-assessment, potentially enhancing applicants' motivation to pursue specific jobs. While some researchers believe this approach reduces bias and improves fairness and transparency, this is a topic of ongoing debate and will be explored further in the subsequent section.

Artificial intelligence (AI) has revolutionised talent selection through the automation and alleged improvement in decision accuracy. AI is employed at various stages of the selection process, including resume screening, assessment analysis and interview evaluations (Campion & Campion, 2024; Stone et.al ., 2024). During the resume screening phase, AI can analyse the content of candidate CVs identifying those whose skills and experiences align with job descriptions (Chen, 2022; Campion & Campion, 2024). AI can scrutinise the words used in CVs, using natural language processing (NLP), a method specifically for analysing text data, to match them with the job description or historical hiring data provided by the employer (Campion & Campion, 2024). From the applicants' perspective, a new use of AI in recruiting process helps to identify jobs that meet their interest and needs (Stone et al., 2024). The system can then provide recommendations in real time, scan applicants' CVs and make recommendations.

In the assessment phase, AI can be utilised to evaluate applicants' skills and personalities using evidence from games, simulations and problem-solving tasks (Stone et al., 2024). Research has also demonstrated AI's capability in analysing applicants' emotions (McStay, 2020) and their facial expression (Stone et al., 2024), analysing applicants' interview videos to provide insights into attributes including integrity or personality (Suen, Hung, and Lin, 2020). These applications of AI can significantly reduce the workload for human HR personnel and are argued to improve the accuracy of recruitment and selection decisions. However, despite its growing popularity, several critical concerns have been raised and will be explored in the subsequent section.

Emergent Issues and Concerns

In this final section we reflect on some overarching concerns that have emerged from exploring the distinct attraction and selection tools.

Faking and Culture

Internet-based testing has enabled cost-effective, high-volume administration of these tools across wider geographical areas. While increasing applicant pools, this application has raised concerns about levels of cheating and faking. Recognising the high stakes involved, the temptation and reward for cheating is high. The increasing proliferation of non-supervised testing has focused recruiters' and test developers' attention on how both to identify and reduce its impact. Solutions include: increasingly sophisticated candidate verification, ranging from photographic to iris recognition systems; two-tier administration with the same form of tests administered in a controlled setting later and the results compared using sophisticated item response and item generation systems, which ensure that while the content of the test is the same, the items are not; additional in-test measurements, such as the applicant's latency of response, which increases with faking. All of these techniques strive to preserve the benefits of large-scale, un-supervised testing while minimising fraud.

However, there is a sensitive, less-discussed aspect of cheating and faking linked to cultural differences. With globalisation, applicant pools from various cultures have different responses to selection processes. In some cultures, using all available means is expected, including having others take tests or claiming others' work. These behaviours shows complex cultural norms around the capacity, willingness and opportunity to fake. For example, in Japan or Greece, where a more socially conditioned response is expected, the item 'I'm always willing to admit when I make mistakes' might elicit very different responses in a high-stakes selection context compared to the UK, where commonly used fake-checking includes items in a personality test. Thus, issues such as honesty and faking can be viewed as socially constructed. Until we have more insight into how cultural dimensions that might colour perceptions of honesty and integrity within selection contexts, we should be cautious of the acceptance of global behavioural dimensions.

Global Systems

A consequence and tension produced by the increasing internationalisation of recruitment and selection is the need to balance systems that can be used across multiple countries with the recognition of local particularities (Schuler et al., 1993). These dilemmas include not only the aforementioned tensions pertinent to assessment centres, but wider issues such as the differences in cultural values, such as individualism and collectivism, power distance and uncertainty avoidance (Han et al., 2016; Ryan et al., 1999), but also the value and acceptance of distinct characteristics and criteria, such as explicit proven job experience in Australia, Canada, Germany and the US, while innate potential and team working is preferred in South Korea, Taiwan and Japan (Huo et al., 2002; Von Glinow et al., 2002).

In addition, the acceptance and value of these multiple-tool selection processes vary across different cultures (Bartram, 2013). While there are no studies that have examined the generalisability of selection procedures criterion-related globally, evidence suggests the universality of selection exercises may be limited. For example, a study on assessment centres in Europe and Japan found support for group exercises as a predictor of future performance amongst Japanese supervisors, but not for presentations (Lievens et al., 2003).

Older Workers

Demographic changes in many countries have altered employment patterns with older workers, through economic necessity or choice, continuing or seeking to re-enter the labour market. The issues of attraction and selection of older workers remains under-researched (Rau et al., 2014). This emergent topic will create further changes with work shifting to a more part-time occupation, becoming just part of how older adults spend their time. In addition, this might influence the criterion space, forcing more organisation-person fit dimensions to the fore as social and esteem requirements of work can become more prominent (Hedge et al., 2006; Kanfer and Ackerman, 2004; Ng and Feldman, 2013). Limited attention has focused on the validity of the assessment and measurement of older workers, but this is changing. Older workers can bring far more knowledge than younger counterparts to a workplace, they can compensate for potential declines through adopting new strategies to optimise their existing skills and abilities (Kanfer and Ackerman, 2004) and, thus, they may, in fact, be doing things far smarter than their younger colleagues. Research is challenging the prevailing narrative of older workers as a disadvantage for employers (Ng and Feldman, 2013). This is likely to be a growth topic in the future.

Trust

At the pre-entry stage, applicants establish their initial trust perceptions through direct and indirect interactions with the hiring organisation and its agents, with such perceptions changing or enduring through subsequent selection experiences (Celani et al., 2008; Klotz et al., 2013; Searle and Billsberry, 2011). Little research has investigated the impact of trust and its breach during recruitment and selection and the role of applicant propensity to trust (Klotz et al., 2013). Research is also needed to explore the factors influencing job applicant decisions (Harold et al., 2016).

Bias and Other Ethical Issues in AI

Inherent in the use of advanced technology, such as AI or ATS, are questions of the quality of the data and the illusion of enhanced objectivity (Scholz, 2019; Davenport, 2014). However, research and practical applications indicate differing results arising from bias in algorithm-driven decisions. Contrary to the belief that computers are more 'bias-free' than humans, bias and discrimination are still reported where automation system are the decision-maker (Lavanchy et al., 2023). For example, Amazon's AI recruiting tool showed gender bias through its training on male-dominated resumes, with women's resumes less likely to be shortlisted (*The Guardian*, 2018). Similarly, a CNN 2023 investigation revealed gender-based job advertisement targeting on Facebook skewing the visibility of certain job advertisements in France and the Netherlands, perpetuating gender imbalances. Despite technology-based recruitment processes' potential to increase objectivity, instead, these merely replicated existing biases because of reliance on biased input data. Köchling and Wehner (2020) highlighted that despite wishing to increase their recruitment's objectivity, instead they resulted in unfair treatment of certain groups, implicit discrimination and unfairness.

Further Critique and Areas for Future Research

The implementation of AI in recruitment and selection can offer some advantages, such as reducing time in the screening process, expanding assessment process and increased efficiency in terms of time and resources (Stone et al., 2024). However, its implementation also generate criticisms and challenge, arising from concerns about bias and fairness, privacy issues, reduced human skills because of reliance on digitisation and inclusivity problems.

The potential for bias remains one of the most significant concerns of AI in selection processes. AI often relies on historical hiring data, which may embed implicit human biases (Scholz, 2019). Without careful design, AI systems can simply perpetuate or even amplify these biases. For example, if a dataset predominantly features successful applicants from specific demographic characteristics, the AI learns to unfavourably score applicants who do not fit the previous profile with discrimination against under-represented groups (Köchling and Wehner, 2020). These errors arise from flawed training data (Andrieux et al., 2024). Therefore, investigating the conditions to create transparent and accountable AI systems is crucial to addressing these concerns.

Accountability and privacy are further concerns from implementing an AI-enabled hiring system. Andrieux et al. (2024) reviewed possible ethical consideration, highlighting the importance of understanding whether the data used are sufficiently free from bias, whether adequate feedback is provided to candidates or whether they are treated equally. AI systems are often referred to as 'black boxes' (Moore and Joyce, 2020), with opaque decision-making that makes it difficult for candidates to understand or challenge hiring decisions that AI makes (Rahman, 2021; Langer and König, 2023). An AI application in selection often involves collecting and analysing substantial amounts of personal data about candidates, raising significant privacy issues, particularly if sensitive data (such as social media activity or biometric data) has been used without explicit consent (Campion & Campion, 2024). This overdependence on technology might result in a workforce that apparently excels in some traits but lacks diversity in their thought and innovation.

An experiment involving 694 professionals found that recruiters trust human advice more, particularly where AI recommendations are inconsistent (Lacroux and Martin-Lacroux, 2022). Applicants' perceptions of the recruitment process are also changed, with automated processes seen as impersonal or unwelcoming, deterring talented individuals from applying for or accepting job offers. Moreover, where applicants perceive that selection processes are unfair or biased, the organisation's reputation and employer brand is harmed. Most studies of AI have used cross-sectional methods, with little longitudinal research. Given the range of concerns, it is crucial for organisations to approach the integration of AI into selection processes with caution. Ongoing research, regular audits and updates of AI systems, along with transparent communication and ethical guidelines, are essential to address these challenges effectively. Engaging with diverse stakeholders, including ethicists, legal experts, technologists and representatives of potential employee groups will be key to refining AI applications in hiring to benefit all parties involved.

References

Abraham, M., Kaliannan, M., Mohan, A. V. and Thomas, S. (2015) 'A Review of SMEs Recruitment and Selection Dilemma: Finding a 'Fit'. *The Journal of Developing Areas* 49 (5), 335–342.

Allen, D., Biggane, J., Pitts, M., Otondo, R. and Van Scotter, J. (2013) 'Reactions to Recruitment Web Sites: Visual and Verbal Attention, Attraction, and Intentions to Pursue Employment.' *Journal of Business and Psychology* 28 (3), 263–285.

Anderson, N., Lievens, F. and van Dam, K. (2004) 'Future Perspectives on Employee Selection: Key Directions for Future Research and Practice'. *Applied Psychology: An International Review* 53 (4), 487–501.

Andrieux, P., Johnson, R. D., Sarabadani, J. and Van Slyke, C. (2024) 'Ethical Considerations of Generative AI-Enabled Human Resource Management'. *Organizational Dynamics*, 53(1). doi:10.1016/j.orgdyn.2024.101032.

Ashforth, B. E., Harrison, S. H. and Sluss, D. M. (2014) 'Becoming. The Interaction of Socialization and Identity in Organizations Over Time', in A. J. Shipp and Y. Fried (Eds.), *Time and Work, Vol. 1: How Time Impacts Individuals*, vol. 1. Hoboken, NJ: Taylor and Francis, pp. 11–39.

Avery, D. R., Volpone, S. D., Stewart, R. W., Luksyte, A., Hernandes, M., Mckay, P. F. and Hebl, M. R. (2013) 'Examining the Draw of Diversity: How Diversity Climate Perceptions Affect Job-Pursuit Intentions'. *Human Resource Management* 52 (2), 175–194.

Avery, R. D. and Campion, J. E. (1982) 'The Employment Interview: A Summary and Review of Research'. *Personnel Psychology* 35, 281–322.

Backhaus, K., & Tikoo, S. (2004). Conceptualizing and researching employer branding. *Career Development International, 9*(5), 501–517.

Baker, E. and Demps II, J. (2009) 'Videoconferencing as a Tool for Recruiting and Interviewing'. *Journal of Business & Economics Research* 7 (10), 9.

Bangerter, A., Roulin, N. and König, C. J. (2012) 'Personnel Selection as a Signaling Game'. *Journal of Applied Psychology* 97 (4), 719–738.

Banks, G. C., Kepes, S., Joshi, M. and Seers, A. (2015) 'Social Identity and Applicant Attraction: Exploring the Role of Multiple Levels of Self'. *Journal of Organizational Behavior 37*(3), 326–345.

Barber, A. E. and Roehling, M. V. (1993) 'Job Postings and the Decision to Interview: A Verbal Protocol Analysis'. *Journal of Applied Psychology* 78 (5), 845.

Barrick, M. R. and Mount, M. K. (1991) 'The Big Five Personality Dimensions and Job Performance: A Meta-Analysis'. *Personnel Psychology* 44, 1–26.

Bartram, D. (2013). 'Scalar Equivalence of OPQ32'. *Journal of Cross-Cultural Psychology* 44 (1), 61–83.

Baum, M. and Kabst, R. (2014) 'The Effectiveness of Recruitment Advertisements and Recruitment Websites: Indirect and Interactive Effects on Applicant Attraction'. *Human Resource Management* 53 (3), 353–378.

Bertolino, M., Truxillo, D. M. and Fraccaroli, F. (2013) 'Age Effects on Perceived Personality and Job Performance'. *Journal of Managerial Psychology* 28 (7/8), 867–885.

Billsberry, J. (2008) *Experiencing Recruitment and Selection*. London: John Wiley & Sons.

Bobko, P., Roth, P. L. and Potosky, D. (1999) 'Derivation and Implications of a Meta-Analytic Matrix Incorporating Cognitive Ability, Alternative Predictors, and Job Performance'. *Personnel Psychology* 52 (3), 561–590.

Borman, W. C., Hanson, M. A. and Hedge, J. W. (1997) 'Personnel Selection'. *Annual Review of Psychology* 48 (1), 299–337.

Bowen, D. E., Ledford G. E. and Nathan, B. R. (1991) 'Hiring for the Organization, Not the Job'. *Academy of Management Executive* 5 (4), 35–51.

Bowers, K. S. (1973) 'Situationism in Psychology: An Analysis and Critique'. *Psychological Review* 80, 307–336.

Breaugh, J. A. (2008) 'Employee Recruitment: Current Knowledge and Important Areas for Future Research'. *Human Resource Management Review* 18 (3), 103–118.

Campion, E. D. and Campion, M. A. (2024) 'Impact of Machine Learning on Personnel Selection'. *Organizational Dynamics* 53, 101035.

Carless, S. A. (2003) 'A Longitudinal Study of Applicant Reactions to Selection Procedures and Job and Organisational Characteristics'. *International Journal of Selection and Assessment* 11, 345–351.

Carless, S. A. (2006) 'Applicant Reactions to Multiple Selection Procedures for the Police Force'. *Applied Psychology* 55 (2), 145–167.

Carless, S. A. and Imber, A. (2007) 'The Influence of Perceived Interviewer and Job and Organizational Characteristics on Applicant Attraction and Job Choice Intentions: The Role of Applicant Anxiety'. *International Journal of Selection and Assessment* 15 (4), 359–371.

Casad, B. J. and Bryant, W. J. (2016) 'Addressing Stereotype Threat is Critical to Diversity and Inclusion in Organizational Psychology'. *Frontiers in Psychology* 7, 1–18.

Celani, A., Deutsch-Salamon, S. and Singh, P. (2008) 'In Justice We Trust: A Model of the Role of Trust in the Organization in Applicant Reactions to the Selection Process'. *Human Resource Management Review* 18 (2), 63–76.

Chan, D. and Schmitt, N. (2002) 'Situational Judgment and Job Performance'. *Human Performance* 15, 233–254.

Chan, D., Schmitt, N., de Shin, R. P., Clause, C. S. and Delbridge, K. (1997) 'Can Racial Difference in Cognitive Test Performance Be Reduced by Presenting Problems in a Social Context?' *Journal of Applied Psychology* 82 (2), 300–310.

Chapman, D. S., Uggerslev, K. L., Carroll, S. A., Piasentin, K. A. and Jones, D. A. (2005) 'Applicant Attraction to Organizations and Job Choice: A Meta-Analytic Review of the Correlates of Recruiting Outcomes'. *Journal of Applied Psychology* 90 (5), 928–944.

Charlier, R. and Kloppenburg, S. (2017) 'Artificial Intelligence in HR: A No-Brainer'. *PwC*. Available at http://www.pwc.nl/nl/assets/documents/artificial-intelligence-in-hr-a-no-brainer.pdf (Accessed 10 October 2021).

Chen, C.-C., Wen-Fen Yang, I. and Lin, W.-C. (2010) 'Applicant Impression Management in Job Interview: The Moderating Role of Interviewer Affectivity'. *Journal of Occupational and Organizational Psychology* 83 (3), 739–757.

Chen, D. (2022). Artificial intelligence (AI) in employee selection: How algorithm-based decision aids influence recruiters' decision-making in resume screening [Doctoral dissertation, University of Texas at Arlington]. UTA ResearchCommons. https://mavmatrix.uta.edu/management_dissertations/71

Chen, Z. (2023). Collaboration among recruiters and artificial intelligence: removing human prejudices in employment. *Cognition, Technology & Work, 25*(1), 135–149.

Chiavaroli, N., Le, L., Parker-Newlyn, L., & Pywell, S. (2024). Should we extend the currency of cognitive ability test scores? Considerations from construct, equity, and psychometric perspectives in medical selection. *International Journal of Selection and Assessment, 32*(1), 138–148.

CIPD (2015) *Resourcing and Talent Planning 2015*. Available at https://www.cipd.co.uk/knowledge/strategy/resourcing/surveys (Accessed 18 May 2017).

Clevenger, J., Pereira, G. M., Wiechmann, D., Schmitt, N. and Harvey, V. S. (2001) 'Incremental Validity of Situational Judgment Tests'. *Journal of Applied Psychology* 86, 410–417.

Costa, P. T. and McCrea, R. R. (1985) *The NEO Personality Inventory Manual.* Odessa, FL: Psychological Assessment Resources.

Cropanzano, R., Bowen, D. E. and Gilliland, S. W. (2007) 'The Management of Organizational Justice'. *Academy of Management Perspective* 21, 34–49.

Davenport, T. (2014) 'How Strategists Use 'Big Data' to Support Internal Business Decisions, Discovery and Production'. *Strategy & Leadership* 42 (4), 45–50.

Derous, E., Pepermans, R. and Ryan, A. M. (2017) 'Ethnic Discrimination during Résumé Screening: Interactive Effects of Applicants' Ethnic Salience with Job Context'. *Human Relations, 70*(7), 860–882.

Dineen, B. R., Ash, S. R. and Noe, R. A. (2002) 'A Web of Applicant Attraction: Person-Organization Fit in the Context of Web-Based Recruitment'. *Journal of Applied Psychology* 87, 723–734.

Doldor, E., Sealy, R. and Vinnicombe, S. (2016) 'Accidental Activists: Headhunters as Marginal Diversity Actors in Institutional Change towards More Women on Boards'. *Human Resource Management Journal* 26 (3), 285–303.

Fisher, C. D., Ilgen, D. R. and Hoyer, W. D. (1979) 'Source Credibility, Information Favorability, and Job Offer Acceptance'. *Academy of Management Journal* 22, 94–103.

Fisher, S. L., Bonaccio, S. and Connelly, C. E. (2024) 'AI-Based Tools in Selection: Considering the Impact on Applicants with Disabilities'. *Organizational Dynamics* 53, 101036.

Gardner, W. L. and Martinko, M. J. (1996) 'Using the Myers-Briggs Type Indicator to Study Managers: A Literature Review and Research Agenda'. *Journal of Management* 22 (1), 45–83.

Gilliland, S. W. (1995) 'Fairness from the Applicants' Perspective: Reactions to Employee Selection Procedures'. *International Journal of Selection and Assessment* 3, 11–19.

Goff, M. and Ackerman, P. L. (1992) 'Typical Intellectual Engagement'. *Journal of Educational Psychology* 84 (4), 537–552.

Guardian (2018) Amazon ditched AI recruiting tool that favored men for technical jobs. Available at: https://www.theguardian.com/technology/2018/oct/10/amazon-hiring-ai-gender-bias-recruiting-engine [Accessed March 10, 2023].

Guest, D. E., Sanders, K., Rodrigues, R. and Oliveira, T. (2021) 'Signalling Theory as a Framework for Analysing Human Resource Management Processes and Integrating Human Resource Attribution Theories: A Conceptual Analysis and Empirical Exploration'. *Human Resource Management Journal* 31 (3), 796–818.

Han, J. and Ling, J. (2016) 'Emotional Appeal in Recruitment Advertising and Applicant Attraction: Unpacking National Cultural Differences'. *Journal of Organizational Behavior* 37 (8), 1202–1223.

Harold, C. M., Holtz, B. C., Griepentrog, B. K., Brewer, L. M. and Marsh, S. M. (2016) 'Investigating the Effects of Applicant Justice Perceptions on Job Offer Acceptance'. *Personnel Psychology* 69 (1), 199–227.

Hausknecht, J. P., Day, D. V. and Thomas, S. C. (2004) 'Applicant Reactions to Selection Procedures: An Updated Model and Meta-Analysis'. *Personnel Psychology* 57 (3), 639–683.

Hedge, J. W., Borman, W. C. and Lammlein, S. E. (Eds.). (2006) *The Aging Workforce.* Washington, DC: American Psychological Association.

Herriot, P. (1987) 'The Selection Interview', in P. Warr (Ed.), *Psychology at Work*, pp. 139–158. London: Penguin Books.

Herriot, P. (1993) 'A Paradigm Bursting at the Seams'. *Journal of Organizational Behavior* 14, 371–375.

Hogan, R. (1992) *Hogan Personality Inventory Manual.* Tulsa, OK: Hogan Assessment Systems.

Holm, A. B. (2012) 'E-recruitment: Towards an Ubiquitous Recruitment Process and Candidate Relationship Management'. *Zeitschrift Für Personal forschung* 26 (3), 241–259.

Holtz, B. C., Ployhart, R. E. and Dominguez, A. (2005) 'Testing the Rules of Justice: The Effects of Frame-of-Reference and Pre-Test Validity Information on Personality Test Responses and Test Perceptions'. *International Journal of Selection and Assessment* 13 (1), 75–86.

Horn, J. L. and Noll, J. (1994) 'A System for Understanding Cognitive Capabilities: A Theory and the Evidence on Which It Is Based', in D. Detterman (Ed.), *Current Topics in Human Intelligence,* vol. 4, *Theories in Intelligence.* Norwood, NJ: Ablex.

Hough, L. M. and Oswald, F. L. (2000) Personnel Selection: Looking toward the Future – Remembering the Past'. *Annual Review of Psychology* 51, 631–664.

Huffcutt, A. I. and Roth, P. L. (1998) 'Racial Group Differences in Employment Interview Evaluations'. *Journal of Applied Psychology* 83 (2), 179–189.

Hunt, E. (1999) Intelligence and Human Resources: Past, Present and Future, in P. L. Ackerman, P. C. Kyllonen and R. D. Roberts (Eds.), *Learning and Individual Difference: Process, Trait and Content Determinants.* Washington, DC: American Psychological Association.

Huo, Y. P., Huang, H. J. and Napier, N. K. (2002) 'Divergence or Convergence: A Cross National Comparison of Personnel Selection Practices'. *Human Resource Management* 41, 31–44.

Imus, A. and Ryan, A. M. (2005) 'The Rigor and Relevance of the Applicant Reactions Literature'. In Evers, A., Anderson, N. and Voskuijl, O (Eds.), *Handbook of Industrial, Work, & Organizational Psychology*, pp. 291–305. Blackwell Publishing.

Ingold, J. and Valizade, D. (2017) 'Employers' Recruitment of Disadvantaged Groups: Exploring the Effect of Active Labour Market Programme Agencies as Labour Market Intermediaries'. *Human Resource Management Journal* 27 (4), 530–547.

Kalokerinos, E. K., von Hippel, C. and Zacher, H. (2014) 'Is Stereotype Threat a Useful Construct for Organizational Psychology Research and Practice?' *Industrial and Organizational Psychology* 7, 381–402.

Kanfer, R. and Ackerman, P. L. (2004) 'Aging, Adult Development, and Work Motivation'. *Academy of Management Review* 29 (3), 440–458.

Kanning, U.P., Grewe, K., Hollenberg, S. and Hadouch, M. (2006) 'From the Subjects' Point of View – Reactions to Different Types of Situational Judgment Items'. *European Journal of Psychological Assessment* 22, 168–176.

Kaplan, D. M., Berkley, R. A. and Fisher, J. E. (2016) 'Applicant Identity Congruence in Selection Decision-Making: Implications for Alejandro & Consuela'. *Human Resource Management* 55 (1), 39–51.

Klehe, U.-C., Kleinmann, M., Nieß, C. and Grazi, J. (2014) 'Impression Management Behavior in Assessment Centers: Artificial Behavior or Much Ado About Nothing?' *Human Performance* 27 (1), 1–24.

Kline, P. (1993). *Handbook of Psychological Testing.* London: Routledge.

Klotz, A. C., Veiga, S. P. D. M., Buckly, M. R. and Gavin, M. B. (2013) 'The Role of Trustworthiness in Recruitment and Selection: A Review and Guide for Future Research'. *Journal of Organizational Behavior* 34 (S1), S104–S119.

Köchling, A. and Wehner, M. C. (2020) 'Discriminated by an Algorithm: A Systematic Review of Discrimination and Fairness by Algorithmic Decision-Making in the Context of HR Recruitment and HR Development'. *Business Research* 13 (3), 795–848. doi:10.1007/s40685-020-00134-w.

Kohn, L. S. and Dipboye, R. L. (1998) 'The Effects of Interview Structure on Recruiting Outcomes'. *Journal of Applied Social Psychology* 28, 821–843.

Krahé, B. (1992) *Personality and Social Psychology*. London: Sage.

Lacroux, A., & Martin-Lacroux, C. (2022). Should I trust the artificial intelligence to recruit? Recruiters' perceptions and behavior when faced with algorithm-based recommendation systems during resume screening. *Frontiers in Psychology, 13*, 895997.

LaHuis, D. M., MacLane, C. N. and Schlessman, B. R. (2007) 'Do Applicants' Perceptions Matter? Investigating Reapplication Behavior Using Fairness Theory'. *International Journal of Selection and Assessment* 15 (4), 383–393.

Landis, R. S., Fogli, L. and Goldberg, E. (1998) 'Future-Oriented Job Analysis: A Description of the Process and Its Organizational Implications'. *International Journal of Selection and Assessment* 6 (3), 192–197.

Langer, M. and König, C. J. (2023) 'Introducing a Multi-Stakeholder Perspective on Opacity, Transparency and Strategies to Reduce Opacity in Algorithm-based Human Resource Management'. *Human Resource Management Review* 33 (1), 100881. doi:10.1016/j.hrmr.2021.100881.

Laumer, S., Eckhardt, A. and Weitzel, T. (2012) 'Online Gaming to Find a New Job–Examining Job Seekers' Intention to Use Serious Games as a Self-Assessment Tool'. *German Journal of Human Resource Management* 26 (3), 218–240.

Laumer, S., Maier, C., & Eckhardt, A. (2015). The impact of business process management and applicant tracking systems on recruiting process performance: an empirical study. *Journal of Business Economics, 85*, 421–453.

Lavanchy, M., Reichert, P., Narayanan, J. and Savani, K. (2023) 'Applicants' Fairness Perceptions of Algorithm-Driven Hiring Procedures'. *Journal of Business Ethics*. doi:10.1007/s10551-022-05320-w.

Levesque, L. L. (2005) 'Opportunistic Hiring and Employee Fit'. *Human Resource Management* 44 (3), 301–317.

Lievens, F. and Klimoski, R. J. (2001) 'Understanding the Assessment Centre Process: Where are We Now?' in C. L. Cooper and I. T. Robertson (Eds.), *International Review of Industrial and Organisational Psychology*, Vol. 16. Chichester: Wiley.

Lievens, F. and Slaughter, J. E. (2016) 'Employer Image and Employer Branding: What We Know and What We Need to Know'. *Annual Review of Organizational Psychology and Organizational Behavior* 3 (1), 407–440.

Lievens, F., Buyse, T. and Sackett, P. R. (2005) 'Retest Effects in Operational Selection Settings: Development and Test of a Framework'. *Personnel Psychology* 58, 981–1007.

Lievens, F., Harris, M.M., Van Keer, E. and Bisqueret, C. (2003) 'Predicting Cross-Cultural Training Performance: The Validity of Personality, Cognitive Ability, and Dimensions Measured by an Assessment Center and a Behavior Description Interview'. *Journal of Applied Psychology* 88 (3), 476.

Lievens, F., Tett, R. and Schleicher, D. J. (2009) 'Assessment Centers at the Crossroads: Toward a Reconceptualization of Assessment Center Exercises'. *Research in Personnel and Human Resources Management* 28, 99–152.

Lin, C., Atkin, D., Cappotto, C., Davis, C., Dean, J., Eisenbaum, J., House, K., Lange, R., Merceron, A., Metzger, J., Mitchum, A., Nicholls, H. and Vidican, S. (2015)

'Ethnicity, Digital Divides and Uses of the Internet for Health Information'. *Computers In Human Behavior* 51 (Pt A), 216–223.

Lopina, E. C., Rogelberg, S. G. and Howell, B. (2012) 'Turnover in Dirty Work Occupations: A Focus on Pre-Entry Individual Characteristics'. *Journal of Occupational and Organizational Psychology* 85 (2), 396–406.

Maurer, S. and Liu, Y. (2007) 'Developing Effective E-Recruiting Websites: Insights for Managers from Marketers'. *Business Horizons* 50 (4), 305–314.

McCarthy, J. M., Bauer, T. N., Truxillo, D. M., Anderson, N. R., Costa, A. C. and Ahmed, S. M. (2017) 'Applicant Perspectives During Selection'. *Journal of Management, 43*(6), 1693–1725.

McFarland, L. A. and Ployhart, R. E. (2015) 'Social Media: A Contextual Framework to Guide Research and Practice'. *Journal of Applied Psychology* 100 (6), 1653–1677.

McStay, A. (2020) 'Emotional AI, Soft Biometrics and the Surveillance of Emotional Life: An Unusual Consensus on Privacy'. *Big Data & Society, 7*(1) January–June 1–12.

Mischel W. (1968) *Personality and Assessment.* New York: Wiley. Republished 1996. Mahwah, NJ: Lawrence Erlbaum.

Moore, P. V. and Joyce, S. (2020) 'Black Box or Hidden Abode? The Expansion and Exposure of Platform Work Managerialism'. *Review of International Political Economy* 27 (4), 926–948. doi:10.1080/09692290.2019.1627569.

Motowidlo, S. J., & Kell, H. J. (2003). Job performance. *Handbook of psychology: Industrial and organizational psychology, 12*(4), 39–53.

Ng, T. W. H. and Feldman, D. C. (2013) 'A Meta-Analysis of the Relationships of Age and Tenure with Innovation-Related Behaviour'. *Journal of Occupational and Organizational Psychology* 86 (4), 585–616.

Nguyen, N. T., Biderman, M. D. and McDaniel, M. A. (2005) 'Effects of Response Instructions on Faking a Situational Judgment Test'. *International Journal of Selection and Assessment* 13 (4), 250–260.

Nikolaou, I. (2014) 'Social Networking Web Sites in Job Search and Employee Recruitment.' *International Journal of Selection and Assessment* 22 (2), 179–189.

O'Boyle Jr., E. H., Forsyth, D. R., Banks, G. C. and McDaniel, M. A. (2012) 'A Meta-Analysis of the Dark Triad and Work Behavior: A Social Exchange Perspective'. *Journal of Applied Psychology* 97 (3), 557– 579.

O'Reilly, C.A., Chatman, J. and Caldwell, D. F. (1991) 'People and Organizational Culture: A Profile Comparison Approach to Assessing Person-Organization Fit'. *Academy of Management Journal* 34, 487–516.

Ones, D. S. and Viswesvaran, C. (1998) 'Gender, Age, and Race Differences on Overt Integrity Tests: Results Across Four Large-Scale Job Applicant Data Sets'. *Journal of Applied Psychology* 83, 34–42.

Pessach, D., Singer, G., Avrahami, D., Ben-Gal, H. C., Shmueli, E. and Ben-Gal, I. (2020) 'Employees Recruitment: A Prescriptive Analytics Approach via Machine Learning and Mathematical Programming'. *Decision Support Systems* 134, 113290.

Pisano, S., Lepore, L. and Lamboglia, R. (2017) 'Corporate Disclosure of Human Capital via LinkedIn and Ownership Structure'. *Journal of Intellectual Capital* 18 (1), 102–127.

Ployhart, R. E. and Ehrhart, M. G. (2002) 'Modelling the Practical Effects of Applicant Reactions: Subgroup Differences in Test-Taking Motivation, Test Performance, and Selection Rates'. *International Journal of Selection and Assessment* 10 (4), 258–270.

Rahman, H. A. (2021) 'The Invisible Cage: Workers' Reactivity to Opaque Algorithmic Evaluations'. *Administrative Science Quarterly* 66 (4), 945–988. doi:10.1177/00018392211010118.

Rau, B. L., Adams, G. A., Yu, K. Y. T. and Cable, D. (2014) 'Recruiting Older Workers: Realities and Needs of the Future Workforce', in D. M. Cable (Ed.), *The Oxford Handbook of Recruitment*, pp. 88–109. Oxford: Oxford University Press.

Reeve, C. L. and Schultz, L. (2004) 'Job-seeker Reactions to Selection Process Information in Job Ads'. *International Journal of Selection and Assessment* 12 (4), 343–355.

Roberson, Q. M. (2019) 'Diversity in the Workplace: A Review, Synthesis, and Future Research Agenda'. *Annual Review of Organizational Psychology and Organizational Behaviour* 6, 69–88.

Robertson, I. T. and Smith, M. (2001) 'Personnel Selection'. *Journal of Occupational and Organizational Psychology* 74, 441–472.

Robertson, I. T., Iles, P. A., Gratton, L. and Sharpley, D. S. (1991) 'The Impact of Personnel Selection and Assessment Methods on Candidates'. *Human Relations* 44, 963–982.

Rockstuhl, T., Ang, S., Ng, K.-Y., Lievens, F. and Van Dyne, L. (2015) 'Putting Judging Situations into Situational Judgment Tests: Evidence from Intercultural Multimedia SJTs'. *Journal of Applied Psychology* 100 (2), 464.

Rupp, D. E. (2009) 'Guidelines and Ethical Considerations for Assessment Center Operations'. *International Journal of Selection and Assessment* 17, 243–254.

Russell, S. and Brannan, M. J. (2016) 'Getting the Right People on the Bus': Recruitment, Selection and Integration for the Branded Organization'. *European Management Journal* 34 (2), 114–124.

Ryan, A. M. (2001) 'Explaining the Black-White Test Score Gap: The Role of Test Perceptions'. *Human Performance* 14 (1), 45–75.

Ryan, A. M. and Derous, E. (2016) 'Highlighting Tensions in Recruitment and Selection Research and Practice'. *International Journal of Selection and Assessment* 24 (1), 54–62.

Ryan, A. M., McFarland, L., Baron, H. and Page, R. (1999) 'An International Look at Selection Practices: Nation and Culture as Explanations for Variability in Practice'. *Personnel Psychology* 52, 359–391.

Ryan, A. M., Sacco, J. M., McFarland, L. A. and Kriska, S. D. (2000) 'Applicant Self-Selection: Correlates of Withdrawal from a Multiple Hurdle Process'. *Journal of Applied Psychology* 85, 163–179.

Rynes, S. L., Giluk, T. L. and Brown, K. G. (2007) 'The Very Separate Worlds of Academic and Practitioner Periodicals in Human Resource Management: Implications for Evidence-Based Management'. *Academy of Management Journal* 50 (5), 987–1008.

Sackett, P. R., Lievens, F., Van Iddekinge, C. H. and Kuncel, N. R. (2017) 'Individual Differences and their Measurement: A Review of 100 Years of Research'. *Journal of Applied Psychology* 102 (3), 254–273.

Sanchez, R. J., Truxillo, D. M. and Bauer, T. N. (2000) 'Development and Examination of an Expectancy-Based Measure of Test-Taking Motivation'. *Journal of Applied Psychology* 85 (5), 739–750.

Sanchiz, M., Chevalier, A. and Amadieu, F. (2017) 'How Do Older and Young Adults Start Searching for Information? Impact of Age, Domain Knowledge and Problem Complexity on the Different Steps of Information Searching'. *Computers in Human Behavior* 72, 67–78.

Saville Consulting (2006) *Saville Consulting Wave Focus. Focus Styles.* Jersey: Saville Consulting Group

Schmidt, F. L. and Hunter, J. E. (1998) 'The Validity and Utility of Selection Methods in Personnel Psychology: Practical and Theoretical Implications of 85 Years of Research Findings'. *Psychological Bulletin* 124, 262–274.

Schmidt, F. L. and Radar, M. (1999) 'Exploring the Boundary Conditions for Interview Validity: Meta-analytic Validity Findings for a New Interview Type'. *Personnel Psychology* 52, 445–464.

Schmidt, N., Godding, R. Z., Noe, R. A. and Kirsch, M. (1984) 'Meta-Analyses of Validity Studies Published between 1964 and 1982 and the Investigation of Study Characteristics'. *Personnel Psychology* 37, 407–422.

Schmitt, N. and Chan, D. (1998) *Personnel Selection: A Theoretical Approach.* Thousand Oaks, CA: Sage Publications.

Schmitt, N. and Coyle, B. W. (1976) 'Applicant Decisions in the Employment Interview'. *Journal of Applied Psychology* 61 (2), 184–192.

Schmitt, N. and Mills, A. E. (2001) 'Traditional Tests and Job Simulations: Minority and Majority Performance and Test Validities'. *Journal of Applied Psychology* 86 (3), 451–458.

Schneider, B., Brent Smith, D., Taylor, S. and Fleenor, J. (1998) 'Personality and Organizations: A Test of the Homogeneity of Personality Hypothesis'. *Journal of Applied Psychology* 83, 462–470

Schneider, B., Kristof-Brown, A. L., Goldstein, H. W. and Smith, D. B. (1997) 'What is this Thing Called Fit?' in N. Anderson and P. Herriot (Eds.), *International Handbook of Selection and Assessment,* 2nd edition, pp. 393–412. Chichester: John Wiley.

Scholz, T. M. (2019). 'Big Data and Human Resource Management', in J. Storm Pederson and A. Wilkinson (Eds.), *Big Data: Promise, Application and Pitfalls,* Edward Elgar , pp. 69–89.

Schuler, R., Dowling, P. and DeCieri, H. (1993) 'An Integrative Framework of Strategic International Human Resource Management'. *Journal of Management* 19, 419–459.

Searle, R. H. (2003) *Selection and Recruitment: A Critical Text.* Milton Keynes: Open University/Palgrave Macmillan.

Searle, R. H. (2006) 'New Technology: The Potential Impact of Surveillance Techniques in Recruitment Practices'. *Personnel Review* 35 (3), 336–351.

Searle, R. H. and Billsberry, J. (2011) 'The Development and Destruction of Organizational Trust during Recruitment and Selection', in R. Searle and D. Skinner (Eds.), *Trust and Human Resource Management,* pp. 67–86. Cheltenham: Edward Elgar Publishing Limited.

Shackleton, V. and Newell, S. (1994) 'European Management Selection Methods: A Comparison of Five Countries'. *International Journal of Selection and Assessment* 2, 91–102.

Siegel, A. I. and Bergman, B. A. (1975) 'A Job Learning Approach to Performance Prediction'. *Personnel Psychology,* 28: 325–339.

Simon, H. A. (1960) *The New Science of Management Decisions.* New York: Harper and Row.

Sissons, P. and Green, A. E. (2017) 'More Than a Match? Assessing the HRM Challenge of Engaging Employers to Support Retention and Progression'. *Human Resource Management Journal* 27 (4), 565–580.

Stewart, C. (2016) 'How Diverse Is Your Pipeline? Developing the Talent Pipeline for Women and Black and Ethnic Minority Employees'. *Industrial and Commercial Training* 48, 61–66.

Stone, D. L., Lukaszewski, K. M. and Johnson, R. D. (2024) 'Will Artificial Intelligence Radically Change Human Resource Management Processes?' *Organizational Dynamics* 53, 101034.

Stoughton, J. W., Thompson, L. F. and Meade, A. W. (2015) 'Examining Applicant Reactions to the Use of Social Networking Websites in Pre-Employment Screening'. *Journal of Business and Psychology* 30 (1), 73–88.

Suen, H. Y., Hung, K. E. and Lin, C. L. (2020) 'Intelligent Video Interview Agent Used to Predict Communication Skill and Perceived Personality Traits'. *Human-Centric Computing and Information Sciences*, 10(1), 3.

Talmage, C. (2012) 'Applicant Quality: Exploring the Differences between Organizational and Third-Party Websites'. *Social Science Computer Review* 30 (2), 240–247.

Uggerslev, K. L., Fassina, N. E. and Kraichy, D. (2012) 'Recruiting through the Stages: A Meta-Analytic Test of Predictors of Applicant Attraction at Different Stages of the Recruiting Process'. *Personnel Psychology* 65 (3), 597–660.

van Deursen, A. and Helsper, E. (2015) 'A Nuanced Understanding of Internet Use and Non-Use among the Elderly'. *European Journal of Communication* 30 (2), 171–187.

Van Hoye, G. and Lievens, F. (2007) 'Recruitment-Related Information Sources and Organizational Attractiveness: Can Something Be Done about Negative Publicity?' *International Journal of Selection and Assessment* 13 (3), 179–187.

Van Iddekinge, C. H., Roth, P. L., Raymark, P. H. and Odle-Dusseau, H. N. (2012) 'The Criterion-Related Validity of Integrity Tests: An Updated Meta-Analysis'. *Journal of Applied Psychology* 97 (3), 499–530.

Von Glinow, M. A., Drost, E. A. and Teagarden, M. B. (2002) 'Converging on IHRM Best Practices: Lessons Learned from a Globally Distributed Consortium on Theory and Practice'. *Human Resource Management* 41 (1), 123–140.

Walker, H. J., Feild, H., Bernerth, J. and Becton, J. (2012) 'Diversity Cues on Recruitment Websites: Investigating the Effects on Job Seekers' Information Processing'. *Journal of Applied Psychology* 97 (1), 214–224.

Walker, H. J., Helmuth, C. A., Feild, H. S. and Bauer, T. N. (2014) 'Watch What You Say: Job Applicants' Justice Perceptions From Initial Organizational Correspondence'. *Human Resource Management, 54*(6), 999–1011.

Wiesner, W. H. and Cronshaw, S. F. (1988) 'The Employment Interview: A Critical Review'. *Personnel Psychology* 2, 17–46.

11 HR Planning

Institutions, Strategy, Tools and Techniques

Zsuzsa Kispal-Vitai and Geoffrey Wood

Introduction

Human resource (HR) planning represents the range of philosophies, tools and techniques that organisations may deploy to monitor and actively mould the ebb and flow of an organisation's people, both in terms of numbers and attributes. As such, it encompasses broad approaches to recruitment, development, advancement reward and termination. This may imply that HR planning represents the entirety of HRM, but, in practice, HR planning has taken to mean the usage of predetermined models, tools and techniques to predict, plan and adjust broad staffing, rather than the day-to-day implementation of the employment contract and the nature and extent of the employee's involvement and participation in the organisation of work (Gold, 2001).

The early 21st century has seen a succession of seemingly unanticipated (even if in reality, there was ample warning) 'Black-Swan' events (Taleb, 2010) that challenged planning the process. These would include the 2008 financial crisis, the COVID-19 pandemic, the Ukraine war, the near collapse of a number of states in the Sahel, and above all, climate change. These supposedly unexpected occurrences had impact around the world. COVID brought the 'Great Resignation', whereby those with alternatives forsook poorly recognised and rewarded jobs or flocked to those offering more flexible and homeworking arrangements. The latter reminded firms to address issues that many deemed less important before, such as mental health and the material conditions and needs of employees. In turn, this challenged the viability of the short-term shareholder value paradigm. In turn, the view that business is responsible not only to the owners, but also the employees, and the external environment, gained renewed currency. HR planning is an activity that may be invaluable to handling unforeseen events and imparting greater sustainability to business activities, even if it is used as a starting point for deviating from a predetermined plan.

As is the case with HRM more generally, HR planning may assume a strategic dimension, aligned with broad organisation-wide strategies or remain a basic administrative tool. It also may be used as a way of deepening implicit contracts, promoting longer term organisational commitment, or as a way

DOI: 10.4324/9781032625560-13

of recasting them and providing *post-hoc* 'scientific' justification for predetermined strategic choices.

This chapter is divided into two parts. In the first, we unpack what HR planning means and how organisations are likely to use HR planning in different contexts and locales. In the second, we provide a broad overview of the different applied tools and techniques of HR planning, their underlying assumptions and their purported benefits and limitations. Here, a caveat is in order. Tools and techniques of HR planning tend to be highly structured and often quantitative: in practice, their effects will reflect not just the nature of the model itself but the information inputted and the manner in which the firm will choose to interpret and disseminate the results.

Philosophies towards and Usages of HR Planning in Comparative Context

HRM, HR Planning, Strategy and the Firm

Human resource planning may be seen as simply a variation of the traditional practice of manpower planning, that is, monitoring and management of the ebb and flow of people within a firm. In more quantitative approaches to manpower planning, the supply of people was managed to meet set targets on the basis of analysing demand, predicting supply and designing interventions to solve any potential mismatches (Iles, 2001: 139). The latter could be done through drawing on the tools and techniques of operations management, using statistical formulas to analyse turnover, service length, etc. (ibid.: 140).

However, more ambitious strategic accounts of HRM have cast it as the crucial linkage between strategic business planning and strategic HRM, whereby the recruitment and selection of key types of employers, job specification, training and retention policies are aligned to the overall strategic vision (Iles, 2001: 139). However, as Gold (2001: 192) cautions, such approaches incorporate an inherent contradiction. Given that overall organisational strategies are likely to be geared towards specific numerical targets, HR planning will inevitably treat people as a factor in production, with the use of numerical models discounting the complexities of the human condition (Gold, 2001: 192).

As with HR more generally, there are hard and soft interpretations of HR planning, with the former founded on an instrumental philosophy regarding the utilisation of people and the latter on an emphasis of issues such as commitment and culture (Gold, 2001: 192; Iles, 2001: 129). Whilst the tendency towards more hard-line employer policies in liberal-market economies may have encouraged the utilisation of ever more sophisticated quantitative HR-planning systems, the credibility of the latter was at the same time undermined both by a lack of evidence as to whether they actually worked and by many organisations prioritising numerical flexibility (Gold, 2001: 193). Quite simply, many organisations opt for short-termist downsizing strategies, making a nonsense of sophisticated HR-planning systems, many of which represent incremental developments of traditional personnel/manpower approaches to planning.

This tension reflects the central challenges and contradictions of HRM. The rise of contemporary HRM mirrored the rise of the shareholder-dominant model that eclipsed the traditional Fordist model of the firm. The latter was about both struggles for control between managers and employees, and also about bargained compromises, permitting both the intensification of production and the deployment of new technologies (Jessop, 2001). During the 1950s and 1960s, the stability of this model allowed for longer-term contracting, both regarding the usage of labour and in relations with customers and suppliers, imparting a predictability to organisational life that had beneficial effects for all parties, with firms enjoying high returns and employees' enhancements in wages and general standards of living (Jessop, 2001). In contrast, the contemporary shareholder-orientated model represents a more experimental approach, aimed at restructuring firms to release resources, often entailing short-term costs to employees and other stakeholders in the interests of owners (Wright and Wood, 2008).

The relatively longer time horizons that characterised traditional Fordism and the use of technologies as a means of refining a particular production paradigm, rather than recasting it, fit well with the manpower planning tradition. On the one hand, much of contemporary people management is still about the administration of existing systems, drawing on whatever proven tools and techniques are available (Storey, 2001: 11). On the other hand, contemporary strategic approaches to HR planning stress issues such as flexibility, which necessitate a radical recasting or at least to rethink ways of doing things (Storey, 2001: 14).

From an employee rights perspective, HR planning is similarly beset with contradictions. Manpower planning – and other consistent long-term models to monitor and adjust the ebb and flow of an organisation's people – imparted a greater predictability to the employment contract and lowering transaction costs (c.f. Marsden, 1999). The implicit duration and trajectory of a job formed part and parcel of a wider implicit contract that allowed for both more harmonious employment relations within the firm and less opportunistic approaches to the external labour market by both employers and employees (c.f. Marsden, 1999; Jessop, 2001). This is not to suggest that manpower planning was unequivocally good for employees: in the end, the choice of what model to opt for generally rested with managers, whilst the abstract and impersonal nature of such models coincided with the formalised and hierarchical nature of the classic Fordist production paradigm (Jessop, 2001).

The shareholder-dominant model challenges such 'predictable' implicit contracts, holding that shorter-term instrumentalism is more conducive to the bottom line. Whilst managers have an interest in predictability and in co-opting employees in the interest of their personal empire building, proponents of the shareholder-dominant model have charged that this is at the expense of their principles, the owners of the firm (Roe, 2003). Does this mean that HR planning is incompatible with the strategic shareholder-orientated approach to HRM? In practice, HR planning may still be desirable for a number of reasons. The first is that both manpower and HR planning represent a technical system that is in some manner removed from bargained terms and conditions of service: whilst employees may expect that a specific approach to manpower planning may make for stability and predictability, its implicit nature gives a greater flexibility to management than an explicitly bargained-employment contract, even if embodied in the latter may be some assumptions regarding the former.

This flexibility gives management some room to manoeuvre: they may, for example, decide to cut back on skills development, decide to view a particular job as an end rather than a stepping stone and/or cut back recruitment as part and parcel of a drive to intensify work among existing staff. In short, whilst management may desire flexibility, they may also have an interest in a planned approach to long-term resourcing, retention and development in order to gradually recast the worth of a job, its trajectory and task intensity.

A second benefit for managers is that HR planning, by its technical and structured nature, may impart legitimacy to what is being done. From a postmodernist perspective, it allows for managers to dominate the knowledge regarding the usage of such systems, deploying abstract statistical models that will be unintelligible to the average worker, yet providing a scientific authority to potentially unpalatable decisions (c.f. Foucault, 1988; Toms, 2008). The authors of this chapter remain sceptical as to the overall worth of postmodernism to studying organisations: the latter discounts the material bases of power imbalances within the firm and the open-ended labour commitment that is exchanged for wages in the employment contract (Kelly, 1988). At the same time, postmodern accounts do help shed some light on why HR planning remains so attractive to managers in contexts characterised by extreme short-termism in hiring and deploying labour. Specific knowledge sets may be harnessed as *post-hoc* justification, rather than determining outcomes in itself (Foucault, 1988): hence, firms may use HR planning in such a way as to support what has already been decided, choosing between applied models and/or adjusting them, in order to support a specific agenda.

Country, Sector, Organisation Type and HR Planning

Before we turn to specific approaches to HR planning, it is worth giving some attention to what broad underlying philosophies regarding HR planning are likely to be encountered in different contexts. For what objectives are HR-planning models likely to be deployed? In other words, where are organisations likely to take a longer-term approach to staffing and where a shorter-term? Where is tenure likely to be more secure? Where are firms more likely to invest in their people? And where less so? Or to put it another way, for what objective are firms likely to use HR planning? Whilst HR planning may presume a longer term 'scientific' way of managing people, as we have seen, it may be used to support an essentially short-termist way of doing things.

The Varieties of Capitalism (VOC) literature has pointed to the persistence of differences in corporate governance and internal firm-level strategies and policies (Dore, 2000; Hall and Soskice, 2001). Central to the VOC literature is the assumption that the shareholder-dominated model is not the only variation of capitalism in the post-1970s era. Whilst liberal-market economies (LMEs) are characterised by the hegemony of the shareholder-dominant paradigm, collaborative markets (CMEs) are defined by a more stakeholder-orientated approach (Dore, 2000). Within the former, employee rights are likely to be weaker, with firms basing their competitiveness on high-tech innovation ('Silicon Valley') or low value-added cost-cutting production ('McDonald's') paradigms (Brewster et al., 2006; Wright and Dwyer, 2006). Meanwhile, in the latter, stronger employee – and other stakeholder – rights impart a more long-term approach to the employment contract, with firms and employees giving more attention to the development of organisation-specific skills as a means of underpinning high value-added incremental innovation in manufacturing and services (Thelen, 2001; Brewster et al., 2006).

Underlying approaches to recruitment may also reflect the wider variety of capitalism. Within LMEs, good supplies both of cheap, unskilled and generic tertiary-level skilled labour are conducive to supporting low cost and 'blue-skies' innovation, respectively. Using the external labour market to meet broadly defined needs makes internal labour more dispensable, weakening the bargaining position of existing staff (Thelen, 2001). In contrast, in CMEs, firms rely on labour with strong vocational, industry-specific skills: through long-term contracting, employees have an incentive to develop and/or supplement these with organisation-specific skills (Thelen, 2001; Harcourt and Wood, 2007).

Within CMEs, firms are thus likely to have an internal orientation, aiming to develop existing staff rather than plug skills gaps externally (Gold, 2001: 208). Employees are likely to enjoy a high degree of task discretion and stable earnings, allowing for a more satisfying work experience, deepening organisational commitment (ibid.). In contrast, in LMEs, a focus on generic skills and/or low skills, both of which may be readily obtained on the external-labour market, lower degrees of task discretion, unstable earnings result in lower organisational commitment, more rapid adjustments to organisational size, and a prioritisation of cost-cutting rather than the engendering of organisation-specific knowledge and wisdom (Gold, 2001: 208).

Harcourt and Wood (2007: 141) shed further light on the relationship between career trajectories, development and varieties of capitalism. They note that during the heyday of neo-liberalism, employment protection was widely believed to be one of the main causes of Europe's poor performance. Yet, the high value-added production paradigms that have sustained the export competitiveness of a number of leading coordinated market economies like Germany remain dependent on high levels of firm-specific human capital made possible by extensive job protection.

In turn, job protection is conducive for human capital development. Employees have more incentives to develop skills specific to their employer, as it is more certain they will be able to use them over the medium and longer terms (rather than face ejection into the external labour market) and will be able to advance their careers by developing them (as adverse to seeking promotion by job-hopping) (Harcourt and Wood, 2007). However, a caveat is in order here: any accommodation between employers and employees will invariably be contested, whilst national economies evolve in a dynamic and non-linear fashion (ibid.; Boyer, 2006; Deeg and Jackson, 2006). This means that in addition to pressures to deepen, refine and strengthen existing collaborative national models, there will be countervailing pressures to greater short-termism, towards more instrumental approaches to HR planning (Harcourt and Wood, 2007). In contrast, within LMEs, excessive short-termism has proved deleterious to many sectors, leading to minorities of firms experimenting with alternatives (Boyer, 2006).

Recent research has also highlighted the nature of internal diversity within specific varieties of capitalism (Streeck and Thelen, 2005; Boyer, 2006; Brewster *et al.*, 2006). Such diversity may be on regional or sectoral grounds, reflecting the uneven nature of systemic change, regional production systems and variations in technology (Lane and Wood, 2009). We have already seen that common in liberal markets are both 'high-tech' and low value-added production paradigms; within collaborative markets, incrementally innovative production coexists with lower value-added strategies. Even within sectors, individual firms may experiment with alternatives: whilst some of the latter may prove unsuccessful, others may throw up unexpected serendipitous complementarities that will be reinforced. In turn, this means that there will be variations in the manner in which firms use HR planning, not only between, but also within national contexts.

It will be apparent from the previous paragraph that not only does the extent and nature of HR planning illuminate broader national, regional, sectoral and organisational philosophies and approaches to people management, but that certain types of organisations are likely to make use of HR-planning systems in particular ways. Organisations may use HR planning as a means of imparting greater stability and predictability into the employment contract and organisational life more generally. Alternatively, they may use HR planning as a means of bringing about and/or justifying more instrumental approaches to recruitment, job tenure and skills development. In the following sections, we review specific tools and techniques of HR planning, with the caveat that each individual technique has more than one application; each may be used in the pursuit of a number of alternative strategies to people management.

Challenges in the Factors Influencing Human Resource Planning

In the subsequent section, we focus on recent developments of salience to HR planning.

HR Analytics – Data, Technologies, Algorithms and Their Consequences

HR Analytics

As noted earlier, developments ranging from COVID-19 to climate change have forced considerable changes in doing work and in managing people. Many of the changes both challenge existing ways of doing things and, indeed, affect how organisations respond to future ones. For example, the COVID-19 pandemic drove the rapid adoption of remote-working technologies. Those businesses that could adapt and change and leverage technology coped much better than those who did not or could not do so. An example would be the case of retail business: many long-standing companies filed for bankruptcy, a few such examples being J.C. Penney, Lord & Taylor, M&Co (Markowitz, 2021; Phillips and Baker, 2022). It might seem that this was simply a product of a move towards online retail, but in reality it also represented a product of past decisions by many traditional high or main-street retailers; many had in past years sought to enhance returns not by offering more enticing products and prices for customers or a better shopping experience, but rather through leveraging debt against property portfolios. This made firms very poorly equipped to cope with downturns and highlighted the follow-up of prioritising debt and distribution over people and products.

More broadly speaking, whole industries were hit hard; services, restaurants, the travel industry, oil and gas (Novicio, 2021). However, those industries and companies that could serve customers even in those adverse conditions thrived during the pandemic. Obvious examples would be platform companies such as Microsoft, Zoom, Shopify, Netflix, Nvidia and Facebook are some of those (Novicio, 2021).

Usage of new technologies has, of course, implications for HRM: data and technology are now inevitable in everyday work. In turn, this meant that the previous cautious approach towards HR analytics has been fading (Murphy, McCarthy, 2021; Polzer, 2022). In 2016, Marler and Boudreau defined HR analytics as

> A HR practice enabled by information technology that uses descriptive, visual, and statistical analyses of data related to HR processes, human capital, organizational performance, and external economic benchmarks to establish business impact and enable data-driven decision-making.

In their review, they found few high-level research-based articles about HR analytics, and they found limited adoption of the same, even if research frequently links it to favourable organisational outcomes (Marler & Boudreau, 2016). After the pandemic and the different approaches towards technology, this has changed.

In broad terms, there can be no HRM without reliable data. In the 21st century, big data may be roughly defined as a mass of information in multiple forms (such as text, videos, blogs and internet sites) having a high volume, high velocity and high variety, which, in turn, allows analysts to capture insights into problems and provides bases for improved decision-making. (Gartner, 2012). There is scepticism as to how much big data is actually used in HRM (Cappelli, 2017), using data for decision-making and advanced analytics supports practicing managers. However, Davenport (2019) argues, HR is one of the most analytics-driven functions of the enterprise. Based on a survey on five continents and 1,510 respondents, 94 per cent of the managers claimed they can predict the likelihood of turnover in crucial roles with confidence (Davenport, 2019). These results were published in 2019 and a year later, the usage of formalised electronic exchange in lieu of informal face-to-face exchanges has placed much more data at the disposal of the firm, for good or ill.

It has been widely argued that the usage of data and technologies is essential in today's HR functions, planning not being an exception (Ledet et al., 2020; Hamilton & Sodeman, 2019). According to Gartner (2020), 33 per cent of HR leaders claimed in 2020 that their organisation effectively used data in workforce planning. PWC's HR tech survey concluded that HR insights and data analytics represented one of the top ten HR challenges and opportunities (PricewaterhouseCoopers, 2022). It might seem that using algorithms in HR sounds like an oxymoron; algorithms are systematic procedures to solve a specific problem (Britannica, 2023). In reality, HR problems often lack optimal solutions, predetermined steps may not provide solutions, and no matter how well meaning, actions may have unintended consequences (Dastin, 2018). An example might be using AI to screen job applicants to reduce bias, when AI itself has bias; in concentrating on one area, it may also neglect others (Dastin, 2018). Cheng and Hackett (2019) suggest that algorithms should be regarded as heuristic computer programmes to create immediate recommendations for HR functions. There are clear issues around how algorithms can and may solve problems both in practice and in research. The issues are manifold, such as the adverse impact of their usage or the accuracy of the suggested solution. There are also clear ethical issues, for example, in employee tracking systems. Data protection and the ethical side of usage is also a crucial issue for both research and practice, including the right to privacy and how much organisations should be able to intrude on the life of their employees (Cheng & Hackett, 2019).

AI in Human Resource Planning

There is much debate and controversy around artificial intelligence, ranging from how to disentangle the reality from the hype (or indeed, if artificial intelligence really exists) to the risks and opportunities it might deliver. Here we deal in more detail only with generative AI and its role in planning, though AI (broadly or charitably defined) already is deployed within many companies (e.g., Oracle 2019, Kaushal et al., 2021; The impact of generative AI on human resources, McKinsey, no date). According to a McKinsey report, one-third of the surveyed 1,684 organisations already use so-called generative

AI. The survey shows that it is used mostly in service operations, product or service development marketing, sales and corporate management.

According to the Oracle survey of 8,000 HR professionals in ten countries, in 2019, AI is part of human resource technology and more companies are using it. The rapid spread of the technology may be due to manifold genuine advantages, such as the fast analysis of data, finding relationships among factors overlooked by managers and more unbiased applicant treatment (though this has not yet been totally achieved and still has deep-rooted issues). Helping in employees' career counselling, identifying strengths and weaknesses in performance evaluation and training and talent development are all fields where AI – when used well – could be a substantial help (ILO, 2023). To proponents, AI's analytic strength, fast response and algorithmic decision-making in scheduling may take away those tasks from humans that are boring, tiresome and repetitive, and it does these much better than any human. One problem with AI, according to one ILO (2023) working paper, is that it takes the human element out of decision-making, and optimisation may not be optimal in certain cases without negotiations with the employees; it may disempower employees and managers alike. In any event, the usage of automation to solve human problems has often led to the reduction of productive jobs and the creation of new 'bullshit' jobs, large numbers of seemingly meaningless administrative roles to keep track of it all and to carry out work for the sake of it (Graeber, 2019).

The other problem with AI, as noted previously, is that of bias. Algorithm bias exists because of how AI was and is trained. It may be that the data it was trained on contained bias or incomplete information or simply to suit the agendas of those who set it up. Ascarza and Israeli (2022) mention a third type of bias when information is complete, but there are correlations in data that lead to biased decision-making because these correlations are based on protected characteristics. There are already approaches and techniques that seek to eliminate or at least mitigate these, but, of course, it is up to those developing the system as to whether these are adopted. In general planning, especially generative AI, can identify data necessary to evaluate the company's position both in the market and inside. It can find industry trends, signs of changes in the institutional environment, data from competitors, correlations and interrelationships that might escape humans. If there is a comprehensive HR database inside the company, AI may identify a fuller range of workforce skills and talent potential for succession. It can identify flight risks and people who might leave based on collected data about their work history (AI in Human Resources The Time is Now, no date).

A concluding thought about technology: there is both hype and potential that are hard to separate. Technology, though, is as good as the people who created it and use it day by day. AI bias is not the machine's problem but a human problem and one with human consequences. Misuse of AI and big data to justify unethical practices is also not caused by technology but by technology users, although, of course, if AI really attains sentience, it would be quite capable of being unethical itself.

Demographics

The changes in the labour force also affect planning strategies. Both in Europe and in the United States, the workforce is ageing. According to Jamet and El-Atillah (2023), many workers work actively past their retirement age in Europe. The reasons are supplementing their income or strengthening their future pension. Eurostat found that 13.2 per cent of the workforce in the age bracket of 65–69 work, and 4.9 per cent of workers in the 70–74 bracket are actively engaged. There are more and more elderly people in the European workforce. In 2001 only 4.5 per cent of the working population was 60 or above; in 2021, over 9 per cent was in that age bracket.

The labour market situation is somewhat starker in the US, where most lack meaningful social protection and retirement security. Employees are active for a longer time, for some by choice, but for many more by necessity. James and Wooten (2022) quote the US Bureau of Labor Statistics that by 2024, a quarter of the workforce will be over 55 years old, and even from this group, a third of the workers will be over 65 or more; this reflects both the ageing population and the need to carry on working to survive. Companies need to consider this in planning as the older worker differs from the traditional employee aged 20 to 50. Older workers bring experience, expertise and reliability more than younger cohorts; also, their needs in the workplace are dissimilar. They have similar needs in terms of interesting work, autonomy and flexibility (Root et al., 2023). On the other hand, because of health issues, the number of unavoidable absences may be higher than for younger workers, even if the rate of unavoidable absences has been proven to be lower (Robbins and Judge, 2017).

Mass migration provides a major new resource of labour: many migrants are relatively youthful and will have obtained some or other level of education elsewhere (and funded by the sender nation). However, the right-wing populist governments in the UK and the US owe their rise to successfully whipping up xenophobia. They are committed to enacting stringent anti-migrancy measures. However, rather than halting migration, the likely outcome will be forcing ever larger numbers of migrants into the underground economy, the main beneficiaries being human traffickers and unprincipled employers who base their competitiveness on cheap – and often unfree – labour.

It is difficult to evaluate the effect of mass migration on the labour market. Migrants face the challenges of adaption and integration in their new country, even if abiding prejudice may make this task more daunting when language skills are limited. It may be hard to evaluate illegal migrants' qualifications. More time and research are needed to evaluate migration's economic and social effects objectively. However, it is worth noting that Germany has successful digested roughly two million immigrants as a result of the Syrian crisis (and those of Iraq, Afghanistan and Libya), with most of the working-age group being successfully reskilled and integrated into the labour market. In the process, the country securing a large number of workers whose basic education and training was paid for elsewhere and who proved willing to perform jobs in those areas where it was difficult to secure local labour. On the other end of the spectrum, the career-starting young workforce 'Millennials' have different work values: it is argued that they are often more family-centric than work-centric and harder to keep and motivate (The Economist , 2008). However, this may simply be due to the diminishing pool of regular, secure and decent jobs in liberal markets such as the US and the UK; it is not clear why people should be committed to a job when it is poorly rewarded and where the firm demonstrates little loyalty to its people. For planning, it means more contingency-based plans, considering a more volatile and higher-maintenance workforce.

Research about demographic values has been challenging. Philip Cohen, a sociologist based at the University of Maryland, has claimed that the Pew Research Center's well known generational labels are arbitrary and not scientific, and he also mentions methodological issues with the generations' research (Cohen, 2021). Even the Pew Research Center warns about over-generalisation and cautions to use labels sparingly (Dimock, 2023). Especially in the age of globalisation and massive migration, employers cannot expect young employees to have the same experiences worldwide. A Generation Z American woman may differ greatly from a Generation Z Indian or Afghan woman. The employer practices should take that into consideration in planning when the company thinks about talent management and succession. Nonetheless, it is clear that baby boomers enjoyed advantages in life (free or cheap education, affordable housing, the assurance of robust economic growth, good terms and conditions of employment and good pensions) that in many national contexts have been denied to future generations, leading to understandable backlashes.

The Human Resource Planning Process

Human resource planning has, as we have seen, links to all of the HR functions of an organisation (Macaleer and Shannon, 2003): no strategy can be accomplished without people.

Assessment of HR Needs to Support Overall Strategies

Although it is widely recognised that human resource allocation should be an integral part of a company's strategic planning process, the evidence on the ground is still mixed. We cannot say companies have a well-thought-of strategic approach towards HR planning, not even in the 21st century. According to a CIPD press release in 2021, 43 per cent of employers did not plan at all. 46 per cent of employers had a workforce planning strategy that was supported by knowing their workforce needs. The same number collected data about organisational skill gaps; even less, 31 per cent, thought about identifying future skill requirements (CIPD, 2021).

According to Komm et al. (2021), the pandemic created new ways for HR to participate in building companies' futures. In this new approach, HR has a role in achieving flexibility and agility to meet the demands of the institutional environment.

As Lussier and Hendon (2019) note, strategic planning in HRM aims at gaining a sustainable competitive advantage. Mathis et al. (2017) argue that the core objective in HR planning is to: 'ensure that the organisation has the *right number of people* with the *right capabilities*, at the *right times*, and in the *right places*'. (p.44.)

In practical terms, the process should start with aligning the organisational strategic plans and the HR plans. In the 1990s, there was a primary emphasis on deriving HR strategies from the master strategic plan of the organisation. After 2000, there has been more interest in integrating closely into the primary strategy, logic dictating that the informational input from HR could significantly improve or, rather, change the overall approach. For example, if the organisation is planning innovation but the talent is lacking inside, then HR must take steps to serve this goal or warn against adopting it at all if resources are not accessible or take too long to acquire.

Besides the strategy it adopts, the organisation's culture also plays a role in the planning process. Many firms (for example, Procter and Gamble) hire most employees for entry-level jobs and those hires must progress through the company to achieve leadership positions. Others hire senior executives with several years of leadership elsewhere; a number of prominent UK and US firms have become noted for hiring celebrity CEOs, who move quite rapidly between assignments. Particularly in the case of firms that rely on the external labour market, the availability of competitive salaries and bonuses, or the lack of those, can either aid or constrain finding and recruiting talent (Mathis & Jackson, 2006).

Setting Priorities in Human Resource Planning: Forecasting

There are many alternative methods for forecasting; the choice management may make is invariably moulded by the wider institutional context and the relationship between management and other stakeholders, including employees. More subjective judgemental models tend to be used more in an uncertain environment, although the accuracy of 'soft methods' is questioned by researchers. Judgement-focused firms can be found in any industry, and the company's size is not an affecting variable. Researchers claim that alternative, more quantitative-focused approaches have lower error rates and more accurate forecasting (Sanders and Manrodt, 2003). However, it can be argued that quantitative methods have their own limitations; they involve managerial judgement on issues such as accountability, the future suitability of a selected employee or the consequences of a layoff. If uncertainty is perceived to be rising, then sophisticated techniques will not be used since they have less value; likewise, if uncertainty decreases to a large extent, then forecasting will no longer be needed at all (Stone and Fiorito, 1986).

Workforce Demand Forecasting Techniques – Judgemental Methods

Direct managerial input or unit forecasting: In this case, each unit or each manager forecasts the future needs of employees. This could be done through so-called 'bottom-up' planning, that is, by unit forecasting, and/or by 'top-down' planning, where each unit is allocated a certain budget for employee payroll expenditure; and this budget is then divided by management to serve their perceptions of desired business needs. Direct managerial input is supposedly based on 'hard' data, that is, on cash flow, rate of return, return on capital employed and discounted cash flow on investment, even if managerial choices and presumptions invariably have a major effect. Although a mathematical method based only on financial data, this has been seen as quite functional if the company wishes to concentrate on decreasing staff numbers, even if it does not take into account the consequences down the line (e.g., the survivor syndrome). Since it does not involve investigating the skills the company needs or the jobs they cut, it may be mechanical and not have the desired effect of enhancing firm performance. If a company reduces staff numbers with the simple aim of reducing the payroll, then it may be counterproductive by inadvertently discarding people they need most and lead to the most talented staff abandoning ship for a more conducive working environment (Ward, 1996a; Mello, 2005).

Unit forecasting: This can be deployed in order to estimate future employee needs in a positive manner when managers at all levels decide how many employees they need for future improvements and new contracts – a 'bottom-up' approach. This technique has been seen as particularly responsive to the market's needs (Mello, 2005) since the responsibility for the decision lies where the decisions on production and services are made. However, it does have the disadvantage of tempting managers to 'hoard' employees for envisaged future needs and not to allocate them to those parts of the organisation that could use them better (Mello, 2005).

Both bottom-up and top-down approaches have advantages: The top-down variety is efficient from the resource allocation perspective, whilst the bottom-up variety addresses the marketplace's requirements. Ideally, an organisation would use both approaches to serve the market (and its own managers) well and to nurture the efficiency of organisational resource allocation (Ward, 1996a; Mello, 2005).

'Best guess' formalised managerial judgement: According to Ward (1996a,b), this was developed by a few companies and is essentially similar to unit forecasting but with the difference that the forecast contains:

- Current headcount requirements
- A 'best-guess' estimate of the impact of expected productivity and technology changes
- The managers' best guesses of headcount changes due to expected business changes

The future employee need may be defined as the sum of the 'best guesses'. In other words, it is a method of approximation, which may or may not be accurate, and assumes that managers correctly forecast, inter alia, the future impact of technology and the marketplace and are able to translate these to HR needs regarding numbers and skills. It also assumes that managers have adequate time to use this method.

Ivanchevich (2007) identifies *trend projection* as finding a relationship between a business-related factor and a desired number of employees. Sales levels are usually related to employment trends, and in trend projection, the planner relates employment to one single factor but which may not take account of changes in productivity.

Historical ratios: Ward (1996a,b) argues that historical ratios can be good predictors if there is a significant correlation between headcount and certain business factors, such as the number of customers served and the number of units manufactured. This method provides a general estimate of all workers, but it cannot differentiate between temporary and permanent workers and cannot handle outsourcing requirements. Skills and other 'soft' issues cannot be considered here, although it is easy to administer and can be used with popular spreadsheets such as Lotus or Excel.

These two methods can also be termed as based on a *rule of thumb* as in Meehan and Basheer's (1990) example: 'one new production worker for every 1,000 additional items produced'.

The hypothetical approach based on process analysis (Business Process Re-engineering): This is mentioned in Ward (1996a,b), although he asserts that it has never actually been used! The concept is seemingly sound since it says that, in process analysis, a detailed analysis of process components of work activities should be developed and human resource needs could be quantified based on each unit. Yet, this concept has never been translated to an operational model, although it could have definite advantages in that qualitative thinking could be incorporated since the analysis could involve aspects of skills and competencies.

The Delphi technique: This technique was originally developed by the RAND Corporation and is characterised by trying to bring experts to a consensus whilst eliciting as many different opinions as possible (Durnham, 1996). However, an important factor of the technique is that it must be used anonymously. The target is problem-solving, planning and decision-making, and the method involves a facilitator who coordinates the process. The physical presence of the participants is not required – and, in fact, a lack of physical presence makes for greater effectiveness. In the first round, the facilitator sends a questionnaire to the participating specialists and collects the answers. All these ideas are incorporated into a new questionnaire for the second round. This iteration process carries on until no new ideas emerge. This procedure allows specialists to change and improve ideas; since it is anonymous, there are no personality or other constraints on participants.

The nominal group technique: Also called 'the alternative way of brainstorming' (Ivanchevich, 2007), it involves a facilitator inviting group members to write down their ideas privately, and then, one by one, each group member presents the ideas, one at a time. These are recorded on a flipchart but with no discussion. Each member can opt out of a round and the ideas need not be from the list written by a member; they could be invented when requested. After all ideas have been listed, the group discusses the ideas for a set period of time. Each member then privately ranks all of the ideas, and their overall ranking will be their aggregate ranking (Nicholson, 1995). This method can incorporate a number of qualitative factors that others might miss. Moreover, to its proponents, it is sufficiently comprehensive and can supposedly eliminate group decision-making problems (such as 'groupthink' or a dominating group member). It can, however, preserve the idea-generating effect that physical presence can have on people (further developing others' ideas). It may also be inaccurate, especially in a fast-changing environment, when specialists in the specific setting cannot consider unexpected occurrences or do not wish to do so.

Scenario analysis: This is a method that is very similar to the other two 'brainstorming' methods, but with the difference that ideas are then built into future workforce scenarios (Ward, 1996a,b). Managers then work backward in order to identify important turning points. The discussions may (at least in theory) be wide-ranging, and participants can identify more crucial factors than otherwise. Scenario-building is commonly used in strategic management. The creation of imaginary, future-event sequences leads to attempts to determine the places in the sequences where managerial intervention is needed and where such intervention might change an unwanted future. Both positive and negative possibilities are weighed up. One problem, however, is that this method cannot provide accurate, quantifiable data; it can merely encourage flexibility and adaptability, which is no novelty to any HR professional but nonetheless may be very welcome.

Balanced Scorecard Approach: This model focuses on the 'human resources deliverables' – factors critical to business success and within the human resources range (Mello, 2005). There are five components as suggested over many articles and publications by Huselid (e.g., online, no date):
Workforce success – goal accomplishment, that is, did the workforce accomplish business objectives in the organisation?Right HR costs – is our investment in the workforce sufficient, do we spend enough on HR in the whole organisation?Right types of HR alignment – do we harmonise our HR activities with the other activities of the organisation, and do we differentiate in different positions when needed?Right HR practices – do we design and use the 'world-class' HR practices in the organisation?Right HR professionals – do we have a HR specialist workforce that is able to implement these practices; do we have the knowledge, skills and abilities to continuously learn, grow and apply what they know?These methods can also be termed judgemental since they all involve managerial decision-making and fallibilities, and are based on a subjective evaluation of facts rather than on quantifiable statistical methods. Accuracy is most certainly an issue in forecasting, but subjective judgement (the 'gut

feeling') can sometimes be more accurate than any statistical method since they can take into account non-quantifiable factors, such as sudden changes in technology and political events, and, indeed, experience and wisdom.

Talent Management

An alternative contemporary approach may be encountered in the literature on talent management. This often emphasises the need for speed in filling gaps through a close linkage between all the different aspects of the HR function (ibid.: 140). It also emphasises the differences in individual talents and the need to consider them. However, the question that emerges is whether or note this is something that HR managers should be doing anyway. Yet, it can be argued that contemporary talent management has much more to do when it comes to planning: calibrating and linking talent to the overall strategy. This can be done through either a resource-based view that links talent to overall results or through an approach that calls for talent to be approached in a similarly quantitative way to financial resources, allowing the latter to be linked to wider organisational decision-making in a scientific fashion (ibid.: 146). In the latter regard, the HC BRidge® Decision Framework developed by Ramstad and Boudreau focuses on critical competencies, key performers who have these competencies and the practices that enable these people to achieve maximum performance. The key elements here are impact, effectiveness and efficiency (Lewis & Heckman, 2006).

Mathis et al. (2017) emphasise competency models as tools to help career planning. Companies may create competency libraries for different jobs, also they can identify a small number of core competencies that are needed in all jobs, along with specific competencies that apply to specific jobs (p. 326)

COVID-19 did not leave talent management untouched. The drastic reorganisation of work and/or loss of people forced theory and practice to re-evaluate how to deal with talent potential (Vaiman et al., 2021). On the one hand, the forced acceptance of remote working facilitated global recruitment, as translocation to the workplace was no longer necessary. On the other hand, those industries that were adversely affected sometimes precipitated downsizing. The pandemic made companies create new talent development programmes in virtual formats and global delivery. The constraints that political changes brought in the world, like Brexit in Europe, also created new challenges in acquiring talent. Restrictions on travel and getting work visas influenced who got permission to work abroad, if that work needed to be done with the employee's physical presence. All these changed the approaches and options of planners.

Assessing Demand – Statistical Methods

Time series analysis: This method examines historical employment patterns and trends in the environment and seeks to extrapolate future employment need. It is effective in a stable environment when the user reasonably expects that trends can be calculated and that the employment pattern will remain the same. It is useful in industries with cyclical peaks and downturns (e.g., in services such as the leisure industry). It is relatively simple, but in large organisations where several job groups are in evidence, the planner has to use more than one time series since the trends can reflect only one job group. It is not useful in small organisations with no historical data or in a dynamic business environment.

The method projects past trends into the future, using time as the independent variable. This analysis can identify long-term trends, seasonal, cyclical and residual effects that emerge from the environment's unpredictability and the randomness of human action. It is especially good for predicting seasonal effects and recurring fluctuations, such as the effects of holidays or other repeated variations. Since the model uses time, it cannot cope with organisational circumstances and cannot be used for scenario analysis; it can, however, be used effectively to identify turning points (Gallagher, 2000).

Work-study: In the absence of historical data present but with a requirement to identify future needs, work-study is an alternative approach. This method is, for example, useful in new businesses. The actual work process is studied, together with the individual activities of the worker. This approach has a long history going back to F. W. Taylor. He monitored how long it took to perform the individual activities that make up a job with a view to closer and better time management, linking pay with output; its track record in terms of production work is controversial: close monitoring and control of output may make it even more unpleasant. It is not a suitable method where work is non-standard, such as some forms of white-collar work. Work-study engineers study the work process and assess rates of employee activity. This is known as 'effort rating'. From this, a formula is created that defines 'standard performance' and, based on this formula, the effort can be rated and the appropriate number of employees calculated.

Time series analysis coupled with productivity trends: This method is best suited to industries where long-term planning is possible. There is no assumption that productivity trends will remain the same and that improvements in productivity are factored into the calculations and projected. It does, however, assume positive changes in staff-productivity ratios.

Regression analysis models: Their usefulness is partly due to the fact that one can evaluate the required mix of employee categories. One can estimate the number of employees required in one category based on the level required in another. For example, how many more checkout staff would be needed if the number of items in a department store were increased? In multiple regression techniques, the variables used in the historical ratio are used as independent variables. Regression models incorporate the rate of change based on historical productivity-improvement trends. Regression analysis is a powerful statistical tool in that it can handle a number of variables and is relatively easy to administer. On the other hand, it has several disadvantages, such as the fact that the models cannot work without historical data. If relationships between the variables change, then the predictive accuracy is weakened. Nevertheless, a number of sophisticated computer packages for regression analysis (Ward, 1996a,b) are widely used.

Additional combined statistical and judgemental models: Integrating models try to consider several factors that influence the organisation. They attempt to simulate the organisation and the environment through efforts to build in the effects of the environment, and they also attempt to simulate the movements of individuals into and out of the organisation, skill requirements and HR activities.

Balancing equations: These are similar to regression models and include variables that are determinants of staffing requirements. Subjective weights are assigned to the determinants based not on statistical relationships but, rather, on expert judgement.

Combination technique – forecasting demand: This model incorporates both managerial judgement and statistical accuracy (Gallagher, 2000):

$$E = \frac{(L+G)\times 1/x}{Y}$$

Where E is the number of staff needed at a specific future date, L is the current turnover (financial), G is the expected growth in turnover, X is the productivity improvement expected during the period and Y is the turnover divided by the number of staff.

Assessing Supply – Supply Analysis Methods

Internal supply: In this case, the planner needs to know the gross number of people and how many are needed for a specific job at the group or organisational level. According to Gallagher (2000), turnover is not a good indicator since it provides only gross numbers, whilst specific turnover data would be more helpful if broken down into categories (job, age, skill set). Internal supply is influenced by other HR processes within the organisation, such as training and development programmes, transfer and promotion policies, retirement, career planning and others (Mathis & Jackson, 2006).

Before any modelling can occur, the HR planner and the organisation's management must have a clear picture of the knowledge, skills and abilities of the members of the organisation in order to be able to plan for the future. Several expressions are used to store these types of workforce data. One such is *skills inventory*, which is the type and quantity of data stored in some organisations. In addition to basic demographics, highly sophisticated data can also be useful. Participation would fall into this category in continuing education, supervisory ranking of employee capabilities, hobbies, personal career goals and objectives, geographical preferences and an indication of the time for retirement (Ivanchevich, 2007). With today's very advanced computerised data-handling methods, virtually all forms of data can be stored and easily accessed when necessary. HRIS systems can be a powerful aid in planning and implementing HR-related action. Data analysis may be done together with help from artificial intelligence to go through big data and find connections that would escape human analysers.

Stock and flow models are used for forecasting supply. These models follow the employee's path through the organisation over time and attempt to predict how many employees will be needed and in which part of the organisation. According to Gallagher (2000), these are not sufficiently useful in forecasting the number of employees at various organisational activity levels.

Wastage analysis: It is a general rule that figure variances may be great within different categories of staff (such as men and women), age groups (wastage declines with age) or unemployment rates (wastage is low) (Gallagher, 2000).

Stability analysis: This concentrates on people who remain rather than examines any loss of personnel.

Replacement charts: These charts list both jobs and individuals and show how key individuals move around the organisation. They list the number of employees and the skills they have, their level of readiness together with their willingness to move into a new job. These charts are then displayed on the organisation chart and offer the possibility of promotion. The time when any selected employee will be ready for promotion is also indicated and is based on the opinions and recommendations of higher-ranking people (Mello, 2005). Some replacement charts are more systematic, showing skills, abilities, competencies and experiences. Therefore, they are more objective and help overcome personal bias and succession-related problems. Replacement charts can be profitably used as a planning tool and could also be used as a component of the whole succession-planning effort (Mello, 2005).

Markov modelling: This model belongs to the stochastic process model sector, which assigns probabilities to future events and tries to incorporate future possible occurrences into models (Parker & Caine, 1996). Examples of this might include the likelihood of securing a contract or of starting or finishing a project on time. The model is named after the Russian mathematician said to have developed the model in 1907. The Markov analysis is a derivative of probability theory and is highly mathematical. In a Markov analysis, the planner attempts to describe the movement of personnel as stochastic possibilities, a series of stocks and flows where each event is decided by a preceding event. In a simple case, the system is closed; but, in reality, in human resource planning, the system has an incoming and an outgoing component. This model is also called a transitional matrix as it examines the overall pattern of movement of people between jobs inside the organisation and outward movement from the organisation. When both incoming and outgoing personnel are featured, Markov modelling is easier to handle by computer. The underlying logic is simple: when employees move from one position to another, they have to be replaced, and this replacement usually comes from a position below the incumbent who is moving on. At the top of the matrix, employees may also leave and disappear from the system.

The value of the approach depends on the mathematical ability of the user. Today sophisticated computer programmes along with artificial intelligence solve these problems. It is interesting to mention that natural language processing and machine learning also use Markov analysis (Brans, 2023).

There are other approaches to describe and predict people movement in an organisation, such as the 'systems approach', also known as *holonic modelling* (Parker & Caine, 1996). It is easier to use, is based on system theory and dynamics and can be handled by less mathematically-oriented planners. It is also said to be more flexible and helpful in the intuitive planning process.

Succession planning: The importance and the unavoidable necessity of succession planning are emphasised in textbooks (for example, Mathis et al., 2017.; Armstrong, 2021; Noe et al., 2023) and professional organisations like the CIPD and SHRM. Also, consulting organisations stress that leadership development should be a priority (Routch et al., 2018; Bennett, 2023).

The function was concentrated on leaders and senior managers (CIPD, 2016); now, a new definition says: 'Succession planning is the process of preparing for inevitable vacancies in the organisation hierarchy' (Mathis et al., 2017, p. 330). The more inclusive definition recognises the need for a strategic mindset and the need for a well-developed system in the organisation to aid decision-makers in identifying and timely placing people in the needed positions. Despite the importance, it is still a field that needs improvement in HR planning. According to Deloitte research, 86 per cent of leaders believe it is important and only 14 per cent say they do it well.

Succession planning logically links to strategy, top management commitment, talent management and development (Mathis et al., 2017).

The SHRM strongly suggests that managers integrate succession-planning tools into their talent management systems. In this process, technology again plays a leading role; software systems are at the aid of managers to identify talent in their organisations for identifying leadership potential. AI may especially become indispensable here, finding employees with potential in unlikely places with linking together characteristics an HR manager might not notice at all.

External supply: The planner at the company has to use outside information, such as statistics concerning the labour market and from the organisation – in other words, external and internal statistics.

Examples of statistics which may be used would include

External Statistics
Unemployment rates
Population density
Number of school-leavers
Proportion with (or in) higher education
Skill levels
Age profile
Number of competitors (Armstrong, 2006).

Internal Statistics
Company growth
Age distribution of employees
Skill levels
Turnover ratios
Overall profile/distribution of employment across job categories (Zeffane and Mayo, 1994).

After general planning is completed, there needs to be specific action regarding what is to be done with supply and demand figures. Mello (2005) has drawn up a table relating to strategies for managing shortages or surpluses in the workforce (see Table 11.1).

Various other options are available, but a detailed analysis is beyond the scope of this work.

Doing Away with the Need for Planning: Gig Working

Temporary work has a bad taste; it implies that the employee will not stay long at the company. The emphasis should be on those who stay on for years because they are the employees who add more value and whom managers can rely upon. With all the changes in the institutional environment, the development of technology and the unforeseen events happening, temporary workers have become vital to organisations (Anima et al., 2020). Even temporary employment decreased during the pandemic, but this tendency has already changed.

Temporary employment means that both the employer and the employee agree to end the employment contract by specific rules, such as the end of a project or at an exact time. In Europe, among the people aged 15–64, the percentage of temporary workers was 12.1 per cent in 2022 (ec.europa.eu,

Table 11.1 Strategies for managing shortages of surpluses in the workforce

Strategies for managing shortages	*Strategies for managing surpluses*
Recruit new permanent employees	Apply a freeze on hiring
Offer incentives to postpone retirement	Do not replace those who leave
Rehire retirees on a part-time basis	Offer incentives for early retirement
Attempt to reduce staff turnover	Reduce working hours
Work current staff overtime	Leave of absence for voluntary service
Subcontract work out	Across-the-board pay cuts
Hire temporary employees	Lay workers off
Redesign job processes so that fewer employees are needed	Reduce outsourced work
	Increase employee training
	Switch to variable pay plan
	Expand operations

Adapted from Mello (2005).

n.d.). In the USA, the picture is very different; according to McKinsey's 2022 American Opportunity Survey, about 58 million employees identified themselves as independent (www.mckinsey.com, n.d.).

The name 'gig economy' gained popularity when temporary positions were filled by freelancers or independent contractors, who gained flexibility in work but almost no job security (see Collings et al. chapter in this volume). It may look tempting to the employer, who does not give benefits to the worker, or only some, or outsources these to external providers. There may be advantages of this arrangement for the worker; flexibility, freedom and accepting tasks that are interesting. The company saves money, also the services may be cheaper for the customer. The drawback is insecurity, no health coverage and on the employer's side, to get the same level and quality of work.

In other words, job seekers commit themselves to being on-call to the employer but are classified as independent contractors with few or no employment rights. The organisation benefits from rapidly responding to changes in demand and few of the fixed costs associated with a regular workforce; there is little need for HR planning, as it is assumed that workers can be readily resourced from the external labour market as and when needed. The downside of the gig is that gig workers are forced to work for very long hours, face strict penalties should they be unavailable and receive wages that barely cover subsistence (Friedman 2014; De Stefano 2015). Still, this type of employment grows fast, and according to surveys, 79 per cent of people who worked this way were more satisfied with their jobs than those who worked full-time (Investopedia, n.d.).

Conclusion

The more critical literature on work and employment relations has tended to neglect HR planning; often the latter has been dismissed as technicist, inflexible, and in some manner, old-fashioned (Gold, 2001: 193; Iles, 2001: 140). However, the rise of gig working may replace established HR-planning tools and techniques with something much worse: firms who are totally uncommitted to their workers, meeting changes in demand and supply through adjusting working time, and, hence, wages at will. On the one hand, any planning process that incorporates an element of long-termism and is based on consistent and predictable assumptions will constrain arbitrary managerial (and, indeed, owner) power, and, indeed, the ability of the firm to rapidly respond to challenges in the pursuit of maximising shareholder value. For employees, this may make for more predictable rights and encourage longer-term approaches to the organisation by themselves. On the other hand, not all HR planning means that good HR management is in place. HR planning may legitimise managerial actions and help redefine implicit contracts. Hence, the manner in which HR planning is used can be seen to be a contested domain. The choice of which set of tools and techniques individual firms use may be less important than the underlying philosophy guiding their usage and the manner in which they are deployed in practice at AI takes a foothold (e.g., Arslan, 2022).

References

Anima, A., Goyal, A., Lietke, B. and Mittal, A. (2020). Taking a fresh look at temporary-labor sourcing amid uncertainty. Available at: https://www.mckinsey.com/capabilities/operations/our-insights/taking-a-fresh-look-at-temporary-labor-sourcing-amid-uncertainty [Accessed 24 August 2023].

Armstrong, M. (2006). *Handbook of Human Resource Management.* London: Kogan Page, pp. 363–388.

Armstrong, M. (2021). *Armstrong's Handbook of Strategic Human Resource Management: Improve Business Performance... Through Strategic People Management.* Berkshire: Mcgraw-Hill Education.

Arslan, A., Cooper, C., Khan, Z., Golgeci, I. and Ali, I. (2022). Artificial intelligence and human workers interaction at team level: A conceptual assessment of the challenges and potential HRM strategies, *International Journal of Manpower*, 43(1): 75–88. doi:10.1108/IJM-01-2021-0052.

Ascarza, E., & Israeli, A. (2022). Eliminating unintended bias in personalized policies using bias-eliminating adapted trees (BEAT). *Proceedings of the National Academy of Sciences, 119*(11), e2115293119.

Bennett, S. (2023). Succession planning statistics 2022 – Everything you need to know. *WebinarCare.* Available at: https://webinarcare.com/best-succession-planning-software/succession-planning-statistics/ [Accessed 24 August 2023].

Boyer, R. (2006). How do institutions cohere and change, in G. Wood and P. James (Eds.), *Institutions and Working Life* (pp. 13–61). Oxford: Oxford University Press.

Brans. P. (2023). What is Markov model? – Definition from WhatIs.com. Available at: https://www.techtarget.com/whatis/definition/Markov-model.

Brewster, C., Brookes, M. and Wood, G. (2006). Varieties of capitalism and varieties of firm, in G. Wood and P. James (Eds), *Institutions, Production and Working Life* (pp. 217–234). Oxford: Oxford University Press.

Britannica. (2023). The editors of encyclopaedia. 'Algorithm'. Encyclopedia Britannica, 30 June. Available at: https://www.britannica.com/science/algorithm [Accessed 7 August 2023].

Cappelli, P. (2017). There's no such thing as big data in HR. *Harvard Business Review.* Available at: https://hbr.org/2017/06/theres-no-such-thing-as-big-data-in-hr [Accessed 7 August 2023].

Cheng, M. M. and Hackett, R. D. (2019). A critical review of algorithms in HRM: Definition, theory, and practice. *Human Resource Management Review*, 31(1): 100698. doi:10.1016/j.hrmr.2019.100698.

CIPD (2021) Resourcing and talent planning survey 2021. Avaiable at: https://www.cipd.org/globalassets/media/knowledge/knowledge-hub/reports/resourcing-and-talent-planning-2021-1_tcm18-100907.pdf. London, CIPD

Cohen, P. (2021). Open letter to the Pew Research Center on generation labels. Family Inequality. Available at: https://familyinequality.wordpress.com/2021/05/26/open-letter-to-the-pew-research-center-on-generation-labels/.

Dastin, J. (2018). Amazon scraps secret AI recruiting tool that showed bias against women. *Reuters.* Available at: https://www.reuters.com/article/us-amazon-com

-jobs-automation-insight/amazon-scraps-secret-ai-recruiting-tool-that-showed-bias-against-women-idUSKCN1MK08G.

Davenport, T. H. (2019). Is HR the most analytics-driven function? *Harvard Business Review*. Available at: https://hbr.org/2019/04/is-hr-the-most-analytics-driven-function [Accessed 7 August 2023].

ec.europa.eu. (n.d.). Temporary employment – Statistics. Available at: https://ec.europa.eu/eurostat/statistics-explained/index.php?title=Temporary_employment_-_statistics#Main_concept [Accessed 24 August 2023].

Deeg, R. and Jackson, G. (2006). Towards a more dynamic theory of capitalist variety, Kings College London, Department of Management Research Paper 40, London.

De Stefano, V. (2015). The rise of the 'just-in-time workforce': On-demand work, crowd work and labour protection in the 'gig-economy'. Available at: https://papers.ssrn.com/sol3/papers.cfm?abstract_id=2682602s.

Dimock, M. (2023). 5 things to keep in mind when you hear about Gen Z, Millennials, Boomers and other generations, Pew Research Center. Available at: https://www.pewresearch.org/short-reads/2023/05/22/5-things-to-keep-in-mind-when-you-hear-about-gen-z-millennials-boomers-and-other-generations/.

Dore, R. (2000). *Stock Market Capitalism: Welfare Capitalism*. Cambridge: Cambridge University Press.

Durnham, R. (1996). The Delphi Technique. Downloaded from http://www.medsch.wisc.edu/adminmed/2002/orgbehav/delphi.pdf.

Foucault, M. (1988). On power, in L. Kritzman (Ed.), *Foucault: Politics, Philosophy, Culture*. New York: Routledge.

Friedman, G. (2014). Workers without employers: Shadow corporations and the rise of the gig economy, *Review of Keynesian Economics*, 2(2): 171–188.

Gallagher, P. (2000). Human resource planning. Scitech Educational, electronic book accessed at Ohio University Ebrary, Ebrary.com, 03. 03. 2008. 12:15 p.m. pp. 23–31.

Gartner. (2012). Big data. Gartner. Available at: https://www.gartner.com/en/information-technology/glossary/big-data. [Accessed 7 August 2023].

Gartner. (2020). How to leverage data for more influential workforce planning. Available at: https://www.gartner.com/en/human-resources/trends/data-for-influential-workforce-planning#:~:text=Build%20a%20catalog%20of%20talent,findings%20in%20a%20visually%20compelling [Accessed 7 August 2023].

Gold, J. (2001). Human resource planning, in J. Bratton and J. Gold (Eds.), *Human Resource Management* (pp. 165–189). London: Palgrave.

Graeber, D. (2019). *Bullshit Jobs: The Rise of Pointless Work, and What We Can Do About It*. London: Penguin Books.

Hall, P. and Soskice, D. (2001). An introduction to the varieties of capitalism, in P. Hall, and D. Soskice (Eds.), *Varieties of Capitalism: The Institutional Basis of Competitive Advantage* (pp. 1–70). Oxford: Oxford University Press.

Hamilton, R. H. and Sodeman, W. A. (2019). The questions we ask: Opportunities and challenges for using big data analytics to strategically manage human capital resources. *Business Horizons*, 63(1). doi:10.1016/j.bushor.2019.10.001.

Harcourt, M. and Wood, G. (2007). The importance of employment protection for skill development in coordinated market economies, *European Journal of Industrial Relations*, 13(2): 141–159.

Huselid, M. (online, no date) The HR Scorecard. Avaiable at: https://www.markhuselid.com/hr.html.

Iles, P. (2001). Employee resourcing, in J. Storey (Ed.), *Human Resource Management.* London: Thomson Learning.

ILO (2023) Artificial intelligence in human resource management: a challenge for the human-centred agenda? Available at: https://www.ilo.org/sites/default/files/wcmsp5/groups/public/%40dgreports/%40inst/documents/publication/wcms_888513.pdf. Geneva, International Labor Organization.

Ivanchevich, J. M. (2007). *Human Resource Management*, 10th edition. New York: McGraw-Hill Irwin.

James, E. and Wooten L. P. (2022). Commentary: Here's what an aging workforce means for America's employers. Available at: https://fortune.com/2022/09/20/labor-shortage-aging-workforce-us-america-employers-talent-job-market-james-wooten/.

Jamet, M. and El-Atillah, I. (2023). The rise of elderly workers: The Europeans defying retirement norms and working past the age of 70. *Euronews.next.* Available at: https://www.euronews.com/next/2023/02/22/the-rise-of-elderly-workers-who-works-beyond-the-age-of-65-or-75-in-europe#:~:text=While%20in%202021%2C%20over%209,per%20cent%2020%20years%20ago.&text=The%20increase%20comes%20mainly%20from%20the%2060%2D64%20age%20group. [Accessed 23 August 2023].

Janet, H. M. and Boudreau, J. W. (2016). An evidence-based review of HR Analytics, *The International Journal of Human Resource Management*, doi:10.1080/09585192.2016.1244699.

Jessop, B. (2001). Series preface, in B. Jessop (Ed.), *Regulation Theory and the Crisis of Capitalism Volume 4 – Developments and Extensions.* London: Edward Elgar.

Kaushal, N., et al. (2021). Artificial intelligence and HRM: Identifying future research agenda using system literature review and bibliometric analysis, *Management Review Quarterly*, doi:10.1007/s11301-021-00249-2.

Kelly, J. (1988). *Rethinking Industrial Relations: Mobilization, Collectivism and Long Waves.* London: Routledge.

Komm, A., et al. (2021). The new possible: How HR can help build the organisation of the future. Edited by B. Tierney. McKinsey. Available at: https://www.mckinsey.com/capabilities/people-and-organisational-performance/our-insights/the-new-possible-how-hr-can-help-build-the-organisation-of-the-future#/ [Accessed 22 August 2023].

Lane, C. and Wood, G. (2009). Introducing diversity in capitalism and capitalist diversity, *Economy and Society*, 38(3): 531–551.

Ledet, E., McNulty, K., Morales, D. and Shandell, E. (2020). How to be great at people analytics. McKinsey. Available at: https://www.mckinsey.com/capabilities/people-and-organisational-performance/our-insights/how-to-be-great-at-people-analytics [Accessed 7 August 2023].

Lewis, R. E. and Heckman, R. J. (2006). Talent management: A critical review, *Human Resource Management Review*, 16: 139–154.

Lussier, R. N., & Hendon, J. R. (2019). *Fundamentals of human resource management: Functions, applications, and skill development.* Sage Publications.

Macaleer, B. and Shannon, J. (2003). Does HRplanning improve business performance? *Industrial Management*, 45(1): 14–21.

Markowitz, A. (2021). *12 Iconic Retailers Sink Into Pandemic Bankruptcy.* AARP. Available at: https://www.aarp.org/money/credit-loans-debt/info-2020/bankrupt-retail-chain-store-list-is-growing.html [Accessed 11 August 2023].

Marsden, D. (1999). *A Theory of Employment Systems.* Oxford: Oxford University Press.

Mathis, R. L. and Jackson, J. H. (2006). *Human Resource Management,* 11th edition. London: Thomson South-Western.

Mathis, R. L., Jackson, J. H., Valentine, S. R. and Meglich, P. (2017). *Human Resource Management,* 15th edition. Boston, MA: Cengage Learning.

Meehan, R. H. and Basheer, A. S. (1990). Forecasting human resources requirements: A demand model, *Human Resource Planning,* 13(4): 297–307.

Mello, J. A. (2005). *Strategic Human Resource Management.* London: Thomson South Western.

Murphy, C. and McCarthy, J. (2021). Human resource analytics, in T. Redman, A. Wilkinson and T. Dundon (Eds.), *Contemporary Human Resource Management: Text and Cases.* 6th edition, pp. 486–508. Harlow: Pearson Education.

Nassim Nicholas Taleb. (2010). *The Black Swan: The Impact of the Highly Improbable.* London: Penguin Random House.

Nicholson, N. (1995). *Blackwell Encyclopedic Dictionary of Organisational Behavior.* Oxford: Blackwell.

Noe, R., Hollenbeck, J., Gerhart, B., & Wright, P. (2006). *Human Resources Management: Gaining a Competitive Advantage.* New York, NY, USA: McGraw-Hill Education.

Novicio, T. (2021). 15 companies that benefited the most from the pandemic. Available at: https://finance.yahoo.com/news/15-companies-benefited-most-pandemic-101257486.html.

Oracle | From Fear to Enthusiasm. (2019). Oracle.com. Available at: https://www.oracle.com/webfolder/s/assets/ebook/ai-work/index.html?source=:em:eo:lpty:pt:RC_PDMK191009P00032:LPD400002437 [Accessed 22 August 2023].

Parker, B. and Caine, D. (1996). Holonic modelling: Human resource planning and the two faces of Janus, *International Journal of Manpower,* 17(8): 30–45.

Phillips, L. and Baker, H. (2022). The UK retailers that have gone bust so far in 2022. *Business Live.* Available at: https://www.business-live.co.uk/retail-consumer/here-retailers-gone-bust-2022-23592469.

Polzer, J. T. (2022). The rise of people analytics and the future of organizational research. *Research in Organizational Behavior, 42,* 100181 – Supplement.

PricewaterhouseCoopers (2022). *PwC HR Tech Survey 2022.* PwC. Available at: https://www.pwc.com/us/en/tech-effect/cloud/hr-tech-survey.html.

Roe, M. (2003). *Political Determinants of Corporate Governance,* Oxford: Oxford University Press.

Robbins, S.P. and Judge, T.A. (2017). Organizational Behavior. Upper Saddle River: Pearson Education Limited.

Root, J., Schwedel, A., Haslett, M. and Bitler, N. (2023). Better with age: The rising importance of older workers. Bain. Available at: https://www.bain.com/insights/better-with-age-the-rising-importance-of-older-workers/ [Accessed 11 August 2023].

Routch, K., Monahan, K. and Doherty, M. (2018). The holy grail of effective leadership succession planning. Deloitte Insights. Available at: https://www2.deloitte.com/us/en/insights/topics/leadership/effective-leadership-succession-planning.html.

Sanders, N. R. and Manrodt, K. B. (2003). The efficacy of using judgmental versus quantitative forecasting methods in practice, *Omega,* 31(6): 511–522.

Stone, T. H. and Fiorito, J. (1986). A perceived uncertainty model of human resource forecasting technique use, *Academy of Management Review*, 11(3): 635–642.

Storey, M. (2001). Human resource management today: An assessment, in M. Storey (Ed.), *Human Resource Management: A Critical Text*. London: Thomson Learning.

Streeck, W. and Thelen, K. (2005). Introduction: institutional change in advanced political economies, in W. Streeck, and K. Thelen (Eds.), *Beyond Continuity. Institutional change in advanced political economies* (pp. 1–39). Oxford: Oxford University Press.

The Economist. (2008). Generation Y Goes to Work: Reality bites for young workers. *The Economist*. Decemeber 30, 2008.

Thelen, K. (2001). Varieties of labor politics in the developed democracies, in P. Hall and D. Soskice (Eds.), *Varieties of Capitalism: The Institutional Basis of Competitive Advantage*. Oxford: Oxford University Press.

Toms, S. (2008). 'Immeasurability': A critique of Hardt and Negri. Paper presented at the Conference of Practical Criticism in the Managerial Social Science, Leicester, January.

Vaiman, V., Cascio, W. F., Collings, D. G., & Swider, B. W. (2021). The shifting boundaries of talent management, *Human Resource Management*, *60*(2), 253–257.

Ward, D. (1996). Workforce demand forecasting techniques, *Human Resource Planning*, 19(1): 54–55.

Wright, E. O. and Dwyer, R. (2006). The American jobs machine, in G. Wood and P. James (Eds.), *Institutions and Working Life*. Oxford: Oxford University Press.

Wright, M. and Wood, G. (2008). Financialization and private equity, Working Paper, University of Sheffield, Sheffield.

Zeffane, R. and Mayo, G. (1994). Planning for human resources in the 1990s: Development of an operational model, *International Journal of Manpower*, 15(6): 36–56.

12 Performance Management

Anthony McDonnell, Patrick Gunnigle and Kevin R. Murphy

Introduction

The evaluation and improvement of job performance is a central concern in modern Human Resource Management. Both performance-appraisal and performance-management systems are commonly believed to be critical to the success of organisations, but they often appear to function poorly and are held in low regard. Performance appraisals have been practised in organisations in one form or another since the 1800s (Murphy and Cleveland, 1995) and over time has become a central plank of organisational life worldwide (Morley, Murphy, Cleveland, Heraty & McCarthy, 2021). In more recent times, some large organisations (e.g., Accenture, Deloitte, Microsoft, GAP, Medtronic) have discussed abandoning or substantially curtailing their use of formal performance-appraisal systems (Buckingham and Goodall, 2015; Culbert and Rout, 2010). This aligns with increasing concerns that both performance-appraisal and performance-management systems regularly fail in many organisations (Aguinis and Burgi-Tian, 2021; Pulakos, Mueller-Hanson, Arad and Moye, 2015; Smith, Hornsby and Shirmeyer, 1996).

There have been calls for organisations to discontinue performance evaluation programmes altogether (Murphy, 2020), mainly on the grounds that organisations rarely act on the results of these evaluations. Nevertheless, most organisations still rely on formal performance-appraisal and performance-management systems (Gunnigle, Turner, Lavelle and McDonnell, 2014; Torrington, Hall, Taylor & Atkinson, 2021). A recent survey of performance appraisal practices in 22 nations suggests that the general patterns reported in previous studies, such as Mercer (2013), are replicated in organisations across the world (Houldsworth et al., 2021; Morley et al., 2021). Virtually all medium- and large-sized organisations employ some sort of performance-management system, although the relations between traditional annual-evaluation systems and performance-management systems vary widely over organisations (Lawler, 2003; Pulakos, 2011).

Performance management has developed from an operational focus to a more strategically-oriented concept, i.e. where it plays an integral role in the formulation and implementation of strategy (Aguinis, 2023;

DOI: 10.4324/9781032625560-14

Scott-Lennon, 1995). It is this strategic impetus that differentiates it from performance appraisal. Performance management seeks to align several processes (e.g., training, performance-related pay systems) with corporate objectives (McKenna and Beech, 2008). Theoretically, it involves a shared process between managers, individuals and teams where goals are agreed and jointly reviewed, although in practice goals are often imposed from above. Furthermore, corporate, divisional, departmental, team and individual objectives should all be integrated. Performance appraisal is a crucial element of the performance-management process, involving a formal review of individual performance. Some have suggested that performance management represents possibly the greatest opportunity for a human resource (HR) system to make an impactful contribution to organisational performance (Cappelli & Tavis, 2016; Sparrow and Hiltrop, 1994). It represents a system that can inform how the firm's human resources contribute to the organisation's strategic objectives. Unfortunately, the extent to which it is an effective and useful system in practice remains open to question (Murphy, 2020). For example, the high use of various facets of performance management does not always correlate with high results regarding perceived effectiveness (DeNisi and Smith, 2014).

This chapter takes a contemporary and critical look at both performance-appraisal and performance-management systems in organisations and asks how and why modern organisations develop systems of this sort to evaluate the performance and effectiveness of employees. We begin by defining performance management and reviewing its evolution. We then consider the performance-management process by applying a critical lens to some of the main approaches set out thus far. We then consider the primary tool used in performance-management systems, namely, performance appraisals, before discussing more contemporary developments in performance management, including the challenge of evaluating the performance of remote workers.

Performance Management: Definition and Evolution

Performance management as a concept can be traced to Anglo-Saxon management (Sparrow and Hiltrop, 1994) but it did not emerge as a standalone concept until the 1980s. In basic terms, performance management is a process that enables employees to perform their roles to the best of their abilities with the aim of achieving or exceeding established targets and standards that are directly linked with the organisation's objectives (Cappelli & Tavis, A. 2016). Performance management is posited as a strategic management technique that supports the overall business goals of the firm through linking each individual's work goals to the overall mission of the firm (Costello, 1994; Sparrow and Hiltrop, 1994). This requires 'the ability to interpret the more abstract goals and objectives at board level into more practical operational goals and objectives at employee level to meet them' (Chase and Fuchs, 2008: 226). Once goals have been developed, it is the supervisor's responsibility to provide frequent and timely feedback on progress towards fulfilling these goals and to assist employees in accomplishing these goals.

Performance management evolved from the *management by objectives* (MBO) approach, first popularised by Peter Drucker (1954). MBO was a scientific-type approach with an emphasis on achieving results that were linked to established targets. It involved management focusing on achievable objectives to produce the best possible results using available resources. Both MBO and performance management hold several similarities, including the requirement for distinguishable job-based goals and development objectives to be achieved (Fowler, 1990). However, performance management has evolved considerably in the interim. MBO tended to only be applied to management, whereas performance management is applied to all staff – it seeks to integrate all organisational actors in the pursuit of improved performance. MBO utilised quantitative performance measures, whereas performance management is more likely to include both quantitative and qualitative measures. This moved organisations away from solely focusing on financial performance and, in parallel, to bring a development focus for employees.

There are four principal normative concerns of performance management (Armstrong, 2022). First, that it aims to improve performance. Second, it endeavours to develop employees. Third, it seeks to satisfy the expectations of the various organisational stakeholders. Finally, communication and involvement are imperative due to the ideology of arriving at jointly agreed goals and objectives. In other words, performance management, in theory, seeks management by agreement rather than dictation. However, whether such lofty expectations play out in practice remain very much open to question. It appears more common that top management unilaterally sets strategic objectives and then attempts to cascade these down the line and translate them into individual performance targets (Aguinis, 2023; Pulakos and O'Leary, 2011; Pulakos, Mueller-Hanson, Arad and Moye, 2015).

The Performance Management Process

Many of the pertinent models on performance management involve a simple four- or five-step process (see Figure 12.1). These models tend to be based on the assertion that all work performance stems from, and is driven by, the corporate objectives. These are then broken into functional/departmental objectives. Individual objectives stem from these and all are monitored and reviewed on an ongoing basis, with a formal review or appraisal conducted at least annually. The results of this appraisal may (or not) be linked to pay; there is a significant body of research arguing for and against linking appraisals to pay. The main argument for doing so is that all parties take the process more seriously. The primary argument against doing so is that pay becomes the central issue, and this is to the detriment of the developmental aspect of performance management. Linking performance to pay is a market-based approach to achieving employee commitment whilst concurrently helping 'to

Stages of a typical performance management system. Adapted from Torrington *et al*, 2021).

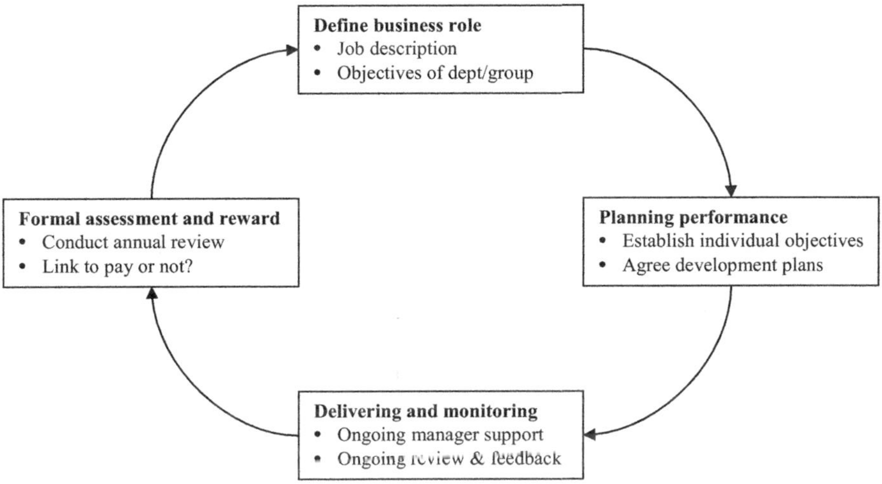

Figure 12.1 Stages of a typical performance management system

align managerial interests with shareholder value and shift downside risk' to the employees (Gospel and Pendleton, 2005: 17).

These models, however, fail to adequately capture the intricacies of applying performance management and elucidate *how* performance management might be employed as an effective means of managing and improving the individual worker and organisational performance. An easy criticism to make of performance management is that it is overly normative. This is largely due to it being rooted in the unitarist ideology. The unitarist perspective 'may represent one of the threats to performance management as it fails to recognize the plurality of interests that are so much a part of organizational reality' (Williams, 2002: 252). For example, little consideration is given to the effect that different markets play on employment-relations systems. Gospel and Pendleton (2005: 10) note that Anglo-Saxon countries (e.g., US and UK) are characterised by 'labour management systems which are essentially based on market signals'. Depending on the conditions of the day, organisations in these countries will adjust recruitment levels and redundancies, pay tends to have a performance element, job tenures will vary and so forth. On the other hand, systems in other countries (e.g., Germany) are influenced less by market conditions. There, jobs are of longer tenure and organisations are more likely to invest in its workforce, with pay tending to be based more towards seniority than performance.

No one best, universally-agreed performance-management model exists and – as already highlighted – those being used tend to be quite simplistic. Buchner (2007) suggests there has been a failure to utilise sufficient theory to support performance management. More specifically, he argues that existent models fail to make explicit linkages between the various elements of the process. For example, it has been claimed that good performance-management systems might aid in the recruitment and retention of top performers (Aguinis, Ryan, Gottfredson and Harry, 2012; Aguinis and Burgi-Tian, 2021), but there have been few empirical demonstrations of how performance management practices influence talent management. Similarly, Bevan and Thompson (1992) suggest a major issue is the lack of integration of activities; some are utilised while others are not. This phenomenon is described by Torrington et al. (2021) as unfortunate since one of the primary espoused advantages of performance management is the integration of activities for managing performance: performance appraisal is integrated with performance planning where individual objectives are linked to the overall organisational objectives. The success of these objectives is, in theory, supported through ongoing feedback and personal-development plans and assessed in order to reward superior performance (Torrington et al., 2021). However, Murphy, Cleveland and Hanscom (2018) question the wisdom of personnel systems that involve giving frequent feedback. They note that there is considerable evidence that feedback is stressful for both the giver and the receiver, and that little evidence exists that identifies feedback as consistently leading to desirable changes in behaviour. If giving and receiving feedback is a negative experience that produces, at best, uncertain results, (Kluger and DeNisi's [1996] review suggests that performance feedback is about as likely to lead to performance decrements as it is to lead to performance improvements), arguments for increasing the frequency of feedback are unconvincing.

Den Hartog et al. (2004) have attempted to redress some criticisms of existing performance-management models by giving greater prominence to the role of the line manager. Much research contends that for performance management to be effective and beneficial, it needs to be owned and driven by line management (cf. Sparrow and Hiltrop, 1994; Williams, 2002; Torrington et al., 2021). Simultaneously, top management must support and be committed to the system (Sparrow and Hiltrop, 1994). As with any system, if there is insufficient support from the top, how can one expect that personnel further down the organisational hierarchy take the system seriously? Line management have a major mediating influence in the implementation of HR practices (Den Hartog et al., 2004), although the line manager also receives far too little support within organisations.

While conceptual models of this sort have much merit, it remains unclear if they connect with the day-to-day reality of performance-management systems. Because they focus so heavily on linking goals at all levels of the organisation and on basing the goals of divisions, departments, work groups and employees on the strategic goals of the organisation, performance management is necessarily a top-down process. Decisions are made by a small set of top executives about the strategic direction of the organisation, and inevitably they drive the goals, plans and strategies of each of the lower levels of the organisation. This often leaves limited scope for line managers to influence the process of performance management.

Performance Management: A Critique

Classically, the starting point of a performance-management system should be setting out the organisation's mission, aims and values. Following this, the organisation's objectives are identified, and these need to be intrinsically linked to, and support, the firm's mission. These objectives should be cascaded down the organisation with strong links to the objectives of all managers and employees. The result should be integrated objectives across all organisational levels and personnel (Fowler, 1990).

In practice, though, converting the business strategy into clear performance objectives is challenging for many reasons. Business strategies do not always result from a rational plan but may – sometimes serendipitously – evolve over time. Mintzberg (1978, 1987) distinguished between 'realised' and 'unrealised' strategies, and 'intended' versus 'emergent' strategies. Deliberate organisational strategies refer to those that are intended and realised. However, there are also 'unrealised' strategies, which for one reason or other are never implemented. In addition, 'realised' strategies may 'emerge' over time without the conscious intervention of strategists. Hence, strategies may emerge that do not follow the traditional planned view; rather they develop in a more incremental fashion. There may be great difficulty in setting measurable objectives unless the firm operates in a relatively stable environment, increasingly rare for organisations.

Furthermore, organisational objectives can conflict with one another. Corporate governance needs to be considered, as managers do not make decisions in a vacuum. For example, if considerable emphasis is placed on shareholder value (Gospel and Pendleton, 2005), management will need to consider the effect any decision they make will have on this aspect. A firm that is downsizing but maintains its commitment to investing in its workforce by not reducing headcount or cutting 'training spend' represents such a scenario. In this instance, commitment towards its employees may conflict with a corporate strategy of cost containment. Likewise, adopting a total quality management (TQM) system sets out to do things right first time, whereas a learning-organisation orientation intimates that mistakes are accepted if one learns from them – two conflicting perspectives (Torrington et al., 2021). The individual versus team dynamic represents another dilemma in performance management. For example, there is a danger that individual objectives could be detrimental to the achievement of team-based objectives and vice versa (Torrington et al., 2021).

There are serious conflicts between the top-down nature of performance management and the broader movement towards developing flatter organisations and empowering workers (Blanchard, Carlos and Randolph, 2001; Murphy et al., 2018). That is, performance management depends heavily on goals that are cascaded down from the top of the organisation, and it puts emphasis on making sure that each employee's behaviours are driven by goals selected by the very top of the organisation. On the other hand, many organisations are moving towards systems that give their employees considerable autonomy and responsibility, a process that can be inconsistent with top-down control. We examine this conflict in more detail in the final section of this chapter.

Performance measurement is a further area of contention. For effective performance management, the organisation needs to know what performance it seeks (Torrington et al., 2021). Fowler (1990) makes an interesting point in suggesting that performance dimensions are chosen by organisations, not because they are the most important or relevant but because they are the most straightforward to measure. It also may lead to a very narrow view of performance being adopted. This links into the much-debated issue of demonstrating a link between human resource management practices and organisational performance (cf. Huselid, 1995; Guest et al., 2003). To date there remains a lack of conclusive evidence on the existence of a link between specific management processes, such as performance management and organisational success (Bevan and Thompson, 1992; DeNisi and Smith, 2014). It is commonly assumed that improved individual performance will lead to better organisational performance. However, this relationship is far more complex. Improvements at lower individual levels may be insufficient in improving organisational performance (DeNisi, 2000; DeNisi and Smith, 2014). For example, improvements at an individual level may not result in improved organisational performance if their objectives are not intrinsically linked with team, departmental and organisational objectives.

Relatedly, the extent to which performance can be solely measured through quantitative measures is open to question (Fowler, 1990). Arriving at crude, quantitative measures (e.g., number of sales in a week or number of products produced) may mean a firm fails to gain a true picture of overall performance. An interesting example is provided by Chase and Fuchs (2008) regarding a teacher who tries exceptionally hard to improve his/her students' learning but the final marks turn out like those of students whose teacher does not make half the effort. Which teacher is doing the most to improve performance? If rewards were based on student performance, it may serve to de-motivate the hard-working teacher. The highly quantitative nature of performance management and worker control in the increasingly important gig economy represents a more novel context where such concerns emerge (Duggan et al., 2023). Further, there is also the phenomenon of unanticipated side effects (see Figure 12.2).

Qualitative measures, such as customer attitude surveys, can also yield vital information. Criticisms of the use of qualitative measures largely relate to their particularly subjective nature. Due to this, appraiser training provides an important tool in reducing subjectivity. Mabey et al. (1998) contend the greatest challenge faced regarding performance management is to ensure that the procedures incorporated in the system can be audited. This helps ensure a fair and effective system is being used. Regular appraisals are often utilised to bring a degree of formalisation to the process of performance management.

A computer salesperson is primarily assessed on his quarterly sales. While he is aware that a current laptop range is being phased out, he focuses his efforts on maximizing sales of this line over the current quarter. He is successful in this regard and receives a substantial bonus for his sales effort. However, he also leaves many dissatisfied customers who soon realize the laptop they purchased was soon after replaced by a superior version at a similar price. The company goal of sales maximization was achieved but to the detriment of arguably more important goals of enhancing customer satisfaction and loyalty.

Figure 12.2 Unanticipated side effects to performance measures

The most important characteristics of performance measures are their validity and reliability (Mabey et al., 1998). Reliability simply refers to whether the same decision reached would be reached if other individuals made it. Validity refers to the extent to which the method used measures what it is supposed to measure. Thus, it is imperative that sufficient time is given to deriving the performance indicators and ensuring they accurately depict the performance that the organisation wants to measure.

The provision of feedback is a major component of effective performance management (Aguinis, 2023; Aguinis, Joo and Gottfredson, 2011). In theory, feedback is frequent and immediate in performance management, though the extent to which this takes place in practice is questionable (Coens and Jenkins, 2000; Fletcher, 2001). As noted earlier, it is far from clear that giving more feedback will result in desirable behaviour changes (Kluger and DeNisi, 1996). Second, there is no clear agreement about the optimal frequency of feedback. Annual performance feedback, such as that provided by traditional performance-appraisal systems may be too little, but daily feedback may be too much. Finally, the challenge of providing performance of timely, ongoing feedback is heightened by the very fact that unforeseen events occur. This may require a reappraisal of objectives. The hallmark of performance management is the idea that goals, plans and strategies at all levels of the organisation can be described and harmonised, but in the fluid and uncertain environments in which organisations function, it is often necessary to modify plans with experience, even if overall organisational strategies do not change.

Performance Management: A System That Confers Organisational Value?

From a normative perspective, the effective and strategic use of performance management provides a means for recognising good performance, as well as clarifying tasks and providing support in undertaking them. It offers the potential to provide a structured means of directing and guiding individual employees, teams and departments towards the pursuit and achievement of corporate objectives. It can also be useful in identifying 'high potentials', thus helping succession planning and management development. Furthermore, it can aid the HR planning process through the identification of training and skills gaps. Through holding review sessions with employees, the opportunity is afforded to set out action plans and to discuss personal and career development. This can be extremely beneficial as it may be construed as showing how valued an employee is to the firm. In addition, it allows the identification of sub-par performers and hopefully can remediate performance shortcomings.

However, the extent to which these benefits are realised appears limited. Dissatisfaction with performance management is well documented (Ellis and Saunier, 2004; Pulakos and O'Leary, 2011), while evidence that performance management works is elusive (DeNisi and Smith, 2014; Pulakos and O'Leary, 2011). It is viewed by some as representing another administration exercise for line managers to allow HR to rate and reward employees (Armstrong, 2014; Ellis and Saunier, 2004). For many organisations performance management is about working out a rating for employees and making pay decisions based on this rating (Ellis and Saunier, 2004), rather than a concerted attempt to improve the organisation's performance and develop employees. Others have suggested that there is often a failure to align performance management with other crucial organisational processes such as strategic planning (Ellis and Saunier, 2004; Torrington et al., 2021). Criticisms abound regarding the extent to which performance management is more a reactive process dealing with external pressures as opposed to being a conscious strategic effort, and the developmental aspect tends to be a decidedly secondary concern relative to the bottom line (Fletcher and Williams, 1992). There also appears to be a feeling among some organisations and managers that performance management brings a low return of investment in terms of the bottom line (Chase and Fuchs, 2008).

Performance Appraisal

The performance appraisal is essentially a formal mechanism of reviewing individual employee performance. Fletcher (2001: 473) defines it as the 'activities through which organisations seek to assess employees and develop their competence, enhance performance and distribute rewards'. It generally involves line managers appraising their subordinate's performance, often on an annual basis. In terms of the content of appraisals, there is no definite 'one best' prescribed approach. For example, job performance will nearly always be reviewed, whilst personality and behaviours may or may not. Performance management is often conflated with performance appraisal and vice versa. Performance appraisals are concerned with individual performance, whereas performance management looks at individual, team and organisational performance. The appraisal may be just another HR technique used by an organisation, while performance management attempts to link the appraisal process to the wider values and objectives of the firm (Foot and Hook, 2008). However, appraisals constitute an integral part of the performance-management process.

One of the critical differences between traditional performance appraisal and modern performance-management systems has to do with the time frame and the perspectives involved. In most organisations, formal performance appraisals are often annual events that are summative and evaluative in nature, in the sense that they provide evaluations of your success or effectiveness in different aspects of your job over the last year. Performance appraisals are often tied to pay and often reflect the assumption that rewarding good performance will motivate employees to improve and to perform well in the future. In contrast, performance management involves feedback that is immediate and that is designed to guide and control performance rather than to motivate it. That is, performance management requires managers to provide feedback on what employees are doing well and poorly now and what they need to do to shape their behaviours in ways that will help the organisation accomplish its strategic goals.

A second important difference between performance appraisal and performance management has to do with an emphasis on consultative vs. directive roles for managers. Most performance appraisal systems include self-ratings of performance and/or goals that are set by employees or through mutual agreement between employees and managers. In contrast, many performance-management systems are directive, in the sense that it is the goals and objectives set by top management that determine the goals, plans and strategies at each lower level of the organisation.

The Effectiveness of Appraisals

Appraisals are believed to enhance managerial and organisational performance as well as positively contributing to employee motivation (Randell, 1989). Conducted effectively, they are credited with several positive benefits (cf. Longenecker, 1997):

1 Performance planning and goal setting
2 Providing feedback and coaching
3 Employee development
4 Linking employee performance to compensation and promotion decisions

Mabey et al. (1998) identified two schools of thought regarding problems with the effectiveness of performance appraisals in evaluating employee performance. The first school focuses on the performance appraisal as a social process (Murphy and Cleveland, 1995). Since an appraisal generally involves one person rating another's performance 'it is impossible to disentangle the social influences which are present' (Mabey et al., 1998: 136). Second, a performance appraisal has a political dimension (cf. Barlow, 1989). Rather than being an objective, neutral process, the performance appraisal represents a political process whereby those involved may pursue personal agendas and strategies (Longenecker, 1997; Mabey et al., 1998). For example, there may be a poor working relationship between employee and appraiser. This may result in appraisees perceiving the appraisal as unfair. This may de-motivate employees, possibly resulting in overt and covert outcomes, including poor performance and higher labour turnover. In addition, the appraiser may not possess enough information to effectively review the employee's performance. This may lead to a situation whereby the appraisee receives incomplete and inaccurate information on their performance. Some firms have tried to negate such issues by having more than one appraiser, with the objective of reducing the potential for bias.

Performance appraisal often suffers from trying to achieve too much (IRS, 2001). For example, performance appraisals may be used to identify poor, good and exceptional performers, spot high potentials, discover training and development needs and decide on appropriate rewards (Cleveland, Murphy and Williams, 1989). Not only are there multiple goals for many performance appraisal systems, there are often also conflicting goals. For example, a recent Cranet-E survey (2003) shows appraisals are most used to identify training and development needs (Chase and Fuchs, 2008). Links to rewards are also strong but there are notable variations in how extensive this is across countries. For example, the link to rewards is far stronger in Germany and Sweden than in the United Kingdom. This is quite interesting given that Germany and Sweden are characterised by high levels of unionisation and the conventional wisdom is that unions may often be averse to systems where pay increases are partially and wholly dependent on performance appraisals (cf. Gunnigle et al., 1998). Utilising appraisals for both developmental needs and for ascribing rewards is particularly interesting because – to all intents and purposes – they are two conflicting approaches. The appraisee might be loath to identify training or developmental needs for fear of it being construed as a sign of weakness which may negatively impact rewards to be received.

Longenecker (1997) found that often it is the fundamentals of the appraisal process that reduce its effectiveness. For example, over eight in ten respondents in his study suggested that the failure to have clear performance criteria negated the potential benefits of conducting an appraisal. The conventional performance management literature is premised on the view that having clear and explicit goals is imperative in eliciting improved employee performance. Whilst ability and motivation are important ingredients, they are not the sole determinant of improved performance (Torrington et al., 2021). It draws from expectancy theory, which basically sets out that employees will be motivated to perform if they believe their goals are achievable and that they will lead to valuable rewards (Vroom, 1964). Hence, if objectives are unclear, the appraisal may do more harm than good. This can include both individual and organisational level outcomes. For example, individual level outcomes may include de-motivation amongst employees and increased tension in the manager–appraisee relationship. Organisational level outcomes may incorporate a loss of credibility for the HR department and a loss of managerial focus.

A key related question is, what type of individual objectives should be set? Should only tightly-defined, results-oriented objectives be set? This often seems to be the case, probably because they provide an easier benchmark against which to measure performance. It is argued that such objectives should follow the SMART (specific, measurable, appropriate, relevant, timed) rules (Torrington et al., 2021). However, setting SMART goals can be problematic if they are not continually reviewed and updated. The business environment is subject to rapid change, possibly rendering pre-set goals a constraint on the firm. Is setting results-oriented objectives sufficient? People are not always necessarily in control of whether they can meet their goals or not. External influences can constrain the achievement of performance. Consequently, it has been suggested that behavioural targets should also be set (Williams, 2002). Almond and Ferner (2006), in their research on US multinational companies in Europe, found that the nature of objectives is changing whereby objective criteria based on job performance were increasingly supplemented with softer, more difficult to quantify objectives such as 'cooperation' within the team.

Contemporary Developments

Recent decades have witnessed considerable evolution in the spheres of performance appraisal and performance management. Three topics that are the focus of current research strike us as especially important for understanding performance management; the use of feedback to influence performance, the role of top-down planning in performance management and the challenges of evaluating performance in remote- or hybrid-work environments.

Feedback

One of the major distinctions between traditional performance appraisal and performance management has to do with the frequency and nature of the feedback that is provided. Performance appraisal provides annual feedback that focuses on how well you did in the past year. Some models of performance management (e.g., Pulakos, 2009) include this type of appraisal, but most of the descriptions of performance management call for a very different approach to performance evaluation. For example, Aguinis (2023) calls for more frequent, if not continuous, evaluations of performance. The assumption here is that summative feedback about what you did well and what you did poorly over the last year is not as valuable for changing behaviour as feedback given at the point that behaviour occurs. Murphy et al. (2018) makes almost the opposite recommendation, that giving more feedback leads to more stress and worse relations between supervisors and subordinates without producing consistent improvements in performance. They argue that frequent feedback produces known losses (e.g., more stress, worse relations between supervisors and subordinates) in exchange for doubtful benefits.

Murphy et al.'s (2018) suggestions notwithstanding, the argument for performance feedback to be more frequent has been echoed by several scholars (e.g., London and Smither, 2002; Steelman et al., 2004). However, it is important to understand that the feedback that is part of performance management is both quantitatively (i.e. it occurs more often) and qualitatively from the type of commentary people receive in their annual appraisals. In traditional performance appraisal, performance feedback is the result of a process of collecting, integrating and evaluating performance relevant in each of the major dimensions of your job. In performance management, feedback is tied to specific tasks or behaviours and is focused on whether or not the behaviour was effective and how it can be improved. The type of frequent or continuous feedback that characterises performance management will necessarily be informal and usually decoupled from administrative decisions (e.g., you are unlikely to get salary adjustments on a daily or weekly basis).

The idea that annual summative feedback might be insufficient and that feedback should be more frequent raises the interesting question of determining the optimal frequency for performance feedback. Very frequent feedback is likely to have the advantage of immediacy, but there is a risk that that same very frequent feedback will become repetitive, especially if it is feedback about behaviours that are difficult to change in the short run. For example, suppose that your mathematical skills are not up to par, rendering one slow in performing. Less frequent feedback loses this immediacy, but it might have the advantage of being based on a potentially large sample of behaviour.

Lukas (2010) developed an analytic model to evaluate the optimal frequency of feedback in systems where performance-contingent pay influences employees' decisions to remain with an organisation or to leave it. His model suggests that more frequent performance evaluations might not be beneficial. The model incorporates several assumptions that are difficult to test, but the results do suggest that more frequent performance feedback might not always be better than less frequent feedback. Frequent feedback about aspects of performance that are difficult to change is likely to feel more like nagging, or even harassment, than like information that is helpful to the employee.

Performance management relies heavily on two assumptions, that employees lack the necessary information to perform their jobs well and that if they are given the right information their performance will improve. Both assumptions are problematic. As noted earlier, the effects of feedback on performance are, at best, inconsistent. About one-third of the time feedback leads to increases in performance, about one-third of the time it seems to lead to decreases in performance and effectiveness, and about one-third of the time it has little effect (Kluger and DeNisi, 1996). More fundamentally, the belief that employees want feedback and that they will incorporate it to improve their job performance is unwarranted (Cleveland, Lim and Murphy, 2007). Supervisors and managers often dread giving feedback and employees often actively avoid it; the faith that proponents of performance management (e.g., Aguinis, 2023) place in the value of feedback is not well-founded.

Questions about whether a particular system gives too much or too little feedback are important, but the more pressing question is *why* organisations give performance feedback. Empirical assessments of the effects of feedback (e.g., Kluger and DeNisi, 1996) suggest that feedback of this sort is unlikely to substantially improve performance or effectiveness. Sometimes it will help, but it is just as likely to hurt. With the rise of algorithmic technologies, additional opportunities and challenges emerge on many aspects of performance feedback. Rather than thinking about feedback as a mechanism for improving employees, it might be more useful to analyse it as a system for controlling the behaviour of employees.

Performance Management as a System of Control

The starting point for the development of most performance-management programmes is a set of decisions that top leaders make about the strategies and objectives of the firm. Subsequent decisions about how the actions of divisions, departments, work groups and even individual employees will contribute to these objectives are, in theory, harmonised with these goals. In this respect, performance management shares much in common with Frederick Taylor's Scientific Management (Murphy et al., 2018). Both systems involve shifting decisions about how to perform work from the individual employee to higher levels in the organisation, presumably in the name of efficiency. In Scientific Management, experts told workers in detail how to perform each task in the most efficient way possible. In performance management, the emphasis is on harmonising the actions of each member of the organisation in service of goals and objectives set by top management. The goal of feedback in these systems is to monitor and enforce the compliance of each employee with goals that have cascaded down from the top of the organisation.

There is some irony in the insistence on top-down planning that appears to characterise many performance-management systems. Contemporary research and business publications place a good deal of emphasis on topics such as empowerment (Blanchard, Carlos and Randolph, 2001; Chen, Lam and Zhong, 2007), employee-centric organisations (Lee-Hoffmann, 2011; Reeves, 2015; Sharma and Sahoo, 2013) and organisational structures that minimise hierarchy. In simple terms, there is a substantial argument for involving employees more directly in planning work, setting goals and objectives and evaluating performance (e.g., Roberston, 2015). The unifying feature of all these trends is the belief that it is important to give employees the tools and the responsibility to design, plan, manage and evaluate their own work. It can be argued that this belief is antithetical to performance management, but highly consistent with contemporary performance appraisal.

Performance management has been criticised on the basis that it attempts to tightly control the behaviour of employees (Winstanley and Stuart-Smith, 1996). Performance management may or may not afford greater autonomy over how work is carried out. It depends largely on how it is administered and the underlying management ethos. At one level, the idea of being appraised can be construed as 'akin to a police state, where the control occurs through the collection of documentation and evidence, a dossier on the individual. Instead of standing over one's shoulder, supervision becomes a matter of spying through keyholes' (Winstanley and Stuart-Smith, 1996: 69). This is an accusation that is particularly noteworthy in certain sectors, such as the call-centre industry. This industry has been characterised by some as a re-creation of the sweatshops, 'dark satanic mills', and the ideal environment for exercising 'panoptican' control over all aspects of employee behaviour (cf. Taylor and Bain, 1999; Kinnie et al., 2000). Call centre agents are often subject to the most in-depth monitoring of their performance through collecting 'hard' quantitative performance measures, including time to answer a call, call length, abandoned call rate, accuracy and adherence to script and wrap-up time. These scenarios can be categorised as a particularly illustrative controlling form of performance management. For some time, there was a view that what was distinctive was the 'overt and pervasive nature' of this management approach in call centres (Holman, 2005: 115), but algorithmic technologies are being employed to some similar effect in different types of work (Duggan et al., 2023).

Performance Management in a Changing Work Environment

The COVID-19 pandemic led to substantial, and possibly lasting, changes in the organisation of work. Many types of office work were done remotely during the pandemic, and there is little likelihood that organisations that had relied substantially on remote work will return to the traditional five-day work week; some hybrid between remote and in-person work appears to be increasingly common (Goldberg, 2023; Miller, 2023). Remote- and hybrid-work systems pose challenges to both traditional performance-appraisal systems and modern performance-management systems, in large part because they provide supervisors with limited opportunities to observe employee behaviour. Overall, the implications of remote and hybrid work are likely to be more disruptive to performance-management systems, which rely on timely and frequent performance feedback. Research on the effects of pandemic-related changes to the organisation of work for performance appraisal and performance management is just starting to emerge (Mitchell et al., 2021; Pasha and Jacobson, 2022; Yang, 2021; see also Staples et al., 1999), and the implications of work arrangements where supervisors have little direct interaction with subordinates for performance evaluation are not yet clear. It is likely, however, that the use of hybrid and remote work will shift the orientation of performance evaluations from work behaviours to the *results* of work behaviours. That is, if a supervisor cannot observe *how* you performed a task or how much time and effort this task involved, evaluations are likely to concentrate on the results of work behaviour (e.g., success and timeliness in completing tasks) rather than the work process. It is also likely that feedback will be more limited and often less necessary. Employees often know whether or not they accomplished key tasks in a timely manner, and there may not be much more a supervisor can tell you when giving performance feedback. All signs point to an end to the traditional five-day, in-person office workweek, but the implications of these changes for performance appraisal and performance management are not yet clearly understood.

Conclusion

Stereotypically, performance management seeks to manage human resources through the establishment of specific objectives for individuals, teams, departments and divisions that tie in with achieving the overall strategic objectives of the firm. It draws together HR policies and practices to form an overall coordinated system in which to manage performance. Performance management draws, in particular, on two theories, namely, expectancy theory and goal-setting theory. Although this integration of theory is welcomed and, indeed, the case for more can be argued, these theories also point towards problems that yet remain unresolved. These include issues regarding setting feasible goals, how performance is measured, should there be a link to rewards and – if so – what type of rewards should be provided and how does feedback work in the system.

Mabey et al. (1998: 149) note that performance management can be 'criticised for relying on a model of management which is more rational than is achievable in practice'. More specific criticisms include the universalistic form it tends to follow. By this, we mean that performance management is often applied with little consideration given to contextual factors such as the differences between organisational roles, cultures and national institutional environments. Performance-management systems invariably incorporate multiple objectives and content including linking objectives to organisational strategy and developing employee skills. As a result, many practices and tools will have to be incorporated, rendering performance-management systems quite complex. In turn, such complexity clearly poses considerable challenges to organisations regarding the design and implementation of performance-management systems. Nor is this complexity likely to diminish any time soon due to pressures for improved performance, technological advances and cultural issues in implementing performance management across borders (cf. Fletcher, 2001; Almond and Ferner, 2006).

In conclusion, whilst performance management has come a long way and may be working effectively in many organisations, there is a need for a more nuanced research agenda regarding the innermost workings of performance management. To date, many of the extant models are too simplistic. We simply do not know whether performance *can* be managed, and if it can, whether performance *should* be managed. Performance management has the potential to contribute to the effectiveness of organisations, but it also has the potential to remove responsibility, autonomy and humanity from work; and we have not yet developed effective ways of creating linkages between top-level goals and the behaviours of individual workers while at the same time empowering workers and giving them a chance to have a meaningful role in determining what they will do and how they will do it when performing their jobs. Not enough credence has been placed on the inherent complexities and potential for contradictions that exist in making performance management an effective system in organisations. These have increased in recent years with the advance of algorithmic technologies and the rise of remote and hybrid forms of work.

References

Aguinis, H. (2023). *Performance Management*, 5th edition, Thousand Oaks, CA: Sage.

Aguinis, H. and Burgi-Tian, J. (2021). Talent management challenges during COVID-19 and beyond: Performance management to the rescue, *Business Research Quarterly*, 4(3): 233–240.

Aguinis, H., Joo, H. and Gottfredson, R. K. (2011). Why we hate performance management – And why we should love it, *Business Horizons*, 54: 503–507.

Aguinis, H., Ryan, K., Gottfredson, R. and Harry, J. (2012). Using performance management to win the talent war, *Business Horizons*, 55(6): 609–616.

Almond, P. and Ferner, A. (2006). *American Multinationals in Europe: Managing Employment Relations Across National Borders*. Oxford: Oxford University Press.

Armstrong, M. (2022). *Armstrong's Handbook of Human Resource Management*, 7th edition, London: Kogan Page Limited.

Barlow, G. (1989). Deficiencies and the perpetuation of power: Latent functions in managerial appraisal, *Journal of Management Studies*, 26(5): 499–517.

Bevan, S. and Thompson, M. (1992). *Personnel Management in the UK: An Analysis of the Issues*. London: IPM.

Blanchard, K., Carlos, J. P. and Randolph, A. (2001). *Empowerment Takes More than a Minute*. San Francisco, CA: Berrett-Koehler.

Buchner, T. W. (2007). Performance management theory: A look from the performer's perspective with implications for HRD, *Human Resource Development International*, 10(1): 59–73.

Buckingham, M. and Goodall, A. (2015). Reinventing performance management, *Harvard Business Review*, 93: 40–50.

Cappelli, P. and Tavis, A. (2016). The performance management revolution, *Harvard Business Review*, 10: 58–67.

Chase, P. and Fuchs, S. (2008). Performance management and appraisal, in M. Muller-Camen, R. Croucher and S. Leigh (Eds.), *Human Resource Management: A Case Study Approach* (pp. 221–241). London: CIPD.

Chen, Z., Lam, W. and Zhong, J. A. (2007). Leader-member exchange and member performance: A new look at individual-level negative feedback-seeking behavior and team-level empowerment climate, *Journal of Applied Psychology*, 92: 202–212.

Cleveland, J. N., Lim, A. and Murphy, K. R. (2007). Feedback phobia? Why employees do not want to give or receive It, in J. Langan-Fox, C. Cooper and R.

Klimoski (Eds.), *Research Companion to the Dysfunctional Workplace: Management Challenges and Symptoms* (pp. 168–186). Cheltenham: Edward Elgar Publishing.

Cleveland, J. N., Murphy, K. R. and Williams, R. (1989). Multiple uses of performance appraisal: Prevalence and correlates, *Journal of Applied Psychology*, 74: 130–135.

Coens, T. and Jenkins, M. (2000). *Abolishing Performance Appraisals.* San Francisco, CA: Berrett-Koehler.

Costello, S. J. (1994). *Effective Performance Management.* New York: Irwin.

Culbert, S. A. and Rout, L. (2010). *Get ,Rid of the Performance Review: How Companies Can Stop Intimidating, Start Managing – And Focus on What Really Matters* New York: Business Plus.

Den Hartog, D. N., Boselie, P. and Paauwe, J. (2004). Performance management: A model and research agenda, *Applied Psychology: An International Review*, 53(4): 556–569.

DeNisi, A. S. (2000). Performance appraisal and performance management, in K. J. Klein and S. Kozlowski (Eds.), *Multilevel Theory, Research and Methods in Organizations.* San Francisco, CA: Jossey-Bass.

DeNisi, A. S. and Smith, C. E. (2014). Performance appraisal, performance management, and firm performance: A review, a proposed model, and new directions for future research, *Academy of Management Annals*, 8: 127–179.

Drucker, P. (1954). *The Practice of Management.* New York: Harper.

Duggan, J., Carbery, R., McDonnell, A. and Sherman, U. (2023). Algorithmic HRM control in the gig economy: The app-worker perspective, *Human Resource Management*, 62(6): 883–899. https://doi.org/10.1002/hrm.22168.

Ellis, C. M. and Saunier, A. M. (2004). Performance appraisal: myth and reality, in L. A. Berger and D. R. Berger (Eds.), *The Talent Management Handbook: Creating Organizational Excellence by Identifying, Developing and Promoting Your Best People.* New York: McGraw-Hill, pp. 104–118.

Fletcher, C. (2001). Performance appraisal and management: the developing research agenda, *Journal of Occupational and Organizational Psychology*, 74(4): 473–487.

Fletcher, C. and Williams, R. (1992). The route to performance management, *Personnel Management*, 24(10): 42–47.

Foot, M. and Hook, C. (2008). *Introducing Human Resource Management*, 5th edition, Essex: Prentice Hall.

Fowler, A. (1990). Performance management: The MBO of the 90s, *Personnel Management*, 22(7): 47–51.

Goldberg, E. (2023). Here's what we know and don't know about the effects of remote work, *New York Times*, 10 October. Available at: https://www.nytimes.com/2023/10/10/business/remote-work-effects.html.

Gospel, H. and Pendelton, A. (2005). *Corporate Governance and Labour Management*, New York: Oxford University Press.

Guest, D. E., Michie, J., Conway, N. and Sheehan, M. (2003). Human resource management and corporate performance in the UK, *British Journal of Industrial Relations*, 41(2): 291–314.

Gunnigle, P., Turner, T. and D'Art, D. (1998). Counterpoising collectivism, performance-related pay and industrial relations in Greenfield sites, *British Journal of Industrial Relations*, 36(4): 565–579.

Gunnigle, P., Turner, T., Lavelle, J. and McDonnell, A. (2014). Pay and performance management in MNCs in Ireland, in B. Harney and K. Monks (Eds.), *Strategic HRM: Research and Practice in Ireland*, Dublin: Orpen Press, pp. 95–116.

Holman, D. (2005). Call centres, in D. Holman, T. D. Wall, C. W. Clegg, P. Sparrow and A. Howard (Eds.), *The Essentials of the New Workplace. A Guide to the Human Impact of Modern Working Practices*, pp. 111–131. Chichester: John Wiley and Sons.

Houldsworth, E., Marra, M., Brewster, C., Brookes, M. and Wood, G. (2021). Performance appraisal and MNEs: The impact of different capitalist archetypes, *International Business Review*, 30(5): 101826.

Huselid, M. A. (1995). The impact of human resource management practices on turnover, productivity, and corporate financial performance, *Academy of Management Journal*, 38(3): 635–672.

IRS. (2001). Performance appraisal must try harder, *IRS Employment Trends*, No. 724, March, pp. 2–3.

Kinnie, N., Hutchinson, S. and Purcell, J. (2000). 'Fun and surveillance': The paradox of high commitment management in call centres, *International Journal of Human Resource Management*, 11(5): 967–985.

Kluger, A. N. and DeNisi, A. S. (1996). The effects of feedback interventions on performance: A historical review, meta-analysis and a preliminary feedback intervention theory, *Psychological Bulletin*, 119: 254–284.

Lawler, E. E. (2003). Reward practices and performance management system effectiveness, *Organizational Dynamics*, 32(4): 396–404.

Lee-Hoffmann, P. (2011). Discover the secrets of becoming a great place to work, *Leader To Leader*, 2011(61): 17–22.

London, M., & Smither, J. W. (2002). Feedback orientation, feedback culture, and the longitudinal performance management process, *Human Resource Management Review*, *12*(1), 81–100.

Longenecker, C. O. (1997). Why managerial performance appraisals are ineffective: Causes and lessons, *Career Development International*, 2(5): 212–218.

Lukas, C. (2010). Optimality of intertemporal aggregation in dynamic agency, *Journal of Management Accounting Research*, 22: 157–174.

Mabey, C., Salaman, G. and Storey, J. (1998). *Human Resource Management: A Strategic Introduction*. Oxford: Blackwell.

McKenna, E. and Beech, N. (2008). *Human Resource Management: A Concise Analysis*, 2nd edition. Essex: Prentice Hall.

Mercer. (2013). Global performance management survey report. Available at: http://www.mercer.com/content/dam/mercer/attachments/global/Talent/Assess-BrochurePerfMgmt.pdf [accessed 21 December 2015].

Miller, C. C. (2023). Is the five-day office week over? *New York Times*, 2 July. Available at: https://www.nytimes.com/2020/07/02/upshot/is-the-five-day-office-week-over.html

Mintzberg, H. (1978). Patterns in strategy formulation, *Management Science*, 24: 934–948.

Mintzberg, H. (1987). The strategy concept I: Five Ps for strategy, *California Management Review*, 30(1): 11–24.

Mitchell, F., Nørreklit, H., Nørreklit, L., Cinquini, L., Koeppe, F., Magnacca, F., Giovanna, S., Jakobsen, M., Korhonen, T., Laine, T. and Liboriussen, J. M. (2021). Evaluating performance management of COVID-19 reality in three European countries: A pragmatic constructivist study, *Accounting, Auditing &Accountability Journal*, 34(6): 1345–1361.

Morley, M., Murphy. K. R., Cleveland, J. N., Heraty, N. and McCarthy, J. (2021). Distal context and performance appraisal: A 22 country study linking three facets of home and host country context to performance appraisal processes and purposes, *Human Resource Management, 60*, 715–736.

Murphy, K. R. (2020). Performance evaluation will not die, but it should, *Human Resource Management Journal*, 30, 13–31.

Murphy, K. R. and Cleveland, J. N. (1995). *Understanding Performance Appraisal: Social, Organizational and Goal-Oriented Perspectives.* Newbury Park, CA: Sage.

Murphy, K. R., Cleveland, J. N. and Hanscom, M. (2018). *Performance Appraisal and Management.* Thousand Oaks, CA: Sage.

Pasha, O. and Jacobson, W. (2022) Municipal performance management during the covid pandemic, *Public Policy and Administration*, OnlineFirst, https://doi.org/10.1177/09520767221141166.

Pulakos. E. D. (2009). *Performance Management: A New Approach for Driving Business Results.* Oxford: Wiley-Blackwell.

Pulakos, E. D., Mueller-Hanson, R. A., Arad, S. and Moye, N. (2015). Performance management can be fixed: An on-the-job experiential learning approach for complex behavior change, *Industrial and Organizational Psychology: Perspectives on Science and Practice*, 8: 51–76.

Pulakos, E. D. and O'Leary, R. S. (2011). Why is performance management so broken? *Industrial and Organizational Psychology: Perspectives on Science and Practice*, 4(2): 146–164.

Randell, G. (1989). Employee appraisal, in K. Sisson (Ed.), *Personnel Management.* Oxford: Blackwell.

Reeves, J. (2015). The Rise of the Employee-Centric Workplace. *Workforce Solutions Review, 6*(1), 15–17.

Robertson, B.J. (2015). *Holocracy: The New Management System for a Rapidly Changing World.* New York: Holt.

Scott-Lennon, F. (1995). *The Appraisals Pocketbook.* Alresford: Management Pocketbooks Limited.

Sharma, R. and Sahoo, C. K. (2013). Regenerating organizational strength: The employee centric way, *Strategic HR Review*, 12(2): 61–69.

Smith, B., Hornsby, J. S. and Shirmeyer, R. (1996). Current trends in performance appraisal: An examination of managerial practice, *SAM Advanced Management Journal,* 61: 10–15.

Sparrow, P. and Hiltrop, J.-M. (1994). *European Human Resource Management in Transition.* Hertfordshire: Prentice Hall.

Staples, S, Hulland, J. and Higgins, C. (1999). A self-efficacy theory explanation for the management of remote workers in virtual organizations, *Organizational Science*, 10: 7580776.

Steelman, L. A., Levy, P. E., & Snell, A. F. (2004). The feedback environment scale: Construct definition, measurement, and validation. *Educational and Psychological Measurement, 64*(1), 165–184.

Taylor, P. and Bain, P. (1999). An assembly line in the head: Work and employee relations in the call centre, *Industrial Relations Journal*, 30(2): 101–117.

Torrington, D., Hall, L., Taylor, S. and Atkinson, C. (2021). *Human Resource Management,* 11th edition. Essex: Pearson Education.

Vroom, V. (1964). *Work and Motivation.* Chichester: John Wiley.

Williams, R. S. (2002). *Managing Employee Performance: Design and Implementation in Organizations*. London: Thomson.

Winstanley, D. and Stuart-Smith, K. (1996). Policing performance: The ethics of performance management, *Personnel Review*, 25(6): 66–84.

Yang, K. (2021). Performance management for a post-covid-19 world, *Public Integrity*, 23: 636–642.

13 Reward Management

Erik Poutsma

Introduction

This chapter is concerned with both the function and form of rewards in the contemporary employment relationship.Together with performance management, reward management systems are concerned with motivating and engaging employees and compelling them to express desired behaviours. Employee rewards are concerned with recruiting, motivating and retaining employees with the required abilities to achieve organisational objectives. Important in this respect is also the strategic emphasis in reward management as to the fit within the wider-organisational strategy, objectives and culture, including ensuring a fit with other elements of HRM and the organisational context.

Reward is defined as all monetary and non-monetary payments that an organisation provides, either intentionally or unintentionally, for its employees in exchange for the employee's potential or actual work contribution and to which employees attach a positive value as a satisfier of certain personal needs (Shields et al., 2015: 12). Typically, a distinction is made between three broad categories of reward: monetary, non-monetary and benefits. Monetary rewards include the financial payment for the performance of the job such as basic wages or salary including any bonuses or other forms of variable compensation that are linked to performance; for example, individual (bonus or merit pay) or collective pay for performance (profit-sharing, stock options, share acquisition).

Non-monetary rewards include the more psychological aspects of rewards related to the nature of the work, the mutual employment relationships and the broader working conditions. Non-monetary rewards include, for example, recognition of the worker's contribution or receiving appreciation. Non-monetary rewards also include obtaining a promotion and the opportunity to develop personally and professionally.

Benefits include those elements that are part of the package of employment conditions, also called secondary employment conditions, such as pension payments, reimbursement of transport costs, healthcare and company car. Other examples of benefits that may be associated with working for the organisation include flexible work arrangements and maternity, paternity and sickness leave.

DOI: 10.4324/9781032625560-15

Following the Ability–Motivation–Opportunity (AMO) framework (Appelbaum et al., 2000), reward management addresses, in particular, the motivation of workers. The focus of this chapter is on the motivation ('M') as influenced by rewards. However, it must be noted that the effects of M may interact with those of A and O. It is clear that Ability ensures the self-efficacy for doing the work and be motivated to perform. One important ability issue not addressed in this chapter, related to motivation, is appraisal. In addition, how work is designed and the constraints it places on the Opportunities can also moderate the effects of motivation. Much literature has devoted considerable attention to the motivating potential of designing jobs that are challenging, interesting, enjoyable and fulfilling (e.g., Deci & Ryan, 1985; Hackman & Oldham, 1976).

Motivation theories provide input for the way incentives may have (or may not have) a motivating effect on expected attitudes and behaviours. Extrinsic motivation, motivation not related to the nature of the work, is stimulated by monetary rewards. Intrinsic motivation includes non-monetary rewards addressing the psychological needs related to the nature of the work and the working conditions.

It is important to recognise that reward management has to do with the employment relationship between two parties, in legal, economic and psychological terms. The legal perspective contractually establishes the rights of the employee as well as the obligations of the employer regarding the terms and conditions of employment. With regard to reward, many things have already been recorded, in particular, basic salary, any social security contributions and pension obligations. This may also relate to forms of contingent pay, although the employer has the discretion to, for example, determine the amount and award of any bonus outside the statutory employment contract. The economic perspective is based on the wage-effort bargain, where reward for the employer is the purchase price to be paid for the employee's effort, while for the employee reward is the price of his labour. In the agreement to be made, both parties will assume a negotiating position in which trade-offs are made between the options offered and any alternatives.

However, the employment relationship is not symmetrical and usually the employee is dependent on the employer, even though there is legal protection in the employment relationship. The use of countervailing powers by representatives and unions try to correct this. In this respect, it is important for reward management to distinguish between individual and collective contracts. Collective contracts are usually concluded with trade unions and relate to the labour terms of most personnel in the company, or in the sector in the case of collective-sector agreements, such as the centralised wage systems of continental Europe and Australia. The result is that with collective agreements, there is a remarkable uniformity in earnings of groups of employees in terms of job grades and pay rates. Individual contracts allow much more variety, and employers are inclined to use that variety to achieve the desired performance. Heightened competitive pressures and the decline of unions has, in many liberal-market economies, resulted in firms placing a greater priority on individually-orientated performance-based reward systems.

The employment relationship is also a social exchange reflecting a wider range of cost-benefit transactions beyond the wage-effort bargain. Reward is an important determinant of a positive (but also negative) psychological contract consisting of the mutual expectations of the parties in more informal terms of reward, such as recognition, promotion opportunities and fairness, equity and trust. Non-monetary rewards play a considerable role in determining either the reinforcement or violation of the psychological contract.

In addition, changes in the labour market may influence the scope and nature of rewards. For instance, in the 2000s, in both the US and the UK, a rise of gig working and platform economy is experienced. Gig working and the platform economy has been criticised for limited security in working time, few employment rights, with possibly wages on (or sometimes below) the legal minima. Meanwhile, top managerial pay sometimes incentivises excessive risk-taking; in the financial services industry, this, along with weak regulatory oversight, was one of the major causes of the 2008 financial crisis. The settlement of pay is, therefore, a continuously contested terrain. Also, the broad definition of rewards suggests complexity in balancing the variety of needs between employer and employees in designing an effective reward system.

Motivation Theories

Extrinsic and Intrinsic Rewards

Distinctions can be made between 'outside the job' or *extrinsic rewards* and other aspects of rewards that stem from the actual content rather than the surrounding context of the work; such rewards constitute *intrinsic rewards*. A brief review of classic motivation theories provides an understanding of the range of human need and, hence, of desired rewards. Key issues in the discussion of motivation theories include the extent to which people are likely to be motivated by money alone or by other issues such as the intrinsic rewards of the job itself.

Efficiency Wage Theory (EWT)

In economics, two theories are central with regard to pay, efficiency wage theory (Akerlof, & Yellen, 1986) and agency theory. Efficiency wage theory assumes that employers vary their pay per worker depending on willingness and ability to work in an effort to ensure a ready and capable workforce. EWT sees the reward level as a motivating factor. The assumption of EWT is that the worker will work to avoid unemployment and will make an effort if the work has a higher pay level than alternatives such as another job. EWT assumes that the worker is, in principle, inclined not to work and that only pay causes the worker to work. If the pay level is not sufficient, then EWT anticipates that there will be a moral hazard problem and that workers will 'shirk', which means they will not be motivated to put forth effort. Of course, it is clear that pay level is important for the choice of a job and that the worker considers alternative options. However, there is more than just pay level or 'extrinsic-rewards level' that matters when choosing work and to be motivated to make the effort. In EWT, there is no direct acknowledgement of factors, other than pay level, acting as motivators.

Agency Theory

In addition to pay level, the focus on pay-for-performance issues has been the agency theory (Eisenhardt, 1989). Agency theory is based on the transactional contract between employer and worker. The question is, which type of contract minimises monitoring costs where the agent (in this case the worker) is motivated in such a way that the worker will act in accordance with the interests of the principal (in this case the employer). Agency theory assumes that the worker acts opportunistically and is not inclined to act in the interest of the principal due to unequal interests and information asymmetry. A contract based on results (output-based contract) links payment to outcomes such as physical output, sales, profit or productivity. The argument is that this contract has a strong motivating effect. However, the contract is not entirely optimal because there is a shift of risk to the worker where it is somewhat uncertain if other factors will influence the output, factors beyond the worker's control. A risk premium is necessary and makes the contract more expensive. In response to criticism of the problem of output measurement due to complex tasks and outcomes, the theory has been expanded to include the behaviour-based contract, in which behaviour is monitored on the basis of, among other ratings, subjective assessment that can include factors that were not covered in the previous output-based contract. However, a risk with behavioural contracts is the chance of subjectivity problems on the part of the supervisor during the job evaluation, which may lead to demotivation of the worker.

While economics predominantly focuses on extrinsic and monetary rewards, psychology focuses more on intrinsic non-monetary rewards. When the psychology literature gives attention to what motivates people, its focus is usually on job characteristics other than pay (e.g., job autonomy). Some of the psychological approaches consider pay as having a detrimental effect on motivating the worker.

Needs Hierarchy and Two Factors

The early work of Maslow (1954) suggests a hierarchy of needs that the individual will aim to satisfy in ascending order, from basic physiological needs through safety and security needs, social or love needs, needs for esteem both from others and from self, and finally self-fulfilment or the realisation of one's own true potential. While this widens the range of potentially motivating rewards, it is very general. Herzberg's motivation theory (1966) provides a more work specific theory. Herzberg makes the distinction between extrinsic (hygiene factors) and intrinsic (motivators) rewards. His theory suggests that the traditional approach of rewarding labour with wages or salary does not result in positive job satisfaction for the individual employee. According to Herzberg (1966), pay, along with other extrinsic factors such as job security and relationships with colleagues, are the factors that, if maintained well, will, at best, keep job dissatisfaction at acceptable levels but will not lead to job satisfaction.

According to Herzberg, prime motivators are the non-monetary intrinsic rewards such as interest in the work itself, achievement, recognition, advancement and growth. The theory suggests that by building the possibility for such intrinsic rewards into employees' work, the employees will be motivated to put in the effort and thus the level of job satisfaction will be increased. While much criticism has been levelled at early content theories in terms of empirical proof and the universalist nature of the findings, they do provide an insight into the importance and complex nature of matching rewards to a variety of individual employee needs.

Expectancy Theory

Next to content theories of motivation, process theories emphasise the complex nature of the action that helps to motivate people to want to put in the work effort to reach goals. Vroom's (1964) expectancy theory suggests that two personal evaluations precede the effort. Firstly the assessment of whether effort is likely to result in achievement of a specific task and, secondly, whether success in the task will lead to the individual's desired personal reward. Important in this theory is that the effort will start only if the employee values the reward, noting that the value of the reward may not be money but could be something else. Expectancy more or less solves the line-of-sight problem of agency theory where the expectancy of the value of the outcome, i.e., the reward, needs to be fully considered beforehand. This has important consequences for reward management due to the necessity to clearly find out what is valued by employees in the economic and psychological contract.

Equity Theory

Another process theory of motivation is Adam's (1965) equity theory. This theory address the importance of feelings of fair treatment, distributive and procedural justice in the workplace and the possible behavioural impact that may result from perceived inequity in the treatment. Feelings of unfair treatment of offering expected motivating rewards (money or not) in comparison with fellow employees may result in withholding effort, restricting output, reducing cooperation and even withdrawal. This has important consequences for reward management and puts emphasis on the need for transparency regarding procedures and distribution of rewards.

Self-Determination Theory, Cognitive Evaluation Theory (CET) and Crowding Out

The psychological theory of motivation that usually assumes a negative view of extrinsic reward is the cognitive evaluation theory (Deci et al., 1999). The argument starts with the self-determination theory. The explanation for a worker's motivation lies not in reward but in self-determination. This theory states that people are intrinsically motivated to develop themselves, but that three basic psychological needs must be met to maintain intrinsic motivation. These three basic needs are: competence, autonomy and relatedness. The CET assumes that performance-oriented material extrinsic rewards undermine the sense of self-efficacy and autonomy, thereby negatively affecting the person's intrinsic motivation. The argument is that monetary pay for performance (PFP) can actually be harmful to a superior-, higher-quality form of motivation: intrinsic motivation (Pink, 2011). The explanation is that 'crowding out' takes place, meaning that when people are given a monetary incentive to engage in a behaviour, what had previously been their source of motivation diminishes.

Psychological Contract

The summaries of motivation theories reflect the possible move away from pay as the primary motivator and even suggest the possibility of detrimental effects of pay on job motivation. The more recent perspective of the psychological contract focuses on a broader view of what motivates the worker and also brings the issue of motivation back to the importance of the employment relationship between the employer and the employee.

Psychological contract theory argues that the employment relationship goes beyond the simple wage-effort bargain and stipulates that the contract basically incorporates the expectations and assumptions, many unwritten, subjective and changing over time, that both employee and employer bring to the relationship (Rousseau, 2001). This more embracing view of the employment relationship presents important implications for reward management, for the motivation of employees' needs to permeate all aspects of the work environment. The need for an integrated system of reward, building motivational factors into all aspects for the management of employees becomes apparent. The recognition of achievements and the provision of interesting work and even the supporting role of line management, where possible, become important aspects of securing motivation.

Nevertheless, a warning about the emphasis on more non-monetary aspects at the expense of pay is in order. Not all work is, and can be, intrinsically rewarding; consider the worldwide occurrence of low-paid jobs in the periphery. Every attempt to make these jobs interesting through a psychological-contract approach (Cullinane & Dundon, 2006) is a form of window dressing that can lead to a distraction from the importance of a decent basic pay in the wage-effort bargain. For those core workers whom the organisation is keen to retain, skills development and career management are essential while, for the unskilled and semi-skilled or peripheral workers, the need for a decent wage and job security through training to enhance future employability may be highly regarded.

Limitations to Motivation Theories

An important limitation is that psychological theories of motivation tend to downplay the subjective effects of social context. Motivational theories often take an individual focus and assume that workers can be simply led or enticed. The theories downplay the importance of social relationship in the workplace, which constitutes, for instance, major problems in the effectivity of collective pay for performance (social loafing and free-riding). Also, in practice, work environments incorporate complex social dynamics: workers may adjust their output to 'fit in', to improve their standing in the eyes of co-workers (which may involve making short bursts of intense activity to impress others), for altruistic reasons (to protect weaker or less effective colleagues), or adjust output to lengthen breaks or to 'reward' or 'punish' supervisors (see Burawoy, 1979). These social dynamics are not the immediate focus of reward strategies.

Reward Strategies

Organisations establish some type of, more or less, developed reward strategies. Central to this strategy is the reward mix, what components of rewards are used in the reward strategy. Given our reporting on motivation theories, the reward mix at the least includes a statement about monetary and non-monetary rewards, indicating what is intended by the mix. The reward mix can range from fairly simple to very integrative and complex, from the use of a simple pay level above the market, to a detailed high-commitment strategy with a mix of variable pay, and involvement and engagement practices.

The Pay Mix

Individual Pay for Performance

With individual pay for performance, employees are rewarded based on their individual performance. Some examples of this are piece-rate pay, where workers are paid by the unit performed (e.g. the number of T-shirts or bricks produced); bonuses where the employee receives an extra amount on top of the basic salary that is paid out when specific goals or targets are achieved; commissions where a percentage of the turnover or profit that an employee generates, for example in the context of a sales job. Merit pay refers to pay for performance which provides base pay increases for employees who hit a target or perform their jobs effectively, according to criteria over a predetermined period of time, usually a year.

In developed societies, the occurrence of piece rates is very low and merit pay is very common (Gerhart, 2017). The global CRANET survey (CRANET Research Network, 2023) reports on average, use of individual PFP is 69.1 per cent of large organisations (large: more than 100 employees). Additionally, the survey found that variable pay is particularly important for management and professionals and less common among administrative staff and manual/operational employees, indicating a high utilisation of individual PFP for key personnel. Also, countries with different institutional arrangements and culture play an important role in the extent to which schemes for individual pay for performance are adopted by companies.

The central problem in motivating through individual pay for performance is the measurability of the output and the evaluation by, usually, the employee's supervisor. With piece rate, the objectivity of the meeting seems guaranteed but with merit pay, the output assessment is often based on a subjective evaluation of more or less complex tasks. Problems with fairness and equity are lurking, especially since supervisors are often also bound by a limited scope for awarding and distributing extra pay among staff. Finally, more collective outcomes might not improve with individual pay for performance, as the worker is more likely to work to achieve outcomes that specifically benefit him than those that lead to broader collective success within the organisation.

Despite these problems, reviews of research report positive associations between individual pay for performance and several outcomes. Only for merit pay is there limited research to conclude such an association (see Gerhart, 2017 for an extensive review).

Collective PFP

Collective PFP consist of pay applied to collectives that are contingent on collective outcomes. We can distinguish between six forms of collective PFPs. At team level we can speak of team PFP where pay of team members depends on the performance of the team as a whole. A second form is called gainsharing, where pay is related to the collective performance of a unit or a facility. In the third form, profit-sharing, pay is based on achieving a collective financial goal on an organisation-wide level. With employee share ownership, employees are offered the opportunity to own shares in the company and receive income in return that is related to the entire performance of the organisation. The fifth form, broad-based stock options, gives employees the right to purchase a company asset for a specified price, with the value related to the company's performance. The last form is top management–team PFP. Distinguishing between team PFP for the rank and file and that for top management is relevant because different types of reward management are applied to both forms and are also treated differently in the research literature.

The global CRANET survey (CRANET, 2023) reports on the average use of team PFP (including for top-management team) among 54.3 per cent of large companies (large: more than 100 employees), 27.7 per cent use profit-sharing,

39.3 per cent use stock options and 33 per cent have employee share schemes in the workplace. Additionally, the survey found that the type of collective PFP is particularly important for management and professionals and less common among administrative staff and manual/operational employees. As with individual pay for performance, countries with different institutional arrangements and culture play an important role in the extent to which schemes for collective pay for performance are adopted by companies. Tax treatment and countries that specifically support regulations appear to be major determinants of the use of these schemes (Ligthart et al., 2018).

Team PFP

The goals of team PFP are generally to promote mutual cooperation and communication, and to improve the outcomes of the team's work. In team PFP, each team member's pay is contingent on the team's aggregate output or performance (Conroy & Gupta, 2016). However, members' pay can be split equally among all team members or divided in proportion to their contribution to the team. There are two opposing perspectives regarding team PFP. According to the first perspective, team PFP leads to better performance through goal setting, knowledge sharing and coordination. On the other hand, the other perspective says that team performance is limited by social loafing and free-rider behaviour (Karau & Wilhau, 2020), a perspective that applies to all forms of collective pay for performance. Social loafing is the tendency for people to perform less well in the presence of others if their individual performance is not or cannot be assessed. To combat this process of social loafing and free-riding, it is important to provide insight into and evaluate individual performance. This often leads to a tendency to link this monitoring to a combination of individual PFP and team PFP, hence, unequal distribution of the team PFP. This mixed PFP can in turn lead to conflicts of perceived inequity related to doubts about the individual evaluation. The possibility of mixed PFP also depends on the extent to which the team members are dependent on each other in the performance of their tasks (Barnes et al., 2011). There are also questions about the possible trade-offs in combinations of various outcomes, such as the trade-off between efficiency and quality. Finally, organisational outcomes also might not improve with better team performance, as the team is more likely to work to achieve outcomes that specifically benefit it than those that lead to broader organisational success. Reviews of research seem to indicate better performance of various outcomes of teams with equal PFP distribution compared with mixed PFP. Team PFP also provides better performance on various outcomes compared with teams with fixed pay (Nyberg et al., 2018).

Gainsharing

Gainsharing links pay to results-based performance at the collective level and involves employee efforts targeted to specific work units. In contrast to profit-sharing, gainsharing is likely to be tied to productivity gains or cost savings rather than profit. Gainsharing plans are likely used in parts of an organisation such as a plant or facility. One possible form of gainsharing is a focus on a performance ratio based on the past year and then compared with the ratio for future years. If the ratio deviates positively, a gain is shared with the workers. Ratios can include all kinds of goals, usually non-financial, such as process improvements, unit sales and productivity, safety, quality and customer satisfaction. The mechanisms that play a role in gainsharing are comparable to team PFP and relate to attitudinal and behavioural effects such as promotion of mutual cooperation and communication in achieving the specific goal or goals. Often gainsharing typically includes employee involvement in developing plans for targeting the specified goals. This can also influence attitudes such as diminishing social loafing and free-riding. Review of studies indicate that gainsharing, indeed, has positive effects on various outcomes (Nyberg et al., 2018).

Profit-Sharing

In contrast to previous forms of collective PFP, profit-sharing is based on collective financial goals at the company level. Profit-sharing usually includes the vast majority of the staff, but usually does not include specific employee involvement in the development and application, such as with gainsharing and team PFP. Following agency reasoning, companies implement profit-sharing to allow employees to focus on profits and cost reductions. It also offers companies some wage flexibility because it is not required to pay out profits if the company performs poorly. However, like other collective PFPs that focus on corporate-level goals, profit-sharing faces the line-of-sight problem where workers cannot directly make the link between profit and their own direct local efforts; profit-sharing is unlikely to motivate employees who cannot see clearly how their performance relates to a firm's profits. The incentive effect on changes in attitude and behaviour will, therefore, be weak. Profit-sharing is usually focused on the distribution of profits in the short term and has a poor relationship with long-term investments and growth. Also, the dependence of part of a worker's income on part of the profit adds a risk to the total income and not every worker will appreciate that as a positive. Therefore, productivity may decrease if the worker does not accept that risk or rejects this type of payment and does not care about it. This is particularly true when such increasing risk is not associated with greater participation in the firm's decision-making or when the firm's performance is poor (Lucifora & Origo, 2015).

Nevertheless, a review of studies points to positive effects on various outcomes such as productivity and wage flexibility, but also attitudinal effects such as knowledge transfer and organisational citizenship behaviour (Nyberg, et al., 2018). However, there is also evidence that the effect decreases over time; the increase in productivity is strongest immediately after implementation, then levels off (Lucifora & Origo, 2015).

Broad-based Stock Options and Employee Share Ownership

Broad-based equity-based PFP plans, such as broad-based stock options and employee share ownership, generally take agency theory as a starting point in which companies try to relate the interests of employees to the interests of shareholders, leading to better performance of the company. These plans also attempt to promote risk-taking and entrepreneurship among employees, as well as to promote a sense of psychological ownership, especially with employee share ownership (Pierce et al., 2003). However, even more than profit-sharing, equity-based schemes face an expectancy theory problem: the line-of-sight problem, where there is a weaker perceived link between employee efforts and outcomes at organisational level. With broad-based stock options in particular, there is still the difficulty of determining the value of the options, which means that research into the effects of equity-based schemes shows mixed results. Nevertheless, meta-review studies generally note positive associations with collective outcomes (O'Boyle, Patel and Gonzalez-Mulé, 2016; Nyberg et al., 2018), such as better financial outcomes (Kaarsemaker et al., 2009), higher productivity (Sesil et al., 2002; Sesil & Lin, 2011), improved social and environmental performance (Braam et al., 2024) and more employee empowerment (Blasi et al., 2016).

Top-Management Team PFP

In top-management teams, PFP follows agency theory predictions and tries to align top-management teams with shareholders' interests. Also, retention of top managers is an option. Usually PFP in top-management teams consists of a pay mix containing bonuses, stock options and shares and constitute a substantial part of the total remuneration, suggesting a large incentive effect. Indeed, TMT PFP relates positively to financial performance, such as return on assets and market-to-book ratios (Nyberg et al., 2018). However, a review of studies notes no positive association with long-term investments and a stronger focus on operational outcomes (Nyberg et al., 2018).

Combining Individual and Collective PFP

Literature suggests that firms may use multiple incentives, and collective PFP schemes may complement individual incentives. The argument is that (groups of) employees typically have multiple tasks with varying levels of problem monitoring and scope; thus, a single incentive may have strong distortion effects. In this type of reasoning, stock plans may mitigate the costs arising from the use of individual incentive pay by encouraging employees to focus on long-term targets and broader interests rather than just short-term financial or output goals. Cooperative behaviour, supported by group incentives, is necessary to counterbalance the self-interested focus of individual incentives (Poutsma & Ligthart, 2017). Thus, various forms of monitoring and incentives may be complementary to each other, and collective PFP may be found where close monitoring and individual incentives are also in use. Indeed, Pendleton (2006) finds that individual incentives are a covariate rather than a substitute for employee share plans. The interpretation of these results is that the merits of employee share plans, in combination with individual PFP, shift the stimuli emanating from stronger incentives in the direction of longer-term time frames, collective performance outcomes and more cooperative behaviour (Pendleton, 2006: 755). However, mixed PFP systems currently receive criticism, supported by empirical outcomes. The argument is that a mixed-pay system sends mixed signals that put team members in a social dilemma, leading them to focus on the individually-based component. Barnes et al. (2011) find that in comparison to team-based-only incentives, mixed-individual/group incentives lead team members to perform faster but less accurately and focus on their own taskwork to the detriment of team-supporting behaviour.

Voice and Employee Financial Participation

Another focus developed in the financial participation literature (financial participation: an umbrella term for profit-sharing, broad-based stock options and employee-share ownership) concerns the complementarities between voice and forms of financial participation, especially regarding equity-based PFP (Croucher et al., 2010; Poutsma & Ligthart, 2017). Voice is defined as a process that allows employees to exert some influence over their work and the conditions under which they work. Employee voice can incorporate a representative voice and various forms of participation developed directly between management and workers. Representative voice covers collective bargaining (which allows influence on the general terms of work) and representative participation works through union representation, work councils and joint consultation committees.

Direct participation may encourage employees to coordinate their work tasks without supervision, thereby saving management time. Joint problem-solving in production/service delivery may facilitate organisational learning, leading to higher-quality human capital and greater efficiency. The consequence of this thinking is a strong ‘consensus orientation’ (in practice and research) (Keegan & Boselie, 2006), and arguments for democratisation have widely become arguments for more efficiency (Boselie, Dietz & Boon, 2005). It has been argued that companies adopt direct participation practices for reasons of ‘dynamic efficiency’ and ‘organisational capabilities’. To sustain and develop these capabilities, collective equity-based PFP may provide for a return on these employee investments in human and social capital. Collective equity-based PFP may be perceived as a reward for becoming more involved in the firm and thus may be seen as a pay-off for direct participation, while involvement in an equity-based PFP scheme may stimulate demand for greater communication and involvement in work decisions (Poutsma & Ligthart, 2017: 27).

Complementarities between financial participation and representative participation are less obvious. To date, there is little evidence of representative involvement in the design of equity-based PFP; collective bargaining and equity-based PFP usually operate independently, even though both may be present. Trade unions are often hostile to financial participation initiatives, which they consider promoting consensus and bypassing union representation (Gollan, Poutsma & Veersma, 2006). The argument for a positive correlation between equity-based PFP and representative participation is based on building commitment and trust. The aligning of interest by equity-based PFP is accompanied by an improvement in management–employee relations. A perceived willingness of management to share information may signal to employees that managerial motives for an equity-based PFP plan are not opportunistic, while the presence of representative participation may ensure that employees are not exposed to excessive risk. A negative correlation between financial participation and voice is based on the argument that management tends not to accept double control of their behaviour through the ownership channel of voice or through the channel of representative participation (Poutsma & Ligthart, 2017: 28).

HRM Commitment or Control Strategies

Advocates of strategic human resource management argue that HRM practices, including rewards, need to be 'bundled' (Lepak et al., 2006) in order to be effective. These bundles may be considered strategies for the effective management of employees. The literature discovers various bundles, of which the distinction between control and commitment strategies (Arthur, 1994) is the most well-known. Financial participation schemes are considered an important complement of these strategies (Poutsma et al., 2017). Together with employee ownership, HR practices such as voice and information sharing theoretically form a 'high-performance work system' that can signal to employees the importance of employee ownership to the firm and its leadership (Kaarsemaker & Poutsma, 2006). Together, these practices may underwrite a 'sharing and ownership culture'.

Organisations that possess such a culture have the strongest impacts of employee ownership on employee attitudes and behaviour (Blasi, Kruse & Bernstein, 2003). Critics of the high-commitment strategy suggest that the related HRM practices may be merely an additional control mechanism for management to increase the effort of employees. Following a neo-Fordist labour-process approach (Friedman 1977), critics argue that financial participation may lead to work intensification, which may reach unhealthy levels (Harley, 1999). An alternative focus is, therefore, on the extent to which key dimensions of the control strategy are associated with financial participation. UK evidence suggests that firms offering share plans are also likely to make use of individual performance-based pay (Pendleton, 2006: 772). Thus, incentives that are open to groups are combined with those operating at an individual level. In sum, the question emerges as to how much financial participation may be found in organisations practising control or commitment HRM and the degree to which financial participation may be a dimension of the latter.

Ligthart et al. (2022) provide evidence that companies adopt financial participation as part of either commitment or control versions of HRM. The scenarios can be interpreted as two pathways to performance: an involvement-orientation/commitment path and a financial-orientation/control path. However, the study also provides evidence that over time, HRM strategy is less important as a determinant than contextual factors such as country and industrial relations. To the extent that financial participation is taking place because of institutional pressures for conformity, this reduces the 'space' for an organisation's strategy or other organisation-level characteristics to have an effect. The study also found that country is a strong determinant of the incidence of financial participation, reflecting large variance between nation states, supporting the divergence perspective. The UK (mainly for equity-based collective pay for performance) and France (mainly for profit-sharing) stand out with relatively high levels of incidence. Both countries have strong traditions of government promoting specific financial participation arrangements. Similar traditions can be found in other countries, although with lower support, causing lower uptakes. The corollary of this support is that management (and employees) may respond to tax exemptions in certain countries and may not particularly target commitment and control strategies with financial participation and performance, but consider financial participation simply as a possible instrument for employee savings (Poutsma et al., 2022: 22).

Managerial Control

Proponents of collective PFP may have different motivations for different schemes and have a variety of beliefs in the targets that are said to be reached by the schemes. These views are related to broader frames of reference on collective PFP that participants may have when considering these schemes. D'Art (1992) summarises these frames of reference nicely. He distinguishes four frames of reference: (1) the traditional philanthropic or altruist perspective, (2) the managerial perspective, where collective PFP is considered a management tool, (3) the neo-liberal perspective, where collective PFP is perceived to resolve the perceived contradiction between capitalism and democracy and (4) the social democratic or union movement perspective, focusing on collective forms of ownership and profit-sharing. Although important, the first and fourth perspectives are not very common in mainstream equity-based PFP. The third perspective is at the heart of the development of the Employee Share Ownership Plan (ESOP) system in the USA, while the second 'managerial' perspective forms the background for mainstream stock purchases, stock options and profit-sharing adoption. This latest perspective can be divided into three subcategories that reflect different managerial intentions. The first is sophisticated managerialism, where management's intention is to bind employees to the firm based not only on an incentive view but also on the offering of additional fringe benefits, representing the company as a preferred employer and enhancing the pool of potential recruits. The second is cost-benefit managerialism, where the intention is to increase the productivity and profitability with a labour cost-reduction perspective of financial participation, focusing mainly on profit-sharing or tax exemption forms of financial participation. The third is what D'Art calls Machiavellian managerialism, where the intention is to develop an individual relationship between the company and its employees, to weaken the appeal of collectivism and, thus, to avoid unionism. Of course, these different intentions may not be played out in full, and though there will probably be a difference between rhetoric and observed practice, they do influence employee reactions and may have unintended consequences. Employees may make positive or negative attributions to the intentions management may have. Rhetoric may observe traditional altruistic objectives, while employees may perceive an exploiting control focus.

Conclusion

Managing reward is a complex business that is difficult to approach objectively. Ultimately, subjective interpretations of employees (either individually or collectively) and supervisors make it difficult to impose reward systems as universal best practices. We can conclude that rewards systems need careful considerations of diverse needs of both employees and the employer to avoid problems and pitfalls. We have also learnt that, for most organisations, reward practices are likely to be bound up with the institutional setting and its own history. Firms are likely to adopt practices broadly in line with its peers, regional and/or national norms and rules, both to adhere to the law and where conventions are taken for granted. Heightened competitive pressures and the decline of unions has, in many liberal-market economies, resulted in firms placing a greater priority on individual and collective pay for performance. However, reward is not only about monetary rewards but also a host of non-monetary rewards and other 'soft motivators' in the workplace. Yet, in the end, the employment contract is about pay and pay-related factors; all emphasis on caring, communication and belonging is likely to be meaningless to employees unless they can count on a decent wage and proper job security.

References

Adams, J. S. (1965). Inequity in social exchange, in L. Berlowitz (Ed.), *Advances in Experimental Social Psychology*, Vol. 2. New York: Academic Press.

Akerlof, G. A., & Yellen, J. L. (Eds.). (1986). *Efficiency wage models of the labor market.* Cambridge: Cambridge University Press.

Appelbaum, E., Bailey, T., Berg, P., & Kalleberg, A.L. (2000). Manufacturing advantage: Why highperformance work systems pay off. London: ILR Press.

Arthur, J. B. (1994). Effects of human resource systems on manufacturing performance and turnover. *Academy of Management Journal*, 37: 670–687.

Barnes, C. M., Hollenbeck, J. R., Jundt, D. K., DeRue, D. S., & Harmon, S. J. (2011). Mixing individual incentives and group incentives: Best of both worlds or social dilemma? *Journal of Management*, 37: 1611–1635.

Blasi, J. R., Freeman, R., & Kruse, D. (2016). Do broad based employee ownership, profit sharing and stock options help the best firms do even better? *British Journal of Industrial Relations*, 54: 5582.–

Blasi, J. R., Kruse, D., & Bernstein, A. (2003). *In the company of owners: The truth about stock options (and why every employee should have them)*. New York: Basic Books.

Boselie, P., Dietz, G., & Boon, C. (2005), Commonalities and contradictions in HRM and performance research. *Human Resource Management Journal*, 15: 67–94.

Braam, G., Poutsma, E., Schouteten, R., & Heijden, B.V.D. (2024) Employee financial participation and corporate social and environmental performance: Evidence from European panel data. *British Journal of Industrial Relations*, 1–29. https://doi.org/10.1111/bjir.12784

Burawoy, M. (1979). *Manufacturing consent*. Chicago, IL: University of Chicago Press.

Conroy, S. A., & Gupta, N. (2016). Team pay-for-performance: The devil is in the details. *Group & Organization Management*, 41: 32–65.

CRANET Research Network. (2023). Cranet executive report on international human resource management: Summary and analysis of 2021-2022 survey data (November 29, 2023). Available at https://ssrn.com/abstract=4647015.

Croucher, R., Brookes, M., Wood, G., & Brewster, C. (2010). Context, strategy and financial participation: A comparative analysis. *Human Relations*, 63(6): 835–855.

Cullinane, N., & Dundon, T. (2006). The psychological contract: A critical review. *International Journal of Management Reviews*, 8: 113–129.

D'Art, D. (1992). *Economic democracy and financial participation: A comparative study*. London: Routledge.

Deci, E. L., Koestner, R., & Ryan, R. M. (1999). A meta-analytic review of experiments examining the effects of extrinsic rewards on intrinsic motivation. *Psychological Bulletin*, 25: 627–668.

Deci, E. L., & Ryan, R. M. (1985). *Intrinsic motivation and self-determination in human behavior*. New York: Plenum Press.

Eisenhardt, K. M. (1989). Agency theory: An assessment and review. *Academy of Management Review*, 14: 57–74.

Friedman, A. (1977). Responsible autonomy versus direct control over the labour process. *Capital & Class*, 1(1): 43–57.

Gerhart, B. (2017). Incentives and pay for performance in the workplace. *Advances in Motivation Science*, 4: 91–140.

Gollan, P. J., Poutsma, E., & Veersma, U. (2006). New roads in organizational participation? *Industrial Relations: A Journal of Economy and Society*, 45(4): 499–512.

Hackman, J. R., & Oldham, G. R. (1976). Motivation through the design of work: Test of a theory. *Organizational Behavior and Human Performance*, 16: 250–279.

Harley, B. (1999). The myth of empowerment: Work organisation, hierarchy and employee autonomy in contemporary Australian workplaces. *Work, Employment & Society*, 13(1): 41–66.

Herzberg, F. (1966). *Work and the nature of man*. Cleveland, OH: World Publishing.

Kaarsemaker, E., Pendleton, A., & Poutsma, E. (2009). *Employee share ownership plans: A review*. Working Paper 44, York Management School, University of York, York.

Kaarsemaker, E., & Poutsma, E. (2006). The fit of employee ownership with other human resource management practices: Theoretical and empirical suggestions regarding the existence of an ownership high-performance work system. *Economic & Industrial Democracy*, 27(2): 669–685.

Karau, S. J., & Wilhau, A. J. (2020). Social loafing and motivation gains in groups: An integrative review, In S. J. Karau *Individual motivation within groups* (pp. 3–51).

Keegan, A., & Boselie, P. (2006). The lack of impact of dissensus inspired analysis on developments in the field of human resource management. *Journal of Management Studies*, 43(7): 1491–1511.

Lepak, D. P., Liao, H., Chung, Y., & Harden, E. E. (2006). A conceptual review of human resource management systems in strategic human resource management research. *Research in Personnel and Human Resources Management*, *25*, 217–271.

Ligthart, P. E., Pendleton, A., & Poutsma, E. (2018). Financial participation: The nature and causes of national variation. In C. Brewster, W. Mayrhofer, and E. Farndale (Eds.), *Handbook of research on comparative human resource management* (pp. 283–302). Edward Elgar Publishing.

Ligthart, P. E., Poutsma, E., & Brewster, C. (2022). The development of financial participation in Europe. *British Journal of Industrial Relations*, 60(3): 479–510.

Lucifora, C., & Origo, F. (2015). Performance-related pay and firm productivity: Evidence from a reform in the structure of collective bargaining. *Industrial and Labor Relations Review*, 68: 606–632.

Maslow, A. (1954). *Motivation and Personality*, New York: Harper Row.

Nyberg, A. J., Maltarich, M. A., Abdulsalam, D. D., Essman, S. M., & Cragun, O. (2018). Collective pay for performance: A cross-disciplinary review and meta-analysis. *Journal of Management*, 44(6): 2433–2472.

O'Boyle, E. H., Patel, P. C., & Gonzalez-Mulé, E. (2016). Employee ownership and firm performance: A meta analysis. *Human Resource Management Journal*, 26(4): 425–448.

Pendleton, A. (2006). Incentives, monitoring, and employee stock ownership plans: New evidence and interpretations. *Industrial Relations: A Journal of Economy and Society*, 45(4): 753–777.

Pierce, J. L., Kostova, T., & Dirks, K. T. (2003). The state of psychological ownership: Integrating and extending a century of research. *Review of General Psychology*, 7(1): 84–107.

Pink, D. H. (2011). *Drive: The surprising truth about what motivates us.* London: Penguin.

Poutsma, E. and Ligthart, P. E. M. (2017). Which companies adopt sharing arrangements and why?, in E. Poutsma and P. E. M. Ligthart (Eds.), *Sharing in the Company* (*Advances in the Economic Analysis of Participatory & Labor-Managed Firms, Vol. 17*) (pp. 23–48). Leeds: Emerald Publishing Limited. https://doi.org/10.1108/S0885-333920160000017005

Poutsma, E., Ligthart, P. E. M., & Kaarsemaker, E. C. (2017). Employee ownership and high-performance work systems in context, in E. Poutsma and P. E. M. Ligthart (Eds.), *Sharing in the Company* (*Advances in the Economic Analysis of Participatory & Labor-Managed Firms, Vol. 17*) (pp. 5–22). Leeds: Emerald Publishing Limited.

Rousseau, D. (2001). 'Schema, promise and mutuality: The building blocks of the psychological contract. *Journal of Occupational and Organisational Psychology*, 74: 511–541.

Sesil, J. C., Kroumova, M. K., Blasi, J. R., & Kruse, D. L. (2002). Broad based employee stock options in US 'new economy' firms. *British Journal of Industrial Relations*, 40: 273–294.

Sesil, J. C., & Lin, Y. P. (2011). The impact of employee stock option adoption and incidence on productivity: Evidence from US panel data. *Industrial Relations*, 50: 514–534.

Shields, J., Brown, M., Kaine, S., Dolle-Samuel, C., North-Samardzic, A., McLean, P., ... & Robinson, J. (2015). *Managing employee performance & reward: Concepts, practices, strategies*. Cambridge: Cambridge University Press.

Vroom, V. H. (1964). *Work and Motivation*. New York: John Wiley.

14 Human Resource Development

Irena Grugulis

Introduction

Human resource development is central to HRM. When experts engage in the contentious task of establishing which HR practices are 'best', or 'core', or result in 'high commitment', the only activity to appear consistently in every list is HRD (Grugulis and Stoyanova 2011b). It is also, possibly, the only HR practice to attract consistent praise, in that 'everybody is for it' (Payne 1991).

Such positive attitudes augur well. Training and development can make a significant difference to the way work is organised, to what workers are paid and to the way organisations and countries compete. Yet despite consensus on its importance from national governments, employers and employees, HRD practice varies considerably. Some organisations do, indeed, do a great deal of training for knowledge and skills development and do it extremely well. Others undertake extensive HRD, but in a way that is divorced from the practicalities of work. Still others operate very successfully on the basis of zero skills, where labour is a cost to be minimised and training, beyond minimum legal requirements, is discouraged.

What this chapter seeks to do, in common with the others in this text, is sift the realities of labour-market practice from the rhetoric of enthusiasm. It starts by differentiating between different types of human resource development and examining the impact that each has. Following Cockburn (1983), the chapter is structured around the ways individuals learn and exercise skills, including the very different approaches taken by different national systems; the ways that jobs can provide space for skilful action or limit it; the impact of the gig economy and organisational fragmentation on skills; and the ways that skills may be judged on the basis of race, sex, class and other social characteristics and the impact this has on workers. It goes on to consider the changing nature of skill and the increasing importance of soft and social skills as well as the problems with these tools.

DOI: 10.4324/9781032625560-16

What Is Human Resource Development?

What is human resource development? Any sensible definition needs to focus on the way individuals learn and develop their skills in and through work, as well as the way that jobs are designed to provide space for discretion and development so that those skills can be exercised. Human resource development and developing resourceful humans is not solely about the activities of corporate training departments (although these certainly play a part). Rather, it involves the skills, knowledge, expertise and experience that individuals possess; the way firms choose to compete, set out their strategies and design jobs; and the way individual workers are seen by society (Cockburn 1983). So, it is about learning, about skills, about jobs and careers, about discretion, employers and the ways work is designed.

Some studies of HRD, having set this out, focus on exemplary organisations and best practice. This can be valuable, since it is always useful to have examples of what to do, but it is also misleading, since it creates the impression that most firms are havens of knowledge work with employee skills prioritised and developed. They are not, and no student of HRM should be required to reshape the world to fit their area of study. Nor is it reasonable to demand that everyone believe that all training is good and all organisations are productive. Instead, this chapter will draw out what actually happens in workplaces, framed around a number of theories about human resource development that will help us to gauge those activities. Some of these examples will be exemplary ones, in which highly-skilled workers are able to exercise discretion and hone their skills. Others will reveal the ways employers limit opportunities to learn.

It is helpful to start by differentiating between types of training. Training, after all, is not generic. It can be used to describe a wide range of different activities, each of which has a varying impact on workers and their workplaces. It may be helpful to classify these in three ways, as *developmental*, *culture-focused* or *statutory*.

Developmental HRD involves building workers' skills in ways that can be used productively in and out of work. It may be linked to qualifications and is likely to both boost pay and prove advantageous when workers are seeking jobs. Higher-level management apprenticeships in the UK combine university-level study with workplace projects and experience leading to masters' level qualifications; in a standard apprenticeship candidates can qualify as gas service and repair engineers through two years of study and work experience; while accountancy firms guide their trainees through up to three years of structured work experience and taught courses to secure their professional accreditation. Each of these vocational qualifications involves a combination of workplace and classroom-based learning, each results in a qualification and each boosts pay. These links to qualifications and pay are not compulsory; a qualified accountant attending a seminar on recent tax changes or an administrator improving their knowledge of spreadsheets would also be developmental. Crucially, developmental training increases people's knowledge, skills or expertise.

Culture-focused development is different. In it, the focus shifts from employees' skills and onto their attitudes or feelings. So firms may organise social events to improve interpersonal relationships, develop a particular organisational culture they wish employees to adopt or focus on desirable attitudes and behaviours. Nick Kinnie and his colleagues (2000) report on two call centres in which the emphasis was on 'fun and surveillance'. Workers were encouraged to name their own teams ('The Untouchables', 'The Pioneers'), were given low-value fun incentives, often wine or chocolates, themed dressing-up days were organised and socialising outside work encouraged. The consultants observed by Grugulis, Dundon and Wilkinson (2000) also participated in dressing-up days, weekends away and fully-funded evening events. Woodcock's (2017) study observed staff taken away from work to play games and engage in quizzes. Management's rationale for these activities were all clearly linked to work. Kinnie et al. (2000) and Grugulis et al.'s (2000) firms were both concerned with commitment and managing an appropriate culture, assuming that higher productivity would stem from positive relations in work. The organisation Woodcock (2017) studied was more cynical, removing poor performers from the call centre floor just before the monthly statistics were collated, to ensure that their performance did not damage the collective effort. Such interventions may be enjoyed or scornfully dismissed, with Storey's (1992: 8) interviewee, as: '[i] t's indoctrination isn't it? Nobody wants to go on all these courses, people find them very boring'. However they are received, and whatever impact they have on organisational culture or commitment, they have little effect on employees' skills; indeed, all of the firms engaged in the culture-focussed training organised separate and often high-quality, work-based training and development.

Statutory and administrative training is different again. In the UK, this tends to cover the general legal obligations of the workplace, so employees may undertake training on general Health and Safety, manual handling of heavy objects or fire safety; categories that cover an estimated one-third of all training provided by employers (ESS 2018). Under administrative training could come helpful information about the firm, changes to the staff website, information on how to book rooms or directions to the canteen. All of these are necessary and useful (no one wants a fire in their workplace and everyone needs to know what to do should this happen), but they do little to develop individuals' skills or to boost workplace productivity.

Each of these types of training is useful, but in different ways, and each produces a different result. If we are evaluating the efficacy of training and HRD, we need these analytical distinctions, together with other information such as what the training is for, its content, duration, any links to outside bodies (for accreditation or certification) and who it benefits. Most training statistics make no attempt to differentiate between different types of training in this way, or at all, so national figures conflate professional training with fire safety and apprenticeships with in-house games. Qualitative studies enable us to see the variation in practice, but tell us little about how widespread the various different types of training are.

This chapter focuses primarily on developmental training, but sets it in the context of the work, the workplace and various different national systems, following Cockburn's (1983) helpful distinction between skill in the person (education, expertise, experience), skill in the job (routines, discretion, standardisation) and skill in the social setting (the value and status put on social groups and the ways this affects perceptions of their skills). It starts by focusing on the workers themselves, skill in the person, development offered in work and some of the different national systems that impact this.

Developing the Workers: Skill in the Person

Skill in the person (Cockburn 1983) is the education, expertise and experience each individual possesses. In work, individual skills can be developed through challenging projects, watching and working with others and formal training (among others). So, workers could enrol on qualifications, undertake internal or external training, observe and collaborate with others, exchange knowledge with their professional community and simply gain experience of their own organisation's systems, people and procedures.

Such skill building can be advantageous. According to Human Capital Theory (HCT) (Becker 1964; Schultz 1961), when individuals invest in themselves, by increasing their education, qualifications, skills, knowledge and health, they will also boost their pay. This is true to an extent, on average higher qualifications do, indeed, provide access to more opportunities at and in work, increase pay and reduce chances of, and duration of, unemployment (Brown, Lauder and Cheung 2021). However, this is on average and a more detailed look at the figures reveal that these premia only apply to the top 10 per cent of earners for each cohort, and that disaggregating data by sex, race, class and occupation reveal considerable and enduring disparities in pay. Skills and qualifications do open up opportunities to workers who might not otherwise have them and can explain some labour market activity but, on its own, HCT is an imperfect explanation (Brown et al. 2021; Grugulis 2023).

Nations approach the challenge of building their workers' skills in very different ways (Bosch 2017). In the USA, firm-level training is erratic but there are pockets of high-skill elites in sectors such as financial services, aero engineering, entertainment, biotechnology and software, supported by excellent educational programmes (Crouch 2005; Rubery and Grimshaw 2003). In Britain, while some industry sectors do have strong traditions of workplace learning, these represent pockets of excellence. Governments of all persuasions have intervened repeatedly, but national vocational-training initiatives have not been completely successful (Grugulis 2003), to the extent that there are concerns about the collapse of technical education (Wolf 2016). Set against this, the proportion of young people staying on at school and progressing to further and higher education has increased markedly, as has the number of people gaining qualifications through work. In 2021, over one-third of the population of England and Wales were qualified to degree level or equivalent, but the second largest category, at 18 per cent (8.8 million people), was those with no qualifications (ONS 2023).

In the USA and Britain, both liberal-market economies, most forms of state intervention are discouraged, many organisations are funded by shareholder capitalism and inter-firm collaboration is strongly discouraged. In co-ordinated market economies, such as Germany, France and the Nordic countries, relations between capital, labour and the state are very different (Ashton 2004). In these regulated nations, employer-groups collaborate to foster innovation and maintain skill levels, organisational capital is more 'patient' and less focused on short-term profits and industrial-relations systems tend to be co-operative rather than adversarial (for a fuller discussion of this see Thelen 2004; Whitley 1999).

Such intervention encourages national provision that is linked to workplace activity, rigorous and often leads to prestigious qualifications, and regulation ensures that employers train and that training is satisfactory. In Germany just over two-thirds of the workforce have successfully undertaken apprenticeships in the area in which they work, jobs tend to be designed to make best use of the skills workers possess and young workers are less likely to be unemployed during recessions because apprenticeship figures remain comparatively stable (Baldi, Brüggemann-Borck and Schlaak 2014; Mason, Van Ark and Wagner 1996; Rubery and Grimshaw 2003). As higher numbers of young people attend university, this system may be challenged (Jacobsen et al. 2016) but work is still organised around learning, with employee problem-solving, on-the-job learning, job discretion and autonomy key to production (Marsden 2015; Roberts 2020). Taiwan provides extensive technical education and training through the education system (Green et al. 1999). French employers are required to support training or pay a levy of 1.5 per cent of turnover plus an apprenticeship tax of 0.5 per cent of turnover to the state (Steedman 2001). According to Harcourt and Wood (2007), while an initial survey of the amount of training reveals little international difference, more detailed enquiry demonstrates that in co-ordinated economies, training is of both higher quality and longer duration.

Clearly the distinction between regulated (or co-ordinated) and liberal-market (or unregulated) economies is a simplistic one. Few nations are prepared to completely abandon the idea of all economic intervention, and even regulated states will not legislate for every activity. Even the USA, which has little to no regulation of skills at workplace level, funds an excellent national and state education system from which skilled workers are drawn (Whitley 1999). The British and Australian governments intervene extensively in attempts to improve the supply of skills (Buchanan, Watson and Briggs 2004; Keep and Ashton 2004). German apprenticeships provide high-quality and widely-recognised qualifications for young people but, after that, much continuing development is as ad hoc and variable as in market economies (Culpepper 1999). And it is difficult to apply either label to Japan where there is little regulation, but extensive economic co-ordination by large firms which affects their internal labour markets and that of their clients and suppliers (Thelen 2004).

Perhaps what is most significant is that both market-based and regulated training can be successful. Some elites fare well in the US where challenging tasks, links to prestigious universities and professional contacts all help to develop expertise (Finegold 1999). However, the majority are often ill-served or neglected. When training is regulated, a great deal of effort is focused on ensuring that the majority of workers are covered, provision is of high quality, workers are challenged to develop valuable skills and programmes are very relevant to the long-term needs of industry sectors. But when most activity is targeted at intermediate-level qualifications or activities, experts may fare less well.

Developing the Work

Education and training are only part of the process: 'skill in the job' (Cockburn 1983:311) is also key to workplace learning. Challenging projects, opportunities to exercise judgement, discretionary space and contacts with informed colleagues all help to develop skills, just as routine work, tightly-timed activities, rules for decisions and limited contact with others restrict them (see Grugulis 2007). Two contrasting examples may serve to illustrate this. Robertson, Scarbrough and Swan (2003) describe 'ScienceCo', a company that specialised in scientific innovations and patenting new work, where 116 of the 140 employees were scientists (most with PhDs), where project teams were unstructured with leaders who were often relatively inexperienced consultants 'emerging' for each project. Personal and divisional-revenue targets were set and employees were described as both competitive and combative; but, there was no onus on them to account rigorously for their time. They could, if they chose, work through weekends, take extended holidays of two or three months or work for 24 hours straight through and take a couple of days off. Work was documented so that the firm could gain patents but most learning took place through experimentation (see also Grugulis et al. 2000; McKinlay 2005).

At the other end of the spectrum, McDonald's famously competes on the basis that a Big Mac is the same, wherever in the world it is bought and that french fries served in Paris are the same as those provided in Dublin, Birmingham and New York. To achieve this, they strip out employee skill and discretion from every aspect of the work process. The Operations and Training Manual (known to staff as 'the bible') provides detailed prescriptions for every aspect of working life. Its 600 pages include full colour photographs illustrating the proper placement of ketchup, mustard and pickle on every type of burger, set out the six steps of counter service and even prescribe the arm motions that should be used in salting a batch of fries. Kitchen and counter technology reinforce these instructions as lights and buzzers tell workers when to turn burgers or take fries out of the fat, ketchup dispensers provide measured amounts of product in the requisite 'flower' pattern and lights on the till remove the need for serving staff to write out orders as well as prompting them to offer additional items (Leidner 1993; Ritzer 1996; Royle 2000). Nor is this codification of work restricted to fast food operatives. Workers on the line in manufacturing companies find their actions timed and monitored to a tenth of a second (Delbridge 1998; Garrahan and Stewart 1992; Pollert 1981); call centre employees are told what to say and how to say it, with calls tightly timed and performance data is displayed on public view during shifts (Taylor and Bain 1999; Taylor et al. 2002); and fitness instructors can work to scripts and choreographed routines so that a keep-fit enthusiast could attend a 'BodyPump' or 'BodyStep' class anywhere in the world and be sure of knowing exactly what to expect (Felstead et al. 2007a). Even 'knowledge work' such as computer programming can be broken down into its constituent parts and cheaper 'coders' hired who need to (and do) know nothing about the whole system but simply write, rewrite and paste their lines of code (Barrett 2004).

This is important. Skill in the job overlaps with skill in the person, since an unskilled person would struggle to perform a skilled job, but only partially. Where jobs are standardised and discretion restricted, individual skill cannot contribute much to the final product. Put a talented chef behind the counter in McDonald's and they would still be required to follow the same rules and procedures to produce the same burgers.

Fuller and Unwin (2004) describe this process as a choice between *expansive* and *restrictive* working environments (see Table 14.1). In an expansive environment, where learning, development and skills are encouraged, workers are more likely to be members of multiple 'communities of practice', with knowledgeable colleagues in the workplace and appropriate professional contacts outside. They may have planned time off the job to apply skills which are valued and opportunities exist for career progression. In a restrictive environment, workers are likely to be confined to a narrow range of tasks with limited opportunities for professional contacts, technical skills may be taken for granted, only key workers have their skills developed, expertise is imposed from the top down and innovation is not considered important.

Yet the way work is designed is not set in stone. Rather, it is a matter of choice exercised by employers. Take retail workers: in Britain this is considered an unskilled job. Staff are rarely required to know much about products sold other than their location, and recruitment often focuses primarily on availability for shift work with single, young women who live with their parents near the store preferred over other candidates. It is, as Gadrey (2000:26) describes, 'tantamount to a personnel strategy based on zero competence', zero qualifications, zero training and zero career. But this is not the case everywhere. In France, customers demand product knowledge of the people who serve them (McGauran 2000, 2001), in Germany, two- and three-year-retail apprenticeships train staff in product knowledge, sales, retail management and other aspects of the work that makes them invaluable 'anchor workers' on the

Table 14.1 Approaches to workforce development

Expansive	*Restrictive*
Participation in multiple communities of practice inside and outside the workplace	Restricted participation in multiple communities of practice
Primary community of practice has shared 'participative memory': cultural inheritance of workforce development	Primary community of practice has little or no 'participative memory': no or little tradition of apprenticeship
Breadth: access to learning fostered by cross-company experience	Narrow: access to learning restricted in terms of tasks/knowledge/location
Access to range of qualifications including knowledge-based vocational qualifications	Little or no access to qualifications
Planned time off-the-job including for knowledge-based courses and for reflection	Virtually all on-the-job: limited opportunities for reflection
Gradual transition to full, rounded participation	Fast – transition as quick as possible
Vision of workplace learning: progression for career	Vision of workplace learning: static for job
Organisational recognition of, and support for, employees as learners	Lack of organisational recognition of, and support for, employees as learners
Workforce development is used as a vehicle for aligning the goals of developing the individual and organisational capability	Workforce development is used to tailor individual capability to organisational need
Workforce development fosters opportunities to extend identity through boundary crossing	Workforce development limits opportunities to extend identity: little boundary crossing experienced
Reification of 'workplace curriculum' highly-developed (eg through documents, symbols, language, tools) and accessible to apprentices	Little reification of 'workplace curriculum' patchy access to reificatory aspects of practice
Widely distributed skills	Polarised distribution of skills
Technical skills valued	Technical skills taken for granted
Knowledge and skills of whole workforce developed and valued	Knowledge and skills of key workers/groups developed and valued
Team work valued	Rigid specialist roles
Cross-boundary communication encouraged	Bounded communication
Managers as facilitators of workforce and individual development	Managers of controllers of workforce and individual development
Chances to learn new skills/jobs	Barriers to learning new skills/jobs
Innovation important	Innovation not important
Multidimensional view of expertise	Uni-dimensional top-down view of expertise

Taken from Fuller and Unwin (2004).

shop floor (Kirsch et al. 2000). In British- and American-owned outlets in China, the combination of high pay, 'frighteningly well-educated' applicants, demanding customers and rapid promotion ensure a ready supply of skilled workers (Gamble 2006). Even for ostensibly simple jobs, there are different ways of designing work and using labour effectively. Lloyd and Payne's (2016) study of low-, medium- and high-skilled workers in Norway, France and the UK reveal substantial national differences between the ways that work was organised and managed, with greater skills and responsibilities consistently demanded from Norwegian and French workers.

National systems of vocational training clearly influence the ways that skills are used in work and the way work is designed. As Bosch (2017) observes, work tasks can be distributed horizontally, among workers at the same level, or vertically, with complex tasks passed to specialists and workers deskilled. Each has implications for the ways organisations are structured; firms that concentrate on a small number of specialists over a larger, unskilled group reduce training costs but lose both flexibility and quality. They also need to employ more managers, supervisors and quality assessors to monitor the workers and control quality (see, for example Jarvis, O'Mahoney and Wessels 2002).

Given this, it should be, and is, possible for a firm to change the way it uses labour; the problem is that few organisations take this as their primary focus. Enda Hannon's (2005, 2006) work in the Irish dairy industry assesses the impact of an official initiative which helped firms to switch from selling milk (an unprocessed staple good) to a more 'value-added' production. The dairies he studied started manufacturing specialist baby foods, cheese sticks for children and 'functional foods' such as yoghurts or probiotic drinks. These certainly helped the companies become more profitable. But the changes to the products did not necessarily increase workers' skills. Most of the knowledge-intensive activities were concentrated at managerial and technical levels, and large numbers of research and development jobs were created, but few shop-floor workers benefitted and one firm actually deskilled its operatives by moving to full automation. High-specification products do not always require high-specification work. Increases to the customer service levels in service industries are often achieved by a simple increase in the number of people employed rather than any rise in skill levels. Even industries with extensive investment in research and development, such as pharmaceuticals, combine small numbers of highly-skilled knowledge workers who develop and test new treatments with much larger numbers of un- or semi-skilled operatives on the factory line producing the pills.

New Forms of Work and the 'Gig' Economy

From the examples noted, it is clear that the way work is structured, organised and managed is important and that these factors have an impact on the skills that workers can develop and exercise. So, in terms of skills and training, much of the restructuring in the new 'gig' economy is a cause for concern.

Traditionally employers have funded skills development because employees are retained on secure, long-term contracts and employers benefit when they are skilled and competent at their work. 'Poaching' of ready-trained employees by rival firms was always seen as a barrier to employer investment. This motivation for funding is challenged by the fragmentation of the public sector and the growth of flexible, zero-hours, temporary and insecure work (Grugulis and Vincent 2005). When an employee is hired by the hour, or by the project, or even by the 'micro task', employers have far less reason to fund their training.

One consequence of this is that responsibility for skills development falls more heavily on the individual employee. Highly-skilled freelance workers are aware of the importance of skills and put considerable effort into ensuring that theirs stay current. Many seek out challenging projects and 'stretch-work', focus on new systems and software that is likely to be in high demand and fund their own training (Barley and Kunda 2004; O'Mahony and Bechky 2006). Skills are often harder to learn or pass on in fragmented workplaces, but highly-skilled professionals know that this is what they are hired for and put effort in to developing systems themselves (Grugulis and Stoyanova 2011a).

Such entrepreneurial skills development is harder for low- and un-skilled workers. By definition, they have less experience of either education or skills development. They are cut off from traditional hierarchies, career ladders and organisational-skill systems in situations where it is often not clear which skills will be rewarded nor how they should be developed (DfE 2021). Ironically, the notionally 'self-employed' workers at Über, Deliveroo and a range of other jobsites are *more* likely to want skills development than their peers on more secure contracts elsewhere, but *less* likely to have any provided for them (CIPD 2017).

Even more worrying, developments in technology and the spread of outsourcing mean that it is not simply the low-skilled 'hand' work that is under pressure on costs. Instead a 'Dutch auction' has developed for much highly-skilled knowledge work with contracts awarded to the lowest bidder, diminishing the rewards which used to be available in exchange for skills (Brown, Lauder and Ashton 2011). A survey of workers at Amazon's Mechanical Turk and Crowdflower revealed professionals who were very highly educated but engaged in low-paid, unregulated work performing 'microtasks'. Most had to spend two hours' job seeking for every hour of paid work, and when their finished work was rejected by the client (which had happened to 94 per cent of the respondents), they had no recourse and no way of getting paid (Berg 2016). Devaluing skills and fragmenting the organisational structures that have traditionally supported development may well have a negative effect on the workforce of the future.

There are positive aspects to the latest developments. Virtual Reality has been used to provide training to surgeons in the developing world, disseminating surgical knowledge and techniques at low cost to surgeons who might otherwise struggle to access it (Please et al. 2024). Nor are outcomes determined by the technology. Lloyd and Payne (2023), in a study of the introduction of robots to food- and drink-processing companies in the UK and Norway, found that the Norwegian system of strong trade unions and consultation resulted in more automation and better outcomes for workers (see also Krzywdzinski 2017).

Managing to Discriminate

Together with skill in the person and skill in the job, we should also consider what Cockburn (1983:113) describes as 'skill in the social setting', the tendency for factors that have nothing to do with skill, such as gender, race, age or appearance, to be used as a proxy for judgements on ability, capacity and achievements. This is not peculiar to skills (see Collinson, Knights and Collinson 1990 for an account of gendered-recruitment practices), rather, skills are subject to such judgements because they are common in wider society and the status in which a particular group is held generally impacts on the skills they are deemed to possess. To the extent that Green and Ashton (1992) argue that there was little point in asking employers whether particular jobs were skilled or unskilled, since the only conclusion the researchers could reach on this evidence was the gender of the workers employed as men's work was consistently rated as skilled and women's unskilled.

These gendered and racialised assumptions are of more than historical significance. Birmingham City Council was successfully sued in the early 2000s for paying 4,000 female workers across 49 different jobs less than men in equivalent jobs, is still using pay systems that discriminate against women (Barber 2023). Breckland Council, whose gender-pay gap narrowed, paid their male staff five times more in bonuses than their female staff (Ali 2019) and the GMB union reported that they were gathering evidence against a further 24 authorities. Stefan Cross KC, a leading barrister, commented that (Murray 2023):

> They might all be using different tactics, but it's always the same outcome, women getting paid less than men for equivalent jobs.

One American bank chose to restructure along highly-gendered lines, effectively demoting its many women managers and promoting male staff (Skuratowicz and Hunter 2004). High flyers are also affected. According to McGuire (2000:518):

> Few white women or people of colour occupy the types of managerial positions … in which they can perform extraordinary tasks, for which they are likely to acquire the label of ***high potential***.
>
> [Emphasis in original]

It seems that, as Reskin and Roos (1990) argue, the labour market is effectively a 'labour queue' in which white men precede both women and black and ethnic minority workers, with judgements often legitimised by being labelled skills. These judgements have two paradoxical effects on skills. Firstly, the skills workers possess and the qualifications they hold are devalued, restricting their access to highly-skilled work. Secondly, such workers are less likely to be offered training and, consequently, are more likely to say that they are under-skilled for the jobs that they do (Rafferty 2020).

'New' Skills and New Opportunities?

This three-fold definition of skills; skill in the person, skill in the job and skill in the social setting, is a useful one. It captures the different aspects of skill well and brings out the way that skill in one area (say, skill in the person) may not necessarily be translated to practice (skill in the job, because of the way work is carried out) or may not be widely recognised (skill in the social setting, because of the gender or race of the person possessing the skill).

It is also useful, when considering how skilled a group of people are, to review the way skills are changing (Payne 2017). Traditionally the word skill was associated with technical work which resulted in physical products. Plumbers, bricklayers, welders and carpenters were (and are) all skilled trades and an individual's skill could be demonstrated by fixing a leak, building a wall or carving out decorative patterns on furnishings. But as Payne (1999) and Keep (2001) observe, in recent years the term skill has been used to describe much more intangible attitudes and attributes. It has effectively been extended to incorporate (among others) communication, problem-solving, customer service, team-working, discipline, punctuality, friendliness and ability to fit in. The lists of desirable qualities are lengthy and vary; from the 'style'-labour markets of boutiques and glamorous hotels, demands for a persona that is 'passionate, stylish, confident, tasty, clever, successful and well-travelled' (Warhurst and Nickson 2001:14) to the more mundane getting-on-with-work mates (Payne 1999).

To a certain extent, this focus on attitudes is not new. Employers have always been interested in the 'type of people' employees are. Ford Motor Company's famous $5 a day was paid only to virtuous employees (Beynon 1975), while Oliver and Turton (1982: 199) dubbed the emphasis on 'stable', 'reliable' and 'responsible' workers the Good Bloke Syndrome. It may be that labour market changes have simply brought this into sharper relief. The dominance of the service sector and the increasing use of team-working in manufacturing have both changed the nature of work. In service work, the process of being served is as much a part of the purchase as any physical product (Noon and Blyton 2007) so an employee's appearance, their feelings about work and the feelings they stimulate in others are now part of the wage-effort bargain to be managed rather than a personal and private matter of no concern to the employer. As a result, flight attendants are expected to be slender, nurturing, attentive and flirtatious; debt collectors 'create alarm' to persuade debtors to pay (Hochschild 1983); and call centre workers must establish rapport then, just as quickly, emotionally disengage (Korczynski 2001). Work is about appearing and feeling as much as about doing.

However, while such attributes have been part of work in the past, they have not previously been labelled as skills. It may be that such a shift is not significant, that what matters is the substance of workplace practice rather than the label attached to it, but this relabelling does have two clear disadvantages. Firstly, it individualises responsibility for the skills. Issues that might previously have been considered part of the remit of the human resource department (demotivation caused by pay rates or poor management practice, high turnover, poor communications) now become problems with individual workers with any reciprocal and relational aspects ignored. Secondly, it conveys the impression that such skills are generic. Yet this is far from being the case. Effective communication, problem-solving or team-working depend on what is being communicated, solved or worked on as well as who is doing it. The person who could communicate the rules of cricket extremely well might struggle to convey those of American football, bridge or ice hockey, not because they had become a less able communicator but because they knew little of what was involved in the games.

With this in mind, it is instructive to see what happens with soft and social skills in practice. Amongst those who are already highly educated and highly skilled, it seems to be an advantage. In computing, greater pay premiums are available when technical knowledge is combined with soft skills and IT experts are able to problem solve or put systems into practice (Green et al. 2007). Most of the main accountancy firms (including KPMG, Coopers and Lybrand, and Ernst and Young) hire image consultants to advise their professional staff (PriceWaterhouse extends this to advice on dining etiquette for prospective partners). The Law Society publishes guidelines on the way that solicitors should dress and Barclays Bank provide grooming sessions for all employees when they introduced a new uniform (Anderson-Gough, et al., 2000; Wellington and Bryson 2001). The problems occur when these new 'soft skills' are not accompanied by technical skills. Despite repeated claims of skill shortages in key areas (such as customer service), there is no pay premium for soft and social skills (Bolton 2004) and there is some evidence that technical-skills training is being sidelined by the focus on attitudes. So in Canada and the USA, return to work training has become a zero-sum game with 'a combination of harsh discipline and hokey motivational seminars' (Butterwick 2003; Lafer 2004:120) replacing more substantive content. Low-skilled workers are effectively being denied access to the traditional career ladders which used to help them out of low-paid jobs.

This concentration on soft skills and neglect of technical skills causes organisational problems too. When London's Heathrow Airport launched its prestigious Terminal 5, the effort that had gone into designing the £4.3 billion project was not matched by technical training for the staff. Repeated workshops showed inspiring computer-generated images of the future of air travel, popcorn was distributed and staff were given mock boarding cards asking 'Are you up for it?' But in the end, employee enthusiasm and commitment were not enough. On the day the terminal officially opened, staff (including senior executives) found that they could not park in the terminal, get into the building, work the computer terminals nor understand the building layout. Flights were cancelled, thousands of people lost their luggage (to the extent that several insurance companies refused to cover items passing through Terminal 5) and both companies involved, BA and BAA, were roundly condemned. Part, though by no means all, of the problem, was that technical and practical training was marginalised and limited to a few days, management refused to meet with unions to discuss their concerns and large numbers of experienced staff took voluntary redundancy before the opening (Doward 2008; Radio4 2008).

How Much Knowledge and How Many Skills Do We Need?

It seems that the developmental picture is a mixed one. Work-based training varies in the extent to which it equips workers with new, valuable skills. Work may assist the learning process but it can also restrict it, confining employees to repetitive and routinised tasks. And social judgements based on an individual's gender or race can both enhance the skills they are assumed to possess and diminish them. Recent changes to the way the word skill is used are just as confusing. Focusing on an individual's attitudes and attributes can provide those who are already highly technically skilled with effective ways of putting their technical skills into practice, but it may also deprive those who lack technical skills of opportunities to develop them and access better paid work.

These complexities reflect the realities of the workplace, where knowledge jobs exist side by side with unskilled work. But they are often ignored by enthusiastic optimists who claim that work is changing and that the new economy will be dominated by knowledge-intensive jobs. If this is true, if *iMac* jobs are set to outnumber and possibly eliminate *McJobs* (Warhurst and Thompson 1998), then such a change will have significant implications for both work and skills so it is worth assessing both existing data and the extent to which we can observe any indications of change.

There are certainly grounds for optimism. The number of people with qualifications is rising and some jobs seem to be becoming more demanding. But while the trend is encouraging, the overall data does not really support predictions about the knowledge society. Rather, the increases in people with qualifications have not been matched with an equivalent growth in jobs for people with qualifications (Felstead and Green 2013:10). Worldwide this trend is more marked, with the number of unskilled jobs growing rapidly and far outstripping knowledge work (Green 2006). Overall demand for skills is stagnating or even reversing (Henseke et al. 2018). Nor does it seem likely that this growth is temporary, a transition phase, as the number of well-paid knowledge jobs grows. Rather, the existence of knowledge work makes many of the unskilled jobs necessary as people outsource their coffeemaking, childcare and cleaning to others. Unlike routine work in manufacturing, person-to-person services are difficult to automate. This mismatch between the skills that people possess and the work they do is not because, as Braverman (1974) argues, jobs are being deskilled. Rather, it is that 'some low skill jobs cannot be further deskilled because they already call for so little skill' (Rose, Penn and Rubery 1994:8).

What are the implications of this? They could be positive. Enhancing the skills and capacity of employees may mean that they are able and willing to take on more demanding tasks, that there will effectively be a grass-roots skills revolution in which workers 'grow' their jobs. However, for that to happen, the jobs need to have discretionary space so that workers can make decisions over work quality, how to do tasks, setting priorities and so on. Such space allows workers to exercise and develop their skills, undertake problem-solving and so on. Yet, this space is becoming more and more restricted. In 1986, 72 per cent of professionals reported having a great deal of discretion over the way they did their jobs. By 2001, this figure had shrunk to 38 per cent (Felstead et al. 2007b). There is some evidence that this is also happening elsewhere. Green (2006) observes similar declines in discretion in Belgium, Denmark, Italy, Ireland and Portugal (although interestingly, Austria and Germany seem to have escaped this general trend). This decline in discretion stopped, just as the increases in skill stopped, in 2001 and the figures afterwards remained stable but while the decline has not continued, there is little evidence that it will be reversed. If more jobs are becoming as tightly codified as call centres and McDonald's, then it is difficult to see how an increase in qualifications will enable individuals to grow their jobs. It may be that we are simply ensuring that more qualified people become more frustrated at the limits set on their talents. That would be extremely unfortunate.

References

Ali, T. 2019. "Council gender pay gap narrows but men receive five times more in bonuses than women." *Eastern Daily Press*. Available at: https://www.edp24.co.uk/news/local-council/20786575.council-gender-pay-gap-narrows-men-receive-five-times-bonuses-women/. Accessed on December 14, 2024.

Anderson-Gough, F., C. Grey, and K. Robson. 2000. "In the name of the client: The service ethic in two professional service firms." *Human Relations* 53(9): 1151–1174.

Ashton, D. 2004. "The political economy of workplace learning." In *Workplace learning in context*, edited by H. Rainbird, A. Fuller, and A. Munro. London and New York: Routledge.

Baldi, G., I. Brüggemann-Borck, and T. Schlaak. 2014. "The effect of the business cycle on apprenticeship training: Evidence from Germany." *Journal of Labor Research* 35(4): 412–422.

Barber, N. 2023. "Birmingham City Council's discriminatory pay practices are indicative of widespread problems." *HR Magazine, November*. Available at: https://www.hrmagazine.co.uk/content/comment/birmingham-city-council-s-discriminatory-pay-practices-are-indicative-of-widespread-problems//. Accessed on November 2 2024.

Barley, S. R. and G. Kunda. 2004. *Gurus, hired guns and warm bodies: Itinerant experts in a knowledge economy.* Princeton, NJ and Oxford: Princeton University Press.

Barrett, R. 2004. "Working at Webboyz: An analysis of control over the software development labour process." *Sociology* 38(4): 777–794.

Becker, G. S. 1964. *Human capital: A theoretical analysis with special reference to education.* New York: Columbia University Press.

Berg, J. 2016. "Income security for crowd workers." In *Precarious work: Causes, consequences and counter measures. Workshop at* Manchester: Hallsworth Foundation and Manchester University. April 21–22, 2016.

Beynon, H. 1975. *Working for Ford.* Wakefield: EP Publishing Ltd.

Bolton, S. C. 2004. "Conceptual confusions: Emotion work as skilled work." Pp. 19–37 in *The skills that matter*, edited by C. Warhurst, I. Grugulis, and E. Keep. Basingstoke: Palgrave Macmillan.

Bosch, G. 2017. "Different national skill systems." Pp. 424–443 in *The Oxford handbook of skills and training*, edited by C. Warhurst, K. Mayhew, D. Finegold, and J. Buchanan. Oxford and New York: Oxford University Press.

Braverman, H. 1974. *Labour and monopoly capital.* New York: Monthly Review Press.

Brown, P., H. Lauder, and D. Ashton. 2011. *The global auction.* Oxford University Press.

Brown, P., H. Lauder, and S. Y. Cheung. 2021. *The death of human capital? Its failed promise and how to renew it in an age of disruption.* New York: Oxford University Press.

Buchanan, J., I. Watson, and C. Briggs. 2004. "Skill and the renewal of labour: The classical wage-earner model and left productivism in Australia." In *The skills that matter*, edited by C. Warhurst, I. Grugulis, and E. Keep. Basingstoke: Palgrave Macmillan.

Butterwick, S. 2003. "Life skills training. "Open for discussion"." Pp. 161–177 in *Training the excluded for work*, edited by M. G. Cohen. Vancouver and Toronto: UBC Press.

CIPD. 2017. "To gig or not to gig? Stories from the modern economy." CIPD Survey Report. London: CIPD.

Cockburn, C. 1983. *Brothers: Male dominance and technological change.* London: Pluto Press.

Collinson, D., D. Knights, and M. Collinson. 1990. *Managing to discriminate.* London and New York: Routledge.

Crouch, C. 2005. "Skill formation systems." In *The Oxford handbook of work and organization*, edited by S. Ackroyd, R. Batt, P. Thompson, and P. S. Tolbert. Oxford and New York: Oxford University Press.

Culpepper, P. D. 1999. "The future of the high-skill equilibrium in Germany." *Oxford Review of Economic Policy* 15(1): 43–59.

Delbridge, R. 1998. *Life on the line in contemporary manufacturing.* Oxford: Oxford University Press.

DfE. 2021. "Decision making of adult learners below Level 2." Research Report. London: Department for Education.

Doward, J. 2008. "Lovely airport, Willie, shame it doesn't work." *Guardian: The Observer.* Available at: https://www.theguardian.com/business/2008/mar/30/theairlineindustry.britishairwaysbusiness. Accessed on March 5 2024.

ESS. 2018. "Employer skills survey 2017 research report." London: Department of Education. Available at: https://assets.publishing.service.gov.uk/government/

uploads/system/uploads/attachment_data/file/746493/ESS_2017_UK_Report _Controlled_v06.00.pdf. Accessed on July 12 2024.

Felstead, A., A. Fuller, N. Jewson, K. Kakavelakis, and L. Unwin. 2007a. "Grooving to the same tunes? Learning, training and productive systems in the aerobics studio." *Work, Employment and Society* 21(2): 189–208.

Felstead, A., D. Gallie, F. Green, and Y. Zhou. 2007b. *Skills at work 1986 – 2006.* Oxford: SKOPE and ESRC.

Felstead, A. and F. Green. 2013. "Skills in focus: Underutilization, over-qualification and skills mis-match, patterns and trends." The Joint Skills Committee. Scottish Funding Council and Skills Development Scotland.

Finegold, D. 1999. "Creating self-sustaining, high-skill ecosystems." *Oxford Review of Economic Policy* 15(1): 60–81.

Fuller, A. and L. Unwin. 2004. "Expansive learning environments: Integrating organisational and personal development." In *Workplace learning in context*, edited by H. Rainbird, A. Fuller, and A. Munro (pp. 142–160). London and New York: Routledge.

Gadrey, J. 2000. "Working time configurations: Theory, methods and assumptions for an international comparison." In *Flexible working in food retailing: A comparison between France, Germany, the UK and Japan*, edited by C. Baret, S. Lehndorff, and L. Sparks. London and New York: Routledge.

Gamble, J. 2006. "Multinational retailers in China: Proliferating 'McJobs' or developing skills." *Journal of Management Studies* 43(7):1463 – 1490.

Garrahan, P. and P. Stewart. 1992. *The Nissan enigma: Flexibility at work in a local economy.* London: Mansett.

Green, F. 2006. *Demanding work: The paradox of job quality in the affluent economy.* Princeton, NJ and Oxford: Princeton University Press.

Green, F. and D. Ashton. 1992. "Skill shortages and skill deficiency: A critique." *Work, Employment and Society* 6(2): 287–301.

Green, F., D. Ashton, D. James, and J. Sung. 1999. "The role of the state in skill formation: Evidence from the Republic of Korea, Singapore and Taiwan." *Oxford Review of Economic Policy* 15(1): 82–96.

Green, F., A. Felstead, D. Gaillie, and Y. Zhou. 2007. "Computers and pay." *National Institute Economic Review* 201(1): 63–75.

Grugulis, I. 2003. "The contribution of NVQs to the growth of skills in the UK." *British Journal of Industrial Relations* 41(3): 457–475.

Grugulis, I. 2007. *Skills, training and human resource development: A critical text.* Basingstoke: Palgrave Macmillan.

Grugulis, I. 2023. "Human Capital Theory." Pp. 93–99 in *A guide to key theories for human resource management research*, edited by K. Hutchings, S. Michailova, and A. Wilkinson. Cheltenham and Northampton, MA: Edward Elgar.

Grugulis, I., T. Dundon, and A. Wilkinson. 2000. "Cultural control and the "culture manager": Employment practices in a consultancy." *Work, Employment and Society* 14(1): 97–116.

Grugulis, I. and D. Stoyanova. 2011a. "The missing middle: Communities of practice in a freelance labour market." *Work, Employment and Society* 25(2): 342 – 351.

Grugulis, I. and D. Stoyanova. 2011b. "Skill and performance." *British Journal of Industrial Relations* 49(3): 515–536.

Grugulis, I. and S. Vincent. 2005. "Changing boundaries, shaping skills: The fragmented organisational form and employee skills." In *Fragmenting work: Blurring organisational boundaries and disordering hierarchies*, edited by M. Marchington, D. Grimshaw, J. Rubery, and H. Willmott. Oxford: Oxford University Press.

Hannon, E. 2005. "Prospects for the upskilling of general workers in liberal market economies." Presented at British Universities Industrial Relations Association, 7th–9th July, Northumbria University, Newcastle upon Tyne.

Hannon, E. 2006. "Interrogating the skills consequences of a strategic industrial policy: Case study evidence from the Irish dairy processing industry." Presented at 24th International Labour Process Conference, 10th–12th April, London.

Harcourt, M. and G. Wood. 2007. "The importance of employment protection for skill development in co-ordinated market economies." *European Journal of Industrial Relations* 13(2): 141–159.

Henseke, G., A. Felstead, D. Gallie, and F. Green. 2018. "Skills trends at work in Britain – First Findings from the skills and employment survey 2017." London: Centre for Learning and Life Chances in Knowledge Economies and Societies, UCL, Institute of Education.

Hochschild, A. R. 1983. *The managed heart: Commercialization of human feeling.* Berkeley, CA: University of California Press.

Jacobsen, H., B. Fitzenberger, M. Knuth, and M. Walwei. 2016. "The German Labour Market 'Miracle': success of skilful institutional recalibration or symptom of creeping erosion of the social system of production." International Labour Process Conference, WZB, Berlin.

Jarvis, V., M. O'Mahoney, and H. Wessels. 2002. "Product quality, productivity and competitiveness: A study of the British and German ceramic and tableware industries." Occasional Paper. London: National Institute of Economic and Social Research.

Keep, E. 2001. "If it moves, it's a skill." Presented at ESRC Seminar on The Changing Nature of Skills and Knowledge, 3rd–4th September, Manchester.

Keep, E. and D. Ashton. 2004. "The state." Presented at SKOPE High Skills Vision Conference, 28th– 29th October, Lumley Castle.

Kinnie, N., S. Hutchinson, and J. Purcell. 2000. "Fun and surveillance: The paradox of high commitment management in call centres." *International Journal of Human Resource Management* 11(5): 967–985.

Kirsch, J., M. Klein, S. Lehndorff, and D. Voss-Dahm. 2000. "The organisation of working time in large German food retail firms." In *Flexible working in food retailing: A comparison between France, Germany, the UK and Japan*, edited by C. Baret, S. Lehndorff, and L. Sparks. London and New York: Routledge.

Korczynski, M. 2001. "The contradictions of service work: Call centre as customer-oriented bureaucracy." Pp. 79–101 in *Customer service: Empowerment and entrapment*, edited by A. Sturdy, I. Grugulis, and H. Willmott. Basingstoke: Palgrave Macmillan.

Krzywdzinski, M. 2017. "Automation, skill requirements and labour- use strategies: High- wage and low- wage approaches to high- tech manufacturing in the automotive industry." *New Technology, Work and Employment* 32(3): 247–267.

Lafer, G. 2004. "What is skill." Pp. 109–127 in *The Skills that Matter*, edited by C. Warhurst, I. Grugulis, and E. Keep. Basingstoke: Palgrave Macmillan.

Leidner, R. 1993. *Fast Food, Fast Talk: Service work and the routinizations of everyday life.* Berkeley and Los Angeles, CA: University of California Press.

Lloyd, C. and J. Payne. 2016. *Skills in the age of over-qualification: Comparing service sector work in Europe.* Oxford: Oxford Univeristy Press.

Lloyd, C. and J. Payne. 2023. "Food for thought: Robots, jobs and skills in food and drink processing in Norway and the UK." *New Technology, Work and Employment* 38(2): 272–290.

Marsden, D. 2015. "The future of the German industrial relations model." *Journal for Labour Market Research* 48(2): 169–187.

Mason, G., B. Van Ark, and K. Wagner. 1996. "Workforce skills, product quality and economic performance." Pp. 175–198 in *Acquiring Skills*, edited by A. Booth and D. J. Snower. Cambridge: Cambridge University Press.

McGauran, A.-M. 2000. "Vive la différence: The gendering of occupational structures in a case study of Irish and French retailing." *Women's Studies International Forum* 23(5): 613–627.

McGauran, A.-M. 2001. "Masculine, feminine or neutral? In-company equal opportunities policies in Irish and French MNC retailing." *International Journal of Human Resource Management* 12(5): 754–771.

McGuire, G. 2000. "Gender, race, ethnicity and networks: The factors affecting the status of employees' network members." *Work and Occupations* 27(4): 501–523.

McKinlay, A. 2005. "Knowledge Management." In *The Oxford handbook of work and organization*, edited by S. Ackroyd, R. Batt, P. Thompson, and P. S. Tolbert. Oxford and New York: Oxford University Press.

Murray, J. 2023. "'It's going to cost billions': UK councils face huge bills over equal pay claims." *The Guardian*.

Noon, M. and P. Blyton. 2007. *The realities of work*. Houndsmills: Palgrave Macmillan.

O'Mahony, S. and B. Bechky. 2006. "Stretchwork: Managing the career progression paradox in external labor markets." *Academy of Management Journal* 49(5): 918–941.

Oliver, J. M. and J. R. Turton. 1982. "Is there a shortage of skilled labour." *British Journal of Industrial Relations* 20(2): 195–200.

ONS. 2023. "Education, England and Wales: Census 2021." London: Office for National Statistics.

Payne, J. 1991. *Women, training and the skills shortage*. London: Policy Studies Institute.

Payne, J. 1999. "All things to all people: Changing perceptions of 'skill' among Britain's policy makers since 1950s and their implications." SKOPE Research Paper No. 1. Coventry: University of Warwick.

Payne, J. 2017. "The changing meaning of skill: Still contested, still important." Pp. 54–71 in *The Oxford Handbook of Skills and Training*, edited by C. Warhurst, K. Mayhew, D. Finegold, and J. Buchanan. Oxford and New York: Oxford University Press.

Please, H., K. Narang, W. Bolton, M. Nsubuga, H. Luweesi, N. B. Richards, J. Dalton, C. Tendo, M. Khan, D. Jjingo, M.F. Bhutta, D. Petrakaki, and J. Dhanda. 2024. "Virtual reality technology for surgical learning: Qualitative outcomes of the first virtual reality training course for emergency and essential surgery delivered by a UK–Uganda partnership." *BMJ Open Quality* 13(1): e002477.

Pollert, A. 1981. *Girls, wives, factory lives*. Basingstoke: Macmillan.

Radio4. 2008. "File on four: A terminal failure." London: BBC Radio. April 29, 2008 (20:00)

Rafferty, A. 2020. "Skill underutilization and under-skilling in Europe: The role of workplace discrimination." *Work, Employment and Society* 34(2): 317–335.

Reskin, B. F. and P. A. Roos. 1990. *Job queues, gender queues: Explaining women's inroads into male occupations.* Philadelphia, PA: Temple University Press.

Ritzer, G. 1996. *The McDonalidization of society.* Thousand Oaks, CA and London: Pine Forge Press.

Roberts, M. F. 2020. "The socio-cultural-political economy of apprenticeships in England and Germany: comparative case studies from the chemical industries." Work and Employment Relations Department, University of Leeds, Leeds.

Robertson, M., H. Scarbrough, and J. Swan. 2003. "Knowledge creation in professional service firms: Institutional effects." *Organization Studies* 24(6): 831–857.

Rose, M., R. Penn, and J. Rubery. 1994. "Introduction, the SCELI skill findings." In *Skill and occupational change*, edited by R. Penn, M. Rose, and J. Rubery. Oxford: Oxford University Press.

Royle, T. 2000. *Working for McDonald's in Europe: The unequal struggle.* London: Routledge.

Rubery, J. and D. Grimshaw. 2003. *The organization of employment.* Basingstoke: Palgrave Macmillan.

Schultz, T. W. 1961. "Investment in human capital: Presidential address to the American Economic Association." *American Economic Review* 51(1): 1–17.

Skuratowicz, E. and L. W. Hunter. 2004. "Where do women's jobs come from? Job resegregation in an American Bank." *Work and Occupations* 31(1): 73–110.

Steedman, H. 2001. *Benchmarking apprenticeship: UK and continental Europe compared.* London: Centre for Economic Performance, LSE.

Storey, J. 1992. *Developments in the management of human resources.* Oxford: Blackwell.

Taylor, P. and P. Bain. 1999. "An assembly line in the head: Work and employee relations in the call centre." *Industrial Relations Journal* 30(2): 101–117.

Taylor, P., G. Mulvey, J. Hyman, and P. Bain. 2002. "Work organisation, control and the experience of work in call centres." *Work, Employment and Society* 16(1): 133–150.

Thelen, K. 2004. *How institutions evolve: The political economy of skills in Germany, Britain the United States and Japan.* Cambridge: Cambridge University Press.

Warhurst, C. and D. Nickson. 2001. *Looking good, sounding right.* London: Industrial Society.

Warhurst, C. and P. Thompson. 1998. "Hands, hearts and minds: changing work and workers at the end of the century." In *Workplaces of the Future*, edited by P. Thompson and C. Warhurst. London: Macmillan.

Wellington, C. A. and J. R. Bryson. 2001. "At face value? Image consultancy, emotional labour and professional work." *Sociology* 35(4): 933–946.

Whitley, R. 1999. *Divergent capitalisms: The social structuring and change of business systems.* Oxford: Oxford University Press.

Wolf, A. 2016. *Remaking tertiary education. Can we create a system that is fair and fit for purpose?* London: Education Policy Institute, King's College London.

Woodcock, J. 2017. *Working the phones: Control and resistance in call centres.* London: Pluto Press.

15 Industrial Relations and Human Resource Management

Gilton Klerck

Introduction

Industrial relations (IR), conceived in narrow terms as the study of the institutions and processes of 'job regulation', has been regarded as an outmoded residue of modernity and industrialism for some time. Developments in managerial thinking, especially human resource management (HRM) in its various iterations, allegedly offer a better account of the 'human factor' in the workplace and, therefore, constitute a grave challenge to IR as a 'discipline' (see Budd, 2008; Ferris *et al.*, 2004; Giles, 2000; Meardi, 2014; Purcell, 1993). To be sure, Godard and Delaney (2000: 484) identify a 'new IR paradigm' in which 'the study and promotion of new work and HRM practices replace research on unions and collective bargaining as the field's core'. Since collective institutions and practices are ostensibly the sole concern of IR scholars, there are 'large conceptually "empty" areas to be colonised by HRM' (Ackers and Wilkinson, 2005: 448). For some, the eclipse of IR by HRM is premised on assumptions of levels and forms of trust and cooperation in the workplace, which are significantly more demanding to (re)produce and considerably more precarious and variable in practice than most HRM scholars are ready to admit. For others, the HRM perspective is intimately connected to the field of IR (see Ackers and Wilkinson, 2008; Boxall and Purcell, 2022; Townsend and Wilkinson, 2014).

Rather than repeating the details of HRM's impact on 'conventional' IR (see Bartram *et al.*, 2015; Harney *et al.*, 2018; Kaufman, 2001, 2014; Kelly, 2003), the focus of this chapter is principally on the demonstrable capacity of the field of study to adapt to changing employment relationships and the critical features of a more expansive conception of IR. The latter conceptualises the employment relationship in its broader socio-economic and political context and contradicts many of the cosy assumptions in the HRM literature about strategic 'integration', employee 'involvement', 'high-commitment' management and the like. In contrast to this literature, which is primarily propelled by an employers' agenda and naturalises capitalist relations of production, the approach adopted here highlights the uncertainties, contradictions

DOI: 10.4324/9781032625560-17

and tensions associated with the changing links between capital accumulation and social regulation.

This chapter considers the analytical purchase of the concept of 'IR' and the explanatory power of its key expressions. The discussion commences with an outline of the employment relationship as a historically-contingent exchange relation that is socially embedded and dependent on institutional mediation for its reproduction. It then turns to an assessment of the 'crisis' of IR in practice, briefly considers theoretical critiques of IR by subjectivist and action-orientated approaches and outlines some of the shortcomings in HRM as revealed by a focus on labour regulation. The chapter concludes by highlighting some of the challenges confronting the future of IR research. Despite long-standing predictions of its fated decline, the field of IR continues to evolve and address a shifting and expanding set of issues related to the employment relationship and its regulation.

The Employment Relationship

IR, as Edwards (2003: 338–9) observes, is 'a field of study rather than an academic discipline ... [that contains] some distinctive perceptions which are more than the sum total of individual disciplines'. The origins of IR lie in a public policy commitment to achieve and maintain a balance between the problems of social welfare and social control in industry (Hyman, 1989; Kaufman, 2008; Wilkinson *et al.*, 2018). For the pioneers of modern IR, such as Dunlop (1958) and Flanders (1965), the 'network of rules' that govern the workplace and how it is formulated, administered and adjusted over time is central to the workings of an 'industrial relations system'. Bain and Clegg (1974: 95) refined the definition of IR to 'the study of all aspects of job regulation – the making and administering of the rules which regulate employment relationships – regardless of whether these are seen as being formal or informal, structured or unstructured'. Sisson (2010: 4) defines IR as the study of

> the institutions involved in governing the employment relationship, the people and organizations that make and administer them, and the rule-making processes that are involved, together with their economic and social outcomes.

With some notable exceptions, however, IR research historically can be located within a narrower conception of the field than that identified by these definitions.

Underlying the concept of 'job regulation' in orthodox or mainstream IR theories is the notion of equilibrium: regulatory mechanisms tend to be in perfect harmony with their environment, and the process of regulation itself is predictable, stable and seemingly trouble-free (Dabscheck, 1993). The bulk of orthodox IR research concentrated on the form of institutions and overlooked the processes through which they are reproduced. The focus was on the status of institutions rather than the maintenance of relations. While important conceptual innovations arose from the research on the institutions of job regulation, the literature was primarily characterised by fact-finding and description rather than theoretical generalisation. The analytical debates that took place centred mainly on the need to establish a conceptual framework for the predominantly pragmatic and empirical concerns of IR, to clarify the boundaries of teaching and research and to establish some degree of intellectual respectability vis-á-vis other applied fields of study and social science disciplines.

Winchester (1983: 101–2) cited several indicators of this trend: examples of successful multidisciplinary research were rare, most research focused on workplace and plant studies in the private manufacturing industry, a somewhat eclectic approach to methodological issues was common and assumptions of policy relevance characterised much of the literature. There is an established and growing consensus that research in IR needs to go beyond a largely functionalist description of the dynamics of job regulation to a theoretically-informed analysis of the expanded reproduction of the inherently unstable and conflict-ridden relationship between capital and labour. Compounding the challenges confronting established IR theory and practice are broader socio-economic and political changes, such as the increasing globalisation of economic activities, the spread of neoliberalism, the deepening of social divisions, the rise of individualism and the increased 'flexibility' in labour markets.

Edwards (1995: 13–16) identifies three levels of analysis within a broader analytical perspective on rules. The first level concerns the immediate balance of cooperation and conflict in the workplace. To avoid the stark choice between whether employers and employees have interests that are shared (human-relations theories) or that conflict (labour-process theories), it is increasingly acknowledged that both are integral features of the employment relationship. The second level focuses on the broader policies underlying the management of the employment relationship. These policies are usually explored in terms of the association between strategic choice and technological determinism. The third level concerns the fundamental nature of the employment relationship. There is an attempt to move beyond simply noting that conflict and cooperation are important. The substantial strengths inherent in the field of IR, which stem from a focus on the employment relationship in its broader context as well as a multidisciplinary perspective that mobilises an array of social scientific concepts, allow us to explain 'the range of change evident in today's workplaces' and to accentuate 'the reciprocal connections between them and other aspects of social and economic development' (Colling and Terry, 2010: 4).

The Object of Inquiry

The fundamental object of inquiry that defines the field of IR is not trade unions, management or industrial conflict but the relationship that generates these phenomena – i.e., the *employment relationship.* As Edwards (1995) points out, the purpose of IR is the control, adaptation and adjustment or regulation of the employment relationship. Likewise, Salamon (1998: 3) regards IR as 'a set of phenomena, both within and outside the workplace, concerned with determining and regulating the employment relationship'. In short, the field of IR is increasingly viewed as encapsulating a study of the regulation or governance of employment relationships. It is possible to discern, Blyton and Turnbull (2004: 37) argue, a growing tendency

> ... to focus on, and define the distinctive characteristics of the ***employment relationship***; to locate that relationship within the ***broader nature of economic activity***; to analyze the ***structural bases*** of conflict and accommodation between employer and employee; to consider the influence of the ***wider society***; and to develop an ***inter-disciplinary approach*** using concepts and ideas derived from sociology, economics, psychology, history and political science.

The employment relationship is one of the great innovations that enabled the rise of the modern business enterprise. It revolutionised the organisation of work, providing managers and workers with a very flexible method of coordination and a basis for investing in skills (Marsden, 1999). In its most basic form, every employment relationship is an economic exchange (an agreement to exchange wages for work) and a power relation (the employee 'agrees' to submit to the employer's authority). While Braverman's (1974) seminal work has been justifiably criticised, what must be retained from his analysis is a rejection of the view of the employment relationship as merely an exchange relationship, as primarily a site of bargaining rather than exploitation. In the 'hidden abode' of production, 'labour and capital come together in a way that is at once a market transaction, a labour process, and a scene of daily life: that is the employment relation' (Storper and Walker, 1989: 168). The employment relationship may be defined as 'the set of conditions determining the exchange, use and reproduction of the labour force' (Michon, 1992: 224). This conception of the employment relationship patently goes beyond the traditional concerns of IR research. In this view, collective bargaining is merely one non-essential aspect of IR.

The employment relationship is not an abstract notion but one of 'practical significance, being the basis of the parties' own interactions and the relationship upon which all other aspects of employee relations develop' (Blyton and Turnbull, 2004: 7). It encompasses the processes through which employees are recruited, rewarded, motivated and disciplined, as well as how the key actors in the labour market respond to these processes. Unlike other factors of production, the employer cannot precisely specify the quantity and quality of tasks to be performed by an employee in advance (Meardi, 2014). Therefore, every workplace must solve an implacable dilemma at the heart of the employment relationship – i.e., converting labour power into actual labour – through negotiating order between employers and employees. The critical point about the indeterminacy of the labour contract and strategies of labour control is that

> managers and workers are locked into a relationship that is contradictory and antagonistic. ... There is thus a relation of "structured antagonism" between employer and worker. This term is used to stress that the antagonism is built into the basis of the relationship, even though on a day-to-day level cooperation is also important.
>
> (Edwards, 1995: 15)

The employee's claim to wages and the employer's claim to performance involve an asymmetrical reciprocity. Consequently, the wage-effort bargain that underlies the employment relationship is subject to a fundamental and continuous antagonism of interest. Management must, therefore, find ways and means of legitimating its authority among workers to gain their cooperation and release their creativity. This indeterminacy encourages management to introduce a 'rule of law' in the form of negotiated policies, practices and procedures of selection, training, appraisal and payment that supplement or replace the direct control by individual managers and the technical controls of machines (Sisson and Marginson, 2003: 161–2). While employers require the consent of their employees, this need has to be tempered by the demands of profitability and requirements of the overall direction of the labour process. The managerial control necessary to regulate the employment relationship and to establish order in the workplace creates a force over and against employees. However, there are practical limits to how far the employer can subordinate the employee and definite disadvantages in the form of potentially reduced levels of worker initiative and collaboration (see Harley, 2015; Smith, 2015; Thompson, 2009). That is, managerial authority and worker obedience are never absolute but rather inherently fluid and open to renegotiation. Any form of stability that does arise in the workplace is thus actively created and sustained. The labour exchange must, in effect, be renewed and re-negotiated in an unremitting cycle.

Such is the intractability of the diverse interests in the workplace that no matter how many managers are appointed, how many rules are formulated and how many organisational changes are made, the problems of productive labour deployment and utilisation will remain. Since a formal employment contract cannot define the relationship between wages and performance in detail, and cost control must be continuously emphasised and achieved, the detail of the wage-effort bargain is subject to on-going and often tacit negotiation. The employment contract is thus a *social* contract endowed with implied expectations and embedded in relations of trust and reciprocity (Streeck, 1992). An important consequence of this open-ended character of the employment contract is that the (re)structuring of the labour market is itself a part of the processes of cultivating labour productivity (Brown and Nolan, 1988).

Given the enormous difficulty in anticipating all the problems that may arise in providing customers with the goods and services they desire, the flexibility of the employment relationship, which builds on workers' agreements to be available to undertake certain types of work as and when their employer directs, is a great advantage. Yet, few workers would agree to give their employers unlimited powers over work assignments. The rise of the employment relationship owes much to 'the development of job rules that square the apparent circle of providing employers with flexible job allocations and employees with limited liability to follow their employer's instructions' (Marsden, 1999: 3–4). Insofar as the employment relationship provides a relatively stable framework for collaboration in the workplace, it reflects the struggles over forms and degrees of control and the nature and extent of autonomy under which people work.

Labour Regulation

Orthodox approaches to IR generally regard employment as a largely self-contained sphere of social activity that leads to a clearly bounded set of labour 'problems' (Hyman, 1994a: 121). In practice, however, the expanded reproduction of the employment relationship is dependent on an ensemble of social structures and practices (such as the law, government policy, collective bargaining, social security, behavioural norms, education and training systems) to mitigate the contradictions inherent in capitalist accumulation. As a set of laws, institutions, practices and customs that control the use of labour, the employment relationship forms an integral part of the broader mode of social regulation (Boyer and Saillard, 1995; Whitley and Kristensen, 1997; Burchell *et al.*, 2003; Rubery and Grimshaw, 2003).

The employment relationship is a product of not just one overarching causal logic but of the (*a priori*) indeterminate intersection of several generative structures. The roots of these structures can be traced to three sets of social processes: the processes of production and the structuring of labour demand; the processes of social reproduction and the structuring of labour supply; and the forces of regulation (Peck, 1996). The ensemble of institutions that regulate the employment relationship (re)produce social relations, connect the processes of production and social reproduction and mediate conflicting interests inside and outside the workplace. The sites and patterns of regulation are characterised by considerable diversity and contingency. In the *régulation* approach, according to Peck (2000: 68), there is 'nothing theoretically pre-ordained or fixed ... about the scale at which regulatory functions are sited'. Labour regulation can occur at more or less mutually coordinated levels (national, sectoral, workplace and occupational group) and comprises more or less mutually integrated forms (market, social and statutory).

As Hyman (1994b: 170) observes, the *régulation* approach has become 'a particularly influential source of innovation in industrial relations analysis in recent years'. The central insight of this approach – that the *relative* stability of specific cycles of capitalist accumulation is secured through the interplay of a whole series of regulatory mechanisms that yields a variety of different propensities and casual liabilities – highlights the recurring instabilities in the processes of valorisation, rooted in antagonistic features of the employment relationship and expressed in imbalances between investment, production and consumption.

The *régulation* approach posits a strong relationship between (a) the *rapport salarial* – the general configuration of the employment relationship in relation to the exchange, utilisation and reproduction of the labour force; and (b) the *fait salarial* – the specific institutional form exhibited by the employment relationship in particular industries, regions and countries (Boyer, 1994). The attributes of a particular mode of labour regulation emerge from the intersection of a localised *fait salarial* with the broader processes of uneven development in the *rapport salarial*. While there is no simple matching process, there is 'a functional concordance between the accumulation system, the mode of social regulation and the mode of labour regulation' (Littler, 1993: 323). Of course, no regulatory system comprises a stable, unified, functionally-integrated totality, but always reflects the antagonistic and contradictory logic of the capital–labour relation (Jessop, 1991: 157).

Underlying this conception of regulation, according to Elger and Edwards (2002: 185), are a series of analytical arguments, which may be summarised as follows. First, the capitalist employment relationship is structured as an antagonistic relationship with a perennial potential to generate conflict. Second, capitalist development is premised on the more or less successful management of this antagonism through a variegated combination of domination and accommodation, freedom and compulsion. Third, labour regulation most directly involves the institutional structuring of the production process, the labour market, collective representation within and beyond the workplace, and the political representation of labour. Fourth, the state is implicated in most forms of regulation, not as a neutral agency or the successful agent of the 'needs' of capitalists but as a more or less adequate manager of the processes of capitalist accumulation. Fifth, labour regulation remains persistently incomplete, recurrently contested and intrinsically contingent, and reflects the complex and varied character of labour utilisation and managerial control.

Labour regulation plays the role that it does because the employment relationship is structured in the way that it is. Since it is inherently open-ended, contested and contradictory, the employment relationship depends on regulatory mechanisms capable of generating the social rules and conventions necessary for its cohesion and durability. At the heart of the employment relationship is a trade-off between effort and wages, control and autonomy, resistance and accommodation, efficiency and equity. These trade-offs, however, are realised and reproduced in a differentiated manner across time, space and occupation.

The various historical and institutional forms of the employment relationship presuppose distinctive, concomitant modes of social regulation.

The competitive capitalism of the nineteenth century was associated with an employment relationship characterised by the primacy of price and market mechanisms. The subsequent development of a monopolistic regulation based on mass production and mass consumption is associated with the stabilisation of earnings, rising state intervention and close ties between production and consumption norms (Michon, 1992: 224–5). Attempts at addressing the crisis of this model of accumulation and regulation, which became organic in the 1970s, did not leave the dominant employment relationship untouched. The regulatory functions of the institutions associated with organised, permanent, full-time employment came under considerable strain with the deepening crisis of Fordism and the proliferation of employment forms that depart from the 'standard' employment relationship.

The claim that the capitalist labour market's inherent and systematic capacity for self-destruction necessitates state, or more broadly, social regulation should not be confused with a crude functionalism in which effective institutional responses are somehow always materialised. Nor are the dilemmas of labour regulation soluble in an absolute sense once an 'appropriate' institutional and policy framework is established. Pressures for regulation do not necessarily result in effective regulation: the effects of institutional interventions cannot be guaranteed. Functionalism is avoided by acknowledging, first, that there are a host of potential institutional responses to the same regulatory dilemma. Second, the form that regulation assumes and the dynamics that it displays are determined in large measure by the structures and propensities of the object of regulation. The contradictions of the employment relationship under capitalism are systemic and ultimately 'resolvable' only in terms of temporary institutional containment. That is, the institutional framework of the employment relationship, while necessary for its continued reproduction, does not fully resolve its underlying contradictions, which are logically (though not temporally) prior to institutional responses (Peck, 1996: 42).

Once established, labour market institutions acquire their own bureaucratic and political momentum, which will only fortuitously happen to coincide with the shifting regulatory requirements of the employment relationship. Although the latter is dependent on some form of social regulation for its reproduction, such interventions are always inherently unstable, partial and contingent on the simultaneous operation of a range of other mediation mechanisms. According to Jessop (2001: 12),

> An adequate account of regulation must not only consider the material preconditions of, and constraints upon, reproduction … but must also take account of the different modes of calculation and the orientations of the various social forces involved in economic and social regulation. An important theoretical development in this context would be a more explicit concern with the 'spatio-temporal fixes' within which capitalist reproduction and regularization occur.

A regime of labour regulation is realised or partially realised through a complex amalgam of regulatory mechanisms geared towards mediating conflicting objectives and managing antagonistic social forces. For instance, essential aspects of labour regulation are shaped through informal workgroup relations, unofficial custom and practice and tacit negotiations. Whereas the traditional concerns of IR are closely associated with 'formal' mechanisms of coordination, 'informal' mechanisms are frequently viewed in static and undifferentiated terms. This error may be avoided by conceptualising the distinction between the formal and informal aspects of IR in terms of different sites and forms or methods of labour regulation that will, by virtue of their respective structures and objects, vary in the extent to which they are based on coercion or consent, are resisted or accepted and so on. Informal practices, such as individualised-pay bargaining, underscore 'the pervasiveness of custom and indeterminacy within the employment relationship' (Ram *et al.*, 2001: 847). The research conducted by these authors shows that all firms combine formality and informality just as they combine control and consent, with the balance varying as conditions differ.

The wide divergence in working practices and the management of labour across time and space reflects the social embeddedness of the employment relationship. Labour regulation is a conjuncturally specific phenomenon that only coalesces under certain spatiotemporal conditions (Peck, 1996). Given the social nature and institutional dependence of labour's production and reproduction, changes in the mechanisms through which it is incorporated, allocated, controlled and reproduced are always partial, contested and highly context-dependent. As Gallie and White (1994: 107) point out, current restructuring is characterised by slow and cautious changes on a trial-and-error basis, a limited and discontinuous search for new employment strategies, a status-quo bias in the efforts to maintain worker commitment and legitimate managerial authority, and an *ad hoc* and piecemeal renewal of policies in response to specific pressures.

Managements' attempts at restructuring the workplace are, therefore, far less conclusive, uniform and purposeful than implied by many proponents of HRM. There is a need for a greater appreciation of the open-ended and complex nature of changes in the workplace. The path dependency of changes in regulatory systems means that regulatory solutions that are effective in one context may not be readily supplanted in others. Establishing a durable form of labour regulation is a contingent process dependent on experimentation and chance discoveries. As a complex and contingently realised 'fit' between social mediation and capital accumulation, labour regulation is inherently unstable and manifests in a myriad of mediation mechanisms. According to Michon (1992: 227), the societal variability of the forms taken by the employment relationship reflects 'the multiple levels that play a significant role in the structuring of the system and that reflect the heterogeneity of economic and social space'.

The 'Crisis' of Industrial Relations in Practice

Orthodox approaches to IR tend to emphasise the collective regulation of employment conditions by management and trade unions at the expense of other modes of regulation (Ackers and Wilkinson, 2008: 59). Common features of collective workplace relations include a history of mutual antagonism between union and management, strong shopfloor organisation that relies on traditional patterns of negotiation underwritten by a formal framework of procedural agreements, the existence of few or no consultative mechanisms and constant disagreements about union rights and management style (Smith, 1994). The processes of collective bargaining are not only extraneous to the experiences of a growing proportion of workers but always contain several inherent limitations. The latter relate to its role as a potential source of managerial control and how it institutionalises conflict, thereby giving it a greater predictability (Sisson, 1987). Collective negotiations also occur within the context of managerial strategies that are *not* part of the bargaining agenda (Hyman, 1975).

Collective bargaining, on its own, is seldom capable of decisively influencing the production, investment and location decisions of capitalist enterprises. The day-to-day management of labour is conducted through different forms of regulation than those involved in wage-determination (Wilkinson *et al.*, 2018). In particular, collective bargaining is not geared towards or designed for managing the organisation of work. The complexity of daily production issues is incapable of regulation by collective agreements, given the contingencies, emergencies and so on that invariably arise. As Bélanger (1994: 62) puts it: 'even in the context of a unionised workplace and once a collective agreement has been struck, shopfloor management and employees still have to make arrangements on the contours and the nature of the numerous tasks to be included in a given job, as well as the volume and quality of actual work to be performed on every shift'.

Unravelling of the Post-War Social Contract

The standard employment relationship of indefinite duration – which came to dominate the labour market in the advanced capitalist economies under relatively favourable economic conditions of continuous growth and full employment during the post-war era – underpins conventional models of IR. This relationship was consolidated at a time when industry commanded the largest share of overall employment; powerful labour movements sustained industry-wide bargaining; governments were committed to corporatist governance of macro-economic policies; industrial organisation was based on more or less stable, predictable and protected domestic markets; and the nation-state enjoyed considerable autonomy in national economic and fiscal policies. The bureaucratic controls associated with Fordism, as Burawoy (1985: 263) shows, established 'constraints on the deployment of capital, whether by tying wages to profits or by creating internal labour markets, collective bargaining and grievance machinery which hamstrung management's domination of the workplace'. Since these constraints stem from the statutory regulation of the labour market and the power of the trade unions, employers and governments increasingly regarded them as unwarranted and unacceptable under conditions of increasing global competition. It is argued that overly protective employment policies and extensive trade union controls have the effect of curbing competition in the labour market. These conditions prevented the downward adjustment of terms and conditions of employment, leading to employment 'rigidity'. Consequently, employers found it challenging to adjust the quantity and the quality of labour supply to rapid changes in labour demand.

Since the 1980s, the 'regionally variable processes of deindustrialisation and disinvestment were pitching "capital against community" in ways that threatened to undermine the post-war social contract' (Herod *et al.*, 2003: 181). The standard employment relationship came under increasing pressure as institutionalised IR faced unparalleled challenges and drastic changes unfolded in the regulatory framework of the labour market. As Hakim (1990: 167) states in her review of workforce restructuring, strategies varied from one country to the next and followed different paths, 'but all pointed in the same general direction of increasing … segmentation of the labour market and exploring new forms of differentiating wage/labour relations'. Therefore, the rise of non-standard or 'precarious' employment relationships is part of a broader process of de-collectivisation and fragmentation in IR. Far from simply being a rational response to changing economic imperatives, the decisions concerning restructuring the employment relationship are political in origin and outcome. The redistributive effects of these decisions involve diverting the costs of restructuring onto the least politically and economically entrenched groups in society.

The Crisis of Fordist Production

By the 1990s, the employment relationship increasingly manifested the signs of the growing internationalisation and volatility of economic activity. Changes in the way that production is organised ruptured existing arrangements in labour regulation by shifting firms' competitive positions, altering the types of skills and aptitudes required, changing the parties' bargaining power and so on. These changes can be explained in large measure as involving a shift in the extent to which the market mediates employment relationships. As Streeck (1992: 66–7) argues:

> [t]he decomposition of the pluralist–corporatist regulation of industrial relations can be interpreted as a decay of the specific balance between status and contract that had underlain the Fordist–Keynesian mode of regulation … [This entails] a polarization in two opposite directions … within national societies between industries, within industries between enterprises, and within enterprises between groups of employees, with

> the emergence of 'good', that is, status-secured, jobs coinciding with growing disparities with a secondary labour market for 'poor', marginal and uncertain employment relationships ... [T]he status-type safeguarding of 'core workforces' not only does not rule out the marginalization of a fringe workforce kept disposable through short-term contracts, but indeed economically presupposes it.

The standard employment relationship was not only rooted in the IR regimes of post-war Europe and North America but was also closely linked to the Taylorist–Fordist organisation of production that prevailed during this period. The mass production of standardised, price-competitive goods for protected domestic markets was characterised by high degrees of capital intensity, the detailed demarcation of jobs and competencies, the vertical integration of production, the centralisation of management and the bureaucratisation of the organisation. The alleged shift from economies of scale (mass production) to economies of scope (flexible or lean production) necessitated a greater emphasis on employee cooperation, multiskilling and a delayering of the managerial hierarchy. The concerted efforts by employers to circumvent shop stewards as a channel of representation and deal directly with the workforce through individualised forms of direct participation generated informal assumptions and modes of behaviour, which put a premium on individualism, consultative managerial styles and a non-antagonistic IR climate.

The establishment of quality circles, just-in-time inventories, semi-autonomous work groups and so on are presented as a move away from the alienating and deskilled employment associated with Fordism towards new forms of employee involvement and high-trust relations in the workplace. Managerial approaches increasingly emphasise

> individualism (rather than collectivism), unitary (rather than pluralism), consultation (rather than negotiation and agreement), flexibility (rather than uniformity), employee commitment (rather than simple compliance) and empowerment and 'responsible' autonomy (rather than direct control). This can be seen as a reassertion of managerial prerogative ... particularly in so far as employees are expected to be committed to management's organisational objectives ... and the process of regulation emphasizes consultation which provides greater management freedom to 'set the agenda' and make decisions.
>
> (Salamon, 1998: 220–2)

Despite the lack of robust empirical evidence, the proponents of 'new' IR regard the employment relationship as increasingly based on polyvalent skills, functional adaptability and high levels of employee discretion and commitment. For these IR scholars, the changes that are unfolding are the product of attempts by employers to reassert their control and to intensify the work process in the context of trade union weakness, a decline in the coverage of collective bargaining, rising unemployment and the rapid spread of new technologies. According to Hyman (1991), these changes merely consolidate or extend the core principles of the traditional patterns of IR. Sengenberger (1992: 139) also notes that 'new opportunities for participation' are accompanied by 'the spectre of new forms of dependency, hierarchisation and unilateral decision-making'. Some emerging regularities, patterns and relationships are consistent with the post-Fordist elements catalogued in the literature. These developments, however, are best viewed as tendencies rather than achievements, occurring within a context of change *and* continuity.

To some extent, these developments are simply a manifestation of the inherent tendencies of capitalism towards crisis, revolutionising the forces of production and extending the division of labour (Pollert, 1991). 'New' IR policies are, therefore, essentially a reactive measure to cope with the uncertainties generated by the economic crisis rather than a proactive means to overcome the crisis itself. As such, employment 'flexibility', 'lean' production and the like are symptoms of, rather than solutions to, the crisis.

Theoretical Critiques of Industrial Relations

Since IR is an area of study with a range of disciplinary inputs, theoretical shifts in these disciplines can have profound implications for conducting research into IR matters. Within IR, we can discern a basic contrast between (a) systems approaches that give precedence to information about patterns and entail an almost exclusive concern with form and universality, and (b) behavioural approaches that prioritise information about processes and embody an overriding commitment to content and variability. While we cannot accept structural and behavioural approaches equally without contradiction, there is room for combining some of their insights. A coherent theoretical synthesis involves not the simple 'joining' of conflicting approaches but rather their transcendence into a new approach in which the whole is greater than the sum of its parts. For example, in their attempt to 'complete the systems framework', Kochan *et al.* (2002: 74) tend to reify society's economic structures and endow management with an inordinate capacity for strategic action. As such, they end up combining, rather than transcending, the errors of determinism and voluntarism.

Structure and Agency

IR scholars, as Edwards (2003: 355) points out, insist that the 'outcomes of policies depend on specific contexts ... [and that] there are continuing features of the employment relationship which hold true across historical eras'. Contrary to post-modernists' claims, the study of IR does not preclude an understanding of instability, fragmentation, uncertainty, identity, consumerism and lifestyle (Eldridge, 2003). Post-modernists, under the guise of anti-essentialism, counterpose essentialism to social constructionism. While realists can accept weak social constructionism (i.e., the socially constructed nature of knowledge and institutions), they do not admit its stronger version that the objects or referents of knowledge are nothing more than social constructions (Bhaskar, 1989). If the world is purely a product of our social constructions, it should be relatively transparent. For realists, the world is relatively inaccessible precisely because it is not reducible to, or a construction of, our concepts of it. If references are unstable, it does not follow that referents are. Moreover, recognising the socially-constructed nature of social phenomena is not a licence for a voluntarism that makes them merely discursively revisable. Social institutions have a structural integrity, which limits and enables what they can and cannot do. In other words, the choice is not simply between a deterministic ontology of essences (empiricism) and one of endless differences (post-modernism).

The post-modernist proclivity for ascribing a primary role to individual values and beliefs will invariably result in granting the strategic dimensions of IR a degree of autonomy that they rarely possess. An emphasis on individual behaviour as the driving force of IR disregards the underlying structural determinations of conflict and accommodation. The assumption is that management simply chooses between clearly marked solutions to the problems of labour regulation. By neglecting the material basis of labour regulation and adopting a voluntaristic model of social action, post-modern approaches cannot account for broader structural determinations and, hence, fail to reveal the complexities, tensions and uncertainties of choice. What is needed is a more expansive, materially-grounded conception of regulation that is consistent with the emphasis on rule-guided behaviour in systems theories and the stress placed on the role of human agency in strategic choice approaches (see Edwards, 2005; Thompson and Vincent, 2010). In line with a commitment to critical realism, the processes of labour regulation are viewed as tendencies that may be realised in various ways in different concrete situations, adding another layer of determination to the idea of the employment relationship as a 'synthesis of multiple determinations'.

Levels of Abstraction

Many of the obstacles that confront the development of theory in IR are, at least in part, 'problems of integrating different levels of generality' (Hyman, 1989: 135). The post-modernist rejection of 'meta-narratives' compounds these problems. The level of generality of abstractions appropriate to determining an adequate explanation will depend on the nature of the structures or mechanisms that are really responsible (Lawson, 1997). Post-modernists are rightfully critical of the inclination to reduce a mode of regulation to national configurations. Such reductionism has encouraged a tendency to reduce intra-national variability (i.e., the forms of regulation associated with particular industries or regions) to a contingent variability around dominant historical–national models. There is a need to bring sub-national regulation out of the shadows, 'not in ritual celebration of diversity and difference but in order to understand *of what* national systems are constituted' (Peck, 1996: 99). To strike a balance between micro- or meso-institutional analysis and the macro-economic focus of the *régulation* approach, labour regulation at the regional or industrial level should be understood not only on its own terms, but also in terms of its articulation with broader national and global regulatory structures. Regional and local systems of regulation cannot be understood simply as derivations from a dominant national model: the latter is itself constituted of a series of regional systems. Hence, we must recognise the complementarities, tensions and conflicts between micro and macro approaches to avoid an eclectic combination of analyses.

By combining a critical realist interpretation of the relationship between labour market processes and space with a regulationist interpretation of the distinctive ways in which labour markets and their regulatory institutions interrelate at the local level, Peck (1996) demonstrates how local labour markets are both constructed (in terms of the concrete working out of generative mechanisms underpinning them) and socially regulated (in terms of the distinctive 'regulatory milieux' formed in and around them) in locally-specific ways. If each local labour market represents a unique geographic conjuncture of regulatory processes, it follows that the institutional form of the employment relationship will also take on a locally distinctive character. A meso-level theorisation of the local labour market is an indispensable component of any explanation of the disjuncture between general processes of social regulation and the variety of local outcomes.

The concept of labour regulation, therefore, is an essential mediation between the theoretical insights of an abstract analysis based on the law of value and concrete empirical reality, as revealed using the methods of social scientific analysis. The dynamics of capitalism define the fundamental tendencies and countertendencies, structural contradictions, strategic dilemmas and overall constraints that shape and are, in turn, shaped by the specific institutional and organisational forms associated with a mode of regulation (Jessop, 1991). Generally, a regulatory mechanism at one level presupposes other, more foundational levels. The regulation of the employment relationship would be impossible in the absence of broader processes and structures of societal regulation, such as the state, the family, schools and the courts. As a site of regulation, however, the workplace is ontologically constituted by sets of relations that are irreducible to these broader processes of social regulation.

Labour regulation, understood as the mediation of power relations, takes place at multiple levels, and each dimension of the employment relationship may be regulated at one or more of these scales. As Bowles and Gintis argue: 'power is heterogeneous, wielding a variety of weapons, yielding to a host of counterpressures, and obeying no single logic' (cited in Spencer, 2000: 556). At the most basic level, we can distinguish between two different planes: the internal and external regulation of the employment relationship. The reductionism in conceptions that emphasise either exogenous or endogenous factors can be avoided once it is recognised that there can be no *a priori* prioritisation of one level at the expense of the other. Whether exogenous or endogenous factors predominate is contingent on a whole host of factors, including the varying degrees to which different regulatory regimes are socially embedded and institutionally mediated. There is a constant tension between the institutionalisation of the employment relationship through collective regulation and the continuous process of negotiating order within the workplace. While the dividing line between internal and external regulation is often blurred, several contemporary workplace changes can be understood as a shift in the balance between external and internal regulation of the employment relationship.

The so-called 'crisis of IR' is merely a crisis of a particular conception of the employment relationship: one that is narrowly focused on mass production and revolves mainly around the experiences of organised, full-time (typically male) workers. In contrast to such a restricted view, an emergent 'labour regulation' approach has been applied effectively to account for non-traditional IR issues such as financialisation, global production networks, non-union firms, non-standard employment, networked organisations, social movements and high-performance work systems (see Ackers and Wilkinson, 2008; Baglioni *et al.*, 2022; Bélanger *et al.*, 1994; Dundon and Rollinson, 2004; Gallie *et al.*, 1998; Giles, 2000; Godard, 2004; Heery *et al.*, 2008; Kelly, 1998; Meardi, 2014; Wilkinson *et al.*, 2018).

Industrial Relations and Human Resource Management

The term 'HRM' became increasingly popular from the 1980s onwards, although its roots can be traced back to personnel management of the 1920s and human relations of the 1950s (Kaufman, 2014). HRM shares with the human relations approach a concern for the internal dynamics of the workgroup, a desire to create social cohesion and value consensus through corporate culture, an attempt to integrate personnel issues within the overall business strategy and an effort to generate higher levels of employee commitment and involvement. According to Salamon (1998: 19), HRM's importance to IR lies in its association with 'a strategic, integrated and highly distinctive managerial approach to the management of people'. It is closely tied to managerial interests and has strong unitarist overtones in its approach to employees as a collective. Storey (1989: 9) suggests that HRM 'eschews the joint regulative approach … places emphasis on utilising labour to its full capacity or potential … [and] is therefore about … exploiting the labour resource more fully'. In fact, Fowler questions whether supporters of HRM are 'genuinely concerned with creating a new, equal partnership between employer and employed, or are they really offering a covert form of employee manipulation dressed up as mutuality' (cited in Salamon, 1998: 19).

Conceptions of HRM range from inclusive (all forms of labour management are included within the broader study of HRM) to exclusive (HRM is contrasted to other forms of labour management) (Storey, 2001: 5). Whereas the former accepts the continued relevance of IR as a study of the collective aspects of employee relations, the latter postulates the eclipse of IR. Exclusive definitions constitute a more significant challenge to the continued relevance of IR. In this view,

> HRM comprises a set of policies designed to maximize organizational integration, employee commitment, flexibility and quality of work. Within this model, collective industrial relations have, at best, only a minor role.
>
> (Guest, 1987: 503)

Several attempts have been made to distinguish HRM from personnel management and IR (see Bacon, 2003; Blyton and Turnbull, 1992; Harney *et al.*, 2018; Kaufman, 2001; Legge, 1995; Storey, 1992). Edwards (2003: 341) suggests that several possible relations between HRM and IR can be identified: (a) HRM and IR can be regarded as co-equal with IR handling collective bargaining and HRM dealing with personnel administration, (b) HRM can be regarded as the generic term, with IR being a subordinate and possibly waning sub-set; (c) HRM can challenge IR by claiming to be more proactive and even strategic; and (d) IR can retain analytical dominance, with HRM being regarded as one particular technique to manage the inherent contradictions of the employment relationship.

Rhetoric and Reality

Insofar as HRM represents a distinctive approach to labour management, it relies primarily on direct communication with employees through mechanisms such as quality circles rather than indirect representation through collective bargaining with trade unions. Despite significant continuities between HRM and personnel management, there are several differences between these two approaches. However, it is essential to remember that personnel management depicts actual practices, while HRM largely portrays normative prescriptions (Guest and Bryson, 2009). As Applebaum and Batt report in their extensive study of workplace reforms: 'despite the reported gains in performance and the apparent acceleration of experiments with innovative practices, the overwhelming majority of US workplaces are traditionally managed' (cited in Milkman, 1997: 144). A significant problem with aspects of the HRM literature is the persistent failure to distinguish between prescription and description, especially in the rhetorical claims of best practice. The prescriptive element is, by definition, open to the challenge that it does not have any bearing on reality. In practice, the emphasis on team working and employee involvement often coincides with conventional forms of authority relations overtly based on an assertion of managerial control (McKinlay and Taylor, 1996; Geary and Dobbins, 2001; Kaufman, 2012).

In many cases, firms could only introduce and maintain these new work arrangements through a more aggressive and hostile managerial style (Steward,

1997). It is, therefore, not surprising to discover that many HRM innovations are either stillborn or have a restricted lifespan (Heckscher and Schurman, 1997). Furthermore, some of the claims regarding the positive impact of HRM innovations on enterprise productivity are (at best) questionable and tend to overlook the effects of new HRM practices on employees, work and society (Godard, 2004; Harley, 2015; Marchington, 2015).

Many, if not all, of the personnel practices associated with HRM (e.g. psychological testing, appraisal, performance-related pay, quality circles and teamwork) are designed to shape employees' beliefs and attitudes and to emphasise individualism. A vital part of HRM is a concerted attempt to avoid, remove or minimise IR practices, such as negotiations with trade unions, to shift the balance between individualism and collectivism (Storey and Bacon, 1993). Given the context of rising economic instability and uncertainty, these strategies have struck a sympathetic chord with employers. Such are the times when cost-cutting is prioritised, the scope for compromise is reduced, and the unions are generally on the defensive. According to Harney *et al.* (2018: 116–9), the critical deficiencies of extant HRM literature, which may be juxtaposed to the insights from IR research, are centred on a poor specification of the 5Cs: complexity (unitarist managerialism and a sterile account of HRM interventions), context (universalistic emphasis and decontextualised prescriptions), contingency (overemphasis on managerial rationality and underemphasis of structural constraints), causality (a Humean quest for event regularities rather than an exploration of underlying generative mechanisms) and critique (a prescriptive and managerial bias reinforced by the neglect of critical trends in the field of IR).

A noteworthy shortcoming in much of the literature on HRM is a failure to canvass the views of employees and their organisations. By contrast, IR scholars do not unreflexively adopt employers' perspectives, and their research on the outcomes of managerial practices considers the impact on the business as well as workers (Barry and Wilkinson, 2016; Godard, 2014; Heery *et al.*, 2008). A study in the British automobile sector found that most workers perceived the changes associated with 'new' IR as 'concrete mechanisms of labour subordination' (Danford, 1997: 109). Quality control and teamworking contain a vital control function aimed at disciplining employees – namely, 'management through blame' (Delbridge and Turnbull, 1992; see also Green, 2006). Teamworking, as Garrahan and Stewart (1992: 106) also point out,

> is a process in which workers control one another's actions. It is this which gives to the autocratic internal regime a spurious air of employee participation and control in work.

The superficial nature of cooperation and empowerment underlying HRM means that the actual experiences of workers will reinforce existing low trust and adversarial IR. Critical studies have shown that the ideology of employee 'involvement' is circumscribed by the real imperative of HRM: namely, getting employees to work harder (Ramsay *et al.*, 2000; Harney *et al.*, 2018). There is a perpetual tension under capitalism between treating workers as commodities to be hired and fired and harnessing their ingenuity and cooperativeness. The emphasis on employee 'involvement' in HRM strategies does not spell the end of control in the workplace but instead signals its reconfiguration. Hence the paradox: 'as workers were given more autonomy they were increasingly coming under tighter managerial control' (Geary, 1994: 648). Achieving and maintaining a balance between control and autonomy in the workplace depends less on the relatively simple task of meeting employees' comparative wage aspirations than on 'the endlessly demanding one of creating and maintaining the institutional forms that will maximise their willingness to work efficiently' (Brown and Nolan, 1988: 353).

Like the postulated links between HRM practices and organisational performance, the decontextualised rhetoric of commitment and cooperation in the HRM literature is readily exposed under empirical scrutiny. The effectiveness of an enterprise depends on the contingent amalgamation of a whole myriad of mediating processes that include managerial style, job demarcation and coordination, the distribution of information, the encouragement of learning and innovation and the mobilisation of consent and cooperation among employees. In their efforts to convert labour power into actual work performance, managers are confronted by a complex set of constraints and opportunities and have access to numerous mechanisms of control and coordination. As Edwards (1986: 41) argues,

> [f]irms will develop their practices of labour control with whatever materials they have available. They are unlikely to have explicit strategies and more likely to react to particular circumstances as best they can. Even when they have fairly clear goals they are unlikely to follow a policy which conforms to an ideal-type: they will proceed according to their own needs. In particular, they are likely to use a variety of means of controlling the labour process and tying workers to the firm.

No matter its strategy, management's primary objective is to maintain a stable, predictable and cost-effective workforce. Hakim's (1990) research shows that employers rely on a blend of IR policies with few sharp distinctions, considerable overlap between types and some ambiguity and variation within types. There is, thus, no clear division between strategies but rather many gradations. Hence, it is necessary to move down a level of abstraction to consider the more concrete dynamics of labour regulation. Descending from the abstract level of analysis means coming to grips with the complexity and indeterminacy of policy change and institutional restructuring. Empirically, strategies may be combined, and the particularities of each case will reflect institutional legacies, conjunctural conditions, the balance of class forces and so on.

Even firms with sophisticated HRM policies rely on negotiation to establish what the rules mean, and managers depend on workers to interpret their instructions intelligently (Edwards, 1994; Marsden, 1999). The negotiability of order in the workplace depends, therefore, on the willingness of workers to interpret the intent of managerial instructions. The need to elicit active cooperation from employees through the provision of material and symbolic rewards stems from the fact that 'no system of regulation is comprehensive enough to achieve complete control over the system to be regulated' (Tsoukas, 2000: 39). In other words, labour power must always, in part, be self-regulating. This underlying contradiction in management's control over labour decisively qualifies management's capacity for strategic action.

Conclusion: The Future of Industrial Relations

A problem that few HRM scholars address explicitly relates to the fact that management's capacity for strategic action is caught on the horns of a dilemma: 'solving' problems of employee involvement and commitment raises issues of managerial control and authority (and vice versa). It is, therefore, not a matter of 'choosing' between control and autonomy, but rather the terms of their resolution. While employers are generally interested in their employees displaying a certain degree of willingness to cooperate, there are definite limits and risks involved in the extent of autonomy that management can concede to any sector of the workforce. IR research has consistently emphasised the conflict, uncertainty and opposition associated with the managerial function. As Edwards (2003: 339) points out:

> the management of labour entails the two principles of control and consent. In particular, any concrete 'industrial relation' will have elements of both, and these elements are necessarily in contradiction … An IR system can never be in equilibrium because it rests on the need to manage actively these contradictory pressures.

Under capitalism, the 'resolution' of regulatory dilemmas in the workplace involves restructuring the employment relationship to (re)assert the priorities of accumulation. That is, the restructuring of production is always also the restructuring of the employment relationship. In the process of restructuring, as Peck (1996: 240) points out, 'the contours of labour control are [continuously] reworked and remade'. We should view the attempts by management to introduce, albeit selectively and partially, aspects of HRM such as performance management, team briefings, quality circles and semi-autonomous workgroups in this light. These mechanisms are geared towards increasing employees' loyalty and commitment to the organisation, changing their attitudes towards management's objectives and priorities, enhancing their willingness to accept change on management's terms and encouraging them to display greater initiative and self-discipline. However, the tentative nature of changes in a transition period means that identifying the directions of change involves more than simply measuring the extent of empirical change. A wide range of potentially disparate changes, for example, does not add up to a shift in the overall direction of IR. We need to identify the types of change involved, determine the reach and pace of these changes, trace the connections between them and then assess which changes (if any) are the more robust or decisive.

Absent from the prescriptions of HRM is an adequate explanation of the processes that constrain or facilitate diversification in regulatory forms. The proponents of HRM have been quick to generalise their findings across occupations, industries and regions, thereby ignoring the constraints and opportunities created by particular forms of mechanisation and labour-market structures. By contrast, IR scholars have long placed the issue of sectoral and occupational variations in workplace restructuring at the centre of their research.

The enduring diversity of national and regional spaces is a product of the 'intricate intertwining of the effects of disparate regulatory regimes and production regimes' (Waddington, 1999: 14). Employers and employees have to act in 'social formations which have already developed distinctive ways of governing work and firms' (Kristensen, 1997: 6). In other words, economic transactions are embedded in different social relations between (as well as within) countries so that they find distinct trade offs between competition and cooperation, efficiency and equity, exclusion and integration. It follows, therefore, that current industrial restructuring is far more problematic for both capital and labour than the technical-organisation discourses of HRM suggest.

The dominant conception of HRM contains few meaningful insights into the bases of social conflict and political power or broader structural determinations in the economy. Theory in HRM is clearly 'not equipped to handle the larger debate in political economy' (Boxall, 2014: 585). In addition, by adopting a unitarist, best-practice orientation that presumes a single source of legitimate workplace authority (Godard, 2014; Harley, 2015; Thompson, 2011), many HRM scholars 'embrace the role of servants of power, suppressing attention to the conflicting interests which underlie the world of work – a conflict which traditional industrial relations scholars recognized as the basis of their studies' (Hyman, cited in Godard and Delaney, 2000: 495). To be sure, the emphasis on economic performance outcomes and the constant refinement of methods for worker control are increasingly qualified by some concern for (a narrowly conceived) notion of employee 'well-being'. Far from being IR's 'potential salvation' (Ackers and Wilkinson, 2008: 59), HRM reflects the decline in social solidarity and labour's collective voice, the ascendancy of individualism and unchecked corporate greed, the predominance of efficiency over equity, the state's servility to globalised capital, the ascendency of neoliberal forms of governance and the consolidation of an uncritical and decontextualised managerial 'science' propagated by business schools.

The prevalence of generalised prescriptions, the penchant for prediction, the dedication to narrow behavioural research into individual motivation and response and the inability to think beyond prevailing economic systems all reflect HRM's underlying disciplinary influences. The unitarist perspectives among both HRM managers and researchers can readily be assimilated into (managerially-orientated) organisational psychology, whereas they sit uneasily with (worker-orientated) industrial sociology (Kelly, 2003; Godard, 2014). From a methodological standpoint, such psychology-based HRM research is grounded in positivist assumptions (Kasyanenko *et al.*, 2014), and its predominance is crowding out critical perspectives (Harley, 2015). Finally, HRM scholarship generally lacks sensitivity to (class) relations of domination and control in the workplace and does not adequately consider the structural imperatives of capitalism (Watson, 2010). Hence, a revitalised IR – which takes seriously the vast disparities in power and wealth as well as social and political diversity that typify the capitalist employment relationship – cannot simply rely on HRM 'to fill in much of what matters in working life today' (Ackers and Wilkinson, 2008: 59).

Grounding an analysis of IR in the labour regulation approach outlined provides a methodological footing that avoids the twin errors of voluntarism versus reification and abstract determinism versus ever-contingent empiricism. By drawing on this approach, we can conceive the drive for profits as the underlying force for change in the workplace, while recognising that it will assume various forms depending on the impact of mediating institutions such as occupational groups, trade unions, employers' associations, regulatory agencies and the like. That is, actors in the labour market regulate the employment relationship in ways that are constrained but not determined by the fundamental features of a capitalist economy and workplace. This approach also encourages a greater sensitivity to the intractability of the object of regulation in IR. Durable regulation, in the form of an essentially stable employment relationship, is unattainable since industrial conflict can never be 'resolved' in any final or absolute sense. In practice, labour regulation is a dialectical and continuous process of challenge and response, cooperation and conflict, control and autonomy. HRM is simply one way of mediating these contradictions, not a means to elude or eradicate them.

References

Ackers, P. and Wilkinson, A. (2005). British industrial relations paradigm: A critical outline history and prognosis. *Journal of Industrial Relations*, 47(4): 443–456.

Ackers, P. and Wilkinson, A. (2008). Industrial relations and the social sciences. In N. Bacon, P. Blyton, J. Fiorito, & E. Heery (Eds.), *The SAGE Handbook of Industrial Relations*. London: Sage Publications.

Bacon, N. (2003). Human resource management and industrial relations. In P. Ackers & A. Wilkinson (Eds.), *Understanding Work and Employment: Industrial Relations in Transition*. Oxford: Oxford University Press.

Baglioni, E., Campling, L., Coe, N. M. and Smith, A. (Eds.). (2022). *Labour Regimes and Global Production*. Newcastle: Agenda Publishing.

Bain, G. S. and Clegg, H. A. (1974). A strategy for industrial relations research in Great Britain. *British Journal of Industrial Relations*, 12(1): 91–113.

Barry, M. and Wilkinson, A. (2016). Pro-social or pro-management? A critique of the conception of employee voice as a pro-social behaviour within organisational behaviour. *British Journal of Industrial Relations*, 54(2): 261–284.

Bartram, T., Boyle, B., Stanton, P., Burgess, J. and McDonnell, A. (2015). Multinational enterprises and industrial relations: A research agenda for the 21st century. *Journal of Industrial Relations*, 57(2): 127–145.

Bélanger, J. (1994). Job controls under different labor relations regimes: A comparison of Canada and Great Britain. In J. Bélanger, P. K. Edwards, & L. Haiven (Eds.), *Workplace Industrial Relations and the Global Challenge*. Ithaca, NY: ILR Press.

Bélanger, J., Edwards, P. K. and Haiven, L. (Eds.). (1994). *Workplace Industrial Relations and the Global Challenge*. Ithaca, NY: ILR Press.

Bhaskar, R. (1989). *Reclaiming Reality: A Critical Introduction to Contemporary Philosophy*. London: Verso Books.

Blyton, P. and Turnbull, P. (1992). *Reassessing Human Resource Management*. London: Sage Publications.

Blyton, P. and Turnbull, P. (2004). *The Dynamics of Employee Relations* (3rd ed.). London: Macmillan.

Boxall, P. (2014). The future of employment relations from the perspective of human resource management. *Journal of Industrial Relations*, 56(4): 578–593.

Boxall, P. and Purcell, J. (2022). *Strategy and Human Resource Management* (5th ed.). London and New York: Bloomsbury Academic.

Boyer, R. (1994). Labour institutions and economic growth: A survey and a 'regulationist' approach. *Labour*, 7(1): 25–72.

Boyer, R. and Saillard, Y. (Eds.). (1995). *Regulation Theory: The State of the Art*. London: Routledge.

Braverman, H. (1974). *Labor and Monopoly Capital: The Degradation of Work in the Twentieth Century*. New York: Monthly Review Press.

Brown, W. and Nolan, P. (1988). Wages and labour productivity: The contribution of industrial relations research to an understanding of pay determination. *British Journal of Industrial Relations*, 26(3): 339–361.

Budd, J. W. (2008). A meta-paradigm for revitalizing industrial relations. In C. J. Whalen (Ed.), *New Directions in the Study of Work and Employment: Revitalizing Industrial Relations as an Academic Enterprise*. Cheltenham: Edward Elgar.

Burawoy, M. (1985). *The Politics of Production. Factory Regimes Under Capitalism and Socialism*. London: Verso Books.

Burchell, B., Deakin, S., Michie, J. and Rubery, J. (Eds.). (2003). *Systems of Production: Markets, Organizations and Performance*. London: Routledge.

Colling, T. and Terry, M. (2010). Work, the employment relationship and the field of industrial relations. In T. Colling and M. Terry (Eds.), *Industrial Relations: Theory and Practice* (3rd ed.). Chichester: John Wiley & Sons.

Dabscheck, B. (1993). Industrial relations and theories of interest group regulation. In R. J. Adams and N. M. Meltz (Eds.), *Industrial Relations Theory: Its Nature, Scope, and Pedagogy*. Lanham, MD: IMLR Press and The Scarecrow Press.

Danford, A. (1997). The 'new industrial relations' and class struggle in the 1990s. *Capital and Class*, 61: 107–112.

Delbridge, R. and Turnbull, P. (1992). Human resource maximization: The management of labour under just-in-time manufacturing systems. In P. Blyton and P. Turnbull (Eds.), *Reassessing Human Resource Management*. London: Sage Publications.

Dundon, T. and Rollinson, D. (2004). *Employment Relations in Non-Union Firms.* London: Routledge.
Dunlop, J. (1958). *Industrial Relations Systems.* New York: Holt.
Edwards, P. (1995). The employment relationship. In P. Edwards (Ed.), *Industrial Relations: Theory and Practice in Britain.* Oxford: Blackwell.
Edwards, P. (2003). The future of industrial relations. In P. Ackers and A. Wilkinson (Eds.), *Understanding Work and Employment: Industrial Relations in Transition.* Oxford: Oxford University Press.
Edwards, P. (2005). The challenging but promising future of industrial relations: Developing theory and method in context sensitive research. *Industrial Relations Journal*, 36(4): 264–282.
Edwards, P. K. (1986). *Conflict at Work: A Materialist Analysis of Workplace Relations.* Oxford: Basil Blackwell.
Edwards, P. K. (1994). Discipline and the creation of order. In K. Sisson (Ed.), *Personnel Management: A Comprehensive Guide to Theory and Practice in Britain.* Oxford: Blackwell.
Eldridge, J. (2003). Post-modernism and industrial relations. In P. Ackers and A. Wilkinson (Eds.), *Understanding Work and Employment: Industrial Relations in Transition.* Oxford: Oxford University Press.
Elger, T. and Edwards, P. (2002). National states and the regulation of labour in the global economy: An introduction. In J. Kelly (Ed.), *Industrial Relations: Critical Perspectives on Business and Management*, Volume III. London: Routledge.
Ferris, G., Hall, A., Royle, M. and Martocchio, J. (2004). Theoretical development in the field of human resources management: Issues and challenges for the future. *Organizational Analysis*, 12(3): 231–254.
Flanders, A. (1965). *Industrial Relations: What's Wrong with the System?* London: Faber and Faber.
Gallie, D. and White, M. (1994). Employer policies, employee contracts, and labour-market structure. In J. Rubery and F. Wilkinson (Eds.), *Employer Strategy and the Labour Market.* Oxford: Oxford University Press.
Gallie, D., White, M. Cheng, Y. and Tomlinson, M. (1998). *Restructuring the Employment Relationship.* Oxford: Clarendon Press.
Garrahan, P. and Stewart, P. (1992). Management control and a new regime of subordination. In N. Gilbert, R. Burrows, & A. Pollert (Eds.), *Fordism and Flexibility: Divisions and Change.* London: Macmillan.
Geary, J. F. (1994). Task participation: Employees' participation enabled or constrained? In K. Sisson (Ed.), *Personnel Management.* Oxford: Blackwell.
Geary, J. F. and Dobbins, T. (2001). Teamworking: A new dynamic in the pursuit of management control, *Human Resource Management Journal*, 11(1): 3–23.
Giles, A. (2000). Industrial relations at the millennium: beyond employment? *Labour/Le Travail*, 46(1): 37–67.
Godard, J. (2004). A critical assessment of the high-performance paradigm. *British Journal of Industrial Relations*, 42(2): 349–378.
Godard, J. (2014). The psychologisation of employment relations? *Human Resource Management Journal*, 24(1): 1–18.
Godard, J. and Delaney, J. T. (2000). Reflections on the 'high performance' paradigm's implications for industrial relations as a field. *Industrial and Labor Relations Review*, 53(3): 482–502.

Green, F. (2006). *Demanding Work: The Paradox of Job Quality in the Affluent Economy.* Princeton, NJ and Oxford: Princeton University Press.
Guest, D. (1987). Human resource management and industrial relations. *Journal of Management Studies*, 24: 503–522.
Guest, D. and Bryson, A. (2009). From industrial relations to human resource management: The changing role of the personnel function. In W. Brown, A. Bryson, J. Forth, and K. Whitfield (Eds.), *The Evolution of the Modern Workplace.* Cambridge: Cambridge University Press.
Hakim, C. (1990). Workforce restructuring in Europe in the 1980s. *International Journal of Comparative Labour Law and Industrial Relations*, 5(4): 167–203.
Harley, B. (2015). The one best way? "Scientific" research on HRM and the threat to critical scholarship. *Human Resource Management Journal*, 25(4): 399–407.
Harney, B., Dundon, T. and Wilkinson, A. (2018). Employment relations and human resource management. In A. Wilkinson, T. Dundon, J. Donaghey, and A. J. S. Colvin (Eds.), *The Routledge Companion to Employment Relations.* London and New York: Routledge.
Heckscher, C. and Schurman, S. (1997). Can labour-management cooperation deliver jobs and justice? *Industrial Relations Journal*, 28(4): 323–330.
Heery, E., Bacon, N., Blyton, P. and Fiorito, J. (2008). Introduction: the field of industrial relations. In N. Bacon, P. Blyton, J. Fiorito, & E. Heery (Eds.), *The SAGE Handbook of Industrial Relations.* London: Sage Publications.
Herod, A., Peck, J. and Wills, J. (2003). Geography and industrial relations. In P. Ackers and A. Wilkinson (Eds.), *Understanding Work and Employment: Industrial Relations in Transition.* Oxford: Oxford University Press.
Hyman, R. (1975). *Industrial Relations. A Marxist Introduction.* London: Macmillan.
Hyman, R. (1989). *The Political Economy of Industrial Relations. Theory and Practice in a Cold Climate.* London: Macmillan.
Hyman, R. (1991). *Plus ça Change?* The theory of production and the production of theory. In A. Pollert (Ed.), *Farewell to Flexibility?* Oxford: Blackwell.
Hyman, R. (1994a). Changing trade union identities and strategies. In R. Hyman and A. Ferner (Eds.), *New Frontiers in European Industrial Relations.* Oxford: Blackwell.
Hyman, R. (1994b). Theory and industrial relations. *British Journal of Industrial Relations*, 32(2): 165–180.
Jessop, B. (1991). Polar bears and class struggle: Much less than a self-criticism. In W. Bonefeld and J. Holloway (Eds.), *Post-Fordism and Social Form. A Marxist Debate on the Post-Fordist State.* London: Macmillan.
Jessop, B. (2001). *Capitalism, the Regulation Approach, and Critical Realism.* Department of Sociology, Lancaster University. Available at: https://www.lancaster.ac.uk/fass/resources/sociology-online-papers/papers/jessop-capitalism-regulation-realism.pdf [Accessed 4/10/2023].
Kasyanenko, T., Nevado, P., Rimmer, M. and Soares, M. E. (2014). The psychologisation of workplace relations: why social context matters. *Asia Pacific Journal of Human Resources*, 52: 393–399.
Kaufman, B. E. (2001). Human resource management and industrial relations: commonalities and differences. *Human Resource Management Review*, 11(4): 339–374.
Kaufman, B. E. (2008). The original industrial relations paradigm: Foundation for revitalizing the field. In C. J. Whalen (Ed.), *New Directions in the Study of Work*

and Employment: Revitalizing Industrial Relations as an Academic Enterprise. Cheltenham: Edward Elgar.

Kaufman, B. E. (2012). Strategic human resource management research in the United States: A failing grade after 30 years? *Academy of Management Perspectives*, 26(2): 12–36.

Kaufman, B. E. (2014). The historical development of American HRM broadly viewed. *Human Resource Management Review*, 24: 196–218.

Kelly, D. (2003). A shock to the system? The impact of HRM on academic IR in Australia in comparison with USA and UK, 1980–95. *Asia Pacific Journal of Human Resources*, 41(2): 149–171.

Kelly, J. (1998). *Rethinking Industrial Relations: Mobilization, Collectivism and Long Waves.* London: Routledge.

Kochan, T. A., McKersie, R. B. and Cappelli, P. (2002). Strategic choice and industrial relations theory. In J. Kelly (Ed.), *Industrial Relations. Critical Perspectives on Business and Management*, Volume I. London: Routledge.

Kristensen, P. H. (1997). National systems of governance and managerial prerogatives in the evolution of work systems: England, Germany and Denmark compared. In R. Whitley and P. H. Kristensen (Eds.), *Governance at Work: The Social Regulation of Economic Relations.* Oxford: Oxford University Press.

Lawson, T. (1997). *Economics and Reality.* London: Routledge.

Legge, K. (1995). *Human Resource Management: Rhetorics and Realities.* London: Macmillan.

Littler, C. R. (1993). Industrial relations theory: A political economy perspective. In R. J. Adams and N. M. Meltz (Eds.), *Industrial Relations Theory: Its Nature, Scope, and Pedagogy.* Lanham, MD: IMLR Press and The Scarecrow Press.

Marchington, M. (2015). Human resource management (HRM): Too busy looking up to see where it is going longer term? *Human Resource Management Review*, 25(2): 176–187.

Marsden, D. (1999). *A Theory of Employment Systems: Micro-foundations of Societal Diversity.* Oxford: Oxford University Press.

McKinlay, A. and Taylor, P. (1996). Power, surveillance and resistance. In P. Ackers, C. Smith, and P. Smith (Eds.), *The New Workplace and Trade Unionism.* London: Routledge.

Meardi, G. (2014). The (claimed) growing irrelevance of employment relations. *Journal of Industrial Relations*, 56(4): 594–605.

Michon, F. (1992). The institutional forms of work and employment: Towards the construction of an international, historical and comparative approach. In A. Castro, P. Méhaut, and J. Rubery (Eds.), *International Integration and Labour Market Organisation.* London: Academic Press.

Milkman, R. (1997). *Farewell to the Factory. Auto Workers in the Late Twentieth Century.* Los Angeles, CA: University of California Press.

Peck, J. (1996). *Workplace: The Social Regulation of Labor Markets.* New York: The Guilford Press.

Peck, J. (2000). Doing regulation. In G. L. Clark, M. P. Feldman, and M. S. Gertler (Eds.), *The Oxford Handbook of Economic Geography.* Oxford: Oxford University Press.

Pollert, A. (1991). The orthodoxy of flexibility. In A. Pollert (Ed.), *Farewell to Flexibility?* Oxford: Blackwell.

Purcell, J. (1993). The challenge of human resource management for industrial relations research and practice. *International Journal of Human Resource Management*, 4(3): 511–527.

Ram, M., Edwards, P., Gilman, M. and Arrowsmith, J. (2001). The dynamics of informality: Employment relations in small firms and the effects of regulatory change. *Work, Employment and Society*, 15(4): 845–861.

Ramsay, H., Scholarios, D. and Harley, B. (2000). Employees in high performance work systems: Testing inside the black box. *British Journal of Industrial Relations*, 38(4): 501–531.

Rubery, J. and Grimshaw, D. (2003). *The Organization of Employment: An International Perspective*. Basingstoke: Palgrave Macmillan.

Salamon, M. (1998). *Industrial Relations: Theory and Practice* (3rd ed.). Hemel Hempstead: Prentice Hall.

Sengenberger, W. (1992). Intensified competition, industrial restructuring and industrial relations. *International Labour Review*, 131(2): 139–153.

Sisson, K. (1987). *The Management of Collective Bargaining. An International Comparison*. Oxford: Basil Blackwell.

Sisson, K. (2010) *Employment Relations Matters*. University of Warwick. Available at: https://warwick.ac.uk/fac/soc/wbs/research/irru/publications/erm/apreface.pdf [Accessed 25/11/2023].

Sisson, K. and Marginson, P. (2003). Management: systems, structures and strategy. In P. Edwards (Ed.), *Industrial Relations: Theory and Practice* (2nd ed.). Oxford: Blackwell Publishing.

Smith, A. (1994). New technology and the process of labor regulation: An international perspective. In J. Bélanger, P. K. Edwards, and L. Haiven (Eds.), *Workplace Industrial Relations and the Global Challenge*. Ithaca, NY: ILR Press.

Smith, C. (2015). Rediscovery of the labour process. In S. Edgell, H. Gottfried, and E. Granter (Eds.), *The SAGE Handbook of the Sociology of Work and Employment*. London: Sage Publications.

Spencer, D. A. (2000). The demise of radical political economics? An essay on the evolution of a theory of capitalist production, *Cambridge Journal of Economics*, 24: 543–564.

Steward, P. (1997). Striking smarter and harder at Vauxhall: The new industrial relations of lean production? *Capital and Class*, 61: 1–12.

Storey, J. (1989). Introduction. In J. Storey (Ed.), *New Perspectives on Human Resource Management*. London: Routledge.

Storey, J. (1992). *Developments in the Management of Human Resources*. Oxford: Blackwell.

Storey, J. (2001). The meaning of strategy in human resource management. In J. Storey (Ed.), *Human Resource Management: A Critical Text*. London: Thomson Learning.

Storey, J. and Bacon, N. (1993). Individualism and collectivism: Into the 1990s. *International Journal of Human Resource Management*, 4(3): 665–684.

Storper, M. and Walker, R. (1989). *The Capitalist Imperative: Territory, Technology, and Industrial Growth*. New York: Basil Blackwell.

Streeck, W. (1992). *Social Institutions and Economic Performance: Studies of Industrial Relations in Advanced Capitalist Economies*. London: Sage Publications.

Thompson, P. (2009). Labour process theory and critical management studies, in M. Alvesson, T. Bridgman and H. Willmott (Eds.), *The Oxford Handbook of Critical Management Studies*. Oxford: Oxford University Press.

Thompson, P. (2011). The trouble with HRM. *Human Resource Management Journal*, 21(4): 355–367.

Thompson, P. and Vincent, S. (2010). Labour process theory and critical realism, in P. Thompson and C. Smith (Eds.), *Working Life: Renewing Labour Process Analysis*. London: Palgrave Macmillan.

Townsend, K. and Wilkinson, A. (2014). Time to reconnect the silos? Similarities and differences in employment relations and human resources. *Human Resource Management*, 53(2): 203–210.

Tsoukas, H. (2000). What is management? An outline of a metatheory, in S. Ackroyd and S. Fleetwood (Eds.), *Realist Perspectives on Management and Organisations*. London: Routledge.

Waddington, J. (1999). Situating labour within the globalization debate, in J. Waddington (Ed.), *Globalization and Patterns of Labour Resistance*. London: Mansell.

Watson, T. J. (2010). Critical social science, pragmatism and the realities of HRM. *International Journal of Human Resource Management*, 21(6): 915–931.

Whitley, R. and Kristensen, P. H. (Eds.). (1997). *Governance at Work: The Social Regulation of Economic Relations*. Oxford: Oxford University Press.

Wilkinson, A., Dundon, T., Donaghey, J. and Colvin, A. J. S. (2018). Employment relations: older reflections and new horizons, in A. Wilkinson, T. Dundon, J. Donaghey, and A. J. S. Colvin (Eds.), *The Routledge Companion to Employment Relations*. London and New York: Routledge.

Winchester, D. (1983). Industrial relations research in Britain. *British Journal of Industrial Relations*, 21(1): 100–114.

16 International Human Resource Management

Kieran M. Conroy and Ashish Malik

Introduction

International human resource management (IHRM) is a well-established body of work within the broader fields of human resource management (HRM) and research on multinational enterprises (MNEs). This chapter explores how IHRM is increasingly confronted with complex challenges that are transforming how HR leaders manage and organise their dispersed workforce on a global scale. First, this chapter begins by introducing the overarching focus of IHRM in MNEs, outlining how rampant turbulence in today's global business environment, characterised by volatility, uncertainty, complexity and ambiguity (VUCA), is rendering conventional methods increasingly obsolete. Second, building on this context, the chapter analyses some main themes that have dominated the IHRM field over the last few decades. We explore three overarching themes: global staffing, HRM practice transfer and global talent management. Looking forward and building on emerging debates on the increased digitisation of work, the chapter discusses how IHRM practitioners and scholars might adopt an artificial intelligence (AI) perspective of IHRM as a comprehensive way to manage an increasingly younger, cross-border workforce in times of a disruptive world of work. We consider how the last decade has witnessed significant growth and adoption of AI-based technologies, transforming the role of the IHRM function, how work is organised in international firms and the critical challenges this presents.

International Human Resource Management in a VUCA World

International HRM can be defined as 'the set of distinct activities, functions and processes that are directed at attracting, developing and maintaining multinational enterprises' human resources' (Taylor, Beechler & Napier,1996: 960). As a scholarly field, it is often depicted as a sub-discipline of international business that shares many overlapping ideas with comparative HRM, international strategy and cross-cultural management studies (Fan et al. 2021). The contemporary role of the IHRM function in the last decade is increasingly challenged by the turbulence arising from greater volatility, uncertainty,

DOI: 10.4324/9781032625560-18

complexity and ambiguity (VUCA) in the global environment (Kelly & Conroy, 2023). Common disruptive trends such as geopolitical instability, populist nationalism, growing terrorist threats, interstate wars and global-health emergencies are creating conditions that can be considered through the VUCA prism (Baran & Woznyj, 2020). Volatility refers to the speed and magnitude of disruption arising from unexpected or unstable events (Bennett & Lemoine, 2014). The Russian invasion of Ukraine or Israel's war on Gaza are examples of highly volatile situations with a global impact characterised by unknown durations. Uncertainty limits the predictability of a situation leading to unknown outcomes. Brexit meant that many firms had to engage in scenario planning when managing their global workforce (Bader et al. 2019). IHRM functions already handle a high level of complexity daily where they manage a multiplicity of unique challenges across countries with contradictory information. Yet, increasingly complex regulations, socio-cultural conflicts and trade tariffs are reducing the interconnectedness of markets and hindering standardised firm responses. Ambiguity results in a lack of clarity or difficulty understanding unfamiliar situations. Operating in emerging markets creates ambiguity, which often challenges IHRM functions to find novel ways to fill talent gaps locally. These VUCA conditions are impacting individual global workers, reducing their willingness and ability to take on cross-border assignments or travel internationally for short periods. Equally, these issues are creating a much more challenging context for global HR leaders, forcing them to rapidly change the role of the IHRM function and how they staff operations, share practices and manage talent.

Yet, this context offers significant opportunities for scholars to explore how IHRM leaders are responding, with many scholars emphasising the increased digitisation of HR through the adoption of AI-enabled applications for achieving HRM effectiveness as well as employee outcomes (Malik et al. 2021, 2022, 2023a, b). For instance, global health emergencies have created a demand for hybrid-work practices where corporate offices in city centres are being vacated while firms are engaging in strong-arm tactics to force employees back into the workplace (Thomason & Gibson, 2024). The rise of a digital nomad culture is another challenge for global firms that are under increased scrutiny to know where their workers are based so they do not breach increasingly strict national regulations (Nichols, 2022). A critical challenge for IHRM involves building a culture of trust, collaboration and knowledge sharing between workers who are co-located and those who are dispersed virtually at home or abroad (Gibson et al. 2023). More recently, scholars have proposed the role of emerging technologies, such as AI, in delivering an AI-mediated knowledge-sharing social exchange not just locally but also in a broader interconnected world of work (Malik et al. 2022b). In this chapter, we suggest that one crucial response is for the IHRM function to adopt new advanced technologies, specifically artificial intelligence (AI). We argue that although the rapid rise of artificial intelligence creates VUCA conditions for firms if managed efficiently, it may also provide them with a way to respond to frequent turbulence and disruption. While the considerable breadth of challenges that VUCA brings means a thorough exploration is beyond the scope of this chapter, we focus on these three key areas of IHRM research and practice that have dominated existing debates.

The next section of this chapter explores three discrete themes of IHRM. These include global staffing, which considers the strategic choices firms make in staffing their global operations; the transfer of HR practices, which considers the extent to which MNEs implement globally-standardised or locally-adapted practices; and global talent management, which focuses on high-performing employees in critical roles. While these themes allow for a critical understanding of traditional IHRM issues, we subsequently present AI as a critical emerging focus that we suggest is going to transform the field.

Global Staffing

Global staffing has been one of the longest-established research streams in IHRM (Conroy & Minbaeva, 2021). Global staffing can be defined as 'the critical issues faced by multinational enterprises regarding the employment of home, host and third-country nationals to fill key positions in their headquarters and subsidiary operations' (Scullion and Collings, 2006: 3). Historically, the literature on global staffing had been dominated by research on expatriation, particularly of parent-country nationals (PCNs) – individuals from the home country of the MNE sent on assignment to subsidiary locations (Takeuchi, 2010). However, the nature of global staffing is becoming more diverse, and host-country nationals (HCNs), as well as third-country nationals (TCNs), are increasingly sent on different types of assignments for a plethora of objectives. Furthermore, the nature of a typical expatriate has also changed, wherein a vast majority of Generation Y or what Pereira et al. (2017) refer to as *Yopatriates*, from HCNs and TCNs, are being assigned expatriate assignments.

The foundations of global staffing are built on Perlmutter's (1969) EPRG framework where four broad types of staffing orientations determine how an MNE mobilises its human resources across borders. These include ethnocentric, polycentric, regiocentric and geocentric staffing. First, an ethnocentric orientation focuses on the global integration of HR systems and policies by sending PCNs from the headquarters' home country to dispersed subsidiaries. Much of this research focuses on corporate expatriates sent to subsidiaries to ensure greater headquarter control (Harzing, 2001), while others consider their role as socialisation agents, focusing on coordination, knowledge sharing and learning across subsidiaries (Harzing, Pudelko & Reiche, 2016). Second, a polycentric orientation focuses more exclusively on localisation or staffing from the bottom up and is driven through the adaptation and subsequent sharing of HR policies and practices from host-country nationals in autonomous subsidiaries. Third, a geocentric staffing orientation seeks to balance global- and local-staffing strategies by mobilising a combination of highly skilled PCNs, HCNs and TCNs, tapping into and sharing knowledge within and across the MNE. Fourth, although less common, a regiocentric orientation involves staffing operations with individuals from given regions and adapting to regional idiosyncrasies rather than global parameters or local adjustments (Heenan & Perlmutter, 1979). We delve deeper into the polycentric orientation as an overlooked staffing strategy and one which we argue is crucial in a VUCA-led world where MNEs are under pressure to adapt to localised conditions that are increasingly hostile. In this context, the escalating uncertainty and volatility from converging global crises are exposing the untenability of relying on expatriates for managing foreign subsidiaries (Caligiuri et al. 2020).

A polycentric-staffing orientation focuses on the deployment of HCNs (subsidiary employees from the local context) that possess knowledge, skills and experiences of local conditions (Michailova et al. 2023), which they can invoke in times of disruption and hostility. Yet, we suggest that IHRM scholars have presented a reductive portrayal of the roles and responsibilities of HCNs. Studies have largely focused on understanding the HCN's role as a *local host* or liaison to expatriates, examining their behaviours and attitudes in supporting or impeding the adjustment of expatriates (Kang & Shen, 2018). For example, Yamao et al. (2020) confine an HCN's value as a source of informational and social support in an expatriate's broader network. Others have examined how HCNs can learn from and enhance their knowledge capacity by building strong relationships with expatriates (Fee & Michailova, 2020) or investigated the impact of corporate HRM practices on HCNs in comparison to expatriates, such as disparities in pay and performance, career development, training, retention and turnover (Bruning, Sonpar & Wang, 2012; Toh & DeNisi, 2003). HCNs, however, are more than mere 'country managers' and are critical staffing options for MNEs as they perform many important functions crucial for combatting local VUCA conditions. These responsibilities include serving as cultural and linguistic interpreters, communication facilitators, resource brokers, translators, talent developers, embedding agents and change partners for the rest of the MNE in understanding locally-adverse circumstances, especially so in the case of cross-border mergers and acquisitions (Malik et al. 2023c).

Another important part of an HCN's role may be to engage in inpatriation, which involves an international assignment to the corporate headquarters for a defined period (Kim, Reiche & Harzing, 2022). Inpatriate assignments are, however, fraught with difficulties and individual inpatriates face challenges owing to factors such as their liability of foreignness, which may impact the effectiveness of knowledge transfer (Harvey et al. 2005). On the one hand, these assignments may be disguised as opportunities for HCNs to develop their careers but in reality, they may serve as a mechanism for headquarters to reinforce power and control over a dispersed network (Conroy et al. 2019). Inpatriates are likely to originate from foreign subsidiaries that have proved themselves credible and trustworthy over time through repeated mandate development (Sarabi, Froese & Hamori, 2017). Indeed, the successful development of a subsidiary's role with the MNE is often driven by key individuals in the subsidiary's top management team (Conroy & Collings, 2016). However, continually exporting key subsidiary talent to the headquarters may disrupt the subsidiary strategy and impact the amount of visibility and influence the subsidiary has built up over time. As such, the continuous use of inpatriation, although rationalised to promote HCNs, may only seek to reinforce the ethnocentric power and control of the headquarters in the long term. Further research is needed to understand the negative implications of inpatriation for HCNs and the localised-staffing strategies of subsidiaries.

In pursuit of greater diversity, and avoiding the typical expatriate-HCN trade-off, global-staffing strategies in practice are inherently much more diverse and complex than portrayed in most IHRM studies. Moreover, MNEs need to be much more agile and adaptable in the type of staffing approaches they implement amid a hostile global environment. For instance, we are increasingly witnessing flexible-staffing arrangements in MNEs over the last two decades with short-term travel and virtual assignments in particular, supplementing or even replacing traditional assignments, changing the requirements of assignees and transforming the role of the IHRM function (Jooss, McDonnell, & Conroy, 2021). Studies have shown that the volatility and uncertainty from COVID-19 changed global-staffing flows with frequent flyers adjusting to virtual work to maintain their cross-border networks (Jooss, Conroy & McDonnell, 2022). As well as these more flexible approaches, it is also likely that subsidiaries will be increasingly staffed through a mix of employees internally from within the MNE (headquarters and other subsidiaries) or individuals externally from the local environment and the host contexts of other subsidiaries (Mäkelä et al. 2009). Equally, rather than focusing on nationality, multicultural employees with no explicitly defined home country and a mix of national identities are also being increasingly utilised in strategic positions when staffing dispersed operations. This agile staffing aligns more closely with a geocentric-staffing orientation, which is often proclaimed as the most desirable approach to staffing a dispersed global workforce, but in practice, this will become an increasingly unrealistic endeavour, particularly given the VUCA conditions. Global-staffing operations have yet to fully embrace or understand how digitisation can create more agile structures and practices.

HRM Practice Transfer

The transfer of HRM practices in MNEs is one of the dominant topics of interest in international HRM (Brewster, Mayrhofer & Smale, 2016). The central idea of these studies is that commonalities and differences exist among HRM practices within MNEs and between countries. Transfer is a process, which involves the movement of HRM practices or policies from one unit (transferring unit) to another (receiving unit) in the MNE. These units typically involve the headquarters and foreign subsidiaries, and the main reason for transferring practices is to enhance the performance and competitiveness of MNEs and their subsidiaries (Rosenzweig and Nohria, 1994). Examples of individual HRM practices that scholars have examined include staffing, career management, performance management, talent management, training and development, or remuneration and compensation. Practice transfer is a complex process as it is influenced by a myriad of internal and external factors, such as home- and host-country contexts and headquarters-subsidiary relations. The transfer of HRM practices may occur vertically from headquarters to subsidiary, horizontally from subsidiary to subsidiary or in reverse from subsidiary to headquarters. Some scholars suggest the 'transfer' of best practices from headquarters to subsidiaries is different to the 'diffusion' of HRM practices from a subsidiary back to the headquarters or the rest of the MNE. A transfer is, therefore, more akin to a one-off event, whereas diffusion implies the gradual flow or dissemination of practices over time (Chiang et al. 2017). Following we outline two key perspectives in the HRM practice transfer literature.

One of the more prominent discussions looks at transfer from an organisational perspective, referred to as the *standardisation versus localisation* of HRM practices in MNEs (Rosenzweig & Nohria, 1994). This debate resembles arguments in international business on integration-responsiveness, in that effective integration relies on the homogenisation of HR practices, whereas heterogeneity signifies a locally-responsive approach. From a standardisation perspective, scholars assume that efficient internalised labour markets require the adoption of a consistent set of HR practices. Standardisation argues that the design of HRM practices should reflect corporate-level strategies that are driven by the headquarters and adopted across subsidiaries (Smale, Bjorkman & Smelius, 2013). The reasons for this are largely due to cost efficiencies, a common corporate culture and the smoother transfer and diffusion of practices globally. This 'forward diffusion' of home-country practices is common in MNEs from developed countries, particularly when entering developing markets. Standardised HRM practices are often transferred, and monitored, through ethnocentric-staffing approaches such as corporate expatriates that control foreign subsidiaries. For instance, US MNE's performance-management practice uses individual employee-appraisal schemes rather than the group. Others have added that standardised practices may resemble headquarters in the home country or they can resemble global 'best' practices that originate from anywhere in the MNE network.

In comparison, localisation focuses on host-country subsidiaries with the autonomy to adapt practices from headquarters to account for local complexities, uncertainties or ambiguities. In this respect, subsidiaries' HRM practices are more likely to be local in design and implementation. Equally, local subsidiaries may play a significant role in the development of new HRM practices, but only if they can be diffused within the MNE. As mentioned previously, a localisation perspective emphasises the importance of host-country nationals leading subsidiaries who are local experts capable of creating new practices that are culturally relevant. The deployment of subsidiary individuals on inpatriate assignments can also enable the reverse diffusion of local practices at headquarters. MNEs from emerging markets (EMNEs) are known to use a more adaptive approach of practice transfer to subsidiaries in developed countries. The reasoning here is that EMNEs leverage the knowledge sourced from developed countries to 'reverse diffuse' 'best' practices to the headquarters.

A more recent perspective proposes a hybridisation of HRM practices which balances standardisation and localisation. This approach sees subsidiaries as capable of balancing internal pressures to standardise HRM practices as well as external pressures to differentiate locally. Hybridisation involves complex- and multifaceted-transfer processes that require highly selective interplay between transfer, adoption and local adaptation within the subsidiary. Chung, Sparrow and Bozkurt (2014) investigate hybridisation in South Korean firms, arguing that their 'liability of origin' results in a lack of dominant HR practices in their home country, increasing the need to develop new practices locally.Ahlvik et al. (2016) consider the importance of alignment between corporate intentions and subsidiary implementation in transferring practices, arguing that an emphasis on centralised HR control may reduce alignment. This work demonstrates the significance of subsidiary HR capabilities to accurately understand corporate transfer intentions and to encourage HQ to adjust these intentions with regard to contextual requirements. In this sense, hybridisation can involve partial adoption or partial modification increasing the potential for the development of new practices locally (Yahiaoui, 2015). Hybrid HRM practices show that the transfer process may be less linear than current studies portray and more iterative. In this sense, HRM practice transfer is often executed and influenced through negotiation between the headquarters and the subsidiary. This may involve back-and-forth adjustment and refinement of HRM practices to satisfy both the transferring and receiving units.

Scholars have also looked at HRM practice transfer from the country-level perspective in the form of the *convergence or divergence* of HRM practices. An important consideration in this context is, do HRM practices follow the dominant model in their home country of origin or do they adhere to their country of domicile. While convergence scholars argue that, due to globalisation, HRM practices will be homogeneous across countries (Fey et al. 2009). This outlook deems that 'best practices' exist which are transferable and universal, and transferring these practices gives MNEs a competitive advantage (Thang et al. 2007). Studies highlight that standardisation is particularly evident in a US context given the economic dominance of home-based institutions and the firm-specific advantages this provides (Edwards et al. 2016). Some research evidences the successful compatibility of a US-based HRM model to different regions (Japan, Korea, EU, New Zealand) (Fan et al. 2021).

On the other hand, a divergence perspective views the transferability of best practices as constrained by a diversity of contextual issues such as cultural, institutional and geographical distance (Bjorkman, Fey & Park, 2007). This approach sees the transfer process as particularly sensitive to social context, and it is commonly accepted that the best-practice transfer approach is most pronounced in US firms that have an ethnocentric orientation, while firms from other countries are generally more flexible. Alternatively, some scholars have suggested a crossvergence approach that is essentially a hybrid- or mixed-HRM model that combines the advantageous traits of each (Farndale et al. 2017). HRM practice transfer is ultimately a complex social process that is influenced by a variety of organisational and institutional factors across MNEs and national contexts (Geary & Aguzzoli, 2016). In a VUCA-led world, it is much more difficult for MNEs to transfer practices and policies that are standardised across a multiplicity of locally-complex conditions with subsidiaries that are struggling to adapt to these challenges.

Global Talent Management

There is little doubt that one of the fastest-growing areas of research in IHRM over the past decade has been global talent management (GTM) (Caligiuri et al. 2024). Global talent management can be defined as initiatives that contribute to attracting, selecting, developing and retaining key talented employees in the most important roles worldwide (Schuler, Jackson & Tarique, 2011). The rise of global talent management research signifies a shift towards understanding how firms cater to a more diversified global workforce (Minbaeva & Collings, 2013). On the one hand, while multinational enterprises (MNEs) can potentially access more diverse employees across the globe, easing some of these tensions, wider challenges are amplified in the global context. A critical challenge is that MNEs must balance consistency in deploying corporate practices, reflecting organisational culture and values, with adapting those practices to account for local-cultural and institutional influences (Stahl et al. 2012). More broadly, the cultural, linguistic, spatial and temporal distances associated with global work create challenges in coordinating work and managing globally-dispersed talent. Thus, while on one level the global environment offers opportunities for efficiency and superior access to talent, it also creates challenges in coordinating and managing talent globally (Caligiuri et al. 2024).

While HRM practice transfer tends to focus on the standardisation–localisation of HR, global talent management scholars examine the nature of a differentiated global workforce through talent systems, talent pools, critical positions and talented individuals. An important component of the GTM system is the idea of differentiation that reflects the fact that GTM is focused on a sub-set of employees globally and does not apply to the entire workforce. This put pressure on costs within firms in the latter part of the last century when HR budgets came under pressure, compared with a greater understanding that investing disproportionately in employees with the greatest potential to add value can add disproportionate value (Collings et al. 2019). The initial focus was on individual employees as the locus of differentiation and this perspective discussed the exploitation of talented stars ‘topgrading’ the firm with high potential and managing out underperformers (Groysberg and Connolly, 2015). Some scholars argue that the specific skills and capabilities of star employees, or the critical positions they are deployed in, are more important for value appropriation than the individuals (Mellahi & Collings, 2010). However, the literature has matured and shifted to critical or pivotal roles and the potential for differential performance in terms of increased quality or quantity of output in these roles (Collings et al. 2019). This recognises that human capital is of little economic value if it is not deployed consistently with the organisation's strategic intent (Becker & Huselid, 2006).

GTM also requires the development of a talent pool of high-performing and high-potential employees to fill these critical roles. The diversity of this talent pool should be determined by the MNE's strategic orientation. For example, if the firm has a geocentric orientation, it is likely to prioritise a diverse talent pool comprising employees with knowledge of both the headquarters (parent-firm human capital) and local context (Morris et al. 2016). However, it is important to recognise that individuals beyond the headquarters often suffer from lower visibility and opportunity to access talent programmes compared to colleagues at headquarters (Mäkelä et al. 2010).

Another important element of GTM is the need for a differentiated HR architecture. This is premised on the recognition that while high levels of human capital (talent) are necessary for superior performance, it is not sufficient to deliver sustainable competitive advantage. As the complexity and dynamism increase, MNEs may need to widen their search to fill these positions, ensuring that subsidiary employees are provided with more opportunities.Collings and Mellahi (2009) argue that MNEs need to develop strategic talent management agendas with differentiated architectures that maximise the potential for exploiting talent pools to fill pivotal positions. The differentiated HR architecture should focus on building a relational-psychological contract instead of a transactional focus on reward, for example.

One key challenge for MNEs is ensuring that global talent can straddle different internal units within the MNE and external stakeholders. This could involve deploying high-potential talent, with international human capital that is relevant both internally in the MNE network and externally beyond its boundaries, in critical positions. For example, GTM can occur through the deployment of talented individuals in global boundary-spanning positions and their international experience, skills and knowledge are leveraged to enhance the coordination of valuable knowledge and resources across a disintegrated subsidiary network. Global boundary-spanning roles can be critical positions that operate at the external boundary of the firm and require talented individuals with the capacity to navigate significant complexity, ambiguity and contradiction when building linkages, sharing knowledge and resolving conflicts with key stakeholders (Schotter, 2021). A major criticism of using boundary-spanning roles is that it often fails to identify the parameters of who may be classified as a boundary spanner, with any individual, role or activity considered a boundary-spanning concern.

A comprehensive understanding of GTM also requires an integrative architecture that combines globally-standardised practices and centralised talent pools from headquarters with local human capital stocks in foreign subsidiaries.

On the one hand, much GTM research examines the corporate GTM function and its role in identifying and exploiting top talent and best practices which flow from the top down (Farndale et al. 2010). However, there is less focus on understanding how GTM unfolds in local subsidiaries with scholars suggesting that high-potential talent in foreign markets is often marginalised and, therefore, underutilised on a global scale (Mellahi & Collings, 2010). Top management teams in foreign subsidiaries represent important stocks of location-specific talent that are disintegrated from the broader GTM architecture, hindering the development of a highly overfed global workforce. Subsidiary managers are strategic leaders in the global MNE structure, engaging with headquarters and a broader subsidiary network while building and leveraging skills, knowledge and resources in their local market (Rickley, 2019). In this sense, subsidiary talent with broader experiential portfolios should be redeployed more consistently to pivotal positions across the MNE as they can process and integrate knowledge, think strategically and remove themselves from any local biases. However, while subsidiaries are gatekeepers to culturally rich and differentiated talent, it is often in their best interests to try and retain their best talent rather than relocating them to headquarters (Kim et al. 2022). Subsidiaries, however, need autonomy to develop talent strategies and tailor to local norms through a process of localising their talent practices. Hiring, training and developing local human capital can lead to the value creation at the subsidiary through a deep-rooted knowledge of idiosyncratic cultural and institutional conditions (Morris, Snell & Bjorkman, 2016).

Another increasingly important line of work considers GTM in developing markets. For instance, on the one hand, firms from developed economies operating in developing markets like China and India will rely on transferring their best practices without much adaptation or local autonomy for subsidiaries (Hartmann et al. 2010). As a result, it is well recognised that Western firms in particular have struggled to tap into or build differentiated workforces in emerging markets, relying instead on standardised GTM practices or talent pools from within the firm's network. On the other hand, the GTM approaches of firms coming from emerging or developing markets are often confronted with greater adaptation challenges, and, hence, they tend to have a more flexible GTM approach (Cooke et al. 2014). For instance, the GTM architecture of Chinese firms involves the exploitation of local human capital when operating in developed countries, but when entering developing markets they will deploy human capital from the headquarters (Zhu, 2019). However, scholars have suggested that the GTM practices of firms from the East, like China, Japan and Korea, are converging with Western-style global best practices (Froese et al. 2020). There is, however, a need for a more inclusive approach to GTM where marginalised groups, particularly in emerging or developing markets, are provided with the appropriate mechanisms to undertake global leadership development opportunities across their firm.

Next, we turn to the need for IHRM scholars and practitioners to respond to the growing influence of advanced technologies and artificial intelligence on the IHRM function. The role of the IHRM function and its leaders is undergoing significant transformation through a myriad of technological influences, such as big data, analytics and artificial intelligence, robotics and automation (Meijerink et al. 2021). The IHRM field has yet to fully appreciate the impact of these technologies on IHRM practices and policies or the broader positive and negative impacts they may have on IHRM in the MNE (Budhwar et al. 2022).

Artificial Intelligence and IHRM

The last decade has seen a geometric growth in the adoption of digital and intelligent technologies, such as AI and related technologies, including generative AI in the domain of HRM (Budhwar et al. 2023; Charlwood & Guenole, 2022; Duggan et al. 2020; Kim et al. 2021; Nguyen & Malik 2022; Malik et al. 2023b). The nature of research on the topic tends to fall into four broad areas: border-level impacts of AI on the world of work, specific impacts of AI on enhancing organisational productivity, efficiency and effectiveness; AI and its impact on micro- or functional-level HRM practices; and AI and its impact on the global organisation of work with a specialist focus on MNCs/MNEs.

First, it tends to focus on broader issues, such as challenges associated with its adoption and how AI-enabled or assisted applications are assimilated into the foray of mainstream HRM (Prikshat, 2023a,b), the debates on whether AI is for automation or augmentation of human capacity and capabilities (Raisch & Krakowski, 2021) or how increasingly employees are witnessing an AI-mediated knowledge-sharing social exchange in both tactical, operational and strategic activities and how this might variously impact on a range of business and employee outcomes (Malik et al. 2022b). Second, an increasing number of studies have attempted to discuss the impact of intelligent technologies, such as robotics and automation, on the nature and extent of HRM effectiveness and productivity (Del Guidice et al. 2022; Malik et al. 2022; Vrontis et al. 2022). Third, scholars have started to examine the impact of specific AI applications in the sub-functional areas of HRM, or on aspects of the HRM employment life cycle and the specific AI technologies that have dominated specific sub-domains (Malik et al. 2023c), including practices, such as recruitment and selection (Allal-Chérif et al. 2021), profiling job seekers (Desiere & Struyven, 2021), training and development (Agrawal et al. 2017; Dutta & Poyil, 2023), teamwork (Arslan et al. 2022), performance management (Bersin & Chamorro-Premuzic, 2019; Sivathanu & Pillai, 2019), and the paradoxical nature of AI leading to both the bright- and dark-side ethical issues in the design, adoption and implementation (Charlwood & Guenole, 2021; Jaiswal et al. 2022; Gligor et al. 2021; Oswald et al. 2020; Wirtz & Zeithaml, 2018), or the nature of HR capabilities needed by HR practitioners to navigate the new terrain of AI-HRM effectively (Deepa et al. 2024). Finally, a select but emerging field of study has tended to focus on the impact of AI in the field of IHRM (Budhwar et al. 2022, 2023; Keegan & Meijerink,

2023; Malik et al. 2022 a,b,c; Pan et al. 2022; Suseno et al. 2022). The following section provides an overview of these themes and the challenges it presents for the field of IHRM.

The nature of research at the intersection of AI and IHRM has focused more on specific MNE sectors, such as information technology software services and product development firms, business services and technology consulting firms, or an eclectic set of gig work or platform firms (Budhwar et al. 2022). IHRM focuses on how these changes impact MNEs' diffusion of their best practices in AI and technology diffusion, which is creating exciting challenges for host-country firms. A global North/West solution may not work in the global South/East geography, and vice versa. Similarly, the adoption of new AI-assisted technologies without nuanced adaptation is only going to bring in issues of biases in the databases from the global North/West to subsidiary operations in the global South/East. The platformisation of work has already seen instances of problems in the bland adoption of gig work platform technologies from the Anglo-Saxon countries in not just emerging markets in Asia and other BRICS nations, but also in some other Rhinish and Mediterranean nations. All this bodes well for an exciting and vibrant stream of inquiry in the field of IHRM, wherein MNE subsidiary operations may exercise significant choices and opportunities for some reverse diffusion of ideas and the development of innovative AI-enabled applications. These aspects were evident in recent studies of AI-enabled employee experience in an extensive subsidiary operation in India that had to create its unique digitalised AI-assisted HR ecosystem, quite distinct from its Anglo-Saxon parent firm (Malik et al. 2023a). Additional evidence in a similar vein was apparent in how the talent experience of IT workers can be enhanced through locally-developed AI applications for a range of HR functional areas and talent acquisition, development and retention (Malik et al. 2021; 2022). The nuances of developing localised AI solutions using local databases are not only logical but they are also legal and ethical, as it will otherwise result in a range of biases and IHRM operational problems. IHRM literature disproportionately focuses on aspects of recruitment, selection and deployment of global teams using various AI-assisted applications for improved business and employee outcomes such as employee commitment, experience and satisfaction, reducing adoption anxiety, improving change readiness and lowering the intention to quit (Malik et al. 2021; 2022; Pan et al. 2022; Suseno et al. 2022). Others have tended to focus on the new nature of skills that managers need to acquire to successfully engage with these new intelligent technologies and maximise their benefits.

A tangential, though related, aspect has been the emergence of workforce ecosystems (Altman et al. 2022; 2023a), in tandem with the HR ecosystems (Snell & Morris, 2021; 2023). From an IHRM perspective, this new and emerging body of literature flags several issues of the overlaps and tensions between local and global workforce and HR ecosystems. It is not clear which functional and strategic aspects of each system are generic and transferable, especially as the workforce ecosystem grows organically and independent of the dynamics of the MNE's HR ecosystem, yet it contributes to the HR delivery and design aspects differently, both domestically but also from an international diffusion of best-practice tools and applications.

Conclusion

IHRM has become an essential body of scholarly work that bridges HRM and international management and has advanced as a critical challenge for HR practitioners. This chapter presented critical themes and emerging issues on how MNEs are managing their global workforce. Staffing globally-dispersed operations remains a central imperative for the IHRM function, although heightened uncertainty across multiple markets may lead to a greater reliance on HCNs and agile structures through digitisation. Coordinating the transfer of HRM practices between headquarters and subsidiaries is also an increasingly complex challenge for IHRM leaders, which is impacted by complexity and ambiguity between home and host countries. Emerging discussions on how to manage a globally-talented workforce of individuals in pivotal roles remain a critical challenge, particularly as MNEs look to grow in emerging markets with potentially greater volatility and instability. Finally, we argued that while the growing digitisation of the global workforce presents immeasurable challenges for MNEs, the adoption of advanced technologies and AI-enabled HRM provides global HR leaders with significant opportunities to rethink their roles in the MNE. Adopting these technologies across local contexts and integrating them into the IHRM function on a global scale may have the potential to transform how MNEs combat the intense VUCA conditions that exist in the contemporary global environment. Applying a critical perspective, with its clear conceptual roots in issues around global staffing, practice transfer and GTM, we argue that the IHRM function will need to urgently adopt and leverage AI-enabled technologies to handle growing VUCA conditions.

References

Agrawal, A., Gans, J., & Goldfarb, A. (2017) What to expect from artificial intelligence. *MIT Sloan Management Review, 58*(3). Retrieved from http://mitsmr.com/2jZdf1Y

Ahlvik, C., Smale, A., & Sumelius, J. (2016). Aligning corporate transfer intentions and subsidiary HRM practice implementation in multinational corporations. *Journal of World Business, 51*(3), 343–355.

Allal-Chérif, O., Aranega, A. Y., & Sánchez, R. C. (2021) Intelligent recruitment: How to identify, select, and retain talents from around the world using artificial intelligence. *Technological Forecasting and Social Change, 169*, 120822.

Altman, E. J., Kiron, D., Jones, R., & Schwartz, J. (2022) Orchestrating workforce ecosystems. *MIT Sloan Management Review*. May 17

Altman, E. J., Kiron, D., Jones, R., Cantrell, S., & Hatfield, S. (2023b) Workforce ecosystem orchestration: A strategic framework. *MIT Sloan Management Review, 64*(3), 1–7.

Altman, E. J., Kiron, D., Schwartz, J., & Jones, R. (2023a). Manage your workforce ecosystem, not just your employees. *MIT Sloan Management Review, 64*(4), 80–84.

Arslan, A., Cooper, C., Khan, Z., Golgeci, I., & Ali, I. (2022). Artificial intelligence and human workers interaction at team level: A conceptual assessment of the challenges and potential HRM strategies. *International Journal of Manpower, 43*(1), 75–88.

Bader, B., Schuster, T., Bader, A. K., & Shaffer, M. (2019). The dark side of expatriation: Dysfunctional relationships, expatriate crises, prejudice and a VUCA world. *Journal of Global Mobility, 7*(2), 126–136.

Baran, B.E., & Woznyj, H.M. (2020). Managing VUCA: The human dynamics of agility. *Organizational dynamics, 50*(2), 100787.

Becker, B. E., & Huselid, M. A. (2006) Strategic human resources management: Where do we go from here? *Journal of Management*, 32(6), 898–925.

Bennett, N., & Lemoine, J. (2014). What VUCA really means for you. *Harvard Business Review, 92*(1/2). 27.

Bersin, J., & Chamorro-Premuzic, T. (2019) New ways to gauge talent and potential. *MIT Sloan Management Review, 60*(2), 1. Retrieved from https://mitsmr.com/2QLPcEN

Bjorkman, I., Fey, C. F., & Park, H. J. (2007). Institutional theory and MNE subsidiary HRM practices: Evidence from a three-country study. *Journal of International Business Studies, 38*(3), 430–446.

Brewster, C., Mayrhofer, W., & Smale, A. (2016). Crossing the streams: HRM in multinational enterprises and comparative HRM. *Human Resource Management Review, 26*(4), 285–297.

Bruning, N. S., Sonpar, K., & Wang, X. (2012). Host-country national networks and expatriate effectiveness: A mixed-methods study. *Journal of International Business Studies, 43*, 444–450.

Budhwar, P., Chowdhury, S., Wood, G., Aguinis, H., Bamber, G. J., Beltran, J. R., Boselie, P., Lee Cooke, F., Decker, S., DeNisi, A., & Dey, P. K. (2023). Human resource management in the age of generative artificial intelligence: Perspectives and research directions on ChatGPT. *Human Resource Management Journal, 33*(3), 606–659.

Budhwar, P., Malik, A., De Silva, T., & Thevisuthan, P. (2022). Artificial intelligence – Challenges and opportunities for International HRM: A review and research agenda, *International Journal of HRM.* https://doi.org/10.1080/09585192.2022.2035161

Caligiuri, P. M., Collings, D. G., DeCieri, H., & Lazarova, M. B. (2024). Global talent management: A critical review and research agenda for the new organizational reality. *Annual Review of Organizational Psychology and Organizational Behavior, 11*(1), 393–421.

Caligiuri, P. M., De Cieri, H., Minbaeva, D., Verbeke, A., & Zimmermann, A. (2020). International HRM insights for navigating the COVID-19 pandemic: Implications for future research and practice. *Journal of International Business Studies, 51*, 697–713.

Charlwood, A., & Guenole, N. (2022). Can HR adapt to the paradoxes of artificial intelligence? *Human Resource Management Journal, 32*(4), 729–742.

Chiang, F. F., Lemański, M. K., & Birtch, T. A. (2017). The transfer and diffusion of HRM practices within MNCs: Lessons learned and future research directions. *The International Journal of Human Resource Management, 28*(1), 234–258.

Chung, C., Sparrow, P., & Bozkurt, Ö. (2014). South Korean MNEs' international HRM approach: Hybridization of global standards and local practices. *Journal of World Business, 49*(4), 549–559.

Collings, D. G., & Mellahi, K. (2009). Strategic talent management: A review and research agenda. *Human Resource Management Review, 19*(4), 304–313.

Collings, D. G., Mellahi, K., & Cascio, W. F. (2019). Global talent management and performance in multinational enterprises: A multilevel perspective. *Journal of Management, 45*(2), 540–566.

Conroy, K. M., & Collings, D. G. (2016). The legitimacy of subsidiary issue selling: Balancing positive & negative attention from corporate headquarters. *Journal of World Business, 51*(4), 612–627.

Conroy, K. M., Collings, D. G., & Clancy, J. (2019). Sowing the seeds of subsidiary influence: Social navigating and political maneuvering of subsidiary actors. *Global Strategy Journal, 9*(4), 502–526.

Conroy, K. M & Minbaeva, D. (2021). New international human resource management approaches and multinational enterprise strategies. In K. Mellahi, K. Meyer, R. Narula, I. Surdu, and A. Verbeke (Eds.), *The Oxford Handbook of International Business Strategy* (pp. 455–473). Oxford: Oxford University Press.

Cooke, F. L., Saini, D. S., & Wang, J. (2014). Talent management in China and India: A comparison of management perceptions and human resource practices. *Journal of World Business, 49*(2), 225–235.

Deepa, R., Sekar, S., Malik, A. Kumar, J., & Attri, R. (2024). Impact of AI-Focussed technologies on social and technical competencies for HR managers – A systematic review and research agenda, *Technological Forecasting and Social Change, 202,* 123301.

Del Giudice, M., Scuotto, V., Ballestra, L. V., & Pironti, M. (2022). Humanoid robot adoption and labour productivity: A perspective on ambidextrous product innovation routines. *The International Journal of Human Resource Management, 33*(6), 1098–1124.

Desiere, S., & Struyven, L. (2021). Using artificial intelligence to classify jobseekers: The accuracy-equity trade-off. *Journal of Social Policy, 50*(2), 367–385.

Duggan, J., Sherman, U., Carbery, R., & McDonnell, A. (2020). Algorithmic management and app-work in the gig economy: A research agenda for employment relations and HRM. *Human Resource Management Journal, 30*(1), 114–132.

Dutta, D., & Poyil, A. (2023). The machine/human agentic impact on practices in learning and development: A study across MSME, NGO and MNC organizations. *Personnel Review, 53*(3), 791–815.

Edwards, T., Sanchez-Mangas, R., Jalette, P., Lavelle, J., & Minbaeva, D. (2016). Global standardization or national differentiation of HRM practices in multinational companies? A comparison of multinationals in five countries. *Journal of International Business Studies, 47*(8), 997–1021.

Fan, D., Zhu, C.J., Huang, X., & Kumar, V. (2021). Mapping the terrain of international human resource management research over the past fifty years: A bibliographic analysis. *Journal of World Business, 56*(2), 101185.

Farndale, E., Brewster, C., Ligthart, P., & Poutsma, E. (2017). The effects of market economy type and foreign MNE subsidiaries on the convergence and divergence of HRM. *Journal of International Business Studies, 48*(9), 1065–1086.

Farndale, E., Scullion, H., & Sparrow, P. (2010). The role of the corporate HR function in global talent management. *Journal of World Business, 45*(2), 161–168.

Fee, A., & Michailova, S. (2020). How host organizations prepare for and learn from expatriate assignments. *Thunderbird International Business Review, 62*(4), 329–342.

Fey, C. F., Morgulis-Yakushev, S., Park, H. J., & Bjorkman, I. (2009). Opening the black box of the relationship between HRM practices and firm performance: A comparison of MNE subsidiaries in the USA, Finland, and Russia. *Journal of International Business Studies, 40*(4), 690–712.

Froese, F. J., Shen, J., Sekiguchi, T., & Davies, S. (2020). Liability of Asianness? Global talent management challenges of Chinese, Japanese, and Korean multinationals. *Human Resource Management Review, 30*(4), 100776.

Geary, J., & Aguzzoli, R. (2016). Miners, politics and institutional caryatids: Accounting for the transfer of HRM practices in the Brazilian multinational enterprise. *Journal of International Business Studies, 47*, 968–996.

Gibson, C. B., Gilson, L. L., Griffith, T. L., & O'Neill, T. A. (2023). Should employees be required to return to the office? *Organizational Dynamics, 52*(2), 100981.

Gligor, D. M., Pillai, K. G., & Golgeci, I. (2021). Theorizing the dark side of business-to-business relationships in the era of AI, big data, and blockchain. *Journal of Business Research, 133*, 79–88.

Groysberg, B., & Connolly, K. (2015). The three things CEOs worry about the most. *Harvard Business Review, 16*. Accessed at: https://hbr.org/2015/03/the-3-things-ceos-worry-about-the-most. March 16.

Hartmann, E., Feisel, E., & Schober, H. (2010). Talent management of western MNEs in China: Balancing global integration and local responsiveness. *Journal of World Business*, 45(2), 169–178.

Harvey, M., Novicevic, M. M., Buckley, M. R., & Fung, H. (2005). Reducing inpatriate managers' 'liability of foreignness' by addressing stigmatization and stereotype threats. *Journal of World Business, 40*(3), 267–280.

Harzing, A. W. (2001). Of bears, bumble-bees, and spiders: The role of expatriates in controlling foreign subsidiaries. *Journal of World Business, 36*(4), 366–379.

Harzing, A.-W., Pudelko, M., & Reiche, B. S. (2016). The bridging role of expatriates and inpatriates in knowledge transfer in multinational corporations. *Human Resource Management, 55*(4), 679–695.

Heenan, D., & Perlmutter, H. (1979). *Multinational Organizational Development: A Social Architecture Perspective*. Reading, MA: Addison-Wesley.

Jaiswal, A., Arun, C. J., & Varma, A. (2022). Rebooting employees: Upskilling for artificial intelligence in multinational corporations. *The International Journal of Human Resource Management, 33*(6), 1179–1208.

Jooss, S., Conroy, K. M., & McDonnell, A. (2022). From travel to virtual work: The transitional experiences of global workers during Covid–19. *International Business Review, 31*(6), 102052.

Jooss, S., McDonnell, A., & Conroy, K. M. (2021). Flexible global working arrangements: An integrative review and future research agenda. *Human Resource Management Review, 31*(4), 100780.

Kang, H., & Shen, J. (2018). Antecedents and consequences of host-country nationals' attitudes and behaviors toward expatriates: What we do and do not know. *Human Resource Management Review, 28*(2), 164–175.

Keegan, A., & Meijerink, J. (2023). Dynamism and realignment in the HR architecture: Online labor platform ecosystems and the key role of contractors. *Human Resource Management, 62*(1), 15–29.

Kelly, G., & Conroy, K. M. (2023). Premature return of self-initiated expatriates in the spectre of a global crisis: A sensemaking perspective. *The International Journal of Human Resource Management*, 35(4), 587–620.

Kim, H., Reiche, B. S., & Harzing, A. W. (2022). How does successive inpatriation contribute to subsidiary capability building and subsidiary evolution? An organizational knowledge creation perspective, *Journal of International Business Studies, 53*(7), 1394–1419.

Kim, S., Wang, Y., & Boon, C. (2021). Sixty years of research on technology and human resource management: Looking back and looking forward. *Human Resource Management, 60*(1), 229–247.

Mäkelä, K., Björkman, I., & Ehrnrooth, M. (2009). MNC subsidiary staffing architecture: Building human and social capital within the organisation. *The International Journal of Human Resource Management, 20*(6), 1273–1290.

Mäkelä, K., Björkman, I., & Ehrnrooth, M. (2010). How do MNCs establish their talent pools? Influences on individuals' likelihood of being labeled as talent. *Journal of World Business, 45*(2), 134–142.

Malik, A., Budhwar, P., & Kazmi, B. A. (2023b). Artificial intelligence (AI) assisted HRM: Towards an extended strategic framework. *Human Resource Management Review, 33*(1), 100940.

Malik, A., Budhwar, P., Mohan, H., & Srikanth, N. R. (2023a). Employee experience – The missing link for engaging employees: Insights from an MNE's AI-based HR ecosystem, *Human Resource Management, 62*(1), 97–115.

Malik, A., Budhwar, P., Patel, C., & Srikanth, N. R. (2022a). May the bots be with you! Delivering HR cost-effectiveness and individualised employee experiences in an MNE. *The International Journal of Human Resource Management, 33*(6), 1148–1178.

Malik, A., De Sliva, T., Budhwar, P., & Srikanth, N. R. (2021). Elevating talents' experience through innovative artificial intelligence-mediated knowledge sharing: Evidence from a multinational enterprise *Journal of International Management, 27*(4), 100871.

Malik, A., Nguyen, M., & Budhwar, P. (2022b). Antecedents and consequences of an artificial intelligence mediated knowledge-sharing social exchange: Towards a conceptual model *IEEE Transactions on Engineering Management*. https://doi.org/10.1109/TEM.2022.3163117

Malik, A., Sinha, P., Budhwar, P., & Pereira, V. (2023c). Managing legitimacy in a cross-border post-merger integration context: The role of language strategies. *The International Journal of Human Resource Management, 34*(21), 4144–4174.

Meijerink, J., Boons, M., Keegan, A., & Marler, J. (2021). Algorithmic human resource management: Synthesizing developments and cross-disciplinary insights on digital HRM. *The International Journal of Human Resource Management, 32*(12), 2545–2562.

Mellahi, K., & Collings, D. G. (2010). The barriers to effective global talent management: The example of corporate elites in MNEs. *Journal of World Business, 45*(2), 143–149.

Michailova, S., Fee, A., & DeNisi, A. (2023). Research on host-country nationals in multinational enterprises: The last five decades and ways forward. *Journal of World Business, 58*(1), 101383.

Minbaeva, D., & Collings, D. G. (2013). Seven myths of global talent management. *The International Journal of Human Resource Management, 24*(9), 1762–1776.

Morris, S., Snell, S., & Björkman, I. (2016). An architectural framework for global talent management. *Journal of International Business Studies, 47*, 723–747.

Nguyen, M., & Malik, A. (2022). A two-wave cross-lagged study on AI service quality: The moderating effects of the job level and job role. *British Journal of Management, 33*(3), 1221–1237.

Nichols, A. (2022). Digital nomads: A savvy enterprise's newest HR frontier. *Strategic HR Review, 21*(6), 185–190.

Oswald, F. L., Behrend, T. S., Putka, D. J., & Sinar, E. (2020). Big data in industrial-organizational psychology and human resource management: Forward progress for organizational research and practice. *Annual Review of Organizational Psychology and Organizational Behavior, 7*, 505–533.

Pan, Y., Froese, F., Liu, N., Hu, Y., & Ye, M. (2022). The adoption of artificial intelligence in employee recruitment: The influence of contextual factors. *The International Journal of Human Resource Management, 33*(6), 1125–1147.

Pereira, V., Malik, A., Howe-Walsh, L., Munjal, S., & Hirekhan, M. (2017). Managing Yopatriates: A longitudinal study of generation Y expatriates in an Indian multi-national corporation. *Journal of International Management, 23*(2), 151–165.

Perlmutter, H. (1969). The tortuous evolution of the multinational corporation. *Columbia Journal of World Business*, January–February, 9–18.

Prikshat, V., Islam, M., Patel, P., Malik, A., Budhwar, P., & Gupta, S. (2023b). AI-Augmented HRM: Literature review and a proposed multilevel framework for future research. *Technological Forecasting and Social Change, 193*, 122645. https://doi.org/10.1016/j.techfore.2023.122645

Prikshat, V., Malik, A., & Budhwar, P. (2023a). AI-augmented HRM: Antecedents, assimilation, and multilevel consequences. *Human Resource Management Review*, 100860. https://doi.org/10.1016/j.hrmr.2021.100860

Raisch, S., & Krakowski, S. (2021). Artificial intelligence and management: The automation–augmentation paradox. *Academy of Management Review, 46*(1), 192–210.

Rickley, M. (2019). Cultural generalists and cultural specialists: Examining international experience portfolios of subsidiary executives in multinational firms. *Journal of Management, 45*(2), 384–416.

Rosenzweig, P. M., & Nohria, N. (1994). Influences on human resource management practices in multinational corporations. *Journal of International Business Studies, 25*(2), 229–251.

Sarabi, A., Froese, F. J., & Hamori, M. (2017). Is inpatriate assignment experience a ticket to the top of a foreign subsidiary? The moderating effect of subsidiary context. *Journal of World Business, 52*(5), 680–690.

Schotter, A. (2021). Resilient or not: boundary-spanning in innovation-focused MNEs during global crises. *Critical Perspectives on International Business, 17*(2), 342–358.

Schuler, R. S., Jackson, S. E., & Tarique, I. (2011). Global talent management and global talent challenges: Strategic opportunities for IHRM. *Journal of World Business, 46*(4), 506–516.

Scullion, H., & Collings, D. G. (Eds.). (2006). *Global Staffing*. London: Routledge.

Sivathanu, B., & Pillai, R. (2019). Technology and talent analytics for talent management – A game changer for organizational performance. *International Journal of Organizational Analysis, 28*(2), 457–473.

Smale, A., Bjorkman, I., & Sumelius, J. (2013). Examining the differential use of global integration mechanisms across HRM practices: Evidence from China. *Journal of World Business, 48*(2), 232–240.

Snell, S. A., & Morris, S. S. (2021). Time for realignment: The HR ecosystem. *Academy of Management Perspectives, 35*(2), 219–236.

Snell, S. A., Swart, J., Morris, S., & Boon, C. (2023). The HR ecosystem: Emerging trends and a future research agenda. *Human Resource Management, 62*(1), 5–14.

Stahl, G., Björkman, I., Farndale, E., Morris, S. S., Paauwe, J., Stiles, P., & Wright, P. (2012). Six principles of effective global talent management. *Sloan Management Review, 53*(2), 25–42.

Suseno, Y., Chang, C., Hudik, M., & Fang, E. S. (2022). Beliefs, anxiety and change readiness for artificial intelligence adoption among human resource managers: The moderating role of high-performance work systems. *The International Journal of Human Resource Management, 33*(6), 1209–1236.

Takeuchi, R. (2010). A critical review of expatriate adjustment research through a multiple stakeholder view: Progress, emerging trends, and prospects. *Journal of Management, 36*(4), 1040–1064.

Taylor, S., Beechler, S., & Napier, N. (1996). Toward an integrative model of strategic international human resource management. *Academy of Management Review, 21*(4), 959–985.

Thang, L.C., Rowley, C., Quang, T., & Warner, M. (2007). To what extent can management practices be transferred between countries?: The case of human resource management in Vietnam. *Journal of World Business, 42*(1), 113–127.

Thomason, B., & Gibson, C. B. (2024). A meta-theory of global work encounters. *Academy of Management Review, 49*(3), 636–661.

Toh, S. M., & Denisi, A. S. (2003). Host country national reactions to expatriate pay policies: A model and implications. *Academy of Management Review, 28*(4), 606–621.

Vrontis, D., Christofi, M., Pereira, V., Tarba, S., Makrides, A., & Trichina, E. (2022). Artificial intelligence, robotics, advanced technologies and human resource management: A systematic review. *The International Journal of Human Resource Management, 33*(6), 1237–1266.

Wirtz, J., & Zeithaml, V. (2018). Cost-effective service excellence. *Journal of the Academy of Marketing Science, 46*(1), 59–80.

Yahiaoui, D. (2015). Hybridization: Striking a balance between adoption and adaptation of human resource management practices in French multinational corporations and their Tunisian subsidiaries. *The International Journal of Human Resource Management, 26*(13), 1665–1693.

Yamao, S., Yoshikawa, T., Choi, D., & Toh, S. (2020). When do host country nationals help expatriates? The roles of identification with the multinational enterprise and career development support by the subsidiary. *Journal of International Management, 26*(3).

Zhu, J. S. (2019). Chinese multinationals' approach to international human resource management: A longitudinal study. *The International Journal of Human Resource Management, 30*(14), 2166–2185.

Section Three

Emerging Trends in HRM Globally

17 HRM – From Digitalisation to AI

Giovanni Oscar Serafini and
Leslie T. Szamosi

The Evolution of HRM towards Digitalisation

The transition of Human Resource Management (HRM) towards digitalisation into what is commonly referred to as e-HRM started in earnest in the 1970s with the aim of attaining strategic advantage (Bondarouk et al., 2016; Theres and Strohmeier, 2023). The emergence of e-HRM signalled the utilisation of technology resulting from the digital revolution, towards the efficient and effective delivery of HR practices (De Alwis, 2010) by virtue of human resource information systems (HRIS), integrated, computerised platforms interfacing with an organisation's workforce via e-HR (Zafar, 2013). In the 1990s, this process accelerated due to significant technological advances (Kambur and Yildirim, 2022) including the digitisation revolution involving the conversion of analogue data into digital format, as exemplified by the data-processing functions of HRM (Votto et al., 2021). This triggered a fundamental reinvention of HRM, characterised by the automation of administrative processes through the integration of HRM and IT (Bondarouk and Ruël, 2009) into human resource management systems (HRMS), representing one of the pillars of an enterprise resource planning system (ERP) (Hoch and Dulebohn, 2013).

The current 'digital age' sees the application of revolutionary technologies, namely, artificial intelligence (AI) and robotics (Vrontis et al., 2021). The integration of AI into HRM is rapidly unfolding and pervasively affecting key HR functions and processes, namely, talent acquisition, benefits and compensation, employee self-service transactions, HRM policies and procedures, as well as people reporting and analytics (Arora et al., 2021). The ensuing enrichment of AI applications in HRM is shifting control of HRM functions and processes from human intelligence to machine-learning-based technologies, partcularly, algorithmic control (AC) (Barati and Ansari, 2022). As Malik et al. (2023) contend, the pressing involvement of AI in multiple facets of organisational-management processes is modifying the nature of work, workers and workplaces (p. 14), ultimately impacting employee well-being (Lee et al., 2023). As competition imperatives require organisations to continuously optimise HRM strategies, AI is being utilised because it is

DOI: 10.4324/9781032625560-20

perceived as instrumental in the elaboration of today's complex and conflicting demands. This development raises, among other issues, fundamental ethical concerns not only in terms of monitoring and privacy, but also in relation to transparency (Chowdhury et al., 2022) and the lack of 'human oversight and intelligibility' (Rodgers et al., 2023, p. 17), ultimately causing the de-skilling of HRM practitioners (Charlwood and Guenole, 2022). Notwithstanding, the AI transformation is signifying a pivotal change in all aspects of HRM due to its pervasiveness (Votto et al., 2021), for instance, in the training function where AI enables its evolution into a full-fledged knowledge organisation thereby securing personalised training offerings (Chen, 2022).

Technological Evolution in HRM and Strategic Adoption in the 4IR Era

These developments need to be understood within the perspective of emerging technological advancements brought by the Fourth Industrial Revolution (4IR/Industry 4.0). Various facets of workplace automation (Bamel et al., 2022) are transforming how organisations operate and manage their human capital (Ali and Zaman, 2023) by virtue of both AI applications and other technologies (e.g., big data, machine learning, mobile technology, the Internet of Things, geo-tagging, virtual reality, speech recognition and biometrics) (Budhwar et al., 2022, p. 1066). Still, researchers highlight that HRM has seen the deployment of such cutting-edge technology, particularly in the recruitment, selection, training and development functions (Chowdhury et al., 2022) due to fears and negative feelings even among HR employees and managers themselves (Palos-Sánchez et al., 2022).

In terms of the application and integration of technology in business processes, there is a positive correlation between company size and early technology adoption (Hsu et al., 2006). In fact, by considering company size as function of number of staff and budget (Rogers, 2010), larger organisations are at a net advantage over small and medium enterprises (SMEs) due to the vastness of resources available (Bolton, 2018; Müller et al., 2018; Sommer, 2015). Given the strategic role of human capital as a source of critical value in attaining and maintaining competitive advantage (Black, 2019; Paschen et al., 2020), the resulting 'war for talent' (Michaels et al., 2001) places recruitment as the key HRM function responsible to attract top-tier talents. Consequently, early adopters of AI technology in HRM have primarily focused on implementing AI-based recruitment solutions over other functions as these technologies assist in bridging the skills gap (Chui, 2017; Ransbotham et al., 2017) by optimising the connection of applicants with the labour market via the internet and web-based tools (Chen, 2023). As suggested by Gratton (2023), organisations feature mostly an exploration, low-stake approach involving experimenting with AI in recruitment, training and performance management.

Cultural and Contextual Factors Influencing Technology Integration in HRM

Parry and Tyson (2011) contend that culture represents a key determining factor according to which organisations would integrate technology in their HRM policies and practices. Current research further highlights the critical role of context in determining the level of technology acceptance. Yadav and Kapoor (2023) identified two contextual factors, internal and external, namely technological competence and regulatory backing that significantly improve HRM practices and e-HRM effectiveness. Consequently, as Schalk et al. (2013) posit, when the deployment of e-HRM is not aligned with strategic planning, it is unlikely that e-HRM will be integrated strategically. From the standpoint of regulatory backing, a case in point is the workforce and job-design evolution triggered by the gig economy and the widespread application of outsourced labour practices (see also Chapter 18 in this volume). In highly-deregulated and liberal-institutional contexts such as that found in Anglo Saxon countries (Wood and Brewster, 2021), labour law facilitates the emergence of employment forms that serve as alternatives to traditional full-time models. These 'advanced' forms of employment deregulation lack benefits, fair wages and job security, and encompass gig work (Bracy and Dark, 2023) and eLancing (Aguinis and Lawal, 2013), for instance. In the first case, gig workers maintain relationships with multiple client organisations, while online free-lancers (eLancers) seeking employment connect with employers through digital platforms to undertake various tasks. Such interconnections require HR to leverage the algorithmic power of AI to manage the highly complex web of resulting work relationships (Connelly et al., 2021). Another case in point is electronic performance monitoring (EPM), where its utilisation in organisations is intimately connected with the contextual legal framework. In fact, the technology featured by EPM tools enables management to pervasively control employee behaviour and expected formal and professional workplace standards both in terms of productivity and alignment (Tomczak et al., 2018). Ultimately, the extensive influence of AI adoption fundamentally changes nearly every aspect related to the HRM domain, including its extension to talent management (TM) activities (Allal-Chérif et al., 2021; Collings and McMackin, 2021; Jaiswal et al., 2021; Nijs et al., 2022; Parent-Rocheleau and Parker, 2022; Prikshat et al., 2023b; Santana and Díaz-Fernández, 2022; Tong et al., 2021).

Revolutionising HRM through AI in the Global Talent Landscape

In today's globalised landscape, attracting and retaining top talent has become a key source of competitive advantage, thus underlining the criticality of talent management (Collings et al., 2015; Dries, 2013; Sparrow and Makram, 2015). Consequently, organisations are increasingly adopting holistic HR systems (Boon et al., 2019) that encompass all aspects of the employee life cycle, from recruitment and onboarding to development and performance management. As an outcome of the 'Fourth Industrial Revolution' or 'Industry 4.0' (Kong et al., 2021), the application of AI in organisations is dramatically shifting the functioning of HR departments, especially at the level of problem-solving and decision-making, based on the unparalleled capacity of AI to analyse and process vast datasets related to complex, structured and unstructured contexts (McCartney and Fu, 2024; Prikshat et al., 2023a). The disruption enacted by AI technology (Haefner et al., 2021), in tandem with the remote-work imperatives induced by the COVID-19 pandemic (Saxena and Khandelwal, 2022; Vahdat, 2022), have spurred the availability of a vast array of human capital management (HCM) tools. With the potential to enhance the efficiency, strategic orientation, and employee-centricity of HR departments, these tools impact the entire spectrum of creating, managing, advancing and retaining the workforce by integrating traditional HR activities with strategic talent management (Rama Shankar et al., 2023). The antecedents of advanced HRM technology adoption and utilisation relate to, firstly, the extent according to which HRM executives receive top management support and are awarded strategic access to the C-Suite; secondly, the amount of exposure to competition; thirdly, the level of employee education that determines user acceptance; and, lastly, organisational culture (Basu et al., 2023; Bondarouk et al., 2016; Lazazzara and Galanaki, 2018).

For the aforementioned reasons, the benefit of harnessing generative AI is primarily evident in the talent acquisition and recruitment function that shows an end-to-end radical overhaul in terms of efficiency and effectiveness (Ali and Zaman, 2023). Namely, AI-powered talent platforms profile key talent attributes, thus automating, shortlisting and pre-screening as well as streamlining candidate sourcing, matching and ranking (Ore and Sposato, 2021), thereby leading to a staggering acceleration of the recruitment process (Yadav and Kapoor, 2023). As demonstrated by best practices leveraging on predictive analytics of top multinational corporations, the development of a centralised automated-assessment system is crucial for facilitating recruitment on a global scale (Nocker and Sena, 2019). Given the impersonality secured by such processing (Sajjadiani et al., 2019), it is claimed that AI algorithms, unlike humans, are not susceptible to personal biases (e.g., emotions, experiences or cultural norms, and expectations around loyalty and reciprocity). Such biases create opportunities for nepotism and favouritism (Kshetri, 2021) while AI-powered analytics supposedly lead to more 'equitable' or 'blind' decision-making (Malik et al., 2020; Ore and Sposato, 2021) and predictions about employee retention and performance patterns that could be missed by human experts (Nguyen and Park, 2022). Hence, AI allows HRM executives to consider a wider range of possibilities and potentially reach more insightful conclusions (Polisetty et al., 2024).

Empowering HR with AI: From Upskilling to Performance Management

In the process of integrating AI into HR functions, such as learning and development and coaching (Upadhyay and Khandelwal, 2019), Malik et al. (2022)

argue that HR leaders and managers need to become active 'co-designers' of digital HR ecosystems and platforms. This requires developing appropriate digital and data science skills and, more importantly, adopting a radically new mindset aimed at securing exceptional employee experience (EX) predicated on cutting-edge HRM core services. A key benefit of educational programmes leveraging AI is thus the possibility to offer personalised upskilling opportunities, thanks to comprehensive learning assistants that handle all aspects of training, from analysing raw learning data to tracking employee progress and generating detailed reports (Chen, 2022). These AI 'teachers' offer real-time feedback and supervision, automatically ranking trainee performance and providing personalised comments and feedback for enhanced learning opportunities (Vrontis et al., 2021). Additionally, AI analyses visual data to gauge understanding and engagement (Upadhyay and Khandelwal, 2019), facilitating the rapid assessment of training effectiveness for both individual learners and the organisation as a whole through the optimisation of return on training investment (ROTI) (Chen, 2022). From the employee standpoint, their own motivation, together with organisational culture and perceived usefulness, is pivotal towards determining not only usage behaviour related to online platforms for continuous learning and knowledge sharing (Nguyen and Malik, 2021), but also the impact on employee productivity (Shaikh et al., 2023). It appears necessary to leverage AI as a strategic alignment resource for employee rebooting and upskilling (Jaiswal et al., 2021) as well as attitude and behaviour modelling (Malik et al., 2021), due to the growing urgency for employees to remain competitive in an increasingly automated workplace, as underscored by the AI job replacement theory (Huang and Rust, 2018). In fact, studies show that firms embracing advanced technologies, alongside investments in employee skills training, achieve double the productivity gains compared to those focusing solely on either technology adoption or isolated skill development (Boothby et al., 2010). What emerges is that companies attracting new generational talent are those that have integrated advanced technology into their HR operations. This highlights the importance for organisations to adopt similar, pervasive, technological advancements to remain competitive in attracting top talent. The distinct workplace expectations of tech-savvy Gen Zs are compelling employers to nurture a flexible, fast-paced workplace offering career development (Barhate and Dirani, 2022; Benítez-Márquez et al., 2022) alongside a strong company culture (Gabrielova and Buchko, 2021) and a leadership inspiring change with empathy (Grow and Shiyu, 2018).

While AI itself is powerful, unlocking its full potential for productivity gains requires fostering a culture of knowledge sharing among employees (Shaikh et al., 2023). This perspective also encompasses the possibility of smart technology being used for employee performance management purposes through the application of EPM systems collecting real-time data, plausibly offering insights for more objective evaluation (Margherita and Braccini, 2023). Research suggests, however, that EPM focused on development, rather than control and deterrence, is associated with higher levels of employee commitment (Tomczak et al., 2018). Since regular performance feedback and evaluation are essential for employee growth and development (Dachner et al., 2021), managers can capitalise on the comprehensive perspective offered by AI data-driven strategic tools. These tools draw upon diverse internal and external data sources, encompassing both behavioural and outcome-based metrics (Cappelli et al., 2018). As long maintained by a stream of research (e.g., Chen et al., 2012), algorithmic decision-making has the potential to reduce subjectivity bias and enhance the overall reliability and accuracy of the performance appraisal process. This is especially possible if not only responsible, bias-proofing and ethical dimensions define the algorithmic HRM context (Delecraz et al., 2022; Rodgers et al., 2023; Vassilopoulou et al., 2024), but also, most importantly, when firms develop appropriate key HRM managerial skills ('managerial cognition, human capital, and social capital' Deepa et al., 2024, p. 11]) for AI to be successfully implemented.

Hybrid Intelligence in Industry 4.0 for Enhanced Employee Engagement and Flexibility

The adoption of Industry 4.0 technologies relies on integrating employees in ways that boost their flexibility and ability to work seamlessly alongside robots and AI (Calitz et al., 2017; Rajnai and Kocsis, 2017). Hence, the rise of Hybrid Intelligence (HI), harnessing the combined power of human creativity and intuition with machine-powered data analysis and automation, promises to revolutionise approaches to complex tasks and deliver substantial competitive advantage to businesses. Beyond mere efficiency gains, HI presents a compelling opportunity for fostering psychological ownership, thereby fuelling employee empowerment, engagement and overall experience (Dornelles et al., 2022). Thus, HI can lead to significant process improvements, enhanced productivity, and crucially, the development of employee 'integrated capabilities' (Abbas et al., 2022, p. 1186) underscoring the transformative impact of AI at both individual and team levels (Dell'Acqua et al., 2023; Webber et al., 2019).

A key prerequisite to attaining this outcome is the formation of a positive employee attitude towards AI adoption that, according to Pillai et al. (2024), gravitates around 'personalisation, interactivity, perceived intelligence and perceived anthropomorphism' (p. 449). To listen more effectively to users' feedback and calibrate to their expectations, HRM can capitalise on AI to produce engagement analytics to measure employee emotional sentiment, identify areas for improvement, as well as predict digital learning preferences (Nocker and Sena, 2019; Vachaspati, 2017). In addition, by effectively leveraging AI to improve the employee experience, organisations may expect positive outcomes such as increased job satisfaction, stronger employee commitment and decreased turnover intentions (Malik et al., 2021). Yet, reliance on quantitative data alone must be balanced by incorporating employee voice, recognising that AI-enabled voice mechanisms purportedly seem to foster a climate of trust and strengthen employee engagement (Dutta et al., 2022).

In sum, from the standpoint of HR operations and administration, AI integration signifies a transformative shift, enhancing company policy alignment and regulatory compliance while promoting a competitive tailoring approach to HR practices (Ekuma, 2023; Huang et al., 2023). This evolution, underscored by the capacity of AI to automate time-consuming administrative tasks, offers a paradigm wherein real-time data analytics foster informed decision-making, thereby streamlining HR functions from payroll processing to employee engagement (Theres and Strohmeier, 2023). Notably, AI-driven systems may have a pivotal role in identifying and mitigating workplace hazards (Patel et al., 2022), underlining their role in bolstering occupational safety and health (Murugesan et al., 2023).

Adapting HRM Practices for a Multigenerational and Remote Workforce in the AI Era

In the current multigenerational work context (Ng and Parry, 2016), digital-native employees, encompassing millennials and Gen Z, are more adaptable towards embracing digital technology while enjoying enhanced employee experience and engagement (Saxena and Mishra, 2023). As suggested by Meret et al. (2018), Gen Zs rate the opportunity to learn and develop as the most important aspect of their future, with trust and security second and third, respectively. Organisations need to consider these fundamental workforce expectations that, not surprisingly, cut across generations (Beier et al., 2022). Thus, besides emphasising user-friendly interfaces (Nguyen and Malik, 2021), organisations are expected to demonstrate credibility in their HRM practices by adopting a holistic approach, as occurs, for instance, in the case of cutting-edge, AI-powered, talent-management applications in the metaverse (Dutta et al., 2023). The same applies to the context of remote work, accelerated by the pandemic (Bloom et al., 2023) and facilitated by digital technology, leading to the emergence of remote intelligence (RI) and further blurring the boundaries between traditional office environments and distributed workforces (Basile and Beauregard, 2016).

While this shift towards an inclusive and technologically-integrated approach to work offers flexibility and efficiency benefits (Charalampous et al., 2018), there are challenges that HRM executives need to consider, namely, the potential for social isolation, disrupted work culture and difficulties in maintaining a sense of belonging in remote settings (Byrd, 2022). Most crucially, organisations must proactively address the pivotal complement–substitution question, balance between RI and AI (Baldwin and Okubo, 2023) and moderate employee anxieties. In fact, besides the compatibility of remote work with career advancement expectations, these concern the genuine risk of job displacement due to AI (Acemoglu et al., 2022; Rampersad, 2020). Hence, the prospect of AI adoption stemming from its positive impact onto HR extended ecosystems that encompass internal and external partners necessitates not only employees who are open and collaborative, but also effective digital leadership, dependable HR data, expert HR partners and comprehensive AI ethical practices (Singh and Pandey, 2024). Against this backdrop, AI-enhanced HR analytics can become crucial in attracting top talents, boosting retention rates, fostering leadership capabilities and predicting talent turnover to guarantee a stable and skilled workforce (Arora et al., 2021; Kiran et al., 2023).

Beyond Efficiency: The Risks of AI Applications in HRM and Key Conclusions

The integration of AI in HRM poses, notwithstanding, complex ethical challenges, fairness concerns as well as fundamental risks of bias, thus necessitating a critical examination of AI deployment and governance. In fact, the emergence of algorithmic control within organisations reflects a technological evolution that, while promising increased efficiency and decision-making capabilities, also amplifies power disparities and introduces new forms of surveillance practices and workplace inequality (Barati and Ansari, 2022; Manroop et al., 2024). This dichotomy underscores the instrumental nature of technology as a tool shaped by and serving the interests of those in positions of power, thereby challenging the notion of technology as an inherently neutral, or equitable, force (Acemoglu et al., 2023). The issue of power asymmetry emerges most alarmingly by algorithmic restrictions and recommendations that seem to be capable of undermining worker autonomy by limiting access to information and guiding employee behaviour through data-driven suggestions. This management form depends on vast behavioural data and exemplifies the intrusive potential of AI in surveilling and influencing worker actions, reflecting concerns over privacy and the subtle 'coercion' of workers (Bracy and Dark, 2023; Negrón and Nguyen, 2023). These practices not only question the ethical boundaries of employers' oversight, but also the broader implications for individual freedom and dignity within the workplace (Robert et al., 2020).

The potential for AI algorithms to perpetuate, and even exacerbate, existing biases presents a significant additional ethical dilemma for HRM. The reliance on historical data, which may inherently reflect societal biases, underscores a critical flaw in the objective façade of algorithmic decision-making (Kelan, 2023; Vassilopoulou et al., 2024). The risk of encoding and reinforcing discriminatory practices through AI in recruitment, selection and performance evaluation necessitates a vigilant and proactive approach to mitigate bias and ensure fairness (Blumen and Cepellos, 2023; Budhwar et al., 2023). Furthermore, the ethical challenges extend to the transparency and accountability of AI systems. The opacity of algorithmic processes, characterised by a lack of understandability and trustworthiness, erodes the foundation of ethical HRM practices (Langer and König, 2023; Leicht-Deobald et al., 2022). Without clear mechanisms for accountability and the ability for both employees and employers to understand and challenge AI-driven decisions, the ethical deployment of AI in HRM remains a contentious issue, especially since AI systems may represent the direct or indirect cause of danger and harm to its users (Kaur et al., 2022). For instance, a case in point is the application of AI in performance management systems (PMS). As most recently revealed by Varma et al. (2024), a significant challenge to implementing AI-enabled performance management systems lies in establishing employee trust. Concerns exist regarding the data used to generate performance evaluations, particularly when supervisors themselves lack a clear understanding of the underlying algorithms. This profound lack of transparency can breed distrust, as employees may question the fairness and accuracy of system-generated assessments. Additionally, ethical considerations arise from the use of specific performance indicators. For instance, relying solely on metrics such as 'the time that an employee spends away from his/her desk' (Varma et al., 2024, p. 4) as a proxy for work ethic might be misleading as an employee's absence could be due to legitimate work-related discussions with colleagues. These concerns highlight the need for careful consideration of data selection and future utilisation within AI-powered performance management systems.

Apart from critical ethical challenges (Lukaszewski and Stone, 2024), the integration of HRM systems with AI imposes a paradigm shift in workforce management involving the re-evaluation of traditional HR processes in the technical and organisational domains (Nawaz et al., 2024). Particularly, a critical bottleneck exists due to the dearth of appropriately-skilled personnel within HR departments for this new era (Nocker and Sena, 2019). The field of talent analytics, which underpins AI-driven HRM, suffers from a general scarcity of IT specialists capable of navigating the complexities of big data analysis. This lack of expertise not only hinders the adoption of AI but also restricts the ability of HR to leverage data analytics for strategic decision-making. Secondly, Singh and Pandey (2024) highlight limitations within HR ecosystems themselves. These limitations include the incapacity of AI systems to replicate human emotional intelligence and the difficulty of fostering collaboration between HR professionals and data experts. These factors can hinder the smooth integration and effective utilisation of AI within HRM functions. Pan et al. (2022) emphasise the economic considerations of AI adoption. In fact, the transaction costs associated with implementing AI in areas such as employee recruitment necessitate the need for comprehensive and meticulous cost-benefit analysis. Thus, the financial and resource investments required for AI integration may act as a deterrent for many organisations. Lastly, there are critical cybersecurity concerns rendering the security and privacy of employee data of paramount importance (Shneiderman, 2020). Hence, the vulnerability of HRIS to data leaks necessitates a proactive approach to HRIS security. To this end, recent high-profile data breaches serve as stark reminders of the potential risks involved (Mayne, 2024; Sadler, 2023), highlighting the fundamental need for robust, flexible security measures (Zafar, 2013) to ensure the integrity and confidentiality of sensitive employee data, mitigating the potential for catastrophic consequences in the event of a breach (Varma et al., 2024).

Employee reactions to AI, ranging from fear and distrust to concerns over job displacement, encapsulate the broader apprehensions surrounding the automation of traditionally human-centric roles (Långstedt and Arrowsmith, 2023; Ljungholm and Popescu, 2023). Colclough and Lappin (2023) argue the crucial role of union power in mitigating the adverse effects of AI on employment, advocating for a concerted effort to harness this collective strength as a counterbalance to technological exploitation. The latter, in fact, is crudely evidenced by the 'gig' economy that, while promising autonomy and flexibility, juxtaposes the precarious nature of such employment models against the backdrop of legal accountability and the quest for fair labour practices (Habig et al., 2023).

To conclude, one cannot avoid addressing this fundamental question: 'What is HRM's role in the relationship with people who are being managed by an algorithm?' (Holland et al., 2022, p. 74). A plausible answer could be that navigating the transformative power of AI requires organisations to ensure that HR leadership spearheads AI integration (Fenwick et al., 2023), and not just the IT department. Through their technological fluency and expertise in AI application, HR leaders need to position themselves as catalysts for change and innovation while providing a framework for evaluating the impact of AI on the workforce. Such activities need to include participation in setting technical requirements for HR technologies, influencing technology investments and enabling the trustworthy adoption of AI throughout the organisation. The aim would be to counter the negative sentiments echoed in the discourse on the dark side of digitalisation, whereby the potential for AI to induce job redundancy is contrasted with the need for strategic HR practices mitigating technostress and fostering a culture of innovation and well-being (Kim and Christensen, 2017; Palumbo, 2022). By closing the digital skills gap, HR can ensure AI adoption aligns with business objectives, solidifying its strategic value. This should also pave the way for the development of 4IR workplace ecosystems where humans and AI work together seamlessly (Einola and Khoreva, 2023).

References

Abbas, S. M., Liu, Z. & Khushnood, M. (2022) When human meets technology: Unlocking hybrid intelligence role in breakthrough innovation engagement via self-extension and social intelligence. *Journal of Computer Information Systems, 63*(5), 1183–1200. doi:10.1080/08874417.2022.2139781

Acemoglu, D., Autor, D., Hazell, J. & Restrepo, P. (2022) Artificial intelligence and jobs: Evidence from online vacancies. *Journal of Labor Economics, 40*(S1), S293–S340.

Acemoglu, D., Johnson, S. & Viswanath, K. (2023) Why the power of technology rarely goes to the people. *MIT Sloan Management Review, 64*(4), 1–4.

Aguinis, H. & Lawal, S. O. (2013) eLancing: A review and research agenda for bridging the science–practice gap. *Human Resource Management Review, 23*(1), 6–17. doi:10.1016/j.hrmr.2012.06.003

Ali, M. J. & Zaman, N. (2023) Unveiling the transformative effects of industry 4.0 on human resource management: A comprehensive review. *Global Media Journal, 21*(63), 1–11.

Allal-Chérif, O., Yela Aránega, A. & Castaño Sánchez, R. (2021) Intelligent recruitment: How to identify, select, and retain talents from around the world using artificial intelligence. *Technological Forecasting and Social Change*, Vol. *169.*

Arora, M., Prakash, A., Mittal, A., & Singh, S. (2021, December). HR analytics and artificial intelligence-transforming human resource management. In *2021 International Conference on Decision Aid Sciences and Application (DASA)* (pp. 288–293). IEEE.

Baldwin, R. & Okubo, T. (2023) Are software automation and teleworker substitutes? Preliminary evidence from Japan. *The World Economy*, 1–26. doi:10.1111/twec.13496

Bamel, U., Kumar, S., Lim, W. M., Bamel, N. & Meyer, N. (2022) Managing the dark side of digitalization in the future of work: A fuzzy TISM approach. *Journal of Innovation & Knowledge, 7*(4).

Barati, M. & Ansari, B. (2022) Effects of algorithmic control on power asymmetry and inequality within organizations. *Journal of Management Control, 33*(4), 525–544.

Barhate, B. & Dirani, K. M. (2022) Career aspirations of generation Z: A systematic literature review. *European Journal of Training and Development, 46*(1/2), 139–157.

Basile, K. A. & Beauregard, T. A. (2016) Strategies for successful telework: How effective employees manage work/home boundaries. *Strategic HR Review, 15*(3), 106–111.

Basu, S., Majumdar, B., Mukherjee, K., Munjal, S. & Palaksha, C. (2023) Artificial intelligence–HRM interactions and outcomes: A systematic review and causal configurational explanation. *Human Resource Management Review, 33*(1).

Beier, M. E., Kanfer, R., Kooij, D. T. A. M. & Truxillo, D. M. (2022) What's age got to do with it? A primer and review of the workplace aging literature. *Personnel Psychology, 75*(4), 779–804.

Benítez-Márquez, M. D., Sánchez-Teba, E. M., Bermúdez-González, G. & Núñez-Rydman, E. S. (2022) Generation Z within the workforce and in the workplace: A bibliometric analysis. *Frontiers in Psychology., 12.*

Black, J. S. (2019) *Competing for and with human capital: It is not just for HR anymore.* Boca Raton, FL: CRC Press.

Bloom, N., Davis, S. J., Hansen, S., Lambert, P. J., Sadun, R. & Taska, B. (2023) *Remote work across jobs, companies and space* (No. dp1935). London, Centre for Economic Performance, LSE.

Blumen, D. & Cepellos, V. M. (2023) Dimensions of the use of technology and Artificial Intelligence (AI) in Recruitment and Selection (R&S): Benefits, trends, and resistance. *Cadernos EBAPE.BR, 21*(2).

Bolton, R. (2018) The future of HR 2019: In the know or in the No. Amstelveen, *KPMG International,* 1–24.

Bondarouk, T., Parry, E. & Furtmueller, E. (2016) Electronic HRM: Four decades of research on adoption and consequences. *The International Journal of Human Resource Management, 28*(1), 98–131.

Bondarouk, T. V. & Ruël, H. J. (2009) Electronic human resource management: Challenges in the digital era. *The International Journal of Human Resource Management, 20*(3), 505–514.

Boon, C., Den Hartog, D. N. & Lepak, D. P. (2019) A systematic review of human resource management systems and their measurement. *Journal of Management, 45*(6), 2498–2537.

Boothby, D., Dufour, A. & Tang, J. (2010) Technology adoption, training and productivity performance. *Research Policy, 39*(5), 650–661.

Bracy, C. & Dark, M. (2023) The ghost workforce the tech industry doesn't want you to think about. *Stanford Social Innovation Review*. Available at https://ssir.org/articles/entry/the_ghost_workforce_the_tech_industry_doesnt_want_you_to_think_about [Accessed 1 April 2024].

Budhwar, P., Chowdhury, S., Wood, G., Aguinis, H., Bamber, G. J., Beltran, J. R., Boselie, P., Lee Cooke, F., Decker, S., DeNisi, A., Dey, P. K., Guest, D., Knoblich, A. J., Malik, A., Paauwe, J., Papagiannidis, S., Patel, C., Pereira, V., Ren, S., Rogelberg, S., Saunders, M. N. K., Tung, R. L. & Varma, A. (2023) Human resource management in the age of generative artificial intelligence: Perspectives and research directions on ChatGPT. *Human Resource Management Journal, 33*(3), 606–659.

Budhwar, P., Malik, A., De Silva, M. T. T. & Thevisuthan, P. (2022) Artificial intelligence – Challenges and opportunities for international HRM: A review and research agenda. *The International Journal of Human Resource Management, 33*(6), 1065–1097.

Byrd, M. Y. (2022) Creating a culture of inclusion and belongingness in remote work environments that sustains meaningful work. *Human Resource Development International, 25*(2), 145–162.

Calitz, A. P., Poisat, P. & Cullen, M. (2017) The future African workplace: The use of collaborative robots in manufacturing. *SA Journal of Human Resource Management, 15*(1), 1–11.

Cappelli, P., Tavis, A., Burrell, L., Barton, D., Carey, D. & Charan, R. (2018) The new rules of talent management. *Harvard Business Review,* March/April, 45–61.

Charalampous, M., Grant, C. A., Tramontano, C. & Michailidis, E. (2018) Systematically reviewing remote e-workers' well-being at work: A multidimensional approach. *European Journal of Work and Organizational Psychology, 28*(1), 51–73.

Charlwood, A. & Guenole, N. (2022) Can HR adapt to the paradoxes of artificial intelligence? *Human Resource Management Journal, 32*(4), 729–742.

Chen, H., Chiang, R. H. L. & Storey, V. C. (2012) Business intelligence and analytics: From big data to big impact. *MIS Quarterly,* 3(2), 1165–1188.

Chen, Z. (2022) Artificial intelligence-virtual trainer: Innovative didactics aimed at personalized training needs. *Journal of the Knowledge Economy, 14*(2), 2007–2025.

Chen, Z. (2023) Collaboration among recruiters and artificial intelligence: Removing human prejudices in employment. *Cognition, Technology & Work, 25*(1), 135–149.

Chowdhury, S., Joel-Edgar, S., Dey, P. K., Bhattacharya, S. & Kharlamov, A. (2022) Embedding transparency in artificial intelligence machine learning models: Managerial implications on predicting and explaining employee turnover. *The International Journal of Human Resource Management, 34*(14), 2732–2764.

Chui, M. (2017) Artificial intelligence the next digital frontier. *McKinsey and Company Global Institute, 47*(3.6), 6–8.

Colclough, C. J. & Lappin, K. (2023) Building union power to rein in the AIi boss. *Stanford Social Innovation Review*. Available at https://ssir.org/articles/entry/building_union_power_to_rein_in_the_ai_boss# [Accessed 1 April 2024].

Collings, D. G. & McMackin, J. (2021) The practices that set learning organizations apart. *MIT Sloan Management Review, 62*(4).

Collings, D. G., Scullion, H., & Vaiman, V. (2015). Talent management: Progress and prospects. *Human Resource Management Review, 25*(3), 233–235.

Connelly, C. E., Fieseler, C., Černe, M., Giessner, S. R. & Wong, S. I. (2021) Working in the digitized economy: HRM theory & practice. *Human Resource Management Review, 31*(1).

Dachner, A. M., Ellingson, J. E., Noe, R. A. & Saxton, B. M. (2021) The future of employee development. *Human Resource Management Review, 31*(2), 100732.

De Alwis, A. C. (2010) The impact of electronic human resource management on the role of human resource managers. *E + M: Ekonomie a Management, 4,* 47–60.

Deepa, R., Sekar, S., Malik, A., Kumar, J. & Attri, R. (2024) Impact of AI-focussed technologies on social and technical competencies for HR managers – A systematic review and research agenda. *Technological Forecasting and Social Change, 202,* 123301.

Delecraz, S., Eltarr, L., Becuwe, M., Bouxin, H., Boutin, N. & Oullier, O. (2022) Responsible artificial intelligence in human resources technology: An innovative inclusive and fair by design matching algorithm for job recruitment purposes. *Journal of Responsible Technology, 11,* 100041.

Dell'Acqua, F., McFowland, E., Mollick, E. R., Lifshitz-Assaf, H., Kellogg, K., Rajendran, S., Krayer, L., Candelon, F. & Lakhani, K. R. (2023) *Navigating the jagged technological frontier: Field experimental evidence of the effects of AI on knowledge worker productivity and quality.* Boston: Harvard Business School Technology & Operations Mgt. Unit Working Paper (24–013).

Dornelles, J., Nestor, A. & Alejandro, F. (2022) Smart working in industry 4.0: How digital technologies enhance manufacturing workers' activities. *Computers & Industrial Engineering, 163,* 107804.

Dries, N. (2013) The psychology of talent management: A review and research agenda. *Human Resource Management Review, 23*(4), 272–285.

Dutta, D., Mishra, S. K. & Tyagi, D. (2022) Augmented employee voice and employee engagement using artificial intelligence-enabled chatbots: A field study. *The International Journal of Human Resource Management, 34*(12), 2451–2480.

Dutta, D., Srivastava, Y. & Singh, E. (2023) Metaverse in the tourism sector for talent management: A technology in practice lens. *Information Technology & Tourism, 25*(3), 331–365.

Einola, K. & Khoreva, V. (2023) Best friend or broken tool? Exploring the co-existence of humans and artificial intelligence in the workplace ecosystem. *Human Resource Management, 62*(1), 117–135.

Ekuma, K. (2023) Artificial intelligence and automation in human resource development: A systematic review. *Human Resource Development Review, 23*(2), 199–229.

Fenwick, A., Molnar, G. & Frangos, P. (2023) Revisiting the role of HR in the age of AI: Bringing humans and machines closer together in the workplace. *Frontiers in Artificial Intelligence, 6.*

Gabrielova, K. & Buchko, A. (2021) Here comes Generation Z: Millennials as managers. *Business Horizons., 64*(4), 489–499.

Gratton, L.(2023) Want more clarity on generative AI? Experiment widely. *MIT Sloan Management Review.* Available at https://sloanreview.mit.edu/article/want-more-clarity-on-generative-ai-experiment-widely/ [Accessed 7 January 2024].

Grow, J. & Shiyu, Y. (2018) Generation-Z enters the advertising workplace: Expectations through a gendered lens. *Journal of Advertising Education, 22*(1), 7–22.

Habig, J., Dubal, V. & Khan, M. (2023) Unrigging the gig economy. *Stanford Social Innovation Review*. Available at https://ssir.org/articles/entry/unrigging_the_gig_economy [Accessed 15 January 2024].

Haefner, N., Wincent, J., Parida, V. & Gassmann, O. (2021) Artificial intelligence and innovation management: A review, framework, and research agenda☆. *Technological Forecasting and Social Change, 162,* 120392.

Hoch, J. E. & Dulebohn, J. H. (2013) Shared leadership in enterprise resource planning and human resource management system implementation. *Human Resource Management Review, 23*(1), 114–125.

Holland, P., Dowling, P. & Brewster, C. (2022) HRM and the smart and dark side of technology. *Asia Pacific Journal of Human Resources, 60*(1), 62–78.

Hsu, P.-F., Kraemer, K. L. & Dunkle, D. (2006) Determinants of E-business use in U.S. firms. *International Journal of Electronic Commerce, 10*(4), 9–45.

Huang, M.-H. & Rust, R. T. (2018) Artificial intelligence in service. *Journal of Service Research, 21*(2), 155–172.

Huang, X., Yang, F., Zheng, J., Feng, C. & Zhang, L. (2023) Personalized human resource management via HR analytics and artificial intelligence: Theory and implications. *Asia Pacific Management Review, 28*(4), 598–610.

Jaiswal, A., Arun, C. J. & Varma, A. (2021) Rebooting employees: Upskilling for artificial intelligence in multinational corporations. *The International Journal of Human Resource Management, 33*(6), 1179–1208.

Kambur, E. & Yildirim, T. (2022) From traditional to smart human resources management. *International Journal of Manpower, 44*(3), 422–452.

Kaur, D., Uslu, S., Rittichier, K. J. & Durresi, A. (2022) Trustworthy artificial intelligence: A review. *ACM computing surveys (CSUR), 55*(2), 1–38.

Kelan, E. K. (2023) Algorithmic inclusion: Shaping the predictive algorithms of artificial intelligence in hiring. *Human Resource Management Journal, 34*(3), 694–707.

Kim, S. & Christensen, A. L. (2017) The dark and bright sides of personal use of technology at work: A job demands–resources model. *Human Resource Development Review, 16*(4), 425–447.

Kiran, P. R., Chaubey, A. & Shastri, R. K. (2023) Role of HR analytics and attrition on organisational performance: A literature review leveraging the SCM-TBFO framework. *Benchmarking: An International Journal, 31*(9), 3102–3129.

Kong, H., Yuan, Y., Baruch, Y., Bu, N., Jiang, X. & Wang, K. (2021) Influences of artificial intelligence (AI) awareness on career competency and job burnout. *International Journal of Contemporary Hospitality Management, 33*(2), 717–734.

Kshetri, N. (2021) Evolving uses of artificial intelligence in human resource management in emerging economies in the global South: Some preliminary evidence. *Management Research Review, 44*(7), 970–990.

Langer, M. & König, C. J. (2023) Introducing a multi-stakeholder perspective on opacity, transparency and strategies to reduce opacity in algorithm-based human resource management. *Human Resource Management Review, 33*(1).

Långstedt, J. & Arrowsmith, J. (2023) Values, work and well-being in artificial intelligence society: Exacerbating dilemmas in human resource management. In M. Filimowicz *Algorithmic ethics* (pp. 22–38). Milton Park, Routledge.

Lazazzara, A., Galanaki, E. (2018). E-HRM Adoption and Usage: A Cross-National Analysis of Enabling Factors. In: Rossignoli, C., Virili, F., Za, S. (eds) Digital Technology and Organizational Change. Lecture Notes in Information Systems and Organisation, vol 23, (pp. 125–140). New York: Springer.

Lee, M. C. M., Scheepers, H., Lui, A. K. H. & Ngai, E. W. T. (2023) The implementation of artificial intelligence in organizations: A systematic literature review. *Information & Management, 60*(5).

Leicht-Deobald, U., Busch, T., Schank, C., Weibel, A., Schafheitle, S., Wildhaber, I. & Kasper, G. (2022) The challenges of algorithm-based HR decision-making for personal integrity. In *Business and the ethical implications of technology* (pp. 71–86). New York: Springer.

Ljungholm, D. P. & Popescu, V. (2023) Generative artificial intelligence algorithms in talent and performance management, job displacement and creation, and employee productivity and well-being. *Contemporary Readings in Law and Social Justice, 15*(2), 9–25.

Lukaszewski, K. M. & Stone, D. L. (2024) Will the use of AI in human resources create a digital Frankenstein? *Organizational Dynamics, 53*(1), 101033

Malik, A., Budhwar, P. & Kazmi, B. A. (2023) Artificial intelligence (AI)-assisted HRM: Towards an extended strategic framework. *Human Resource Management Review, 33*(1).

Malik, A., Budhwar, P., Mohan, H. & N. R, S. (2022) Employee experience The missing link for engaging employees: Insights from an MNE's AI-based HR ecosystem. *Human Resource Management, 62*(1), 97–115.

Malik, A., Budhwar, P., Patel, C. & Srikanth, N. R. (2020) May the bots be with you! Delivering HR cost-effectiveness and individualised employee experiences in an MNE. *The International Journal of Human Resource Management, 33*(6), 1148–1178.

Malik, A., De Silva, M. T. T., Budhwar, P. & Srikanth, N. R. (2021) Elevating talents' experience through innovative artificial intelligence-mediated knowledge sharing: Evidence from an IT-multinational enterprise. *Journal of International Management, 27*(4).

Manroop, L., Malik, A. & Milner, M. (2024) The ethical implications of big data in human resource management. *Human Resource Management Review, 34*(2), 101012.

Margherita, E. G. & Braccini, A. M. (2023) Industry 4.0 technologies in flexible manufacturing for sustainable organizational value: Reflections from a multiple case study of italian manufacturers. *Information Systems Frontiers: A Journal of Research and Innovation., 25*(3), 995–1016.

Mayne, M. (2024) *What does the Manchester United data error teach us about workplace breaches?* People Management. Available at https://www.peoplemanagement.co.uk/article/1866108/does-manchester-united-data-error-teach-us-workplace-breaches [Accessed 22 March 2024].

McCartney, S. & Fu, N. (2024) Enacting people analytics: Exploring the direct and complementary effects of analytical and storytelling skills. *Human Resource Management, 63*(2), 187–205,

Meret, C., Fioravanti, S., Iannotta, M. & Gatti, M. (2018) The digital employee experience: Discovering generation Z. In C. Rossignoli, F. Virili, and S. Za (Eds.), *Digital technology and organizational change: Reshaping technology, people, and organizations towards a global society* (pp. 241–256).

Michaels, E., Handfield-Jones, H. & Axelrod, B. (2001) *The war for talent*. Brighton, MA: Harvard Business Press.

Müller, J. M., Kiel, D. & Voigt, K.-I. (2018) What drives the implementation of Industry 4.0? The role of opportunities and challenges in the context of sustainability. *Sustainability, 10*(1), 247.

Murugesan, U., Subramanian, P., Srivastava, S. & Dwivedi, A. (2023) A study of artificial intelligence impacts on human resource digitalization in industry 4.0. *Decision Analytics Journal, 7,* 100249.

Nawaz, N., Arunachalam, H., Pathi, B. K. & Gajenderan, V. (2024) The adoption of artificial intelligence in human resources management practices. *International Journal of Information Management Data Insights, 4*(1).

Negrón, W. & Nguyen, A. (2023) The long shadow of workplace surveillance. *Stanford Social Innovation Review, September 6.* Available at: https://ssir.org/articles/entry/the_long_shadow_of_workplace_surveillance#.

Ng, E. S. & Parry, E. (2016) Multigenerational research in human resource management. In M.R. Buckely, J.R.B. Halbesleben, and A.R. Wheeler (Eds.), *Research in personnel and human resources management* (pp. 1–41). Emerald Group Publishing Limited.

Nguyen, L. A. & Park, M. (2022) Artificial intelligence in staffing. *Vision: The Journal of Business Perspective*, 1–13.

Nguyen, T.-M. & Malik, A. (2021) Employee acceptance of online platforms for knowledge sharing: Exploring differences in usage behaviour. *Journal of Knowledge Management, 26*(8), 1985–2006.

Nijs, S., Dries, N., Van Vlasselaer, V. & Sels, L. (2022) Reframing talent identification as a status-organising process: Examining talent hierarchies through data mining. *Human Resource Management Journal, 32*(1), 169–193.

Nocker, M. & Sena, V. (2019) Big data and human resources management: The rise of talent analytics. *Social Sciences, 8*(10), 273.

Ore, O. & Sposato, M. (2021) Opportunities and risks of artificial intelligence in recruitment and selection. *International Journal of Organizational Analysis, 30*(6), 1771–1782.

Palos-Sánchez, P. R., Baena-Luna, P., Badicu, A. & Infante-Moro, J. C. (2022) Artificial intelligence and human resources management: A bibliometric analysis. *Applied Artificial Intelligence, 36*(1).

Palumbo, R. (2022) Does digitizing involve desensitizing? Strategic insights into the side effects of workplace digitization. *Public Management Review, 24*(7), 975–1000.

Pan, Y., Froese, F., Liu, N., Hu, Y. & Ye, M. (2022) The adoption of artificial intelligence in employee recruitment: The influence of contextual factors. *The International Journal of Human Resource Management, 33*(6), 1125–1147.

Parent-Rocheleau, X. & Parker, S. K. (2022) Algorithms as work designers: How algorithmic management influences the design of jobs. *Human Resource Management Review, 32*(3), 100838.

Parry, E. & Tyson, S. (2011) Desired goals and actual outcomes of e-HRM. *Human Resource Management Journal, 21*(3), 335–354.

Paschen, U., Pitt, C. & Kietzmann, J. (2020) Artificial intelligence: Building blocks and an innovation typology. *Business Horizons, 63*(2), 147–155.

Patel, V., Chesmore, A., Legner, C. M. & Pandey, S. (2022) Trends in workplace wearable technologies and connected-worker solutions for next-generation occupational safety, health, and productivity. *Advanced Intelligent Systems, 4*(1), 2100099.

Pillai, R., Ghanghorkar, Y., Sivathanu, B., Algharabat, R. & Rana, N. P. (2024) Adoption of artificial intelligence (AI) based employee experience (EEX) chatbots. *Information Technology & People, 37*(1), 449–478.

Polisetty, A., Sowdamini, T., Lakshmi, R. S. & Athota, V. S. (2024) Transformation of human resources: Future of workforce analytics. In V. Garg, R. Goel, P. Tiwari, & E. S. Döngül (Eds.), *Handbook of artificial intelligence applications for industrial sustainability* (pp. 144–156). Boca Raton, FL: CRC Press.

Prikshat, V., Islam, M., Patel, P., Malik, A., Budhwar, P. & Gupta, S. (2023a) AI-Augmented HRM: Literature review and a proposed multilevel framework for future research. *Technological Forecasting and Social Change, 193*, 122645.

Prikshat, V., Malik, A. & Budhwar, P. (2023b) AI-augmented HRM: Antecedents, assimilation and multilevel consequences. *Human Resource Management Review, 33*(1), 100860.

Rajnai, Z. & Kocsis, I.(2017) *Labor market risks of industry 4.0, digitization, robots and AI.* Conference.: IEEE, 000343-000346.

Rama Shankar, Y., Sema Kayapinar, K., Abhay, P. & Anurag, T. (2023) AI-enabled human capital management (HCM) software adoption using full consistency method (FUCOM): Evidence from banking industry. *Global Knowledge, Memory and Communicatio*n, Emerald.

Rampersad, G. (2020) Robot will take your job: Innovation for an era of artificial intelligence. *Journal of Business Research, 116*, 68–74.

Ransbotham, S., Kiron, D., Gerbert, P. & Reeves, M. (2017) Reshaping business with artificial intelligence: Closing the gap between ambition and action. *MIT Sloan Management Review, 59*(1).

Robert, L. P., Pierce, C., Marquis, L., Kim, S. & Alahmad, R. (2020) Designing fair AI for managing employees in organizations: A review, critique, and design agenda. *Human–Computer Interaction, 35*(5–6), 545–575.

Rodgers, W., Murray, J. M., Stefanidis, A., Degbey, W. Y. & Tarba, S. Y. (2023) An artificial intelligence algorithmic approach to ethical decision-making in human resource management processes. *Human Resource Management Review, 33*(1), 100925.

Rogers, E. (2010) *Diffusion of innovations.* 4th ed. New York: The Free Press.

Sadler, R. (2023) *Live company data breaches and stats for 2024.* Independent Advisor. Available at https://www.independent.co.uk/advisor/vpn/live-data-breaches-and-stats [Accessed 1 March 2024].

Sajjadiani, S., Sojourner, A. J., Kammeyer-Mueller, J. D. & Mykerezi, E. (2019) Using machine learning to translate applicant work history into predictors of performance and turnover. *Journal of Applied Psychology, 104*(10), 1207–1225.

Santana, M. & Díaz-Fernández, M. (2022) Competencies for the artificial intelligence age: Visualisation of the state of the art and future perspectives. *Review of Managerial Science, 17*(6), 1971–2004.

Saxena, M. & Mishra, D. K. (2023) Artificial intelligence: The way ahead for employee engagement in corporate India. *Global Knowledge, Memory and Communication, 74*(1/2), 111–127.

Saxena, N. & Khandelwal, A. R. (2022) Effectiveness of E-HRM tools using the functionalities of artificial intelligence during remote working in lockdown period. In S. Balamurugan, S. Pathak, A. Jain, S. Gupta, S. Sharma, and S. Duggal (Eds.), *Impact of artificial intelligence on organizational transformation.* New York: Wiley (pp. 387–397).

Schalk, R., Timmerman, V. & den Heuvel, S. v. (2013) How strategic considerations influence decision making on e-HRM applications. *Human Resource Management Review, 23*(1), 84–92.

Shaikh, F., Afshan, G., Anwar, R. S., Abbas, Z. & Chana, K. A. (2023) Analyzing the impact of artificial intelligence on employee productivity: The mediating effect of knowledge sharing and well-being. *Asia Pacific Journal of Human Resources, 61*(4), 794–820.

Shneiderman, B. (2020) Bridging the gap between ethics and practice: Guidelines for reliable, safe, and trustworthy human-centered AI systems. *ACM Transactions on Interactive Intelligent Systems (TiiS), 10*(4), 1–31.

Singh, A. & Pandey, J. (2024) Artificial intelligence adoption in extended HR ecosystems: Enablers and barriers. An abductive case research. *Frontiers in Psychology, 14*, 1339782.

Sommer, L. (2015) Industrial revolution-industry 4.0: Are German manufacturing SMEs the first victims of this revolution? *Journal of Industrial Engineering and Management, 8*(5), 1512–1532.

Sparrow, P. R. & Makram, H. (2015) What is the value of talent management? Building value-driven processes within a talent management architecture. *Human Resource Management Review, 25*(3), 249–263.

Theres, C. & Strohmeier, S. (2023) Met the expectations? A meta-analysis of the performance consequences of digital HRM. *The International Journal of Human Resource Management, 34*(20), 3857–3892.

Tomczak, D. L., Lanzo, L. A. & Aguinis, H. (2018) Evidence-based recommendations for employee performance monitoring. *Business Horizons, 61*(2), 251–259.

Tong, S., Jia, N., Luo, X. & Fang, Z. (2021) The Janus face of artificial intelligence feedback: Deployment versus disclosure effects on employee performance. *Strategic Management Journal, 42*(9), 1600–1631.

Upadhyay, A. K. & Khandelwal, K. (2019) Artificial intelligence-based training learning from application. *Development and Learning in Organizations: An International Journal, 33*(2), 20–23.

Vachaspati, S. (2017) HR analytics in IBM: Employee engagement index and the digital learning marketplace. *NHRD Network Journal, 10*(3), 44–53.

Vahdat, S. (2022) The role of IT-based technologies on the management of human resources in the COVID-19 era. *Kybernetes, 51*(6), 2065–2088.

Varma, A., Pereira, V. & Patel, P. (2024) Artificial intelligence and performance management. *Organizational dynamics., 53*(1), 101037.

Vassilopoulou, J., Kyriakidou, O., Ozbilgin, M. F. & Groutsis, D. (2024) Scientism as illusio in HR algorithms: Towards a framework for algorithmic hygiene for bias proofing. *Human Resource Management Journal, 34*(2), 311–325.

Votto, A. M., Valecha, R., Najafirad, P. & Rao, H. R. (2021) Artificial intelligence in tactical human resource management: A systematic literature review. *International Journal of Information Management Data Insights, 1*(2), 100047.

Vrontis, D., Christofi, M., Pereira, V., Tarba, S., Makrides, A. & Trichina, E. (2021) Artificial intelligence, robotics, advanced technologies and human resource management: A systematic review. *The International Journal of Human Resource Management, 33*(6), 1237–1266.

Webber, S. S., Detjen, J., MacLean, T. L. & Thomas, D. (2019) Team challenges: Is artificial intelligence the solution? *Business Horizons, 62*(6), 741–750.

Wood, G. & Brewster, C. (2021) Human resource management in the Anglo-Saxon countries. In M. J. M. Emma Parry & C. Brewster (Eds.), *The Oxford handbook of contextual approaches to human resource management* (pp. 159–176). Oxford: Oxford University Press.

Yadav, S. & Kapoor, S. (2023) Adopting artificial intelligence (AI) for employee recruitment: The influence of contextual factors. *International Journal of System Assurance Engineering and Management, 15*(5), 1828–1840.

Zafar, H. (2013) Human resource information systems: Information security concerns for organizations. *Human Resource Management Review, 23*(1), 105–113.

18 The End of Jobs

How Gig Work and Job Deconstruction Are Transforming the World of Work

David G. Collings, James Duggan and Philip Rogiers[*1]

Introduction

Work is a central part of life for most working-age adults. It accounts for a significant percentage of their waking hours, and it provides income to support their lives. Indeed, we know that unemployment, or the lack of work, can have significant negative consequences for individuals, highlighting the value work brings to an individual's identity (McKee-Ryan et al., 2005).

How work is organised had been relatively stable since the early 20th century. Individuals typically worked in jobs based in organisations, and enjoyed the benefits of employment. This included protection through legislation around how employment was managed. These positions typically sat in career structures where individuals entered at the lower levels of organisational hierarchies and often progressed their careers by moving up through a career path in the organisation. Over time there was somewhat of a breakdown in internal careers as individuals no longer considered one's job as being for life and instead moved between organisations to build their careers (Arthur & Rousseau, 2001). However, occupations remained a relatively constant reference point for individuals in their careers. In this chapter, we consider this historical context of jobs and how recent years have witnessed a breakdown in how we think about and understand employment. We highlight the gig economy and internal job deconstruction as key examples of this breakdown and consider what this means for work and employment. We conclude by considering the implications of these changes for individuals, organisations and society.

Jobs and Organisations

How people are organised in the workplace is generally traced to the first industrial revolution in the mid-18th century and rooted in the operational capabilities of the factory. This coincided with the transfer of work from homes and farms to factories, with cottage industries and agrarian societies being displaced by the industrial revolution (Thompson, 1967). Driven by mechanisation and enabled through the use of steam and waterpower, factory managers

DOI: 10.4324/9781032625560-21

focused on fragmenting skilled artisans' work into sequences of tasks that could be mechanised and scaled (Winsor & Paik, 2024). The implementation of FW Taylor's (1911) theory of scientific management took these trends to another level and was supported by a greater experience through hiring, training, evaluating and compensating large numbers of employees in these factories. At this time, work became more structured as a bureaucratic hierarchy, with people almost exclusively being hired at the bottom of that hierarchy and progressing through a career ladder based on relatively transparent rules and procedures and supported by increasingly formalised HR functions (Burton et al, 2016; Baron, Dobbin & Jennings, 1986).

Jobs became the essential building blocks of organisations. Jobs are defined as 'bundles of tasks performed by employees under administrative job titles' (Cohen, 2013: 432). Jobs are fundamental to the structure of organisations and also to individuals' experience of work. Reflecting on their research on job design, Oldham and Hackman's (2010: 465) summarised the nature of jobs in the following manner:

> Organizational work generally was organized as a linked set of specific jobs, each set up to be performed by individuals who worked mostly independently of one another in bounded, stand-alone organizations. These jobs were carefully analyzed and defined, both to establish pay rates and to remove any ambiguity about what job holders are supposed to do.

Indeed, jobs are so central that how they are designed determines the level of variety and complexity, as well as the meaningfulness and desirability of a position, and this in turn determines employee motivation, productivity and satisfaction (Hackman & Oldham, 1975). While supervisory roles emerged in early factories, as organisations became more complex, such as in the railroads, the demands for standardisation and coordination led to the creation of senior management or executive jobs, which in turn created an internal hierarchy of jobs which individuals could aspire to progress through. Thus, with increasing complexity, individual jobs were combined into an organisational job structure – 'the collective set of individual jobs in an organisation bundled into levels, departments, and hierarchies' (Cohen, 2016: 29).

Given this context, much of our understanding of work and individuals' experience of work is considered though the lens of jobs. However, over recent years, the very notion of jobs has come under increasing pressure. Writing over a decade ago, Cappelli and Keller (2013) argued that alternatives to traditional employment, such as independent contracting, accounted for up to 20 per cent of individuals doing economic work in the US and potentially a higher percentage elsewhere, pointing to growing fragmentation of traditional job structures. Gig work is a primary example of such alternatives, referring to the provision of services by contractors mediated by online platforms. High-profile examples of platform organisations found in gig work include Uber,

Deliveroo and Fiverr. Contractors working on these platforms are digitally matched with consumers seeking their services and subsequently do not hold jobs in these organisations, nor do they automatically receive the protections of employment afforded to conventional employees (Duggan et al., 2020). Indeed, one of the key challenges of gig work for workers is that the legal rights and obligations, such as labour standards, fair wages, hours and the regulation of health and safety that have been hard fought for over many years, all depend on shared understandings of work being under a single employer, with a clear structure of how work is offered, performed and compensated (Alexander, 2016; Burton et al., 2016). When the nature and structure of work changes, existing laws and policies may no longer be effective or appropriate (Weil, 2014), thereby creating challenges for governments, trade unions and workers alike.

We will now discuss gig work in more detail before turning to wider trends in job deconstruction, where organisations are increasingly exploring more dynamic ways of matching employees with work in the internal labour market.

The Gig Economy

Viewed as a transformative force in the global economic landscape, the gig economy has become the subject of widespread discussion and scrutiny in scholarly, practitioner and policy-making circles (Cropanzano et al., 2023; De Stefano, 2016). Broadly defined as an economic system utilising online labour platforms to digitally connect freelance workers with clients for fixed-term tasks, the gig economy harnesses the information and connectivity properties made possible by modern technology (Cennamo, 2021). Specific definitions of gig work range from focusing exclusively on tasks performed through online platforms and crowdsourcing marketplaces, to encompassing all forms of non-traditional work arrangements – essentially, any labour form that falls beyond the norms of traditional, permanent employment (Adamson & Roper, 2019; Ashford et al., 2018). The key principle and differentiator, however, is that in the gig economy, work is digitally outsourced and offered to contractors on a hyper-flexible and highly-precarious basis. The various manifestations of gig work across multiple industries and sectors underscore its significance in the evolving labour market.

Since its origin around the time of the 2008 global financial crisis, which precipitated more fragmented and precarious working arrangements (Cropanzano et al., 2023; Reiche, 2023), several major players have emerged in building the gig economy. For example, online platforms such as Uber, Lyft and Deliveroo exemplify the local market presence of the gig economy through the provision of on-demand services that can be requested and paid for via smartphone applications (i.e. 'app-work'), including transportation, food-delivery and home repair services (Duggan et al., 2020; Veen et al., 2020). Likewise, online platforms such as Fiverr, Upwork and Amazon Mechanical Turk showcase the gig economy's capacity for remote, computer-based 'crowdwork', offering a diverse range of services such as translation, coding and graphic design (De Stefano, 2016). Combined, these examples illustrate the dynamic economic model found in gig work, essentially reshaping and reimagining how individuals can engage with work and organisations. In all scenarios, the work tasks are contingent and heavily transactional, being completed on an ad-hoc basis without any commitment to an on-going relationship between the gig worker and the platform organisation.

For platform organisations, the gig economy presents a unique approach to navigating an increasingly dynamic and competitive global business environment. Unlike traditional employment models, gig work enables organisations to reduce labour costs significantly and to increase agility in hiring practices operating beyond traditional-employment frameworks (Keegan & Meijerink, 2022). Importantly, in doing so, these organisations typically emphasise their role as digital infrastructure providers rather than conventional service providers or employers. Hence, the role of the platform organisation is pitched as simply matching gig workers – who are positioned as independent service providers – with clients or customers. Consequently, any physical assets required for the service provision (e.g. motor vehicles for transportation, bicycles for food-delivery) must be owned or supplied by workers themselves rather than the platform organisation (Duggan et al., 2022). By leveraging non-core workers for roles typically held by salaried employees, gig work fosters a unique flexibility amongst a workforce of self-employed contractors, devoid of commitment or considerations for past or future employment (Graham et al., 2017). By relegating gig workers to peripheral roles beyond core organisational boundaries, platform organisations shift the risk of economic fluctuations almost entirely onto workers, that is, the piece-rate remuneration system determines that if demand is low at a given time, it is workers who absorb the consequences by earning less income (Caza et al., 2022; Duggan et al., 2023).

For workers, gig work is positioned as offering a range of benefits, many of which are heavily promoted by platform organisations in attracting potential workers. Most significant is the ability for workers to exert increased autonomy over scheduling their work activities. Gig workers can exert a degree of control over when, where and how often they work, a feature that distinguishes this form of labour from traditional employment and potentially appeals to those seeking a greater work-life balance (Keegan & Meijerink, 2022; Reiche, 2023). Likewise, the absence of hierarchical reporting relationships, the ability to work for multiple platform organisations simultaneously and the minimal thresholds for accessing work further enhance the appeal of gig work by offering individuals the opportunity to diversify their working opportunities and income sources (Duggan et al., 2022). For example, the adaptability of gig work is likely to be particularly appealing for those who lack full-time roles, desire control over their schedules or seek to supplement their existing income from other roles. Hence, engaging in gig work can act as a safety net of sorts, ensuring alternatives are available if they are needed.

Yet, critics have consistently highlighted the darker side of gig work, arguing that it presents important risks for workers by replacing stable, benefitted roles with precarious, short-term work, wherein individuals lack the protections enjoyed by employees and are heavily monitored while undertaking their work (Caza et al., 2022). The inherent job insecurity, reduced commitment and diminished loyalty between gig workers and organisations raise concerns about the long-term viability and quality of these roles for those who partake, and particularly for those who may be reliant on the income derived from gig work (Ayentimi et al., 2023). The absence of labour protections contributes to the notion that gig work can be exploitative, offering extrinsic monetary rewards but limiting opportunities for skill development and meaningful work (Petriglieri et al., 2019). Likewise, the use of algorithms to comprehensively monitor, coordinate and control gig workers' activities has raised concern (Duggan et al., 2023), particularly because these workers are self-employed and remain on the periphery of platform organisations. By relying on technological infrastructures for almost all interactions and aspects of their roles, gig workers are likely to feel isolated due to their limited human interaction with management and fellow workers, thereby hindering the development of anything resembling a more traditional working relationship (Cropanzano et al., 2023). In essence, while gig work offers heightened autonomy and flexibility for workers, its potential risks and downsides underscore the nuanced and complex nature of this evolving labour model.

Several tensions dominate research and debates on gig work. Controversies surrounding gig work have sparked debates on issues such as the potential erosion of employment standards (Adams-Prassl, 2022), the role and influence of algorithmic technologies in managing gig workers (Duggan et al., 2023) and the overall quality of jobs in this domain (Adamson & Roper, 2019). Despite its advantages as a mode of matching workers with work in terms of cost reduction and flexibility, the gig economy's impact on workers and employment standards has become a focal point of global discussions and regulatory considerations. The classification of workers as contractors, while beneficial for platform organisations, generates significant complexity. Gig workers, despite being labelled as self-employed, typically experience high levels of monitoring and control from platform organisations, thereby challenging the delineation between independent contractors and employees (Keegan & Meijerink, 2022). This has resulted in numerous legal challenges related to the legal status of gig workers as employees across the globe. This ambiguity in classification has also fuelled discussions about the need for a new, hybrid status – essentially, falling somewhere between 'employee' and 'independent contractor' – that accommodates the unique dynamics of work in the gig economy (Taylor et al., 2017). The inherent tension lies in the conflicting narratives presented by platform organisations, who continue to position gig work as mutually beneficial, while gig workers and unions contest the independent contractor status in ongoing legal challenges and protests (Adams-Prassl, 2022; Ayentimi et al., 2023).

The gig economy's reliance on digital platforms to facilitate work emphasises the important role of algorithms in coordinating and managing workers, and this represents another key tension for workers. The use of these algorithms, collectively known as algorithmic management or algorithmic HRM, facilitates the automation of core HR and managerial functions such as task allocation, performance evaluation and reward management (Duggan et al., 2020). In line with the previous tension around classification, algorithmic management further blurs the lines between determining whether gig workers are, indeed, independent contractors or whether the prescriptive nature of these tools mean that gig workers are more akin to employees of the platform organisation. Research has also considered the implications of algorithmic management for workers, particularly where it signifies a departure from the conventional human-managed relationships associated with employment (Charlwood & Guenole, 2022). Indeed, research has highlighted the controlling nature of these technologies (Duggan et al., 2023) and how workers may perceive and react to the use of algorithmic management in such contexts (Caza et al., 2022; Cropanzano et al., 2023).

The lived experiences of gig workers represent another important dimension of tension within the gig economy. Despite not being classified as employees, gig work demands a level of social connection and motivation, as workers must ultimately provide services to requestors and often do so in a pressurised, time-bound environment (Petriglieri et al., 2019). Hence, the motivation, satisfaction and well-being of gig workers are critical concerns, especially given the precarious nature of their roles. The scalability and disposability of gig workers, compensated on a 'pay-as-you-go' basis, foster a high level of vulnerability to job insecurity and a lack of occupational health protections (Ayentimi et al., 2023; Cropanzano et al., 2023). This precariousness underscores the multifaceted risks faced by this cohort of 'invisible' workers who navigate challenges that extend beyond the economic realm to encompass psychological and well-being aspects, and, hence, emphasising the need for a comprehensive understanding of their experiences within the gig economy.

Given the perviousness of the gig economy combined with the challenges that organisations face in attracting and retaining the quality and quantity of skills they require, and the requirement for more agile approaches to the matching of skills and work, it is not surprising that we are witnessing the increasing prevalence of the deconstruction of jobs within organisations with approaches similar to gig work. This is significant as it impacts traditional employees within organisations who have largely been isolated from the tensions of the gig economy. We now consider emerging trends in job deconstruction.

Internal Job Deconstruction

The gig economy is extending its grip within contemporary organisations too. Organisations are increasingly experimenting with a form of 'internal gigs' or deconstructed jobs, wherein traditional jobs are unbundled into discrete job elements (e.g., tasks and skills) and matched with the knowledge, skills and abilities of employees in the internal labour market (Rogiers & Collings, 2024). Job deconstruction initiatives range from short-term projects, stretch assignments and side gigs, to a portfolio of temporary team roles in organisations (including holacratic forms of organising; Bernstein, Bunch, Canner and Lee, 2016). What differentiates workers in deconstructed jobs from gig workers is that they continue to have a long-term employment relationship with their employer, receiving a monthly stipend and employment benefits like regular employees. At the same time, however, their experience of work is similar to that of gig workers as they transition between temporary and often ambiguously-defined roles, actively searching and bidding for projects and lacking a predefined career template.

This new way of working is not limited to organisations wherein employees are accustomed to taking on varied temporary projects (such as consulting firms) but is being implemented in a wide variety of organisations, ranging from manufacturing, retail, financial, healthcare and public sector organisations (Schrage, Schwartz, Kiron, Jones, & Buckley, 2020). An example is Mastercard, which started matching employees to high-priority tasks through an internal programme titled 'Project Possible' (Mastercard, 2020). This experimental initiative eventually resulted in the rollout of a fully-fledged, internal-talent marketplace for deconstructed work named 'Unlocked'. While specific figures regarding employee participation in Unlocked remain undisclosed, Mastercard reportedly now 'empowers' its 21,000 employees 'to expand their horizons' (Gloat, 2020) by engaging with deconstructed work opportunities through this programme.

The creation of an internal labour market of deconstructed jobs has several benefits. For organisations, it provides flexibility to deploy the right people to the right place at the right time. It creates a pool of mobile talent who can surge to the demands of the business as needed. This flexibility allows organisations to better meet changing business conditions and respond to critical skills gaps (Jesuthasan & Boudreau, 2022). During the pandemic, the US government, for instance, used its internal marketplace, Open Opportunities, to facilitate matches between medical personnel and public hospitals. What was in regular times a platform where federal employees could find various short- or longer-term stretch assignments in other federal government departments (Rogiers, De Stobbeleir, & Viaene, 2021) thus quickly became a matching platform wherein available personnel could surge to meet the urgent public health crisis that was unfolding. While pioneering cases like Open Opportunities were often custom-built platforms developed within an organisation, technology vendors have started to step into this emerging space to provide off-the-shelf solutions. An example is Microsoft's Viva Skills, a skills-based learning system featuring 'an employee development platform, and an internal mobility tool that looks like a talent marketplace' (Bersin, 2023). Viva Skills testifies to how job deconstruction and skills-based organising is becoming an integral feature of mainstream technology solutions, facilitating employee mobility and experiential learning in contemporary organisations.

From the employee perspective, deconstructing traditional jobs into more nimble, internal gig opportunities offers the possibility to practice new skills unavailable in one's regular job or career path. Rogiers and colleagues' (2021) study illuminates the experience of an analyst in the US Navy who gained access to a new work experience by using artificial intelligence and data analysis to match patients to clinical trials. This became possible by working on a standalone project a few hours a week, outside her main job duties. Additionally, deconstructed job opportunities can be a valuable outlet to make new connections, widen one's professional network and forge relationships that can give rise to new career opportunities. Anecdotally, conversations with individuals in organisations with internal gig platforms described how the contacts they had established throughout these experiences eventually led to more permanent career opportunities in the groups they had worked with.

Finally, amid the liminality of fragmented temporary work, there is an opportunity for identity experimentation. Specifically, moving beyond the rigidity of a traditional full-time job creates new degrees of freedom, enabling wider experimentation with the content (tasks) of the work, the people one works with, and the motivation and meaning derived from the work. Thus, the transient and dynamic nature of deconstructed job opportunities creates space for personal reinvention, helping people to break out of predefined career moulds and paving the way for new identities to emerge.

Further, while job deconstruction is often portrayed (and sold) as uniformly positive for organisations and their workers, there are important tensions to consider. Rogiers and Collings (2024) identify three key paradoxes in this regard, highlighting the disconnect between a popularised narrative where organisational benefits are prioritised and worker benefits automatically assumed, and the lived experiences workers have. The paradoxes the authors identify – the autonomy-control paradox, the detachment-inclusion paradox and the growth-stability paradox – show that when left unchecked, deconstructed jobs can disempower rather than empower employees. Specifically, the autonomy-control paradox highlights that without countermeasures, increased instrumentality and control over work may occur in organisations, as deconstructed jobs prompt both formal and normative control over individual activity in deconstructed jobs. The detachment-inclusion paradox shows that these new work arrangements may contribute to a growing marginalisation and exclusion of vulnerable employee groups, such as women or minority employee groups – by facilitating discriminatory patterns and taking away safeguards built into traditional jobs, such as a clear-role identity and interaction scripts. The growth-stability paradox emphasises how worker anxieties and uncertainty may intensify in deconstructed jobs, potentially leading to a bifurcated labour market situated between those realising progressive self-change and those who are not. Collectively, these insights highlight the ensuing tensions that persist in deconstructed job initiatives, and the need to balance corporate appetite for enhanced workforce flexibility with a profound understanding of how these new work models can be implemented to allow for positive and sustainable outcomes for employees.

Thus, as deconstructed job arrangements take hold in organisations, important challenges emerge for organisational leaders in thoughtfully implementing these models. One important priority for HR and talent leaders is to design policies and processes that support workers in such an environment. This could include customised career guidance, evaluation systems and administrative and practical support for workers shifting between varied work tasks and roles. At the same time, there is a need to ask bolder, broader questions about the structure of organisations and the shifts needed to unlock the full potential of deconstructed work models. For example, how could organisations make sure that teams can smoothly form, operate and disband while ensuring that knowledge and expertise are effectively transferred within a fluid workforce? One might further ponder where we are headed as organisational jobs become deconstructed and employees compete internally for deconstructed work opportunities. Is the future of organisations set to be a fusion of traditional and deconstructed job elements– a blend of hierarchy and decentralised self-management? Alternatively, will unbridled market forces eventually erode organisations as we know them, as employees effectively become free agents? In the age-old tension between bureaucracy and market (Ouchi, 1980), what is the role of communities in binding people together around a shared purpose? These questions warrant further exploration and require the collective insight of both practitioners and scholars alike.

We now consider the broader impacts of trends in gig work and job deconstruction for workers, organisations and society.

How Gig Work and Job Deconstruction Are Transforming the World of Work

Implications for Workers

There is little doubt that the trends we identify in both gig work and job deconstruction have significant implications for workers.

Positively, both offer workers the opportunity to develop skills beyond their domain specialism. For example, international data suggest that much gig work is not an individual's sole, or even major, income stream (Duggan et al., 2022; Sessions et al., 2021). Gig work may offer a side-hustle for individuals, presenting an opportunity to boost their income or experiment in an area beyond their day job. In these ways, gig work can positively impact the meaning, value and impact people derive from work (Ashford et al., 2018; Cropanzano et al., 2023). Indeed, some gig workers experience heightened feelings of purpose, authenticity and vitality from their work, as they are no longer tied to organisationally determined jobs and can, instead, build a portfolio of roles akin to a form of micro-entrepreneurship (Petriglieri, Ashford, & Wrzesniewski, 2019). In a similar vein, one of the key advantages of job deconstruction is in offering employees the opportunity to work on projects beyond their day job (Rogiers & Collings, 2024). Online platforms like internal-talent marketplaces provide a tool for these employees to identify opportunities and put themselves forward for consideration.

Both gig work and job deconstruction offer employees some flexibility and autonomy over the hours they work and the projects they work. Unilever's U-Work programme is a good example of how job deconstruction can facilitate such flexibility. U-Work facilitates workers in working flexibly across projects. These workers do not have a fixed job role but do enjoy the benefits and security that permanent workers typically have, including, for example, a monthly retainer and a benefits package. Thus, for individual employees, it brings the benefit of crafting their work patterns to suit their personal circumstances, while exploring new opportunities across the organisation (Unilever, 2023). However, as we noted previously, gig work in particular is highly precarious, and the scheduling flexibility granted to workers comes at the heavy cost of having almost no continuity of employment or a guaranteed minimum income. For gig workers, striving to build an income from a range of ad hoc, sometimes competitive, and often poorly compensated gigs is potentially detrimental to their professional identity and well-being (Petriglieri et al, 2019). The demise of organisational jobs also potentially disempowers employees rather than bringing the empowerment that many advocates argue for (Cappelli, 2020). For many critics, job deconstruction is, in effect, a 20th-century work optimisation logic penetrating modern-day institutions, with employees at risk of being no more than 'cogs' in a larger machinery of commodified work tasks (Anicich, 2022; Frischmann & Selinger, 2018; Rogiers & Collings, 2024).

Implications for Organisations

As outlined earlier, both gig work and job deconstruction bring considerable benefits in terms of more flexible and agile deployment of workers for organisations. One of the key benefits of gig work for platform organisations is the easing of what they perceive as the restrictions surrounding employment. Workers are positioned as independent contractors and, hence, the organisation can almost always avoid the costs of employment, including social welfare, holiday pay, redundancy payments, the costs of work equipment and so on. Yet, through the use of algorithmic technologies, platform organisations can, nonetheless, retain a significant degree of control over the design of work and supply of labour, despite not directly employing gig workers (Duggan et al., 2023). Hence, the hyper-flexible operational structure of gig work seemingly represents several strategic benefits for platform organisations, even if these benefits may be at the detriment of workers.

A key distinction with job deconstruction is that workers are employees and, hence, they enjoy the protections and rights that come with employment. Thus, organisations do not gain the same degree of flexibility as gig platforms do. Yet they do have the potential to much more agilely deploy talent to meet demands within the organisation. As illustrated, through Unilever's U-work programme, the organisation enjoys the benefits of on-demand, skilled talent who are already socialised into the organisation, while avoiding some of the challenges that come with external freelancers who lack an understanding of internal processes and systems.

Implications for Society

There is little doubt that the gig economy and wider trends in job deconstruction have significant implications for society more broadly. Davis (2016), for example, laments the 'ubiquitous Uberisation, in which jobs are completely decomposed into tasks that are staffed on demand' (pp. 273). More broadly, the marketisation of work is argued to break down the relationship between corporations and workers, which has, in turn, been argued to be a key factor influencing the growing economic polarisation and social instability that is evident across the globe (Davis, 2016; Hacker, 2019). Thus, while these trends offer organisations, and arguably workers, some immediate benefits, longer-term considerations about the viability and sustainability of careers, social welfare and employment relations have largely been left out of the picture. The rapid advancement of generative AI and algorithmic technologies, coupled with the allure of short-term productivity gains by 'gigifying' employment relations, has created a perfect storm that threatens to shake up the labour standards and security that workers and unions have built for over a century, potentially undermining the job structures that form the very fabric of our society. As we navigate this uncharted territory, it is imperative that we prioritise sustainable, human-centric solutions that enable both organisations and their workers to thrive in a brave new world of work.

We have witnessed a global rebalancing of labour legislation as national governments and legal establishments seek to keep pace with the changing nature of work in the gig economy (Alexander, 2016). The options to strengthen and expand the regulatory framework governing gig work being pursued by regulators and legislators in different national contexts range from: the enforcement of existing laws; to clarifying or expanding definitions of 'employment'; creating a new category of 'independent worker'; creating rights for 'workers', not employees; and reconsidering the concept of an 'employer' (Stewart & Stanford, 2017). This is a complex and fluid area and we have witnessed ebbs and flows in the balance of power between gig platforms and workers in many developed nations as the regulatory and legislative context evolves. It appears that establishing a floor of rights for workers beyond those provided by employment legislation is one key means by which the rights of workers could be established in such relationships.

The short-term societal implications of job deconstruction are less profound, but it is imperative that regulators and legislators keep a watchful eye on trends in employment to ensure that the extremes of job deconstruction do not lead to ubiquitous Uberisation that Gerry Davis (2016) cautions against. Regulation and legislation cannot stand still and must evolve to keep pace with emerging changes in the workplace. Additionally, given one of the drivers of job deconstruction is the pace of change of skills (Rogiers & Collings, 2024), a further societal challenge should be in ensuring that governments have a perspective on skills within national economies and ensure there is investment in identifying workers at risk of skills' redundancies and ensuring that these workers have the opportunity to reskill and upskill to ensure their continued employability.

Conclusions

Work plays a key role in people's lives. It accounts for a significant percentage of how we spend our waking hours and provides an income to support individuals' lives. How work is designed has been broadly stable for almost two centuries. However, we have witnessed considerable disruption to work design over recent decades. This emerged with the growth of the gig economy and we are now seeing elements of gig work transposed in organisations as evidenced through job deconstruction. While both gig work and job deconstruction offer opportunities for individuals and organisations alike, we also point to some significant challenges that should be considered for both stakeholders. Regulators and legislators also play an important role, and it is critical that regulation and legislation keep pace with the evolving landscape of work and employment.

Note

1 Authors are listed alphabetically and contributed equally to this chapter.

References

Adams-Prassl, J. 2022. Regulating algorithms at work: Lessons for a 'European approach to artificial intelligence. *European Labour Law Journal*, 13, 30–50.

Adamson, M., & Roper, I. 2019. Good jobs and bad jobs: Contemplating job quality in different contexts. *Work, Employment and Society*, 33(4), 551–559.

Alexander, C. S. 2016. Legal avoidance and the restructuring of work. In L. E. Cohen, M. D. Burton, & M. Lounsbury (Eds.), *The structuring of work in organizations*. Research in the Sociology of Organizations (Vol. 47). Bingley: Emerald Group.

Anicich, E. M. 2022. Flexing and floundering in the on-demand economy: Narrative identity construction under algorithmic management. *Organizational Behavior and Human Decision Processes*, 169, 104138.

Arthur, M. B., & Rousseau, D. M. (Eds.). 2001. *The boundaryless career: A new employment principle for a new organizational era*. Oxford: Oxford University Press.

Ashford, S. J., Caza, B. B., & Reid, E. M. 2018. From surviving to thriving in the gig economy: A research agenda for individuals in the new world of work. *Research in Organizational Behavior*, 38, 23–41.

Ayentimi, D. T., Abadi, H. A., & Burgess, J. 2023. Decent gig work in Sub Sahara Africa? *Journal of Industrial Relations*, 65(1), 112–125.

Baron, J. N., Dobbin, F. R., & Jennings, P. D. 1986. War and peace: The evolution of modern personnel administration in US industry. *American Journal of Sociology,* 92, 350–383.

Bernstein, E., Bunch, J., Canner, N., & Lee, M. 2016. Beyond the holacracy hype. *Harvard Business Review*, 94(7), 8.

Bersin, J. 2023. *Why Microsoft viva skills could disrupt the HR tech market.* https://joshbersin.com/2023/10/why-microsoft-viva-skills-could-disrupt-the-hr-tech-market/.

Burton, M. D., Cohen, L. E., & Lounsbury, M. 2016. Introduction: Bringing jobs back in: Toward a new multi-level approach to the study of work and organizations. *Research in the Sociology of Organizations,* 47, 1–22.

Cappelli, P. 2020. Stop overengineering people management. *Harvard Business Review*, 98(5), 56–63.

Cappelli, P., & Keller, J. R. 2013. Classifying work in the new economy. *Academy of Management Review*, 38(4), 575–596.

Caza, B. B., Reid, E. M., Ashford, S. J., & Granger, S. 2022. Working on my own: Measuring the challenges of gig work. *Human Relations,* 75(11), 2122–2159.

Cennamo, C. 2021. Competing in digital markets: A platform-based perspective. *Academy of Management Perspectives*, 35(2), 265–291.

Charlwood, A., & Guenole, N. 2022. Can HR adapt to the paradoxes of artificial intelligence? *Human Resource Management Journal*, 32(4), 729–742.

Cohen, L. E. 2013. Assembling jobs: A model of how tasks are bundled into and across jobs. *Organization Science,* 24, 432–454.

Cohen, L. E. 2016. Jobs as Gordian knots: A new perspective linking individuals, tasks, organisations, and institutions. In. L. E. Cohen, M. D. Burton, & M. Lounsbury (Eds.), *The structuring of work in organizations* (pp. 25–59). Bingley: Emerald Group Publishing Limited.

Cropanzano, R., Keplinger, K., Lambert, B. K., Caza, B. B., & Ashford, S. J. 2023. The organizational psychology of gig work: An integrative conceptual review. *Journal of Applied Psychology,* 108, 492–519.

Davis, G. F. 2016. *The vanishing American corporation: Navigating the hazards of the new economy.* Oakland, CA: Berrett-Koehler.

De Stefano, V. 2016. The rise of the 'just-in-time' workforce: On-demand work, crowdwork and labour protection in the gig economy. *International Labour Office: Conditions of Work and Employment Series, 71.* Geneva: ILO.

Duggan, J., Carbery, R., McDonnell, A., & Sherman, U. 2023. Algorithmic HRM control in the gig economy: The app-worker perspective. *Human Resource Management,* 62(6), 883–899.

Duggan, J., Sherman, U., Carbery, R., & McDonnell, A. 2020. Algorithmic management and app-work in the gig economy: A research agenda for employment relations and HRM. *Human Resource Management Journal*, 30(1), 114–132.

Duggan, J., Sherman, U., Carbery, R., & McDonnell, A. 2022. Boundaryless careers and algorithmic constraints in the gig economy. *The International Journal of Human Resource Management, 33*(22), 4468–4498.

Frischmann, B., & Selinger, E. 2018. *Re-engineering humanity.* Cambridge: Cambridge University Press.

Gloat. 2020. *How Mastercard created priceless career development opportunities.* https://resources.gloat.com/resources/mastercard-customer-success-story/.

Graham, M., Hjorth, I., & Lehdonvirta, V. 2017. Digital labour and development: Impacts of global digital labour platforms and the gig economy on worker livelihoods. *Transfer: European Review of Labour and Research*, 23(2), 135–162.

Hacker, J. S. 2019. *The great risk shift: The new economic insecurity and the decline of the American dream.* Oxford University Press.

Hackman, J. R., & Oldham, G. R. 1975. Development of the job diagnostic survey. *Journal of Applied Psychology*, 60(2), 159–170.

Jesuthasan, R., & Boudreau, J. W. 2022. *Work without jobs: How to reboot your organization's work operating system.* Cambridge, MA: MIT Press.

Keegan, A., & Meijerink, J. 2022. Dynamism and realignment in the HR architecture: Online labor platform ecosystems and the key role of contractors. *Human Resource Management*, 62, 15–29.

Mastercard. 2020. *Project possible: How this employee answered a CEO's call during the pandemic.* https://www.mastercard.com/news/perspectives/2020/project-possible-how-this-employee-answered-a-ceo-s-call-during-the-pandemic/.

McKee-Ryan, F., Song, Z., Wanberg, C. R., & Kinicki, A. J. 2005. Psychological and physical well-being during unemployment: A meta-analytic study. *Journal of Applied Psychology*, 90(1), 53.

Oldham, G. R., & Hackman, J. R. 2010. Not what it was and not what it will be: The future of job design research. *Journal of Organizational Behavior*, 31, 463–479.

Ouchi, W. 1980. Markets, bureaucracies, and clans. *Administrative Science Quarterly*, 25(1), 129–141.

Petriglieri, G., Ashford, S. J., & Wrzesniewski, A. 2019. Agony and ecstasy in the gig economy: Cultivating holding environments for precarious and personalized work identities. *Administrative Science Quarterly*, 64, 124–170.

Reiche, B. S. 2023. Between interdependence and autonomy: Toward a typology of work design modes in the new world of work. *Human Resource Management Journal, 33*(4), 1001–1017.

Rogiers, P., & Collings, D. G. 2024. The end of jobs? Paradoxes of job deconstruction in organizations. *Academy of Management Perspectives*, 38(2), 177–196.

Rogiers, P., De Stobbeleir, K., & Viaene, S. 2021. Stretch yourself: Benefits and burdens of job crafting that goes beyond the job. *Academy of Management Discoveries*, 7(3), 367–380.

Schrage, M., Schwartz, J., Kiron, D., Jones, R., & Buckley, N. 2020. Opportunity marketplaces: Aligning workforce investment and value creation in the digital enterprise. *MIT Sloan Management Review*. https://sloanreview.mit.edu/projects/opportunity-marketplaces/.

Sessions, H., Nahrgang, J. D., Vaulont, M. J., Williams, R., & Bartels, A. L. 2021. Do the hustle! Empowerment from side-hustles and its effects on full-time work performance. *Academy of Management Journal*, 64(1), 235–264.

Stewart, A., & Stanford, J. 2017. Regulating work in the gig economy: What are the options? *The Economic and Labour Relations Review*, 28(3), 420–437.

Taylor, F. W. 1911. *The principles of scientific management.* New York: Norton.

Taylor, M., Marsh, G., Nicol, D., & Broadbent, P. 2017. *Good work: The Taylor review of modern working practices.* London: Department of Business, Energy, and Industry.

Thompson, E. P. 1967. Time, work-discipline, and industrial capitalism. *Past and Present*, 38, 56–97.

Unilever. 2023. *Future workplace.* https://www.unilever.com/planet-and-society/future-of-work/future-workplace.

Veen, A., Barratt, T., & Goods, C. 2020. Platform-capital's app-etite for control: A labor process analysis of food-delivery work in Australia. *Work, Employment & Society,* 34, 388–406.

Weil, D. 2014. *The fissured workplace: Why work became so bad for so many and what can be done to improve it.* Cambridge, MA: Harvard Business School Press.

Winsor, J. & Paik, J. H. 2024. *Open talent: Leveraging the global workforce to solve your biggest challenges.* Harvard Business Review Press.

19 Sustainable HRM – A Critical and Commons-Centric Perspective

Brian Matthews and Michael Muller-Camen

Introduction

There is growing awareness that the adoption of sustainable strategies can contribute to organisational competitive advantage (Ahmadi-Gh and Bello-Pintado, 2022) and that HRM is optimally suited to implement such strategies (Voegtlin and Greenwood, 2016). As a result, whether and how HRM as a strategic function can meet demands for more ethical decision-making and effectively address grand societal challenges such as environmental degradation, poverty and growing inequality is a major (if not yet the predominating) concern amongst current HR management and organisational researchers (Ren, Cooke, Stahl, Fan and Timming, 2023). This academic interest reflects the growing importance of sustainability within the discipline culminating with the recent new conceptualisation of Sustainable HRM (SustHRM) (Aust, Matthews and Muller-Camen, 2020). But it can also be interpreted as a past lack of reflectivity of the socio-ecological limitations of a pro-market and commodifying business model and HRM paradigm characterised by an inherent institutionalised economic and shareholder bias – a dilemma of sustainability that has still to be resolved (Kaufman, 2020). It, therefore, remains unclear how a fiscal-driven Strategic HRM (SHRM) can reassess its purpose, rethink its role, revalue stakeholders and reform practices to break free from an overtly strategic and unsustainable straitjacket (Pfeffer, 2016). As a result, there is still a lot of conflicting opinion, division, conceptual ambiguity and paradox regarding the antecedents and core components of a future SustHRM (Poon and Law, 2022).

Due to rapidly changing global circumstances and shifting consumer values and expectations, organisations and HRM have, however, increasingly limited time and leeway to develop credible and responsible answers to negative externalities (Podgorodnichenko, Edgar and McAndrew, 2020). Because of the urgency of the issue, this chapter aims to give an overview of the field, identify research gaps and provide some suggestions to drive the SustHRM debate forward.

After revisiting our past critique of the status quo (Matthews, Obereder, Aust and Müller-Camen, 2018), and positioning the debate in the context of

DOI: 10.4324/9781032625560-22

more recent developments, we discuss the SHRM–SustHRM nexus and then analyse our original conclusions from the viewpoint of a growing interest in the SDGs as a normative HRM framework. We then explore the implications of the new emerging influence of common good values (CGVs) and relational collective action approaches in management (Sarasvathy and Ramesh, 2019; Souza, 2023), before finally discussing remaining tensions and issues of SustHRM implementation. By doing so, we hope to offer innovative insights regarding the future role which HRM can play in unifying the discipline towards a sustainable agenda focused on achieving the SDGs and which more authentically reflects the original integrated Brundtland Commission sustainable development (SD) conceptualisation of transgenerational socio-ecological fairness (Hajian and Kashani, 2021). This supports our expressed hope that HRM actors would reorientate to 'critically reassess and redesign their role as mere administrators and managers of human capital towards authentic, trustful, convincing leaders and nurturers of real holistic organisational change' (Matthews et al, 2018, p. 128).

Competing Paradigms

SustHRM has been defined as 'the adoption of HRM strategies and practices that enable the achievement of financial, social and ecological goals, with an impact inside and outside the organisation and over a long-term time horizon' (Ehnert, Parsa, Roper, Wagner and Muller-Camen, 2016, p. 90). This requires a shift beyond traditional market-centric SHRM-business norms and conventions, which has proved a challenge for most organisations in a very competitive environment (Heras-Saizarbitoria, Urbieta and Boiral, 2022). The difficulty of how to balance the requirements of multiple (economic, social, ecological) stakeholders and maintain our social responsibility to future generations all within a narrow capitalist framework of maximising shareholder value is, however, not new to HRM. For example, the need to critically reflect on the sustainable compatibility and strength of the long-dominating SHRM paradigm was a core element of our earlier critical and questioning text 'Competing paradigms-status quo and alternative approaches in HRM' (Matthews, Obereder, Aust and Müller-Camen, 2018). With a specific focus on the concept of 'Green HRM' (Renwick et al., 2016), then considered a best-practice option in promoting (environmental) sustainable actions in organisations, we somewhat controversially implied that firm-centric sustainable approaches aimed at changing individual attitudes and behaviour were proving not only to be ineffective but also lacking in wider societal engagement and trans-generational commitment. A more transformative and relational approach would, therefore, be needed.

Our line of reasoning was based on the conviction that long-term organisational sustainability and social legitimacy is inherently linked with the strategic operational context (Farndale and Paauwe, 2018), but also a managerial ability to move beyond the traditional HRM-performance paradigm and the established assumption that internal stakeholders contribute most to organisational value and, therefore, need to always be prioritised (Beer, Boselie and Brewster, 2015; Reynolds, Shoss and Jundt, 2015). As an overemphasis on shareholder primacy has long been considered a barrier to more CSR and stakeholder plurality (Smith and Rönnegard, 2016), we concluded that

> the discipline of HR will need to do far more to develop employee organisational commitment, participation and organisational citizen behaviour towards a sustainable agenda and implement procedures which accommodate both internal (employees) and external stakeholder (customers, health and environmental legislators) needs.
>
> (Matthews et al, 2018, p. 128)

Recently scholars have reciprocated this critique and lack of communality and drawn attention to how power regimes of economic efficiency act to deepen social inequalities by shifting the responsibility for change to the level of the individual (Vincent, Lopes, Meliou and Özbilgin, 2024). We similarly argued that an over-psychological and individualised HRM (Kaufman, 2020) needs to repurpose itself towards the creation of more relational and empowering practices of stakeholder inclusion supported by new democratic structures of HR management and leadership (Souza, 2023). We also optimistically proclaimed that concerns of sustainability and growing pressure from internal and external stakeholders would increase awareness of the need for more stakeholder-friendly approaches (Matthews et al, 2018, p.121). However, and although the challenge of sustainable development (incorporating both non-economic concerns of social justice and climate change), has gained an unprecedented urgency in the succeeding years, the goal of a more contextual and unified SustHRM model remains as distant as ever.

Nevertheless, at the same time, three major developments centred on social equality, global governance and stakeholder democracy have introduced a new dynamic and optimism to the discussion. Firstly, an alternative SustHRM narrative has emerged (Kramar, 2022), which challenges the status quo; secondly, a normative framework of global governance, the United Nation's Sustainable Development Goals (SDGs), is in the process of being adopted by HRM (Aust, Cooke, Muller-Camen and Wood, 2024); and thirdly, a renewed ethical orientation towards CGVs has recently begun to exert its influence (Järlström et al, 2024; Lu, Zhang, Yang and Wang, 2023). At first sight, these developments (with their multidisciplinary, idiosyncratic limitations and strengths) could be seen as a source for further uncertainty and disagreement. We argue, however, that in combination there lies a multilevel potential to develop an integrative SustHRM perspective. Transforming HRM research, policy and processes demands a critical reappraisal of the utilitarian, profit-centric strategic model and a managerial openness for an alternative value-driven and more democratic and ecological SustHRM paradigm. From this socio-ecological perspective, an inherent paradox between SHRM and SustHRM becomes more apparent – which needs to be addressed.

Strategic HRM

The success of the capitalist business model is based on an understanding that economic advancement and societal progress is best achieved in a system of free-market competition and production efficiency optimised in hierarchical models of organisational control and performance (Madden, 2023). Paradoxically, despite years of global economic growth and the neo-liberal promise of prosperity and self-determination through an open-society of market-liberalisation, the world has unmistakeably experienced increased job-precarity, inequality, worker exploitation and human rights violations (Cruz-Del Rosario and Rigg, 2019). We argue that performance-orientated business models and 'hard' types of HRM strategy cannot be divorced from the economic assumptions, the (utilitarian, behavioural) theories of the firm and the profit-maximising managerial philosophies on which they are built (Riaz, Townsend and Woods, 2021), nor from the responsibility for the negative multilevel socio-economic and ecological consequences. For example, how recent economic-driven, neo-liberal policies of austerity, state pension reforms, growing energy-poverty and the deepening institutional discrimination and economic marginalisation of minorities and migrant-workers even in developed countries, points to a structural, systemic, global decline in intra-generational equality (Krause and Li, 2022). HR research has, however, mostly failed to capture how social inequalities are often (if not intentionally) mirrored in harmful HRM recruiting training and development practices (Guerci, Hauff, Panichella and Radaelli, 2023). Not all strategic scholars would agree, but from our critical perspective, SustHRM as a new paradigm can, therefore, be considered an antidote to the dominance of a pro-market, alienating and decontextualised SHRM. To date, SHRM lacks an awareness of the conflicting outcomes (Van de Voorde, Veldhoven and Veld, 2016), and 'dark side' of many high-involvement HR practices (Mariappanadar, 2020) – and, therefore, has resisted a need for change. This ideological inflexibility has a historical background and has resulted in continued ambiguity and tension regarding HR role and purpose (Cayrat and Boxall, 2023).

SHRM, which was introduced in the early 1990s (e.g., Wright and McMahan, 1992), has become well established and accepted as a model that links HRM policy and practices to organisational efficiency and capital performance outcomes (Jiang and Messersmith, 2018). Much of the model's strength and popularity is based on the assumption that organisational performance results from a strategic fit between 'best practice' HRM interventions in core areas (e.g., recruitment, training, development), and organisational goals (McClean and Collins, 2019). As a result, HRM has gained professional legitimacy for the development of high-performance-work-systems, bundles of SHRM practices aimed at increasing organisational capital outcomes by engaging and motivating employees to commit to 'shared' organisational goals (Boxall and Macky, 2009). The resulting organisational-desired positive behaviour and increases in efficiency and productivity, although good for the fiscal bottom-line, can, however, at the same time produce the side-effects of excessive overtime, work intensification and stress, all which impact negatively on overall individual health and, indirectly, societal well-being (Mariappanadar, 2020). Particularly regarding the human impact and wider negative societal or common good outcomes, more critical voices argue that

> The SHRM approach, however, is fraught with difficulties, including failing to take into account a variety of stakeholder requirements, the reality of HRM inconsistencies within organisations, the ambiguities, paradoxes and dilemmas of HRM practice and inadequate account of external influences.
>
> (Van Buren III, 2022, p 687)

For example, there is increasing evidence that SHRM underplays the significance of economic factors and externalities on management decisions and firm performance, is missing a worker perspective and has become dependent on reductionist, over-psychological explanations (Boxall, 2018; Kaufman, 2020; Paauwe and Boselie, 2005). An adherence to a firm-centric, inward focus on capital performance outcomes, therefore, lacks an awareness of the interdependent and reciprocal nature of successful business activity and the important role of external institutions (e.g., the state, trade unions, NGOs, communities), and this can be problematic when organisations are confronted with stakeholder concerns of well-being and mental health and larger questions of governance, such as how HRM can implement the SDGs (Aust et al, 2020).

Despite the present strategic asymmetry towards economic actors and outcomes, scholars have long debated the role that HRM can play in contributing to human and societal well-being and continually make creative suggestions for multilevel change (Beer, Boselie and Brewster, 2015). However, from the early days of SHRM, a fundamental difference in approach was observable that still has consequences for developing a unified SustHRM agenda. For example, the 'Harvard model' (Beer, Spector, Lawrence, Mills and Walton, 1984), took a multistakeholder approach, arguing that HRM needs to include contextual and institutional variables (difference in working conditions, voice, misalignment of perceptions), when exploring the link between organisational performance and employee well-being and engagement (Boxall, 2021). In contrast, the 'Michigan model' (Fombrun, Tichy and Devanna, 1984) adopted a much harder approach, arguing that the sole purpose of HRM is to contribute to shareholder value by establishing a 'tight fit' between HRM strategies and business goals. This is achieved through high-performance-work-systems and the development of 'best practices' in all areas of HR responsibility. It is this single-purpose model (where strategic goals and managerial decisions inform HRM practices) that has come to dominate (an increasingly unitarian) HRM over the last 30 years. As a result, a short-term, firm-centric orientation has led to a number of reductionist theoretical models, the most influential being the resource-based-view (RBV), which argues that in order to remain competitive, companies should concentrate on developing their internal strengths and protecting unique valuable, rare, inimitable, non-substitutable resources and assets while controlling for negative external threats (Barney, 1991; Barney, Ketchen and Wright, 2011). However, from the perspective of sustainability, this narrow reactive and protectionist understanding of HR purpose and strategy fails to understand the need for organisations (as embedded social actors) to build cooperative capabilities and to pro-actively interact with the external (social and natural) environment, and where long-term survival is based on an 'ability to cooperate with other companies and other stakeholders to jointly address sustainability challenges' (da Cunha Bezerra, Gohr and Morioka, 2020, p. 9).

Sustainable HRM

It is in the context of a missing societal purpose and engagement, and in response to a paradigm shift towards sustainability (Boudreau & Ramstad, 2005) within society, business and HRM, that the alternative (or more realistically, complementary) concept of SustHRM that gives more consideration to social and ecological outcomes has evolved. As a multistakeholder approach, and a counterbalance to prevailing short-term, one-dimensional mindsets, it aims to improve the quality of workers' lives and reduce the health harm of modern HRM workplace practices (Mariappanadar, 2020). SustHRM, in addition, can be differentiated from SHRM by an increased recognition of the tensions between managerial and employee goals, a focus on increasing stakeholder capabilities rather than protecting and utilising (human capital) resources and by a foundation based on ethical and not just economic considerations (Kramar, 2022). Although this perspective is slowly gaining traction, it remains far less established than SHRM (Brewster and Brookes, 2024) and is thus lacking in legitimacy and acceptance. Furthermore, as SustHRM basically grew out of the strategic perspective, much early research was still focused mainly on firm-centric concerns and how strategic HRM practices can help manage the human capital base sustainability to maintain the continued achievement of organisational goals in the future (Ehnert, 2009). SustHRM, for example, was mostly understood in terms of a defensive 'survival strategy' to secure the availability of highly-skilled talents vital for organisational competitive advantage, especially in times of growing crisis and demographic change (Ehnert and Harry, 2012, p.223). And many scholars still view SustHRM as a type of 'business sustainability' and strategic HRM agenda attempting to maintain, or better still, to increase profit margins within a new 'Green HRM' agenda of pro-environmental employee behaviour (Ren, Cooke, Stahl, Fan and Timming, 2023). However, scholars argue that a business orientation will not suffice and 'for sustainable HRM to realise this promise and to advance organisational sustainability in all of its dimensions, employee perspectives and participation are essential' (Van Buren III, 2022, p.694) – a multistakeholder approach.

The narrative has, however, not remained static and although the academic debate around SustHRM is still developing, wide-ranging and fragmented, several research trends can be observed (Macke and Genari, 2019). The first is a concern with sustainable HR leadership and the role of the HRM function in developing corporate sustainability. The second explores the relationship between ecological sustainability and organisational performance. A third, focuses on the inherent conflict between sustainability and strategic goals of profitability. And finally, and more recently, a renewed interest is emerging about issues of social responsibility and the impact on external stakeholders and the common good (Aust et al. 2020). SustHRM research has, therefore, experienced a shift from initially studying sustainable work systems and organisational practices (Gollan, 2006), towards contextual antecedents (Kramar, 2014), and external negativities (Mariappanadar, 2014), and more recently, the social dimensions and implications for broader stakeholders (Stahl, Brewster, Collings and Hajro, 2020). This development from a firm-centric 'inside-in' towards a societal 'outside-in' approach (Dyllick and Muff, 2016) was recently shown in a typography of SustHRM types (Socially Responsible HRM, Green HRM, Triple Bottom Line HRM and Common Good HRM) (Aust et al, 2020). The fourth type Common Good HRM (CGHRM) being considered the most stakeholder inclusive.

In addition to this new categorisation and characterisation, as a useful moral compass, scholars suggest that SustHRM (as an umbrella term) has certain core defining characteristics that differentiates it from SHRM (Kramar, 2022), offering some welcome SustHRM convergence. For example, a heightened awareness that the interests of shareholders and stakeholders can often be conflicting and that an inherent contradiction can exist between business and sustainable outcomes (Podgorodnichenko, Edgar and McAndrew, 2020), and between short-term and long-term organisational goals. Following this is a recognition that HR can have a 'dark side' and decisions and practices can have both a positive and negative impact on internal and external stakeholders, something that is often missing in the unitarist SHRM perspective with a narrow focus on positive employee behaviour and firm performance (Van Buren III, 2022). A future ethically concerned SustHRM, in contrast, would recognise and respect tensions, accommodate different stakeholder perceptions and needs, be committed to the development of employee capabilities and creating opportunities for participation and view human, social and environmental well-being as a determinant factor for organisational legitimacy and commercial success (Kramar, 2022). However, although a stronger conceptual framework is now beginning to emerge, SustHRM as a whole still remains fragmented and lacks an all-comprehensive theory (Chams, and García-Blandón, 2019), which can convince managers to make a paradigm change. At the same time, the SDGs could provide a badly needed unifying frame of reference and catalyst (Aust, Cooke, Muller-Camen and Wood 2024).

SDGs – Institutional Barriers

A growing literature supports the SDGs as a normative business framework of global development that can help bridge the gap between theory (intent) and practice (action) (Baldassari, Muller-Camen and Aust, 2024; Pizzi, Caputo, Corvino and Venturelli, 2020). In reality, despite the SDGs' aim to provide prosperity and peace for both people and the planet, across the globe and for our and future generations, the economic and human cost and suffering caused by the impact of environmental destruction and exploitive economic practices has actually deepened and has been also over-proportionally paid for by the poor, the marginalised and people in developing and emerging economies (Khan, Parvaiz, Tohirovich, Iqbal and Junghan, 2022). Progress has, therefore, been relatively slow regarding both impact and increased business social and ecological responsibility, and uncertainty remains about the strategic role of businesses in reaching the SDGs (Mio, Panfilo and Blundo, 2020). The question thus arises about this continued gap between theory and practice, about board-level commitment to a transformation of governance and, therefore, the utility of the SDGs as a benchmark for achieving the goal of SustHRM, which 'takes into account long-term influences such as climate change, biodiversity, urbanization and workforce demographics rather than simply quarterly returns and market-driven, short-term financial issues' (Aust et al, 2020, p2). And indeed, scholars have highlighted several weaknesses of the SDGs as a tool for socio-ecological transformation, such a failure to recognize the systemic cause of inequality and structural barriers to progress inherent in the neo-liberal capitalist model. A closer examination of the building blocks of the SDGs shows, for example, that the (pro-economic) definition of sustainability used diverges considerably from the traditional, more societal understanding of sustainable development (SD) based on social equality. In addition, questions regarding stakeholder inclusion and agency, the role of regulatory bodies and the obligations of businesses are inadequately answered (Spangenberg, 2017). Despite these reservations, we argue, however, that (at the level of the organisation) the problem is not the SDGs per se, but rather the dominance of a neo-liberal business ideology from which SHRM derives its power and which continues to influence the SustHRM debate in a number of counterproductive ways. As a result, the aim of developing HRM sustainably has long faced a range of external barriers (gaining institutional funding, finding strategic partners), organisational problems (short-term planning, structural rigidity) and strategic difficulties (lack of board support, strategic power and alignment) (Russ-Eft, 2014) – all which remain relevant. Moreover, recently Brewster and Brookes (2024) have raised doubts that HRM will reach the goals of the SDGs, and certainly within the given timeframe to 2030. But they also argue that the SDGs have some value in reminding HRM managers of the need to rethink their role and purpose in the context of increasing precarity, inequality and environmental destruction. We also agree that the SDGs should be considered a compass for sustainable governance or at best, a 'litmus test' of stakeholder inclusion, which needs to be accompanied by an awareness of the limitations of the strategic economic model and a critical reassessment of self-centred business practices and myopic understandings of HRM purpose. For example, adding CGVs would be one way to address institutional barriers and to improve the humanistic and ethical credentials and socio-ecological authenticity of SustHRM (Järlström, Saru, Viitasaari and Akrivou, 2024).

Sustainable HRM and Common Good Values

The recent tendency to equate the aim of Sustainability and SustHRM with the adoption of the SDGs as an 'all-encompassing' strategic solution to the dilemma of business-societal purpose has generated some critique both with regard to conceptual validity and operational practicality (Brewster and Brookes, 2024). Furthermore, and similar to the historical development of SHRM and the eclipse of more humanistic approaches, we argue that there is a danger that a SustHRM strategy, void of the necessary critical lens and which lacks a strong foundation embedded in CGVs, will meet the same fate of economic appropriation (Ritala, Albareda and Bocken, 2021) as earlier SustHRM models. Although we agree that companies have to meet short-term targets of profitability and maintain strategic command, we argue from a critical perspective that the continued dominance of shareholder primacy and the use of management regimes of control, mirrored in standardised SHRM systems of high-performance, work intensification and flexibilisation (Neirotti, 2020) have resulted in repressive workplace cultures (Laaser, 2016), and a loss of autonomy, trust and motivation (Ho and Kuvaas, 2020), which all combine to make acceptance and the shift to sustainability an even bigger challenge.

On the other hand, by drawing on established common good theory from business ethics (Frémeaux and Michelson, 2017) and heterodox economics (Ostrom, 1990), and redefining purpose through CGVs such as solidarity, trust, dignity, respect, subsidiarity and reciprocity, organisations can become a 'generator of trust' (Hollensbe, Wookey, Hickey, George, Nichols, 2014, p. 1227), influence behaviour and make gains in sustainability, which 'value-free' strategic frameworks have failed to achieve. This return to morals and a 'language of the commons' (Meyer and Hudon, 2019) means revaluing and, when possible, giving priority to collective forms of organising, distribution and ownership (Albareda and Sison, 2020). This alternative worldview has implications for addressing a range of HR-related everyday challenges. If we take, for example, the long and on-going dilemma of inclusion and diversity, Frémeaux (2020), follows Oswick and Noon's (2014) suggestion, 'Rather than seeing the rationales for equality, diversity and inclusion as mutually exclusive, it could be more constructive to focus upon the points of commonality, overlap and compatibility' (p.36), and implies that a common good paradigm could offer a more effective integrative method than previous segregated models that focus on group membership, economic situation or individual contexts.

From a common good perspective, instead of utilising stakeholders as a means to a (purely business) end, organisational resources are used to create value for wider society (including capital gains that can finance pay, job creation and reinvestments). However, importantly, purpose drives productivity and profits rather than profits determining (business) purpose. This is the optimistic (critical–pragmatic) assumption of the values-based emerging CGHRM model (Aust et al, 2020), which challenges the positivist managerial ideology behind strategic HRM (Omidi, Dal Zotto and Gandini, 2023). The CGHRM model goes beyond a traditional triple bottom line and resource-based approaches with the ultimate aim of individual human dignity and collective economic, social and ecological flourishing (***eudaimonia***). In culmination, CGHRM proposes the alternative idea that, 1) organisational purpose needs to reflect an 'outside-in' commitment to contributing to the common good, 2) that business decisions need to be value-driven and be sensitive to wider social and ecological impact, 3) that HR strategies and practices should be stakeholder-inclusive, human-centric, focused on workplace democracy and 4) aimed at reducing employee harm while enhancing human capabilities to flourish (Aust et al, 2020). Considering these points and with advertence to HR literature on the continued importance of voice and positive employment relations (Bratton and Paulet, 2022), we newly define CGHRM as

> Common-Good Human Resource Management (CGHRM) is a critical–pragmatic and relational multistakeholder approach to work and employment relations, characterized by an outside-in perspective that emphasizes the importance of common good values and the societal purpose of Human Resource Management (HRM) in enabling maximum stakeholder empowerment. This approach aims to enhance an organisation's socio-ecological impact by fostering and encouraging individual and collective engagement and action.

The CGHRM communal approach that 'encourages organisations to move beyond a focus on individual goals to give higher importance to collective interests' (Cooke, Dickmann and Parry, 2022. p.11) may seem somewhat utopian within an individualistic and competitive market-based system and SHRM. However, regarding the limitations of performative HRM models to make sustainable progress, models of collective action that provide stakeholders with maximal agency and opportunities for co-creation and self-organisation might be better suited to creating long-term sustainable solutions, especially in challenging and uncertain times and situations of limited and depleting common resources (Sarasvathy and Ramesh, 2019). In addition, scholars have recently indicated that CGHRM (apart from the moral obligation) could have long-term consequences for organisational success. For example, by enhancing employee well-being, engagement and performance

(Lu, Zhang, Yang and Wang, 2023), by diminishing the harmful effects of rapid workplace digitalisation (Dabić, Maley, Švarc and Poček, 2023), or by encouraging ethical and organisational citizenship employee behaviours (Pham, Jabbour, Pereira, Usman, Ali and Vo-Thanh, 2023). As a result, we argue that CGHRM as a new orientation towards common good purpose and societal benefit could be a core factor in helping organisations maintain legitimacy and worker motivation, to commit to more stakeholder plurality in HRM and to realise the long-term benefit of implementing the SDGs (Kramar, 2022).

At the same time, due to its alternative nature, a lack of empirical data regarding antecedents, and a developed and proven system of measurement, CGHRM faces difficulties of validation and implementation. Therefore, we argue that CGHRM (at least in the meantime) needs a strong complementary framework of governance such as the SDGs, which it, in return, can enrich with an explicit commitment to moral values and a socio-ontological foundation.

Concluding Discussion

Even though HRM is ideally situated to address growing shareholder–stakeholder tensions within organisations caused by the challenge of sustainability, a continued allegiance to strategic-capital performance business models acts as a hurdle (e.g., to implementing the SDGs) that has proved difficult to straddle. Although in recent years a new SustHRM perspective has developed and a range of different types categorised, a universally accepted and effective SustHRM framework and explication remains elusive. Therefore, we provide a new CGHRM definition based on pro-societal awareness, stakeholder empowerment, positive employee relationships and coordinated collective action.

Furthermore, despite the initial success of the SDGs as a compass for sustainable governance, a core issue of contention that remains is whether and how HRM can redesign purpose, policy and practices to meet growing employee demands for increased voice and recognition and also promote socio-ecological flourishing within the institutional constraints of normative understandings of HRM's role as a strategic managerial partner. To break this impasse, in this chapter we argue that a sustainable progress requires a leap of faith and a new openness regarding the opportunities that an alternative purpose-driven and socially-engaged HRM mindset can create to help grow both profits and people. For example, how the adoption of a critical-reflective 'outside-in' and a return to CGVs (which inevitably means increasing workplace democracy and stakeholder empowerment), rather than acting to weaken the business legitimacy and capabilities of HRM can, in fact, act as a motor for enduring sustainable change and usher in the constructive (social and environmental sensitive) renewal of an ideologically fragmented and strategically isolated HRM.

References

Albareda, L., & Sison, A. J. G. (2020). Commons organizing: Embedding common good and institutions for collective action. Insights from ethics and economics. *Journal of Business Ethics, 166*(4), 727–743.

Ahmadi-Gh, Z., & Bello-Pintado, A. (2022). Why is manufacturing not more sustainable? The effects of different sustainability practices on sustainability outcomes and competitive advantage. *Journal of Cleaner Production, 337*, 130392.

Aust, I., Cooke, F. L., Muller-Camen, M., & Wood, G. (2024), Achieving sustainable development goals through common-good HRM: Context, approach and practice *German Journal of Human Resource Management, 38*(2), 93–110.

Aust, I., Matthews, B., & Muller-Camen, M. (2020). Common good HRM: A paradigm shift in sustainable HRM?. *Human Resource Management Review, 30*(3), 100705.

Baldassari, P., Muller-Camen, M., & Aust, I. (2024). The Sustainable HRM-SDG nexus: Contributions to global sustainable development. In K. Lueg & S. Jebsen (Eds.). *Social sustainability and good work in organizations* (pp. 173–198). Routledge.

Barney, J. (1991). Firm resources and sustained competitive advantage. *Journal of Management, 17*(1), 99–120.

Barney, J. B., Ketchen Jr, D. J., & Wright, M. (2011). The future of resource-based theory: revitalization or decline? *Journal of Management, 37*(5), 1299–1315.

Beer, M., Boselie, P., & Brewster, C. (2015). Back to the future: Implications for the field of HRM of the multi-stakeholder perspective proposed 30 years ago. *Human Resource Management, 54*, 427–438.

Beer, M., Spector, B., Lawrence, P. R., Mills, D. Q., & Walton, R. E. (1984). *Managing human assets.* Simon and Schuster.

Boudreau, J. W., & Ramstad, P. M. (2005). Talentship, talent segmentation, and sustainability: A new HR decision science paradigm for a new strategy definition. *Human Resource Management, 44*(2), 129–136.

Boxall, P. (2018). The development of strategic HRM: Reflections on a 30-year journey. *Labour & Industry, 28*(1), 21–30.

Boxall, P. (2021). Studying mutuality and perversity in the impacts of human resource management on societal well-being: Advancing a pluralist agenda. *Human Resource Management Journal, 31*(4), 834–846.

Boxall, P., & Macky, K. (2009). Research and theory on high-performance work systems: progressing the high-involvement stream. *Human Resource Management Journal, 19*(1), 3–23.

Bratton, A., & Paulet, R. (2022). Sustainable human resource management and organisational sustainability. In P. Holland, T. Bartra, T. Garavan, and K. Grant (Eds.), *The Emerald handbook of work, workplaces and disruptive issues in HRM* (pp. 149–169). Emerald Publishing Limited.

Brewster, C., & Brookes, M. (2024). Sustainable development goals and new approaches to HRM: Why HRM specialists will not reach the sustainable development goals and why it matters. *German Journal of Human Resource Management, 38*(2), 183–201.

Cayrat, C., & Boxall, P. (2023). The roles of the HR function: A systematic review of tensions, continuity, and change. *Human Resource Management Review, 33*, 100984.

Chams, N., & García-Blandón, J. (2019) On the importance of sustainable human resource management for the adoption of sustainable development goals. *Resources, Conservation and Recycling, 141*, 109–122

Cooke, F. L., Dickmann, M., & Parry, E. (2022). Building sustainable societies through human-centred human resource management: Emerging issues and research opportunities. *The International Journal of Human Resource Management, 33*(1), 1–15.

Cruz-Del Rosario, T., & Rigg, J. (2019). Living in an age of precarity in 21st century Asia. *Journal of Contemporary Asia, 49*(4), 517–527.

da Cunha Bezerra, M. C., Gohr, C. F., & Morioka, S. N. (2020). Organizational capabilities towards corporate sustainability benefits: A systematic literature review and an integrative framework proposal. *Journal of Cleaner Production, 247*, 119114.

Dabić, M., Maley, J. F., Švarc, J., & Poček, J. (2023). Future of digital work: Challenges for sustainable human resources management. *Journal of Innovation & Knowledge, 8*(2), 100353.

Dyllick, T., & Muff, K. (2016). Clarifying the meaning of sustainable business: Introducing a typology from business-as-usual to true business sustainability. *Organization & Environment, 29*(2), 156–174.

Ehnert, I. (2009). Sustainability and human resource management: Reasoning and applications on corporate websites. *European Journal of International Management, 3*(4), 419–438.

Ehnert, I., & Harry, W. (2012). Recent developments and future prospects on sustainable human resource management: Introduction to the special issue. *Management Revue, 23*, 221–238.

Ehnert, I., Parsa, S., Roper, I., Wagner, M., & Muller-Camen, M. (2016). Reporting on sustainability and HRM: A comparative study of sustainability reporting practices by the world's largest companies. *The International Journal of Human Resource Management, 27*(1), 88–108.

Farndale, E., & Paauwe, J. (2018). SHRM and context: Why firms want to be as different as legitimately possible. *Journal of Organizational Effectiveness: People and Performance, 5*(3), 202–210.

Fombrun, C. J., Tichy, N. M., & Devanna, M. A. (1984). *Strategic human resource management*. Wiley.

Frémeaux, S. (2020). A common good perspective on diversity. *Business Ethics Quarterly, 30*(2), 200–228.

Frémeaux, S., & Michelson, G. (2017). The common good of the firm and humanistic management: Conscious capitalism and economy of communion. *Journal of Business Ethics, 145*, 701–709.

Gollan, P. J. (2006). Sustainable strategies towards human resources: A way forward. In D. Marinova, D. Annandale, J. Phillimore (Eds.), *International handbook on environmental technology management* (pp. 104–118). Edward Elgar.

Guerci, M., Hauff, S., Panichella, N., & Radaelli, G. (2023). Sustainable HRM and class-based inequality. *Personnel Review, 52*(5), 1597–1613.

Hajian, M., & Kashani, S. J. (2021). Evolution of the concept of sustainability. From Brundtland Report to sustainable development goals. In C. M. Hussain & J. F. Velasco-Muñoz (Eds.), *Sustainable resource management* (pp. 1–24). Elsevier.

Heras-Saizarbitoria, I., Urbieta, L., & Boiral, O. (2022). Organizations' engagement with sustainable development goals: From cherry-picking to SDG-washing? *Corporate Social Responsibility and Environmental Management, 29*(2), 316–328.

Ho, H., & Kuvaas, B. (2020). Human resource management systems, employee well-being, and firm performance from the mutual gains and critical perspectives: The well-being paradox. *Human Resource Management*, *59*(3), 235–253.

Hollensbe, E., Wookey, C., Hickey, L., George, G., & Nichols, C. V. (2014). Organizations with purpose. *Academy of Management Journal*, *57*(5), 1227–1234.

Järlström, M., Saru, E., Viitasaari, M., & Akrivou, K. (2024). Integrating 'common good' authenticity for sustainable human resource management reporting. *German Journal of Human Resource Management*, *38*(2), 159–182.

Jiang, K., & Messersmith, J. (2018). On the shoulders of giants: A meta-review of strategic human resource management. *The International Journal of Human Resource Management*, *29*(1), 6–33.

Kaufman, B. E. (2020). The real problem: The deadly combination of psychologisation, scientism, and normative promotionalism takes strategic human resource management down a 30-year dead end. *Human Resource Management Journal*, *30*(1), 49–72.

Khan, M., Parvaiz, G. S., Tohirovich Dedahanov, A., Iqbal, M., & Junghan, B. (2022). Research trends in humanitarian logistics and sustainable development: A bibliometric analysis. *Cogent Business & Management*, *9*(1), 2143071.

Kramar, R. (2014). Beyond strategic human resource management: Is sustainable human resource management the next approach? *The International Journal of Human Resource Management*, *25*(8), 1069–1089.

Kramar, R. (2022). Sustainable human resource management: Six defining characteristics. *Asia Pacific Journal of Human Resources*, *60*(1), 146–170.

Krause, E. L., & Li, Y. (2022). Out of place: Everyday forms of marginalization, racism, and resistance among Chinese migrants in Italy. *Journal of Ethnic and Migration Studies*, *48*(9), 2037–2055.

Laaser, K. (2016). 'If you are having a go at me, I am going to have a go at you': The changing nature of social relationships of bank work under performance management. *Work, Employment and Society*, *30*(6), 1000–1016.

Lu, Y., Zhang, M. M., Yang, M. M., & Wang, Y. (2023). Sustainable human resource management practices, employee resilience, and employee outcomes: Toward common good values. *Human Resource Management*, *62*(3), 331–353.

Macke, J., & Genari, D. (2019). Systematic literature review on sustainable human resource management. *Journal of Cleaner Production*, *208*, 806–815.

Madden, B. J. (2023). Understanding the benefits of capitalism through the lens of a new theory of the firm. *Capitalism & Society*, *7*(1).

Mariappanadar, S. (2014). Stakeholder harm index: A framework to review work intensification from the critical HRM perspective. *Human Resource Management Review*, *24*(4), 313–329.

Mariappanadar, S. (2020). Do HRM systems impose restrictions on employee quality of life? Evidence from a sustainable HRM perspective. *Journal of Business Research*, *118*, 38–48.

Matthews, B., Obereder, L., Aust, I., & Müller-Camen, M. (2018). Competing paradigms: Status quo and alternative approaches in HRM. In D. Renwick (Ed.), *Contemporary developments in Green human resource management research* (pp. 116–134). Routledge.

Meyer, C., & Hudon, M. (2019). Money and the commons: An investigation of complementary currencies and their ethical implications. *Journal of Business Ethics*, *160*, 277–292.

McClean, E., & Collins, C. J. (2019). Expanding the concept of fit in strategic human resource management: An examination of the relationship between human resource practices and charismatic leadership on organizational outcomes. *Human Resource Management*, *58*(2), 187–202.

Mio, C., Panfilo, S., & Blundo, B. (2020). Sustainable development goals and the strategic role of business: A systematic literature review. *Business Strategy and the Environment*, *29*(8), 3220–3245.

Neirotti, P. (2020). Work intensification and employee involvement in lean production: New light on a classic dilemma. *The International Journal of Human Resource Management*, *31*(15), 1958–1983.

Omidi, A., Dal Zotto, C., & Gandini, A. (2023). Labor process theory and critical HRM: A systematic review and agenda for future research. *European Management Journal*, *41*(6), 899–913.

Ostrom, E. (1990). *Governing the commons: The evolution of institutions for collective action*. Cambridge University Press.

Oswick, C., & Noon, M. (2014). Discourses of diversity, equality and inclusion: Trenchant formulations or transient fashions? *British Journal of Management*, *25*(1), 23–39.

Paauwe, J., & Boselie, P. (2005). HRM and performance: What next? *Human Resource Management Journal*, *15*(4), 68–83.

Pfeffer, J. (2016). Why the assholes are winning: Money trumps all. *Journal of Management Studies*, *53*(4), 663–669.

Pham, N. T., Jabbour, C. J. C., Pereira, V., Usman, M., Ali, M., & Vo-Thanh, T. (2023). Common good human resource management, ethical employee behaviors, and organizational citizenship behaviors toward the individual. *Human Resource Management Journal*, *33*(4), 977–1000.

Pizzi, S., Caputo, A., Corvino, A., & Venturelli, A. (2020). Management research and the UN sustainable development goals (SDGs): A bibliometric investigation and systematic review. *Journal of Cleaner Production*, *276*, 124033.

Podgorodnichenko, N., Edgar, F., & McAndrew, I. (2020). The role of HRM in developing sustainable organizations: Contemporary challenges and contradictions. *Human Resource Management Review*, *30*(3), 100685.

Poon, T. S. C., & Law, K. K. (2022). Sustainable HRM: An extension of the paradox perspective. *Human Resource Management Review*, *32*(2), 100818.

Ren, S., Cooke, F. L., Stahl, G. K., Fan, D., & Timming, A. R. (2023). Advancing the sustainability agenda through strategic human resource management: Insights and suggestions for future research. *Human Resource Management*, *62*(3), 251–265.

Renwick, D. W., Jabbour, C. J., Muller-Camen, M., Redman, T., & Wilkinson, A. (2016). Contemporary developments in Green (environmental) HRM scholarship. *The International Journal of Human Resource Management*, *27*(2), 114–128.

Reynolds, C. A., Shoss, M. K., & Jundt, D. K. (2015). In the eye of the beholder: A multi-stakeholder perspective of organizational citizenship and counterproductive work behaviors. *Human Resource Management Review*, *25*(1), 80–93.

Riaz, S., Townsend, K., & Woods, P. (2021). Understanding HRM philosophy for HPWS and employees' perceptions. *Personnel Review*, *50*(3), 812–828.

Ritala, P., Albareda, L., & Bocken, N. (2021). Value creation and appropriation in economic, social, and environmental domains: Recognizing and resolving the institutionalized asymmetries. *Journal of Cleaner Production*, *290*, 125796.

Russ-Eft, D. F. (2014). Human resource development, evaluation, and sustainability: What are the relationships? *Human Resource Development International, 17*(5), 545–559.

Sarasvathy, S. D., & Ramesh, A. (2019). An effectual model of collective action for addressing sustainability challenges. *Academy of Management Perspectives, 33*(4), 405–424.

Spangenberg, J. H. (2017). Hot air or comprehensive progress? A critical assessment of the SDGs. *Sustainable Development, 25*(4), 311–321.

Stahl, G. K., Brewster, C. J., Collings, D. G., & Hajro, A. (2020). Enhancing the role of human resource management in corporate sustainability and social responsibility: A multi-stakeholder, multidimensional approach to HRM. *Human Resource Management Review, 30*(3), 100708.

Smith, N. C., & Rönnegard, D. (2016). Shareholder primacy, corporate social responsibility, and the role of business schools. *Journal of Business Ethics, 134*(3), 463–478.

Souza, R. (2023). Beyond the individualised organisation: The role of HRM in the (non) emergence of organisational and leadership practices for impact. *Scandinavian Journal of Management, 39*(4), 101300.

Van Buren III, H. J. (2022). The value of including employees: A pluralist perspective on sustainable HRM. *Employee Relations, 44*(3), 686–701.

Van de Voorde, K., Veldhoven, M. V., & Veld, M. (2016). Connecting empowerment focused HRM and labour productivity to work engagement: The mediating role of job demands and resources. *Human Resource Management Journal, 26*(2), 192–210.

Vincent, S., Lopes, A., Meliou, E., & Özbilgin, M. (2024). Relational responsibilisation and diversity management in the 21st century: The case for reframing equality regulation. *Work, Employment and Society, 38*(6), 1549–1568.

Voegtlin, C., & Greenwood, M. (2016). Corporate social responsibility and human resource management: A systematic review and conceptual analysis. *Human Resource Management Review, 26*(3), 181–197.

Wright, P. M., & McMahan, G. C. (1992). Theoretical perspectives for strategic human resource management. *Journal of Management, 18*(2), 295–320.

20 Worker Well-Being in the Context of Human Resource Management

Karina Van De Voorde, Steven Kilroy and Riccardo Peccei

Introduction

From its inception, the strategic Human Resource Management (HRM) field has emphasised the importance of aligning worker interests with managerial interests in HRM by prioritising individual well-being and organisational effectiveness (Beer et al., 1984). The most extensive stream of strategic HRM research, however, centres on the effect of HR systems on organisational performance. This includes exploring worker well-being as a key mechanism that may help to explain this positive relationship. Additionally, there has also been a rapidly growing stream of employee-centred HRM research, exploring the effect that HR systems have on various dimensions of worker well-being as a critical outcome in its own right (Peccei & Van De Voorde, 2019a).

Organisations are currently facing mounting pressures from regulatory bodies and social stakeholders to strongly govern their social impact, including their impact on the health and well-being of their workforce (Corporate Sustainability Reporting Directive, n.d.; Holmes et al., 2022). Especially in the midst of a dynamic and disruptive business environment, this is an increasingly challenging but crucial endeavour (Collings et al., 2021). Focusing solely on meeting financial goals can have detrimental effects on individuals and society, such as reduced life satisfaction, impoverished worker health and higher social welfare expenses. However, investing in progressive HRM may increase worker well-being, but usually, this can come with financial costs. Therefore, it is important, relevant and timely to provide an overview of our understanding of worker well-being in the context of HRM.

This chapter aims to critically examine the extant research on worker well-being in the context of HRM. To begin with, we will define worker well-being. In this regard, we will link it to the broader discussion of hedonic and eudaimonic well-being while elucidating the aspects of well-being at work that are of particular interest from a managerial perspective. We then set out how HRM can influence worker well-being by qualitatively reviewing the evolution of employee-centred HRM research. The rest of the chapter will then focus on four contemporary developments that aim to provide a more nuanced understanding of worker well-being in the context of HRM: the exploration of

DOI: 10.4324/9781032625560-23

trade-offs between different aspects of employee well-being, curvilinear HRM effects, the role of context in the HRM-well-being link and examining HRM interventions to enhance workers' well-being to decipher the benefits involved.

Worker Well-Being

Broadly speaking, well-being at work refers to the overall quality of a worker's experience and functioning in the workplace (Warr 1987). Looking across the management, economics, philosophy, applied psychology and occupational health psychology literature, various concepts have been proposed to describe the experiences and functioning of employees at work; including job satisfaction, perceived meaningfulness at work, quality of social functioning and absence of burnout symptoms. In addition, different taxonomies have been developed to classify worker well-being concepts (e.g., Taris & Schaufeli, 2015). In this regard, we focus on three main distinctions commonly identified in the HRM literature (Grant et al., 2007; Van De Voorde et al., 2012).

1. The first dimension of well-being at work is psychological well-being, which is centred around an individual's subjective experiences at work and comprises two aspects – hedonic and eudaimonic (Ryan & Deci, 2001). The hedonic or happiness component relates to an individual's experience of pleasure at work. It includes overall job satisfaction, as well as positive and negative work-related affect. On the other hand, the eudaimonic aspect focuses on human fulfilment and how individuals realise their potential at work, including concepts like work engagement and finding meaning in their work.
2. The second dimension is concerned with health at work and focuses on both physiological and psychological aspects (Danna & Griffin, 1999). Psychological aspects refer to subjective experiences of bodily health, such as job-related anxiety, stress, burnout and exhaustion. On the other hand, physiological aspects concern objective measures of bodily health, including occupational-related cardiovascular diseases and work-related sleeping problems, backache and headaches, etc.
3. The third dimension is relationship well-being. While psychological and health-related well-being are centred around the individual, relationship well-being is centred around relationships and the quality of interactions among employees (such as cooperation) or between employees and their supervisor or the organisation they work for (such as organisational trust and organisational support).

Research on strategic HRM has primarily focused on hedonic or relationship well-being (Peccei & Van De Voorde 2019b). However, it is equally important to consider work-related eudaimonic and health-related well-being as outcomes of HRM. This is apposite because of potential trade-offs that can emerge between different types of worker well-being (Grant et al., 2007) invoked by HRM, which we will discuss later in this chapter. Extensive evidence has shown that an individual's well-being at work is linked to their overall satisfaction with life and general health (e.g., Cole et al., 2012; Erdogan et al., 2012; Faragher et al., 2005). Therefore, identifying initiatives that can help workers to maintain and improve their well-being at work helps them lead a better life. It also improves the performance of organisations, including their financial performance and social legitimacy, and contributes to societal economic and social development.

A focus on the well-being of workers is becoming increasingly important in the field of HRM. Many top executives of corporations in the United States have recognised that companies should no longer solely focus on the interests of shareholders but also invest in their employees (Gelles & Yaffe-Bellany, 2019). Similarly, Chief HR officers from international companies headquartered in Europe have emphasised the important transition to creating value for multiple stakeholders, including workers, rather than just focusing on profits (Neicu et al., 2023). Organisations are also facing increasing pressures from regulatory and social stakeholders to rethink their business practices to ensure economic viability and promote positive worker well-being and health (e.g., Corporate Sustainability Reporting Directive, n.d.; United Nations Sustainable Goal #8; Holmes et al., 2022). In the next section, we will explore the academic literature in the strategic HRM field pertaining to managing employee well-being in the workplace.

The Impact of HRM on Worker Well-Being

Although the Harvard model by Beer et al. (1984) long ago emphasised the importance of considering the interests of various stakeholders, including managers and employees, most HRM research has focused on the financial benefits of implementing coherent and interconnected sets of HR practices (i.e., HR systems) designed to achieve high-performance, high-commitment or high-involvement. In particular, these studies empirically explored the performance effects of systems of HR practices, such as sophisticated recruitment and selection processes, comprehensive training, career development and promotion opportunities, systematic performance management, competitive compensation and benefits, job security guarantees, welfare practices, flexible job design, extensive employee involvement, participation and information sharing. Since 2000, research has shifted focus to include the employee's perspective, exploring the impact of HR systems on employee-centred outcomes, such as worker well-being (Peccei & Van De Voorde, 2019a). This stream of research has been informed by seminal work in the UK (Guest, 1999; Peccei, 2004; Ramsay et al., 2000), Canada (Godard, 2001) and the USA (Appelbaum et al., 2000).

Early Employee-Centred HRM Research

In a study titled 'The Workers Verdict of HRM', Guest (1999) investigated the impact of high-commitment HR practices on the well-being of workers in the UK. The study found that workers who experienced a higher number of high-commitment HR practices reported higher levels of hedonic and relationship well-being, such as job satisfaction, trust in management and organisational fairness. However, when it came to employee health, specifically feelings of being under excessive pressure at work, the results were more equivocal. Workers who reported very few high-commitment HR practices and those who reported experiencing many of these practices both reported experiencing excessive pressures at work. This result suggested the possibility of a curvilinear relationship between high-commitment HR systems and employee health, whereby the impact of HR practices depended on their levels.

In their study using a national representative matched employer–employee dataset, the British Workforce Employee Relations Survey (WERS) from 1998, Ramsay and colleagues (2000) found that high-performance work systems (HPWS) have a positive impact on pay satisfaction, management relations and organisational and financial performance. However, they also found that these systems are linked to higher levels of job strain among employees. Also, using the British WERS (1998) data, Peccei (2004) carried out a study to explore the impact of 33 HR practices on employee well-being (composed of job satisfaction and job stress), and the findings essentially extended those of Ramsay et al. (2000). Indeed, it was concluded that workplaces with more full-time permanent employees and where employees do not have to work long hours or overtime are more likely to have high levels of job satisfaction combined with low levels of work stress. Such workplaces have jobs that are loosely structured and defined but not pressurised and a core focus is placed on multiskilling. In addition, they offer comparatively high rates of pay, a fair degree of internal dispersion in pay, additional benefits, extensive management communication and a range of family-friendly and work-life balance policies. Importantly, Ramsay et al (2000) concluded that the HR practices that maximise employee well-being are not necessarily the same as those that make up HPWS.

Godard (2001) conducted a telephone survey among Canadian workers to assess the effect of alternative work practices (such as employee participation, group-based compensation and work design) linked with the high-performance model of HRM on outcomes. He found that moderate levels of adopting these alternative work practices resulted in increased job satisfaction. However, higher levels of adoption were associated with negative outcomes. Furthermore, such alternative work practices were also linked with more stressful work.

Finally, Appelbaum et al. (2000) conducted a study to investigate the influence of HPWS on employees in 40 manufacturing facilities across the United States. The results indicated that manufacturing plants that implemented HPWS tended to have better operational and financial performance. Furthermore, these practices also contributed to increased trust in management and job satisfaction among employees. Interestingly, the study found that HPWS did not have any negative effects on workers' stress levels. However, employees who reported having more opportunities to participate in decision-making indicated high levels of perceived workload.

In summary, the early studies on the effects of HRM on worker well-being have shown that various (sets) of HR practices have an impact on dimensions of employee well-being. The findings were somewhat inconsistent but generally supported the idea that certain sets of HR practices enhance aspects of psychological (hedonic) and relationship well-being but seem to impair health-related well-being. These findings, along with previous critical management scholarship in the area (e.g., Keenoy, 1990; Legge, 1995, 1998), sparked a lively debate about the impact of HRM on firms and on workers reflected in two perspectives on these relationships. The mutual gains or optimistic perspective suggests that both organisations and workers benefit from HRM, creating a win-win situation for both parties. Rooted in the behavioural perspective on HRM, this mainstream perspective argues that HR practices contribute positively to organisational performance via positive worker outcomes such as employee well-being. On the other hand, the conflicting outcomes or pessimistic perspective suggests that HR practices that maximise organisational performance do so at the expense of individual worker well-being, creating a win-lose situation. Drawing on the labour process theory, the adoption of sophisticated HR practices is believed to increase work effort and higher output expectations, thereby negatively impacting workers' well-being. Reviewing the research on the impact of HRM on employee well-being, as well as organisational performance, Van De Voorde et al. (2012) and Peccei and Van De Voorde (2019) concluded that HRM positively impacts psychological and relationship well-being. While the number of studies focusing on health well-being is limited, the reviews of the empirical articles tend to support a negative effect of HRM on health well-being, i.e., they have deleterious effects.

Studies of the Effects of HRM on Worker Well-Being

To better understand the relationship between HRM and worker well-being, we will review some of the salient empirical research that explores this link. Before that, we will briefly discuss the conceptual mechanisms through which HR systems affect well-being at work and explain these mechanisms based on key theoretical perspectives that have been integrated into HRM research, including social exchange theory (SET) (Blau, 1964), the Job Demands-Resources model (JD-R) (Demerouti et al., 2001), Conservation of Resources theory (COR) (Hobfoll, 1989), Self-Determination Theory (SDT) (Deci & Ryan, 2000T) and attribution theory (e.g., Kelley, 1967). In general, we propose two counteracting pathways: (a) HR systems may help to make the organisation and work be perceived as more resourceful and serving employee interests, and (b) HR systems may help to make the organisation and work be perceived as more exploitative and demanding.

Following the SET, HR systems signal organisations' commitment and support to its employees and provides them with valued resources and rewards at work, thereby enhancing their well-being at work (e.g., job satisfaction, positive affect, etc.). The JD-R theory postulates that job resources that are shaped by HR systems have a positive influence on worker well-being, such as work engagement. The COR theory also recognises that work-related resources, such as those provided through HR systems, help workers deal with stressful situations, thus positively impacting their health, for example, mitigating burnout. In addition, following the SDT theory, HR systems can foster psychological well-being by satisfying workers' basic needs, i.e., needs for autonomy, competence and meaningfulness. Finally, based on attribution theory, when employees perceive that management has designed the HR system to enhance their well-being, it does positively have an impact on their well-being. Following the JD-R theory, HR systems can also result in increased job demands, thereby negatively impacting workers' well-being at work, such as increasing their levels of burnout. Along similar lines, following the COR theory, HR systems may activate resource losses and thereby reduce workers' well-being. The SDT also helps to explain the potential negative effect of HR systems on worker well-being. Some HR systems have the ability to stimulate extrinsic motivation, which might result in impaired health at work, such as feelings of burnout. Lastly, in accordance with attribution theory, when employees believe that the HR system is designed based on management interests in cost reduction and exploiting employees, it negatively impacts their well-being at work. Illustrative recent empirical studies examining the positive and negative effects of HR systems on worker well-being based on these theories are reviewed following.

Ogbonnaya and Messersmith (2019) integrated the JD-R theory into the HRM literature to explore the effects of HR systems on worker health-related well-being. Specifically, they examined the proposition that demands trigger a health-impairment process. Using data from the Finnish 2012 Practices of Working Life survey, they found that employee perceptions of HPWS were associated with increased time demands, which contributed to higher levels of stress. Van De Voorde et al. (2016) conducted a multilevel study among hospital employees and their line managers. They found that a set of HR practices that focused on empowerment did not affect work demands in terms of quantity and speed. However, these practices positively influenced job resources, which, in turn, stimulated a motivational process, resulting in higher levels of work engagement. Also testing the JD-R motivational and health-impairment processes in a study of employees in South Korean organisations, Kim et al. (2023) found that HPWS are positively associated with employee mental health via employee perceptions of empowerment but negatively associated with employee mental health through perceptions of work-role overload. In addition, these authors also found support for an extension of the JD-R model by integrating a personal resource (e.g., occupational identification) that attenuates the relationship between HPWS and mental health. Consistent with Kim et al. (2023), the results of a two-way study of 223 Chinese healthcare workers (Wang et al., 2021) show that personal resources such as core self-evaluations and job resources like servant leadership can buffer the effect of HPWS on mental- and physical-health problems.

Li et al. (2023) conducted a study based on the resource spiral proposition of the COR theory. The study investigated how time pressure and workload act as mediators in the relationship between job resource-oriented HRM (participation and autonomy) and demand-oriented HRM (training and pay for performance) and exhaustion and workplace relations. Using data from a National Workplace Survey of Employees conducted in Ireland, they show that job resource-oriented HR practices foster relationship well-being and health by reducing challenge demands; demand-oriented HR practices impair health and relationship well-being by increasing challenge demands. Building on the COR theory and the notion of resource caravans and gain spirals, Bartram et al. (2023) studied how well-being-oriented HR practices can serve as organisational resources that support individual resources (i.e., thriving) and mitigate the effects of burnout (a resource drain). Using a time-lagged study, well-being-oriented HR practices were positively associated with feelings of thriving and negatively with feelings of burnout. Building on similar COR logic, Huettermann and Bruch (2019) hypothesise that an HR system aimed at creating a healthy workplace facilitates collective employee well being by signalling organisational support. Results from a multisource study in 88 organisations in Germany revealed that this health-related HR system, as rated by HR representatives, is indirectly related to lower levels of collective emotional exhaustion and higher levels of collective engagement through employees' positive stress mindset.

Drawing on (HRM-specific) attribution arguments, Van De Voorde and Beijer (2015) explored the signalling impact of HPWS on well-being and performance attributions and how these influence employee outcomes. Using multisource, multilevel data collected in the Netherlands (1,065 employees and 150 line managers), it was revealed that when HPWS covers a larger proportion of employees within a work unit, this facilitates these two types of attributions. More specifically, consistent with the JD-R (motivational and health impairment pathways) and SET propositions, when employees perceive that the practices inherent to an HPWS in their workplace are intended to care for and support them, they are more likely to show commitment and feel less job strain. Conversely, if employees feel that the HPWS practices are solely motivated by maximising their performance, they tend to experience higher levels of job strain. Extending these findings by integrating SDT arguments, Cao et al. (2023), using multisource and multilevel data (36 team leaders and 181 employees) from China, showed that HPWS positively affect psychological availability when employees attribute these HPWS to a more well-being-focused management approach, which promotes thriving at work. However, performance-oriented attributions did not interact to influence role overload and emotional exhaustion. Goštautaite et al. (2022) tested the SDT propositions more directly by examining the mediating role of basic need satisfaction in the link between HR systems and work engagement among healthcare professionals. They found that employee perceptions of HRM systems have a positive effect on work engagement through the satisfaction of three basic needs: autonomy, relatedness and competence.

Collectively, this selective review of research suggests that various theory-informed mechanisms play a role in explaining how HR systems exert their impact on worker well-being. Across studies, findings are somewhat inconsistent but generally support the idea that performance-oriented HR systems signal care and support for employees and make work more resourceful but also more challenging and demanding, and signal that increased work effort is expected, which can facilitate or diminish well-being at work. In contrast, systems aimed at fostering well-being primarily show positive well-being effects. This emerging literature is promising as it integrates ideas and arguments from various theories to comprehend how and why HR systems relate to employee well-being in the workplace. For instance, multiple key propositions from the JD-R theory or JD-R with SET and attribution theory are applied to explain opposite effects for well-being, indicating mixed effects of HR systems on well-being at work. Finally, (some of) the theories also point out that the mechanisms explaining the effect of HR systems on worker well-being are likely to vary depending on circumstances; they allow for examination of theory-informed moderators of the HRM–worker well-being link.

Contemporary Developments

The relationship between HRM and worker well-being is difficult to predict and complex (Peccei et al., 2013), highlighting the need for more fine-grained approaches and theoretical perspectives to understand this topic in all its intricacy. In this regard, a number of key themes have surfaced in the literature aiming to provide a more nuanced understanding of the HRM and employee well-being link. While not exhaustive, some of the key themes we highlight as particularly important include 1) trade-offs, 2) curvilinearity, 3) the role of context and 4) intervention studies. We now turn to these key themes and discuss why they are particularly important from a theoretical and practical perspective, while at the same time pointing out particular research directions in each theme that may be important to advance the strategic HRM field.

Trade-Offs

Trade-offs, as the name implies, means that achieving a gain in one aspect typically involves incurring a loss or drawback in another aspect. As mentioned earlier, employee well-being can be broadly categorised into psychological, relationship and health components. Grant and colleagues (2007), in advocating their multidimensional view of well-being, also make apparent that there might be trade-offs that emerge in different aspects of well-being as a result of various managerial practices. For the field of HRM, this is informative because it shows that to fully understand the impact of HRM on worker well-being, it may be imperative to incorporate multiple or all of the key components of well-being. To illustrate, empowerment or other forms of enriched job design, which foster improved responsibility and variety at work, might lead to improved psychological well-being (since employees' jobs are more cognitively stimulating and experience psychological growth). Simultaneously, however, employees may also experience strain due to the increased expectations and accountability accompanying enlarged responsibility (Wang et al., 2019). Therefore, while psychological well-being might improve among workers, their health-related well-being could be compromised. Other examples include training as well as compensation and performance management. Indeed, while training could increase job complexity, and compensation and performance management practices may be satisfying and engaging for workers because of the challenge involved, such practices at the same time can demand high efforts from employees, thereby leading to strain (Hauff et al., 2022).

Despite these possibilities for trade-offs in worker well-being arising from HRM, it has been acknowledged that most research to date, when exploring the impact of HRM on well-being, has failed to incorporate multiple aspects of well-being to ascertain such effects (Guerci et al., 2019). The importance of considering trade-offs in well-being dimensions arising from HRM was brought to the fore in the review of Van De Voorde et al. (2012). The author's review of empirical studies revealed that the impact of HRM on workers' well-being depended on the actual type of well-being outcome included; support was found for a mutual gains perspective (win-win for employees and employer) when it comes to psychological well-being and relationship well-being, while support for a conflicting outcomes perspective (employers win and employees lose) for health well-being. Building on this research, Guerci and colleagues (2019) tested the impact of different HRM practices (ability-enhancing, motivation-enhancing and opportunity-enhancing HR practices) on different components of worker well-being using secondary data from the European Working Conditions Survey (EWCS). Incentive compensation was revealed to decrease employees' health and relationship well-being, although at the same time, hedonic well-being increased. Autonomy was also found to be damaging to employees' health well-being but at the same was beneficial for employees' psychological and relationship well-being. Finally, working in a self-directed team was damaging for employees' health well-being but beneficial for employees' psychological well-being. The study of Guerci et al. (2019) is a welcome development since it shows how HRM can have divergent effects on different aspects of well-being, thereby empirically substantiating the notion of trade-offs in action. Hauff and colleagues (2022) followed up on this research, also revealing that HRM more generally was beneficial for psychological well-being (engagement and job satisfaction), while at the same time harmful for health well-being (sleep quality). While the majority of research in HRM focuses on an integrationist perspective whereby HR practices are included as an overall 'bundle' or 'system' of practices (reflective of their additive or synergistic effects) (Ogbonnaya & Ayree, 2021), the findings of Guerci et al. (2019), in which the HR practices are treated separately, and where divergent effects of such practices are found, adds an additional layer of complexity to understanding the HRM–well-being relationship. Indeed, while the notion of different HR practices pushing in different and competing directions has been acknowledged, when applied to trade-offs, their findings show that different types of HRM practices also lead to corresponding trade-offs between different aspects of well-being; some practices were positively related to one or multiple well-being dimensions, whereas others were negatively related or not related at all. As such, future researchers may need to disentangle the effects of individual HRM practices (consistent with an isolationist perspective) on different components of well-being for a more robust understanding. Important here, for example, would be to gain a better understanding of the mechanisms underlying different types or combinations of trade-offs, as well as of the dynamics of these trade-offs and how they develop over time.

Curvilinearity

Another key theme which elucidates the complexity of HRM (and especially in terms of its relationship with well-being) concerns the issue of curvilinearity. As highlighted in the previous-mentioned review of studies, most of the relationships between HRM and worker well-being are tested in a linear fashion. By doing so, the implicit assumption is that increases (or investments) in HRM either increases or decreases various aspects of well-being. However, it is plausible that the impact of HRM on well-being might depend on the amount or intensity of the practices actually employed. Such reckoning is consistent with the so-called 'too-much-of-a-good-thing effect' (TMGT effect) principle, a meta-theory which has gained significant popularity in the management literature in recent years (Pierce & Aguinis, 2011). In this regard, Pierce and Aguinis (2011) argued that the impact of various management practices on workers can often reach a saturation (or inflection) point, whereby continued investments in such practices provide either no additional benefits or potentially damaging effects for workers. Indeed, in advancing the TMGT effect principle, the authors acknowledge that such potential for curvilinearity in relationships may account for paradoxical or seemingly contradictory findings that dominate much of the management literature. As highlighted in the review of studies, contradictory findings permeate much of the literature on HRM and well-being (Peccei & Van de Voorde, 2019b). Consequently, acknowledging the reality that linear relations don't always materialise is essential to advance HRM theory and practice (Ho & Kuvaas, 2020).

Although not specifically focusing on HRM practices, the potential for non-linear relations between various job characteristics and employee well-being has been previously acknowledged in the influential vitamin model of Warr (1987). This model stipulates that the presence of job characteristics initially has a beneficial effect on employees' well-being, whereas their absence impairs well-being. Beyond a certain point, however, vitamin intake (job characteristics) has no positive effect anymore; a plateau has been reached and the level of well-being tends to remain constant. Then, a further increase in job characteristics may either continue to produce either (1) a constant effect (analogously to vitamins C and E) whereby they neither harm nor improve well-being or (2) an additional decrement (analogously to vitamins A and D), whereby increased intake can be damaging for well-being. As such, both the vitamin model and the TMGT effect share similar assumptions and advocate the need to move away from considering monotonic relationships between core management constructs.

Putting together the logic inherent to the principle of the TMGT effect (Pierce & Aguinis, 2011) as well as the vitamin model (Warr, 1987), it is conceivable to suggest that HRM might initially be beneficial for employees, but when implemented at high or extremely high levels, this positive association might essentially diminish and thereby turn into a negative effect. Given that HRM can potentially yield contradictory effects on worker well-being, one way in which researchers have tended to reconcile this reality is to conceive HRM as either a job demand or a job resource (Kilroy, 2024). More specifically, whether HRM is perceived to be beneficial or harmful depends on employees' reactions in terms of whether they experience them as a *job demand* or *job resource* (Ho & Kuvaas, 2020) in accordance with the JD-R model. In the context of understanding curvilinear relations between HRM and well-being, one line of reasoning could be that HRM is initially perceived by employees as a job resource when implemented at moderate levels. However, when perceived beyond a certain point or extremely high levels, the HRM practices ultimately transpire into being perceived as demands.

Based on these theories and examples, and to develop a more complete understanding of the relationship between HRM and worker well-being, it is critical to move away from the 'more is better' assumption that predominates the HRM field (Ho & Kuvaas, 2020). Some scholars have heeded such advice, albeit looking at broader relations between HRM and performance. For example, Lee and Cogin (2022), drawing from the economics principle of the law of diminishing returns, investigated the curvilinear relationship between HRM and organisational performance measures. Their study, in an attempt to showcase the tension between investments and costs, revealed that the relationship between HRM and firm marginal benefit is non-linear in the shape of an S-curve. More specifically, there was no relationship between HRM and well-being using linear effects but at low and high levels of investment in HRM, the marginal benefit began to decline. More specifically related to employee well-being, only in recent years has this focus on curvilinearity gained traction. Ho and Kuvaas (2020) investigated and found support for a curvilinear effect between HRM and job satisfaction (psychological well-being).

Given this discussion and to resolve the paradoxical findings on HRM and well-being, testing for curvilinearity should be centre stage to advance HRM research. Based on this early evidence of Ho and Kuvaas (2020), a central question warranting investigation concerns, to what extent do curvilinear relationships exist between HRM and other dimensions of well-being (e.g., health and relationship)? Moreover, the extent to which different bundles of HRM practices (e.g., ability-enhancing, motivation-enhancing and opportunity-enhancing practices) differentially exert effects (linear or non-linear) on various aspects of well-being would vastly enrich our knowledge of the TMGT effect in the realm of HRM research. Another central focus could be geared towards understanding at what levels or stages do relationships between HRM and various aspects of well-being reach a context inflection point (Pierce & Aguinis, 2011), thereby having either no effect (constant effect or asymptotic pattern) or damaging effect (additional decrement or U-shaped pattern)? In this regard, exploring whether the same saturation point for performance (Lee & Cogin, 2020) also applies to the outcome of well-being would be insightful. Enriching our understanding of what types of employees (by exploring various traits and states) are likely to experience the aforementioned patterns (constant versus additional decrement), as well as testing broader contextual factors that shed light on the likelihood of such patterns, would also be a welcome development. These questions can potentially enable HR and management professionals to know when inflection points are likely to occur with respect to various HRM practices and thus know when not to intensify or keep investing in them and/or to take measures that will mitigate any adverse effects (Pierce & Aguinis, 2011; Lee & Cogin, 2020). From a return-on-investment perspective, this may end up enabling organisations to be more frugal with their resources (since any increase in HRM may not be necessary or, in fact, be counterproductive).

The Role of 'Context'

A third theme that we cover that is also critical in the field of HRM, especially in terms of reconciling the inconsistent and paradoxical findings that often emerge in studies investigating the relationship between HRM and worker well-being, is the role of context. According to Johns (2006, p.386), context represents the 'situational opportunities and limitations that influence the incidence and significance of organisational behaviour and the functional link between variables'. In the field of HRM, scholars have vigorously argued that the impact of managerial practices on various employee and organisational outcomes cannot be understood without taking into account the context (Schuler & Jackson, 1987). HRM practices are unlikely to universally improve employees' working conditions and well-being because of the complexity involved (Peccei et al., 2013). There may be differences linked to the individual (i.e., personal dispositions), the job itself (i.e., autonomy, workload), the workers' managers (i.e., leadership style) and, more broadly, to the internal and external organisational setting (i.e., management systems, national cultures) that moderate the relationship between HRM and well-being (Peccei et al., 2013). However, the full spectrum of these contextual factors has not yet received sufficient attention in the literature, and scholars have often investigated them for the specific purpose of making sense of the contradicting findings in the extant literature concerning the impact of HRM on well-being (Jensen et al., 2011; Jensen & Van De Voorde, 2016).

To illustrate the importance of contextual factors in reconciling such inconsistent findings, and in particular, the conditions under which HRM is likely to yield optimistic or pessimistic outcomes, the JD-R model is particularly fruitful (Kilroy & Flood, 2021; Kilroy, 2024; Jensen & Van De Voorde, 2016; Wang et al., 2021). Indeed, as previously mentioned, HRM can be either conceived of as a job demand (Wang et al., 2021) or a job resource (Kilroy et al., 2020). Therefore, should HRM practices be considered as a job demand by workers, it is possible that there are other resources that an organisation might provide (or an individual may possess) to help them overcome their strain-inducing effects (Jensen et al., 2011; Wang et al., 2021). This is consistent with the 'buffer hypothesis' inherent to the JD-R model. Likewise, when HRM is conceived as a job resource by workers, it is possible that an organisation might also provide other resources (or an individual may possess), thereby complementing or enhancing the positive effect of HRM on well-being (Kilroy et al., 2020). At the same time, there are many demands that employees encounter that could either counteract the positive effects of HRM on well-being or, indeed, consistent with the 'resource salience' hypothesis, amplify their positive impact on well-being (De Reuver et al., 2021).

As such, the JD-R model provides a useful theoretical lens to help understand the often contradictory findings with respect to the impact of managerial practices (including HRM) on well-being (Kilroy & Flood, 2021). For empirical research, this naturally involves testing interactions between HRM and a multitude of other factors in terms of how they relate to worker well-being. A plethora of studies have already been conducted to shed light on the role of contextual factors, including investigating contextual factors concerning individual and occupational characteristics and the nature of the employee–supervisor relationship (Kilroy, 2024). Next, we highlight a flavour of studies under each of these increasingly explored categories for the purpose of illustration.

Individual dispositions or personal resources can have a profound impact on how employees perceive HRM. For example, Kilroy and colleagues (2020) found that psychological detachment (conceived as a personal resource) moderated the relationship between high-involvement HRM and employee burnout, such that the beneficial effects of high-involvement HRM in fostering lower levels of burnout were more pronounced when employees were able to psychologically detach from work when they go home. In terms of occupational differences, research in the healthcare domain found that the experience of HRM was lower for medical and support service workers in comparison to nurses and administrative staff (Bartram et al., 2014) while HRM was more important for administrative staff than nurses (Shantz et al., 2016). Together, these findings emphasise that there are different occupational groups and different types of workers for which HRM may be more or less beneficial.

Concerning employee and supervisor relationships, a number of studies have explored the interactive role of various leadership styles in the relationship between HRM and well-being. This is in accordance with the view that both HRM and leadership are engaged in people management and critical for well-being (Guest, 2017) and should, therefore, consistent with the 'supplementary fit perspective', be seen as complementary in nature (Leroy et al., 2018). Supporting this notion, Kilroy et al. (2022) found that high-involvement HRM was associated with improved health well-being (burnout) via reducing demands and increasing resources (consistent with the optimistic perspective) and this relationship was further strengthened when engaging leadership was high rather than low. However, the indirect effect was no longer significant when engaging leadership was low. As such, these findings show that HRM can be beneficial for employee well-being, but under conditions whereby leadership behaviours are not enacted, this relationship can dissipate. In line with this finding, a number of studies have also shown that while HRM may be harmful in the first instance for employees, this effect is attenuated when leadership behaviours are enacted fully. For example, Hauff and colleagues (2022) found that HPWS impaired health well-being (sleep quality) among workers (consistent with the pessimistic perspective), although this relationship was weakened when the levels of supportive leadership was high. Also consistent with the pessimistic perspective, Wang et al. (2021) found that HPWS was associated with impaired worker well-being under conditions of low servant leadership. However, demonstrating the ability of leadership to counteract such effects, this aforementioned negative effect turned non-significant when servant leadership was high. These findings suggest that the demanding nature of HRM can be counteracted when servant leadership is exhibited by employees' line managers.

Taken together, the presented studies emphasise that context plays a key role in unearthing the potential impact of HRM on worker well-being from a theoretical and practical perspective. In terms of future research directions, there is a specific need to decipher the extent to which personal resources and dispositions interact with HRM practices because this will dictate what types of employees are more prone to different types of HRM perceptions, i.e., either as demands or resources (Kilroy et al., 2020). Moreover, given the salience of leaders in the implementation of HRM (Purcell & Hutchinson, 2007), and based on the growing number of studies exploring leadership behaviour as a moderator of the HRM-well-being relationship (e.g., Hauff et al., 2022; Kilroy et al., 2022; Wang et al., 2021), future research could uncover the relative importance of leadership styles for successful HRM implementation. This could enable leadership development interventions to focus on a tried-and-tested leadership style that would complement HRM in fostering well-being and/or ameliorating their potential negative effects (Leroy et al, 2018). The role of context is also essential for the other research themes presented earlier. Indeed, for the theme of trade-offs, the identification of potent contextual factors could enable possible trade-offs with respect to certain aspects of well-being to be minimised. Moreover, for the theme of curvilinearity, research could identify potent contextual factors that prevent context-specific inflection points from materialising and thereby help to avoid the potentially beneficial linear relationships turning into non-linear relationships.

HRM-Related Interventions and Field Experiments

In this last section, we turn briefly to a consideration of HRM-related structured interventions and field experiments, SIFEs for short, aimed at improving worker well-being. Although relatively rare compared to survey-based observational studies of the HRM–well-being relationship, workplace interventions and field experiments are central to further advance both HRM research and practice. In particular, these kinds of studies can make a significant contribution, over and above the contribution that is made by observational studies, in terms of building the store of evidence-based knowledge in the area. When looking at SIFE studies aimed at improving employee well-being, it is important to note that, from a disciplinary point of view, they mainly originate from outside the field of HRM itself – emanating from organisational and occupational psychology, organisational behaviour and management research more generally. The vast majority of these studies, however, are directly concerned with key HR practices in organisations including, for example, interventions and field experiments that focus on training, coaching and employee development, job redesign, communication, work hours and flexible work schedules, health and safety, work-family practices, diversity and inclusion programmes, and employee participation and voice. As such, the bulk of SIFE studies are related in important ways to the field of HRM and are of direct relevance to the analysis and understanding of the impact of HRM on well-being.

This broader SIFE literature includes hundreds of individual studies, as well as dozens of meta-analyses and systematic reviews of the area (e.g., Daniels et al., 2017; Fox et al., 2021; Sonnentag et al., 2023; Vîrgă et al., 2022). The focus here is not to provide a detailed review of this vast literature. Rather, we aim to (1) highlight the importance of workplace interventions and field experiments for our understanding of the impact of HRM on well-being, (2) distinguish between different types of interventions and field experimental studies and, (3) provide a brief overview of what selective studies tell us about the HRM–well-being relationship. In doing so, we also highlight some of the potential limitations of SIFE studies and, hence, the importance, going forward, of finding better ways of integrating SIFE and observational-based approaches in HRM research.

The Importance of SIFE Studies

The vast majority of survey-based observational HRM–well-being studies, like HRM-performance ones, are essentially cross-sectional, using either what Wright et al. (2005) refer to as 'contemporaneous' or 'retrospective' research designs. As is widely recognised, cross-sectional studies of this kind are not able to test for causality in the sense of showing that a set of HR practices, when adopted, actually leads to better well-being outcomes for workers. Longitudinal studies, especially ones using repeated measures like cross-lagged panel designs, are in a much better position to explore causal effects over time and draw causal inferences from data (Wright et al., 2005; Zyphur et al., 2019).

Despite the undoubted advantages of longitudinal designs, however, demonstrating causality with longitudinal data is by no means straightforward. In particular, drawing causal inferences from longitudinal data in the presence of time-varying confounders is notoriously challenging (Clare et al., 2018). For instance, organisational performance can be a time-varying confounder in the relationship between a system of HR practices and worker well-being in that prior performance can affect both current levels of investment in HRM and worker well-being, but investments in HRM can, in turn, affect subsequent levels of performance, and so on, over time. Although there are various analytical methods that have been proposed for handling time-varying confounding factors (Rohrer & Murayama, 2023; Zyphur et al., 2019), modelling and analysing complex dynamic relationships over time is highly challenging, particularly if the models involved include multiple well-being outcomes, mediators and boundary conditions.

In this context, the core value and benefit of SIFE studies, compared to observational ones, is their greater ability to test for causality by controlling for or ruling out alternative explanations for possible cause–effect connections (Eden, 2017; Shadish & Cook, 2009). This is true, especially of field experiments that use randomised control trials (RCT) to enhance causal inference. RCTs, the universally recognised gold standard for establishing causation (Eden, 2017), involve the random assignment of participants to control and treatment groups to examine the effects of an HR-related intervention on their subsequent health and well-being. Equally important, if more limited in their ability to test for causality, are non-randomised quasi-experiments that are similar to RCTs but without the random assignment of participants to control and treatment groups. The weakest form of SIFE studies are so-called 'pre-post' interventions that measure well-being levels of participants before and after an intervention but have no control groups (Eden, 2017). RCTs and quasi-experiments are commonly classified as high-quality interventions. Therefore, the key point is that, because of randomisation and the use of control groups, these more rigorous types of SIFE studies can significantly add to our understanding of the impact of HRM on employee well-being, over and above what can be learnt from either cross-sectional or longitudinal survey-based observational studies.

Types of SIFE Studies

Apart from the rigour of their research design, structured interventions and field experiments also vary along a number of other dimensions, including, for example, their scope, duration and focus (Fox et al., 2021; Van Woerkom, 2021). Perhaps the main distinction that is commonly made here is between individual-level SIFEs designed to influence worker behaviours that are relevant to well-being, and workplace/organisational-level SIFEs designed to protect and/or improve well-being by targeting workplace and organisational factors and changing aspects of the work environment (Fleming, 2024; LaMontagne et al., 2007; Sonnentag et al., 2023). This distinction is sometimes referred to as the difference between interventions aimed at changing the worker versus those aimed at changing the workplace (Fox et al., 2021).

Individual-Level Interventions

SIFEs that target the individual typically aim to improve well-being by building personal resources that help workers better to cope, respond and flourish at work. They include a wide variety of interventions, ranging from counselling and stress management programmes of various kinds, to resource-building, strength-based mindfulness and resilience interventions, to programmes designed to promote healthy lifestyles (Fleming, 2024; Sonnentag et al., 2023). The outcomes involved also vary, including various aspects of hedonic and eudaimonic well-being, as well as exhaustion, stress and other components of physical well-being. Not surprisingly, given the heterogeneity of these interventions in terms of both content and outcomes, evidence about their effectiveness is mixed. Meta-analytic results of high quality SIFEs, for example, indicate small to moderate positive effects of mindfulness interventions on both hedonic and eudaimonic well-being (Monzani et al., 2021), but deleterious effects on burnout of interventions that support prevention-focused job-crafting (Lichtenthaler & Fischbach, 2018). Overall, however, and in line with JD-R theory arguments about the importance of personal resources for well-being at work, the summary of meta-analytic results reported by Sonnentag and her colleagues (2023) suggests a generally positive effect of individual-level SIFEs on various aspects of worker well-being. The effects involved, however, only tend to be small to moderate. It is also unclear how long these positive effects last and the extent to which they are, in any case, affected by the broader organisational context in which the interventions took place, thereby raising questions both about the longer-term benefits of these individual-level interventions and their generalisability (Fleming, 2024; Nielsen & Miraglia, 2017). More generally, a number of researchers, while acknowledging the potential benefits of individual-level interventions, have questioned the value of strategies to improve worker health and well-being that focus purely on 'changing the worker', emphasising instead, and/or in addition, the importance of workplace-level interventions designed to change factors that are at the root of the negative health and well-being outcomes experienced by individuals at work in the first place (Fleming, 2024; Fox at al., 2021; Sonnentag et al., 2023).

Workplace-Level Interventions

Workplace-level SIFEs are commonly defined as interventions 'that aim to improve employee health and well-being through changing the way work is designed, organised and planned' (Nielsen & Abildgaard, 2013:278). Like individual-level interventions, they vary greatly in terms of their content and scope, as well as in terms of the well-being outcomes they target and their measurement. In their systematic review of high-quality workplace SIFEs, Fox and her colleagues (2021) identify four main types of interventions, namely, those focusing on flexible work and scheduling changes, job redesign, relational and team dynamics and employee participation and voice. The picture that emerges from their review is quite complex. The results are generally positive, indicating that workplace-level interventions, by increasing job resources like work autonomy and flexibility, and modulating job demands, can indeed help to enhance various aspects of well-being. Once again, however, the results are mixed, varying both between and within types of interventions (Fox et al., 2021; see also the summary meta-analytic review by Sonnentag et al., 2023). On balance, flexible work interventions have the strongest and most consistent positive effects, while the effects in other areas are more mixed. Work redesign interventions that increase job control and autonomy, for example, tend to have a positive impact on well-being, while lean production initiatives that involve reorganisation of work but prioritise productivity and increase job pressures and demands have a negative effect (Fox et al., 2021).

Positive but mixed results for job redesign and other types of workplace-level interventions are also reported by Daniels and his colleagues (Daniels et al., 2017; Daniels et al., 2021) and by Sonnentag et al. (2023). A number of reasons have been proposed for this variability in results and, in particular, for why workplace-level interventions often fail to improve workers' well-being. In this context, two key boundary conditions linked to the quality of the implementation process and the existence of supportive employment practices have been highlighted as especially important for the success of workplace-level interventions. In terms of the implementation process, a number of factors stand out as particularly important for success including, for example, managerial commitment to the intervention and worker participation and engagement in the process (Daniels et al., 2017; Nielsen, 2013). In terms of the existence of supportive employment practices, job redesign interventions coupled with, for example, training for employees to improve their own jobs and, more generally, system-wide approaches that simultaneously enhance job design and a range of other HR practices, have been found to improve well-being outcomes more effectively than single-focused work design interventions (Daniels et al., 2017).

Potential Limitations of SIFE Studies and the Way Forward

In sum, SIFE studies can, and do, add significantly to our knowledge and understanding of the effects of HRM on worker well-being. In particular, they show that even though the effects involved are generally not all that strong, the adoption of a variety of both individually- and workplace-oriented HR-related practices leads to a range of better well-being outcomes for workers. At the same time, however, the supportive employment practices boundary conditions highlighted previously point to the importance of focusing not simply on individual HR practices, but rather on broader combinations of practices and/or on the HR system as a whole for the more effective promotion of well-being at work. This is consistent with key arguments from the wider HRM literature about the importance of synergistic effects between HR practices for both organisational performance and worker well-being and goes to highlight one of the key potential limitations of SIFE studies. This is the fact that the ultimate value of such studies lies in their rigour. Rigorous field experimental methods, however, can be more easily applied to look at the effects of narrower interventions focused on single practices than at more complex systemic interventions involving changes in multiple combinations of practices (e.g., the introduction of bundles of new high-involvement or high-performance practices). Yet, it is precisely the combined effect of HR systems that may be the most important for worker well-being. Here, therefore, is where it is more difficult for SIFE studies to make a contribution and where rigorous longitudinal studies of the effects of bundles and systems of HR practices are particularly valuable. More generally, this highlights the complementary contribution that longitudinal observational studies and SIFEs can make to our understanding of the impact of HRM on well-being and, therefore, the importance of systematically integrating SIFE and observational-based approaches in HRM research to make further progress in this area.

In Conclusion

In this chapter, we have critically examined extant research on worker well-being in the context of HRM. Specifically, we provided insights into what well-being consists of, the key debates on the role of HRM in influencing worker well-being (and, in this regard, the inconsistent empirical evidence in the existing literature to date), as well as the key theories and underlying mechanisms that account for the reported positive and negative effects of HRM on well-being. We believe that there is a need for more fine-grained approaches to understand this relationship in all its complexity and thereby advance HRM scholarship. Specifically, we recommend exploring trade-offs between different aspects of well-being and curvilinear effects invoked by HRM, as well as the conditions that influence them and further engaging in HRM-related structured interventions and field experiments aimed at improving worker well-being. This will contribute to the evidence-based theoretical knowledge in this area and, in the process, help HRM scholars to respond more effectively and convincingly to the growing demands from organisations, governments and regulatory bodies for actionable knowledge that can better inform efforts to improve the health and well-being of people at work.

References

Appelbaum, E., Bailey, T., Berg, P., & Kalleberg, A. (2000). *Manufacturing advantage: Why high-performance work systems pay off.* Cornell University Press.

Bartram, T., Cooper, B., Cooke, F. L., & Wang, J. (2023). Thriving in the face of burnout? The effects of wellbeing-oriented HRM on the relationship between workload, burnout, thriving and performance. *Employee Relations: The International Journal, 45*(5), 1234–1253.

Bartram, T., Karimi, L., Leggat, S. G., & Stanton, P. (2014). Social identification: Linking high-performance work systems, psychological empowerment and patient care. *International Journal of Human Resource Management, 25*(17), 2401–2419.

Beer, M., Spector, B., Lawrence, P., Mills, D. Q., & Walton, R. (1984). *Human resource management: A general manager's perspective.* Free Press.

Blau, P. M. (1964). *Exchange and power in social life.* John Wiley and Sons.

Cao, M., Zhao, S., Chen, J., & Lv, H. (2023). Employees' HR attributions count: the effects of high-performance work systems on employees' thriving at work and emotional exhaustion. *Personnel Review, 53*(4), 835–856.

Clare, P., Dobbins, T., & Mattick, R. P. (2018). Causal models adjusting for time-varying confounding—A systematic review of the literature. *International Journal of Epidemiology, 48*(1), 254–265.

Cole, M., Walter, F., Bedeian, A., & O'Boyle, E. (2012). Job burnout and employee engagement: A meta-analytic examination of construct proliferation. *Journal of Management, 38*(5), 1550–1581.

Collings, D. G., Nyberg, A. J., Wright, P. M., & McMackin, J. (2021). Leading through paradox in a COVID-19 world: Human resources comes of age. *Human Resource Management Journal, 31*(4), 819–833.

Corporate Sustainability Reporting. (n.d.). *Finance.* https://finance.ec.europa.eu/capital-markets-union-and-financial-markets/company-reporting-and-auditing/company-reporting/corporate-sustainability-reporting_en

Daniels, K., Gedikli, C., Watson, D., Semkina, A., & Vaughn, O. (2017). Job design, employment practices and well-being: A systematic review of intervention studies. *Ergonomics, 60*(9), 1177–1196.

Daniels, K., Watson, D., Nayani, R., Tregaskis, O., Hogg, M., Etuknwa, A., & Semkina, A. (2021). Implementing practices focused on workplace health and psychological wellbeing: A systematic review. *Social Science & Medicine, 277*, 113888.

Danna, K., & Griffin, R. W. (1999). Health and well-being in the workplace: A review and synthesis of the literature. *Journal of Management, 25*(3), 357–384.

Deci, E. L., & Ryan, R. M. (2000). Self-determination theory and the facilitation of intrinsic motivation, social development, and well-being. *American Psychologist, 55*(1), 68–78.

Demerouti, E., Bakker, A. B., Nachreiner, F., & Schaufeli, W. B. (2001). The job demands-resources model of burnout. *Journal of Applied Psychology, 86*(3), 499–512.

Eden, D. (2017). Field experiments in organisations. *Annual Review of Organizational Psychology and Organizational Behavior, 4*(1), 91–122.

Erdogan, B., Bauer, T. N., Truxillo, D. M., & Mansfield, L. R. (2012). Whistle while you work: A review of the life satisfaction literature. *Journal of Management, 38*(4), 1038–1083.

Faragher, E.B., Cass, M., & Cooper, C.L. (2005). The relationship between job satisfaction and health: A meta-analysis. *Occupational and Environmental Medicine, 62*(1), 105–112.

Fleming, W. J. (2024). Employee well-being outcomes from individual-level mental health interventions: Cross-sectional evidence from the UK. *Industrial Relations Journal, 55*, 162–182.

Fox, K., Johnson, S., Berkman, L. F., Sianoja, M., Soh, Y., Kubzansky, L. D., & Kelly, E. (2021). Organisational- and group-level workplace interventions and their effect on multiple domains of worker well-being: A systematic review. *Work & Stress, 36*(1), 30–59.

Gelles, D., & Yaffe-Bellany, D. (2019, August 19). Shareholder value is no longer everything, top CEOs say. *The New York Times.* Available at: https://www.nytimes.com/2019/08/19/business/business-roundtable-ceos-corporations.html. Accessed on March 30, 2024

Godard, J. 2001: Beyond the high-performance paradigm? An analysis of variation in Canadian managerial perceptions of reform program effectiveness, *British Journal of Industrial Relations, 39*, 25–52.

Goštautaitė, B., Bučiūnienė, I., & Milašauskienė, Ž. (2022). HRM and work outcomes: The role of basic need satisfaction and age. *The International Journal of Human Resource Management, 33*(2), 169–202.

Grant, A. M., Christianson, M. K., & Price, R. H. (2007). Happiness, health, or relationships? Managerial practices and employee well-being tradeoffs. *Academy of Management* Perspectives, *21*(3), 51–63.

Guerci, M., Hauff, S., & Gilardi, S. (2019). High performance work practices and their associations with health, happiness and relational well-being: Are there any tradeoffs? *International Journal of Human Resource Management, 33*(2), 329–359.

Guest, D. E. (2017). Human resource management and employee well-being: Towards a new analytic framework. *Human Resource Management Journal, 27*(1), 22–38.

Hauff, S., Felfe, J., & Klug, K. (2022). High-performance work practices, well-being, and supportive leadership: spillover mechanisms and boundary conditions between HRM and leadership behavior. *International Journal of Human Resource Management, 33*(10), 2109–2137.

Ho, H., & Kuvaas, B. (2020). Human resource management systems, employee well-being, and firm performance from the mutual gains and critical perspectives: The well-being paradox. *Human Resource Management, 59*(3), 235–253.

Hobfoll, S. E. (1989). Conservation of resources: A new attempt at conceptualizing stress. *American Psychologist, 44*(3), 513–524.

Holmes, R. M., Waldman, D. A., Siegel, D. S., & Pepe, J. (2022). Declining trust in capitalism: Managerial, research, and public policy implications. *Academy of Management Perspectives, 36*(4), 984–1006.

Huettermann, H., & Bruch, H. (2019). Mutual gains? Health-related HRM, collective well-being and organisational performance. *Journal of Management Studies, 56*(6), 1045–1072.

Jensen, J. M., Patel, P. C., & Messersmith, J. G. (2011). High-performance work systems and job control. *Journal of Management, 39*(6), 1699–1724.

Jensen, J. M., & Van De Voorde, K. (2016). High performance at the expense of employee health? Reconciling the dark side of high-performance work systems. In N. M. Ashkanasy, R. J. Bennet, & M. Martinko (Eds.), *Understanding the high-performance workplace* pp. 81–102, Routledge.

Johns, G. (2006). The essential impact of context on organisational behavior. *Academy of Management Review, 31*(2), 386–408.

Keenoy, T. (1990). HRM: A case of the wolf in sheep's clothing? *International Journal of Manpower, 11*(5), 4–10.

Kelley, H. H. (1967) Attribution theory in social psychology. In D. Levine (Ed.), *Nebraska symposium on motivation* (pp. 192–238). University of Nebraska Press.

Kilroy, S. (2024). High-performance work practices in health care: Progress on key themes and prospects for future research. In A. McDermott, A. Avgar, P. Hyde, & L. Fitzgerald (Eds.), *Research handbook on contemporary human resource management for health care* (pp. 255–272). Edward Elgar.

Kilroy, S., Bosak, J., Flood, P. C., & Peccei, R. (2020). Time to Recover: The moderating role of psychological detachment in the link between high-involvement work practices and burnout. *Journal of Business Research, 108*, 52–61.

Kilroy, S., & Flood, P. C. (2021). Lean management and employee well-being. In P. Brough, E. Gardiner, and K. Daniels (Eds.), *Handbook series in occupational health sciences*, pp. 1–19. Springer.

Kilroy, S., Fu, N., Bosak, J., Hayes, R., & Schaufeli, W. B. (2022). Reducing day-level emotional exhaustion: The complementary role of high involvement work systems and engaging leadership. *Human Resource Management Journal, 33*(4), 846–867.

Kim, K. Y., Messersmith, J. G., Pieper, J. R., Baik, K., & Fu, S. (2023). High-performance work systems and employee mental health: The roles of psychological empowerment, work role overload, and organisational identification. *Human Resource Management, 62*(6), 791–810.

LaMontagne, A. D., Keegel, T., Louie, A., Ostry, A., & Landsbergis, P. (2007). A systematic review of the job-stress intervention evaluation literature, 1990–2005. *International Journal of Occupational and Environmental Health, 13*(3), 268–280.

Lee, I., & Cogin, J. (2022). Formalizing the HRM and firm performance link: The S-curve hypothesis. *The International Journal of Human Resource Management, 33*(5), 898–929.

Legge, K. (1995). *Human resource management: Rhetorics and realities.* Macmillan.

Legge, K. (1998). The morality of HRM. In C. Mabey, D. Skinner, & T. Clark (Eds.), *Experiencing human resource management*, pp. 14–32, Sage.

Leroy, H., Segers, J., Van Dierendonck, D., & Den Hartog, D. (2018). Managing people in organisations: Integrating the study of HRM and leadership. *Human Resource Management Review, 28*(3), 249–257.

Li, M., Fu, N., Chadwick, C., & Harney, B. (2023). Untangling human resource management and employee wellbeing relationships: Differentiating job resource HR practices from challenge demand HR practices. *Human Resource Management Journal, 34*(1), 214–235.

Lichtenthaler, P. W., & Fischbach, A. (2018). A meta-analysis on promotion- and prevention-focused job crafting. *European Journal of Work and Organizational Psychology, 28*(1), 30–50.

Monzani, L., Escartín, J., Ceja, L., & Bakker, A. B. (2021). Blending mindfulness practices and character strengths increases employee well-being: A second-order meta-analysis and a follow-up field experiment. *Human Resource Management Journal, 31*(4), 1025–1062.

Neicu, M., Beets, J., Van den Brink, F., Hoes, B., & Pajic, E. (2023). *Humanized growth and multi-stakeholder value creation.* KennedyFitch. www.kennedyfitch.com.

Nielsen, K. (2013). Review Article: How can we make organisational interventions work? Employees and line managers as actively crafting interventions. *Human Relations*, *66*(8), 1029–1050.

Nielsen, K., & Abildgaard, J. S. (2013). Organizational interventions: A research-based framework for the evaluation of both process and effects. *Work & Stress*, *27*(3), 278–297.

Nielsen, K., & Miraglia, M. (2017). What works for whom in which circumstances? On the need to move beyond the 'what works?' Question in organisational intervention research. *Human Relations*, *70*(1), 40–62.

Ogbonnaya, C., & Aryee, S. (2021). HRM practices, employee well-being, and organizational performance. In P. Brough, E. Gardiner, & K. Daniels (Eds.), *Handbook on management and employment practices.* Handbook Series in Occupational Health Sciences, pp. 369–391, Springer.

Ogbonnaya, C., & Messersmith, J. (2019). Employee performance, well-being, and differential effects of human resource management subdimensions: Mutual gains or conflicting outcomes?. *Human Resource Management Journal*, *29*(3), 509–526.

Peccei, R. (2004) *Human resource management and the search for the happy workplace, Inaugural address*. Erasmus Research Institute of Management (ERIM).

Peccei, R., & Van De Voorde, K. (2019a). The application of the multilevel paradigm in HRM–outcomes research: Taking stock and going forward. *Journal of Management*, *45*(2), 786–818.

Peccei, R., & Van De Voorde, K. (2019b). HRM–well-being–performance research revisited: Past, present, and future. *Human Resource Management Journal*, *29*(4), 539–563.

Peccei, R., Van de Voorde, K., & Van Veldhoven, M. (2013). HRM well-being and performance: A theoretical and empirical review. In D. Guest, J. Paauwe, & P. Wright (Eds.), *HRM and performance: Achievements and challenges* (pp. 26–46). John Wiley & Sons.

Purcell, J., & Hutchinson, S. (2007). Front-line managers as agents in the HRM-performance causal chain: Theory, analysis and evidence. *Human Resource Management Journal*, *17*(1), 3–20.

Pierce, J. R., & Aguinis, H. (2011). The too-much-of-a-good-thing effect in management. *Journal of Management*, *39*(2), 313–338.

Ramsay, H., Scholarios, D., & Harley, B. (2000). Employees and high-performance work systems: Testing inside the black box. *British Journal of Industrial Relations*, *38*(4), 501–531.

Rohrer, J. M., & Murayama, K. (2023). These are not the effects you are looking for: Causality and the within-/between-person distinction in longitudinal data analysis. *Advances in Methods And Practices in Psychological Science*, *6*(1), 1–14.

De Reuver, R., Van de Voorde, K., & Kilroy, S. (2021). When do bundles of high-performance work systems reduce employee absenteeism? The moderating role of workload. *International Journal of Human Resource Management*, *32*(13), 2889–2909.

Ryan, R. M., & Deci, E. L. (2001). On happiness and human potentials: A review of research on hedonic and eudaimonic well-being. *Annual Review of Psychology*, *52*(1), 141–166.

Schuler, R. S., & Jackson, S. E. (1987). Linking competitive strategies with human resource management practices. *Academy of Management Perspectives*, *1*(3), 207–219.

Shadish, W. R., & Cook, T. D. (2009). The renaissance of field experimentation in evaluating interventions. *Annual Review of Psychology*, *60*(1), 607–629.

Shantz, A., Alfes, K., & Whiley, L. (2016). HRM in healthcare: The role of work engagement. *Personnel Review*, *45*(2), 274–295.

Sonnentag, S., Tay, L., & Shoshan, H. N. (2023). A review on health and well-being at work: More than stressors and strains. *Personnel Psychology*, *76*(2), 473–510.

Taris, T. W., & Schaufeli, W. (2015). Individual well-being and performance at work: A conceptual and theoretical overview. In M. Van Veldhoven & R. Peccei (Eds.), *Well-being and performance at work: The role of context* (pp. 24–43). Psychology Press.

Van De Voorde, K., & Beijer, S. (2015). The role of employee HR attributions in the relationship between high-performance work systems and employee outcomes. *Human Resource Management Journal*, *25*(1), 62–78.

Van De Voorde, K., Paauwe, J., & Van Veldhoven, M. (2012). Employee well-being and the HRM–organizational performance relationship: A review of quantitative studies. *International Journal of Management Reviews*, *14*(4), 391–407.

Van De Voorde, K., Veld, M., & Van Veldhoven, M. (2016). Connecting empowerment-focused HRM and labour productivity to work engagement: The mediating role of job demands and resources. *Human Resource Management Journal*, *26*(2), 192–210.

Van Woerkom, M. (2021). Building positive organisations: A typology of positive psychology interventions. *Frontiers in Psychology*, *12*, 769782.

Vîrgă, D., Rusu, A., Pap, Z., Maricuțoiu, L. P., & Tisu, L. (2022). Effectiveness of strengths use interventions in organisations: A pre-registered meta-analysis of controlled trials. *Applied Psychology*, *72*(4), 1653–1693.

Wang, Z., Lu, X., & Zhang, Y. (2019). Do high-performance work systems harm employees' health? An investigation of service-oriented HPWS in the Chinese healthcare sector. *International Journal of Human Resource Management*, *32*(10), 2264–2297.

Wang, Z., Xing, L., & Zhang, Y. (2021). Do high-performance work systems harm employees' health? An investigation of service-oriented HPWS in the Chinese healthcare sector. *International Journal of Human Resource Management*, *32*(10), 2264–2297.

Warr, P. (1987). *Work, unemployment, and mental health*. Oxford University Press.

Wright, P., Gardner, T.., Moynihan, L., & Allen, M. (2005). The relationship between HR practices and firm performance: Examining causal order. *Personnel Psychology*, *58*(2), 409–446.

Zyphur, M., Allison, P., Tay, L., Voelkle, M., Preacher, K., Zhang, Z., Hamaker, E., Shamsollahi, A., Pierides, D., Koval, P., & Diener, E. (2019). From data to causes I: Building a general Cross-Lagged Panel Model (GCLM). *Organizational Research Methods*, *23*(4), 651–687.

Index

Page numbers in italics indicate figures, while page numbers in bold indicate tables

For Product Safety Concerns and Information please contact our EU representative GPSR@taylorandfrancis.com Taylor & Francis Verlag GmbH, Kaufingerstraße 24, 80331 München, Germany

Printed and bound by CPI Group (UK) Ltd, Croydon, CR0 4YY

20/05/2025

01877149-0003